PHILOSOPHY AND CONTEMPORARY PROBLEMS
A Reader

PHILOSOPHY AND CONTEMPORARY PROBLEMS
A Reader

Richard H. Popkin

Washington University

Avrum Stroll

University of California, San Diego

Holt, Rinehart and Winston

New York   Chicago   San Francisco   Philadelphia
Montreal   Toronto   London   Sydney
Tokyo   Mexico City   Rio de Janeiro   Madrid

Library of Congress Cataloging in Publication Data
Main entry under title:

Philosophy and contemporary problems.

1. Philosophy—Addresses, essays, lectures.
2. Ethics—Addresses, essays, lectures.   3. Political
science—Addresses, essays, lectures.   4. Religion—
Philosophy—Addresses, essays, lectures.   I. Popkin,
Richard Henry, 1923–   .   II. Stroll, Avrum,
1921–   .
BD41.P472 1984   100   83–18682

ISBN 0-03-061701-4

4 5 6 7   090   9 8 7 6 5 4 3 2 1

CBS COLLEGE PUBLISHING
  Holt, Rinehart and Winston
  The Dryden Press
  Saunders College Publishing

Acknowledgment of permission to use copyrighted material appears on page 541.

Book composition by York Graphic Services, Inc., York, Pennsylvania

CONTENTS

3 *ETHICS* · *270*

A. Is Abortion Ever Morally Justified?

B. Is Pleasure the Main Goal of Life?

4 *POLITICAL PHILOSOPHY* *351*

A. Do Citizens Have the Right to Revolt Against Their Government?

B. Are There Justifiable Limits to Free Speech and Publication?

5 *PHILOSOPHY OF RELIGION* *453*

A. Does God Exist?

B. How Can Evil Exist If God Is All-Wise, All-Powerful, and All-Good?

PHILOSOPHY AND CONTEMPORARY PROBLEMS
A Reader

GENERAL
INTRODUCTION

On November 22, 1963, at 12:31 P.M. in Dealey Plaza, Dallas, Texas, one of the most dramatic events of the twentieth century occurred. President John F. Kennedy was shot and killed while riding in a motorcade. The event took place in broad daylight. Photographs taken at the time indicate that about six hundred spectators saw what happened. In the motorcade were quite a few experts on firearms and crime, the sheriff, the police chief, and several Secret Service officers, and many policemen from a nearby police station. Numerous newspapermen and news photographers were present, as well as private citizens taking pictures of the parade. All in all, it was a very public event.

But what actually happened? Photographs taken at the time and eyewitness reports indicate that when most people heard the shots they immediately thought the bullets were being fired from a "grassy knoll" on the right side of the motorcade. This was the immediate reaction of the sheriff, the police chief, the Secret Service people, and most of the policemen. Photographs show a massive movement of law-enforcement personnel toward the "grassy knoll" and spectators running away from it or dropping to the ground between the "grassy knoll" and the motorcade.

One policeman on a motorcycle well behind the President's car was riding directly toward the Texas Book Depository Building, located at the corner where the motorcade was turning down to the freeway, when the President was hit. This policeman, on hearing the shots, also saw birds flying off the roof of the building. He immediately inferred that the bullets were being fired from an upper floor of the building and he rushed in. He met Lee Harvey Oswald on the second floor of the building while running up to the top floors. This policeman's activities led within forty-five minutes to others locating a rifle, three gun cartridges, and a likely place from which shots could have been fired.

The FBI agents interrogated around two hundred spectators and obtained signed statements from many of them. In these statements there was little agreement about the number of shots (three to six), their direction, or the sequence of events.

How does one determine what actually happened? In this case there were far

1

more ordinary and expert witnesses than are usually present at an event. One spectator, Abraham Zapruder, was taking a movie of the motorcade. His film turned out to record much of the sequence of events from the time the President showed a reaction to being shot until an explosion blew off a large portion of his skull.

Because Zapruder's camera ran at a fairly uniform rate, it was possible to time the sequence of events. Another timetable was given by then Governor John Connally of Texas. Connally was seated in front of the President in a jump seat in the limousine. Connally was a hunter, used to the sound of firing guns. He said that when he heard the first shot he turned to his right, looking behind for the source of the firing, and then was turning his head to the left to look toward the President when he himself felt a strong force hitting him, and he collapsed. Governor Connally was badly wounded. A bullet hit him in the back, fractured a rib, smashed his wrist, and ended up in his thigh. It took three hours of emergency surgery to save him. Connally's testimony coupled with what appears on the Zapruder film indicates a time interval of less than two seconds between the first shot and the shot that hit the Governor.

By mid-afternoon Lee Harvey Oswald had been arrested in a movie theater far from the scene of the President's assassination, where police found him when they were looking for the killer of a patrolman, Officer J. B. Tippitt, who was killed about forty minutes after the President was shot. Officer Tippitt was shot on a public street by someone using a revolver. Several people were nearby, again giving differing information as to what they saw and heard.

By mid-afternoon the Dallas police had also located on the sixth floor of the Texas Book Depository what turned out to be Oswald's rifle, as well as three shell casings near a window. By that night an autopsy had been performed on the late President at Bethesda Naval Hospital in Washington, D.C., by leading doctors from the army, navy, and air force, in the presence of several Secret Service men and FBI men who expected to testify at the trial of the President's assassin and were at the autopsy to witness the facts.

After the autopsy it became apparent that the facts as uncovered by the doctors in Washington did not coincide with what was reported by the doctors at Parkland Hospital in Dallas who had treated the President shortly after the shooting. One of the latter group had seen what he claimed was an entry wound in Kennedy's throat. He had made an incision there to enable Kennedy to breathe. The Bethesda doctors saw no evidence of a throat wound but found an entry wound on Kennedy's upper back. They could discover no path of the bullet through the President's body.

After the autopsy they learned that a bullet (called Exhibit #399 thereafter) had been found on a stretcher at Parkland Hospital and that this bullet, which was in almost pristine condition, had been fired from Oswald's gun.

With all of these data and quite a bit more, the Dallas police and the FBI tried to figure out what had happened. They decided within about twelve hours of the event that Lee Harvey Oswald had fired three rifle shots at the President from the sixth floor of the Book Depository, that two of these shots had hit the President, and that one of these two shots also had hit Governor Connally. (There was evidence that a bullet had hit a manhole cover some distance from the President's car and that a fragment had bounced up and injured a spectator.)

From the outset there was much disagreement with this official theory of Oswald as the lone assassin. The only eyewitness who claimed to have seen the firing could not pick Oswald out in a lineup. (The same was the case with regard to the Tippitt shooting.) Various people insisted they saw evidence of firing from the "grassy knoll." No one saw Oswald on the sixth floor of the Book Depository, and he was on the second floor drinking a bottled beverage when Patrolman Baker ran into him. There were no fingerprints on the firing mechanism of Oswald's gun, and no gloves were found.

Oswald denied any connection with the shooting during the thirteen hours of interrogation by the Dallas police, the FBI, and the Secret Service. After Oswald was shot and killed the following day by Jack Ruby, President Johnson decided that since there were so many rumors and divergent reports about what had happened, and since there would be no trial in which the facts would be aired, he would appoint a special commission to answer the questions about the event. This commission, headed by Chief Justice Earl Warren and including former CIA chief Allen Dulles and later President Gerald Ford, set to work with the assistance of the FBI to ascertain what had in fact occurred. They started out less than two months after the event with all of the FBI and other police reports and the medical data. Using Zapruder's pictures they determined that the shots that hit the President were fired in about 5.8 seconds. Testing Oswald's rifle, they learned that it took at least 2.3 seconds to pull the bolt and fire the gun without aiming it. The ballistics evidence indicated three bullets fired. Three casings were found in the Book Depository. Fragments of one bullet were found in the car. Another bullet missed and hit a manhole cover and a spectator, and a third (#399) was found on a stretcher at Parkland Hospital.

But these facts were difficult to reconcile with some others. Governor Connally and his wife both were sure that the Governor had been struck by a bullet other than the first one that hit the President. Zapruder's pictures agreed with the recollections of the Connallys and showed Connally reacting to his wounds less than two seconds after the President was first struck. Since Oswald's gun could not be reloaded and fired that fast, this seemed to contradict the official account. Further, there was no ballistics evidence of a fourth bullet fired from Oswald's gun (only three casings were found in the Book Depository).

Still more baffling was bullet #399. The FBI ballistics expert had no doubt that it had been fired from Oswald's rifle. Someone had found it when he pushed some stretchers aside and it fell off one of them. But it could never be determined whether the stretcher had held the President, the Governor, or someone else. Since no bullet was found in the President's body, the prevailing explanation, in view of all of the other data, was that bullet #399 had been the first bullet fired and that it had passed cleanly through the President's body without striking any bone and then struck Governor Connally. This only raised more problems. First, the evidence from Kennedy's clothes and from some of the autopsy data was that the first bullet could not have entered his upper back, come out of his throat, and then hit Governor Connally in his back unless it had been deflected a couple of times. Second, this explanation could not account for the time interval—almost two seconds—between the woundings of the President and the Governor. Third and probably most significant, bullet #399 had suffered no appreciable loss of material and weight and had no blood on it after supposedly traversing two bodies and leaving many fragments in the Governor.

As a result of these problems many people questioned the findings of the Warren Commission, which filed its report that Lee Harvey Oswald had been the lone assassin and had fired three shots. After September 30, 1964, when the Warren Commission Report was filed, many books and articles appeared questioning the account of the commission. Gun experts, pathologists, and eyewitnesses challenged its facts and conclusions. Several additional autopsy studies were made and many independent tests were run, some disputing, some confirming or at least not contradicting the findings of the Warren Commission.

Were it not for the trauma of President Kennedy's assassination and its political importance, the dispute about it might have died down (though people are still arguing about the events surrounding President Abraham Lincoln's assassination, and recently questions have been raised about the case concerning the kidnapping and killing of Charles A. Lindbergh's infant child). What the dispute indicates is the problem of ascertaining facts. Although we possess far more data about the events that took place in Dealey Plaza on November 22, 1963, than we do about most historical events, even some of the most basic facts are still being questioned: the number, order, and direction of the shots.

When eyewitnesses and "earwitnesses" disagree, how do we determine who is right? We can investigate the witnesses and examine the condition of their faculties. If some have poor eyesight or hearing, we tend to take their reports less seriously than those of people with unimpaired faculties. Some people are trained observers: policemen, FBI agents, Secret Service men, newspaper reporters, hunters. We might consider their evidence more credible than that of others. Some people have no reason to falsify or deceive, others may. We usually employ a whole set of beliefs in order to sort out the apparent conflicts in the data we receive. These enable us to dismiss crank reports, claims of "crackpots," idiosyncratic interpretations of events. However, when we have employed all these standards and beliefs, we still find that great disagreements remain in the accounts of the events in Dallas.

Next, we turn to physical evidence that has lasted beyond the fleeting few seconds in which the President was shot. This includes the physical evidence of the bullet fragments; the medical findings; the damage to the car, the manhole, and the spectator; the Zapruder pictures; and many other photographs taken at the time. Experts in pathology, firearms, and photographic analysis dispute the reliability and interpretation of this evidence. For example, people have questioned whether bullet #399 was part of the sequence of shots or claim that it was planted in order to implicate Oswald.

The tremendous interest in the Kennedy assassination has made people aware of the difficulty of ascertaining facts. The problems involved introduce some of the basic issues in philosophy concerning the nature, sources, and reliability of our knowledge. The Kennedy case shows how elusive the bare facts are and how even with the best technical equipment experts can disagree. Even quite outrageous possibilities can seem to fit with many of the facts. For example, one person who made an exhaustive study of the available data hypothesized that a body other than Kennedy's was examined at the Bethesda autopsy.

The problems faced in ascertaining the facts in Kennedy's assassination are similar to problems of verification that we face all the time. The Kennedy case provides a lesson for the foundation of our knowledge. If the leader of our country could be shot in broad daylight before six hundred people, with all sorts of ocular and photographic evidence, and after exhaustive examination of the data the facts are still in dispute, then what *can* we be sure of?

The Kennedy problem so haunted our country that investigations were made of the investigators, revealing reasons for doubting the findings of the FBI and the CIA. The work done by the Dallas police turned out to be highly questionable. The records of the Warren Commission revealed a lack of thoroughness, unwillingness to consider conflicting data, and hasty and biased investigations. The case raised so much doubt (polls repeatedly showed that about two thirds of the American population and most of the Europeans questioned doubted the findings of the Warren Commission) that the credibility of our institutions was being undermined. Congress finally decided to conduct its own investigation in 1977.

In the course of this investigation, fourteen years after the event, new data were discovered. A sound record of the sequence of events was uncovered, made from the radio on a police motorcycle believed by some to be located near the car in which Kennedy was riding. Some acoustics experts analyzed the sounds and reported they believed that shots came from two directions. Under questioning, the experts admitted they could be wrong. Other acoustics experts specializing in submarine detection reported they were certain the shots came from two directions and that at least one shot came from the "grassy knoll." The FBI experts and the Dallas police both disputed this. The congressional committee ended its investigations and early in 1979 announced that President Kennedy had been killed by two gunmen, but they had no theory about the nature of the plot. In the meantime new criticisms of the acoustical analysis have been made. The National Academy of Science carried on its own investigation and reported that the recording began at least one second after the shooting and therefore throws no light on the sequence of events. But will that finding end the controversy?

Is there any way we can find out what actually happened? The raw data are confusing, and the expert evaluation conflicting. So our knowledge about this and similar observable events is open to question. Can we find guaranteed ways of resolving these questions? We will see in the first chapter some of the basic problems of philosophy that are raised by such inquiries, problems that force us to look into the foundations of our claims to knowledge.

Suppose we accept either the Warren Commission view or the congressional one. In either case, further questions of motivation arise. Why did the events happen? Who was responsible? The Warren Commission never found satisfactory motive for Oswald. He seemed to have admired Kennedy as a president. In his book on the case, Gerald Ford tried to find a motive in Oswald's purported Communist political beliefs. Others gave weight to his psychological problems. It was even suggested that Oswald was a "Manchurian candidate," a brainwashed killer programed by some group that wanted to eliminate the President. If there were two gunmen acting in concert, the motivational possibilities are far greater. Since there was never a trial, there was no opportunity to explore questions of motivation under rigorous courtroom conditions. From the conflicts of data and interpretation and the lack of a known motive, one can imagine a clever lawyer having a field day defending Oswald.

In the case of the assassination of Robert F. Kennedy (also a public event with conflicts of eyewitnesses and experts), the trial of the purported assassin, Sirhan Sirhan, dealt chiefly with motive and responsibility. The central issue was whether the defendant could be held responsible for his acts. Was he insane? Did he have diminished ability to tell what he was doing or to control himself as a result of being drugged, drunk, or hypnotized? The trial was more a battle of psychiatrists offering differing analyses of Sirhan's mental condition than an examination of the external facts. Involved in evaluating these analyses are fundamental philosophical issues that we will explore in some of the chapters, such as the following: What is the relationship between mental events and physical ones? What responsibility do we have for our actions? If we have no power to make a choice, can we be said to have done something right or wrong, good or bad?

One psychiatrist at the Sirhan trial claimed that Sirhan's experience as a child in Palestine during the Arab-Israeli conflict and his relationship with his father led to his destructive act. This raises the possibility that Sirhan did not have free will but was caused to act in a certain way because of circumstances in his life beyond his control. Does such an evaluation extend to the entire human condition? Are our actions no more than the sum of the effects upon us of the environment in which we live? Or does our nature have some component that enables us to make independent decisions that produce various consequences? Put more generally, are we and all other living beings just complicated physical and biochemical entities that act in obedience to physical laws, or are we to some extent free agents?

(As we shall see, recent scientific work concerning biochemical treatment of certain mental conditions forces us to consider carefully the nature of a person. Dependent upon such consideration are the questions of human responsibility. The question of what constitutes personality and when it emerges significantly in our biological nature is, of course, at the heart of the controversy over abortion. Is a fetus a person? Is it a person at conception, three months after conception, six months after conception, or at birth?)

Assuming that human beings are free agents, what rights and responsibilities do they have? Taking the matter beyond ethical into political philosophy, what rights do people have as members of a society? Are there limits to what people should be allowed to say or do in a society?

Obviously trying someone like Sirhan Sirhan for murder, or John Hinckley for the attempted murder of President Reagan, assumes that people should not be allowed to destroy other people. But is this always the case? Can killing be justified in self-defense or during warfare? Is mercy killing valid? These issues require careful philosophical consideration of the proper role of the individual in society.

A murder trial raises the question of human responsibility. One does not put cars or guns or poisons on trial, but the human agents who used them. But what is a human agent? A defense often raised is that a person was not responsible at the moment of the commission of the crime because of circumstances beyond her or his control. Premeditation seems to indicate the person was responsible. A premeditated killing is assigned a special category—murder in the first degree. But if we are the products of biochemical states within us, of environmental conditioning, do we decide what we do, or are we forced to do it, in the same way a gun is forced to fire when the trigger mechanism is squeezed? The man who killed Mayor Moscone of San Francisco in 1978 offered as a defense that his consumption of large quantities of fast-food desserts and sweet drinks caused chemical effects on his brain, making him very depressed and leading him to shoot the mayor. Reputable scientists supported this claim. He was still found guilty because the jury felt that regardless of what he ate and how it affected him, he was responsible for his actions and that his actions were morally and legally wrong. The jury also found that because of his circumstances he had diminished responsibility for his actions, and they gave him a moderate sentence. (The question of the nature of our moral behavior will be taken up in the third chapter, and of our social and political status in the fourth chapter. The final chapter on the philosophy of religion will deal with overall religious evaluations of the human and physical world.)

This new collection of readings provides an unusual approach to the traditional problems of philosophy that have arisen from the efforts of thinkers to develop sets of rational, consistent, and broad-ranging principles for understanding the world and for providing sensible guidelines for acting in it.

Roughly speaking, such problems fall into two categories. The first concerns the nature of reality. Typical questions in this area that philosophers have asked include: What is the world really like? What are its ultimate constituents? How can we speak about the world consistently and significantly? How can we obtain knowledge of it, and what is such knowledge like? Democritus, Plato, Aristotle, Descartes, Spinoza, and Kant are among the distinguished figures of the past who offered theoretical answers to these questions. Other philosophers looked on the possibility of reaching any such answers with skepticism. Bishop Berkeley, for example, suggested that there are reasonable grounds for doubting that an external world, a world independent of our conception of it, exists or that anyone could acquire knowledge of it if it did exist. With the passage of time, the kinds of issues in this general category have come to be treated more specifically in such areas as *metaphysics*, which focuses on the nature of reality; *epistemology*, which treats the nature of knowledge; *logic*, which deals with our ability to reason coherently; and the *philosophy of language*, which studies how we can speak meaningfully about the world. A good example of a problem in philosophy of language is the following. In order to speak about the world, our words must refer to something. There must be a direct connection between words and corresponding objects in the world. We can talk about cats, for example, because they are the referents of the word *cat*. But how can we speak significantly and truly about things that do not or cannot exist? We can say that Julius Caesar was a Roman general and that he crossed the Rubicon. We can say that there are no round squares. Yet how can we talk about Caesar and about round squares if such "things" do not exist? What do our words refer to in such cases? In classical times this was called the problem of non-being. It has remained a puzzle into the twentieth century and is the main topic of a theory developed by Bertrand Russell called "the theory of descriptions."

The second category of problems is quite different. It presupposes that the sorts of epistemological and logical puzzles belonging to the first category have been settled in their broad outlines. It takes as given that there is an external world of which human beings can acquire knowledge and about which significant discourse is possible. This second category also assumes that the world is inhabited by many human beings with minds, the content of which is knowable to other human beings—for example, that we can know when another person is in pain. The kinds of issues dealt with in the first category are thus moved into the background or regarded as irrelevant. The problems dealt with in this second category are practical and applied and revolve around two broad sets of questions: Which of the main features of the world are valuable, desirable, or good; which are not; and why? Are there better or worse types of relationships between people; if so, what are they; and why are they better or worse? The specific areas of philosophy that treat such questions are *ethics*, which examines issues of good and bad, right and wrong; and *political theory*, which seeks to discover desirable forms of human social association. Plato, Hobbes, Locke, and Mill are among the eminent theorists who have advanced answers to these difficult questions. To be sure, issues of skepticism arise in this second general category, as in the first, but the thrust of this skepticism is different. Here the issue is whether objectivity is possible in morals, aesthetics, and politics, or, on the contrary, whether one person's opinion is as good as another's. Is the life of a drug addict provably inferior to the life of someone who shuns drugs? Can the pursuit of pleasure for oneself be shown to be a worthwhile way of life? Is it objectively right for some persons to exercise authority and control over others in society? This skepticism regarding values, often called "philosophical relativism," is captured in a memorable phrase by the Greek sophist Protagoras, who said that "man is the measure of all things."

The readings that follow belong to both categories. Like most traditional approaches to the fundamental issues of philosophy, ours deal both with questions about the nature of reality and with questions about the proper evaluations of its features. It is a well-founded opinion among philosophers that if reflective persons pursue a conceptual issue long enough, no matter how trivial the question from which they start, they will ultimately find themselves discussing the kinds of questions that fall into these two categories. People who wish to buy a new car may at some stage ask themselves whether the car is worth the money it costs, what they are giving up in other areas of life to purchase it, and whether in terms of ultimate values it is really worth having a car. Of course, most persons faced with this sort of practical problem do not pursue these reflections systematically or at length, but if they did, such questions would lead to fundamental issues about what is valuable in human life and how one ought to order one's priorities in living. The deepest questions of philosophy in fact begin from such relatively trivial matters; with a little persistence one may find oneself suddenly immersed in conceptual waters that seem to have no bottom.

Of course, most textbooks in philosophy are written or edited by professional philosophers. As sophisticated thinkers, they tend not to focus on the trivial, practical, or mundane concerns of daily living but instead to plunge into the deepest waters of theory. If we were to follow this practice, we believe that our readers would not understand why philosophy is an important subject and why it is worth pursuing. They might not appreciate how ordinary practical issues are ultimately connected with the abstract and often abstruse deliberations of professional philosophers. Issues about the existence of the external world or access to the mind of another seem remote compared with the urgent and pressing practical conundrums that most of us face daily.

This new collection of readings provides an unusual approach to the main issues in philosophy. In contrast to the organization of a traditional textbook, which might begin with Descartes' proofs of his own existence or Berkeley's sophisticated arguments that mind is the only reality, we start from current issues that are grist for the ordinary person's mill. We first examine the assassination of President John F. Kennedy and the deep epistemological issues that the event raises concerning the nature of human testimony and the kind of knowledge upon which it is based. We then discuss the main ethical issues surrounding abortion, concentrating on the question of whether it is ever justified to kill an innocent person and how this question deepens into the recondite issues discussed in utilitarian moral theory. Our book thus *arrives* at the views of Plato, Descartes, Mill, and so on, rather than immediately plunging the reader into these views. Like all such texts in philosophy, ours aims to present the reader with the central issues of the discipline, but it also tries to fill in the steps from the mundane to the theoretical in a way seldom found in such literature today.

Each of the chapters that follow presents a series of views from leading thinkers. We start with a present-day statement concerning the basic issues involved, and then turn back to some of the significant discussions of these issues in the writings of great philosophers from ancient times to the present day. Letting the philosophers speak for themselves, we trust that students will find their writings stimulating, will consider the philosophers' views, and will seek to find their own answers to these basic questions about ourselves and our place in the cosmos.

R. H. Popkin
Avrum Stroll

1
EPISTEMOLOGY

We all find that people disagree with us about what we experience, how we interpret an experience, and what we believe based on an experience. Sometimes we explain these disagreements as a result of different conditions of sense organs or different situations in which the experience takes place. For instance, we say that some people are color-blind and hence do not see what we see; some are tone-deaf and do not hear what we hear; some are nearsighted, others hard of hearing, and so on. We also explain that people may disagree because they have too much alcohol in their systems or have been affected by drugs. And we explain that there are disagreements because people have not tried hard enough to see, hear, taste, smell, or feel certain qualities, or have tried to experience them under strange conditions—for example, tasting something when it is too hot, looking at a picture when there is not enough light, and so on.

We find that some of these disagreements can be accounted for by different backgrounds, customs, education, and geography. For example, Finns are more adept than southern Californians at noticing differences in types of snowflakes. People like or dislike various experiences in part because of their upbringing and the attitudes of those around them.

As we find ways of accounting for our disagreements, we also find that some people are so persistently opposed to our view of experience that we cannot explain our differences by these physiological, cultural, and sociological factors. In some cases we decide that the disagreements are due to some fault in the other person that is more than physiological and declare that he or she is crazy, that his or her mental equipment is not functioning properly.

This distinction between the sane and the insane goes back to ancient literature. The Greeks had a saying that "Those whom the gods would destroy, they first make mad." Various people in the Bible are described as being "out of their mind." We also read about a more positive kind of madness that Plato called "divine madness." The prophet, the inspired person appears to have experience beyond that of normal people. Joan of Arc claimed to have heard voices that led her to save her country. Various religious people claim to have had mystical experiences or revelations. And then we also find various types of antisocial people who justify their aberrant behavior because of their private experiences or private interpretations of experiences.

On what basis do we distinguish the sane from the insane? Does any objective standard of insanity exist, or only subjective measures that we use to push aside those who are too different from ourselves? Tolstoy asked in his novel *Resurrection*, Am I mad because the world looks like this to me, or is the world mad because it looks like this to me?

In the present age, when the treatment of insanity as mental illness has become part of general medical practice and when psychiatrists and psychoanalysts are trained to specialize in the treatment of mental disorders, is it clear who is sane and who is insane? Do we at last have objective, scientific standards?

Day after day, as people are arrested for various kinds of antisocial behavior ranging from child abuse, to rape, to robbery, to assault, the question is raised as to whether the defendant is criminally insane, or was temporarily insane at the time of the commission of the crime. Should the defendant be sent to a mental hospital for treatment or to a jail for punishment? We find little agreement among psychiatrists and other experts. The trial of John Hinckley, who shot President Reagan, brought out sharply the conflicting opinions of experts over the definition of sanity.

Further questions about the reliability or scientific objectivity of the standards for judging sanity are raised by the case of persons who convince military doctors they are insane when they are about to be drafted, and who then revert to normal behavior as soon as the military is no longer interested in them. Experiments have been made in which a normal, sane person is admitted to a mental hospital and then feigns symptoms usually associated with insanity in order to see how the psychiatrists diagnose his or her case. The usual result of the experiment is that the doctors accept the false clues and classify the person as suffering from some kind of mental illness, whereas the patients in the hospital are not misled.

All of this begins to make one doubt whether we can really tell who is sane and who is not. The treatment of Soviet dissidents as insane indicates that the classification may be political rather than medical. We can also see echoes of this in our own country. During the Vietnam War, some students who burned their draft cards in protest against the war were sent to the Federal Mental Facility in Springfield, Missouri, for mental examination and observation before they were tried. It was assumed that their protest represented some mental aberration or illness. People who make threats—verbal or written—against the President of the United States are sent for psychiatric examination. This happened immediately to John Hinckley after he shot at President Ronald Reagan.

Diagnosis of insanity has changed so much throughout the ages that we should hesitate to think of our present practice as indisputably correct. People have been accused of being witches or being possessed by the devil for what we would now consider minor deviations from normal behavior. People were put in mental hospitals fifty or a hundred years ago for behavior that is now accepted or that can be altered by taking a pill. Epileptics were once considered insane because of their seizures, which we now know to be physiologically produced and medically controllable.

A contemporary psychoanalyst, Thomas Szasz, has questioned the framework in which the distinction between sanity and insanity is made. Szasz has challenged the very basis of abnormal psychology. On the first page of his book *The Myth of Mental Illness* (1961) he declares, "I submit that the traditional definition of psychiatry, which is still in vogue, places it alongside such things as alchemy, and astrology, and commits it to the category of pseudo-science. Psychiatry is said to be a medical speciality concerned with the study and treatment of mental illness. Similarly, astrology was the study of the influence of planetary movements and positions on human behavior and destiny." In each case Szasz argues that there is nothing to study. Examining the history of the development of the study of mental illness over the last century, Szasz contends that types of human behavior have been interpreted as manifestations of illnesses and a whole branch of medicine, "psychiatry," has developed to treat these illnesses. Actually, he claims, the deviant behavior results from different ethical and cultural norms and is not a medical condition at all.

If there is no mental illness, madness or insanity may be culturally conditioned classifications to justify restricting some kinds of behavior. Michel Foucault's *Madness and Civilization: A History of Insanity in the Age of Reason* has put into sharp focus how the post-Renaissance world developed the distinction between rationality and madness. By studying this historical and cultural setting, one is forced to see that the distinction represents a way society deals with an aspect of human experience by creating a whole social apparatus of doctors, hospitals, drugs, and insane asylums that may have no ultimate justification.

This returns us to the fundamental issue of whether we can *know*, with genuine certainty, what is going on in our world. Is there at least some degree of doubt about all of our purported knowledge? Earlier philosophers, including Plato, Descartes, Pascal, and Hume, implied that one of the major reasons for taking skepticism seriously is that our so-called knowledge may just be a form of madness. We conclude that other people are insane, but what we take as our own sanity may be just another form of insanity. Unless we can find an objective criterion for sanity, our best rational efforts may degenerate into personal madness.

Josef Breuer and Sigmund Freud claimed to have found just such a criterion in their studies on hysteria, from which a major modern treatment for mental illness developed. Freud and his followers have given us categories for classifying people as mentally ill: schizophrenia, paranoid schizophrenia, manic depression. Most recently, as we see in the next chapter, attempts have been made to reduce these categories of mental illness to biochemical conditions, thereby giving a more objective measure. But a measure of what? Are we assessing mental health, balance, and accuracy, or are we measuring certain biochemical conditions on the same level as sugar content in urine or blood pressure? Arne Naess, a contemporary thinker, has argued that adopting complete skepticism leads to mental health. Some ancient Greek skeptics known as the Pyrrhonists, presented skepticism as a form of medical therapy, claiming most people suffer from anxiety, worrying about whether what they believe is true or false. They may carry these worries to the point of insanity. However, if people doubt and question their beliefs and suspend judgment as to their truth or falsity, they will find peace of mind.

In opposition to obsessive doubt we have been offered a panacea, scientific knowledge, which purports to be objective and subject to verification. It is said that such knowledge can give us a genuine basis for describing our world and its operation. The success of modern science—pure and applied—in solving our problems and answering our questions has been so impressive that it has taken over most of our educational system. From Copernicus and Galileo to Newton, Einstein, the atomic bomb, space travel, and DNA, some of the most baffling aspects of human experience have been examined and found to be intelligible in terms of scientific concepts. The discovery of lawful relationships between those concepts has enabled us to change our environment, cure many diseases, mechanize our labor, improve our means of killing each other, and increase our agricultural yields.

Amid the triumphs of scientific achievement in the second half of this century, two kinds of doubts have been raised about the entire scientific enterprise, one by the philosopher Paul Feyerabend, harking back to Szasz's view, and the other by a historian of science, Thomas Kuhn. Szasz had questioned whether psychoanalysis was any better than pseudo-sciences like astrology and alchemy. Feyerabend went many steps further by asking whether one can tell the difference between science and pseudo-science with any accuracy or whether any intellectually justifiable standard can be offered for distinguishing scientific from unscientific or pseudo-scientific assertions.

Feyerabend was stimulated to raise this question by the skeptical implications in an essay entitled "Proofs and Refutations," by the brilliant Hungarian philosopher Imre Lakatos. Lakatos had traced the history of a mathematical theorem set down by the great eighteenth-century Swiss mathematician Leonhard Euler. Almost immediately after he published this theorem, evidence was offered that it was false. Mathematicians for more than two hundred years have been rescuing Euler's theorem by strategies that Lakatos called "concept-stretching" and "monster-barring." No amount of refutation has sufficed to dismiss the theorem.

Lakatos' article suggested that the same is the case with scientific claims. Although scientists assert that their results were testable while pseudo-scientific ones were not, in fact how does one decide when a sufficient test has occurred or if a supposed test was really a test? Feyerabend developed these sorts of questions into a systematic skeptical attack on scientific reasoning, arguing that it is not possible to give an adequate rationally justifiable basis for counting some results as scientific and others as not.

A different kind of skepticism about science arose from the work of Thomas Kuhn, an important historian of science. In studying the controversy in the sixteenth and seventeenth centuries over the acceptance of Copernican and Galilean astronomy, Kuhn found that not only did the opponents of this new astronomy have good scientific reasons for their opposition, but, more important, that the acceptance of the new astronomy and Newtonian physics was based on social and cultural, rather than scientific, factors. Kuhn argued that scientific theories do not get refuted, they get replaced. The reasons for their replacement relate to the role science plays in a society and especially to the social, economic, and cultural forces affecting scientific research. We may not be able to tell what is true scientific knowledge, but only what the state of science represents in a given society.

Feyerabend and Kuhn challenged in their own ways the vaunted achievements of modern science and raised skeptical questions about the possibility of genuine scientific knowledge. If we turn back to the beginning of scientific efforts in the Western world in ancient Greece, we find Plato and Aristotle each attempting to determine what genuine scientific knowledge is possible. After the radical challenge against medieval Aristotelian science by Galileo, the great French mathematician, physicist, and philosopher René Descartes tried to offer a basis for modern science that would be so certain that none of the doubts of the skeptics could shake it. A century later, the skeptical Scottish philosopher David Hume questioned some of the basic assumptions of scientific reasoning and concluded that we cannot know the causal relations between events or whether future events will occur in the same fashion as past or present events, that the basis for our believing scientific laws was psychological rather than logical.

A generation after Hume, Immanuel Kant sought to show that we can find true knowledge about experience. This, he maintained, does not mean that we can gain scientific knowledge about reality, but rather that we can discover the necessary conditions under which to gain scientific knowledge. These conditions apply only to our experience, and we have no way of telling if they apply beyond this area. Kant contended that all our experience has to take place spatially and temporally. Therefore, we can be certain that the theorems of Euclidean geometry apply to our experience. The interior angles of every experienced triangle will add up to 180 degrees. But we have no way of knowing if this is true of *real* triangles, those existing independent of our experience.

The evaluations of scientific knowledge by Hume and Kant have shaped the interpretation of science ever since. Most scientists accept the tentative nature of their own findings and grant that they may have to be revised or even rejected in the light of future information. These scientists probably also grant that science does not and cannot achieve the kind of ultimate knowledge Plato, Aristotle, and Descartes sought.

Two important twentieth-century discussions of scientific knowledge have been presented by Bertrand Russell and Karl Popper. Russell tended to accept and intensify the skeptical problems raised by Hume. He sought to describe what our scientific activities could amount to in light of what we now know about mental activities. Popper tried to transcend the skeptical impasse that resulted from the thinking of Hume and Kant. He sought to show that scientific investigation can continue without overcoming the skeptical doubts about its methods and principles. Some feel, however, that he has avoided rather than answered the question of whether genuine scientific knowledge is possible.

While research goes on in astronomy, astrophysics, physics, chemistry, bio-chemistry, biology, psychology, and the other sciences, the debate about the cognitive value of new scientific discoveries continues. Do these discoveries tell us any ultimate truths? Or do they just provide techniques that are socially useful for dealing with our experience?

We also find that in spite of the careful specification of experimental method and evaluation and interpretations of results, scientific scandals still occur. Well-trained, seemingly reliable scientists sometimes admit to faking their data. Politics also enters into science. Certain results and interpretations desired by the scientific community are easily published and disseminated, while others get little hearing. Long after the fact, we find out why certain clues were not followed up, why certain theories were taught and accepted long after they became outdated.

In the selections that follow we look at the two overriding questions raised in this introductory discussion: How does one tell who is mad and who is sane? and Is there genuine scientific knowledge? With regard to the first question, we first present the challenge to accepted criteria presently being made by Szasz. Then we turn to earlier discussions of this issue, starting in antiquity with Plato and moving on to Descartes, Pascal, and Hume. Then we examine part of the seminal study on hysteria by Sigmund Freud and Josef Breuer that launched the psychoanalytic movement and eventually led to the current scientific means of determining sanity and insanity. Finally we look at Arne Naess' views on the relation of skepticism to mental health.

We move on to consideration of the second question. Selections by Paul Feyerabend and Thomas Kuhn indicate reasons presently being offered by serious critics to challenge the possibility of genuine scientific knowledge. Then we again turn back to the classics to see Plato's and Aristotle's views of scientific knowledge and how it is obtained. Descartes, one of the theoreticians of modern science, suggests that genuine scientific knowledge can be obtained and that it is guaranteed by God. The skeptical questioning of this kind of assurance by Hume and a proposed solution to skeptical difficulties by Kant follow.

We conclude by looking at a twentieth-century formulation by Sir Karl Popper, who recognized the uncertainty of scientific knowledge but sought to show that this did not prevent the continuation of rational activity.

We hope that in examining the readings that follow the student will understand some of the basic problems in epistemology and will begin to work out her or his own solutions to them.

A. HOW DO WE TELL WHO IS MAD?

Thomas Szasz

THE MYTH OF MENTAL ILLNESS

Thomas S. Szasz (b. 1920), a Hungarian-born psychiatrist, has written many works challenging accepted medical and psycho-analytic views.

Hysteria as a typical example of mental illness was chosen as the starting point for our inquiry into the nature of self-experience and personal conduct. Charcot, Breuer, Freud, and many of their contemporaries observed that certain patterns of human behavior—or, more precisely, certain modes of nonverbal communication—resembled neurological illnesses, yet differed from them in crucial ways. For historical and social reasons, the phenomena in question were *defined* and *classified* as members of the class "disease." Thus, hysteria as a quasi-neurological illness formed the nucleus around which the vast structure of "psychopathology" gradually crystallized.

ORIGIN OF THE MODERN CONCEPT OF MENTAL ILLNESS

Hysteria and the Concept of Illness

The error of classifying hysteria as an illness, with emphasis on its similarities to known neurological diseases, is attributable mainly to the nineteenth-century reductionist conception of personal conduct. According to this view, all behavior was regarded as a problem in muscle and nerve physiology. As a tabetic ataxia was explained by certain nerve lesions, it was assumed that normal behavior too could be adequately explained by describing its neuroanatomical and neurophysiological correlates. This approach rested on the

18

erroneous belief that there were no significant differences between complex items of learned behavior on the one hand, and the behavioral manifestations of *defects of the body* on the other hand. It followed that whenever defective functioning of the body was encountered it was regarded as *prima facie* evidence of illness. In view of the practical task of the neurologist, it is easy to see why he should have been especially prone to make this mistake. It often happens that diseases of the nervous system (for example, multiple sclerosis, brain tumor) first manifest themselves by peculiarities in personal conduct. It was tempting to conclude from such occurrences that brain and behavior stand in a simple type of cause-and-effect relationship to each other.

This approach was consistent with the prevalent philosophical preconceptions of medical workers concerning the principles of their science. It allowed them to treat as medical problems all manner of complicated human situations that found overt expression in the patient's belief that he was ill. If known methods of physiochemical examination failed to reveal the presence of bodily disease, this was of no great concern. The late nineteenth-century physician's model of disease was derived from his experiences with tuberculosis, syphilis, and typhoid fever. As the causes of these illnesses had been discovered by medical science, so it would be with hysteria and mental illnesses.

Charcot succeeded in making hysteria acceptable to the medical profession. This achievement, however, was in the nature of a social reform, not a scientific discovery. Although some members of suffering humanity were promoted, as it were, to higher social rank, this was attained at the cost of obscuring the logical character of the observed phenomena.

Because of the conceptual make-up of late nineteenth-century psychiatry, hysteria was compared and contrasted with malingering on the one hand, and with "real illness" on the other. The persistent medical and psychiatric opinion that behavior which imitated illness was an effort to cheat or fool doctors made it necessary to condemn it. Hence, physicians who wished to prevent the condemnation of people exhibiting this type of behavior had to insist that such patients *were* "ill." In this way their behavior could still be described as essentially illness-imitating—and could be studied scientifically—while at the same time the pejorative diagnosis of malingering could be avoided. This strategy contained a hidden danger. The notion of illness, at first used mainly with a socially promotive aim in mind, rapidly became accepted as the correct description of "facts." The expression "mental illness" was not understood in a metaphorical sense as it should have been, but attained a high degree of concretization and began to lead a life of its own. Now it is a *panchreston* (Hardin, 1956), a word that is supposed to explain everything, whereas it explains nothing and serves only to hinder our critical understanding. In modern psychiatry this thesis is exemplified by the persistent denial that a person may *wish* to imitate sickness and *play the role* of a disabled person without necessarily being sick. The nosological categorization of every possible feature of malingering as a manifestation of mental illness is a result of this tendency.

Sociology of the Physician–Patient Relationship

In late nineteenth-century Europe and America, medical care could be obtained by purchase and owned, much as private property. Private medical practice became an integral part of capitalistic, individualistic society. Those who could not afford to buy this commodity were forced to obtain it—as they did many other things in life—through the charity of others. The private practice type of relationship between physician and patient was a crucial antecedent of the psychoanalytic situation. In both, the therapist was the patient's agent, in contrast to being the agent of some other person or group.

Nineteenth-century medical practice may be profitably compared to contemporary Western practices. Today, medical practice is characterized by a mixture of *private* and *insured* situations. The insurance scheme introduces third (and fourth, etc.) parties into the transaction between sufferer and healer. Finally, in the Soviet system of medical practice the physician is an agent of the state. Depending on the type of disability the patient has, the Soviet medical system readily leads to various conflicts between physician, patient, and state. The concept of malingering is very much in vogue in Russia, whereas in Western countries it has largely been displaced by the concepts of hysteria, neurosis, and mental illness. None of these terms denotes or describes a "disease entity." Actually, they arise from and reflect characteristic features of the social matrix of the therapeutic situation. They point to covert preferences of individualistic or collectivistic ethics and their attendant notions concerning the duties and privileges of citizen and state in regard to each other.

What Is Psychiatry?

It is customary to define psychiatry as a medical specialty concerned with the study, diagnosis, and treatment of mental illnesses. This is a worthless and misleading definition. Mental illness is a myth. Psychiatrists are not concerned with mental illnesses and their treatments. In actual practice they deal with personal, social, and ethical problems in living.

I have argued that, today, the notion of a person "having mental illness" is scientifically crippling. It provides professional assent to a popular rationalization, namely, that problems in human living experienced and expressed in terms of bodily feelings or signs (or in terms of other "psychiatric symptoms") are significantly similar to *diseases of the body*. It also undermines the principle of personal responsibility, upon which a democratic political system is necessarily based, by assigning to an external source (i.e., the "illness") the blame for antisocial behavior. We know that for the individual patient this attitude precludes an inquiring, psychoanalytic approach to problems which "symptoms" at once hide and express. Codifying every type of occurrence that takes place in a medical setting as, *ipso facto*, a medical problem makes about as much sense as suggesting that when physicists quarrel their argument constitutes a problem in physics. . . .

SEMIOTICAL ANALYSIS OF BEHAVIOR

The bodily signs of conversion hysteria—for example, an hysterical seizure or paralysis—were chosen as typical examples of at least one type of so-called psychiatric symptom. Our inquiry was focused on the following questions: (1) What type of language, or communication system, is employed by persons exhibiting this kind of behavior? (2) What type of object relationship is secured and maintained by means of hysterical communications? (3) What are the specific interpersonal functions of indirect communications in general, and of dreams and certain "psychiatric symptoms" in particular?

The "Psychiatric Symptom" as a Form of Picture Language

It was found that a sign relation of iconicity was the chief characteristic of signs typically encountered in hysterical symptom-communications. An iconic sign is defined as an object, X, which because of its similarity to another object, Y, is used to denote the latter. The relation of similarity (iconicity) is usually based on appearance, as for example in a photograph. It may also be based on function. Thus, animals may symbolize (represent) people, as in cartoons, because both exhibit manifestations of life.

The observation that hysterical symptoms depict certain occurrences was originally made by Freud. He asserted that hysteria was like a pantomime, or dumb-show, in which the patient expressed a message by means of nonverbal signs. Pseudocyesis is a good example. It is a pictorial representation of the idea "I am pregnant." Hysterical body language therefore consists essentially of pictures. As such, it is similar to other picture languages, such as *picture puzzles* or *charades*. In each of these, communication is achieved by means of pictures (iconic signs) instead of words (conventional signs). In a picture puzzle, the name "Forrestal" may be depicted by showing a picture of several trees to the right of which is placed a tall man. Given such a puzzle, the task is to translate from picture language to word language. Similarly, in the game of charades, a proverb, quotation, or almost anything "spelled out" in words must be so "acted out" by one of the players that his teammates shall recognize the message. In both of the examples cited, there is a two-way process of translation or sign-transformation. In charades, the person who acts out the message must translate from English (or some other ordinary language) to pantomime, while his teammates must reverse the process by transforming pantomime back into English. In hysteria, and in many other behavioral phenomena as well, the task of the psychiatrist is similar to that confronting a person who tries to unravel a picture puzzle. The meaning of hysteria—stated in the form of a picture language, or, more precisely, in the form of a language composed of iconic signs—must be rendered into everyday verbal language.

The logical character of communications composed of iconic body signs was then compared to other types of communications. Since hysterical body language constitutes a mode of communication logically inferior to that of object and metalanguages, it was designated a protolanguage. Ordinary object language stands in a meta relation to protolanguage.

The Functions of Protolanguage

Protolanguage may serve all the cognitive and instrumental uses of ordinary language. The differences in usefulness between an iconic sign language and a conventional symbol language lie in the degree to which the various language functions may be exercised by means of each. Thus, for purely cognitive purposes, protolanguage is greatly inferior to object and metalanguages. It is superior, however, for purposes of affective and promotive communication. Thus, the facial expression of grave suffering, perhaps accompanied by tears and groans, usually is more effective in imparting a mood and in inducing a wished-for action, than the simple statement "I am in pain."

Protolanguage is relatively nondiscursive. This is inherent in its being composed of iconic rather than conventional signs. The former mode of symbolization embodies a more idiosyncratic or private sign relationship than does the latter. The most public or impersonal language systems (for example, mathematics, the Morse code) are the most discursive, while the typically private or personal idioms (for example, an "hysterical" or "schizophrenic" symptom) are relatively nondiscursive. Because of the iconicity and nondiscursiveness of hysterical body language, it affords vast possibilities for mistakes and misunderstandings in cognitive communication. Exploration of the cognitive or informative use of iconic body signs made it possible to ask whether such communication might be similar to mistakes and lies in everyday language. An analysis of this problem disclosed that there is a compelling parallelism between the concepts of malingering, hysteria, and (ordinary "organic") illness on the one hand and the concepts of lying, making a mistake, and telling the truth on the other.

Considerations of the uses of iconic body signs in a psychiatric context led, finally, to highlighting an hitherto unrecognized function of this mode of communicative behavior. The object-seeking and relationship-maintaining function of any type of communication was arrived at by a combined semiotical and object relations approach to problems of communication in psychiatry. This point of view lends special force to the interpretation of such things as the dance, religious ritual, and the representative arts. In each of these, the participant or the viewer is enabled *to enter into a significant human relationship by means of a particular system of communication.* The same is true, of course, for logically higher levels of language, such as mathematics. Scientists achieve and maintain object contact with their colleagues by means of special languages, just as members of primitive tribes may gratify similar needs by means of a ritual dance. It is significant, however, that the language of science has, in addition to its object-relations aspect, a cognitive facet as well, and that this is largely, although not entirely, absent in the more primitive communicative modes. Still, considerations of object contact are at least potentially relevant in connection with all sign-using functions.

The Uses of Indirect Communications

Hysteria or any mental illness may also be considered an indirect communication or language that is used ambiguously, usually in order to give the recipient of the message a choice between several alternative replies. Hints, allusions, and metaphorical expressions of all kinds are everyday examples of indirect communications. The need for this mode of communication arises typically in the family. The social conditions of this unit make it necessary that family members curb their wishes and hence also the explicit symbolic representations of them. This leads to the inhibition ("repression") of direct forms of communication and provides the stimulus for the development of relatively more devious, or indirect, forms of need-communicative behavior. The function of hinting was illustrated by an analysis of dream communication. The "hysterical symptom" may also be regarded as a hint addressed to the patient's significant objects or to physicians.

The chief advantages of hinting—and hence of hysteria—are the following: (1) It provides a mode of sending a message whose effect is feared, either because the communication pertains to the expression of an ego-alien wish or because it is an aggressive reproach against a loved but needed person. (2) It permits the expression of a communication without full commitment to it. In other words, it provides an escape route should the message misfire or backfire. (3) It makes it possible for a person to be granted what he desires without having to ask for it explicitly. It thus protects the help-seeking person from being humiliated should his request be denied. This is an exceedingly important mechanism, commonly used by children. It is also employed by adults, either because they have retained certain childish ideals (for example, "I should not need anything or anybody"), or because they find themselves in a situation in which they feel more strongly committed to a person than the "objective conditions" would warrant (for example, "love at first sight"). In these situations, hinting—whether by means of socially acceptable metaphors or "mental symptoms"—provides an exploratory mode of communication.

Situations of close personal interdependence favor indirect communications, whereas certain more impersonal, functional types of social relations foster direct communications. In the psychoanalytic situation, the hinting functions of hysteria, dreams, and other "mental symptoms" are subjected to persistent scrutiny. Indeed, it may be said that one of the aims of the analytic process is to induce the patient to relinquish his indirect ("symptomatic," "transference") communications and to substitute for them direct messages framed in the straightforward idiom of ordinary English. This is accomplished by placing him in a situation in which hinting is not rewarded, as it might be in ordinary life, but direct communication is. This is inherent in the conditions of the analytic situation, in which an explicit positive value is placed on direct communication (absolute truthfulness, privacy of the two-person situation, etc.). Thus, the interpersonal conditions of analysis are such as to favor a process of change in regard to the patient's (habitual) sign-using behavior.

In this regard, being in analysis could be compared to going to a foreign country for purposes of study. By means of this analogy, the double impact of psychoanalysis on the patient's sign-using behavior may be illustrated. First, it induces him to give up his habitual mode of communicating (mother tongue, symptom language) and to substitute for it a *new language* (foreign language, direct communication in ordinary language). To accomplish this alone, however, might be merely a "transference cure." Ideally, psychoanalysis accomplishes more than this, just as going abroad to study physics enables the student to learn a foreign language *and* physics. Similarly, in the psychoanalytic situation the analysand is not only induced to shift from symptom-language to ordinary verbal communication but is *also taught to examine and understand the particular patterns of object relationships which he has had and the communicative patterns to which these gave rise.* Thus, the basic aim of psychoanalytic treatment is to enable the patient to learn about his object relationships and communicative behavior. A shift from protolanguage to object and metalanguage must be successfully achieved before mastery of the more far-reaching task of self-knowledge can be attempted.

The chief purpose of iconic body language may be merely to make contact with objects. For some people, sometimes, no verbal language may be available with which legitimately to address their fellow man. If all else fails, there still remains the language of illness—a language that virtually everyone the world over knows how to speak and understand. This is the idiom which the lonely, the downcast, the poor, and the uneducated can still use and thereby hope to "get something" which they had failed to obtain in other ways. Thus, the language of illness—and of social deviance, too—constitutes the last, and perhaps the firmest, bastion on the grounds of which unsatisfied and "regressed" man can make a last stand and claim his share of human "love." For the average layman, or for the therapeutically dedicated physician or psychiatrist, this message of nonspecific help-seeking may, of course, be difficult to hear, since all labor under the assumption that what they see and hear are manifestations of "illness." This leaves them no choice but to endeavor to "cure" or at least "ameliorate" the "disease." Yet, it seems that this whole imagery is false. The spectacle that faces us is simply an aspect of the *human condition*—call it fate, destiny, life style, character, existence, or what you will—and what we hear and see are *the cries for help* and their *pictorial representations*.

THE RULE-FOLLOWING MODEL OF BEHAVIOR

"Social life," as Peters (1958) reminded us, "is never like the jungle life popularized by evolutionary theories, a matter of mere survival; it is a matter of surviving in a certain sort of way" (p. 127). To ask, then, "In what sort of way?" and to provide answers to this question, is the task of the sciences concerned with man as a social being. Since survival by means of exhibiting "hysteria" (or "mental illness") is one distinctively human form of survival, it is necessary to study the factors that contribute to this pattern of human existence.

Classification of Rules

Three broad categories of rules may be distinguished. In the first group, designated as natural laws or biological rules, belong the regularities that must be obeyed lest sheer physical survival be jeopardized. Examples are the need to satisfy hunger or thirst and the prevention of injuries from falling, drowning, burning, and the like. Prescriptive laws constitute the next group. These are the rules—whether social, religious, or moral—that govern social life among particular groups of men. The Bible or the American Constitution and Bill of Rights are typical examples. They define the rules of the game by which social living in a given community shall be played. The third group, named "imitative or interpersonal rules," is composed of those patterns of action which must be copied by children, more or less accurately, from the behavior of the adults about them, if they are to partake of the social life of the group: for example, the learning of one's mother tongue, the use of household items, patterns of eating, and the like. Biological rules are of the utmost importance for the survival of the human (and animal) body and species. The exploration, the elucidation, and sometimes the alteration of these rules are the aims of the basic medical sciences (physiology, biochemistry, genetics, etc.) and of clinical medicine. Social and interpersonal rules, on the other hand, constitute the core-subject of the sciences of man (anthropology, psychiatry, psychoanalysis, psychology, sociology, etc.).

The Family Situation, Religion, and the Rules for Getting and Giving Help

Childhood patterns of help-seeking and help-getting form the core of a system of rules that in later life may foster the seeking or imitating of illness or disability in order to induce others to care for one. This communicative, coercive feature of disabilities of all sorts is often enhanced by Jewish and Christian religious teachings. In this connection, an examination of the Bible as a rule-book was undertaken. It was shown that the Judaeo-Christian religions contain numerous incentives to being ill or disabled. States of distress and failure—whether because of stupidity, poverty, sickness, or what not—may be interpreted as potentially desirable goals, for as the hungry infant is given the mother's breast, so the disabled human being is promised God's all-embracing helpfulness and benevolence. This pattern of human interaction and communication is regarded as the main source of a vast number of rules, all of which conspire, as it were, to foster man's infantilism and dependence. These may be contrasted with rules emphasizing the need for man's striving for mastery, responsibility, self-reliance, and mutually cooperative interdependence.

Witchcraft and Hysteria

The specific effects of certain Biblical rules on human conduct were illustrated by means of the social phenomenon of medieval witchcraft. The psychiatric and the rule-following theories of witchcraft were compared. According to the former, witches were misdiagnosed hysterics. According to the latter, they were persons sacrificed as scapegoats in a real-life game in which the activities of God and devil were taken too literally and too seriously.

Witchcraft existed as an integral part of the medieval Christian game of life. This game was theologically defined, and demanded that the players conduct themselves according to rules which were impossible to follow. Violation of the game-rules—that is, cheating—was thus unavoidable. Hence, virtually everyone was a cheat. In general, persons of high social status could cheat much more easily and safely than persons of low status. Poor old women were especially expendable and most of the witches were recruited from among their ranks. High officials of the Roman Catholic Church—who themselves disobeyed the rules of the game most flagrantly and whose activities sparked the Protestant Reformation—fostered the persecution of those who were alleged to cheat.

In the language of chess, the persecution of witches meant that poor, unimportant people (pawns) were sacrificed to insure the safety and well-being of the ruling classes (king and queen). By this maneuver, victory for God (the master player) was assured. In addition to insuring God's continued glory, this operation also served to preserve the social *status quo*. Witch-hunts and witch-trials were, accordingly, a safety valve of society. Some aspects of contemporary psychiatric practices—especially psychiatric operations involving involuntary patients and legal actions—appear to serve a function analogous to that served by the medieval witch-trials.

The contest between theological persecutor and witch is closely paralleled by the contest between institutional psychiatrist and involuntary mental patient. The former is always the victor, the latter forever the vanquished. The concept of mental illness and the social actions taken in its name serve the self-seeking interests of the medical and psychiatric professions, just as the notion of witchcraft served the interests of the theologians, acting in the name of God. As the theological game was the "opiate of the people" in past ages, so the medical-psychiatric game is the opiate of contemporary peoples. By draining interpersonal and group tensions, each game fulfills the function of social tranquilization. . . .

Ethics, Games, and Psychiatry

As long as the socioethical values of psychiatric theories and therapies remain obscure and inexplicit, their scientific worth is bound to be rather limited. This is simply because human social behavior is fundamentally ethical behavior. It is difficult to see, therefore, how such behavior could be described, or how modifications of it could be advocated, without at the same time coming to grips with the issue of ethical values. Psychoanalytic descriptions of behavior and of therapy, for example, have emphasized instinctual forces, pathogenic occurrences, and mental mechanisms at the expense of explicitly specifying norms and values. . . .

In the theory of personal conduct which I have put forward—and implicitly, in the theory of psychotherapy that may be based upon it—I have endeavored to correct this deficiency, emphasizing the urgent need to clearly specify norms and values first and techniques of behavior second. This approach was illustrated by emphasizing the end-goals of the hysterical game which were identified as domination or interpersonal control. It follows from this goal that coercing strategies may be employed in pursuit of it. In contrast, one might espouse the goals of self-reliant competence and dignified human interdependence. It is evident that these goals could not be secured by coercive techniques, for pursuing them in this fashion would conflict with the very ends that are sought. Since the ends determine, within a certain range, the means that may be used to attain them, failure to specify clearly and to bear in mind end-goals cannot be corrected by concentration on, or training in, specific techniques of living.

Impersonation and Cheating

. . . I refer here to the *credo* of most contemporary psychiatrists, that psychiatry—including psychotherapy—is significantly similar to other branches of medicine, and belongs to it. It seems to me, however, that medical psychotherapists, having had a medical training, only look like other doctors—just as hysterics only look like organically sick persons. The difference between the purely communicational interventions of the psychotherapist and the physicochemical actions of the physician represents an instrumental gulf between the two groups that no institutional resemblance can convincingly close. It is common knowledge that when clinical psychologists press their claims to practice independent psychotherapy, they tend to be regarded (especially by physicians) as impersonators of the medical role of "taking care of sick people." But the same could be said for medically trained psychotherapists whose work also differs in crucial ways from that of the surgeon or internist.

Until now, this impersonation has served the apparent interests of both mental patients and psychiatrists. Thus, no one really protested against this variation on the theme of the myth of the emperor's clothes. I think the time is now ripe to consider seriously the possibility that the medical aspects of psychotherapy are about as substantial as the legendary emperor's cloak which was so finely woven that only the wisest and most perspicacious men could perceive it. To claim that he was naked was, therefore, tantamount to self-confessed stupidity, as well as an affront against a powerful personage. . . .

Games, Objects, and Values

In conclusion, some connections between the theories of object relationships and game-playing were presented. For adults (and probably also for children after the age of ten to twelve years), games and their constituent rules often function as objects. In other words, loss of game—that is, the inability to play a game, either because of the unavailability of other players or because of changes in one's own game-playing propensities—no less than loss of object, leads to serious disequilibrium within the personality, requiring adaptive, reparative measures. Indeed, objects and games are interdependent, since the players are of necessity *people*. Hence, psychology and sociology are interlocking and interdependent.

The game model of human behavior appears well suited for unifying psychology, sociology, and ethics. For example, the sociological concept of anomie—a state of social unrest resulting from the dissolution of established rules—could readily be integrated with the psychoanalytic concepts of object loss, anxiety-depression, and ego identity. Loss of a sense of satisfying personal identity is linked to *modern man's inevitable loss of the "games" learned early in life*. In other words, modern man, if he is at all educated, cannot play the same sorts of games which he played as a youngster, or which his parents played, and remain satisfied with them. Cultural conditions are changing so rapidly that everyone tends to share the problem of the immigrant who *must* change games because he has moved from one country to another. Even those who stay put geographically find themselves in a world other than that of their parents. Indeed, as they grow older they usually find themselves in a world other than that of their youth. In this dilemma, man is confronted by the imperative need to relinquish old games and to learn to play new ones. Failing this, he is forced to play new games by old rules, the old games being the only ones he knows how to play. *This fundamental game-conflict leads to various problems in living. It is these that the modern psychotherapist is usually called on to "treat."*

Three general types of game-conflict may be distinguished. One is characterized by the person's inability to forget the old rules, or by his outright unwillingness to relinquish playing the old game. This may result in a refusal to play any of the games that others play: It is a kind of "strike" against living. Various so-called disability states—malingering, hysteria, and "dependency reactions"—illustrate such a "strike" or revolt against the challenge to learn. A second type of game-conflict consists of the superimposition of old goals and rules upon new games. Illustrative is the "transference neurosis" or reaction, the "neurotic character structure," the foreign accent, and so on; in each of these, we are confronted by a pattern of behavior that is the result of mixing different, to some extent mutually incompatible, games. Finally, a third type of game-conflict, manifested in a general disappointment-reaction, develops from the realization that man can play no transcendentally valid (God-given) game. Many react to this insight with the feeling that, in this case, *no game is worth playing!* The significance of this condition—namely, *that no game is really worth playing*—appears to be especially great for contemporary Western man.

Plato

PHAEDRUS

Plato (427?–347? B.C.) came from an aristocratic family in Athens. He was a student of Socrates who, after the death of his teacher, wrote dialogues in which Socrates was portrayed developing various themes. This selection is from his dialogue *Phaedrus.*

SOCRATES: Where is that boy I was talking to? He must listen to me once more, and not rush off to yield to his nonlover before he hears what I have to say.

PHAEDRUS: Here he is, quite close beside you, whenever you want him.

SOCRATES: Now you must understand, fair boy, that whereas the preceding discourse was by Phaedrus, son of Pythocles, of Myrrhinus, that which I shall now pronounce is by Stesichorus, son of Euphemus, of Himera. This then is how it must run.

"False is the tale" that when a lover is at hand favor ought rather to be accorded to one who does not love, on the ground that the former is mad, and the latter sound of mind. That would be right if it were an invariable truth that madness is an evil, but in reality, the greatest blessings come by way of madness, indeed of madness that is heaven-sent. It was when they were mad that the prophetess at Delphi and the priestesses at Dodona achieved so much for which both states and individuals in Greece are thankful; when sane they did little or nothing. As for the Sibyl and others who by the power of inspired prophecy have so often foretold the future to so many, and guided them aright, I need not dwell on what is obvious to everyone. Yet it is in place to appeal to the fact that madness was accounted no shame nor disgrace by the men of old who gave things their names; otherwise they would not have connected that greatest of arts, whereby the future is discerned, with this very word "madness," and named it accordingly. No, it was because they held madness to be a valuable gift, when due to divine dispensation, that they named that art as they did, though the men of today, having no sense of values, have put in an extra letter, making it not *manic* but *mantic*. That is borne out by the name they gave to the art of those sane prophets who inquire into the future by means of birds and other signs; the name was "*oionoistic*," which by its components indicated that the prophet attained understanding and information by a purely human activity of thought belonging to his own intelligence, though a younger generation has come to call it "*oionistic*," lengthening the quantity of the *o* to make it sound impressive. You see then what this ancient evidence attests. Corresponding to the superior perfection and value of the prophecy of inspiration over that of omen reading, both in name and in fact, is the superiority of heaven-sent madness over man-made sanity.

And in the second place, when grievous maladies and afflictions have beset certain families by reason of some ancient sin, madness has appeared among them, and breaking out into prophecy has secured relief by finding the means thereto, namely by recourse to prayer and worship, and in consequence thereof rites and means of purification were established, and the sufferer was brought out of danger, alike for the present and for the future. Thus did madness secure, for him that was maddened aright and possessed, deliverance from his troubles.

There is a third form of possession or madness, of which the Muses are the source. This seizes a tender, virgin soul and stimulates it to rapt passionate expression, especially in lyric poetry, glorifying the countless mighty deeds of ancient times for the instruction of posterity. But if any man come to the gates of poetry without the madness of the Muses, persuaded that skill alone will make him a good poet, then shall he and his works of sanity with him be brought to nought by the poetry of madness, and behold, their place is nowhere to be found.

Such then is the tale, though I have not told it fully, of the achievements wrought by madness that comes from the gods. So let us have no fears simply on that score; let us not be disturbed by an argument that seeks to scare us into preferring the friendship of the sane to that of the passionate. For there is something more that it must prove if it is to carry the day, namely that love is not a thing sent from heaven for the advantage both of lover and beloved. What we have to prove is the opposite, namely that this sort of madness is a gift of the gods, fraught with the highest bliss. And our proof assuredly will prevail with the wise, though not with the learned.

Now our first step toward attaining the truth of the matter is to discern the nature of soul, divine and human, its experiences, and its activities. Here then our proof begins.

All soul is immortal, for that which is ever in motion is immortal. But that which while imparting motion is itself moved by something else can cease to be in motion, and therefore can cease to live; it is only that which moves itself that never intermits its motion, inasmuch as it cannot abandon its own nature; moreover this self-mover is the source and first principle of motion for all other things that are moved. Now a first principle cannot come into being, for while anything that comes to be must come to be from a first principle, the latter itself cannot come to be from anything whatsoever; if it did, it would cease any longer to be a first principle. Furthermore, since it does not come into being, it must be imperishable, for assuredly if a first principle were to be destroyed, nothing could come to be out of it, nor could anything bring the principle itself back into existence, seeing that a first principle is needed for anything to come into being.

The self-mover, then, is the first principle of motion, and it is as impossible that it should be destroyed as that it should come into being; were it otherwise, the whole universe, the whole of that which comes to be, would collapse into immobility, and never find another source of motion to bring it back into being.

And now that we have seen that that which is moved by itself is immortal, we shall feel no scruple in affirming that precisely that is the essence and definition of soul, to wit, self-motion. Any body that has an external source of motion is soulless, but a body deriving its motion from a source within itself is animate or *besouled*, which implies that the nature of soul is what has been said.

And if this last assertion is correct, namely that "that which moves itself" is precisely identifiable with soul, it must follow that soul is not born and does not die.

René Descartes

MEDITATIONS ON THE FIRST PHILOSOPHY

René Descartes (1596–1650) was a French mathematician, scientist, and philosopher. His *Meditations on the First Philosophy in Which the Existence of God and the Distinction Between Mind and Body Are Demonstrated* (1640) has been influential in the development of modern philosophy. At the beginning of this work, he tried to show how dubious all our beliefs are.

MEDITATION I

Of the things which may be brought within the sphere of the doubtful

It is now some years since I detected how many were the false beliefs that I had from my earliest youth admitted as true, and how doubtful was everything I had since constructed on this basis; and from that time I was convinced that I must once for all seriously undertake to rid myself of all the opinions which I had formerly accepted, and commence to build anew from the foundation, if I wanted to establish any firm and permanent structure in the sciences. But as this enterprise appeared to be a very great one, I waited until I had attained an age so mature that I could not hope that at any later date I should be better fitted to execute my design. This reason caused me to delay so long that I should feel that I was doing wrong were I to occupy in deliberation the time that yet remains to me for action. Today, then, since very opportunely for the plan I have in view I have delivered my mind from every care [and am happily agitated by no passions] and since I have procured for myself an assured leisure in a peaceable retirement, I shall at last seriously and freely address myself to the general upheaval of all my former opinions.

   Now for this object it is not necessary that I should show that all of these are false—I shall perhaps never arrive at this end. But inasmuch as reason already persuades me that I ought no less carefully to withhold my assent from matters which are not entirely certain and indubitable than from those which appear to me manifestly to be false, if I am able to find in each one some reason to doubt, this will suffice to justify my rejecting the whole. And for that end it will not be requisite that I should examine each in particular, which would be an endless undertaking; for owing to the fact that the destruction of the foundations of necessity brings with it the downfall of the rest of the edifice, I shall only in the first place attack those principles upon which all my former opinions rested.

All that up to the present time I have accepted as most true and certain I have learned either from the senses or through the senses; but it is sometimes proved to me that these senses are deceptive, and it is wiser not to trust entirely to any thing by which we have once been deceived.

But it may be that although the senses sometimes deceive us concerning things which are hardly perceptible, or very far away, there are yet many others to be met with as to which we cannot reasonably have any doubt, although we recognise them by their means. For example, there is the fact that I am here, seated by the fire, attired in a dressing gown, having this paper in my hands and other similar matters. And how could I deny that these hands and this body are mine, were it not perhaps that I compare myself to certain persons, devoid of sense, whose cerebella are so troubled and clouded by the violent vapours of black bile, that they constantly assure us that they think they are kings when they are really quite poor, or that they are clothed in purple when they are really without covering, or who imagine that they have an earthenware head or are nothing but pumpkins or are made of glass. But they are mad, and I should not be any the less insane were I to follow examples so extravagant.

At the same time I must remember that I am a man, and that consequently I am in the habit of sleeping, and in my dreams representing to myself the same things or sometimes even less probable things, than do those who are insane in their waking moments. How often has it happened to me that in the night I dreamt that I found myself in this particular place, that I was dressed and seated near the fire, whilst in reality I was lying undressed in bed! At this moment it does indeed seem to me that it is with eyes awake that I am looking at this paper, that this head which I move is not asleep, that it is deliberately and of set purpose that I extend my hand and perceive it; what happens in sleep does not appear so clear nor so distinct as does all this. But in thinking over this I remind myself that on many occasions I have in sleep been deceived by similar illusions, and in dwelling carefully on this reflection I see so manifestly that there are no certain indications by which we may clearly distinguish wakefulness from sleep that I am lost in astonishment. And my astonishment is such that it is almost capable of persuading me that I now dream.

Now let us assume that we are asleep and that all these particulars, e.g. that we open our eyes, shake our head, extend our hands, and so on, are but false delusions; and let us reflect that possibly neither our hands nor our whole body are such as they appear to us to be. At the same time we must at least confess that the things which are represented to us in sleep are like painted representations which can only have been formed as the counterparts of something real and true, and that in this way those general things at least, i.e. eyes, a head, hands, and a whole body, are not imaginary things, but things really existent. For, as a matter of fact, painters, even when they study with the greatest skill to represent sirens and satyrs by forms the most strange and extraordinary, cannot give them natures which are entirely new, but merely make a certain medley of the members of different animals; or if their imagination is extravagant enough to invent something so novel that nothing similar has ever before been seen, and that then their work represents a thing purely fictitious and absolutely false, it is certain all the same that the colours of which this is composed are necessarily real. And for the same reason, although these general things, to wit, |a body|, eyes, a head, hands, and such like, may be imaginary, we are bound at the same time to confess that there are at least some other objects yet more simple and more universal, which are real and true; and of these just in the same way as with certain real colours, all these images of things which dwell in our thoughts, whether true and real or false and fantastic, are formed.

To such a class of things pertains corporeal nature in general, and its extension, the figure of extended things, their quantity or magnitude and number, as also the place in which they are, the time which measures their duration, and so on.

That is possibly why our reasoning is not unjust when we conclude from this that Physics, Astronomy, Medicine and all other sciences which have as their end the consideration of composite things, are very dubious and uncertain; but that Arithmetic, Geometry and other sciences of that kind which only treat of things that are very simple and very general, without taking great trouble to ascertain whether they are actually existent or not, contain some measure of certainty and an element of the indubitable. For whether I am awake or asleep, two and three together always form five, and the square can never have more than four sides, and it does not seem possible that truths so clear and apparent can be suspected of any falsity |or uncertainty|.

Nevertheless I have long had fixed in my mind the belief that an all-powerful God existed by whom I have been created such as I am. But how do I know that He has not brought it to pass that there is no earth, no heaven, no extended body, no magnitude, no place, and that nevertheless |I possess the perceptions of all these things and that| they seem to me to exist just exactly as I now see them? And, besides, as I sometimes imagine that others deceive themselves in the things which they think they know best, how do I know that I am not deceived every time that I add two and three, or count the sides of a square, or judge of things yet simpler, if anything simpler can be imagined? But possibly God has not desired that I should be thus deceived, for He is said to be supremely good. If, however, it is contrary to His goodness to have made me such that I constantly deceive myself, it would also appear to be contrary to His goodness to permit me to be sometimes deceived, and nevertheless I cannot doubt that He does permit this.

There may indeed be those who would prefer to deny the existence of a God so powerful, rather than believe that all other things are uncertain. But let us not oppose them for the present, and grant that all that is here said of a God is a fable; nevertheless in whatever way they suppose that I have arrived at the state of being that I have reached—whether they attribute it to fate or to accident, or make out that it is by a continual succession of antecedents, or by some other method—since to err and deceive oneself is a defect, it is clear that the greater will be the probability of my being so imperfect as to deceive myself ever, as is the Author to whom they assign my origin the less powerful. To these reasons I have certainly nothing to reply, but at the end I feel constrained to confess that there is nothing in all that I formerly believed to be true, of which I cannot in some measure doubt, and that not merely through want of thought or through levity, but for reasons which are very powerful and maturely considered; so that henceforth I ought not the less carefully to refrain from giving credence to these opinions than to that which is manifestly false, if I desire to arrive at any certainty [in the sciences].

But it is not sufficient to have made these remarks, we must also be careful to keep them in mind. For these ancient and commonly held opinions still revert frequently to my mind, long and familiar custom having given them the right to occupy my mind against my inclination and rendered them almost masters of my belief; nor will I ever lose the habit of deferring to them or of placing my confidence in them, so long as I consider them as they really are, i.e. opinions in some measure doubtful, as I have just shown, and at the same time highly probable, so that there is much more reason to believe in than to deny them. That is why I consider that I shall not be acting amiss, if, taking of set purpose a contrary belief, I allow myself to be deceived, and for a certain time pretend that all these opinions are entirely false and imaginary, until at last, having thus balanced my former prejudices with my latter [so that they cannot divert my opinions more to one side than to the other], my judgment will no longer be dominated by bad usage or turned away from the right knowledge of the truth. For I am assured that there can be neither peril nor error in this course, and that I cannot at present yield too much to distrust, since I am not considering the question of action, but only of knowledge.

I shall then suppose, not that God who is supremely good and the fountain of truth, but some evil genius not less powerful than deceitful, has employed his whole energies in deceiving me; I shall consider that the heavens, the earth, colours, figures, sound, and all other external things are nought but the illusions and dreams of which this genius has availed himself in order to lay traps for my credulity; I shall consider myself as having no hands, no eyes, no flesh, no blood, nor any senses, yet falsely believing myself to possess all these things; I shall remain obstinately attached to this idea, and if by this means it is not in my power to arrive at the knowledge of any truth, I may at least do what is in my power [i.e. suspend my judgment], and with firm purpose avoid giving credence to any false thing, or being imposed upon by this arch deceiver, however powerful and deceptive he may be. But this task is a laborious one, and insensibly a certain lassitude leads me into the course of my ordinary life. And just as a captive who in sleep enjoys an imaginary liberty, when he begins to suspect that his liberty is but a dream, fears to awaken, and conspires with these agreeable illusions that the deception may be prolonged, so insensibly of my own accord I fall back into my former opinions, and I dread awakening from this slumber, lest the laborious wakefulness which would follow the tranquillity of this repose should have to be spent not in daylight, but in the excessive darkness of the difficulties which have just been discussed.

Blaise Pascal

PENSÉES

The great French mathematician and scientist Blaise Pascal (1623–1662) had a religious conversion and retired to the Port-Royal monastery, where he wrote his *Pensées* (*Thoughts*), depicting the human condition.

432

Scepticism is true; for, after all, men before Jesus Christ did not know where they were, nor whether they were great or small. And those who have said the one or the other, knew nothing about it, and guessed without reason and by chance. They also erred always in excluding the one or the other. . . .

434

The chief arguments of the sceptics—I pass over the lesser ones—are that we have no certainty of the truth of these principles apart from faith and revelation, except in so far as we naturally perceive them in ourselves. Now this natural intuition is not a convincing proof of their truth; since, having no certainty, apart from faith, whether man was created by a good God, or by a wicked demon, or by chance, it is doubtful whether these principles given to us are true, or false, or uncertain, according to our origin. Again, no person is certain, apart from faith, whether he is awake or sleeps, seeing that during sleep we believe that we are awake as firmly as we do when we *are* awake; we believe that we see space, figure, and motion; we are aware of the passage of time, we measure it; and in fact we act as if we were awake. So that half of our life being passed in sleep, we have on our own admission no idea of truth, whatever we may imagine. As all our intuitions are then illusions, who knows whether the other half of our life, in which we think we are awake, is not another sleep a little different from the former, from which we awake when we suppose ourselves asleep?

And who doubts that, if we dreamt in company, and the dreams chanced to agree, which is common enough, and if we were always alone when awake, we should believe that matters were reversed? In short, as we often dream that we dream, heaping dream upon dream, may it not be that this half of our life, wherein we think ourselves awake, is itself only a dream on which the others are grafted, from which we wake at death, during which we have as few principles of truth and good as during natural sleep, these different thoughts which disturb us being perhaps only illusions like the flight of time and the vain fancies of our dreams?

These are the chief arguments on one side and the other.

I omit minor ones, such as the sceptical talk against the impressions of custom, education, manners, country, and the like. Though these influence the majority of common folk, who dogmatise only on shallow foundations, they are upset by the least breath of the sceptics. We have only to see their books if we are not sufficiently convinced of this, and we shall very quickly become so, perhaps too much.

I notice the only strong point of the dogmatists, namely, that, speaking in good faith and sincerely, we cannot doubt natural principles. Against this the sceptics set up in one word the uncertainty of our origin, which includes that of our nature. The dogmatists have been trying to answer this objection ever since the world began.

So there is open war among men, in which each must take a part, and side either with dogmatism or scepticism. For he who thinks to remain neutral is above all a sceptic. This neutrality is the essence of the sect; he who is not against them is essentially for them. In this appears their advantage. They are not for themselves; they are neutral, indifferent, in suspense as to all things, even themselves being no exception.

What then shall man do in this state? Shall he doubt everything? Shall he doubt whether he is awake, whether he is being pinched, or whether he is being burned? Shall he doubt whether he doubts? Shall he doubt whether he exists? We cannot go so far as that; and I lay it down as a fact that there never has been a real complete sceptic. Nature sustains our feeble reason, and prevents it raving to this extent.

Shall he then say, on the contrary, that he certainly possesses truth—he who, when pressed ever so little, can show no title to it, and is forced to let go his hold?

What a chimera then is man! What a novelty! What a monster, what a chaos, what a contradiction, what a prodigy! Judge of all things, imbecile worm of the earth; depositary of truth, a sink of uncertainty and error; the pride and refuse of the universe!

Who will unravel this tangle? Nature confutes the sceptics, and reason confutes the dogmatists. What then will you become, O men! who try to find out by your natural reason what is your true condition? You cannot avoid one of these sects, nor adhere to one of them.

Know then, proud man, what a paradox you are to yourself. Humble yourself, weak reason; be silent, foolish nature; learn that man infinitely transcends man, and learn from your Master your true condition, of which you are ignorant. Hear God.

For in fact, if man had never been corrupt, he would enjoy in his innocence both truth and happiness with assurance; and if man had always been corrupt, he would have no idea of truth or bliss. But, wretched as we are, and more so than if there were no greatness in our condition, we have an idea of happiness, and cannot reach it. We perceive an image of truth, and possess only a lie. Incapable of absolute ignorance and of certain knowledge, we have thus been manifestly in a degree of perfection from which we have unhappily fallen. . . .

Whence it clearly seems that man by grace is made like unto God, and a partaker in His divinity, and that without grace he is like unto the brute beasts.

David Hume

A TREATISE OF HUMAN NATURE

The Scottish skeptical philosopher David Hume (1711–1776) ended the first volume of his first book, A *Treatise of Human Nature* (1737–1740), as follows.

. . . Can I be sure, that in leaving all establish'd opinions I am following truth; and by what criterion shall I distinguish her, even if fortune shou'd at last guide me on her foot-steps? After the most accurate and exact of my reasonings, I can give no reason why I shou'd assent to it; and feel nothing but a *strong* propensity to consider objects *strongly* in that view, under which they appear to me. Experience is a principle, which instructs me in the several conjunctions of objects for the past. Habit is another principle, which determines me to expect the same for the future; and both of them conspiring to operate upon the imagination, make me form certain ideas in a more intense and lively manner, than others, which are not attended with the same advantages. Without this quality, by which the mind enlivens some ideas beyond others (which seemingly is so trivial, and so little founded on reason) we cou'd never assent to any argument, nor carry our view beyond those few objects, which are present to our senses. Nay, even to these objects we cou'd never attribute any existence, but what was dependent on the senses; and must comprehend them entirely in that succession of perceptions, which constitutes our self or person. Nay farther, even with relation to that succession, we cou'd only admit of those perceptions, which are immediately present to our consciousness, nor cou'd those lively images, with which the memory presents us, be ever receiv'd as true pictures of past perceptions. The memory, senses, and understanding are, therefore, all of them founded on the imagination, or the vivacity of our ideas.
    . . . When we trace up the human understanding to its first principles, we find it to lead us into such sentiments, as seem to turn into ridicule all our past pains and industry, and to discourage us from future enquiries. Nothing is more curiously enquir'd after by the mind of man, than the causes of every

phænomenon; nor are we content with knowing the immediate causes, but push on our enquiries, till we arrive at the original and ultimate principle. We wou'd not willingly stop before we are acquainted with that energy in the cause, by which it operates on its effect; that tie, which connects them together; and that efficacious quality, on which the tie depends. This is our aim in all our studies and reflections: And how must we be disappointed, when we learn, that this connexion, tie, or energy lies merely in ourselves, and is nothing but that determination of the mind, which is acquir'd by custom, and causes us to make a transition from an object to its usual attendant, and from the impression of one to the lively idea of the other? Such a discovery not only cuts off all hope of ever attaining satisfaction, but even prevents our very wishes; since it appears, that when we say we desire to know the ultimate and operating principle, as something, which resides in the external object, we either contradict ourselves, or talk without a meaning.

This deficiency in our ideas is not, indeed, perceiv'd in common life, nor are we sensible, that in the most usual conjunctions of cause and effect we are as ignorant of the ultimate principle, which binds them together, as in the most unusual and extraordinary. But this proceeds merely from an illusion of the imagination; and the question is, how far we ought to yield to these illusions. This question is very difficult, and reduces us to a very dangerous dilemma, whichever way we answer it. For if we assent to every trivial suggestion of the fancy; beside that these suggestions are often contrary to each other; they lead us into such errors, absurdities, and obscurities, that we must at last become asham'd of our credulity. Nothing is more dangerous to reason than the flights of the imagination, and nothing has been the occasion of more mistakes among philosophers. Men of bright fancies may in this respect be compar'd to those angels, whom the scripture represents as covering their eyes with their wings. This has already appear'd in so many instances, that we may spare ourselves the trouble of enlarging upon it any farther.

But on the other hand, if the consideration of these instances makes us take a resolution to reject all the trivial suggestions of the fancy, and adhere to the understanding, that is, to the general and more establish'd properties of the imagination; even this resolution, if steadily executed, wou'd be dangerous, and attended with the most fatal consequences. For I have already shewn, that the understanding, when it acts alone, and according to its most general principles, entirely subverts itself, and leaves not the lowest degree of evidence in any proposition, either in philosophy or common life. We save ourselves from this total scepticism only by means of that singular and seemingly trivial property of the fancy, by which we enter with difficulty into remote views of things, and are not able to accompany them with so sensible an impression, as we do those, which are more easy and natural. Shall we, then, establish it for a general maxim, that no refin'd or elaborate reasoning is ever to be receiv'd? Consider well the consequences of such a principle. By this means you cut off entirely all science and philosophy: You proceed upon one singular quality of the imagination, and by a parity of reason must embrace all of them: And you expresly contradict yourself; since this maxim must be built on the preceding reasoning, which will be allow'd to be sufficiently refin'd and metaphysical. What party, then, shall we choose among these difficulties? If we embrace this principle, and condemn all refin'd reasoning, we run into the most manifest absurdities. If we reject it in favour of these reasonings, we subvert entirely the human understanding. We have, therefore, no choice left but betwixt a false reason and none at all. For my part, I know not what ought to be done in the present case. I can only observe what is commonly done; which is, that this difficulty is seldom or never thought of; and even where it has once been present to the mind, is quickly forgot, and leaves but a small impression behind it. Very refin'd reflections have little or no influence upon us; and yet we do not, and cannot establish it for a rule, that they ought not to have any influence; which implies a manifest contradiction.

But what have I here said, that reflections very refin'd and metaphysical have little or no influence upon us? This opinion I can scarce forbear retracting, and condemning from my present feeling and experience. The *intense* view of these manifold contradictions and imperfections in human reason has so wrought upon me, and heated my brain, that I am ready to reject all belief and reasoning, and can look upon no opinion even as more probable or likely than another. Where am I, or what? From what causes do I derive my existence, and to what condition shall I return? Whose favour shall I court, and whose anger must I dread? What beings surround me? and on whom have I any influence, or who have any influence on me? I am confounded with all these questions, and begin to fancy myself in the most deplorable condition imaginable, inviron'd with the deepest darkness, and utterly depriv'd of the use of every member and faculty.

Most fortunately it happens, that since reason is incapable of dispelling these clouds, nature herself suffices to that purpose, and cures me of this philosophical melancholy and delirium, either by relaxing this bent of mind, or by some avocation, and lively impression of my senses, which obliterate all these chimeras. I dine, I play a game of back-gammon, I converse, and am merry with my friends; and when after three or four hours' amusement, I wou'd return to these speculations, they appear so cold, and strain'd, and ridiculous, that I cannot find in my heart to enter into them any farther.

Here then I find myself absolutely and necessarily determin'd to live, and talk, and act like other people in the common affairs of life. But notwithstanding that my natural propensity, and the course of my animal spirits and passions reduce me to this indolent belief in the general maxims of the world, I still feel such remains of my former disposition, that I am ready to throw all my books and papers into the fire, and resolve never more to renounce the pleasures of life for the sake of reasoning and philosophy. For those are my sentiments in that splenetic humour, which governs me at present. I may, nay I must yield to the current of nature, in submitting to my senses and understanding;

and in this blind submission I shew most perfectly my sceptical disposition and principles. But does it follow, that I must strive against the current of nature, which leads me to indolence and pleasure; that I must seclude myself, in some measure, from the commerce and society of men, which is so agreeable; and that I must torture my brain with subtilities and sophistries, at the very time that I cannot satisfy myself concerning the reasonableness of so painful an application, nor have any tolerable prospect of arriving by its means at truth and certainty. Under what obligation do I lie of making such an abuse of time? And to what end can it serve either for the service of mankind, or for my own private interest? No: If I must be a fool, as all those who reason or believe any thing *certainly* are, my follies shall at least be natural and agreeable. Where I strive against my inclination, I shall have a good reason for my resistance; and will no more be led a wandering into such dreary solitudes, and rough passages, as I have hitherto met with.

These are the sentiments of my spleen and indolence; and indeed I must confess, that philosophy has nothing to oppose to them, and expects a victory more from the returns of a serious good-humour'd disposition, than from the force of reason and conviction. In all the incidents of life we ought still to preserve our scepticism. If we believe, that fire warms, or water refreshes, 'tis only because it costs us too much pains to think otherwise. Nay if we are philosophers, it ought only to be upon sceptical principles, and from an inclination, which we feel to the employing ourselves after that manner. Where reason is lively, and mixes itself with some propensity, it ought to be assented to. Where it does not, it never can have any title to operate upon us.

. . . Human Nature is the only science of man; and yet has been hitherto the most neglected. 'Twill be sufficient for me, if I can bring it a little more into fashion; and the hope of this serves to compose my temper from that spleen, and invigorate it from that indolence, which sometimes prevail upon me. If the reader finds himself in the same easy disposition, let him follow me in my future speculations. If not, let him follow his inclination, and wait the returns of application and good humour. The conduct of a man, who studies philosophy in this careless manner, is more truly sceptical than that of one, who feeling in himself an inclination to it, is yet so over-whelm'd with doubts and scruples, as totally to reject it. A true sceptic will be diffident of his philosophical doubts, as well as of his philosophical conviction; and will never refuse any innocent satisfaction, which offers itself, upon account of either of them.

Nor is it only proper we shou'd in general indulge our inclination in the most elaborate philosophical researches, notwithstanding our sceptical principles, but also that we shou'd yield to that propensity, which inclines us to be positive and certain in *particular points*, according to the light, in which we survey them in any *particular instant*. 'Tis easier to forbear all examination and enquiry, than to check ourselves in so natural a propensity, and guard against that assurance, which always arises from an exact and full survey of an object. On such an occasion we are apt not only to forget our scepticism, but even our modesty too; and make use of such terms as these, *'tis evident, 'tis certain, 'tis undeniable*; which a due deference to the public ought, perhaps, to prevent. I may have fallen into this fault after the example of others; but I here enter a *caveat* against any objections, which may be offer'd on that head; and declare that such expressions were extorted from me by the present view of the object, and imply no dogmatical spirit, nor conceited idea of my own judgment, which are sentiments that I am sensible can become no body, and a sceptic still less than any other.

Josef Breuer and Sigmund Freud

STUDIES IN HYSTERIA

Sigmund Freud (1856–1939), the founder of psychoanalysis, was a prominent Viennese doctor. With his colleague Josef Breuer (1842–1925) he studied how to treat hysteria. Their work was summarized in *Studies in Hysteria*, of which this selection is from the first chapter.

THE PSYCHIC MECHANISM OF HYSTERICAL PHENOMENA

(Preliminary Communication)

Actuated by a number of accidental observations, we have investigated over a period of years the different forms and symptoms of hysteria for the purpose of discovering the cause and the process which first provoked the phenomena in question, and which in a great many of our cases frequently appeared years before. In the great majority of cases we did not succeed in elucidating this starting point from the mere history, no matter how detailed it might have been, partly because we had to deal with experiences about which discussion was disagreeable to the patients, but mainly because they really could not recall anything. Often they had no inkling of the causal connection between the causative process and the pathological phenomenon. It was generally necessary to hypnotize the patients and reawaken the memory of the time in which the symptom first appeared, but we thus succeeded in exposing that connection in a most precise and convincing manner.

This method of examination in a great number of cases has furnished us with results which seem to be of theoretical as well as of practical value.

It is of *theoretical value* because it has shown us that in the determination of the pathology of hysteria the accidental factor plays a much greater part than is generally known and recognized. It is quite evident that in "*traumatic*" hysteria it is the accident which evokes the syndrome. Moreover, in hysterical crises, if the patients state that in each attack they hallucinate the same process which evoked the first attack, here, too, the causal connection seems quite clear. But the situation is more obscure in the other phenomena.

Our experiences have shown us *that the most varied symptoms which pass as spontaneous, or, as it were, as idiopathic attainments of hysteria, stand in just as stringent connection with the causal trauma as the transparent phenomena mentioned.* To such causal factors we are able to refer neuralgias as well as the different kind of anesthesias, often of years' duration, contractures and paralyses, hysterical attacks and epileptiform convulsions, which every observer has taken for real epilepsy, *petit mal* and tic-like affections, persistent vomiting and anorexia, even up to the refusal of nourishment, all kinds of visual disturbances, constantly recurring visual hallucinations, and similar affections. The disproportion between the hysterical symptom of years' duration and the former cause is the same as the one we are regularly accustomed to see in the traumatic neuroses. Very often they are experiences of childhood which have established more or less intensive morbid phenomena for all succeeding years.

The connection is often so clear that it is perfectly manifest how the causal event produced just this and no other phenomenon. It is quite clearly determined by the cause. Thus, let us take the most banal example: if a painful affect originates while eating, and is repressed, it may produce nausea and vomiting, and then continue for months as an hysterical symptom. The following examples will illustrate what we mean:

A very distressed young girl, while anxiously watching at a sick bed, fell into a dreamy state, had terrifying hallucinations, and her right arm, which was at the time hanging over the back of the chair, became numb. This resulted in a paralysis, contracture, and anesthesia of that arm. She wanted to pray, but could find no words, but finally succeeded in uttering an English children's prayer. Later, on developing a very grave and most complicated hysteria, she spoke, wrote, and understood only English, whereas her native tongue was incomprehensible to her for a year and a half.

A very sick child finally fell asleep. The mother exerted all her will power to make no noise to awaken it, but because she resolved to do so, she emitted a clicking sound with her tongue ("hysterical counter-will"). This was later repeated on another occasion when she wished to be absolutely quiet, and developed into a tic, which in the form of tongue clicking accompanied every excitement for years.

A very intelligent man was present while his brother was anesthetized and his ankylosed hip stretched. At the moment when the joint yielded and crackled, he perceived severe pain in his own hip, which continued for almost a year.

In other cases the connection is not so simple, there being only, as it were, a symbolic relation between the cause and the pathological phenomenon, just as in the normal dream. Thus, psychic pain may result in neuralgia, or the affect of moral disgust may cause vomiting. We have studied patients, who were wont to make the most prolific use of such symbolization. In still other cases such a determination is at first sight incomprehensible, yet in this group we find the typical hysterical symptoms, such as hemianesthesia, contraction of the visual field, epileptiform convulsions, and similar symptoms. The explanation of our views concerning this group must be deferred for a more detailed discussion of the subject.

Such observations seem to demonstrate the pathogenic analogy between simple hysteria and traumatic neurosis, and justify a broader conception of "traumatic hysteria." The active etiological factor in traumatic neurosis is really not the insignificant bodily injury, but the affect of the fright; that is, the *psychic trauma*. In an analogous manner our investigations show that the causes of many, if not of all, cases of hysteria can be designated as psychic traumas. Every experience which produces the painful affect of fear, anxiety, shame, or of psychic pain may act as a trauma. Whether an experience becomes of traumatic importance naturally depends on the person affected, as well as on the condition which will be mentioned later. In ordinary hysterias we frequently find, instead of one large trauma, many partial traumas, grouped causes which can be of traumatic significance only when summarized, and which belong together insofar as they form small fragments of the sorrowful tale. In still other cases a connection with a real efficacious event or with a period of time of special excitability raises seemingly indifferent situations to traumatic dignity, which they would not have attained otherwise, but which they retain ever after.

But the causal connection of the causative psychic trauma with the hysterical phenomena does not mean that the trauma, as an *agent provocateur* would release the symptom which would then become independent and continue as such. On the contrary, we must maintain that the psychic trauma or the memory of the same acts like a foreign body which even long after its penetration must be considered as an agent of the present, the proof of which we see in a most remarkable phenomenon, which at the same time adds to our discoveries a distinctly practical interest.

We found, at first to our greatest surprise, that the *individual hysterical symptoms immediately disappeared without returning if we succeeded in thoroughly awakening the memories of the causal process with its accompanying affect, and if the patient circumstantially discussed the process in the most detailed manner and gave verbal expression to the affect.* Recollections without affects are almost utterly useless. The psychic process, which originally elapsed, must be reproduced as vividly as possible so as to bring it back into the *statum nascendi*, and then thoroughly "talked out." If it concerns such irritating manifestations as convulsions, neuralgias, and hallucinations, they are once more brought to the surface with their full intensity, and they then vanish forever. Functional attacks like paralyses and anesthesias likewise disappear, but naturally without any appreciable distinctness of their momentary aggravation.

Arne Naess

SCEPTICISM

Arne Naess (b. 1912), a leading Norwegian philosopher, has written on many themes in contemporary philosophy. In his book *Scepticism* (1968) he sought to show the value of a skeptical attitude in attempting to understand mental health.

ENCOURAGING A SCEPTICAL BENT OF MIND: CAN IT EVER BE RIGHT?

In cases of deep and painful doubt and oscillation between opposite views, the therapist should, it seems, represent the dogmatist rather than the sceptic. That is, he or she must help the patient towards a stable view, a valid positive conclusion, whether or not valid in the eyes of the therapist. This may also apply to young people drifting along the stream, and with little feeling of identity, or of anything that is truly expressive of themselves. They may look like potential (Pyrrhonian) sceptics, but they are not likely to become so. They have not gone through the presceptical stage of asking 'What is truth?' with strength and endurance. And therefore the sceptic's peace of mind cannot be theirs.

Admitting, however, that in many cases a tendency towards scepticism should *not* be encouraged, what are the cases in which it should or at least might?

Let us consider a young man called Max. He is brought up in a highly intellectual atmosphere with stress on articulated opinions justifying attitudes and actions. It is never enough for him to say "That's the way I feel now," "I cannot help valuing this higher than that," "I just like it," "This, not that, is my duty," and so on; there must be reasons and claims of objective truth and validity. For various reasons Max has early developed a keen critical sense, *contra*-argument coming to him more naturally than *pro*-argument. And this criticalness, owing to a not too greatly developed sense of superiority, comes as easily to him in respect of his *own* tentative positions as in respect of those of others.

Without being intellectually inferior, Max is constantly in trouble because he cannot form enduring verbalized convictions and because his father and others who try to press him into certain beliefs are largely immune to counterarguments relating to their own positions. When Max has to make decisions in school, as a student, as a friend, and in relation to the other sex, he insists on making positions conscious, and on justifying them intellectually. He demands that his own actions should always be based on considerations of truth, correctness, and worthwhile consequences.

Any effort to change the old trait Max has of coming to see two sides of a thing, and his tendency towards detached objectivity and valid reasoning, is liable to fail just because this feature is so deeply engrained. And, of course, few therapists would have the audacity to interfere with it, since from many points of view such a trait is an asset. However, the case is one in which help towards a more complete scepticism is warranted. What Max lacks may be said to be the courage to oppose those who make him feel that the intellectual articulation and justification of impulses is necessary, and who have implanted in him a distrust of action or attitude-formation without an accompaniment of intellectual justification in terms of truth and general validity. The sceptical outlook involves a mistrust in such justifications and a capacity to see their hollowness from the point of view of intellectual detachment and honesty. Instead of feeling that this ability to see counterarguments is shameful and expressive of inferiority, Max will be encouraged to exercise his ability and to stick to his resulting intellectual indecision and suspension of judgment.

It will perhaps be objected that Max's cure is basically one not of being led to accept and develop further his sceptical bent of mind but of being led to trust his own impulses.

However, the term "scepticism" has been introduced in this text as it was by Sextus, that is, in terms of the genesis of a kind of personality. Essential in Sextus's narrative is his "impression" that indecision, or rather suspension of judgment, as to truth and falsity does not result in inactivity. Natural impulses lead to action. Upbringing, social institutions, teachers in the arts provide a sufficient basis for adjustment, both for the passive component, the accommodation, and the active, the assimilation, in the terminology of Piaget. Thus trust in one's own impulses is an integral part of the scepticism expressed by Sextus Empiricus.

An essential kind of question for Max is "*How did* I come to think that in order to decide whether to go to college or not I would have to *solve* the question whether an interesting or lucrative job is best for me? Or whether there is a duty for intelligent men today to go to college in order that in 1980 the United States may have more able engineers than the Soviet Union and China put together?" Max would have to train himself to have a sharp awareness of his own inclinations, develop his sensitivity, get his impulses co-ordinated, and use his intellectual acumen to reveal for himself the unwarranted jumps from particular, concrete personal questions to more general and abstract ones, and to distinguish innocent verbalizations ("What beautiful places some college campuses are!") from more formidable articulations in terms of truth and validity.

Let us, once more, look for personality traits correlated with a profoundly sceptical bend of mind. Let us consider a middle-aged intellectually gifted person called Adam. Adam has long had a need for a unified outlook on life of the kind which Gordon Allport takes to be a sign of health. And as far as we, his psychologist friends, are able to judge, he *had* a highly unified all-pervading outlook when he was twenty-five years old. When he had that outlook he seemed to thrive. Then he became married to a headstrong girl, Mary, with a different outlook. Unhappily there developed much friction and Adam was gradually led to *carefully articulate his own outlook*, articulation functioning mainly as a defence mechanism.

Articulation presupposes a certain degree of alienation from oneself, a dangerous kind of objectivity. Adam was led to look at himself from the outside and to make clear other possibilities than his own outlook. There now developed a profound indecision and general doubt, and Adam proceeded to undergo an analysis of a somewhat orthodox Freudian kind. It was soon clear that the need of a unified outlook developed out of earlier conflicts, when he was torn between father and mother. His outlook represented a victory of the father image, but there must be something left over, something incompletely integrated in his personality. This explains why his infatuation for Mary had the serious consequence of marriage, in spite of the incongruence between the two in the matter of outlook.

The analysis was highly successful. To put it in terms of symbols, the main result was that he saw that he no longer needed to choose between mother and father. On the contrary, he felt the arbitrariness of any choice of that kind. Transferred to the field of conscious behaviour, it meant a rejection of unified outlooks, a natural disinclination to let himself fasten on to any decision in terms of outlooks on life or anything else. Confronted with believers in the truth of any religion, philosophy, or political ideology, counterarguments developed, in a natural way, in his mind. Having William James as a distant relative, he often justified his renunciation of knowledge in terms of pragmatism, but he did not really believe in pragmatism. He used pragmatic patterns of argumentation because they were the most convenient way of cutting off reflections leading nowhere.

Whatever the genesis of a definite general outlook, it cannot be shed like a coat. It is therefore not surprising to hear from the psychologist friends of Adam that his social and physical perceptions still have a peculiar tone or colour consistent with his former highly integrated outlook. The difference is that he will not stand up and defend his impressions and reactions as any more valid or true than any other. He trusts his impulses but his intellectualizations have disintegrated, leaving only the minimum necessary for adjustment to his social environment.

Today I surmise that there are many psychotherapists who are not far from scepticism in their basic attitudes, however full of certainty they may sometimes be in their speech. This makes it easier to help unburden over-intellectualized minds of unnecessary, unending reflections about truth and falsity, validity and invalidity. I should think therefore that scepticism of the radical kind we are discussing should not be wholly without practical importance for psychotherapy, hence that here at least is one context in which it may be considered practically desirable. The relevance in wider contexts of a conclusion about the practical value of scepticism in this one field must be left to those who would consider in more detail the connection between mental health and community, and the importance of a sceptical attitude among those who would seek to influence the development of society. One might reasonably predict important social implications of widespread scepticism, even of the fragmentary, unphilosophical kind. It should effectively undermine closed societies with their demands for explicit adherence to certain doctrines and the systematic rejection of counterargument. And in more or less open societies scepticism should help both in the reshuffling of political priorities and in the elimination of rigid ideological reasoning that lacks any basis in spontaneous thought and feeling.

B. IS THERE GENUINE SCIENTIFIC KNOWLEDGE?

Paul Feyerabend
AGAINST METHOD

Paul Feyerabend was born in Vienna in 1924 and came to the United States in 1958. He is currently a professor of philosophy at the University of California at Berkeley. In *Against Method* he has raised some striking challenges to claims that we possess genuine scientific knowledge.

INTRODUCTION

Science is an essentially anarchistic enterprise: theoretical anarchism is more humanitarian and more likely to encourage progress than its law-and-order alternatives.

The following essay is written in the conviction that *anarchism*, while perhaps not the most attractive *political* philosophy, is certainly excellent medicine for *epistemology*, and for the *philosophy of science*.

The reason is not difficult to find.

"History generally, and the history of revolutions in particular, is always richer in content, more varied, more many-sided, more lively and subtle than even" the best historian and the best methodologist can imagine.[1] History is full of "accidents and conjunctures and curious juxtapositions of events"[2] and it demonstrates to us the "complexity of human change and the unpredictable character of the ultimate consequences of any given act or decision of men."[3] Are we really to believe that the naive and simple-minded rules which

[1]"History as a whole, and the history of revolutions in particular, is always richer in content, more varied, more multiform, more lively and ingenious than is imagined by even the best parties, the most conscious vanguards of the most advanced classes" (V. I. Lenin, "Left-Wing Communism— An Infantile Disorder," *Selected Works*, Vol. 3, London, 1967, p. 401). Lenin is addressing parties and revolutionary vanguards rather than scientists and methodologists; the lesson, however, is the same. cf. footnote 5.

[2]Herbert Butterfield, *The Whig Interpretation of History*, New York, 1965, p. 66.

[3]ibid., p. 21.

methodologists take as their guide are capable of accounting for such a "maze of interactions?"[4] And is it not clear that successful *participation* in a process of this kind is possible only for a ruthless opportunist who is not tied to any particular philosophy and who adopts whatever procedure seems to fit the occasion?

This is indeed the conclusion that has been drawn by intelligent and thoughtful observers. "Two very important practical conclusions follow from this [character of the historical process]," writes Lenin,[5] continuing the passage from which I have just quoted. "First, that in order to fulfil its task, the revolutionary class [i.e. the class of those who want to change either a part of society such as science, or society as a whole] must be able to master *all* forms or aspects of social activity without exception [it must be able to understand, and to apply, not only one particular methodology, but any methodology, and any variation thereof it can imagine] . . . ; second [it] must be ready to pass from one to another in the quickest and most unexpected manner." "The external conditions," writes Einstein,[6] "which are set for [the scientist] by the facts of experience do not permit him to let himself be too much restricted, in the construction of his conceptual world, by the adherence to an epistemological system. He therefore, must appear to the systematic epistemologist as a type of unscrupulous opportunist. . . ." A complex medium containing surprising and unforeseen developments demands complex procedures and defies analysis on the basis of rules which have been set up in advance and without regard to the ever-changing conditions of history.

Now it is, of course, possible to simplify the medium in which a scientist works by simplifying its main actors. The history of science, after all, does not just consist of facts and conclusions drawn from facts. It also contains ideas, interpretations of facts; problems created by conflicting interpretations, mistakes, and so on. On closer analysis we even find that science knows no "bare facts" at all but that the "facts" that enter our knowledge are already viewed in a certain way and are, therefore, essentially ideational. This being the case, the history of science will be as complex, chaotic, full of mistakes, and entertaining

[4]ibid., p. 25, cf. Hegel, *Philosophie der Geschichte, Werke*, Vol. 9, ed. Edward Gans, Berlin, 1837, p. 9: "But what experience and history teach us is this, that nations and governments have never learned anything from history, or acted according to rules that might have derived from it. Every period has such peculiar circumstances, is in such an individual state, that decisions will have to be made, and decisions *can* only be made, in it and out of it." "Very clever"; "shrewd and very clever"; "NB" writes Lenin in his marginal notes to this passage. (*Collected Works*, Vol. 38, London, 1961, p. 307.)

[5]ibid. We see here very clearly how a few substitutions can turn a political lesson into a lesson for *methodology*. This is not at all surprising. Methodology and politics are both means for moving from one historical stage to another. The only difference is that the standard methodologies disregard the fact that history constantly produces new features. We also see how an individual, such as Lenin, who is not intimidated by traditional boundaries and whose thought is not tied to the ideology of a profession, can give useful advice to everyone, philosophers of science included.

[6]Albert Einstein, *Albert Einstein: Philosopher Scientist*, ed. P. A. Schilpp, New York, 1951, pp. 683f.

as the ideas it contains, and these ideas in turn will be as complex, chaotic, full of mistakes, and entertaining as are the minds of those who invented them. Conversely, a little brainwashing will go a long way in making the history of science duller, simpler, more uniform, more "objective" and more easily accessible to treatment by strict and unchangeable rules.

Scientific education as we know it today has precisely this aim. It simplifies "science" by simplifying its participants: first, a domain of research is defined. The domain is separated from the rest of history (physics, for example, is separated from metaphysics and from theology) and given a "logic" of its own. A thorough training in such a "logic" then conditions those working in the domain; it makes *their actions* more uniform and it freezes large parts of the *historical process* as well. Stable "facts" arise and persevere despite the vicissitudes of history. An essential part of the training that makes such facts appear consists in the attempt to inhibit intuitions that might lead to a blurring of boundaries. A person's religion, for example, or his metaphysics, or his sense of humour (his *natural* sense of humour and not the inbred and always rather nasty kind of jocularity one finds in specialized professions) must not have the slightest connection with his scientific activity. His imagination is restrained, and even his language ceases to be his own.[7] This is again reflected in the nature of scientific "facts" which are experienced as being independent of opinion, belief, and cultural background.

It is thus *possible* to create a tradition that is held together by strict rules, and that is also successful to some extent. But is it *desirable* to support such a tradition to the exclusion of everything else? Should we transfer to it the sole rights for dealing in knowledge, so that any result that has been obtained by other methods is at once ruled out of court? This is the question I intend to ask in the present essay. And to this question my answer will be a firm and resounding NO.

There are two reasons why such an answer seems to be appropriate. The first reason is that the world which we want to explore is a largely unknown entity. We must, therefore, keep our options open and we must not restrict ourselves in advance. Epistemological prescriptions may look splendid when compared with other epistemological prescriptions, or with general principles—but who can guarantee that they are the best way to discover, not just a few isolated "facts," but also some deep-lying secrets of nature? The second reason is that a scientific education as described above (and as practised in our schools) cannot be reconciled with a humanitarian attitude. It is in conflict "with the cultivation of individuality which alone produces, or can produce, well-developed human beings";[8] it "maims by compression, like a Chinese lady's foot, every

---

[7]For the deterioration of language that follows any increase of professionalism cf. my essay "Experts in a Free Society," *The Critic*, November/December 1970.

[8]John Stuart Mill, "On Liberty," *The Philosophy of John Stuart Mill*, ed. Marshall Cohen, New York, 1961, p. 258.

part of human nature which stands out prominently, and tends to make a person markedly different in outline"[9] from the ideals of rationality that happen to be fashionable in science, or in the philosophy of science. The attempt to increase liberty, to lead a full and rewarding life, and the corresponding attempt to discover the secrets of nature and of man entails, therefore, the rejection of all universal standards and of all rigid traditions. (Naturally, it also entails the rejection of a large part of contemporary science.)

It is surprising to see how rarely the stultifying effect of "the Laws of Reason" or of scientific practice is examined by professional anarchists. Professional anarchists oppose any kind of restriction and they demand that the individual be permitted to develop freely, unhampered by laws, duties or obligations. And yet they swallow without protest all the severe standards which scientists and logicians impose upon research and upon any kind of knowledge-creating and knowledge-changing activity. Occasionally, the laws of scientific method, or what are thought to be the laws of scientific method by a particular writer, are even integrated into anarchism itself. "Anarchism is a world concept based upon a mechanical explanation of all phenomena," writes Kropotkin.[10] "Its method of investigation is that of the exact natural sciences . . . the method of induction and deduction." "It is not clear," writes a modern "radical" professor at Columbia,[11] "that scientific research demands an absolute freedom of speech and debate. Rather the evidence suggests that certain kinds of unfreedom place no obstacle in the way of science. . . ."

There are certainly some people to whom this is "not so clear." Let us, therefore, start with our outline of an anarchistic methodology and a corresponding anarchistic science.[12] There is no need to fear that the diminished concern for law and order in science and society that characterizes an anarchism of this kind will lead to chaos. The human nervous system is too well organized for that.[13] There may, of course, come a time when it will be necessary to give reason a temporary advantage and when it will be wise to defend its rules to the exclusion of everything else. I do not think that we are living in such a time today.

[9]ibid., p. 265.

[10]Peter Alexeivich Kropotkin, "Modern Science and Anarchism," *Kropotkin's Revolutionary Pámphlets*, ed. R. W. Baldwin, New York, 1970, pp. 150–2. "It is one of Ibsen's great distinctions that nothing was valid for him but science." B. Shaw, *Back to Methuselah*, New York, 1921, xcvii. Commenting on these and similar phenomena Strindberg writes (*Antibarbarus*): "A generation that had the courage to get rid of God, to crush the state and church, and to overthrow society and morality, still bowed before Science. And in Science, where freedom ought to reign, the order of the day was 'believe in the authorities or off with your head.'"

[11]R. P. Wolff, *The Poverty of Liberalism*, Boston, 1968, p. 15. For a more detailed criticism of Wolff see footnote 52 of my essay "Against Method" in *Minnesota Studies in the Philosophy of Science*, Vol. 4, Minneapolis, 1970.

1

This is shown both by an examination of historical episodes and by an abstract analysis of the relation between idea and action. The only principle that does not inhibit progress is: anything goes.

The idea of a method that contains firm, unchanging, and absolutely binding principles for conducting the business of science meets considerable difficulty when confronted with the results of historical research. We find then, that there is not a single rule, however plausible, and however firmly grounded in epistemology, that is not violated at some time or other. It becomes evident that such violations are not accidental events, they are not results of insufficient knowledge or of inattention which might have been avoided. On the contrary, we see that they are necessary for progress. Indeed, one of the most striking features of recent discussions in the history and philosophy of science is the realization that events and developments, such as the invention of atomism in antiquity, the Copernican Revolution, the rise of modern atomism (kinetic theory; dispersion theory; stereochemistry; quantum theory), the gradual emergence of the wave theory of light, occurred only because some thinkers either *decided* not to be bound by certain "obvious" methodological rules, or because they *unwittingly broke* them.

This liberal practice, I repeat, is not just a *fact* of the history of science. It is both reasonable and *absolutely necessary* for the growth of knowledge. More specifically, one can show the following: given any rule, however "fundamental" or "necessary" for science, there are always circumstances when it is advisable not only to ignore the rule, but to adopt its opposite. For example, there are

[12]When choosing the term "anarchism" for my enterprise I simply followed general usage. However anarchism, as it has been practised in the past and as it is being practised today by an ever increasing number of people has features I am not prepared to support. It cares little for human lives and human happiness (except for the lives and the happiness of those who belong to some special group); and it contains precisely the kind of Puritanical dedication and seriousness which I detest. (There are some exquisite exceptions such as Cohn-Bendit, but they are in the minority.) It is for these reasons that I now prefer to use the term *Dadaism*. A Dadaist would not hurt a fly—let alone a human being. A Dadaist is utterly unimpressed by any serious enterprise and he smells a rat whenever people stop smiling and assume that attitude and those facial expressions which indicate that something important is about to be said. A Dadaist is convinced that a worthwhile life will arise only when we start taking things *lightly* and when we remove from our speech the profound but already putrid meanings it has accumulated over the centuries ("search for truth"; "defence of justice"; "passionate concern"; etc., etc.) A Dadaist is prepared to initiate joyful experiments even in those domains where change and experimentation seem to be out of the question (example: the basic functions of language). I hope that having read the pamphlet the reader will remember me as a flippant Dadaist and *not* as a serious anarchist.

[13]Even in undetermined and ambiguous situations, uniformity of action is soon achieved and adhered to tenaciously. See Muzafer Sherif, *The Psychology of Social Norms*, New York, 1964.

circumstances when it is advisable to introduce, elaborate, and defend *ad hoc* hypotheses, or hypotheses which contradict well-established and generally accepted experimental results, or hypotheses whose content is smaller than the content of the existing and empirically adequate alternative, or self-inconsistent hypotheses, and so on.[14]

There are even circumstances—and they occur rather frequently—when *argument* loses its forward-looking aspect and becomes a hindrance to progress. Nobody would claim that the teaching of *small children* is exclusively a matter of argument (though argument may enter into it, and should enter into it to a larger extent than is customary), and almost everyone now agrees that what looks like a result of reason—the mastery of a language, the existence of a richly articulated perceptual world, logical ability—is due partly to indoctrination and partly to a process of *growth* that proceeds with the force of natural law. And where arguments *do* seem to have an effect, this is more often due to their *physical repetition* than to their *semantic content*.

Having admitted this much, we must also concede the possibility of non-argumentative growth in the *adult* as well as in (the theoretical parts of) *institutions* such as science, religion, prostitution, and so on. We certainly cannot take it for granted that what is possible for a small child—to acquire new modes of behaviour on the slightest provocation, to slide into them without any noticeable effort—is beyond the reach of his elders. One should rather expect that catastrophic changes in the physical environment, wars, the breakdown of encompassing systems of morality, political revolutions, will transform adult reaction patterns as well, including important patterns of argumentation. Such a transformation may again be an entirely natural process and the only function of a rational argument may lie in the fact that it increases the mental tension that precedes *and causes* the behavioural outburst.

Now, if there are events, not necessarily arguments which *cause* us to adopt new standards, including new and more complex forms of argumentation, is it then not up to the defenders of the *status quo* to provide, not just counter-arguments, but also contrary *causes*? ("Virtue without terror is ineffective," says Robespierre.) And if the old forms of argumentation turn out to be too weak a cause, must not these defenders either give up or resort to stronger and more "irrational" means? (It is very difficult, and perhaps entirely impossible, to

[14]One of the few thinkers to understand this feature of the development of knowledge was Niels Bohr: ". . . he would never try to outline any finished picture, but would patiently go through all the phases of the development of a problem, starting from some apparent paradox, and gradually leading to its elucidation. In fact, he never regarded achieved results in any other light than as starting points for further exploration. In speculating about the prospects of some line of investigation, he would dismiss the usual consideration of simplicity, elegance or even consistency with the remark that such qualities can only be properly judged *after* |my italics| the event. . . ." L. Rosenfeld in *Niels Bohr, His Life and Work as seen by his Friends and Colleagues*, ed. S. Rosental, New York, 1967, p. 117. Now science is never a completed process, therefore it is always "before" the event. Hence simplicity, elegance or consistency are *never* necessary conditions of (scientific) practice.

combat the effects of brainwashing by argument.) Even the most puritanical rationalist will then be forced to stop reasoning and to use *propaganda* and *coercion*, not because some of his *reasons* have ceased to be valid, but because the *psychological conditions* which make them effective, and capable of influencing others, have disappeared. And what is the use of an argument that leaves people unmoved?

Of course, the problem never arises quite in this form. The teaching of standards and their defence never consists merely in putting them before the mind of the student and making them as *clear* as possible. The standards are supposed to have maximal *causal efficacy* as well. This makes it very difficult indeed to distinguish between the *logical force* and the *material effect* of an argument. Just as a well-trained pet will obey his master no matter how great the confusion in which he finds himself, and no matter how urgent the need to adopt new patterns of behaviour, so in the very same way a well-trained rationalist will obey the mental image of *his* master, he will conform to the standards of argumentation he has learned, he will adhere to these standards no matter how great the confusion in which he finds himself, and he will be quite incapable of realizing that what he regards as the "voice of reason" is but a *causal after-effect* of the training he has received. He will be quite unable to discover that the appeal to reason to which he succumbs so readily is nothing but a *political manoeuvre*.

That interests, forces, propaganda and brainwashing techniques play a much greater role than is commonly believed in the growth of our knowledge and in the growth of science, can also be seen from an analysis of the *relation between idea and action*. It is often taken for granted that a clear and distinct understanding of new ideas precedes, and should precede, their formulation and their institutional expression. (An investigation starts with a problem, says Popper.) *First*, we have an idea, or a problem, *then* we act, i.e. either speak, or build, or destroy. Yet this is certainly not the way in which small children develop. They use words, they combine them, they play with them, until they grasp a meaning that has so far been beyond their reach. And the initial playful activity is an essential prerequisite of the final act of understanding. There is no reason why this mechanism should cease to function in the adult. We must expect, for example, that the *idea* of liberty could be made clear only by means of the very same actions, which were supposed to *create* liberty. Creation of a *thing*, and creation plus full understanding of a *correct idea* of the thing, *are very often parts of one and the same indivisible process* and cannot be separated without bringing the process to a stop. The process itself is not guided by a well-defined programme, and cannot be guided by such a programme, for it contains the conditions for the realization of all possible programmes. It is guided rather by a vague urge, by a "passion" (Kierkegaard). The passion gives rise to specific behaviour which in turn creates the circumstances and the ideas necessary for analysing and explaining the process, for making it "rational."

The development of the Copernican point of view from Galileo to the 20th century is a perfect example of the situation I want to describe. We start with a strong belief that runs counter to contemporary reason and contemporary experience. The belief spreads and finds support in other beliefs which are equally unreasonable, if not more so (law of inertia; the telescope). Research now gets deflected in new directions, new kinds of instruments are built, "evidence" is related to theories in new ways until there arises an ideology that is rich enough to provide independent arguments for any particular part of it and mobile enough to find such arguments whenever they seem to be required. We can say today that Galileo was on the right track, for his persistent pursuit of what once seemed to be a silly cosmology has by now created the material needed to defend it against all those who will accept a view only if it is told in a certain way and who will trust it only if it contains certain magical phrases, called "observational reports." And this is not an exception—it is the normal case: theories become clear and "reasonable" only *after* incoherent parts of them have been used for a long time. Such unreasonable, nonsensical, unmethodical foreplay thus turns out to be an unavoidable precondition of clarity and of empirical success.

Now, when we attempt to describe and to understand developments of this kind in a general way, we are, of course, obliged to appeal to the existing forms of speech which do not take them into account and which must be distorted, misused, beaten into new patterns in order to fit unforeseen situations (without a constant misuse of language there can not be any discovery, any progress). "Moreover, since the traditional categories are the gospel of everyday thinking (including ordinary scientific thinking) and of everyday practice, |such an attempt at understanding| in effect presents rules and forms of false thinking and action—false, that is, from the standpoint of (scientific) common sense."[15] This is how *dialectical thinking* arises as a form of thought that "dissolves into nothing the detailed determinations of the understanding,"[16] formal logic included.

(Incidentally, it should be pointed out that my frequent use of such words as "progress," "advance," "improvement," etc., does not mean that I claim to possess special knowledge about what is good and what is bad in the sciences and that I want to impose this knowledge upon my readers. *Everyone can read the terms in his own way* and in accordance with the tradition to which he belongs. Thus for an empiricist, "progress" will mean transition to a theory that provides direct empirical tests for most of its basic assumptions. Some people believe the quantum theory to be a theory of this kind. For others, "progress" may mean unification and harmony, perhaps even at the expense of empirical adequacy. This is how Einstein viewed the general theory of relativity. *And my thesis is that anarchism helps to achieve progress in any one of the senses one cares to choose.* Even a

[15]Herbert Marcuse, *Reason and Revolution*, London, 1941, p. 130.

[16]Hegel, *Wissenschaft der Logik*, Vol. 1, Meiner, Hamburg, 1965, p. 6.

law-and-order science will succeed only if anarchistic moves are occasionally allowed to take place.)

It is clear, then, that the idea of a fixed method, or of a fixed theory of rationality, rests on too naive a view of man and his social surroundings. To those who look at the rich material provided by history, and who are not intent on impoverishing it in order to please their lower instincts, their craving for intellectual security in the form of clarity, precision, "objectivity," "truth," it will become clear that there is only *one* principle that can be defended under *all* circumstances and in *all* stages of human development. It is the principle: *anything goes.* . . .

Thomas Kuhn

THE STRUCTURE OF SCIENTIFIC KNOWLEDGE

Thomas Kuhn (b. 1922) is professor of the history of science at Princeton. He has tried to show that cultural and social conditions affect what is taken to be scientific knowledge.

I. INTRODUCTION: A ROLE FOR HISTORY

History, if viewed as a repository for more than anecdote or chronology, could produce a decisive transformation in the image of science by which we are now possessed. That image has previously been drawn, even by scientists themselves, mainly from the study of finished scientific achievements as these are recorded in the classics and, more recently, in the textbooks from which each new scientific generation learns to practice its trade. Inevitably, however, the aim of such books is persuasive and pedagogic; a concept of science drawn from them is no more likely to fit the enterprise that produced them than an image of a national culture drawn from a tourist brochure or a language text. This essay attempts to show that we have been misled by them in fundamental ways. Its aim is a sketch of the quite different concept of science that can emerge from the historical record of the research activity itself.

Even from history, however, that new concept will not be forthcoming if historical data continue to be sought and scrutinized mainly to answer questions posed by the unhistorical stereotype drawn from science texts. Those texts have, for example, often seemed to imply that the content of science is uniquely exemplified by the observations, laws, and theories described in their pages. Almost as regularly, the same books have been read as saying that scientific methods are simply the ones illustrated by the manipulative techniques used in gathering textbook data, together with the logical operations employed when relating those data to the textbook's theoretical generalizations. The result has been a concept of science with profound implications about its nature and development.

If science is the constellation of facts, theories, and methods collected in current texts, then scientists are the men who, successfully or not, have striven to contribute one or another element to that particular constellation. Scientific development becomes the piecemeal process by which these items have been added, singly and in combination, to the ever growing stockpile that constitutes scientific technique and knowledge. And history of science becomes the discipline that chronicles both these successive increments and the obstacles that have inhibited their accumulation. Concerned with scientific development, the historian then appears to have two main tasks. On the one hand, he must determine by what man and at what point in time each contemporary scientific fact, law, and theory was discovered or invented. On the other, he must describe and explain the congeries of error, myth, and superstition that have inhibited the more rapid accumulation of the constituents of the modern science text. Much research has been directed to these ends, and some still is.

In recent years, however, a few historians of science have been finding it more and more difficult to fulfil the functions that the concept of development-by-accumulation assigns to them. As chroniclers of an incremental process, they discover that additional research makes it harder, not easier, to answer questions like: When was oxygen discovered? Who first conceived of energy conservation? Increasingly, a few of them suspect that these are simply the wrong sorts of questions to ask. Perhaps science does not develop by the accumulation of individual discoveries and inventions. Simultaneously, these same historians confront growing difficulties in distinguishing the "scientific" component of past observation and belief from what their predecessors had readily labeled "error" and "superstition." The more carefully they study, say, Aristotelian dynamics, phlogistic chemistry, or caloric thermodynamics, the more certain they feel that those once current views of nature were, as a whole, neither less scientific nor more the product of human idiosyncrasy than those current today. If these out-of-date beliefs are to be called myths, then myths can be produced by the same sorts of methods and held for the same sorts of reasons that now lead to scientific knowledge. If, on the other hand, they are to be called science, then science has included bodies of belief quite incompatible with the ones we hold today. Given these alternatives, the historian must choose the latter. Out-of-date theories are not in principle unscientific because they have been discarded. That choice, however, makes it difficult to see scientific development as a process of accretion. The same historical research that displays the difficulties in isolating individual inventions and discoveries gives ground for profound doubts about the cumulative process through which these individual contributions to science were thought to have been compounded.

The result of all these doubts and difficulties is a historiographic revolution in the study of science, though one that is still in its early stages. Gradually, and often without entirely realizing they are doing so, historians of science have begun to ask new sorts of questions and to trace different, and often less than cumulative, developmental lines for the sciences. Rather than seeking the permanent contributions of an older science to our present vantage, they attempt to display the historical integrity of that science in its own time. They ask, for example, not about the relation of Galileo's views to those of modern science, but rather about the relationship between his views and those of his group, i.e., his teachers, contemporaries, and immediate successors in the sciences. Furthermore, they insist upon studying the opinions of that group and other similar ones from the viewpoint—usually very different from that of modern science—that gives those opinions the maximum internal coherence and the closest possible fit to nature. Seen through the works that result, works perhaps best exemplified in the writings of Alexandre Koyré, science does not seem altogether the same enterprise as the one discussed by writers in the older historiographic tradition. By implication, at least, these historical studies suggest the possibility of a new image of science. This essay aims to delineate that image by making explicit some of the new historiography's implications.

What aspect of science will emerge to prominence in the course of this effort? First, at least in order of presentation, is the insufficiency of methodological directives, by themselves, to dictate a unique substantive conclusion to many sorts of scientific questions. Instructed to examine electrical or chemical phenomena, the man who is ignorant of these fields but who knows what it is to be scientific may legitimately reach any one of a number of incompatible conclusions. Among those legitimate possibilities, the particular conclusions he does arrive at are probably determined by his prior experience in other fields, by the accidents of his investigation, and by his own individual makeup. What beliefs about the stars, for example, does he bring to the study of chemistry or electricity? Which of the many conceivable experiments relevant to the new field does he elect to perform first? And what aspects of the complex phenomenon that then results strike him as particularly relevant to an elucidation of the nature of chemical change or of electrical affinity? For the individual, at least, and sometimes for the scientific community as well, answers to questions like these are often essential determinants of scientific development. . . . For example, . . . the early developmental stages of most sciences have been characterized by continual competition between a number of distinct views of nature, each partially derived from, and all roughly compatible with, the dictates of scientific observation and method. What differentiated these various schools was not one or another failure of method—they were all "scientific"—but what we shall come to call their incommensurable ways of seeing the world and of practicing science in it. Observation and experience can and must drastically restrict the range of admissible scientific belief, else there would be no science. But they cannot alone determine a particular body of such belief. An apparently arbitrary element, compounded of personal and historical accident, is always a formative ingredient of the beliefs espoused by a given scientific community at a given time.

That element of arbitrariness does not, however, indicate that any scientific group could practice its trade without some set of received beliefs. Nor does it make less consequential the particular constellation to which the group, at a given time, is in fact committed. Effective research scarcely begins before a scientific community thinks it has acquired firm answers to questions like the following: What are the fundamental entities of which the universe is composed? How do these interact with each other and with the senses? What questions may legitimately be asked about such entities and what techniques employed in seeking solutions? At least in the mature sciences, answers (or full substitutes for answers) to questions like these are firmly embedded in the educational initiation that prepares and licenses the student for professional practice. Because that education is both rigorous and rigid, these answers come to exert a deep hold on the scientific mind. That they can do so does much to account both for the peculiar efficiency of the normal research activity and for the direction in which it proceeds at any given time. . . .

Yet that element of arbitrariness is present, and it too has an important effect on scientific development. . . . Normal science, the activity in which most scientists inevitably spend almost all their time, is predicated on the assumption that the scientific community knows what the world is like. Much of the success of the enterprise derives from the community's willingness to defend that assumption, if necessary at considerable cost. Normal science, for example, often suppresses fundamental novelties because they are necessarily subversive of its basic commitments. Nevertheless, so long as those commitments retain an element of the arbitrary, the very nature of normal research ensures that novelty shall not be suppressed for very long. Sometimes a normal problem, one that ought to be solvable by known rules and procedures, resists the reiterated onslaught of the ablest members of the group within whose competence it falls. On other occasions a piece of equipment designed and constructed for the purpose of normal research fails to perform in the anticipated manner, revealing an anomaly that cannot, despite repeated effort, be aligned with professional expectation. In these and other ways besides, normal science repeatedly goes astray. And when it does—when, that is, the profession can no longer evade anomalies that subvert the existing tradition of scientific practice—then begin the extraordinary investigations that lead the profession at last to a new set of commitments, a new basis for the practice of science. The extraordinary episodes in which that shift of professional commitments occurs are the ones known in this essay as scientific revolutions. They are the tradition-shattering complements to the tradition-bound activity of normal science.

The most obvious examples of scientific revolutions are those famous episodes in scientific development that have often been labeled revolutions before . . . [, such as] the major turning points . . . associated with the names of Copernicus, Newton, Lavoisier, and Einstein. More clearly than most other episodes in the history of at least the physical sciences, these display what all scientific revolutions are about. Each of them necessitated the community's rejection of one time-honored scientific theory in favor of another incompatible with it. Each produced a consequent shift in the problems available for scientific scrutiny and in the standards by which the profession determined what should count as an admissible problem or as a legitimate problem-solution. And each transformed the scientific imagination in ways that we shall ultimately need to describe as a transformation of the world within which scientific work was done. Such changes, together with the controversies that almost always accompany them, are the defining characteristics of scientific revolutions.

These characteristics emerge with particular clarity from a study of, say, the Newtonian or the chemical revolution. It is, however, a fundamental thesis of this essay that they can also be retrieved from the study of many other episodes that were not so obviously revolutionary. For the far smaller professional group affected by them, Maxwell's equations were as revolutionary as Einstein's, and they were resisted accordingly. The invention of other new theories regularly, and appropriately, evokes the same response from some of the specialists on whose area of special competence they impinge. For these men the new theory implies a change in the rules governing the prior practice of normal science. Inevitably, therefore, it reflects upon much scientific work they have already successfully completed. That is why a new theory, however special its range of application, is seldom or never just an increment to what is already known. Its assimilation requires the reconstruction of prior theory and the re-evaluation of prior fact, an intrinsically revolutionary process that is seldom completed by a single man and never overnight. No wonder historians have had difficulty in dating precisely this extended process that their vocabulary impels them to view as an isolated event.

Nor are new inventions of theory the only scientific events that have revolutionary impact upon the specialists in whose domain they occur. The commitments that govern normal science specify not only what sorts of entities the universe does contain, but also, by implication, those that it does not. It follows, though the point will require extended discussion, that a discovery like that of oxygen or X-rays does not simply add one more item to the population of the scientist's world. Ultimately it has that effect, but not until the professional community has re-evaluated traditional experimental procedures, altered its conception of entities with which it has long been familiar, and, in the process, shifted the network of theory through which it deals with the world. Scientific fact and theory are not categorically separable, except perhaps within a single tradition of normal-scientific practice. That is why the unexpected discovery is not simply factual in its import and why the scientist's world is qualitatively transformed as well as quantitatively enriched by fundamental novelties of either fact or theory. . . .

Undoubtedly, some readers will already have wondered whether historical study can possibly effect the sort of conceptual transformation aimed at here. An entire arsenal of dichotomies is available to suggest that it cannot properly do so. History, we too often say, is a purely descriptive discipline. The theses suggested above are, however, often interpretive and sometimes normative. Again, many of my generalizations are about the sociology or social psychology of scientists; yet at least a few of my conclusions belong traditionally to logic or epistemology. . . . I may even seem to have violated the very influential contemporary distinction between "the context of discovery" and "the context of justification." Can anything more than profound confusion be indicated by this admixture of diverse fields and concerns?

Having been weaned intellectually on these distinctions and others like them, I could scarcely be more aware of their import and force. For many years I took them to be about the nature of knowledge, and I still suppose that, appropriately recast, they have something important to tell us. Yet my attempts to apply them, even *grosso modo*, to the actual situations in which knowledge is gained, accepted, and assimilated have made them seem extraordinarily problematic. Rather than being elementary logical or methodological distinctions, which would thus be prior to the analysis of scientific knowledge, they now seem integral parts of a traditional set of substantive answers to the very questions upon which they have been deployed. That circularity does not at all invalidate them. But it does make them parts of a theory and, by doing so, subjects them to the same scrutiny regularly applied to theories in other fields. If they are to have more than pure abstraction as their content, then that content must be discovered by observing them in application to the data they are meant to elucidate. How could history of science fail to be a source of phenomena to which theories about knowledge may legitimately be asked to apply?

Plato

REPUBLIC

The following selection is from Plato's major dialogue, the *Republic*, Books v–vii, in which he sets forth his view of what constitutes complete knowledge. Socrates is speaking as the selection begins.

I think I said, that there might be a reform of the State if only one change were made, which is not a slight or easy though still a possible one.

What is it? he said.

Now then, I said, I go to meet that which I liken to the greatest of the waves; yet shall the word be spoken, even though the wave break and drown me in laughter and dishonour; and do you mark my words.

Proceed.

I said: *Until philosophers are kings, or the kings and princes of this world have the spirit and power of philosophy, and political greatness and wisdom meet in one, and those commoner natures who pursue either to the exclusion of the other are compelled to stand aside, cities will never have rest from their evils,—no, nor the human race, as I believe,—and then only will this our State have a possibility of life and behold the light of day.* Such was the thought, my dear Glaucon, which I would fain have uttered if it had not seemed too extravagant; for to be convinced that in no other State can there be happiness private or public is indeed a hard thing.

Socrates, what do you mean? I would have you consider that the word which you have uttered is one at which numerous persons, and very respectable persons too, in a figure pulling off their coats all in a moment, and seizing any weapon that comes to hand, will run at you might and main, before you know where you are, intending to do heaven knows what; and if you don't prepare an answer, and put yourself in motion, you will be "pared by their fine wits," and no mistake.

You got me into the scrape, I said.

And I was quite right; however, I will do all I can to get you out of it; but I can only give you good-will and good advice, and, perhaps, I may be able to fit answers to your questions better than another—that is all. And now, having such an auxiliary, you must do your best to show the unbelievers that you are right.

I ought to try, I said, since you offer me such invaluable assistance. And I think that, if there is to be a chance of our escaping, we must explain to them whom we mean when we say that philosophers are to rule in the State; then we shall be able to defend ourselves: There will be discovered to be some natures who ought to study philosophy and to be leaders in the State; and others who are not born to be philosophers, and are meant to be followers rather than leaders.

And may we not say of the philosopher that he is a lover, not of a part of wisdom only, but of the whole?

Yes, of the whole.

And he who dislikes learning, especially in youth, when he has no power of judging what is good and what is not, such an one we maintain not to be a philosopher or a lover of knowledge, just as he who refuses his food is not hungry, and may be said to have a bad appetite and not a good one?

Very true, he said.

Whereas he who has a taste for every sort of knowledge and who is curious to learn and is never satisfied, may be justly termed a philosopher? Am I not right?

Glaucon said: If curiosity makes a philosopher, you will find many a strange being will have a title to the name. All the lovers of sights have a delight in learning, and must therefore be included. Musical amateurs, too, are a folk strangely out of place among philosophers, for they are the last persons in the world who would come to anything like a philosophical discussion, if they could help, while they run about at the Dionysiac festivals as if they had let out their ears to hear every chorus; whether the performance is in town or country—that makes no difference—they are there. Now are we to maintain that all these and any who have similar tastes, as well as the professors of quite minor arts, are philosophers?

Certainly not, I replied; they are only an imitation.

He said: Who then are the true philosophers?

Those, I said, who are lovers of the vision of truth.

That is also good, he said; but I should like to know what you mean?

To another, I replied, I might have a difficulty in explaining; but I am sure that you will admit a proposition which I am about to make.

What is the proposition?

That since beauty is the opposite of ugliness, they are two?

Certainly.

And inasmuch as they are two, each of them is one?

True again.

And of just and unjust, good and evil, and of every other class, the same remark holds: taken singly, each of them is one; but from the various combinations of them with actions and things and with one another, they are seen in all sorts of lights and appear many?

Very true.

And this is the distinction which I draw between the sight-loving, art-loving, practical class and those of whom I am speaking, and who are alone worthy of the name of philosophers.

How do you distinguish them? he said.

The lovers of sounds and sights, I replied, are, as I conceive, fond of fine tones and colours and forms and all the artificial products that are made out of them, but their mind is incapable of seeing or loving absolute beauty.

True, he replied.

Few are they who are able to attain to the sight of this.

Very true.

And he who, having a sense of beautiful things has no sense of absolute beauty, or who, if another lead him to a knowledge of that beauty is unable to follow—of such an one I ask, Is he awake or in a dream only? Reflect: is not the dreamer, sleeping or waking, one who likens dissimilar things, who puts the copy in the place of the real object?

I should certainly say that such an one was dreaming.

But take the case of the other, who recognises the existence of absolute beauty and is able to distinguish the idea from the objects which participate in the idea, neither putting the objects in the place of the idea nor the idea in the place of the objects—is he a dreamer, or is he awake?

He is wide awake.

And may we not say that the mind of the one who knows has knowledge, and that the mind of the other, who opines only, has opinion?

Certainly.

But suppose that the latter should quarrel with us and dispute our statement, can we administer any soothing cordial or advice to him, without revealing to him that there is sad disorder in his wits?

We must certainly offer him some good advice, he replied.

Come, then, and let us think of something to say to him. Shall we begin by assuring him that he is welcome to any knowledge which he may have, and that we are rejoiced at his having it? But we should like to ask him a question: Does he who has knowledge know something or nothing? (You must answer for him.)

I answer that he knows something.

Something that is or is not?

Something that is; for how can that which is not ever be known?

And are we assured, after looking at the matter from many points of view, that absolute being is or may be absolutely known, but that the utterly nonexistent is utterly unknown?

Nothing can be more certain.

Good. But if there be anything which is of such a nature as to be and not to be, that will have a place intermediate between pure being and the absolute negation of being?

Yes, between them.

And, as knowledge corresponded to being and ignorance of necessity to not-being, for that intermediate between being and not-being there has to be discovered a corresponding intermediate between ignorance and knowledge, if there be such?

Certainly.

Do we admit the existence of opinion?

Undoubtedly.

As being the same with knowledge, or another faculty?

Another faculty.

Then opinion and knowledge have to do with different kinds of matter corresponding to this difference of faculties?

Yes.

And knowledge is relative to being and knows being. But before I proceed further I will make a division.

What division?

I will begin by placing faculties in a class by themselves: they are powers in us, and in all other things, by which we do as we do. Sight and hearing, for example, I should call faculties. Have I clearly explained the class which I mean?

Yes, I quite understand.

Then let me tell you my view about them. I do not see them, and therefore the distinctions of figure, colour, and the like, which enable me to discern the differences of some things, do not apply to them. In speaking of a faculty I think only of its sphere and its result; and that which has the same sphere and the same result I call the same faculty, but that which has another sphere and another result I call different. Would that be your way of speaking?

Yes.

And will you be so very good as to answer one more question? Would you say that knowledge is a faculty, or in what class would you place it?

Certainly knowledge is a faculty, and the mightiest of all faculties.

And is opinion also a faculty?

Certainly, he said; for opinion is that with which we are able to form an opinion.

And yet you were acknowledging a little while ago that knowledge is not the same as opinion?

Why, yes, he said: how can any reasonable being ever identify that which is infallible with that which errs?

An excellent answer, proving, I said, that we are quite conscious of a distinction between them.

Yes.

Then knowledge and opinion having distinct powers have also distinct spheres or subject-matters?

That is certain.

Being is the sphere or subject-matter of knowledge, and knowledge is to know the nature of being?

Yes.

And opinion is to have an opinion?

Yes.

And do we know what we opine? or is the subject-matter of opinion the same as the subject-matter of knowledge?

Nay, he replied, that has been already disproven; if difference in faculty implies difference in the sphere or subject-matter, and if, as we were saying, opinion and knowledge are distinct faculties, then the sphere of knowledge and of opinion cannot be the same.

Then if being is the subject-matter of knowledge, something else must be the subject-matter of opinion?

Yes, something else.

Well then, is not-being the subject-matter of opinion? or, rather, how can there be an opinion at all about not-being? Reflect: when a man has an opinion, has he not an opinion about something? Can he have an opinion which is an opinion about nothing?

Impossible.

He who has an opinion has an opinion about some one thing?

Yes.

And not-being is not one thing but, properly speaking, nothing?

True.

Of not-being, ignorance was assumed to be the necessary correlative; of being, knowledge?

True, he said.

Then opinion is not concerned either with being or with not-being?

Not with either.

And can therefore neither be ignorance nor knowledge?

That seems to be true.

But is opinion to be sought without and beyond either of them, in a greater clearness than knowledge, or in a greater darkness than ignorance?

In neither.

Then I suppose that opinion appears to you to be darker than knowledge, but lighter than ignorance?

Both; and in no small degree.

And also to be within and between them?

Yes.

Then you would infer that opinion is intermediate?

No question.

But were we not saying before, that if anything appeared to be of a sort which is and is not at the same time, that sort of thing would appear also to lie in the interval between pure being and absolute not-being; and that the corresponding faculty is neither knowledge nor ignorance, but will be found in the interval between them?

True.

And in that interval there has now been discovered something which we call opinion?

There has.

Then what remains to be discovered is the object which partakes equally of the nature of being and not-being, and cannot rightly be termed either, pure and simple; this unknown term, when discovered, we may truly call the subject of opinion, and assign each to their proper faculty,—the extremes to the faculties of the extremes and the mean to the faculty of the mean.

True.

This being premised, I would ask the gentleman who is of opinion that there is no absolute or unchangeable idea of beauty—in whose opinion the beautiful is the manifold—he, I say, your lover of beautiful sights, who cannot bear to be told that the beautiful is one, and the just is one, or that anything is one—to him I would appeal, saying, Will you be so very kind, sir, as to tell us whether, of all these beautiful things, there is one which will not be found ugly; or of the just, which will not be found unjust; or of the holy, which will not also be unholy?

No, he replied; the beautiful will in some point of view be found ugly; and the same is true of the rest.

And may not the many which are doubles be also halves?—doubles, that is, of one thing, and halves of another?

Quite true.

And things great and small, heavy and light, as they are termed, will not be denoted by these any more than by the opposite names?

True; both these and the opposite names will always attach to all of them.

And can any one of those many things which are called by particular names be said to be this rather than not to be this?

He replied: They are like the punning riddles which are asked at feasts or the children's puzzle about the eunuch aiming at the bat, with what he hit him, as they say in the puzzle, and upon what the bat was sitting. The individual objects of which I am speaking are also a riddle, and have a double sense: nor can you fix them in your mind, either as being or not-being, or both, or neither.

Then what will you do with them? I said. Can they have a better place than between being and not-being? For they are clearly not in greater darkness or negation than not-being, or more full of light and existence than being.

That is quite true, he said.

Thus then we seem to have discovered that the many ideas which the multitude entertain about the beautiful and about all other things are tossing about in some region which is half-way between pure being and pure not-being?

We have.

Yes; and we had before agreed that anything of this kind which we might find was to be described as matter of opinion, and not as matter of knowledge; being the intermediate flux which is caught and detained by the intermediate faculty.

Quite true.

Then those who see the many beautiful, and who yet neither see absolute beauty, nor can follow any guide who points the way thither; who see the many just, and not absolute justice, and the like,—such persons may be said to have opinion but not knowledge?

That is certain.

But those who see the absolute and eternal and immutable may be said to know, and not to have opinion only?

Neither can that be denied.

The one love and embrace the subjects of knowledge, the other those of opinion? The latter are the same, as I dare say you will remember, who listened to sweet sounds and gazed upon fair colours, but would not tolerate the existence of absolute beauty.

Yes, I remember.

Shall we then be guilty of any impropriety in calling them lovers of opinion rather than lovers of wisdom, and will they be very angry with us for thus describing them?

I shall tell them not to be angry; no man should be angry at what is true.

But those who love the truth in each thing are to be called lovers of wisdom and not lovers of opinion.

Assuredly. . . .

Will you be a little more explicit? he said.

Why, you know, I said, that the eyes, when a person directs them towards objects on which the light of day is no longer shining, but the moon and stars only, see dimly, and are nearly blind; they seem to have no clearness of vision in them?

Very true.

But when they are directed towards objects on which the sun shines, they see clearly and there is sight in them?

Certainly.

And the soul is like the eye: when resting upon that on which truth and being shine, the soul perceives and understands and is radiant with intelligence; but when turned towards the twilight of becoming and perishing, then she has opinion only, and goes blinking about, and is first of one opinion and then of another, and seems to have no intelligence?

Just so.

Now, that which imparts truth to the known and the power of knowing to the knower is what I would have you term the idea of good, and this you will deem to be the cause of science, and of truth in so far as the latter becomes the subject of knowledge; beautiful too, as are both truth and knowledge, you will be right in esteeming this other nature as more beautiful than either; and, as in the previous instance, light and sight may be truly said to be like the sun, and yet not to be the sun, so in this other sphere, science and truth may be deemed to be like the good, but not the good; the good has a place of honour yet higher.

What a wonder of beauty that must be, he said, which is the author of science and truth, and yet surpasses them in beauty; for you surely cannot mean to say that pleasure is the good?

God forbid, I replied; but may I ask you to consider the image in another point of view.

In what point of view?

You would say, would you not, that the sun is not only the author of visibility in all visible things, but of generation and nourishment and growth, though he himself is not generation?

Certainly.

In like manner the good may be said to be not only the author of knowledge to all things known, but of their being and essence, and yet the good is not essence, but far exceeds essence in dignity and power.

Glaucon said, with a ludicrous earnestness: By the light of heaven, how amazing!

Yes, I said, and the exaggeration may be set down to you; for you made me utter my fancies.

And pray continue to utter them; at any rate let us hear if there is anything more to be said about the similitude of the sun.

Yes, I said, there is a great deal more.

Then omit nothing, however slight.

I will do my best, I said; but I should think that a great deal will have to be omitted.

You have to imagine, then, that there are two ruling powers, and that one of them is set over the intellectual world, the other over the visible. I do not say heaven, lest you should fancy that I am playing upon the name (σὐρανός, ὁρατος). May I suppose that you have this distinction of the visible and intelligible fixed in your mind?

I have.

Now take a line which has been cut into two unequal parts, and divide each of them again in the same proportion, and suppose the two main divisions to answer, one to the visible and the other to the intelligible, and then compare the subdivisions in respect of their clearness and want of clearness, and you will find that the first section in the sphere of the visible consists of images. And by images I mean, in the first place, shadows, and in the second place, reflections in water and in solid, smooth and polished bodies and the like: Do you understand?

Yes, I understand.

Imagine, now, the other section, of which this is only the resemblance, to include the animals which we see, and everything that grows or is made.

Very good.

Would you not admit that both the sections of this division have different degrees of truth, and that the copy is to the original as the sphere of opinion is to the sphere of knowledge?

Most undoubtedly.

Next proceed to consider the manner in which the sphere of the intellectual is to be divided.

In what manner?

Thus:—There are two subdivisions, in the lower of which the soul uses the figures given by the former division as images; the enquiry can only be hypothetical, and instead of going upwards to a principle descends to the other end; in the higher of the two, the soul passes out of hypotheses, and goes up to a principle which is above hypotheses, making no use of images as in the former case, but proceeding only in and through the ideas themselves.

I do not quite understand your meaning, he said.

Then I will try again; you will understand me better when I have made some preliminary remarks. You are aware that students of geometry, arithmetic, and the kindred sciences assume the odd and the even and the figures and three kinds of angles and the like in their several branches of science; these are their hypotheses, which they and every body are supposed to know, and therefore they do not deign to give any account of them either to themselves or others; but they begin with them, and go on until they arrive at last, and in a consistent manner, at their conclusion?

Yes, he said, I know.

And do you not know also that although they make use of the visible forms and reason about them, they are thinking not of these, but of the ideals which they resemble; not of the figures which they draw, but of the absolute square and the absolute diameter, and so on—the forms which they draw or make, and which have shadows and reflections in water of their own, are converted by them into images, but they are really seeking to behold the things themselves, which can only be seen with the eye of the mind?

That is true.

And of this kind I spoke as the intelligible, although in the search after it the soul is compelled to use hypotheses; not ascending to a first principle, because she is unable to rise above the region of hypothesis, but employing the objects of which the shadows below are resemblances in their turn as images, they having in relation to the shadows and reflections of them a greater distinctness, and therefore a higher value.

I understand, he said, that you are speaking of the province of geometry and the sister arts.

And when I speak of the other division of the intelligible, you will understand me to speak of that other sort of knowledge which reason herself attains by the power of dialectic, using the hypotheses not as first principles, but only as hypotheses—that is to say, as steps and points of departure into a world which is above hypotheses, in order that she may soar beyond them to the first principle of the whole; and clinging to this and then to that which depends on this, by successive steps she descends again without the aid of any sensible object, from ideas through ideas, and in ideas she ends.

I understand you, he replied; not perfectly, for you seem to me to be describing a task which is really tremendous; but, at any rate, I understand you to say that knowledge and being, which the science of dialectic contemplates, are clearer than the notions of the arts, as they are termed, which proceed from hypotheses only: these are also contemplated by the understanding, and not by the senses: yet, because they start from hypotheses and do not ascend to a principle, those who contemplate them appear to you not to exercise the higher reason upon them, although when a first principle is added to them they are cognizable by the higher reason. And the habit which is concerned with geometry and the cognate sciences I suppose that you would term understanding and not reason, as being intermediate between opinion and reason.

You have quite conceived my meaning, I said; and now, corresponding to these four divisions, let there be four faculties in the soul—reason answering to the highest, understanding to the second, faith (or conviction) to the third, and perception of shadows to the last—and let there be a scale of them, and let us suppose that the several faculties have clearness in the same degree that their objects have truth.

I understand, he replied, and give my assent, and accept your arrangement. . . .

And now, I said, let me show in a figure how far our nature is enlightened or unenlightened:—Behold! human beings living in an underground den, which has a mouth open towards the light and reaching all along the den; here they have been from their childhood, and have their legs and necks chained so that they cannot move, and can only see before them, being prevented by the chains from turning round their heads. Above and behind them a fire is blazing at a distance, and between the fire and the prisoners there is a raised way; and you will see, if you look, a low wall built along the way, like the screen which marionette players have in front of them, over which they show the puppets.

I see.

And do you see, I said, men passing along the wall carrying all sorts of vessels, and statues and figures of animals made of wood and stone and various materials, which appear over the wall? Some of them are talking, others silent.

You have shown me a strange image, and they are strange prisoners.

Like ourselves, I replied; and they see only their own shadows, or the shadows of one another, which the fire throws on the opposite wall of the cave?

True, he said; how could they see anything but the shadows if they were never allowed to move their heads?

And of the objects which are being carried in like manner they would only see the shadows?

Yes, he said.

And if they were able to converse with one another, would they not suppose that they were naming what was actually before them?

Very true.

And suppose further that the prison had an echo which came from the other side, would they not be sure to fancy when one of the passers-by spoke that the voice which they heard came from the passing shadow?

No question, he replied.

To them, I said, the truth would be literally nothing but the shadows of the images.

That is certain.

And now look again, and see what will naturally follow if the prisoners are released and disabused of their error. At first, when any of them is liberated and compelled suddenly to stand up and turn his neck round and walk and look towards the light, he will suffer sharp pains; the glare will distress him, and he will be unable to see the realities of which in his former state he had seen the shadows; and then conceive some one saying to him, that what he saw before was an illusion, but that now, when he is approaching nearer to being and his eye is turned towards more real existence, he has a clearer vision,—what will be his reply? And you may further imagine that his instructor is pointing to the objects as they pass and requiring him to name them,—will he not be perplexed? Will he not fancy that the shadows which he formerly saw are truer than the objects which are now shown to him?

Far truer.

And if he is compelled to look straight at the light, will he not have a pain in his eyes which will make him turn away to take refuge in the objects of vision which he can see, and which he will conceive to be in reality clearer than the things which are now being shown to him?

True, he said.

And suppose once more, that he is reluctantly dragged up a steep and rugged ascent, and held fast until he is forced into the presence of the sun himself, is he not likely to be pained and irritated? When he approaches the light his eyes will be dazzled, and he will not be able to see anything at all of what are now called realities.

Not all in a moment, he said.

He will require to grow accustomed to the sight of the upper world. And first he will see the shadows best, next the reflections of men and other objects in the water, and then the objects themselves; then he will gaze upon the light of the moon and the stars and the spangled heaven; and he will see the sky and the stars by night better than the sun or the light of the sun by day?

Certainly.

Last of all he will be able to see the sun, and not mere reflections of him in the water, but he will see him in his own proper place, and not in another; and he will contemplate him as he is.

Certainly.

He will then proceed to argue that this is he who gives the season and the years, and is the guardian of all that is in the visible world, and in a certain way the cause of all things which he and his fellows have been accustomed to behold?

Clearly, he said, he would first see the sun and then reason about him.

And when he remembered his old habitation, and the wisdom of the den and his fellow-prisoners, do you not suppose that he would felicitate himself on the change, and pity them?

Certainly, he would.

And if they were in the habit of conferring honours among themselves on those who were quickest to observe the passing shadows and to remark which of them went before, and which followed after, and which were together; and who were therefore best able to draw conclusions as to the future, do you think that he would care for such honours and glories, or envy the possessors of them? Would he not say with Homer, "Better to be the poor servant of a poor master," and to endure anything, rather than think as they do and live after their manner?

Yes, he said, I think that he would rather suffer anything than entertain these false notions and live in this miserable manner.

Imagine once more, I said, such an one coming suddenly out of the sun to be replaced in his old situation; would he not be certain to have his eyes full of darkness?

To be sure, he said.

And if there were a contest, and he had to compete in measuring the shadows with the prisoners who had never moved out of the den, while his sight was still weak, and before his eyes had become steady (and the time which would be needed to acquire this new habit of sight might be very considerable), would he not be ridiculous? Men would say of him that up he went and down he came without his eyes; and that it was better not even to think of ascending; and if any one tried to loose another and lead him up to the light, let them only catch the offender, and they would put him to death.

No question, he said.

This entire allegory, I said, you may now append, dear Glaucon, to the previous argument; the prison-house is the world of sight, the light of the fire is the sun, and you will not misapprehend me if you interpret the journey upwards to be the ascent of the soul into the intellectual world according to my poor belief, which, at your desire, I have expressed—whether rightly or wrongly God knows. But, whether true or false, my opinion is that in the world of knowledge the idea of good appears last of all, and is seen only with an effort; and, when seen, is also inferred to be the universal author of all things beautiful and right, parent of light and of the lord of light in this visible world, and the immediate source of reason and truth in the intellectual; and that this is the power upon which he who would act rationally either in public or private life must have his eye fixed.

I agree, he said, as far as I am able to understand you.

Moreover, I said, you must not wonder that those who attain to this beatific vision are unwilling to descend to human affairs; for their souls are ever hastening into the upper world where they desire to dwell; which desire of theirs is very natural, if our allegory may be trusted.

Yes, very natural.

And is there anything surprising in one who passes from divine contemplations to the evil state of man, misbehaving himself in a ridiculous manner; if, while his eyes are blinking and before he has become accustomed to the surrounding darkness, he is compelled to fight in courts of law, or in other places, about the images or the shadows of images of justice, and is endeavouring to meet the conceptions of those who have never yet seen absolute justice?

Anything but surprising, he replied.

Any one who has common sense will remember that the bewilderments of the eyes are of two kinds, and arise from two causes, either from coming out of the light or from going into the light, which is true of the mind's eye, quite as much as of the bodily eye; and he who remembers this when he sees any one whose vision is perplexed and weak, will not be too ready to laugh; he will first ask whether that soul of man has come out of the brighter life, and is unable to see because unaccustomed to the dark, or having turned from darkness to the day is dazzled by excess of light. And he will count the one happy in his condition and state of being, and he will pity the other; or, if he have a mind to laugh at the soul which comes from below into the light, there will be more reason in this than in the laugh which greets him who returns from above out of the light into the den.

That, he said, is a very just distinction.

But then, if I am right, certain professors of education must be wrong when they say that they can put a knowledge into the soul which was not there before, like sight into blind eyes.

They undoubtedly say this, he replied.

Whereas, our argument shows that the power and capacity of learning exists in the soul already; and that just as the eye was unable to turn from darkness to light without the whole body, so too the instrument of knowledge can only by the movement of the whole soul be turned from the world of becoming into that of being, and learn by degrees to endure the sight of being, and of the brightest and best of being, or in other words, of the good.

Very true.

And must there not be some art which will effect conversion in the easiest and quickest manner; not implanting the faculty of sight, for that exists already, but has been turned in the wrong direction, and is looking away from the truth?

Yes, he said, such an art may be presumed.

And whereas the other so-called virtues of the soul seem to be akin to bodily qualities, for even when they are not originally innate they can be implanted later by habit and exercise, the virtue of wisdom more than anything else contains a divine element which always remains, and by this conversion is rendered useful and profitable; or, on the other hand, hurtful and useless. Did you never observe the narrow intelligence flashing from the keen eye of a clever rogue—how eager he is, how clearly his paltry soul sees the way to his end; he is the reverse of blind, but his keen eye-sight is forced into the service of evil, and he is mischievous in proportion to his cleverness?

Very true, he said.

But what if there had been a circumcision of such natures in the days of their youth; and they had been severed from those sensual pleasures, such as eating and drinking, which, like leaden weights, were attached to them at their birth, and which drag them down and turn the vision of their souls upon the things that are below—if, I say, they had been released from these impediments and turned in the opposite direction, the very same faculty in them would have seen the truth as keenly as they see what their eyes are turned to now.

Very likely.

Yes, I said; and there is another thing which is likely, or rather a necessary inference from what has preceded, that neither the uneducated and uniformed of the truth, nor yet those who never make an end of their education, will be able ministers of State; not the former, because they have no single aim of duty which is the rule of all their actions, private as well as public; nor the latter, because they will not act at all except upon compulsion, fancying that they are already dwelling apart in the islands of the blest.

Very true, he replied.

Then, I said; the business of us who are the founders of the State will be to compel the best minds to attain that knowledge which we have already shown to be the greatest of all—they must continue to ascend until they arrive at the good; but when they have ascended and seen enough we must not allow them to do as they do now.

What do you mean?

I mean that they remain in the upper world: but this must not be allowed; they must be made to descend again among the prisoners in the den, and partake of their labours and honours, whether they are worth having or not.

But is not this unjust? he said; ought we to give them a worse life, when they might have a better?

You have again forgotten, my friend, I said, the intention of the legislator, who did not aim at making any one class in the State happy above the rest; the happiness was to be in the whole State. And he held the citizens together by persuasion and necessity, making them benefactors of the State, and therefore benefactors of one another; to this end he created them, not to please themselves, but to be his instruments in binding up the State.

True, he said, I had forgotten.

Observe, Glaucon, that there will be no injustice in compelling our philosophers to have a care and providence of others; we shall explain to them that in other States, men of their class are not obliged to share in the toils of politics: and this is reasonable, for they grow up at their own sweet will, and the government would rather not have them. Being self-taught, they cannot be expected to show any gratitude for a culture which they have never received. But we have brought you into the world to be rulers of the hive, kings of yourselves and of the other citizens, and have educated you far better and more perfectly than they have been educated, and you are better able to share in the double duty. Wherefore each of you, when his turn comes, must go down to the general underground abode, and get the habit of seeing in the dark. When you have acquired the habit, you will see ten thousand times better than the inhabitants of the den, and you will know what the several images are, and what they represent, because you have seen the beautiful and just and good in their truth. And thus our State which is also yours will be a reality, and not a dream only, and will be administered in a spirit unlike that of other States, in which men fight with one another about shadows only and are distracted in the struggle for power, which in their eyes is a great good. Whereas the truth is that the State in which the rulers are most reluctant to govern is always the best and most quietly governed, and the State in which they are most eager, the worst.

Quite true, he replied.

And will our pupils, when they hear this, refuse to take their turn at the toils of State, when they are allowed to spend the greater part of their time with one another in the heavenly light?

Impossible, he answered; for they are just men, and the commands which we impose upon them are just; there can be no doubt that every one of them will take office as a stern necessity, and not after the fashion of our present rulers of State.

Yes, my friend, I said; and there lies the point. You must contrive for your future rulers another and a better life than that of a ruler, and then you may have a well-ordered State; for only in the State which offers this, will they rule who are truly rich, not in silver and gold, but in virtue and wisdom, which are the true blessings of life. Whereas if they go to the administration of public affairs, poor and hungering after their own private advantage, thinking that hence they are to snatch the chief good, order there can never be; for they will be fighting about office, and the civil and domestic broils which thus arise will be the ruin of the rulers themselves and of the whole State.

Most true, he replied.

And the only life which looks down upon the life of political ambition is that of true philosophy. Do you know of any other?

Indeed, I do not, he said.

And those who govern ought not to be lovers of the task? For, if they are, there will be rival lovers, and they will fight.

No question.

Who then are those whom we shall compel to be guardians? Surely they will be the men who are wisest about affairs of State, and by whom the State is best administered, and who at the same time have other honours and another and a better life than that of politics?

They are the men, and I will choose them, he replied.

Now, when all these studies reach the point of inter-communion and con-nection with one another, and come to be considered in their mutual affinities, then, I think, but not till then, will the pursuit of them have a value for our objects; otherwise there is no profit in them.

I suspect so; but you are speaking, Socrates, of a vast work.

What do you mean? I said; the prelude or what? Do you not know that all this is but the prelude to the actual strain which we have to learn? For you surely would not regard the skilled mathematician as a dialectician?

Assuredly not, he said; I have hardly ever known a mathematician who was capable of reasoning.

But do you imagine that men who are unable to give and take a reason will have the knowledge which we require of them?

Neither can this be supposed.

And so, Glaucon, I said, we have at last arrived at the hymn of dialectic. This is that strain which is of the intellect only, but which the faculty of sight will nevertheless be found to imitate; for sight, as you may remember, was imag-ined by us after a while to behold the real animals and stars, and last of all the sun himself. And so with dialectic; when a person starts on the discovery of the absolute by the light of reason only, and without any assistance of sense, and perseveres until by pure intelligence he arrives at the perception of the abso-lute good, he at last finds himself at the end of the intellectual world, as in the case of sight at the end of the visible.

Exactly, he said.

Then this is the progress which you call dialectic?

True.

But the release of the prisoners from chains, and their translation from the shadows to the images and to the light, and the ascent from the underground den to the sun, while in his presence they are vainly trying to look on animals and plants and the light of the sun, but are able to perceive even with their weak eyes the images in the water [which are divine], and are the shadows of true existence (not shadows of images cast by a light of fire, which compared with the sun is only an image)—this power of elevating the highest principle in the soul to the contemplation of that which is best in existence, with which we may compare the raising of that faculty which is the very light of the body to the sight of that which is brightest in the material and visible world—this power is given, as I was saying, by all that study and pursuit of the arts which has been described.

I agree in what you are saying, he replied, which may be hard to believe, yet, from another point of view, is harder still to deny. This however is not a theme to be treated of in passing only, but will have to be discussed again and again. And so, whether our conclusion be true or false, let us assume all this, and proceed at once from the prelude or preamble to the chief strain, and describe that in like manner. Say, then, what is the nature and what are the divisions of dialectic, and what are the paths which lead thither; for these paths will also lead to our final rest.

Dear Glaucon, I said, you will not be able to follow me here, though I would do my best, and you should behold not an image only but the absolute truth, according to my notion. Whether what I told you would or would not have been a reality I cannot venture to say; but you would have seen something like reality; of that I am confident.

Doubtless, he replied.

But I must also remind you, that the power of dialectic alone can reveal this, and only to one who is a disciple of the previous sciences.

Of that assertion you may be as confident as of the last.

And assuredly no one will argue that there is any other method of comprehending by any regular process all true existence or of ascertaining what each thing is in its own nature; for the arts in general are concerned with the desires or opinions of men, or are cultivated with a view to production and construction, or for the preservation of such productions and constructions; and as to the mathematical sciences which, as we were saying, have some apprehension of being true—geometry and the like—they only dream about being, but never can they behold the waking reality so long as they leave the hypotheses which they use unexamined, and are unable to give an account of them. For when a man knows not his own first principle, and when the conclusion and intermediate steps are also constructed out of he knows not what, how can he imagine that such a fabric of convention can ever become science?

Impossible, he said.

Then dialectic, and dialectic alone, goes directly to the first principle and is the only science which does away with hypotheses in order to make her ground secure; the eye of the soul, which is literally buried in an outlandish slough, is by her gentle aid lifted upwards; and she uses as handmaids and helpers in the work of conversion, the sciences which we have been discussing. Custom terms them sciences, but they ought to have some other name, implying greater clearness than opinion and less clearness than science: and this, in our previous sketch, was called understanding. But why should we dispute about names when we have realities of such importance to consider?

Why indeed, he said, when any name will do which expresses the thought of the mind with clearness?

At any rate, we are satisfied, as before, to have four divisions; two for intellect and two for opinion, and to call the first division science, the second understanding, the third belief, and the fourth perception of shadows, opinion being concerned with becoming, and intellect with being; and so to make a proportion:—

As being is to becoming, so is pure intellect to opinion.

And as intellect is to opinion, so is science to belief, and understanding to the perception of shadows.

But let us defer the further correlation and subdivision of the subjects of opinion and of intellect, for it will be a long enquiry, many times longer than this has been.

As far as I understand, he said, I agree.

And do you also agree, I said, in describing the dialectician as one who attains a conception of the essence of each thing? And he who does not possess and is therefore unable to impart this conception, in whatever degree he fails, may in that degree also be said to fail in intelligence? Will you admit so much?

Yes, he said; how can I deny it?

And you would say the same of the conception of the good? Until the person is able to abstract and define rationally the idea of good, and unless he can run the gauntlet of all objections, and is ready to disprove them, not by appeals to opinion, but to absolute truth, never faltering at any step of the argument— unless he can do all this, you would say that he knows neither the idea of good nor any other good; he apprehends only a shadow, if anything at all, which is given by opinion and not by science;—dreaming and slumbering in this life, before he is well awake here, he arrives at the world below, and has his final quietus.

In all that I should most certainly agree with you.

And surely you would not have the children of your ideal State, whom you are nurturing and educating—if the ideal ever becomes a reality—you would not allow the future rulers to be like posts, having no reason in them, and yet to be set in authority over the highest matters?

Certainly not.

Then you will make a law that they shall have such an education as will enable them to attain the greatest skill in asking and answering questions?

Yes, he said, you and I together will make it.

Dialectic, then, as you will agree, is the coping-stone of the sciences, and is set over them; no other science can be placed higher—the nature of knowledge can no further go?

I agree, he said.

Aristotle

POSTERIOR ANALYTICS

Aristotle (384–322 B.C.) had been Plato's student. He rejected his teacher's philosophy and developed his own theory. In Book I of the *Posterior Analytics* he presented his theory of scientific knowledge.

9 . . . It is hard to be sure whether one knows or not; for it is hard to be sure whether one's knowledge is based on the basic truths appropriate to each attribute—the differentia of true knowledge. We think we have scientific knowledge if we have reasoned from true and primary premisses. But that is not so: the conclusion must be homogeneous with the basic facts of the science.

10 I call the basic truths of every genus those elements in it the existence of which cannot be proved. As regards both these primary truths and the attributes dependent on them the meaning of the name is assumed. The fact of their existence as regards the primary truths must be assumed; but it has to be proved of the remainder, the attributes. Thus we assume the meaning alike of unity, straight, and triangular; but while as regards unity and magnitude we assume also the fact of their existence, in the case of the remainder proof is required.

Of the basic truths used in the demonstrative sciences some are peculiar to each science, and some are common, but common only in the sense of analogous, being of use only in so far as they fall within the genus constituting the province of the science in question.

Peculiar truths are, e.g., the definitions of line and straight; common truths are such as "take equals from equals and equals remain." Only so much of these common truths is required as falls within the genus in question: for a truth of this kind will have the same force even if not used generally but applied by the geometer only to magnitudes, or by the arithmetician only to numbers. Also peculiar to a science are the subjects the existence as well as the meaning of which it assumes, and the essential attributes of which it investigates, e.g. in arithmetic units, in geometry points and lines. Both the existence and the meaning of the subjects are assumed by these sciences; but of their essential attributes only the meaning is assumed. For example arithmetic assumes the meaning of odd and even, square and cube, geometry that of incommensurable, or of deflection or verging of lines, whereas the existence of these attributes is demonstrated by means of the axioms and from previous conclusions as premises. Astronomy too proceeds in the same way. For indeed every demonstrative science has three elements: (1) that which it posits, the subject genus whose essential attributes it examines; (2) the so-called axioms, which are primary premises of its demonstration; (3) the attributes, the meaning of which it assumes. Yet some sciences may very well pass over some of these elements; e.g. we might not expressly posit the existence of the genus if its existence were obvious (for instance, the existence of hot and cold is more evident than that of number); or we might omit to assume expressly the meaning of the attributes if it were well understood. In the same way the meaning of axioms, such as "Take equals from equals and equals remain," is well known and so not expressly assumed. Nevertheless in the nature of the case the essential elements of demonstration are three: the subject, the attributes, and the basic premises.

That which expresses necessary self-grounded fact, and which we must necessarily believe,[1] is distinct both from the hypotheses of a science and from illegitimate postulate—I say "must believe," because all syllogism, and therefore *a fortiori* demonstration, is addressed not to the spoken word, but to the discourse within the soul,[2] and though we can always raise objections to the spoken word, to the inward discourse we cannot always object. That which is capable of proof but assumed by the teacher without proof is, if the pupil believes and accepts it, hypothesis, though only in a limited sense hypothesis—that is, relatively to the pupil; if the pupil has no opinion or a contrary opinion on the matter, the same assumption is an illegitimate postulate: the latter is the contrary of the pupil's opinion, demonstrable, but assumed and used without demonstration.

The definitions—viz. those which are not expressed as statements that anything is or is not—are not hypotheses: but it is in the premises of a science that its hypotheses are contained. Definitions require only to be understood, and this is not hypothesis—unless it be contended that the pupil's hearing is also an hypothesis required by the teacher. Hypotheses, on the contrary, postulate facts on the being of which depends the being of the fact inferred. Nor are the geometer's hypotheses false, as some have held, urging that one must not employ falsehood and that the geometer is uttering falsehood in stating that the line which he draws is a foot long or straight, when it is actually

---

[1] *sc.* axioms.

[2] Cf. Plato, *Theaetetus,* 189 E ff.

neither. The truth is that the geometer does not draw any conclusion from the being of the particular line of which he speaks, but from what his diagrams symbolize. A further distinction is that all hypotheses and illegitimate postulates are either universal or particular, whereas a definition is neither.

11 So demonstration does not necessarily imply the being of Forms nor a One beside a Many, but it does necessarily imply the possibility of truly predicating one of many; since without this possibility we cannot save the universal, and if the universal goes, the middle term goes with it, and so demonstration becomes impossible. We conclude, then, that there must be a single identical term unequivocally predicable of a number of individuals.

The law that it is impossible to affirm and deny simultaneously the same predicate of the same subject is not expressly posited by any demonstration except when the conclusion also has to be expressed in that form; in which case the proof lays down as its major premiss that the major is truly affirmed of the middle but falsely denied. It makes no difference, however, if we add to the middle, or again to the minor term, the corresponding negative. For grant a minor term of which it is true to predicate man—even if it be also true to predicate not-man of it—still grant simply that man is animal and not not-animal, and the conclusion follows: for it will still be true to say that Callias—even if it be also true to say that not-Callias—is animal and not not-animal. The reason is that the major term is predicable not only of the middle, but of something other than the middle as well, being of wider application; so that the conclusion is not affected even if the middle is extended to cover the original middle term and also what is not the original middle term.[3]

The law that every predicate can be either truly affirmed or truly denied of every subject is posited by such demonstration as uses *reductio ad impossibile*, and then not always universally, but so far as it is requisite; within the limits, that is, of the genus—the genus, I mean (as I have already explained[4]), to which the man of science applies his demonstrations. In virtue of the common elements of demonstration—I mean the common axioms which are used as premisses of demonstration, not the subjects or the attributes demonstrated as belonging to them—all the sciences have communion with one another, and in communion with them all is dialectic and any science which might attempt a universal proof of axioms such as the law of excluded middle, the law that the subtraction of equals from equals leaves equal remainders, or other axioms of the same kind. Dialectic has no definite sphere of this kind, not being confined to a single genus. Otherwise its method would not be interrogative; for the interrogative method is barred to the demonstrator, who cannot use the

---

[3]Lit. "even if the middle is itself and also what is not itself"; i.e. you may pass from the middle term man to include not-man without affecting the conclusion.

[4]Cf. 75[a] 42 ff. and 76[b] 13.

opposite facts to prove the same *nexus*. This was shown in my work on the syllogism.[5]

12   If a syllogistic question[6] is equivalent to a proposition embodying one of the two sides of a contradiction, and if each science has its peculiar propositions from which its peculiar conclusion is developed, then there is such a thing as a distinctively scientific question, and it is the interrogative form of the premises from which the "appropriate" conclusion of each science is developed. Hence it is clear that not every question will be relevant to geometry, nor to medicine, nor to any other science: only those questions will be geometrical which form premises for the proof of the theorems of geometry or of any other science, such as optics, which uses the same basic truths as geometry. Of the other sciences the like is true. Of these questions the geometer is bound to give his account, using the basic truths of geometry in conjunction with his previous conclusions; of the basic truths the geometer, as such, is not bound to give any account. The like is true of the other sciences. There is a limit, then, to the questions which we may put to each man of science; nor is each man of science bound to answer all inquiries on each several subject, but only such as fall within the defined field of his own science. If, then, in controversy with a geometer *qua* geometer the disputant confines himself to geometry and proves anything from geometrical premises, he is clearly to be applauded; if he goes outside these he will be at fault, and obviously cannot even refute the geometer except accidentally. One should therefore not discuss geometry among those who are not geometers, for in such a company an unsound argument will pass unnoticed. This is correspondingly true in the other sciences.

Since there are "geometrical" questions, does it follow that there are also distinctively "ungeometrical" questions? Further, in each special science—geometry for instance—what kind of error is it that may vitiate questions, and yet not exclude them from that science? Again, is the erroneous conclusion one constructed from premises opposite to the true premises, or is it formal fallacy though drawn from geometrical premises? Or, perhaps, the erroneous conclusion is due to the drawing of premises from another science; e.g. in a geometrical controversy a musical question is distinctively ungeometrical, whereas the notion that parallels meet is in one sense geometrical, being ungeometrical in a different fashion: the reason being that "ungeometrical," like "unrhythmical," is equivocal, meaning in the one case not geometry at all, in the other bad geometry? It is this error, i.e. error based on premises of this kind—"of" the science but false—that is the contrary of science. In mathemat-

---

[5]*An. Pr.* i. 1. The "opposite facts" are those which would be expressed in the alternatively possible answers to the dialectical question, the dialectician's aim being to refute his interlocutor whether the latter answers the question put to him affirmatively or in the negative.

[6]i.e. a premiss put in the form of a question.

ics the formal fallacy is not so common, because it is the middle term in which the ambiguity lies, since the major is predicated of the whole of the middle and the middle of the whole of the minor (the *predicate* of course never has the prefix "all"); and in mathematics one can, so to speak, see these middle terms with an intellectual vision, while in dialectic the ambiguity may escape detection. E.g. "Is every circle a figure?" A diagram shows that this is so, but the minor premiss "Are epics circles?" is shown by the diagram to be false.

If a proof has an inductive minor premiss, one should not bring an "objection" against it. For since every premiss must be applicable to a number of cases (otherwise it will not be true in every instance, which, since the syllogism proceeds from universals, it must be), then assuredly the same is true of an "objection"; since premisses and "objections" are so far the same that anything which can be validly advanced as an "objection" must be such that it could take the form of a premiss, either demonstrative or dialectical. On the other hand arguments formally illogical do sometimes occur through taking as middles mere attributes of the major and minor terms. An instance of this is Caeneus' proof that fire increases in geometrical proportion: "Fire," he argues, "increases rapidly, and so does geometrical proportion." There is no syllogism so, but there is a syllogism if the most rapidly increasing proportion is geometrical and the most rapidly increasing proportion is attributable to fire in its motion. Sometimes, no doubt, it is impossible to reason from premisses predicating mere attributes: but sometimes it is possible, though the possibility is overlooked. If false premisses could never give true conclusions "resolution" would be easy, for premisses and conclusion would in that case inevitably reciprocate. I might then argue thus: let A be an existing fact; let the existence of A imply such and such facts actually known to me to exist, which we may call B. I can now, since they reciprocate, infer A from B.

Reciprocation of premisses and conclusion is more frequent in mathematics, because mathematics takes definitions, but never an accident, for its premisses—a second characteristic distinguishing mathematical reasoning from dialectical disputations.

A science expands not by the interposition of fresh middle terms, but by the apposition of fresh extreme terms. E.g. A is predicated of B, B of C, C of D, and so indefinitely. Or the expansion may be lateral: e.g. one major, A, may be proved of two minors, C and E. Thus let A represent number—*a* number or *number* taken indeterminately; B determinate odd number; C any particular odd number. We can then predicate A of C. Next let D represent determinate even number, and E even number. Then A is predicable of E.

13 Knowledge of the fact differs from knowledge of the reasoned fact. To begin with, they differ within the same science and in two ways: (1) when the premisses of the syllogism are not immediate (for then the proximate cause is not contained in them—a necessary condition of knowledge of the reasoned fact): (2) when the premisses are immediate, but instead of the cause the

better known of the two reciprocals is taken as the middle; for of two recipro-cally predicable terms the one which is not the cause the better known of the two reciprocals is taken as the middle; for of two reciprocally predicable terms the one which is not the cause may quite easily be the better known and so become the middle term of the demonstration. Thus (2) (a) you might prove as follows that the planets are near because they do not twinkle: let C be the planets, B not twinkling, A proximity. Then B is predicable of C; for the planets do not twinkle. But A is also predicable of B, since that which does not twinkle is near—we must take this truth as having been reached by induction or sense-perception. Therefore A is a necessary predicate of C; so that we have demonstrated that the planets are near. This syllogism, then, proves not the reasoned fact but only the fact; since they are not near because they do not twinkle, but, because they are near, do not twinkle. The major and middle of the proof, however, may be reversed, and then the demonstration will be of the reasoned fact. Thus: let C be the planets, B proximity, A not twinkling. Then B is an attribute of C, and A—not twinkling—of B. Consequently A is predicable of C, and the syllogism proves the reasoned fact, since its middle term is the proximate cause. Another example is the inference that the moon is spherical from its manner of waxing. Thus: since that which so waxes is spherical, and since the moon so waxes, clearly the moon is spherical. Put in this form, the syllogism turns out to be proof of the fact, but if the middle and major be reversed it is proof of the reasoned fact; since the moon is not spherical be-cause it waxes in a certain manner, but waxes in such a manner because it is spherical. (Let C be the moon, B spherical, and A waxing.) Again (b), in cases where the cause and the effect are not reciprocal and the effect is the better known, the fact is demonstrated but not the reasoned fact. This also occurs (1) when the middle falls outside the major and minor, for here too the strict cause is not given, and so the demonstration is of the fact, not of the reasoned fact. For example, the question "Why does not a wall breathe?" might be answered, "Because it is not an animal"; but that answer would not give the strict cause, because if not being an animal causes the absence of respiration, then being an animal should be the cause of respiration, according to the rule that if the negation of x causes the noninherence of y, the affirmation of x causes the inherence of y; e.g. if the disproportion of the hot and cold elements is the cause of ill health, their proportion is the cause of health; and conversely, if the assertion of x causes the inherence of y, the negation of x must cause y's noninherence. But in the case given this consequence does not result; for not every animal breathes. A syllogism with this kind of cause takes place in the second figure. Thus: let A be animal, B respiration, C wall. Then A is predicable of all B (for all that breathes is animal), but of no C; and consequently B is predicable of no C; that is, the wall does not breathe. Such causes are like far-fetched explanations which precisely consist in making the cause too re-mote, as in Anacharsis' account of why the Scythians have no flute-players; namely because they have no vines.

Thus, then, do the syllogism of the fact and the syllogism of the reasoned fact differ within one science and according to the position of the middle terms. But there is another way too in which the fact and the reasoned fact differ, and that is when they are investigated respectively by different sciences. This occurs in the case of problems related to one another as subordinate and superior, as when optical problems are subordinated to geometry, mechanical problems to stereometry, harmonic problems to arithmetic, the data of observation to astronomy. (Some of these sciences bear almost the same name; e.g. mathematical and nautical astronomy, mathematical and acoustical harmonics.) Here it is the business of the empirical observers to know the fact, of the mathematicians to know the reasoned fact; for the latter are in possession of the demonstrations giving the causes, and are often ignorant of the fact: just as we have often a clear insight into a universal, but through lack of observation are ignorant of some of its particular instances. These connexions[7] have a perceptible existence though they are manifestations of forms. For the mathematical sciences concern forms: they do not demonstrate properties of a substratum, since, even though the geometrical subjects are predicable as properties of a perceptible substratum, it is not as thus predicable that the mathematician demonstrates properties of them. As optics is related to geometry, so another science is related to optics, namely the theory of the rainbow. Here knowledge of the fact is within the province of the natural philosopher, knowledge of the reasoned fact within that of the optician, either *qua* optician or *qua* mathematical optician. Many sciences not standing in this mutual relation enter into it at points; e.g. medicine and geometry: it is the physician's business to know that circular wounds heal more slowly, the geometer's to know the reason why.

14   Of all the figures the most scientific is the first. Thus, it is the vehicle of the demonstrations of all the mathematical sciences, such as arithmetic, geometry, and optics, and practically of all sciences that investigate causes: for the syllogism of the reasoned fact is either exclusively or generally speaking and in most cases in this figure—a second proof that this figure is the most scientific; for grasp of a reasoned conclusion is the primary condition of knowledge. Thirdly, the first is the only figure which enables us to pursue knowledge of the essence of a thing. In the second figure no affirmative conclusion is possible, and knowledge of a thing's essence must be affirmative; while in the third figure the conclusion can be affirmative, but cannot be universal, and essence must have a universal character: e.g. man is not two-footed animal in any qualified sense, but universally. Finally, the first figure has no need of the others, while it is by means of the first that the other two figures are developed, and have their intervals close-packed until immediate premisses are reached. Clearly, therefore, the first figure is the primary condition of knowledge.

[7]*sc.* "which require two sciences for their proof." Cf. 78[b] 35.

René Descartes

MEDITATIONS ON FIRST PHILOSOPHY

This selection sets forth Descartes' theory of the basis for guaranteed true scientific knowledge.

MEDITATION IV

Of Truth and Error

I have been habituated these bygone days to detach my mind from the senses, and I have accurately observed that there is exceedingly little which is known with certainty respecting corporeal objects,—that we know much more of the human mind, and still more of God himself. I am thus able now without difficulty to abstract my mind from the contemplation of sensible or imaginable objects, and apply it to those which, as disengaged from all matter, are purely intelligible. And certainly the idea I have of the human mind in so far as it is a thinking thing, and not extended in length, breadth, and depth, and participating in none of the properties of body, is incomparably more distinct than the idea of any corporeal object; and when I consider that I doubt, in other words, that I am an incomplete and dependent being, the idea of a complete and independent being, that is to say of God, occurs to my mind with so much clearness and distinctness,—and from the fact alone that this idea is found in me, or that I who possess it exist, the conclusions that God exists, and that my own existence, each moment of its continuance, is absolutely dependent upon him, are so manifest,—as to lead me to believe it impossible that the human mind can know anything with more clearness and certitude. And now I seem to discover a path that will conduct us from the contemplation of the true God, in whom are contained all the treasures of science and wisdom, to the knowledge of the other things in the universe.

For, in the first place, I discover that it is impossible for him ever to deceive me, for in all fraud and deceit there is a certain imperfection: and although it may seem that the ability to deceive is a mark of subtlety or power, yet the will testifies without doubt of malice and weakness; and such, accordingly, cannot be found in God. In the next place, I am conscious that I possess a certain faculty of judging or discerning truth from error, which I doubtless received from God, along with whatever else is mine; and since it is impossible that he should will to deceive me, it is likewise certain that he has not given me a faculty that will ever lead me into error, provided I use it aright.

And certainly this can be no other than what I have now explained: for as often as I so restrain my will within the limits of my knowledge, that it forms no judgment except regarding objects which are clearly and distinctly represented to it by the understanding, I can never be deceived; because every clear and distinct conception is doubtless something, and as such cannot owe its origin to nothing, but must of necessity have God for its author—God, I say, who, as supremely perfect, cannot, without a contradiction, be the cause of any error; and consequently it is necessary to conclude that every such conception or judgment is true. Nor have I merely learned to-day what I must avoid to escape error, but also what I must do to arrive at the knowledge of truth; for I will assuredly reach truth if I only fix my attention sufficiently on all the things I conceive perfectly, and separate these from others which I conceive more confusedly and obscurely: to which for the future I shall give diligent heed.

But, indeed, whatever mode of probation I in the end adopt, it always returns to this, that it is only the things I clearly and distinctly conceive which have the power of completely persuading me. And although, of the objects I conceive in this manner, some, indeed, are obvious to everyone, while others are only discovered after close and careful investigation; nevertheless, after they are once discovered, the latter are not esteemed less certain than the former. Thus, for example, to take the case of a right-angled triangle, although it is not so manifest at first that the square of the base is equal to the squares of the other two sides, as that the base is opposite to the greatest angle; nevertheless, after it is once apprehended, we are as firmly persuaded of the truth of the former as of the latter. And, with respect to God, if I were not pre-occupied by prejudices, and my thought beset on all sides by the continual presence of the images of sensible objects, I should know nothing sooner or more easily than the fact of his being. For is there any truth more clear than the existence of a Supreme Being, or of God, seeing it is to his essence alone that necessary and eternal existence pertains? And although the right conception of this truth has cost me much close thinking, nevertheless at present I feel not only as assured of it as of what I deem most certain, but I remark further that the certitude of all other truths is so absolutely dependent on it, that without this knowledge it is impossible ever to know anything perfectly.

For although I am of such a nature as to be unable, while I possess a very clear and distinct apprehension of a matter, to resist the conviction of its truth, yet because my constitution is also such as to incapacitate me from keeping my mind continually fixed on the same object, and as I frequently recollect a past judgment without at the same time being able to recall the grounds of it, it may happen meanwhile that other reasons are presented to me which would readily cause me to change my opinion, if I did not know that God existed; and thus I should possess no true and certain knowledge, but merely vague and vacillating opinions. Thus, for example, when I consider the nature of the recti-lineal triangle, it most clearly appears to me, who have been instructed in the principles of geometry, that its three angles are equal to two right angles, and I find it impossible to believe otherwise, while I apply my mind to the demon-stration; but as soon as I cease from attending to the process of proof, al-though I still remember that I had a clear comprehension of it, yet I may readily come to doubt of the truth demonstrated, if I do not know that there is a God: for I may persuade myself that I have been so constituted by nature as to be sometimes deceived, even in matters which I think I apprehend with the great-est evidence and certitude, especially when I recollect that I frequently consid-ered many things to be true and certain which other reasons afterwards con-strained me to reckon as wholly false.

But after I have discovered that God exists, seeing I also at the same time observed that all things depend on him, and that he is no deceiver, and thence inferred that all which I clearly and distinctly perceive is of necessity true: although I no longer attend to the grounds of a judgment, no opposite reason can be alleged sufficient to lead me to doubt of its truth, provided only I remember that I once possessed a clear and distinct comprehension of it. My knowledge of it thus becomes true and certain. And this same knowledge ex-tends likewise to whatever I remember to have formerly demonstrated, as the truths of geometry and the like: for what can be alleged against them to lead me to doubt of them? Will it be that my nature is such that I may be frequently deceived? But I already know that I cannot be deceived in judgments of the grounds of which I possess a clear knowledge. Will it be that I formerly deemed things to be true and certain which I afterwards discovered to be false? But I had no clear and distinct knowledge of any of those things, and, being as yet ignorant of the rule by which I am assured of the truth of a judgment, I was led to give my assent to them on grounds which I afterwards discovered were less strong than at the time I imagined them to be. What further objection, then, is there? Will it be said that perhaps I am dreaming (an objection I lately myself raised), or that all the thoughts of which I am now conscious have no more truth than the reveries of my dreams? But although, in truth, I should be dreaming, the rule still holds that all which is clearly presented to my intellect is indisputably true.

And thus I very clearly see that the certitude and truth of all science depends on the knowledge alone of the true God, insomuch that, before I knew him, I could have no perfect knowledge of any other thing. And now that I know him, I possess the means of acquiring a perfect knowledge respecting innumerable matters, as well relative to God himself and other intellectual objects as to corporeal nature, in so far as it is the object of pure mathematics which do not consider whether it exists or not.

David Hume

A TREATISE OF HUMAN NATURE

These selections from Book I of Hume's A *Treatise of Human Nature* present his analysis of our claims to knowledge of causes and effects.

SECTION VI
Of the inference from the impression to the idea

'Tis easy to observe, that in tracing this relation, the inference we draw from cause to effect, is not deriv'd merely from a survey of these particular objects, and from such a penetration into their essences as may discover the dependance of the one upon the other. There is no object, which implies the existence of any other if we consider these objects in themselves, and never look beyond the ideas which we form of them. Such an inference wou'd amount to knowledge, and wou'd imply the absolute contradiction and impossibility of conceiving any thing different. But as all distinct ideas are separable, 'tis evident there can be no impossibility of that kind. When we pass from a present impression to the idea of any object, we might possibly have separated the idea from the impression, and have substituted any other idea in its room.

'Tis therefore by EXPERIENCE only, that we can infer the existence of one object from that of another. The nature of experience is this. We remember to have had frequent instances of the existence of one species of objects; and also remember, that the individuals of another species of objects have always attended them, and have existed in a regular order of contiguity and succession with regard to them. Thus we remember to have seen that species of object we call *flame*, and to have felt that species of sensation we call *heat*. We likewise call to mind their constant conjunction in all past instances. Without any farther ceremony, we call the one *cause* and the other *effect*, and infer the existence of the one from that of the other. In all those instances, from which we learn the conjunction of particular causes and effects, both the causes and effects have been perceiv'd by the senses, and are remember'd: But in all cases, wherein we reason concerning them, there is only one perceiv'd or remember'd, and the other is supply'd in conformity to our past experience.

Thus in advancing we have insensibly discover'd a new relation betwixt cause and effect, when we least expected it, and were entirely employ'd upon another subject. This relation is their CONSTANT CONJUNCTION. Contiguity and succession are not sufficient to make us pronounce any two objects to be cause and effect, unless we perceive, that these two relations are preserv'd in several instances. We may now see the advantage of quitting the direct survey of this relation, in order to discover the nature of that *necessary connexion*, which makes so essential a part of it. . . .

Since it appears, that the transition from an impression present to the memory or senses to the idea of an object, which we call cause or effect, is founded on past *experience*, and on our remembrance of their *constant conjunction*, the next question is, Whether experience produces the idea by means of the understanding or of the imagination; whether we are determin'd by reason to make the transition, or by a certain association and relation of perceptions. If reason determin'd us, it wou'd proceed upon that principle, *that instances, of which we have had no experience, must resemble those, of which we have had experience, and that the course of nature continues always uniformly the same.* In order therefore to clear up this matter, let us consider all the arguments, upon which such a proposition may be suppos'd to be founded; and as these must be deriv'd either from *knowledge* or *probability*, let us cast our eye on each of these degrees of evidence, and see whether they afford any just conclusion of this nature.

Our foregoing method of reasoning will easily convince us, that there can be no *demonstrative* arguments to prove, *that those instances, of which we have had no experience, resemble those, of which we have had experience.* We can at least conceive a change in the course of nature; which sufficiently proves, that such a change is not absolutely impossible. To form a clear idea of any thing, is an undeniable argument for its possibility, and is alone a refutation of any pretended demonstration against it. . . .

Thus not only our reason fails us in the discovery of the *ultimate connexion* of causes and effects, but even after experience has inform'd us of their *constant conjunction*, 'tis impossible for us to satisfy ourselves by our reason, why we shou'd extend that experience beyond those particular instances, which have fallen under our observation. We suppose, but are never able to prove, that there must be a resemblance betwixt those objects, of which we have had experience, and those which lie beyond the reach of our discovery. . . .

We have no other notion of cause and effect, but that of certain objects, which have been *always conjoin'd* together, and which in all past instances have been found inseparable. We cannot penetrate into the reason of the conjunction. We only observe the thing itself, and always find that from the constant conjunction the objects acquire an union in the imagination. When the impression of one becomes present to us, we immediately form an idea of its usual attendant; and consequently we may establish this as one part of the definition of an opinion or belief, that 'tis *an idea related to or associated with a present impression*.

SECTION VIII
Of the causes of belief

Having thus explain'd the nature of belief, and shewn that it consists in a lively idea related to a present impression; let us now proceed to examine from what principles it is deriv'd, and what bestows the vivacity on the idea.

I wou'd willingly establish it as a general maxim in the science of human nature, *that when any impression becomes present to us, it not only transports the mind to such ideas as are related to it, but likewise communicates to them a share of its force and vivacity*. All the operations of the mind depend in a great measure on its disposition, when it performs them; and according as the spirits are more or less elevated, and the attention more or less fix'd, the action will always have more or less vigour and vivacity. When therefore any object is presented, which elevates and enlivens the thought, every action, to which the mind applies itself, will be more strong and vivid, as long as that disposition continues. Now 'tis evident the continuance of the disposition depends entirely on the objects, about which the mind is employ'd; and that any new object naturally gives a new direction to the spirits, and changes the disposition; as on the contrary, when the mind fixes constantly on the same object, or passes easily and insensibly along related objects, the disposition has a much longer duration. Hence it happens, that when the mind is once inliven'd by a present impression, it proceeds to form a more lively idea of the related objects, by a natural transition of the disposition from the one to the other. The change of the objects is so easy, that the mind is scarce sensible of it, but applies itself to the conception of the related idea with all the force and vivacity it acquir'd from the present impression.

If in considering the nature of relation, and that facility of transition, which is essential to it, we can satisfy ourselves concerning the reality of this phæ-nomenon, 'tis well: But I must confess I place my chief confidence in experience to prove so material a principle. We may, therefore, observe, as the first experiment to our present purpose, that upon the appearance of the picture of an absent friend, our idea of him is evidently inliven'd by the *resemblance*, and that every passion, which that idea occasions, whether of joy or sorrow, acquires new force and vigour. In producing this effect there concur both a relation and a present impression. Where the picture bears him no resemblance, or at least was not intended for him, it never so much as conveys our thought to him: And where it is absent, as well as the person; tho' the mind may pass from the thought of the one to that of the other; it feels its idea to be rather weaken'd than inliven'd by that transition. We take a pleasure in viewing the picture of a friend, when 'tis set before us; but when 'tis remov'd, rather choose to consider him directly, than by reflexion in an image, which is equally distant and obscure.

The ceremonies of the *Roman Catholic* religion may be consider'd as experiments of the same nature. The devotees of that strange superstition usually plead in excuse of the mummeries, with which they are upbraided, that they feel the good effect of those external motions, and postures, and actions, in inlivening their devotion, and quickening their fervour, which otherwise wou'd decay away, if directed entirely to distant and immaterial objects. We shadow out the objects of our faith, say they, in sensible types and images, and render them more present to us by the immediate presence of these types, than 'tis possible for us to do, merely by an intellectual view and contemplation. Sensible objects have always a greater influence on the fancy than any other; and this influence they readily convey to those ideas, to which they are related, and which they resemble. I shall only infer from these practices, and this reasoning, that the effect of resemblance in inlivening the idea is very common; and as in every case a resemblance and a present impression must concur, we are abundantly supply'd with experiments to prove the reality of the foregoing principle.

We may add force to these experiments by others of a different kind, in considering the effects of *contiguity*, as well as of *resemblance*. 'Tis certain, that distance diminishes the force of every idea, and that upon our approach to any object; tho' it does not discover itself to our senses; it operates upon the mind with an influence that imitates an immediate impression. The thinking on any object readily transports the mind to what is contiguous; but 'tis only the actual presence of an object that transports it with a superior vivacity. When I am a few miles from home, whatever relates to it touches me more nearly than when I am two hundred leagues distant; tho' even at that distance the reflecting on any thing in the neighbourhood of my friends and family naturally produces an idea of them. But as in this latter case, both the objects of the mind are ideas; notwithstanding there is an easy transition betwixt them; that transition alone is not able to give a superior vivacity to any of the ideas, for want of some immediate impression.

No one can doubt but causation has the same influence as the other two relations of resemblance and contiguity. Superstitious people are fond of the relicts of saints and holy men, for the same reason that they seek after types and images, in order to inliven their devotion, and give them a more intimate and strong conception of those exemplary lives, which they desire to imitate. Now 'tis evident, one of the best relicks a devotee cou'd procure, wou'd be the handywork of a saint; and if his cloaths and furniture are ever to be consider'd in this light, 'tis because they were once at his disposal, and were mov'd and affected by him; in which respect they are to be consider'd as imperfect effects, and as connected with him by a shorter chain of consequences than any of those, from which we learn the reality of his existence. This phænomenon clearly proves, that a present impression with a relation of causation may enliven any idea, and consequently produce belief or assent, according to the precedent definition of it.

But why need we seek for other arguments to prove, that a present impression with a relation or transition of the fancy may inliven any idea, when this very instance of our reasonings from cause and effect will alone suffice to that purpose? 'Tis certain we must have an idea of every matter of fact, which we believe. 'Tis certain, that this idea arises only from a relation to a present impression. 'Tis certain, that the belief super-adds nothing to the idea, but only changes our manner of conceiving it, and renders it more strong and lively. The present conclusion concerning the influence of relation is the immediate consequence of all these steps; and every step appears to me sure and infallible. There enters nothing into this operation of the mind but a present impression, a lively idea, and a relation or association in the fancy betwixt the impression and idea; so that there can be no suspicion of mistake.

In order to put this whole affair in a fuller light, let us consider it as a question in natural philosophy, which we must determine by experience and observation. I suppose there is an object presented, from which I draw a certain conclusion, and form to myself ideas, which I am said to believe or assent to. Here 'tis evident, that however that object, which is present to my senses, and that other, whose existence I infer by reasoning, may be thought to influence each other by their particular powers or qualities; yet as the phænomenon of belief, which we at present examine, is merely internal, these powers and qualities, being entirely unknown, can have no hand in producing it. 'Tis the present impression, which is to be consider'd as the true and real cause of the idea, and of the belief which attends it. We must therefore endeavour to discover by experiments the particular qualities, by which 'tis enabled to produce so extraordinary an effect.

First then I observe, that the present impression has not this effect by its own proper power and efficacy, and when consider'd alone, as a single perception, limited to the present moment. I find, that an impression, from which, on its first appearance, I can draw no conclusion, may afterwards become the foundation of belief, when I have had experience of its usual consequences. We must in every case have observ'd the same impression in past instances, and have found it to be constantly conjoin'd with some other impression. This is confirm'd by such a multitude of experiments, that it admits not of the smallest doubt.

From a second observation I conclude, that the belief, which attends the present impression, and is produc'd by a number of past impressions and conjunctions; that this belief, I say, arises immediately, without any new operation of the reason or imagination. Of this I can be certain, because I never am conscious of any such operation, and find nothing in the subject, on which it can be founded. Now as we call every thing CUSTOM, which proceeds from a past repetition, without any new reasoning or conclusion, we may establish it as a certain truth, that all the belief, which follows upon any present impression, is deriv'd solely from that origin. When we are accustom'd to see two impressions conjoin'd together, the appearance or idea of the one immediately carries us to the idea of the other.

Being fully satisfy'd on this head, I make a third set of experiments, in order to know, whether any thing be requisite, beside the customary transition, towards the production of this phænomenon of belief. I therefore change the first impression into an idea; and observe, that tho' the customary transition to the correlative idea still remains, yet there is in reality no belief nor perswasion. A present impression, then, is absolutely requisite to this whole operation; and when after this I compare an impression with an idea, and find that their only difference consists in their different degrees of force and vivacity, I conclude upon the whole, that belief is a more vivid and intense conception of an idea, proceeding from its relation to a present impression.

Thus all probable reasoning is nothing but a species of sensation. 'Tis not solely in poetry and music, we must follow our taste and sentiment, but likewise in philosophy. When I am convinc'd of any principle, 'tis only an idea, which strikes more strongly upon me. When I give the preference to one set of arguments above another, I do nothing but decide from my feeling concerning the superiority of their influence. Objects have no discoverable connexion together; nor is it from any other principle but custom operating upon the imagination, that we can draw any inference from the appearance of one to the existence of another.

'Twill here be worth our observation, that the past experience, on which all our judgments concerning cause and effect depend, may operate on our mind in such an insensible manner as never to be taken notice of, and may even in some measure be unknown to us. A person, who stops short in his journey upon meeting a river in his way, foresees the consequences of his proceeding forward; and his knowledge of these consequences is convey'd to him by past experience, which informs him of such certain conjunctions of causes and effects. But can we think, that on this occasion he reflects on any past experience, and calls to remembrance instances, that he has seen or heard of, in order to discover the effects of water on animal bodies? No surely; this is not the method in which he proceeds in his reasoning. The idea of sinking is so closely connected with that of water, and the idea of suffocating with that of sinking, that the mind makes the transition without the assistance of the memory. The custom operates before we have time for reflexion. The objects seem so inseparable, that we interpose not a moment's delay in passing from the one to the other. But as this transition proceeds from experience, and not from any primary connexion betwixt the ideas, we must necessarily acknowledge, that experience may produce a belief and a judgment of causes and effects by a secret operation, and without being once thought of. This removes all pretext, if there yet remains any, for asserting that the mind is convinc'd by reasoning of that principle, *that instances of which we have no experience, must necessarily resemble those, of which we have.* For we here find, that the understanding or imagination can draw inferences from past experience, without reflecting on it; much more without forming any principle concerning it, or reasoning upon that principle.

In general we may observe, that in all the most establish'd and uniform conjunctions of causes and effects, such as those of gravity, impulse, solidity, &c., the mind never carries its view expressly to consider any past experience: Tho' in other associations of objects, which are more rare and unusual, it may assist the custom and transition of ideas by this reflexion. Nay we find in some cases, that the reflexion produces the belief without the custom; or more properly speaking, that the reflexion produces the custom in an *oblique* and *artificial* manner. I explain myself. 'Tis certain, that not only in philosophy, but even in common life, we may attain the knowledge of a particular cause merely by one experiment, provided it be made with judgment, and after a careful removal of all foreign and superfluous circumstances. Now as after one experiment of this kind, the mind, upon the appearance either of the cause or the effect, can draw an inference concerning the existence of its correlative; and as a habit can never be acquir'd merely by one instance; it may be thought, that belief cannot in this case be esteem'd the effect of custom. But this difficulty will vanish, if we consider, that tho' we are here suppos'd to have had only one experiment of a particular effect, yet we have many millions to convince us of this principle; *that like objects, plac'd in like circumstances, will always produce like effects*; and as this principle has establish'd itself by a sufficient custom, it bestows an evidence and firmness on any opinion, to which it can be apply'd. The connexion of the ideas is not habitual after one experiment; but this connexion is comprehended under another principle, that is habitual; which brings us back to our hypothesis. In all cases we transfer our experience to instances, of which we have no experience, either *expressly* or *tacitly*, either *directly* or *indirectly*.

I must not conclude this subject without observing, that 'tis very difficult to talk of the operations of the mind with perfect propriety and exactness; because common language has seldom made any very nice distinctions among them, but has generally call'd by the same term all such as nearly resemble each other. And as this is a source almost inevitable of obscurity and confusion in the author; so it may frequently give rise to doubts and objections in the reader, which otherwise he wou'd never have dream'd of. Thus my general position, that an opinion or belief is *nothing but a strong and lively idea deriv'd from a present impression related to it*, may be liable to the following objection, by reason of a little ambiguity in those words *strong and lively*. It may be said, that not only an impression may give rise to reasoning, but that an idea may also have the same influence; especially upon my principle, *that all our ideas are deriv'd from correspondent impressions*. For suppose I form at present an idea, of which I have forgot the correspondent impression, I am able to conclude from this idea, that such an impression did once exist; and as this conclusion is attended with belief, it may be ask'd, from whence are the qualities of force and vivacity deriv'd, which constitute this belief? And to this I answer very readily, *from the present idea*. For as this idea is not here consider'd as the representation of any absent object, but as a real perception in the mind, of which we are intimately conscious, it must be able to bestow on whatever is related to it the same quality, call it *firmness, or solidity, or force, or vivacity*, with which the mind reflects upon it, and is assur'd of its present existence. The idea here supplies the place of an impression, and is entirely the same, so far as regards our present purpose.

Upon the same principles we need not be surpriz'd to hear of the remembrance of an idea; that is, of the idea of an idea, and of its force and vivacity superior to the loose conceptions of the imagination. In thinking of our past thoughts we not only delineate out the objects, of which we were thinking, but also conceive the action of the mind in the meditation, that certain *je-ne-scai-quoi*, of which 'tis impossible to give any definition or description, but which every one sufficiently understands. When the memory offers an idea of this, and represents it as past, 'tis easily conceiv'd how that idea may have more vigour and firmness, than when we think of a past thought, of which we have no remembrance.

After this any one will understand how we may form the idea of an impression and of an idea, and how we may believe the existence of an impression and of an idea.

SECTION XIV
Of the idea of necessary connexion

Having thus explain'd the manner, *in which we reason beyond our immediate impressions, and conclude that such particular causes must have such particular effects*; we must now return upon our footsteps to examine that question, which first occur'd to us, and which we dropt in our way, viz. *What is our idea of necessity, when we say that two objects are necessarily connected together.* Upon this head I repeat what I have often had occasion to observe, that as we have no idea, that is not deriv'd from an impression, we must find some impression, that gives rise to this idea of necessity, if we assert we have really such an idea. In order to this I consider, in what objects necessity is commonly suppos'd to lie; and finding that it is always ascrib'd to causes and effects, I turn my eye to two objects suppos'd to be plac'd in that relation; and examine them in all the situations, of which they are susceptible. I immediately perceive, that they are *contiguous* in time and place, and that the object we call cause *precedes* the other we call effect. In no one instance can I go any farther, nor is it possible for me to discover any third relation betwixt these objects. I therefore enlarge my view to comprehend several instances; where I find like objects always existing in like relations of contiguity and succession. At first sight this seems to serve but little to my purpose. The reflection on several instances only repeats the same objects; and therefore can never give rise to a new idea. But upon farther enquiry I find, that the repetition is not in every particular the same, but produces a new impression, and by that means the idea, which I at present examine. For after a frequent repetition, I find, that upon the appearance of one of the objects, the mind is *determin'd* by custom to consider its usual attendant, and to consider it in a stronger light upon account of its relation to the first object. 'Tis this impression, then, or *determination*, which affords me the idea of necessity.

I doubt not but these consequences will at first sight be receiv'd without difficulty, as being evident deductions from principles, which we have already establish'd, and which we have often employ'd in our reasonings. This evidence both in the first principles, and in the deductions, may seduce us unwarily into the conclusion, and make us imagine it contains nothing extraordinary, nor worthy of our curiosity. But tho' such an inadvertence may facilitate the reception of this reasoning, 'twill make it be the more easily forgot; for which reason I think it proper to give warning, that I have just now examin'd one of the most sublime questions in philosophy, *viz. that concerning the power and efficacy of causes*; where all the sciences seem so much interested. Such a warning will naturally rouze up the attention of the reader, and make him desire a more full account of my doctrine, as well as of the arguments, on which it is founded. This request is so reasonable, that I cannot refuse complying with it; especially as I am hopeful that these principles, the more they are examin'd, will acquire the more force and evidence.

There is no question, which on account of its importance, as well as difficulty, has caus'd more disputes both among antient and modern philosophers, than this concerning the efficacy of causes, or that quality which makes them be followed by their effects. But before they enter'd upon these disputes, methinks it wou'd not have been improper to have examin'd what idea we have of that efficacy, which is the subject of the controversy. This is what I find principally wanting in their reasonings, and what I shall here endeavour to supply.

I begin with observing that the terms of *efficacy, agency, power, force, energy, necessity, connexion,* and *productive quality,* are all nearly synonimous; and therefore 'tis an absurdity to employ any of them in defining the rest. By this observation we reject at once all the vulgar definitions, which philosophers have given of power and efficacy; and instead of searching for the idea in these definitions, must look for it in the impressions, from which it is originally deriv'd. If it be a compound idea, it must arise from compound impressions. If simple, from simple impressions.

I believe the most general and most popular explication of this matter, is to say, that finding from experience, that there are several new productions in matter, such as the motions and variations of body, and concluding that there must somewhere be a power capable of producing them, we arrive at last by this reasoning at the idea of power and efficacy. But to be convinc'd that this explication is more popular than philosophical, we need but reflect on two very obvious principles. *First,* That reason alone can never give rise to any original idea, and *secondly,* that reason, as distinguish'd from experience, can never make us conclude, that a cause or productive quality is absolutely requisite to every beginning of existence. Both these considerations have been sufficiently explain'd; and therefore shall not at present be any farther insisted on.

I shall only infer from them, that since reason can never give rise to the idea of efficacy, that idea must be deriv'd from experience, and from some particular instances of this efficacy, which make their passage into the mind by the common channels of sensation or reflection. Ideas always represent their objects or impressions; and *vice versa*, there are some objects necessary to give rise to every idea. If we pretend, therefore, to have any just idea of this efficacy, we must produce some instance, wherein the efficacy is plainly discoverable to the mind, and its operations obvious to our consciousness or sensation. By the refusal of this, we acknowledge, that the idea is impossible and imaginary; since the principle of innate ideas, which alone can save us from this dilemma, has been already refuted, and is now almost universally rejected in the learned world. Our present business, then, must be to find some natural production, where the operation and efficacy of a cause can be clearly conceiv'd and comprehended by the mind, without any danger of obscurity or mistake.

In this research we meet with very little encouragement from that prodigious diversity, which is found in the opinions of those philosophers, who have pretended to explain the secret force and energy of causes. There are some, who maintain, that bodies operate by their substantial form; others, by their accidents or qualities; several, by their matter and form; some, by their form and accidents; others, by certain virtues and faculties distinct from all this. All these sentiments again are mix'd and vary'd in a thousand different ways; and form a strong presumption, that none of them have any solidity or evidence, and that the supposition of an efficacy in any of the known qualities of matter is entirely without foundation. This presumption must encrease upon us, when we consider, that these principles of substantial forms, and accidents, and faculties, are not in reality any of the known properties of bodies, but are perfectly unintelligible and inexplicable. For 'tis evident philosophers wou'd never have had recourse to such obscure and uncertain principles had they met with any satisfaction in such as are clear and intelligible; especially in such an affair as this, which must be an object of the simplest understanding, if not of the senses. Upon the whole, we may conclude, that 'tis impossible in any one instance to shew the principle, in which the force and agency of a cause is plac'd; and that the most refin'd and most vulgar understandings are equally at a loss in this particular. If any one think proper to refute this assertion, he need not put himself to the trouble of inventing any long reasonings; but may at once shew us an instance of a cause, where we discover the power or operating principle. This defiance we are oblig'd frequently to make use of, as being almost the only means of proving a negative in philosophy.

The small success, which has been met with in all the attempts to fix this power, has at last oblig'd philosophers to conclude, that the ultimate force and efficacy of nature is perfectly unknown to us, and that 'tis in vain we search for it in all the known qualities of matter. In this opinion they are almost unanimous; and 'tis only in the inference they draw from it, that they discover any difference in their sentiments. For some of them, as the *Cartesians* in particular, having establish'd it as a principle, that we are perfectly acquainted with the essence of matter, have very naturally inferr'd, that it is endow'd with no efficacy, and that 'tis impossible for it of itself to communicate motion, or produce any of those effects, which we ascribe to it. As the essence of matter consists in extension, and as extension implies not actual motion, but only mobility; they conclude, that the energy, which produces the motion, cannot lie in the extension.

This conclusion leads them into another, which they regard as perfectly unavoidable. Matter, say they, is in itself entirely unactive, and depriv'd of any power, by which it may produce, or continue, or communicate motion: But since these effects are evident to our senses, and since the power, that produces them, must be plac'd somewhere, it must lie in the DEITY, or that divine being, who contains in his nature all excellency and perfection. 'Tis the deity, therefore, who is the prime mover of the universe, and who not only first created matter, and gave it it's original impulse, but likewise by a continu'd exertion of omnipotence, supports its existence, and successively bestows on it all those motions, and configurations, and qualities, with which it is endow'd.

This opinion is certainly very curious, and well worth our attention; but 'twill appear superfluous to examine it in this place, if we reflect a moment on our present purpose in taking notice of it. We have establish'd it as a principle, that as all ideas are deriv'd from impressions, or some precedent *perceptions*, 'tis impossible we can have any idea of power and efficacy, unless some instances can be produc'd, wherein this power *is perceiv'd* to exert itself. Now as these instances can never be discover'd in body, the *Cartesians*, proceeding upon their principle of innate ideas, have had recourse to a supreme spirit or deity, whom they consider as the only active being in the universe, and as the immediate cause of every alteration in matter. But the principle of innate ideas being allow'd to be false, it follows, that the supposition of a deity can serve us in no stead, in accounting for that idea of agency, which we search for in vain in all the objects, which are presented to our senses, or which we are internally conscious of in our own minds. For if every idea be deriv'd from an impression, the idea of a deity proceeds from the same origin; and if no impression, either of sensation or reflection, implies any force of efficacy, 'tis equally impossible to discover or even imagine any such active principle in the deity. Since these philosophers, therefore, have concluded, that matter cannot be endow'd with any efficacious principle, because 'tis impossible to discover in it such a principle; the same course of reasoning shou'd determine them to exclude it from the supreme being. Or if they estem that opinion absurd and impious, as it really is, I shall tell them how they may avoid it; and that is, by concluding from the very first, that they have no adequate idea of power or efficacy in any object; since neither in body nor spirit, neither in superior nor inferior natures, are they able to discover one single instance of it.

The same conclusion is unavoidable upon the hypothesis of those, who maintain the efficacy of second causes, and attribute a derivative, but a real power and energy to matter. For as they confess, that this energy lies not in any of the known qualities of matter, the difficulty still remains concerning the origin of its idea. If we have really an idea of power, we may attribute power to an unknown quality: But as 'tis impossible, that that idea can be deriv'd from such a quality, and as there is nothing in known qualities, which can produce it; it follows that we deceive ourselves, when we imagine we are possest of any idea of this kind, after the manner we commonly understand it. All ideas are deriv'd from, and represent impressions. We never have any impression, that contains any power or efficacy. We never therefore have any idea of power. . . .

Suppose two objects to be presented to us, of which the one is the cause and the other the effect; 'tis plain, that from the simple consideration of one, or both these objects we never shall perceive the tie, by which they are united, or be able certainly to pronounce, that there is a connexion betwixt them. 'Tis not, therefore, from any one instance, that we arrive at the idea of cause and effect, of a necessary connexion of power, of force, of energy, and of efficacy. Did we never see any but particular conjunctions of objects, entirely different from each other, we shou'd never be able to form any such ideas.

But again; suppose we observe several instances, in which the same objects are always conjoin'd together, we immediately conceive a connexion betwixt them, and begin to draw an inference from one to another. This multiplicity of resembling instances, therefore, constitutes the very essence of power or connexion, and is the source, from which the idea of it arises. In order, then, to understand the idea of power, we must consider that multiplicity; nor do I ask more to give a solution of that difficulty, which has so long perplex'd us. For thus I reason. The repetition of perfectly similar instances can never *alone* give rise to an original idea, different from what is to be found in any particular instance, as has been observ'd, and as evidently follows from our fundamental principle, *that all ideas are copy'd from impressions*. Since therefore the idea of power is a new original idea, not to be found in any one instance, and which yet arises from the repetition of several instances, it follows, that the repetition *alone* has not that effect, but must either *discover* or *produce* something new, which is the source of that idea. Did the repetition neither discover nor produce any thing new, our ideas might be multiply'd by it, but wou'd not be enlarg'd above what they are upon the observation of one single instance. Every enlargement, therefore, (such as the idea of power or connexion) which arises from the multiplicity of similar instances, is copy'd from some effects of the multiplicity, and will be perfectly understood by understanding these effects. Wherever we find any thing new to be discover'd or produc'd by the repetition, there we must place the power, and must never look for it in any other object.

But 'tis evident, in the first place, that the repetition of like objects in like relations of succession and contiguity *discovers* nothing new in any one of them; since we can draw no inference from it, nor make it a subject either of our demonstrative or probable reasonings;[1] as has been already prov'd. Nay suppose we cou'd draw an inference, 'twou'd be of no consequence in the present case; since no kind of reasoning can give rise to a new idea, such as this of power is; but wherever we reason, we must antecedently be possest of clear ideas, which may be the objects of our reasoning. The conception always precedes the understanding; and where the one is obscure, the other is uncertain; where the one fails, the other must fail also.

Secondly, 'Tis certain that this repetition of similar objects in similar situations *produces* nothing new either in these objects, or in any external body. For 'twill readily be allow'd, that the several instances we have of the conjunction of resembling causes and effects are in themselves entirely independent, and that the communication of motion, which I see result at present from the shock of two billiard-balls, is totally distinct from that which I saw result from such an impulse a twelve-month ago. These impulses have no influence on each other. They are entirely divided by time and place; and the one might have existed and communicated motion, tho' the other never had been in being.

There is, then, nothing new either discover'd or produc'd in any objects by their constant conjunction, and by the uninterrupted resemblance of their relations of succession and contiguity. But 'tis from this resemblance, that the ideas of necessity, of power, and of efficacy, are deriv'd. These ideas, therefore, represent not any thing, that does or can belong to the objects, which are constantly conjoin'd. This is an argument, which, in every view we can examine it, will be found perfectly unanswerable. Similar instances are still the first source of our idea of power or necessity; at the same time that they have no influence by their similarity either on each other, or on any external object. We must therefore, turn ourselves to some other quarter to seek the origin of that idea.

Tho' the several resembling instances, which give rise to the idea of power, have no influence on each other, and can never produce any new quality *in the object*, which can be the model of that idea, yet the *observation* of this resemblance produces a new impression *in the mind*, which is its real model. For after we have observ'd the resemblance in a sufficient number of instances, we immediately feel a determination of the mind to pass from one object to its usual attendant, and to conceive it in a stronger light upon account of that relation. This determination is the only effect of the resemblance; and therefore must be the same with power or efficacy, whose idea is deriv'd from the resemblance. The several instances of resembling conjunctions leads us into the notion of power and necessity. These instances are in themselves totally distinct from each other, and have no union but in the mind, which observes them, and collects their ideas. Necessity, then, is the effect of this observation, and is nothing but an internal impression of the mind, or a determination to carry our thoughts from one object to another. Without considering it in this

---

[1]Sect. 6.

view, we can never arrive at the most distant notion of it, or be able to attribute it either to external or internal objects, to spirit or body, to causes or effects.

The necessary connexion betwixt causes and effects is the foundation of our inference from one to the other. The foundation of our inference is the transition arising from the accustom'd union. These are, therefore, the same.

The idea of necessity arises from some impression. There is no impression convey'd by our senses, which can give rise to that idea. It must, therefore, be deriv'd from some internal impression, or impression of reflexion. There is no internal impression, which has any relation to the present business, but that propensity, which custom produces, to pass from an object to the idea of its usual attendant. This therefore is the essence of necessity. Upon the whole, necessity is something, that exists in the mind, not in objects; nor is it possible for us ever to form the most distant idea of it, consider'd as a quality in bodies. Either we have no idea of necessity, or necessity is nothing but that determination of the thought to pass from causes to effects and from effects to causes, according to their experienc'd union.

Thus as the necessity, which makes two times two equal to four, or three angles of a triangle equal to two right ones, lies only in the act of the understanding, by which we consider and compare these ideas; in like manner the necessity or power, which unites causes and effects, lies in the determination of the mind to pass from the one to the other. The efficacy or energy of causes is neither plac'd in the causes themselves, nor in the deity, nor in the concurrence of these two principles; but belongs entirely to the soul, which considers the union of two or more objects in all past instances. 'Tis here that the real power of causes is plac'd, along with their connexion and necessity.

I am sensible, that of all the paradoxes, which I have had, or shall hereafter have occasion to advance in the course of this treatise, the present one is the most violent, and that 'tis merely by dint of solid proof and reasoning I can ever hope it will have admission, and overcome the inveterate prejudices of mankind. Before we are reconcil'd to this doctrine, how often must we repeat to ourselves, *that* the simple view of any two objects or actions, however related, can never give us any idea of power, or of a connexion betwixt them: *that* this idea arises from the repetition of their union: *that* the repetition neither discovers nor causes any thing in the objects, but has an influence only on the mind, by that customary transition it produces: *that* this customary transition is, therefore, the same with the power and necessity; which are consequently qualities of perceptions, not of objects, and are internally felt by the soul, and not perceiv'd externally in bodies? There is commonly an astonishment attending every thing extraordinary; and this astonishment changes immediately into the highest degree of esteem or contempt, according as we approve or disapprove of the subject. I am much afraid, that tho' the foregoing reasoning appears to me the shortest and most decisive imaginable; yet with the generality of readers the biass of the mind will prevail, and give them a prejudice against the present doctrine.

'Tis now time to collect all the different parts of this reasoning, and by joining them together form an exact definition of the relation of cause and effect, which makes the subject of the present enquiry. This order wou'd not have been excusable, of first examining our inference from the relation before we had explain'd the relation itself, had it been possible to proceed in a different method. But as the nature of the relation depends so much on that of the inference, we have been oblig'd to advance in this seemingly preposterous manner, and make use of terms before we were able exactly to define them, or fix their meaning. We shall now correct this fault by giving a precise definition of cause and effect.

There may two definitions be given of this relation, which are only different, by their presenting a different view of the same object, and making us consider it either as a *philosophical* or as a *natural* relation; either as a comparison of two ideas, or as an association betwixt them. We may define a CAUSE to be "An object precedent and contiguous to another, and where all the objects resembling the former are plac'd in like relations of precedency and contiguity to those objects, that resemble the latter." If this definition be esteem'd defective, because drawn from objects foreign to the cause, we may substitute this other definition in its place, *viz.* "A CAUSE is an object precedent and contiguous to another, and so united with it, that the idea of the one determines the mind to form the idea of the other, and the impression of the one to form a more lively idea of the other."

SECTION XV
Rules by which to judge of causes and effects

According to the precedent doctrine, there are no objects, which by the mere survey, without consulting experience, we can determine to be the causes of any other; and no objects, which we can certainly determine in the same manner not to be the causes. Any thing may produce any thing. Creation, annihilation, motion, reason, volition; all these may arise from one another, or from any other object we can imagine. Nor will this appear strange, if we compare two principles explain'd above, *that the constant conjunction of objects determines their causation*, and *that properly speaking, no objects are contrary to each other, but existence and nonexistence*. Where objects are not contrary, nothing hinders them from having that constant conjunction, on which the relation of cause and effect totally depends.

Since therefore 'tis possible for all objects to become causes or effects to each other, it may be proper to fix some general rules, by which we may know when they really are so.

1. The cause and effect must be contiguous in space and time.
2. The cause must be prior to the effect.

3. There must be a constant union betwixt the cause and effect. 'Tis chiefly this quality, that constitutes the relation.

4. The same cause always produces the same effect, and the same effect never arises but from the same cause. This principle we derive from experience, and is the source of most of our philosophical reasonings. For when by any clear experiment we have discover'd the causes or effects of any phænomenon, we immediately extend our observation to every phænomenon of the same kind, without waiting for that constant repetition, from which the first idea of this relation is deriv'd.

5. There is another principle, which hangs upon this, *viz.* that where several different objects produce the same effect, it must be by means of some quality, which we discover to be common amongst them. For as like effects imply like causes, we must always ascribe the causation to the circumstance, wherein we discover the resemblance.

6. The following principle is founded on the same reason. The difference in the effects of two resembling objects must proceed from that particular, in which they differ. For as like causes always produce like effects, when in any instance we find our expectation to be disappointed, we must conclude that this irregularity proceeds from some difference in the causes.

7. When any object encreases or diminishes with the encrease or diminution of its cause, 'tis to be regarded as a compounded effect, deriv'd from the union of the several different effects, which arise from the several different parts of the cause. The absence or presence of one part of the cause is here suppos'd to be always attended with the absence or presence of a proportionable part of the effect. This constant conjunction sufficiently proves, that the one part is the cause of the other. We must, however, beware not to draw such a conclusion from a few experiments. A certain degree of heat gives pleasure; if you diminish that heat, the pleasure diminishes; but it does not follow, that if you augment it beyond a certain degree, the pleasure will likewise augment; for we find that it degenerates into pain.

8. The eighth and last rule I shall take notice of is, that an object, which exists for any time in its full perfection without any effect, is not the sole cause of that effect, but requires to be assisted by some other principle, which may forward its influence and operation. For as like effects necessarily follow from like causes, and in a contiguous time and place, their separation for a moment shews, that these causes are not compleat ones.

Immanuel Kant

CRITIQUE OF PURE REASON

Immanuel Kant (1724–1804) sought to overcome the skeptical consequences of Hume's analysis of scientific knowledge. In this selection from his *Critique of Pure Reason* (1781), Kant outlines his theory of how necessary knowledge about causality is possible.

III. ANALOGIES OF EXPERIENCE

Their principle is: Experience is possible only through the representation of a necessary connection of perceptions.

Proof

Experience is empirical knowledge, that is, knowledge which determines an object by means of perceptions. It is, therefore, a synthesis of perceptions, which synthesis itself is not contained in the perception, but contains the synthetical unity of the manifold of the perceptions in a consciousness, that unity constituting the essential of our knowledge of the objects of the senses, i.e. of experience (not only of intuition or of sensation of the senses). In experience perceptions come together contingently only, so that no necessity of their connection could be discovered in the perceptions themselves, apprehension being only a composition of the manifold of empirical intuition,but containing no representation of the necessity of the connected existence, in space and time, of the phenomena which it places together. Experience, on the contrary, is a knowledge of objects by perceptions, in which therefore the relation in the existence of the manifold is to be represented, not as it is put together in time, but as it is in time, objectively. Now, as time itself cannot be perceived, the determination of the existence of objects in time can take place only by their connection in time in general, that is, through concepts connecting them *a priori*. As these concepts always imply necessity, we are justified in saying that experience is possible only through a representation of the necessary connection of perceptions. . . .

The three modi of time are *permanence, succession*, and *coexistence*. There will therefore be three rules of all relations of phenomena in time, by which the existence of every phenomenon with regard to the unity of time is determined, and these rules will precede all experience, nay, render experience possible.

The general principle of the three analogies depends on the necessary unity of apperception with reference to every possible empirical consciousness (perception) *at every time*, and, consequently, as that unity forms an *a priori* ground, on the synthetical unity of all phenomena, according to their relation in time. For the original apperception refers to the internal sense (comprehending all representations), and it does so *a priori* to its form, that is, to the relation of the manifold of the empirical consciousness in time. The original apperception is intended to combine all this manifold according to its relations in time, for this is what is meant by its transcendental unity *a priori*, to which all is subject which is to belong to my own and my uniform knowledge, and thus to become an object for me. This synthetical unity in the time relations of all perceptions, which is determined *a priori*, is expressed therefore in the law, that all empirical determinations of time must be subject to rules of the general determination of time; and the analogies of experience, of which we are now going to treat, are exactly rules of this kind. . . .

What has been remarked of all synthetical principles and must be enjoined here more particularly is this, that these analogies have their meaning and validity, not as principles of the transcendent, but only as principles of the empirical use of the understanding. They can be established in this character only, nor can phenomena ever be comprehended under the categories directly, but only under their schemata. If the objects to which these principles refer were things by themselves, it would be perfectly impossible to know anything of them *a priori* and synthetically. But they are nothing but phenomena, and our whole knowledge of them, to which, after all, all principles *a priori* must relate, is only our possible experience of them. Those principles therefore can aim at nothing but the conditions of the unity of empirical knowledge in the synthesis of phenomena, which synthesis is represented only in the schema of the pure concepts of the understanding, while the category contains the function, restricted by no sensuous condition, of the unity of that synthesis as synthesis in general. Those principles will therefore authorise us only to connect phenomena, according to analogy, with the logical and universal unity of concepts, so that, though in using the principle we use the category, yet in practice (in the application to phenomena) we put the schema of the category, as a practical key, in its place, or rather put it by the side of the category as a restrictive condition, or, as what may be called, a formula of the category.

FIRST ANALOGY
Principle of Permanence

All phenomena contain the permanent (substance) as the object itself, and the changeable as its determination only, that is, as a mode in which the object exists.

SECOND ANALOGY
Principle of Production

Everything that happens (begins to be), presupposes something on which it follows according to a rule.

Proof

The apprehension of the manifold of phenomena is always successive. The representations of the parts follow one upon another. Whether they also follow one upon the other in the object is a second point for reflection, not contained in the former. We may indeed call everything, even every representation, so far as we are conscious of it, an object; but it requires a more profound investigation to discover what this word may mean with regard to phenomena, not in so far as they (as representations) are objects, but in so far as they only signify an object. So far as they, as representations only, are at the same time objects of consciousness, they cannot be distinguished from our apprehension, that is from their being received in the synthesis of our imagination, and we must therefore say, that the manifold of phenomena is always produced in the mind successively. If phenomena were things by themselves, the succession of the representations of their manifold would never enable us to judge how that manifold is connected in the object. We have always to deal with our representations only; how things may be by themselves (without reference to the representations by which they affect us) is completely beyond the sphere of our knowledge. Since, therefore, phenomena are not things by themselves, and are yet the only thing that can be given to us to know, I am asked to say what kind of connection in time belongs to the manifold of the phenomena itself, when the representation of it in our apprehension is always successive. Thus, for instance, the apprehension of the manifold in the phenomenal appearance of a house that stands before me, is successive. The question then arises, whether the manifold of the house itself be successive by itself, which of course no one would admit. Whenever I ask for the transcendental meaning of my concepts of an object, I find that a house is not a thing by itself, but a phenomenon only, that is, a representation the transcendental object of which is unknown. What then can be the meaning of the question, how the manifold in the phenomenon itself (which is not a thing by itself) may be connected? Here that which is contained in our successive apprehension is considered as representation, and the given phenomenon, though it is nothing but the whole of those representations, as their object, with which my concept, drawn from the representations of my apprehension, is to accord. As the accord between knowledge and its object is truth, it is easily seen, that we can ask here only for the formal conditions of empirical truth, and that the phenomenon, in contradistinction to the representations of our apprehension, can only be represented as the object different from them, if it is subject to a rule distinguishing it from every other apprehension, and necessitating a certain kind of conjunction of the manifold. That which in the phenomenon contains the condition of this necessary rule of apprehension is *the object.*

Let us now proceed to our task. That something takes place, that is, that something, or some state, which did not exist before, begins to exist, cannot be perceived empirically, unless there exists antecedently a phenomenon which does not contain that state; for a reality, following on empty time, that is a beginning of existence, preceded by no state of things, can be apprehended as little as empty time itself. Every apprehension of an event is therefore a perception following on another perception. But as this applies to all synthesis of apprehension, as I showed before in the phenomenal appearance of a house, that apprehension would not thereby be different from any other. But I observe at the same time, that if in a phenomenon which contains an event I call the antecedent state of perception A, and the subsequent B, B can only follow A in my apprehension, while the perception A can never follow B, but can only precede it. I see, for instance, a ship gliding down a stream. My perception of its place below follows my perception of its place higher up in the course of the stream, and it is impossible in the apprehension of this phenomenon that the ship should be perceived first below and then higher up. We see therefore that the order in the succession of perceptions in our apprehension is here determined, and our apprehension regulated by that order. In the former example of a house my perceptions could begin in the apprehension at the roof and end in the basement, or begin below and end above: they could apprehend the manifold of the empirical intuition from right to left or from left to right. There was therefore no determined order in the succession of these perceptions, determining the point where I had to begin in apprehension, in order to connect the manifold empirically; while in the apprehension of an event there is always a rule, which makes the order of the successive perceptions (in the apprehension of this phenomenon) necessary.

In our case, therefore, we shall have to derive the subjective succession in our apprehension from the objective succession of the phenomena, because otherwise the former would be entirely undetermined, and unable to distinguish one phenomenon from another. The former alone proves nothing as to the connection of the manifold in the object, because it is quite arbitrary. The latter must therefore consist in the order of the manifold in a phenomenon, according to which the apprehension of what is happening follows upon the apprehension of what has happened, in conformity with a rule. Thus only can I be justified in saying, not only of my apprehension, but of the phenomenon itself, that there exists in it a succession, which is the same as to say that I cannot arrange the apprehension otherwise than in that very succession.

In conformity with this, there must exist in that which always precedes an event the condition of a rule, by which this event follows at all times, and necessarily; but I cannot go back from the event and determine by apprehension that which precedes. For no phenomenon goes back from the succeeding to the preceding point of time, though it is related to some preceding point of time, while the progress from a given time to a determined following time is necessary. Therefore, as there certainly is something that follows, I must necessarily refer it to something else which precedes, and upon which it follows by rule, that is, by necessity. So that the event, as being conditional, affords a safe indication of some kind of condition, while that condition itself determines the event. . . .

It is necessary therefore to show by examples that we never, even in experience, ascribe the sequence or consequence (of an event or something happening that did not exist before) to the object, and distinguish it from the subjective sequence of our apprehension, except when there is a rule which forces us to observe a certain order of perceptions, and no other; nay, that it is this force which from the first renders the representation of a succession in the object possible.

We have representations within us, and can become conscious of them; but however far that consciousness may extend, and however accurate and minute it may be, yet the representations are always representations only, that is, internal determinations of our mind in this or that relation of time. What right have we then to add to these representations an object, or to ascribe to these modifications, beyond their subjective reality, another objective one? Their objective character cannot consist in their relation to another representation (of that which one wished to predicate of the object), for thus the question would only arise again, how that representation could again go beyond itself, and receive an objective character in addition to the subjective one, which belongs to it, as a determination of our mind. If we try to find out what new quality or dignity is imparted to our representations by their relation to an *object*, we find that it consists in nothing but the rendering necessary the connection of representations in a certain way, and subjecting them to a rule; and that on the other hand they receive their objective character only because a certain order is necessary in the time relations of our representations.

In the synthesis of phenomena the manifold of our representations is always successive. No object can thus be represented, because through the succession which is common to all apprehensions, nothing can be distinguished from anything else. But as soon as I perceive or anticipate that there is in this succession a relation to an antecedent state from which the representation follows by rule, then something is represented as an event, or as something that happens: that is to say, I know an object to which I must assign a certain position in time, which, after the preceding state, cannot be different from what it is. If therefore I perceive that something happens, this representation involves that something preceded, because the phenomenon receives its position in time with reference to what preceded, that is, it exists after a time in which it did not exist. Its definite position in time can only be assigned to it, if in the antecedent state something is presupposed on which it always follows by rule. It thus follows that, first of all, I cannot invert the order, and place that which happens before that on which it follows; secondly, that whenever the antecedent state is there, the other event must follow inevitably and necessarily. Thus it happens that there arises an order among our representations, in which the present state (as having come to be), points to an antecedent state, as a correlative of the event that is given; a correlative which, though as yet indefinite, refers as determining to the event, as its result, and connects that event with itself by necessity, in the succession of time. . . .

What is required for all experience and renders it possible is the understanding, and the first that is added by it is not that it renders the representation of objects clear, but that it really renders the representation of any object for the first time possible. This takes place by the understanding transferring the order of time to the phenomena and their existence, and by assigning to each of them as to a consequence a certain *a priori* determined place in time, with reference to antecedent phenomena, without which place phenomena would not be in accord with time, which determines *a priori* their places to all its parts. This determination of place cannot be derived from the relation in which phenomena stand to absolute time (for that can never be an object of perception); but, on the contrary, phenomena must themselves determine to each other their places in time, and render them necessary in the series of time. In other words, what happens or follows must follow according to a general rule on that which was contained in a previous state. We thus get a series of phenomena which, by means of the understanding, produces and makes necessary in the series of possible perceptions the same order and continuous coherence which exists *a priori* in the form of internal intuition (time), in which all perceptions must have their place.

That something happens is therefore a perception which belongs to a possible experience, and this experience becomes real when I consider the phenomenon as determined with regard to its place in time, that is to say, as an object which can always be found, according to a rule, in the connection of perceptions. This rule, by which we determine everything according to the succession of time, is this: the condition under which an event follows at all times (necessarily) is to be found in what precedes. All possible experience therefore, that is, all objective knowledge of phenomena with regard to their relation in the succession of time, depends on "the principle of sufficient reason."

The proof of this principle rests entirely on the following considerations. All empirical knowledge requires synthesis of the manifold by imagination, which is always successive, one representation following upon the other. That succession, however, in the imagination is not at all determined with regard to the order in which something precedes and something follows, and the series of successive representations may be taken as retrogressive as well as progressive. If that synthesis, however, is a synthesis of apperception (of the manifold in a given phenomenon), then the order is determined in the object, or, to speak more accurately, there is then in it an order of successive synthesis which determines the object, and according to which something must necessarily precede, and, when it is once there, something else must necessarily follow. If therefore my perception is to contain the knowledge of an event, or something that really happens, it must consist of an empirical judgment, by which the succession is supposed to be determined, so that the event presupposes another phenomenon in time on which it follows necessarily and according to a rule. If it were different, if the antecedent phenomenon were there, and the event did not follow on it necessarily, it would become to me a mere play of my subjective imaginations, or if I thought it to be objective, I should call it a dream. It is therefore the relation of phenomena (as possible perceptions) according to which the existence of the subsequent (what happens) is determined in time by something antecedent necessarily and by rule, or, in other words, the relation of cause and effect, which forms the condition of the objective validity of our empirical judgments with regard to the series of perceptions, and therefore also the condition of the empirical truth of them, and of experience. The principle of the causal relation in the succession of phenomena is valid therefore for all objects of experience, also (under the conditions of succession), because that principle is itself the ground of the possibility of such experience.

Karl Popper

CONJECTURES AND REFUTATIONS

Sir Karl Popper (b. 1902), one of the leading philosophers of science today, was born in Vienna. He was professor of philosophy in New Zealand and at the London School of Economics. One of his most important works is *Conjectures and Refutations: The Growth of Scientific Knowledge* (1963), from which the following selection is taken.

ON THE SOURCES OF KNOWLEDGE AND OF IGNORANCE

It follows, therefore, that truth manifests itself . . .

BENEDICTUS DE SPINOZA

Every man carries about him a touchstone . . . to distinguish . . . truth from appearances.

JOHN LOCKE

. . . it is impossible for us to think of any thing, which we have not antecedently felt, either by our external or internal senses.

DAVID HUME

I

The problem which I wish to examine afresh in this lecture, and which I hope not only to examine but to solve, may perhaps be described as an aspect of the old quarrel between the British and the Continental schools of philosophy— the quarrel between the classical empiricism of Bacon, Locke, Berkeley, Hume, and Mill, and the classical rationalism or intellectualism of Descartes, Spinoza, and Leibniz. In this quarrel the British school insisted that the ultimate source of all knowledge was observation, while the Continental school insisted that it was the intellectual intuition of clear and distinct ideas.

Most of these issues are still very much alive. Not only has empiricism, still the ruling doctrine in England, conquered the United States, but it is now widely accepted even on the European Continent as the true theory of *scientific* knowledge. Cartesian intellectualism, alas, has been only too often distorted into one or another of the various forms of modern irrationalism.

I shall try to show in this lecture that the differences between classical empiricism and rationalism are much smaller than their similarities, and that both are mistaken. I hold that they are mistaken although I am myself both an empiricist and a rationalist of sorts. But I believe that, though observation and reason have each an important role to play, these roles hardly resemble those which their classical defenders attributed to them. More especially, I shall try to show that neither observation nor reason can be described as a source of knowledge, in the sense in which they have been claimed to be sources of knowledge, down to the present day. . . .

III

The great movement of liberation which started in the Renaissance and led through the many vicissitudes of the reformation and the religious and revolutionary wars to the free societies in which the English-speaking peoples are privileged to live, this movement was inspired throughout by an unparalleled epistemological optimism: by a most optimistic view of man's power to discern truth and to acquire knowledge.

At the heart of this new optimistic view of the possibility of knowledge lies the doctrine that *truth is manifest*. Truth may perhaps be veiled. But it may reveal itself.[1] And if it does not reveal itself, it may be revealed by us. Removing the veil may not be easy. But once the naked truth stands revealed before our eyes, we have the power to see it, to distinguish it from falsehood, and to know that it *is* truth.

The birth of modern science and modern technology was inspired by this optimistic epistemology whose main spokesmen were Bacon and Descartes. They taught that there was no need for any man to appeal to authority in matters of truth because each man carried the sources of knowledge in himself; either in his power of sense-perception which he may use for the careful observation of nature, or in his power of intellectual intuition which he may use to distinguish truth from falsehood by refusing to accept any idea which is not clearly and distinctly perceived by the intellect. . . .

V

In examining the optimistic epistemology inherent in certain ideas of liberal-

---

[1]See my mottoes: Spinoza, *Of God, Man, and Human Happiness*, ch. 15 (parallel passages are: *Ethics*, ii, *scholium* to *propos.* 43 ("Indeed, as light manifests itself and darkness, so with truth: it is its own standard, and that of falsity."); *De intell. emend.*, 35, 36; 74th letter, end of para. 7); Locke, *Conduc. Underst.*, 3. (Cp. also *Romans*, i, 19.)

ism, I found a cluster of doctrines which, although often accepted implicitly, have not, to my knowledge, been explicitly discussed or even noticed by philosophers or historians. The most fundamental of them is one which I have already mentioned—the doctrine that truth is manifest. The strangest of them is the conspiracy theory of ignorance, which is a curious outgrowth from the doctrine of manifest truth.

By the doctrine that truth is manifest I mean, you will recall, the optimistic view that truth, if put before us naked, is always recognizable as truth. Thus truth, if it does not reveal itself, has only to be unveiled, or dis-covered. Once this is done, there is no need for further argument. We have been given eyes to see the truth, and the "natural light" of reason to see it by.

This doctrine is at the heart of the teaching of both Descartes and Bacon. Descartes based his optimistic epistemology on the important theory of the *veracitas dei*. What we clearly and distinctly see to be true must indeed be true; for otherwise God would be deceiving us. Thus the truthfulness of God must make truth manifest.

In Bacon we have a similar doctrine. It might be described as the doctrine of the *veracitas naturae*, the truthfulness of Nature. Nature is an open book. He who reads it with a pure mind cannot misread it. Only if his mind is poisoned by prejudice can he fall into error.

This last remark shows that the doctrine that truth is manifest creates the need to explain falsehood. Knowledge, the possession of truth, need not be explained. But how can we ever fall into error if truth is manifest? The answer is: through our own sinful refusal to see the manifest truth; or because our minds harbour prejudices inculcated by education and tradition, or other evil influences which have perverted our originally pure and innocent minds. Ignorance may be the work of powers conspiring to keep us in ignorance, to poison our minds by filling them with falsehood, and to blind our eyes so that they cannot see the manifest truth. Such prejudices and such powers, then, are sources of ignorance. . . .

For the simple truth is that truth is often hard to come by, and that once found it may easily be lost again. Erroneous beliefs may have an astonishing power to survive, for thousands of years, in defiance of experience, and without the aid of any conspiracy. The history of science, and especially of medicine, could furnish us with a number of good examples. One example is, indeed, the general conspiracy theory itself. I mean the erroneous view that whenever something evil happens it must be due to the evil will of an evil power. Various forms of this view have survived down to our own day.

Thus the optimistic epistemology of Bacon and of Descartes cannot be true. Yet perhaps the strangest thing in this story is that this false epistemology was the major inspiration of an intellectual and moral revolution without parallel in history. It encouraged men to think for themselves. It gave them hope that through knowledge they might free themselves and others from servitude and misery. It made modern science possible. It became the basis of the fight against censorship and the suppression of free thought. It became the basis of the nonconformist conscience, of individualism, and of a new sense of man's dignity; of a demand for universal education, and of a new dream of a free society. It made men feel responsible for themselves and for others, and eager to improve not only their own condition but also that of their fellow men. It is a case of a bad idea inspiring many good ones. . . .

How can we prepare ourselves to read the book of Nature properly or truly? Bacon's answer is: by purging our minds of all anticipations or conjectures or guesses or prejudices (*Nov. Org.* i, 68, 69 end). There are various things to be done in order so to purge our minds. We have to get rid of all sorts of "idols," or generally held false beliefs; for these distort our observations (*Nov. Org.* i, 97). But we have also, like Socrates, to look out for all sorts of counter-instances by which to destroy our prejudices concerning the kind of thing whose true essence or nature we wish to ascertain. Like Socrates, we must, by purifying our intellects, prepare our souls to face the eternal light of essences or natures (cf. St Augustine, *Civ. Dei*, VIII, 3): our impure prejudices must be exorcised by the invocation of counter-instances (*Nov. Org.* ii, 16 ff).

Only after our souls have been cleansed in this way may we begin the work of spelling out diligently the open book of Nature, the manifest truth.

In view of all this I suggest that Baconian (and also Aristotelian) induction is the same, fundamentally, as Socratic *maieutic*; that is to say, the preparation of the mind by cleansing it of prejudices, in order to enable it to recognize the manifest truth, or to read the open book of Nature.

Descartes' method of systematic doubt is also fundamentally the same: it is a method of destroying all false prejudices of the mind, in order to arrive at the unshakable basis of self-evident truth.

We can now see more clearly how, in this optimistic epistemology, the state of knowledge is the natural or the pure state of man, the state of the innocent eye which can see the truth, while the state of ignorance has its source in the injury suffered by the innocent eye in man's fall from grace; an injury which can be partially healed by a course of purification. And we can see more clearly why this epistemology, not only in Descartes' but also in Bacon's form, remains essentially a religious doctrine in which the source of all knowledge is divine authority. . . .

X

In spite of the religious character of their epistemologies, Bacon's and Descartes' attacks upon prejudice, and upon traditional beliefs which we carelessly or recklessly harbour, are clearly anti-authoritarian and anti-traditionalist. For they require us to shed all beliefs except those whose truth we have perceived ourselves. And their attacks were certainly intended to be attacks upon authority and tradition. They were part of the war against authority which it was the fashion of the time to wage, the war against the authority of Aristotle and the tradition of the schools. Men do not need such authorities if they can perceive the truth themselves.

But I do not think that Bacon and Descartes succeeded in freeing their epistemologies from authority; not so much because they appealed to religious authority—to Nature or to God—but for an even deeper reason.

In spite of their individualistic tendencies, they did not dare to appeal to our critical judgment—to your judgment, or to mine; perhaps because they felt that this might lead to subjectivism and to arbitrariness. Yet whatever the reason may have been, they certainly were unable to give up thinking in terms of authority, much as they wanted to do so. They could only replace one authority—that of Aristotle and the Bible—by another. Each of them appealed to a new authority; the one to *the authority of the senses*, and the other to *the authority of the intellect*.

This means that they failed to solve the great problem: How can we admit that our knowledge is a human—an all too human—affair, without at the same time implying that it is all individual whim and arbitrariness?

Yet this problem had been seen and solved long ago; first, it appears, by Xenophanes, and then by Democritus, and by Socrates (the Socrates of the *Apology* rather than of the *Meno*). The solution lies in the realization that all of us may and often do err, singly and collectively, but that this very idea of error and human fallibility involves another one—the idea of *objective truth*: the standard which we may fall short of. Thus the doctrine of fallibility should not be regarded as part of a pessimistic epistemology. This doctrine implies that we may seek for truth, for objective truth, though more often than not we may miss it by a wide margin. And it implies that if we respect truth, we must search for it by persistently searching for our errors: by indefatigable rational criticism, and self-criticism. . . .

XI

Bacon and Descartes set up observation and reason as new authorities, and they set them up within each individual man. But in doing so they split man into two parts, into a higher part which had authority with respect to truth—Bacon's observations, Descartes' intellect—and a lower part. It is this lower part which constitutes our ordinary selves, the old Adam in us. For it is always "we ourselves" who are alone responsible for error, if truth is manifest. It is we, with *our* prejudices, *our* negligence, *our* pigheadedness, who are to blame; it is we ourselves who are the sources of our ignorance.

Thus we are split into a human part, we ourselves, the part which is the source of our fallible opinions (*doxa*), of our errors, and of our ignorance; and a super-human part, such as the senses or the intellect, the part which is the source of real knowledge (*epistēmē*), and which has an almost divine authority over us.

But this will not do. For we know that Descartes' physics, admirable as it was in many ways, was mistaken; yet it was based only upon ideas which, he thought, were clear and distinct, and which therefore should have been true. And that the senses were not reliable either, and thus had no authority, was known to the ancients even before Parmenides, for example to Xenophanes and Heraclitus, and to Democritus and Plato. . . .

XIII

. . . The problem of the source of our knowledge has recently been restated as follows. If we make an assertion, we must justify it; but this means that we must be able to answer the following questions.

"*How do you know? What are the sources of your assertion?*"

This, the empiricist holds, amounts in its turn to the question,

"*What observations* (or memories of observations) *underlie your assertion?*"

I find this string of questions quite unsatisfactory.

First of all, most of our assertions are not based upon observations, but upon all kinds of other sources. "I read it in *The Times*" or perhaps "I read it in the *Encyclopaedia Britannica*" is a more likely and a more definite answer to the question "How do you know?" than "I have observed it" or "I know it from an observation I made last year."

"But," the empiricist will reply, "how do you think that *The Times* or the *Encyclopaedia Britannica* got their information? Surely, if you only carry on your inquiry long enough, you will end up with *reports of the observations of eyewitnesses* (sometimes called 'protocol sentences' or—by yourself—'basic statements'). Admittedly," the empiricist will continue, "books are largely made from other books. Admittedly, a historian, for example, will work from documents. But ultimately, in the last analysis, these other books, or these documents, must have been based upon observations. Otherwise they would have to be described as poetry, or invention, or lies, but not as testimony. It is in this sense that we empiricists assert that observation must be the ultimate source of our knowledge."

Here we have the empiricist's case, as it is still put by some of my positivist friends.

I shall try to show that this case is as little valid as Bacon's; that the answer to the question of the sources of knowledge goes against the empiricist; and, finally, that this whole question of ultimate sources—sources to which one may appeal, as one might to a higher court or a higher authority—must be rejected as based upon a mistake.

First I want to show that if you actually went on questioning *The Times* and its correspondents about the sources of their knowledge, you would in fact never arrive at all those observations by eyewitnesses in the existence of which the empiricist believes. You would find, rather, that with every single step you take, the need for further steps increases in snowball-like fashion.

Take as an example the sort of assertion for which reasonable people might simply accept as sufficient the answer "I read it in *The Times*"; let us say the assertion "The Prime Minister has decided to return to London several days ahead of schedule." Now assume for a moment that somebody doubts this assertion, or feels the need to investigate its truth. What shall he do? If he has a friend in the Prime Minister's office, the simplest and most direct way would be to ring him up; and if this friend corroborates the message, then that is that.

In other words, the investigator will, if possible, try to check, or to examine, *the asserted fact itself*, rather than trace the source of the information. But according to the empiricist theory, the assertion "I have read it in *The Times*" is merely a first step in a justification procedure consisting in tracing the ultimate source. What is the next step?

There are at least two next steps. One would be to reflect that "I have read it in *The Times*" is also an assertion, and that we might ask "What is the source of your knowledge that you read it in *The Times* and not, say, in a paper looking very similar to *The Times*?" The other is to ask *The Times* for the sources of its knowledge. The answer to the first question may be "But we have only *The Times* on order and we always get it in the morning" which gives rise to a host of further questions about sources which we shall not pursue. The second question may elicit from the editor of *The Times* the answer: "We had a telephone call from the Prime Minister's Office." Now according to the empiricist procedure, we should at this stage ask next: "Who is the gentleman who received the telephone call?" and then get his observation report; but we should also have to ask that gentleman: "What is the source of your knowledge that the voice you heard came from an official in the Prime Minister's office," and so on.

There is a simple reason why this tedious sequence of questions never comes to a satisfactory conclusion. It is this. Every witness must always make ample use, in his report, of his knowledge of persons, places, things, linguistic usages, social conventions, and so on. He cannot rely merely upon his eyes or ears, especially if his report is to be of use in justifying any assertion worth justifying. But this fact must of course always raise new questions as to the sources of those elements of his knowledge which are not immediately observational.

That is why the programme of tracing back all knowledge to its ultimate source in observation is logically impossible to carry through: it leads to an infinite regress. (The doctrine that truth is manifest cuts off the regress. This is interesting because it may help to explain the attractiveness of that doctrine.)

I wish to mention, in parenthesis, that this argument is closely related to another—that all observation involves interpretation in the light of our theoretical knowledge,[2] or that pure observational knowledge, unadulterated by theory, would, if at all possible, be utterly barren and futile.

The most striking thing about the observationalist programme of asking for sources—apart from its tediousness—is its stark violation of common sense. For if we are doubtful about an assertion, then the normal procedure is to test it, rather than to ask for its source; and if we find independent corroboration, then we shall often accept the assertion without bothering at all about sources.

---

[2]See my *Logic of Scientific Discovery*, last paragraph of section 24, and new appendix *x, (2).

Of course there are cases in which the situation is different. Testing an *historical* assertion always means going back to sources; but not, as a rule, to the reports of eyewitnesses.

Clearly, no historian will accept the evidence of documents uncritically. There are problems of genuineness, there are problems of bias, and there are also such problems as the reconstruction of earlier sources. There are, of course, also problems such as: was the writer present when these events happened? But this is not one of the characteristic problems of the historian. He may worry about the reliability of a report, but he will rarely worry about whether or not the writer of a document was an eyewitness of the event in question, even assuming that this event was of the nature of an observable event. A letter saying "I changed my mind yesterday on this question" may be most valuable historical evidence, even though changes of mind are unobservable (and even though we may conjecture, in view of other evidence, that the writer was lying).

As to eyewitnesses, they are important almost exclusively in a court of law where they can be cross-examined. As most lawyers know, eyewitnesses often err. This has been experimentally investigated, with the most striking results. Witnesses most anxious to describe an event as it happened are liable to make scores of mistakes, especially if some exciting things happen in a hurry; and if an event suggests some tempting interpretation, then this interpretation, more often than not, is allowed to distort what has actually been seen.

Hume's view of historical knowledge was different: ". . . we believe," he writes in the *Treatise* (Book I, Part III, Section iv; Selby-Bigge, p. 83), "that Caesar was kill'd in the Senate-house on the *ides of March* . . . because this fact is establish'd on the unanimous testimony of historians, who agree to assign this precise time and place to that event. Here are certain characters and letters present either to our memory or senses; which characters we likewise remember to have been us'd as the signs of certain ideas; and these ideas were either in the minds of such as were immediately present at that action, and receiv'd the ideas directly from its existence; or they were deriv'd from the testimony of others, and that again from another testimony . . . 'till we arrive at those who were eyewitnesses and spectators of the event." (See also E*nquiry*, Section x; Selby-Bigge, pp. 111 ff.)

It seems to me that this view must lead to the infinite regress described above. For the problem is, of course, whether "the unanimous testimony of historians" is to be accepted, or whether it is, perhaps, to be rejected as the result of their reliance on a common yet spurious source. The appeal to "letters present to our memory or our senses" cannot have any bearing on this or on any other relevant problem of historiography.

XIV

But what, then, are the sources of our knowledge?

The answer, I think, is this: there are all kinds of sources of our knowledge; but *none has authority.*

We may say that *The Times* can be a source of knowledge, or the Encyclopaedia *Britannica*. We may say that certain papers in the *Physical Review* about a problem in physics have more authority, and are more of the character of a source, than an article about the same problem in *The Times* or the Encyclopaedia. But it would be quite wrong to say that the source of the article in the *Physical Review* must have been wholly, or even partly, observation. The source may well be the discovery of an inconsistency in another paper, or say, the discovery of the fact that a hypothesis proposed in another paper could be tested by such and such an experiment; all these non-observational discoveries are "sources" in the sense that they all add to our knowledge.

I do not, of course, deny that an experiment may also add to our knowledge, and in a most important manner. But it is not a source in any ultimate sense. It has always to be checked: as in the example of the news in *The Times* we do not, as a rule, question the eyewitness of an experiment, but, if we doubt the result, we may repeat the experiment, or ask somebody else to repeat it.

The fundamental mistake made by the philosophical theory of the ultimate sources of our knowledge is that it does not distinguish clearly enough between questions of origin and questions of validity. Admittedly, in the case of historiography, these two questions may sometimes coincide. The question of the validity of an historical assertion may be testable only, or mainly, in the light of the origin of certain sources. But in general the two questions are different; and in general we do not test the validity of an assertion or information by tracing its sources or its origin, but we test it, much more directly, by a critical examination of what has been asserted—of the asserted facts themselves.

Thus the empiricist's questions "How do you know? What is the source of your assertion?" are wrongly put. They are not formulated in an inexact or slovenly manner, but *they are entirely misconceived*: they are questions that beg for an authoritarian answer.

XV

The traditional systems of epistemology may be said to result from yes-answers or no-answers to questions about the sources of our knowledge. *They never challenge these questions, or dispute their legitimacy*; the questions are taken as perfectly natural, and nobody seems to see any harm in them.

This is quite interesting, for these questions are clearly authoritarian in spirit. They can be compared with that traditional question of political theory, "Who should rule?" which begs for an authoritarian answer such as "the best," or "the wisest," or "the people," or "the majority." (It suggests, incidentally, such silly alternatives as "Who should be our rulers: the capitalists or the workers?" analogous to "What is the ultimate source of knowledge: the intellect or the senses?") This political question is wrongly put and the answers which it elicits are paradoxical (as I have tried to show in chapter 7 of my *Open Society*). It should be replaced by a completely different question such as "*How can we organize our political institutions so that bad or incompetent rulers* (whom we should try not to get, but whom we so easily might get all the same) *cannot do too much damage?"* I believe that only by changing our question in this way can we hope to proceed towards a reasonable theory of political institutions.

The question about the sources of our knowledge can be replaced in a similar way. It has always been asked in the spirit of: "What are the best sources of our knowledge—the most reliable ones, those which will not lead us into error, and those to which we can and must turn, in case of doubt, as the last court of appeal?" I propose to assume, instead, that no such ideal sources exist—no more than ideal rulers—and that *all* "sources" are liable to lead us into error at times. And I propose to replace, therefore, the question of the sources of our knowledge by the entirely different question: *"How can we hope to detect and eliminate error?"*

The question of the sources of our knowledge, like so many authoritarian questions, is a *genetic* one. It asks for the origin of our knowledge, in the belief that knowledge may legitimize itself by its pedigree. The nobility of the racially pure knowledge, the untainted knowledge, the knowledge which derives from the highest authority, if possible from God: these are the (often unconscious) metaphysical ideas behind the question. My modified question, "How can we hope to detect error?" may be said to derive from the view that such pure, untainted and certain sources do not exist, and that questions of origin or of purity should not be confounded with questions of validity, or of truth. This view may be said to be as old as Xenophanes. Xenophanes knew that our knowledge is guesswork, opinion—*doxa* rather than *epistēmē*—as shown by his verses (DK, B, 18 and 34):

> The gods did not reveal, from the beginning,
> All things to us; but in the course of time,
> Through seeking, men find that which is the better.
>
> But as for certain truth, no man has known it,
> Nor will he know it; neither of the gods,
> Nor yet of all the things of which I speak.
> And even if by chance he were to utter
> The final truth, he would himself not know it;
> For all is but a woven web of guesses.

Yet the traditional question of the authoritative sources of knowledge is repeated even today—and very often by positivists and by other philosophers who believe themselves to be in revolt against authority.

The proper answer to my question "How can we hope to detect and eliminate error?" is, I believe, "By *criticizing* the theories or guesses of others and—if we can train ourselves to do so—by *criticizing* our own theories or guesses." (The latter point is highly desirable, but not indispensable; for if we fail to criticize our own theories, there may be others to do it for us.) This answer sums up a position which I propose to call "critical rationalism." It is a view, an attitude, and a tradition, which we owe to the Greeks. It is very different from the "rationalism" or "intellectualism" of Descartes and his school, and very different even from the epistemology of Kant. Yet in the field of ethics, of moral knowledge, it was approached by Kant with his *principle of autonomy*. This principle expresses his realization that we must not accept the command of an authority, however exalted, as the basis of ethics. For whenever we are faced with a command by an authority, it is for us to judge, critically, whether it is moral or immoral to obey. The authority may have power to enforce its commands, and we may be powerless to resist. But if we have the physical power of choice, then the ultimate responsibility remains with us. It is our own critical decision whether to obey a command; whether to submit to an authority.

Kant boldly carried this idea into the field of religion: ". . . in whatever way," he writes, "the Deity should be made known to you, and even . . . if He should reveal Himself to you: it is you . . . who must judge whether you are permitted to believe in Him, and to worship Him."[3]

In view of this bold statement, it seems strange that in his philosophy of science Kant did not adopt the same attitude of critical rationalism, of the critical search for error. I feel certain that it was only his acceptance of the authority of Newton's cosmology—a result of its almost unbelievable success in passing the most severe tests—which prevented Kant from doing so. If this interpretation of Kant is correct, then the critical rationalism (and also the critical empiricism) which I advocate merely puts the finishing touch to Kant's own critical philosophy. And this was made possible by Einstein, who taught us that Newton's theory may well be mistaken in spite of its overwhelming success.

So my answer to the questions "How do you know? What is the source or the basis of your assertion? What observations have led you to it?" would be: "I do *not* know: my assertion was merely a guess. Never mind the source, or the sources, from which it may spring—there are many possible sources, and I may not be aware of half of them; and origins or pedigrees have in any case little bearing upon truth. But if you are interested in the problem which I tried to solve by my tentative assertion, you may help me by criticizing it as severely as you can; and if you can design some experimental test which you think might refute my assertion, I shall gladly, and to the best of my powers, help you to refute it."

This answer applies, strictly speaking, only if the question is asked about some scientific assertion as distinct from an historical one. If my conjecture was an historical one, sources (in the non-ultimate sense) will of course come into the critical discussion of its validity. Yet fundamentally, my answer will be the same, as we have seen.

---

[3]See Immanuel Kant, *Religion Within the Limits of Pure Reason*, 2nd edition (1794), Fourth Chapter, Part II, § 1, the first footnote.

XVI

It is high time now, I think, to formulate the epistemological results of this discussion. I will put them in the form of nine theses.

1. There are no ultimate sources of knowledge. Every source, every suggestion, is welcome; and every source, every suggestion, is open to critical examination. Except in history, we usually examine the facts themselves rather than the sources of our information.

2. The proper epistemological question is not one about sources; rather, we ask whether the assertion made is true—that is to say, whether it agrees with the facts. . . . And we try to find this out, as well as we can, by examining or testing the assertion itself; either in a direct way, or by examining or testing its consequences.

3. In connection with this examination, all kinds of arguments may be relevant. A typical procedure is to examine whether our theories are consistent with our observations. But we may also examine, for example, whether our historical sources are mutually and internally consistent.

4. Quantitatively and qualitatively by far the most important source of our knowledge—apart from inborn knowledge—is tradition. Most things we know we have learned by example, by being told, by reading books, by learning how to criticize, how to take and to accept criticism, how to respect truth.

5. The fact that most of the sources of our knowledge are traditional condemns anti-traditionalism as futile. But this fact must not be held to support a traditionalist attitude: every bit of our traditional knowledge (and even our inborn knowledge) is open to critical examination and may be overthrown. Nevertheless, without tradition, knowledge would be impossible.

6. Knowledge cannot start from nothing—from a *tabula rasa*—nor yet from observation. The advance of knowledge consists, mainly, in the modification of earlier knowledge. Although we may sometimes, for example in archaeology, advance through a chance observation, the significance of the discovery will usually depend upon its power to modify our earlier theories.

7. Pessimistic and optimistic epistemologies are about equally mistaken. The pessimistic cave story of Plato is the true one, and not his optimistic story of *anamnēsis* (even though we should admit that all men, like all other animals, and even all plants, possess inborn knowledge). But although the world of appearances is indeed a world of mere shadows on the walls of our cave, we all constantly reach out beyond it; and although, as Democritus said, the truth is hidden in the deep, we can probe into the deep. There is no criterion of truth at our disposal, and this fact supports pessimism. But we do possess criteria which, *if we are lucky*, may allow us to recognize error and falsity. Clarity and distinctness are not criteria of truth, but such things as obscurity or confusion *may* indicate error. Similarly coherence cannot establish truth, but incoherence and inconsistency do establish falsehood. And, when they are recognized, our

own errors provide the dim red lights which help us in groping our way out of the darkness of our cave.

8. Neither observation nor reason are authorities. Intellectual intuition and imagination are most important, but they are not reliable: they may show us things very clearly, and yet they may mislead us. They are indispensable as the main sources of our theories; but most of our theories are false anyway. The most important function of observation and reasoning, and even of intuition and imagination, is to help us in the critical examination of those bold conjectures which are the means by which we probe into the unknown.

9. Every solution of a problem raises new unsolved problems; the more so the deeper the original problem and the bolder its solution. The more we learn about the world, and the deeper our learning, the more conscious, specific, and articulate will be our knowledge of what we do not know, our knowledge of our ignorance. For this, indeed, is the main source of our ignorance—the fact that our knowledge can be only finite, while our ignorance must necessarily be infinite.

We may get a glimpse of the vastness of our ignorance when we contemplate the vastness of the heavens: though the mere size of the universe is not the deepest cause of our ignorance, it is one of its causes. "Where I seem to differ from some of my friends," F. P. Ramsey wrote in a charming passage of his *Foundations of Mathematics* (p. 291), "is in attaching little importance to physical size. I don't feel in the least humble before the vastness of the heavens. The stars may be large but they cannot think or love; and these are qualities which impress me far more than size does. I take no credit for weighing nearly seventeen stone." I suspect that Ramsey's friends would have agreed with him about the insignificance of sheer physical size; and I suspect that if they felt humble before the vastness of the heavens, this was because they saw in it a symbol of their ignorance.

I believe that it would be worth trying to learn something about the world even if in trying to do so we should merely learn that we do not know much. This state of learned ignorance might be a help in many of our troubles. It might be well for all of us to remember that, while differing widely in the various little bits we know, in our infinite ignorance we are all equal.

XVII

There is a last question I wish to raise.

If only we look for it we can often find a true idea, worthy of being preserved, in a philosophical theory which must be rejected as false. Can we find an idea like this in one of the theories of the ultimate sources of our knowledge?

I believe we can; and I suggest that it is one of the two main ideas which underlie the doctrine that the source of all our knowledge is super-natural. The first of these ideas is false, I believe, while the second is true.

The first, the false idea, is that we must *justify* our knowledge, or our theories, by *positive* reasons, that is, by reasons capable of establishing them, or at least of making them highly probable; at any rate, by better reasons than that they have so far withstood criticism. This idea implies, I suggested, that we must appeal to some ultimate or authoritative source of true knowledge; which still leaves open the character of that authority—whether it is human, like observation or reason, or super-human (and therefore super-natural).

The second idea—whose vital importance has been stressed by Russell—is that no man's authority can establish truth by decree; that we should submit to truth; that *truth is above human authority*.

Taken together these two ideas almost immediately yield the conclusion that the sources from which our knowledge derives must be super-human; a conclusion which tends to encourage self-righteousness and the use of force against those who refuse to see the divine truth.

Some who rightly reject this conclusion do not, unhappily, reject the first idea—the belief in the existence of ultimate sources of knowledge. Instead they reject the second idea—the thesis that truth is above human authority. They thereby endanger the idea of the objectivity of knowledge, and of common standards of criticism or rationality.

What we should do, I suggest, is to give up the idea of ultimate sources of knowledge, and admit that all knowledge is human; that it is mixed with our errors, our prejudices, our dreams, and our hopes; that all we can do is to grope for truth even though it be beyond our reach. We may admit that our groping is often inspired, but we must be on our guard against the belief, however deeply felt, that our inspiration carries any authority, divine or otherwise. If we thus admit that there is no authority beyond the reach of criticism to be found within the whole province of our knowledge, however far it may have penetrated into the unknown, then we can retain, without danger, the idea that truth is beyond human authority. And we must retain it. For without this idea there can be no objective standards of inquiry; no criticism of our conjectures; no groping for the unknown; no quest for knowledge.

2
METAPHYSICS

The Judeo-Christian tradition has long held that the mental or spiritual part of a person is different from the physical part. Most leading Jewish and Christian theologians in the last two millennia have claimed that some portion of the mental or spiritual aspect can and does survive the decay of the physical aspect. In our ordinary conception of a person, we seem to believe that a "person" is to some extent more than the sum of her or his parts. At the other end of life, arguments are going on as to when a human being becomes a person. Is it when certain physical features exist, or when some mental ones begin to appear? We seem to want to view the beginning and the continuous identity of personality as involving something more than mere physical components. The traditional religious view, and aspects of our ordinary views, suggest that a person has at least some aspect, mind, that is more than a physical feature, and that this aspect might be separable from the body.

In spite of traditional views that the mind is separate from the body, it is commonly asserted that the mind can be influenced by bodily events, such as the consumption of alcohol or the smoking of marijuana. More recently we have learned that one's mental outlook, reasoning processes, and beliefs can be altered, temporarily or permanently, by brainwashing, that is, by various kinds of psychological conditioning. Conversely, doctors have learned to diagnose and treat psychosomatic ailments, in which various mental states and stresses result in bodily ailments, such as ulcers.

One area of scientific research in which tremendous advances have been claimed in the last decade is in the treatment of mental diseases, especially manic depression and schizophrenia. Through the use of drugs the symptoms of these ailments have been eliminated and some patients have been able to function normally in society. In the case of manic depression, where the results have been most spectacular, research has found that administering lithium, a chemical element not normally found in the human body, reduces symptoms of mania very rapidly. Regular doses seem to prevent the occurrence of manic-depressive cycles in many patients. Thousands of people who had been hospitalized for long periods of time have been sent home as a result of lithium treatment. It is still somewhat of a mystery how and why lithium works for manic depressives, since the precise biochemical changes that lithium produces are only slowly being pinpointed.

Some researchers in this field believe that they have discovered a chemical link between physical and mental events in human beings. The discovery of lithium and other drugs, such as LSD and Valium, that appear to bring about changes in people's mental states has reinforced the view frequently held by medical and biological scientists that the mind is related to the body through biochemical processes in the nervous system and the brain. The exact nature of the relationship has not yet been discovered.

Nonetheless, some medical scientists are already claiming that the long-sought link between the mental and the physical sides of human nature has been found and that the problem of how a separate mind and body can affect each other is about to be resolved. Along with this accomplishment, it is claimed, will come the cure of all sorts of mental illnesses. On December 27, 1981, the *Los Angeles Times* proudly informed its readers that MIND-BODY SEPARATION HAS BECOME OBSOLETE and then explained HOW THE MIND-BODY RIDDLE WAS SOLVED through recent discoveries in the biochemistry of the nervous system.

On another front, researchers in parapsychology have been claiming that there is growing evidence of mental powers that cannot be explained by any known physical, chemical, or biological process. They claim that some people possess extrasensory perception, also called telepathy, and that others possess telekinesis, or the ability to effect physical events through what appears to be purely mental efforts.

For several decades experiments have been carried out that indicate the uncanny ability of some people to know about events far beyond their field of sensory perception, such as the arrangement of cards in a deck placed face down in a room quite distant from the perceiver. Some experiments placed the subject in a capsule underwater, where he perceived events occurring above the surface. Similarly, experiments have been carried out to ascertain if a person can determine through mental effort which faces of dice turn up, and, more spectacularly, if a person can bend a spoon by sheer will power.

Even though experts disagree about the significance and interpretations of these kinds of experiments, the proponents of parapsychology insist that their results indicate the existence of a mental force active in the universe that is different from the kinds of forces so far recognized and analyzed by modern science. If there is such a mental force, then we will have to recognize that the mind has features beyond those studied by present-day physiological psychologists and discussed by present-day philosophers, scientists, and theologians.

Another developing field of research that is contributing to our understanding of the relation of mind and body is artificial intelligence. As the computer has been improved to perform increasingly complex tasks, such as playing chess at the level of a grand master or translating a text into another language, some experts have claimed that they are on the verge of creating a machine with artificial intelligence. These experts say it is just a matter of time before computers can do creative intellectual tasks, such as writing poetry and designing computer problems. If this proves to be the case, it could be argued that the supposedly unique mental feature of a human being is just the property of a very complex machine. In that event, two questions arise: Are we essentially machines that perform functions of which a computer is capable (walking, talking, thinking)? And, is it only our emotional reactions that distinguish us from computers?

Philosophers have been trying for well over two thousand years to find a satisfactory explanation for the difference between the mental and physical features of human beings. Many psychiatrists and psychoanalysts now try to account for both aspects in terms of some physical explanation. Parapsychologists contend that there must be a special mental feature of human beings not explicable in terms of our present knowledge of the physical world. Some computer experts offer another form of physical explanation of mental features by analogy with the mental activities that computers can duplicate. These differing theories elaborate ideas proposed earlier in the writings of philosophers.

One of these theories follows from a part of Plato's philosophy. Plato saw the soul as a prisoner within the body. The body restricted the soul's ability to participate in the pure world of ideas or forms. St. Augustine used this view as the basis for a theology that separated the body and the soul. The soul, or spiritual part of human nature, could exist after and apart from the body. Aristotle sought for a more naturalistic relationship. The soul, the intellectual capacity of mankind, was the "form" of a human being. It was that feature that organized the physical parts of a human being into its functional state. It was not a separate entity, but rather an organizing principle within a human being that made it human. With the beginnings of modern science, Descartes sought to develop a new version of the Augustinian view. Mind and matter were two separate substances with totally distinct attributes. Matter could be characterized solely in physical terms by a mind employing clear and distinct mathematical ideas. However, Descartes saw that it was obvious that matter and mind interacted. What became the Achilles heel of Cartesian metaphysics was the attempt to explain how two totally unrelated substances could interact. Baruch Spinoza and Gottfried Leibniz each developed theories of the nature of mind and matter to overcome Descartes' difficulties. Spinoza proposed that the mental and the physical were two aspects of one substance, God or Nature, and hence did not have to interact. Leibniz proposed that no actual interaction takes place between mind and matter. They have each been created in terms of a pre-established harmony, so that their activities keep in tune. Hume challenged the very distinction between mental and physical events and thereby sought to eliminate the problem by removing the fundamental assumptions upon which it rested.

Various positions offered from Descartes onward have been categorized as follows:

1.   *Dualism.* Mind and body are separate substances that somehow interact. (Descartes)

2.   *Occasionalism.* Mind and body are separate substances that do not interact. Whenever an event occurs in one substance, it is the occasion of God acting on the other substance. (Malebranche)

3.   *The double-aspect theory, or psycho-physical parallelism.* Mind and body are just two aspects of, or ways of looking at, the same substance. Every event can be described either in physical or mental terms. (Spinoza)

4.   *The pre-established harmony.* Everything is a separate substance. These substances have been created so that there is a pre-established harmony among them and no interaction. (Leibniz)

5.   *Monism.* There is only one substance, and all events can be explained in terms of it:

      a.   The only substance is material; all events are either physical or caused by physical events. (Hobbes and many present-day researchers in psychobiochemistry)

      b.   The only substance is mental; all events are ideas. (Berkeley)

6.   *Skepticism.* Mental and physical events are just part of the sequence of experience and can be described without recourse to any substantial categories. (Hume)

The various ways of treating mental and physical events involve, of course, an original conception of what the world is composed of. Are the world's fundamental ingredients entirely physical entities, or entirely nonphysical entities, or some combination? If we limit ourselves to considerations of the basic components of the external world (leaving the internal one aside for the time being), the prevailing scientific view is that these components are entirely physical, consisting of material particles and various kinds of forces not all of which we may know at this time. Scientists generally believe that the entire external world can be explained in terms of these ultimate particles and their interactions. The various spiritual and supernatural entities found in ancient mythology, in various Judeo-Christian theologies, and in witchcraft and spiritualist theories have been banished from the pure scientific vision. One of its most forceful statements was presented by the eminent twentieth-century philosopher Bertrand Russell in the essay "The Free Man's Worship," in which he asserted that the physical world is deterministically going on its way according to its natural laws, with no purpose and no direction.

Russell's picture reflects the results of over two thousand years of theorizing about the nature of the external world. The earliest Greek thinkers that we know of—Thales, Anaximander, and Anaximenes—sought to find some ultimate material, such as water or air, that underlies all of nature. After more than a century of deliberation by these early thinkers starting around 600 B.C., Democritus offered a theory that the world was made up of indivisible physical units of various sizes and shapes. These units, called atoms, moved downward at varying speeds and in so doing, either combined or collided, changed directions, and set off more collisions. All physical phenomena that we experience can be explained, according to Democritus, as the results of these atomic combinations and collisions. The actual external world, composed of all of the atoms, which have neither color, nor sound, nor smell, nor taste, nor feeling. In the Democritean picture of the world, nothing happens for any purpose, but only because of the blind actions of atoms following the natural laws of motion.

This Greek atomism did not become a particularly successful scientific theory. The atoms, according to the theory, were too small to be observed and verified. No experimental equipment existed to test any of the hypotheses about atomic behavior. In addition, the brilliant Greek logician, Zeno of Elea, presented certain paradoxes that seemed to show that an indivisible unit of space, time, or matter was impossible. If every line can be divided (as a theorem in Euclidean geometry declares), why can't an atom be divided? It either has some size, or no size. If the latter, then it is nothing. If the former, it should be divisible. Further, Zeno argued, if anything has two parts, it must have three parts, the third being that which divides the first two, and thus it must have four, five, six, and an infinite number of parts.

Zeno's paradoxes forced thinkers to develop new theories about the nature of the external world. Aristotle sought to avoid Zeno's problems by denying that the process of division can actually be carried on indefinitely. Rather, one can carry on the process of division as long as one liked but there will still be potentially further divisions that can be made. Therefore no ultimate units will be found by dividing matter. The basic ingredients of the world were material entities undergoing constant change. These entities had goals that they were trying to achieve, namely some permanent state. They moved naturally toward these goals if not interfered with by other objects. Thus natural change is a purposeful process. It involves a material base progressing from form to form. The universe consists of a graded scale of different kinds of material objects, each seeking its natural goal. The ultimate goal is to be like the Unmoved Mover, the perfect being that cannot change.

Aristotle offered a way of analyzing all facets of the external world—inanimate material objects like stones, animate beings like animals and plants, and even psychological and astronomical entities—in terms of purposeful changes of forms. His scientific view dominated medieval Europe and was the prevailing theory until the seventeenth century. With the rise of modern science Aristotle's picture was found wanting on many counts, but principally because of its teleology (its explanation in terms of purpose). The theories of Hobbes,

Gassendi, and Descartes all sought to explain the external world without introducing goal-seeking accounts.

Hobbes and Gassendi, who were friends, offered completely materialistic views. Hobbes thought that everything from the movement of physical bodies to the actions of individual people and their social organizations could be explained in terms of matter in motion. Gassendi, a Catholic priest, was quite skeptical of any ultimate explanations but felt the best hypothesis for accounting for events was that of ancient atomism. He revived the atomic theory of Democritus and Epicurus, and tried to make it fit modern scientific knowledge. As a Christian he rejected the implication that the world was always and always will be just collections of atoms in motion. Instead he Christianized the theory by making God the creator and initiator of atoms and their motion.

Descartes, a contemporary and strong opponent of both Gassendi and Hobbes, offered a dualistic theory. For him mental events and physical events were completely different. The former consisted of ideas, sensations, and feelings that belonged to a mind. The latter consisted of geometrically measurable extended parts pushing each other. The material world could be studied purely in terms of mathematical properties and any element of purpose discarded. The mental world was distinct from the material one, but somehow they interacted, as we learn from experience.

The Cartesian picture involved finding out about the external world by "the way of ideas," that is, through using our clear and distinct ideas of extension, those of geometry. Critics raised the problem of how we could learn about the external material world from internal mental mathematical ideas. If all we know are ideas, then how can we know about some realm not composed of ideas? The dramatic possibilities resulting from such questioning were put forth in the daring theory of Bishop George Berkeley. He argued that any theory that separated ideas from things made knowledge of things dubious, if not impossible. Accepting Descartes' subjective starting point that we only know our own ideas, Berkeley insisted that ideas *are* reality, that the being of anything consists in its being perceived. What we call the external world is a set of ideas that we perceive and live with.

If everything consists of ideas, this doesn't mean that it is fictional or unreal. Its reality, Berkeley insisted, lies in its being perceived. But does the world jump into and out of existence when a person starts and stops perceiving it? No, the good bishop insisted, because there is a universal perceiver, God, who keeps all ideas in His consciousness.

Berkeley's rather startling view indicates a basic problem. If our knowledge of the external world comes to us from sensory experience of one kind or another, can we really know something called matter that is independent of, and beyond, our experience? Partly as a result of Berkeley's analysis, many modern philosophers of science have tried to frame their picture of what we know of the external world in terms of empirical constructs, concepts based on experience.

Most have rejected Berkeley's idealistic metaphysics, which maintains that the world consists of nothing but minds, ideas, and God, the universal perceiver. However, a leading twentieth-century astronomer and physicist, Sir Arthur Eddington, has tried to present a picture of the modern scientific world in terms much like those of Berkeley but incorporating our present understanding of physical relationships.

In contrast, Russell, with whom we started our discussion, formulated a materialistic view in empirical terms. The developments in physics and chemistry over the last fifty years have caused a serious revision of traditional atomism. Modern atomic physics is not about indivisible entities, but about entities with many parts. The ultimate constituents of matter have not yet been discovered. Physical relationships that had not previously been conceived have been introduced. Scientists are continuously finding new facets of the world that call for explanation. Empirical thinkers like Russell remain convinced that these facets can be fully described in empirical terms, requiring no non-material entities. The religious implications of Berkeley's or Eddington's views are still excluded by most present-day empiricists. Whether scientific materialism or naturalism can satisfactorily account for the external world remains to be seen in terms of the further development of scientific knowledge. Some philosophers disagree with Russell and contend that no amount of scientific information, couched in empirical terms, can totally explain all human experience. They point out that each time scientists claim that they have nearly discovered the secrets of the universe, still more questions arise.

The following selections deal with the two basic metaphysical questions we have discussed: How do mind and body relate? What is the nature of the external world? Consideration of the first will begin with a statement by Dr. Ronald Fieve about the dramatic effects of lithium on the treatment of mental illness. This is followed by a statement concerning extrasensory perception taken from the *Encyclopedia of Psychic Science*. Then we consider the psychoanalytic explanation of mental events offered by Freud and Breuer in their pioneering study of hysteria.

From these modern accounts, we turn back to classical statements about the relation between the mind or soul and the body offered by Plato, Aristotle, and St. Augustine. Then we look at Descartes' proffered solution in terms of his new metaphysics and at Leibniz's alternative in terms of the pre-established harmony of monads. Finally we see how Hume tried to resolve the difficulties involved in previous theories by denying the basis for the distinction between mental and physical events.

Our consideration of the second question concerning the nature of the external world begins with Russell's statement of what the world looks like to someone who accepts scientific explanations as providing a complete account of reality. We then turn back to the original formulation of the atomic theory by the early Greek philosophers, Leucippus and Democritus. This theory was criticized by Zeno of Elea in his famous paradoxes, which we include, along with Aristotle's attempt to offer a different conception of the external world (based on its continuous rather than its atomic character) to avoid these difficulties.

Moving to modern thinkers we consider Gassendi's presentation of atomic theory in the seventeenth century, Descartes' answer to Gassendi, and a statement of Descartes' own theory. Next we turn to Berkeley's startling attack on the new theories about the nature of the material world, in which he denied that we can know anything about such a world. Finally, we close this section with Russell's discussion of modern science's view of the external world.

A. HOW DO MIND AND BODY RELATE?

Ronald Fieve

MOODSWING: THE THIRD REVOLUTION IN PSYCHIATRY

Dr. Ronald R. Fieve (b. 1930) is the medical director of the Foundation for Depression and Manic Depression and professor of psychiatry at the College of Physicians and Surgeons of Columbia University. He was one of the pioneers in the use of lithium therapy. His book *Moodswing: The Third Revolution in Psychiatry* (1975) presents his views about recent progress in drug therapy for mental illnesses.

THE THIRD REVOLUTION

What is being done today for people who are overcome by feelings of low energy and depression? What happens to the superachievers in business, politics, and the arts whose extremes of elation become irrational and psychotic? What is the promise of the revolutionary chemical treatments now available in psychiatry for depression and elation?

Depression is the most common psychiatric problem for which people seek help, and it may have caused more anguish and suffering throughout the world than any other medical or psychiatric illness. Because of its pleasurable aspect, elation has been less talked about, and regarded as an illness only in its most immoderate forms.

Moods of deep depression and elation were described by Old Testament writers and by early Greeks and Romans. Philosophers, historians, poets, and novelists have accepted mental depression that returns from time to time as a part of the human condition, ranging from inexplicable moments of misery or joy to prolonged periods of extreme despondency or elation indicating serious mental derangement. Disorders of mood throughout the centuries have been misdiagnosed and, at the very least, unsuccessfully treated until recently.

141

Those that have not led to suicide have often remained uncontrollable, even in the hands of experts.

What I have to say in the pages to follow may startle many who believe primarily or exclusively in the psychological approaches to depression. Anyone who has kept abreast of the new chemical advances for treatment and prevention of mood disorders, however, will know that we are now undergoing our third and most spectacular revolution in the treatment of emotional states. In particular, we are witnessing for the first time a major chemical breakthrough with the lithium treatment and prevention of manic depression and recurrent depression. These chemically treatable mood disorders can now be easily recognized in normal people, and are characterized by what I refer to as a recurrent *moodswing*.

From 1959 until mid-1970 I was in charge of the acute psychiatric service at the New York State Psychiatric Institute, and word had spread from Australia and Denmark of promising results from the use of lithium carbonate in treating manic depression. Researching the world literature on lithium was a relatively easy task in 1959, since it consisted of only a few reports from abroad. I soon read that lithium carbonate was a simple white powder found in mineral water and rocks, a naturally occurring salt similar to table salt. I found that it could be given to excited manic patients by mouth in capsule form. And according to the reports by its Australian discoverer, John F. Cade, it would calm manic excitement in five to ten days.

My first research trials of this drug on hyperactive and elated manics resulted in a dramatic calming of their symptoms. Furthermore, with the correct dosage of lithium, there seemed to be no side effects, unlike the chemical straitjacketing of the patient which often resulted from use of the major tranquilizers. I had seen this latter effect in acutely agitated patients for whom massive doses of tranquilizers were required, to slow them down and induce sleep. In the process, side effects—retarded body movement, a masklike face with little expression, a zombielike appearance—were usually evident. Manic patients calmed on lithium, in contrast, were perfectly normal. Their overactivity, talkativeness, seductiveness, playful tie pulling, and high energy levels were quickly dampened, and they were ready for discharge in a few weeks. Previously, these same patients had received months and years of electroshock therapy, multiple drugs, psychotherapy, and psychoanalysis. During the three years I spent in psychiatric training, the additional five years of formal psychoanalytic training, and the years I have spent in psychiatric research, I have not found another treatment in psychiatry that works so quickly, so specifically, and so permanently as lithium for recurrent manic and depressive mood states. . . .

Over the years, my experience with lithium in treating mild to severe manic-depressives and patients with simple recurrent depression has convinced me that lithium not only effectively normalizes the manic state, but also prevents or dampens many future lows of manic depression and recurrent depression.

Lithium is the first truly prophylactic agent in psychiatry to control, prevent, or stabilize the future lifetime course of a major mental illness.

The first revolution in psychiatry began with the work of Philippe Pinel in 1791. Later, as chief psychiatrist and neurologist of the Salpêtrière Hospital in Paris, he reformed the treatment of the mentally insane by introducing liberal principles in the organization and administration of mental hospitals. For the first time in history, through Pinel's efforts, the mental hospital became the main therapeutic tool for helping mental patients. Pinel rejected the use of chains and beatings as methods of treating mental illness, measures which had been employed liberally since early Roman times. Bloodletting and sudden ducking in ice-cold water, he felt, induced a medical delirium more serious than the delirium of the mentally ill patients themselves. Excited manic patients, in particular, were subjected to these treatments until Pinel's revolutionary changes began to occur. Pinel's humane approach and his theories of hospital management are still valid today in the contemporary community mental-health center. His primary contribution was to change society's attitude toward the insane so that patients were considered sick human beings, deserving and requiring medical treatment. He asserted that it was impossible to determine whether mental symptoms resulted from the mental disease itself or from the effects of the chains on the patient.

Even though the mentally ill had not been tortured at the stake for some time, their condition during most of Pinel's life—in "the Century of Enlightenment"—was still agonizing. If mental patients were not hospitalized, they could be seen wandering aimlessly through the countryside, beaten and ridiculed. In England as early as 1403, the insane were frequently interned and brutalized at Bethlehem Hospital, or "Bedlam," as it was called. This famous insane asylum was a favorite Sunday excursion spot for Londoners who came to peer through the iron gates at the unfortunate patients.

Whether in Paris, London, Philadelphia, or New Orleans, if a dangerous madman had no relatives he would be placed in prison. The inhumanity with which the mentally ill were treated was probably due to complete ignorance of the nature of mental illness, deep dread of the insane, and the belief that mental disease was incurable. Excited patients were locked naked in narrow closets and fed through holes from copperware attached to chains. Straitjackets attached to walls or beds were used to restrain patients, since it was believed that the more painful the restraint, the better the results, particularly with obstinate psychotics. Attendants were often sadistic individuals of low intelligence who could find no other employment. Pinel revolutionized this state of horror for the mentally ill.

Around 1900, when Sigmund Freud ushered in the second revolution in psychiatry, the role of the psychiatrist remained frustrating. He could classify the psychoses and predict their course better than his predecessors a century before, but he still suffered from the same ignorance of the causes of mental illness and basically had to resort to crude and miserable methods of treatment. Freud (1856–1936) was undoubtedly the most renowned of all psychotherapists and psychoanalysts of the late nineteenth century. Originally he had been a neurologist, and he never gave up the idea that all psychological illness must in the end be attributable to an organic process that would one day be treatable with chemical therapy.

Since at that time in history basic research in the neuroses and psychoses had not yielded any positive biological clues, Freud resolved to confine his work to the purely psychological level. As a young psychotherapist, Freud made a pilgrimage to the French town of Nancy to learn the method of hypnosis for treating the neuroses and investigating them. Freud synthesized the ideas of the great neurologists and hypnotists of France into a theory of personality which soon became an international movement. He developed the theory of the unconscious and the concept of mental repression and its role in neurosis. For him symptoms were substitute gratifications. The psychotherapist's task was to get the patient to express unconscious feelings and uncover repressed memories which were causing the neurotic conflict. His new technique of uncovering the unconscious through the process of free association of thoughts and the analysis of dreams he called *psychoanalysis*. He soon became convinced that all neuroses had at their basis sexual problems and experiences in childhood. Freud invented the concept of *libido*, a vague term that referred to sexual energy. He also formed the concept of the *Oedipal complex*, the key to all neuroses, in which the unconscious problem of a neurotic male was an unresolved sexual attachment to his mother. A similar problem in neurotic females was termed the *Electra complex*.

Freud felt that the therapeutic force in analytic treatment was the phenomenon of *transference*, in which the patient redirected toward the psychoanalyst many of his previous feelings and ideas associated with his parents and other significant figures of his past. Freud attempted to apply psychoanalysis to the psychoses, but he found that they were not very accessible. He also attempted to apply psychoanalysis to explain art and religion as well as war and culture. Soon in some countries psychoanalysis became a substitute religion, a church with a dogma, like other scientific movements such as Marxism and Darwinism.

Although it is easy now to look back and mention only the shortcomings of the psychoanalytic revolution in psychiatry, it was of fundamental importance, if only because doctors began to listen to what their patients had to say. Furthermore, the psychoanalytic movement represented important progress beyond simply observing, describing, and listing the outward symptoms of mental illness, in which the causes were so poorly understood and the treatments unavailable. It was in large part responsible for the development of a feeling of expectancy and optimism on the part of psychiatrists, patients, and society throughout the early decades of the twentieth century.

The third revolution in psychiatry was initiated in the 1950s, with the introduction of the potent antipsychotic phenothiazine tranquilizers and reserpine treatment of the emotionally ill. Psychiatric hospitals that began to employ these chemical treatments reported a decrease in the use of physical restraints, electroshock therapy, hydrotherapy, insulin coma, and other physical methods of treatment. A reduction in patients' violence and agitation and an increase in the discharge rate of chronic patients hitherto considered hopeless cases began to be achieved. The widespread success with chemical agents in the late Fifties precipitated government and private funding for intensive research to find additional psychoactive drugs—and the new science of *psychopharmacology*, the chemical treatment of emotional states, was born.

In 1955, for the first time in 100 years, the number of patients admitted to psychiatric hospitals in the United States began to decline. Since then, despite a steady increase in the admission rates, a decrease in the mental-hospital populations in America continued, to an all-time low of about three hundred thousand patients in 1973. This number would have doubled had it not been for the introduction of the antipsychotic phenothiazine tranquilizers in the early Fifties. . . .

The lithium breakthrough has brought all of these fascinating pieces of the puzzle together. It has clarified the fact that major mood disorders—which may at times be advantageous and productive—are stabilized by a simple, naturally occurring substance. Furthermore, findings point to the fact that mania and mental depression must be due to biochemical causes handed down through the genes, since they are correctable so rapidly by chemical rather than talking therapy.

This revelation, which is now gaining wide acceptance in most scientific circles around the world, also calls for social change. It is bound to change the diagnostic styles and treatments in modern American psychiatry and bring psychiatry back into medicine, from which is has strayed for seventy years. Diagnoses of manic depression and recurrent depression are already on the increase. Millions of cyclically depressed people if stabilized on lithium could lead normal lives after years of waste and suffering. Most young manic-depressives could look forward to normal lives if maintained on lithium, just as diabetics and cardiacs can when maintained on insulin or digitalis.

TELEPATHY

The following article comes from the *Encyclopaedia of Psychic Science*.

TELEPATHY, the word was coined by F. W. H. Myers in 1882 as the outcome of his joint investigation with Gurney, Sidgwick and Prof. Barrett into the possibilities of thought transference. It was meant as a name for a fact: "a coincidence between two person's thoughts which requires a causal explanation," and it was defined as "transmission of thought independently of the recognised channels of sense." The name involved no attempt at explanation, yet it was soon construed as such and from the comparatively simple fact of experimentally demonstrated thought-transference a mighty jump was made to the portentous claim that it is an agency of communication between mind and mind even when consciously no such attempt is thought of, that it is a mysterious link between conscious and subconscious minds, that it is endowed with an intelligence by which incidents either from the memory of the person present or from the memories of distant and unknown persons can be selected, in fact that telepathy is a rival of the spirit theory. This conception spread so widely that many people conceive it now as something distinct from thought-transference and claim a line of division with the following argument: in telepathy the transmitter is often unaware that he acts as an agent and the receiver does not consciously prepare himself for the reception. Telepathy cannot be made a subject of experiments while thought-transference can. Thought-transference is a rudimentary faculty. Telepathy is a well-developed mode of supernormal perception and is usually brought into play by the influence of very strong emotions.

The need of differentiation is acknowledged by the old school of telepathists, too, when they speak of spontaneous and experimental telepathy. An as hardened sceptic as Frank Podmore believed that "whilst the attempt to correlate the two kinds of phenomena is perhaps legitimate, we can hardly be justified in making the spontaneous phenomena the basis of a theory of telepathy." (*The Newer Spiritualism*, p. 26).

Myers pointed out that telepathy as a faculty must absolutely exist in the universe if the universe contains any unembodied intelligences at all. Social life requires a method for the exchange of thought. The belief in telepathy is age old. Prayer is telepathic communion with higher beings. The basis of sympathy and antipathy may be telepathy. The monitions of approach appear to be telepathic messages. The knowledge of victory or disaster which so unexplainably spread in ancient Greece may have been telepathically acquired.

The working of telepathy is apparently demonstrated in suggestion. The case is quite clear when the hypnotisation is effected through a distance. Myers called it "telepathic hypnotism."

A good instance of audibly received telepathy is the following (*Proc.* S.P.R. I. p. 6.): "On September 9, 1848, at the siege of Mooltan, Major-General R——, C.B., then adjutant of his regiment, was severely wounded, and thought himself to be dying, and requested that his ring be taken off and sent to his wife. At the same time she was in Ferozepore (150 miles distant), lying on her bed between sleeping and waking, and distinctly saw her husband being carried off the field, and heard his voice saying "Take this ring off my finger and send it to my wife."

The case was fully verified. All the names were known to the Society.

William T. Stead often received automatic writing from the living. Thinking of a lady with whom he was in such communication more than once, his hand wrote: "I am very sorry to tell you that I have had a very painful experience of which I am almost ashamed to speak. I left Haslemere at 2.27 p.m. in a second-class carriage, in which there were two ladies and one gentleman. When the train stopped at Godalming, the ladies got out, and I was left alone with the man. After the train started he left his seat and came close to me. I was alarmed, and repelled him. He refused to go away and tried to kiss me. I was furious. We had a struggle. I seized his umbrella and struck him, but it broke, and I was beginning to fear that he would master me, when the train began to slow up before arriving at Guildford Station. He got frightened, let go of me, and before the train reached the platform he jumped out and ran away. I was very much upset. But I have the umbrella."

Stead sent his secretary to the lady with a note that he was very sorry to hear what had happened and added: "Be sure and bring the man's umbrella on Wednesday." She wrote in reply: "I am very sorry you know anything about it. I had made up my mind to tell nobody. I will bring the broken umbrella, but it was my umbrella, not his."

The determination of the lady not to tell of the painful evidence apparently indicates that a telepathic message may not only be unconscious, but may directly counteract the conscious mind. . . .

The Wave Theory

In his Presidential Address to the British Association for the Advancement of Science, Sir William Crookes said: "If telepathy takes place we have two physi-

cal facts—the physical change in the brain of A, the suggester, and the analogous change in the brain of B, the recipient of the suggestion. Between these
two physical events there must exist a train of physical causes." He further
argued that "with every fresh advance of knowledge it is shown that ether
vibrations have powers and attributes abundantly equal to any demand—even
to the transmission of thought."

He believed that these ether waves are of small amplitude and greater frequency than the X-rays, continually passing between human brains and arous-
ing a similar image in the second brain to the first. Against this is that the
intensity of waves diminishes with the square of distance and that the telepathic image may not only be very vivid despite the remoteness of the agent
but that the picture is often modified and symbolical. A dying man may appear
in normal state of health, unsuffering. "Mr. L.," quotes Myers, "dies of heart
disease when in the act of lying down undressed in bed. At or about the same
time Mr. N. J. S. sees Mr. L. standing beside him with a cheerful air, dressed for
walking and with a cane in his hand. One does not see how a system of undula-
tions could have transmuted the physical facts in this way."

In cases of collective reception an added difficulty is presented. Why should
only a few people in a room be sensitive to the waves and other strangers
outside the room not? Take the case of the crystal gazer. Why should he get a
telepathic message at the time of his own choosing, when he happens to look
into the crystal. How can the pictures in the crystal be sometimes seen to
others if they are only produced in his brain by telepathic impact?

In *The Survival of Man*, 1908, Sir Oliver Lodge was of the opinion that the
experimental evidence is not sufficient to substantiate the non-physical nature
of thought-transference. Of its reality he had no doubt and as early as 1903
stated in an interview to the *Pall Mall Magazine*: "What we can take before the
Royal Society, and what we can challenge the judgment of the world upon, is
Telepathy."

Dr. Hereward Carrington suggests that telepathic manifestations may take
place through a superconscious mind, that there may be a mentiferous ether as
some writers have suggested which carries telepathic waves, and that there is a
species of spiritual gravitation, uniting life, throughout the universe, as physical gravity binds together all matter. . . .

William J. Long, in his *How Animals Talk*, produces many instances in evidence
of a telepathic faculty in animals. He noticed for instance that if a mother
she-wolf cannot head off a cub which rushes away because of the distance
which he has already put between himself and her, she simply stops quiet, lifts
her head high and looks steadily at the running cub. He will suddenly waver,
halt, whirl and speed back to the pack. The famous case of the Elberfeld horses
also furnished good evidence that telepathy may operate between animals and
the human mind. Edmund Selous in *Thought Transference in Birds* records many
curious observations on the subject from bird life.

Telepathy versus Survival

Obviously telepathy as a fact is of tremendous importance. But those who tried to find in it an all-inclusive solution of supernormal manifestations faced very great difficulties. If a telepathic message is followed by major movements, for instance, the automatic announcement of the death of somebody in writing the question is who executes the movements: the subconscious self or the agent himself who sends the message? The similar uncertainty applies if the reception of a telepathic message is accompanied by telekinetic movements.

An attempt was made to explain all apparitions as telepathic hallucinations. Frank Podmore was the greatest exponent of this theory. He was the author of the first book which, published in 1894, under the title: *Apparitions and Thought Transference*, dealt with the accumulated evidence for telepathy.

Myers was the first to admit the insufficiency of telepathy as an explanation of apparitions. Being forced to concede that collective perception of phantasmal appearances militates for something objective, he worked out a theory of psychical invasion, the creation of a phantasmogenetic centre in the percipient's surroundings. The theory is a halfway house between telepathy and disembodied spirits and its real value is that it covers many freakish phantasmal manifestations for which no satisfactory solution has yet been offered.

The problem whether telepathy should not be admitted both from the living and the dead forced itself on the attention with an ever-increasing moment.

Apparitions of the dying are on the borderland between telepathy with the living and telepathy with the dead. A similar borderland phenomenon which lacks all the conditions for the evidence of telepathy is visions of the dead appearing to the dying.

The strain of the telepathic theory was growing with instances which made, on one hand the acquisition of certain knowledge by telepathic process wildly improbable but were, on the other hand, easily understood on the basis of the survival theory. The question that awaited answer was not only how certain information could have been acquired but also why should it be associated with definite personalities or be disclosed in a personified form. . . .

There are many cases on record in which missing wills, the whereabouts of which was not known to anyone living, have been found through what alleged to be spirit communication. There are others in which the supposition of the latent information, subconsciously received, must be stretched over ages and successive generations. Such is the case of the finding of Edgar Chapel, Glastonbury Abbey, as narrated in Mr. Bligh Bond's *The Gate of Remembrance*. The abbey was in ruins, every trace of the Chapel was lost, very little was known as to its location and precise dimensions. Nevertheless, in automatic writing series of communications came through, giving the most precise measurement. When excavations were undertaken in 1908, a year after the receipt of the communications, every statement was verified and the chapel was found.

The personal element puts insurmountable obstacles in the way of telepathic explanation in the following case recorded by Bozzano in notes on the July 14, 1928, sitting at Millesimo Castle. "An unknown voice, in Genoese dialect, addresses Gino Gibelli, one of the presents: 'I am Stefano's father. You must tell my son that I insist on his giving the message to Maria with which I entrusted him. He has not carried out my request in the slightest degree.'" Signor Gibelli explained that a month before he had been present in Genoa. The father communicated with the son and charged him with a message to his mother. Very probably the young man had not dared to carry out this request. Gibelli stated that he had completely forgotten this incident, it had nothing to do with him personally nor did it interest him in the slightest degree. He was not thinking of Stefano's father, whom he did not know in life, and was unaware of the fact that the request which the father had made to his son had not been carried out.

The technical side of communication also disproves telepathy as the means of the medium for gaining knowledge. Telepathy has no allowance for false or confused information, it does not explain the loss of the idea of time, nor the individual style of the different communicators, i.e., the Biblical manner of Imperator, his haughtiness, Pelham's impatience, etc. Names are often inaccurately spelt, giving for instance Margaret instead of Maggie. Telepathy cannot reveal coming events, nor can it explain how children who if recently dead ask for their toys and act childishly, behave years after as grown ups, though no such memory is retained in any living mind. . . .

The real insufficiency of the telepathic explanation has been amply demonstrated by hundreds of strange cross-correspondences and book and newspaper-tests.

The post-mortem letters, many of which are preserved by the S.P.R., and wait for opening until after a communication revealing their contents, comes through a medium after the writer's death, show as yet no complete success and it is doubtful whether this evidence will ever be conclusive in view of the fact that in one instance the content of the letter was revealed, apparently as a result of telepathic operation, by the medium while the writer was yet alive. The telepathist may always argue that the contents of the letter were subconsciously transferred into another brain while the writer was preparing it.

The "Hannah Wild" case is a well-known failure. Mrs. Blodgett, the sister of the deceased, obtained communications through Mrs. Piper which purported to come from Hannah Wild. The communicator, however, could not explain the words in a letter which she left behind and which no one understood. The idea of these post-mortem letters was originated by Myers. As a proof of survival, cross-correspondences are far more conclusive as the part messages coming through several mediums are by themselves nonsensical and they could only be explained away by the supposition of a tremendous conspiracy between several subconscious minds for the purposes of deceit. In the newspaper tests recorded by the Rev. Drayton Thomas such a subconscious conspiracy will have to be stretched to the utmost as at the time when the contents of a certain column in the next day's paper was indicated neither the editor nor the compositor could tell what particular text would occupy the column in question.

The Arguments of Prof. Hyslop

The original confusion in the ideas which assigned telepathy a rival importance to the spirit theory was, according to Prof. Hyslop—due to the word "transmission," in the first definition of telepathy. He prefers to define it as "a coincidence excluding normal perception, between the thoughts of two minds." It was the word transmission which gave telepathy the implication that "it is a process exclusively between living people and not permitting the intervention of the dead, if the discarnate exist and can act on the living." Hyslop's definition permits the employment of the term to describe the action of discarnate as well as incarnate minds. Hyslop was certainly right in saying: "We are not entitled to assume the larger meaning of telepathy to be a fact because we are not sure of its limitations. Here is where we have been negligent of the maxims of scientific methods and the legitimate formation of convictions."

"Mediumistic phenomena," he writes in *Contact with the Other World*, "too often suggest the action of spirits, to be cited as direct evidence for telepathy. The possibility of spirits and the fact that an incident is appropriate to illustrate the personal identity of a deceased person forbids using it as positive evidence for telepathy. One can only insist that one theory is as good as the other to account for the facts."

For selective telepathy "no evidence has been adduced . . . and I do not see how it would be possible to adduce such evidence. Every extension of the term beyond coincidences between the mental states of two persons is wholly without warrant. The introduction of the assumption that this coincidence is due to a direct transmission from one living mind to another has never been justified, and as there is no known process whatever associated with the coincidences we are permitted to use the term only in a descriptive, not in an explanatory sense.

". . . There is no scientific evidence for any of the following conceptions of it (1) Telepathy as a process of selecting from the contents of the subconscious of any person in the presence of the percipient; (2) Telepathy as a process of selecting from the contents of the mind of some distant person by the percipient and constructing these acquired facts into a complete simulation of a given personality; (3) Telepathy as a process of selecting memories from any living people to impersonate the dead; (4) Telepathy as implying the transmission of the thoughts of all living people to all others individually, with the selection of the necessary facts for impersonation from the present sitter; (5) Telepathy as involving a direct process between agent and percipient; (6) Telepathy as explanatory in any sense whatever, implying any known cause.

"The failures in experiments to read the present active states of the agent and the inability to verify any thoughts outside those states, in the opinion of science is so finite that its very existence is doubted, while the extended hypothesis requires us to believe in its infinity without evidence.

"As a name for facts, with suspended judgment regarding explanation, it is tolerable, but there can be no doubt that spirits explain certain facts, while telepathy explains nothing. At least as a hypothesis, therefore, the spiritistic theory has the priority and the burden of proof rests upon the telepathic theory."

Dr. Hodgson similarly concluded in his second Piper report: "having tried the hypothesis of telepathy from the living for several years, and the spirit hypothesis also for several years, I have no hesitation in affirming with the most absolute assurance that the spirit hypothesis is justified by its fruits, and the other hypothesis is not."

Telepathy—The Result of Spirit Agency?

Hyslop was not averse to the possibility that spirits may furnish the explanation of telepathy between the living. He says that Myers saw this implication at the very outset of the investigations into telepathy. . . .

The dividing line between clairvoyance and telepathy is vague. The telepathic message may take the form of visual or auditory sensation. If the content indicates future events clairvoyance should be suspected at work. Past events may be both telepathic communications and the result of psychometric reading.

Sigmund Freud

STUDIES IN HYSTERIA

This selection from Chapter 4 of Freud and Breuer's *Studies in Hysteria* shows how Freud (who wrote this chapter) thought mental events and physical events are related.

THE PSYCHOTHERAPY OF HYSTERIA

In our "Preliminary Communication" we have stated that while investigating the etiology of hysterical symptoms, we have also discovered a therapeutic method which we consider of practical significance. "*We found, at first to our greatest surprise, that the individual hysterical symptoms immediately disappeared without returning if we succeeded in thoroughly awakening the memories of the causal process with its accompanying affect, and if the patient circumstantially discussed the process in the most detailed manner and gave verbal expression to the affect*" (p. 3).

We furthermore attempted to explain how our psychotherapeutic method acts: "*It abrogates the efficacy of the original non-abreacted ideas by affording an outlet to their strangulated affects through speech. It brings them to associative correction by drawing them into normal consciousness (in mild hypnosis) or by eliminating them through medical suggestion in the same way as in somnambulism with amnesia*" (p. 12).

Although the essential features of this method have been enumerated in the preceding pages, a repetition is unavoidable, and I shall now attempt to show connectedly how far-reaching this method is, its superiority over others, its technique, and its difficulties. . . .

In this way it was found that *neurasthenia* really corresponds to a monotonous morbid picture in which, as shown by analysis, "psychic mechanisms" play no part. From neurasthenia we sharply distinguished the compulsion neurosis (obsessions, doubts, impulses), the neurosis of genuine obsessions, in which we can recognize a complicated psychic mechanism, an etiology resembling the one of hysteria, and a far-reaching possibility of its reduction by psychotherapy. On the other hand, it seemed to me absolutely imperative to separate from neurasthenia a neurotic symptom complex which depends on a totally divergent, indeed, strictly speaking, on a contrary etiology, the partial symptoms of this complex have already been recognized by E. Hecker as having a common character. They are either symptoms, or equivalents, or rudiments of *anxiety manifestations*, and it is for that reason that in order to distinguish this complex from neurasthenia, that I have called it *anxiety neurosis*. I maintained that it originates from an accumulation of physical tension, which is in turn of sexual origin. This neurosis, too, has no psychic mechanism, but regularly influences the psychic life, so that among its regular manifestations we have "anxious expectation," phobias, hyperesthesias to pain, and other symptoms. This anxiety neurosis, as I take it, certainly corresponds in part to the neurosis called "hypochondria," which in some features resembles hysteria and neurasthenia. Yet, I cannot consider the demarcation of this neurosis in the existing works as correct, and moreover, I find that the usefulness of the name hypochondria is impaired by its close relation to the symptom of "nosophobia."

After I had thus constructed for myself the simple picture of neurasthenia, anxiety neuroses, and obsessions, I turned my attention to the commonly occurring cases of neuroses which enter into consideration in the diagnosis of hysteria. I now had to say to myself that it would not do to mark a neurosis as a whole hysterical, merely because its symptom complex evinced some hysterical features. I could readily explain this practice by the fact that hysteria is the oldest, the most familiar, and the most striking neurosis under consideration, but it was an abuse none-the-less to put so many characteristics of perversion and degeneration under the caption of hysteria. Whenever an hysterical symptom, such as anesthesia or a characteristic attack, could be discovered in a complicated case of psychic degeneration, the whole thing was called "hysteria," and hence, one could naturally find united under this same trade mark the worst and most contradictory features. As certain as this diagnosis was incorrect, it is also certain that our classification must be made on neurotic lines, and as we knew neurasthenia, anxiety neurosis, and similar conditions in the pure state, there was no need of overlooking them in combination.

It seemed, therefore, that the following conception was more warrantable: The neuroses usually occurring, are generally to be designated as "mixed." Neurasthenia and anxiety neurosis can be found without effort in pure forms, and most frequently in young persons. Pure cases of hysteria and compulsion neurosis are rare, they are usually combined with an anxiety neurosis. This frequent occurrence of mixed neuroses is due to the fact that their etiological factors are frequently mixed, now only accidentally, and now in consequence of a causal relation between the processes which give rise to the etiological factors of the neuroses. This can be sustained and proven in the individual cases without any difficulty. But it follows from this that for the purpose of examination it is hardly possible to take hysteria out of its association with the sexual neuroses, that hysteria, as a rule, presents only one side, one aspect of the complicated neurotic case, and that only, as it were, in the borderline case can it be found and treated as an isolated neurosis. In a series of cases we can perhaps say *a potiori fit denominatio.*

I shall now examine the cases reported to see whether they speak in favor of my view of the clinical dependence of hysteria. Breuer's patient, Anna O., seems to contradict this and exemplifies a pure hysterical disease. Yet, this case, which became so fruitful for the knowledge of hysteria, was never considered by its observer under the guise of a sexual neurosis and hence, cannot at present be utilized as such. When I began to analyze the second patient, Mrs. Emmy v. N., the idea of a sexual neurosis on an hysterical basis was far from my mind. I had just returned from the Charcot school, and considered the connection of hysteria with the sexual theme as a sort of insult—just as my patients were wont to do. But when I now review my notes on this case, there is absolutely no doubt that I have to consider it as a severe case of anxiety neurosis with anxious expectations and phobias, due to sexual abstinence, which was combined with hysteria.

The third case, Miss Lucy R., could perhaps more than any other be called a borderline case of pure hysteria. It is a short episodic hysteria based on an unmistakably sexual etiology, which would correspond to an anxiety neurosis in an over-ripe, amorous girl, whose love was too rapidly awakened through a misunderstanding. Yet, the anxiety neurosis could either not be demonstrated or had escaped me. Case IV, Katharina, is really a model of what I have called virginal anxiety; it is a combination of an anxiety neurosis and hysteria, the former creates the symptoms, while the latter repeats them and works with them. At all events, it is a typical case of many juvenile neuroses called "hysteria." Case V, Miss Elisabeth v. R., was again not investigated as a sexual neurosis. I could only suspect that there was a spinal neurasthenia at its basis, but I could not confirm it. I must, however, add that since then pure hysterias have become still rarer in my experience. That in grouping together these four cases of hysteria I could disregard in the discussion the decisive factors of sexual neuroses, was due to the fact that they were older cases in which I had not as yet carried out the intentional and urgent investigation for the neurotic sexual subsoil. Moreover, the reason for my reporting four instead of twelve cases of hysteria, the analyses of which would confirm our claims of the psychic mechanism of hysterical phenomena, is due to one circumstance, namely, that the analysis reveals these cases simultaneously as sexual neuroses, though there is no doubt that any diagnostician would have denied them the name "hysteria." However, the discussion of such sexual neuroses would have overstepped the limits of our joint publication.

I do not wish to be misunderstood and give the impression that I refuse to accept hysteria as an independent neurotic affection, that I conceive it only as a psychic manifestation of the anxiety neurosis, that I ascribe it to only "ideogenous" symptoms, and that I attribute the somatic symptoms, like hysterogenic points and anesthesia, to the anxiety neurosis. None of these statements are true. I believe that hysteria, purified of all admixtures, can be treated independently in every respect except in therapy. For in the treatment we deal with a practical purpose, namely, we have to do away with the whole diseased state, and if hysteria occurs in most cases as a component of a mixed neurosis, the case merely resembles a mixed infection, where the task is to preserve life and not merely to combat the effect of one inciting cause of the disease.

I, therefore, find it important to separate the hysterical part in the pictures of the mixed neuroses from neurasthenia, anxiety neurosis, etc., for after this separation I can express concisely the therapeutic value of the cathartic method. Similarly I would venture to assert that—principally—it can readily dispose of any hysterical symptom, whereas, as can be easily understood, it is perfectly powerless in the presence of neurasthenic phenomena, and can only seldom and only through detours, influence the psychic results of the anxiety neurosis. Its therapeutic efficacy in the individual case will depend on whether or not the hysterical components of the morbid picture can claim a practical and significant position in comparison to the other neurotic components.

I will now attempt to give a series of examples which will show the excellent achievements of this procedure. I treated a young lady who suffered for six years from an intolerable and protracted nervous cough, which apparently was nurtured by every common catarrh, but must have had its strong psychic motives. Every other remedy had long since shown itself powerless, and I, therefore, attempted to remove the symptom by psychic analysis. All that she could remember was that the nervous cough began at the age of fourteen while she boarded with her aunt. She remembered absolutely no psychic excitement during that time, and did not believe that there was a motive for her suffering. Under the pressure of my hand, she at first recalled a large dog. She then recognized the memory picture; it was her aunt's dog which was attached to her, and used to accompany her everywhere, and without any further aid it occurred to her that this dog died and that the children buried it solemnly; and on the return from this funeral her cough appeared. I asked her why she began to cough, and the following thought occurred to her: "Now I am all alone in this world; no one loves me here; this animal was my only friend, and now I have lost it." She then continued her story. "The cough disappeared when I left my aunt, but reappeared a year and a half later."—"What was the reason for it?"—"I do not know."—I again exerted some pressure on the forehead and she recalled the news of her uncle's death during which the cough again manifested itself, and also recalled a train of thought similar to the former. The uncle was apparently the only one in the family who sympathized with her and loved her. That was, therefore, the pathogenic idea: People do not love her, everybody else is preferred; she really does not deserve to be loved, etc. To the idea of love there clung something which caused a marked resistance to the communication. The analysis was interrupted before this explanation was obtained.

Some time ago I attempted to relieve an elderly lady of her anxiety attacks, which, considering their characteristic qualities, were hardly suitable for such treatment. Since her menopause she had become extremely religious, and always received me as if I were the Devil, she was always armed with a small ivory crucifix which she hid in her hand. Her attacks of anxiety, which bore a hysterical character, could be traced to her early girlhood, and were supposed to have originated from the application of an iodine preparation to reduce a moderate swelling of the thyroid. I naturally repudiated this origin, and sought to substitute it by another which was in better harmony with my views concerning the etiology of neurotic symptoms. To the first question for an impression of her youth, which would stand in causal connection to the attacks of anxiety, there appeared the reminiscences of reading a so-called devotional book wherein piously enough there was some mention of the sexual processes. The passage in question made an impression on this girl, which was contrary to the intention of the author. She burst into tears and flung the book away. That was before the first attack of anxiety. The next reminiscence referred to her brother's teacher, who showed her great respect and for whom she entertained a warmer feeling. This reminiscence culminated in the reproduction of an evening in her parents' home during which they all sat around the table with the young man, and delightfully enjoyed themselves in a lively conversation. During the night following this evening, she was awakened by the first attack of anxiety which surely had more to do with some resistance against a sensual feeling than perhaps with the coincidental use of iodine. In what other way could I have succeeded in revealing in this obstinate patient, prejudiced against me and every worldly remedy, such a connection contrary to her own opinion and assertion?

On another occasion I had to deal with a young happily married woman, who as early as in the first years of her girlhood, was found every morning for some time in a state of lethargy, with rigid limbs, opened mouth, and protruding tongue. Similar attacks, though not so marked, recurred at the present time on awakening. A deep hypnosis could not be produced, so that I began my investigation in a state of concentration, and assured her during the first pressure that she would see something that would be directly connected with the cause of her condition during her childhood. She acted calmly and willingly, she again saw the residence in which she had passed her early girlhood, her room, the position of the bed, the grandmother who lived with them at the time, and one of her governesses whom she dearly loved. Then there was a succession of small scenes in these rooms and among these quite indifferent persons, the conclusion of which was the leavetaking of the governess who married from the home. I did not know what to start with these reminiscences; I could not bring about any connection between them and the etiology of the attacks. To be sure, the various circumstances were recognized as having occurred at the same time as the attacks first appeared.

Before I could continue the analysis, I had occasion to talk to a colleague, who, in former years, was my patient's family physician. From him I obtained the following explanation: At the time that he treated the mature and physically well developed girl for these first attacks, he was struck by the excessive affection in the relations between her and the governess. He became suspicious and caused the grandmother to watch these relations. After a short while the old lady informed him that the governess was wont to pay nightly visits to the child's bed, and that quite regularly after such visits the child was found in the morning in an attack. She did not hesitate to bring about the quiet removal of this corruptress of youth. The children, as well as the mother, were made to believe that the governess left the house in order to get married.

The treatment, which was above all successful, consisted in informing the young woman of the explanations given to me. . . .

I now believe that I have sufficiently indicated how such analyses should be executed, and the experiences gained from them. They perhaps make some things appear more complicated than they are, for many things really result by themselves during such work. I have not enumerated the difficulties of the work in order to give the impression that in view of such requirements it does not pay the physician or patient to undertake a cathartic analysis except in the rarest cases. However, in my medical activities I am influenced by contrary suppositions.—To be sure, I am unable to formulate the most definite indications for the application of the therapeutic method discussed here without entering into the valuation of the more significant and more comprehensive theme of the therapy of the neuroses in general. I have often compared the cathartic psychotherapy to surgical measures, and designated my cures as psychotherapeutic operations; the analogies follow the opening of a pus pocket, the curetting of a carious location, etc. Such an analogy finds its justification, not so much in the removal of the morbid material as in the production of better curative conditions for the issue of the process.

When I promised my patients help and relief through the cathartic method, I was often obliged to hear the following objections, "You say, yourself, that my suffering has probably much to do with my own relation and destinies. You cannot change any of that. In what manner, then, can you help me?" To this I could always answer: "I do not doubt at all that it would be easier for fate than for me to remove your sufferings, but you will be convinced that much will be gained if we succeed in transforming your hysterical misery into everyday unhappiness, against which you will be better able to defend yourself with a restored nervous system."

Plato

MENO

One of the best-known presentations of Plato's theory of the operation of the mind appears in the *Meno*, where Socrates seeks to indicate how knowledge is acquired.

SOCRATES: Then begin again, and answer me, What, according to you and your friend Gorgias, is the definition of virtue?

MENO: O Socrates, I used to be told, before I knew you, that you were always doubting yourself and making others doubt; and now you are casting your spells over me, and I am simply getting bewitched and enchanted, and am at my wits' end. And if I may venture to make a jest upon you, you seem to me both in your appearance and in your power over others to be very like the flat torpedo fish, who torpifies those who come near him and touch him, as you have now torpified me, I think. For my soul and my tongue are really torpid, and I do not know how to answer you; and though I have been delivered of an infinite variety of speeches about virtue before now, and to many persons—and very good ones they were, as I thought—at this moment I cannot even say what virtue is. And I think that you are very wise in not voyaging and going away from home, for if you did in other places as you do in Athens, you would be cast into prison as a magician.

SOCRATES: You are a rogue, Meno, and had all but caught me.

MENO: What do you mean, Socrates?

SOCRATES: I can tell why you made a simile about me.

MENO: Why?

SOCRATES: In order that I might make another simile about you. For I know that all pretty young gentlemen like to have pretty similes made about them—as well they may—but I shall not return the compliment. As to my being a torpedo, if the torpedo is torpid as well as the cause of torpidity in others, then indeed I am a torpedo, but not otherwise; for I perplex others, not because I am clear, but because I am utterly perplexed myself. And now I know not what virtue is, and you seem to be in the same case, although you did once perhaps know before you touched me. However, I have no objection to join with you in the enquiry.

MENO: And how will you enquire, Socrates, into that which you do not know? What will you put forth as the subject of enquiry? And if you find what you want, how will you ever know that this is the thing which you did not know?

SOCRATES: I know, Meno, what you mean; but just see what a tiresome dispute you are introducing. You argue that a man cannot enquire either about that which he knows, or about that which he does not know; for if he knows, he has no need to enquire; and if not, he cannot; for he does not know the very subject about which he is to enquire.

MENO: Well, Socrates, and is not the argument sound?

SOCRATES: I think not.

MENO: Why not?

SOCRATES: I will tell you why: I have heard from certain wise men and women who spoke of things divine that—

MENO: What did they say?

SOCRATES: They spoke of a glorious truth, as I conceive.

MENO: What was it? and who were they?

SOCRATES: Some of them were priests and priestesses, who had studied how they might be able to give a reason of their profession: there have been poets also, who spoke of these things by inspiration, like Pindar, and many others who were inspired. And they say—mark, now, and see whether their words are true—they say that the soul of man is immortal, and at one time has an end, which is termed dying, and at another time is born again, but is never destroyed. And the moral is, that a man ought to live always in perfect holiness. "*For in the ninth year Persephone sends the souls of those from whom she has received the penalty of ancient crime back again from beneath into the light of the sun above, and these are they who become noble kings and mighty men and great in wisdom and are called saintly heroes in after ages.*" The soul, then, as being immortal, and having been born again many times, and having seen all things that exist, whether in this world or in the world below, has knowledge of them all; and it is no wonder that she should be able to call to remembrance all that she ever knew about virtue, and about everything; for as all nature is akin, and the soul has learned all things, there is no difficulty in her eliciting or as men say learning, out of a single recollection all the rest, if a man is strenuous and does not faint; for all enquiry and all learning is but recollection. And therefore we ought not to listen to this sophistical argument about the impossibility of enquiry: for it will make us idle, and is sweet only to the sluggard; but the other saying will make us active and inquisitive. In that confiding, I will gladly enquire with you into the nature of virtue.

MENO: Yes, Socrates; but what do you mean by saying that we do not learn, and that what we call learning is only a process of recollection? Can you teach me how this is?

SOCRATES: I told you, Meno, just now that you were a rogue, and now you ask whether I can teach you, when I am saying that there is no teaching, but only recollection; and thus you imagine that you will involve me in a contradiction.

MENO: Indeed, Socrates, I protest that I had no such intention. I only asked the question from habit; but if you can prove to me that what you say is true, I wish that you would.

SOCRATES: It will be no easy matter, but I will try to please you to the utmost of my power. Suppose that you call one of your numerous attendants, that I may demonstrate on him.

MENO: Certainly. Come hither, boy.

SOCRATES: He is Greek, and speaks Greek does he not?

MENO: Yes, indeed; he was born in the house.

SOCRATES: Attend now to the questions which I ask him, and observe whether he learns of me or only remembers.

MENO: I will.

SOCRATES: Tell me, boy, do you know that a figure like this is a square?

BOY: I do.

SOCRATES: And you know that a square figure has these four lines equal?

BOY: Certainly.

SOCRATES: And these lines which I have drawn through the middle of the square are also equal?

BOY: Yes.

SOCRATES: A square may be of any size?

BOY: Certainly.

SOCRATES: And if one side of the figure be of two feet, and the other side be of two feet, how much will the whole be? Let me explain: if in one direction the space was of two feet, and in the other direction of one foot, the whole would be of two feet taken once?

BOY: Yes.

SOCRATES: But since this side is also of two feet, there are twice two feet?

BOY: There are.

SOCRATES: Then the square is of twice two feet?

BOY: Yes.

SOCRATES: And how many are twice two feet? count and tell me.

BOY: Four, Socrates.

SOCRATES: And might there not be another square twice as large as this, and having like this the lines equal?

BOY:	Yes.
SOCRATES:	And of how many feet will that be?
BOY:	Of eight feet.
SOCRATES:	And now try and tell me the length of the line which forms the side of that double square: this is two feet—what will that be?
BOY:	Clearly, Socrates, it will be double.
SOCRATES:	Do you observe, Meno, that I am not teaching the boy anything, but only asking him questions; and now he fancies that he knows how long a line is necessary in order to produce a figure of eight square feet; does he not?
MENO:	Yes.
SOCRATES:	And does he really know?
MENO:	Certainly not.
SOCRATES:	He only guesses that because the square is double, the line is double.
MENO:	True.
SOCRATES:	Observe him while he recalls the steps in regular order. (*To the Boy.*) Tell me, boy, do you assert that a double space comes from a double line? Remember that I am not speaking of an oblong, but of a figure equal every way, and twice the size of this—that is to say of eight feet; and I want to know whether you still say that a double square comes from a double line?
BOY:	Yes.
SOCRATES:	But does not this line become doubled if we add another such line here?
BOY:	Certainly.
SOCRATES:	And four such lines will make a space containing eight feet?
BOY:	Yes.
SOCRATES:	Let us describe such a figure: Would you not say that this is the figure of eight feet?
BOY:	Yes.
SOCRATES:	And are there not these four divisions in the figure, each of which is equal to the figure of four feet?
BOY:	True.
SOCRATES:	And is not that four times four?
BOY:	Certainly.
SOCRATES:	And four times is not double?
BOY:	No, indeed.
SOCRATES:	But how much?
BOY:	Four times as much.
SOCRATES:	Therefore the double line, boy, has given a space, not twice, but four times as much.
BOY:	True.
SOCRATES:	Four times four are sixteen—are they not?

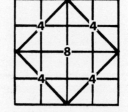

BOY:	Yes.
SOCRATES:	What line would give you a space of eight feet, as this gives one of sixteen feet;—do you see?
BOY:	Yes.
SOCRATES:	And the space of four feet is made from this half line?
BOY:	Yes.
SOCRATES:	Good; and is not a space of eight feet twice the size of this, and half the size of the other?
BOY:	Certainly.
SOCRATES:	Such a space, then, will be made out of a line greater than this one, and less than that one?
BOY:	Yes, I think so.
SOCRATES:	Very good; I like to hear you say what you think. And now tell me, is not this a line of two feet and that of four?
BOY:	Yes.
SOCRATES:	Then the line which forms the side of eight feet ought to be more than this line of two feet, and less than the other of four feet?
BOY:	It ought.
SOCRATES:	Try and see if you can tell me how much it will be.
BOY:	Three feet.
SOCRATES:	Then if we add a half to this line of two, that will be the line of three. Here are two and there is one; and on the other side, here are two also and there is one: and that makes the figure of which you speak?
BOY:	Yes.
SOCRATES:	But if there are three feet this way and three feet that way, the whole space will be three times three feet?
BOY:	That is evident.
SOCRATES:	And how much are three times three feet?
BOY:	Nine.
SOCRATES:	And how much is the double of four?
BOY:	Eight.
SOCRATES:	Then the figure of eight is not made out of a line of three?
BOY:	No.
SOCRATES:	But from what line?—tell me exactly; and if you would rather not reckon, try and show me the line.
BOY:	Indeed, Socrates, I do not know.
SOCRATES:	Do you see, Meno, what advances he has made in his power of recollection? He did not know at first, and he does not know now, what is the side of a figure of eight feet: but then he thought that he knew, and answered confidently as if he knew, and had no difficulty; now he has a difficulty, and neither knows nor fancies that he knows.
MENO:	True.

SOCRATES:	Is he not better off in knowing his ignorance?
MENO:	I think that he is.
SOCRATES:	If we have made him doubt, and given him the "torpedo's shock," have we done him any harm?
MENO:	I think not.
SOCRATES:	We have certainly, as would seem, assisted him in some degree to the discovery of the truth; and now he will wish to remedy his ignorance, but then he would have been ready to tell all the world again and again that the double space should have a double side.
MENO:	True.
SOCRATES:	But do you suppose that he would ever have enquired into or learned what he fancied that he knew, though he was really ignorant of it, until he had fallen into perplexity under the idea that he did not know, and had desired to know?
MENO:	I think not, Socrates.
SOCRATES:	Then he was the better for the torpedo's touch?
MENO:	I think so.
SOCRATES:	Mark now the farther development. I shall only ask him, and not teach him, and he shall share the enquiry with me: and do you watch and see if you find me telling or explaining anything to him, instead of eliciting his opinion. Tell me, boy, is not this a square of four feet which I have drawn?
BOY:	Yes.
SOCRATES:	And now I add another square equal to the former one?
BOY:	Yes.
SOCRATES:	And a third, which is equal to either of them?
BOY:	Yes.
SOCRATES:	Suppose that we fill up the vacant corner?
BOY:	Very good.
SOCRATES:	Here, then, there are four equal spaces?
BOY:	Yes.
SOCRATES:	And how many times larger is this space than this other?
BOY:	Four times.
SOCRATES:	But it ought to have been twice only, as you will remember.
BOY:	True.
SOCRATES:	And does not this line, reaching from corner to corner, bisect each of these spaces?
BOY:	Yes.
SOCRATES:	And are there four equal lines which contain this space?
BOY:	There are.
SOCRATES:	Look and see how much this space is.
BOY:	I do not understand.
SOCRATES:	Has not each interior line cut off half of the four spaces?
BOY:	Yes.

SOCRATES:	And how many spaces are there in this section?
BOY:	Four.
SOCRATES:	And how many in this?
BOY:	Two.
SOCRATES:	And four is how many times two?
BOY:	Twice.
SOCRATES:	And this space is of how many feet?
BOY:	Of eight feet.
SOCRATES:	And from what line do you get this figure?
BOY:	From this.
SOCRATES:	That is, from the line which extends from corner to corner of the figure of four feet?
BOY:	Yes.
SOCRATES:	And that is the line which the learned call the diagonal. And if this is the proper name, then you, Meno's slave, are prepared to affirm that the double space is the square of the diagonal?
BOY:	Certainly, Socrates.
SOCRATES:	What do you say of him, Meno? Were not all these answers given out of his own head?
MENO:	Yes, they were all his own.
SOCRATES:	And yet, as we were just now saying, he did not know?
MENO:	True.
SOCRATES:	But still he had in him those notions of his—had he not?
MENO:	Yes.
SOCRATES:	Then he who does not know may still have true notions of that which he does not know?
MENO:	He has.
SOCRATES:	And at present these notions have just been stirred up in him, as in a dream; but if he were frequently asked the same questions, in different forms, he would know as well as any one at last?
MENO:	I dare say.
SOCRATES:	Without any one teaching him he will recover his knowledge for himself, if he is only asked questions?
MENO:	Yes.
SOCRATES:	And this spontaneous recovery of knowledge in him is recollection?
MENO:	True.
SOCRATES:	And this knowledge which he now has must he not either have acquired or always possessed?
MENO:	Yes.
SOCRATES:	But if he always possessed this knowledge he would always have known; or if he has acquired the knowledge he could not have acquired it in this life, unless he has been taught geometry; for he may be made to do the same with all geometry and every other

branch of knowledge. Now, has any one ever taught him all this? You must know about him, if, as you say, he was born and bred in your house.

MENO: And I am certain that no one ever did teach him.

SOCRATES: And yet he has the knowledge?

MENO: The fact, Socrates, is undeniable.

SOCRATES: But if he did not acquire the knowledge in this life, then he must have had and learned it at some other time?

MENO: Clearly he must.

SOCRATES: Which must have been the time when he was not a man?

MENO: Yes.

SOCRATES: And if there have been always true thoughts in him, both at the time when he was and was not a man, which only need to be awakened into knowledge by putting questions to him, his soul must have always possessed this knowledge, for he always either was or was not a man?

MENO: Obviously.

SOCRATES: And if the truth of all things always existed in the soul, then the soul is immortal. Wherefore be of good cheer, and try to recollect what you do not know, or rather what you do not remember.

MENO: I feel, somehow, that I like what you are saying.

SOCRATES: And I, Meno, like what I am saying. Some things I have said of which I am not altogether confident. But that we shall be better and braver and less helpless if we think that we ought to enquire, than we should have been if we indulged in the idle fancy that there was no knowing and no use in seeking to know what we do not know;—that is a theme upon which I am ready to fight, in word and deed, to the utmost of my power.

MENO: There again, Socrates, your words seem to me excellent.

St. Augustine

ON THE IMMORTALITY OF THE SOUL

St. Augustine (A.D. 354–430) the Bishop of Hippo, formulated
one of the basic Christian interpretations of the relation of the
body and soul in On the Immortality of the Soul, from which the
following selection is taken.

CHAPTER I
THE FIRST REASON WHY THE SOUL IS IMMORTAL: IT IS THE SUBJECT OF SCIENCE WHICH IS ETERNAL

If science [disciplina] exists anywhere, and cannot exist except in that which
lives; and if it is eternal, and nothing in which an eternal thing exists can be
non-eternal; then that in which science exists lives eternally. If we exist who
reason, that is, if our mind does, and if our mind cannot reason rightly without
science, and if without science no mind can exist except as a mind without
science, then science is in the mind of man. Science, moreover, is somewhere,
for it exists, and whatever exists cannot be nowhere. Further, science cannot
exist except in that which lives. For nothing which is not alive learns anything,
and science cannot be in a thing which does not learn.

Again, science is eternal. For what exists and is unchangeable must be eternal. But no one denies that science exists. And whoever admits that it is impossible that a line drawn through the midpoint of a circle is not greater than all
lines which are not drawn through the midpoint, and admits that this is a part
of science, does not deny that science is unchangeable. Further, nothing in
which an eternal thing exists can be non-eternal. For nothing which is eternal
ever allows to be taken from it that in which it exists eternally.

Now, truly, when we reason it is the mind which reasons. For only he who
thinks reasons. Neither does the body think, nor does the mind receive the
help of the body in thinking, since when the mind wishes to think it turns away
from the body. For what is thought is thus eternal, and nothing pertaining to

the body is thus eternal, therefore the body cannot help the mind as it strives to understand; for it is sufficient if the body does not hamper the mind. Again, without science [*disciplina*] nobody reasons rightly. For thought is right reasoning moving from things certain to the investigation of things uncertain, and there is nothing certain in an ignorant mind. All that the mind knows, moreover, it contains within itself, nor does knowledge consist in anything which does not pertain to some science. For science is the knowledge of any things whatsoever. Therefore the human mind always lives.

CHAPTER II
ANOTHER REASON: IT IS THE SUBJECT OF REASON WHICH IS NOT CHANGED

Surely, reason either is the mind or is in the mind. Our reason, moreover, is better than our body, and body is a substance, and it is better to be a substance than to be nothing. Therefore, reason is not nothing.

Again, whatever the harmony of the body is, it must be in the body inseparably as in a subject; and nothing may be held to be in the harmony unless it is also necessarily in that body inseparably as in a subject. But the human body is mutable and reason is immutable. For all which does not exist always in the same mode is mutable, but that two and two are four exists always in the same mode, and also that four contains two and two exists always in the same mode, but two does not contain four, therefore two is not four. This sort of reasoning, then, is immutable. Therefore, reason is immutable.

Moreover, if the subject is changed, there is no way in which that which is in the subject remains unchanged. Hence, it follows that the mind is not a harmony of the body. Nor can death befall unchangeable things. Consequently, the mind always lives, and either the mind is reason itself or has reason in it inseparably.

CHAPTER III
MIND IS LIVING SUBSTANCE AND IMMUTABLE; AND IF IT IS IN SOME MODE MUTABLE, IT DOES NOT ON THAT ACCOUNT BECOME MORTAL

Some power [*virtus*] is constant, and all constancy is unchangeable, and all power can act, nor does it cease to be power when it acts. Further, all action is moved or moves. Therefore, not all which is moved, or surely not all which moves, is changeable. But all which is moved by another and does not move itself is a mortal thing. Nor is anything immutable which is mortal. Hence, certainly and without any disjunction, it is concluded that not all which moves is changed.

There is, moreover, no motion without substance, and any substance either is alive or is not alive, and all which does not live is inanimate. But no action is inanimate. Therefore, that which moves so as not to be changed can be only living substance. Any action, moreover, moves the body through a number of steps; therefore, not all which moves the body is changeable. The body, moreover, is not moved except in time; and to the body pertains being moved faster and slower; therefore, there is shown to be a certain thing which moves in time and is not changed. Moreover, every body which moves in time, although it tends towards one end, yet can neither accomplish simultaneously all the steps which lead to this end, nor can avoid the several steps. For by whatever impulse it is moved, a body cannot be perfectly one, because it can be divided into parts; and there is no body without parts, as there is no time without an interval of delay, even if it is expressed by a very short syllable of which you hear neither the beginning nor the end. Further, what occurs thus needs expectation that it may be accomplished and memory that it may be understood as much as possible. And expectation is of future things, while memory is of things past. But intention to act belongs to present time, through which the future moves into the past. And without memory we cannot expect the end of a motion which has begun. For how can that be expected to cease which forgets either that it has begun or that it is in motion? Again, the intention of accomplishing which is present cannot be without expectation of the end which is future: nor does anything exist which does not yet exist or which has already ceased to exist. Therefore, there can be something in acting which pertains to those things which do not yet exist. There can be several things simultaneously in the agent, although these several acts when executed cannot exist simultaneously. Likewise, they can exist simultaneously in the mover, although they cannot in the thing moved. But whatever things cannot exist simultaneously in time, and yet are transmitted from future into past, must of necessity be mutable.

From the above we have already gathered that there can be a certain thing which is not changed when it moves changeable things. For when the intention of the mover to bring the body which it moves to the end it desires is not changed, while the body which is acted upon is changed by this motion from moment to moment, and when that intention of accomplishment, which obviously remains unchanged, moves both the members of the artificer and the wood or stone which are subject to the artificer, who may doubt that what we have said follows as a logical consequence? Therefore, if any change in bodies be effected by the mind as mover, however intent upon the change the mind may be, we should not think that the mind is changed necessarily by this, or that the mind dies. For along with this intention it can have memory of past things and expectation of future things, none of which can exist without life. And even if there be no destruction without change, and no change without motion, yet not all change is engaged in destruction, nor is all motion engaged in change. For we can say that this body of ours has been for the most part moved by an action, and that it has undoubtedly been changed especially by age; still it has not yet perished, that is, is not without life. Therefore, from this it follows immediately that the mind is not deprived of life, even though some change does perchance occur to it through motion.

CHAPTER IV
ART AND THE UNCHANGEABLE PRINCIPLE OF NUMBERS, WHICH DO NOT INHERE IN THE MIND WITHOUT LIFE

For if there persists anything in the mind unchangeable, which cannot exist without life, then life must also remain in the mind eternally. For indeed the mind is so constituted that if the antecedent is true, the consequent is true. Moreover, the antecedent is true. For who dares say, not to mention other things, either that the principle [ratio] of number is changeable or that there is any art which does not depend upon this principle [ratio]; or that an art is not in the artist even if he be not applying it; or that it is in him other than as being in the mind; or that it can be where there is no life; or that what is unchangeable cannot be anywhere; or that art is other than a principle [ratio]? For although an art is said to be a sort of assemblage of many principles [rationes], yet an art can in truth be called one principle [ratio] and can be so thought. But whether it be the former or the latter, it follows none the less that art is unchangeable. Moreover, it is clear not only that an art is in the mind of the artist, but also that it is nowhere else except in the mind, and in it inseparably. For if art is separated from the mind it will be other than in the mind, or will be nowhere, or will pass immediately from the mind. But just as there is no seat of art without life, so there is no life according to a principle [ratio] anywhere except in the soul. Further, that which is cannot be nowhere nor can that which is immutable be non-existent at any time. But if art passes from mind to mind, it would leave one mind and abide in another; in this case nobody would teach an art except by losing it, or further, nobody would become skilled except through the forgetting of his teacher, or by the teacher's death. If these things are utterly absurd and false, as they are, then the human mind is immortal.

And if indeed art exists at some time, it does not so exist in a mind which is conspicuous for its forgetfulness and ignorance. The conclusion of this argument adds nothing to the mind's immortality unless the preceding be denied in the following way. Either there is something in the mind which is not in present thought or else the art of music is not in the educated mind when it thinks of geometry alone. And this latter is false. Hence the former is true.

Moreover, the mind does not perceive that it contains anything except what comes into thought. Therefore, there can be something in the mind, which the mind itself does not perceive to be in it. But as long as it is there, this makes no difference. For if the mind has been occupied with other things too long to be able to turn its attention back to things thought of before, this is called forgetting or ignorance. But since, when we reason with ourselves or when we are skillfully questioned by another concerning certain liberal arts, we then discover the things which we discover nowhere else but in the mind; and since to discover is not to make or to cause, as otherwise the mind would cause eternal things through temporal discovery (for it often discovers eternal things, as the principle [ratio] of the circle, or anything else of this sort in the arts, which is not understood either to have been non-existent at some time or ever to be about to be); hence it is also evident that the human mind is immortal, and all true principles [rationes] are in its hidden places, although, either because of ignorance or forgetting, it seems not to contain them or to have lost them.

CHAPTER V
MIND IS NOT CHANGED SO THAT
IT CEASES TO BE MIND

But now let us see to what extent we should accept the statement that the mind changes. For if the mind is the subject, with art existing in the subject, and if a subject cannot be changed unless that which is in it as in a subject be changed also, who can hold that art and principle [ratio] are unchangeable in the mind if the mind in which they exist is shown to be changeable? Moreover, where is there greater change than that in contraries? And who denies that the mind is, to say the least, at times stupid and at other times wise? Therefore, let us see in how many ways that which is called change of the soul may be taken. Of these I think there are found two genera quite evident or at least quite clear to us, though there are found several species. For the soul is said to be changed either according to passions of the body or according to its own passions. According to the passions of the body, as through age, disease, sorrow, work, hatred, or carnal desires; according to its own passions, however, as by desiring, enjoying, fearing, worrying, striving, or learning.

All these changes, if they are not necessarily proof that the soul dies, ought not to be feared at all taken separately each by each; but it should be seen whether they oppose our reasoning in which we said that when a subject is changed all which is in the subject is necessarily changed. But they do not oppose it. For this is said of a subject according to such a change as makes the name change entirely. For if wax changes to a black color from white, it is none the less wax; and also if it assumes a round shape after being square, becomes hard when it has been soft, cools after being hot. These are all in the subject, and wax is the subject. But wax remains not more or less wax when these things are changed. Therefore, some change of the things in the subject can occur, when the subject itself is not changed with regard to what it is and is called. But if so much change occurs in those things which are in the subject that that which was said to be the subject cannot any longer be so called, as, for example, when from the heat of fire wax disappears into the air, and suffers such change that it may rightly be understood that the subject is changed, since it was wax, and is no longer wax; then by no reasoning of any kind whatever would we think that any of those things would remain, which were in that subject because it was what it was.

Consequently, if, as we said above, the soul is a subject in which reason is inseparably (by that necessity also by which it is shown to be in the subject) neither can there be any soul except a living soul, nor can reason be in a soul without life, and reason is immortal; hence, the soul is immortal. For in absolutely no way could the soul remain immutable if its subject did not exist. This would happen if so great a change should befall the soul as would make it not a soul, that is, would compel it to die. Moreover, not one of those changes which occur to the soul, either through the body or through itself (although there is not a little question whether any occur through itself, that is, of which it is itself the cause) causes the soul not to be a soul. Therefore, they need not be feared *per se*; nor because they may oppose our reasoning.

CHAPTER VI
UNCHANGEABLE REASON, WHETHER IT BE IN THE MIND OR WITH THE MIND, OR WHETHER THE MIND BE IN IT, CANNOT BE SEPARATED FROM THE VERY SAME MIND

Hence I see that all men of reason ought to take pains to know what reason is and in how many ways it can be defined, so that it may remain firm according to all modes and with regard to the immortality of the soul. Reason is the aspect of the mind which perceives the true *per se* and not through the body; or it is the contemplation of the true, not through the body; or it is the true itself which is contemplated. Nobody doubts that the first of these is in the mind. There can be a question about the second and third; but even the second cannot exist without the mind. Concerning the third the great question is whether the true which is perceived by the mind without the instrument of the body exists *per se*, and is not in the mind, or whether it can exist without the mind. Moreover, in whatever mode the true may be, the mind cannot contemplate it *per se* except through some connection with it. For all that we contemplate we either perceive through cogitation [*cogitatio*], or through a sense or through the intellect. But those things which are perceived through sense we also sense to be outside us, and to be contained in places apart from which it is established that they cannot be perceived. But those things which are thought are not thought as being in another place other than the very mind which thinks them: for at the same time they also are thought as not being contained in any place.

Consequently, the connection between the mind which perceives and the true which it perceives is either such that the mind is the subject with the true in it as in a subject; or on the other hand the true is the subject with the mind in it as in a subject; or else each is a substance. Moreover, if the connection is of the first sort, the mind is as immortal as reason, according to the preceding argument, since reason can be in nothing but a living thing. The same necessity lies in the second sort of connection. For if the true, which is called reason, contains nothing which is changeable, as it appears, then nothing can be changed which is in it as in a subject. Therefore, all the struggle is left to the third. For if mind is one substance and reason another substance to which it is joined, he is not absurd who would think it possible for the former to remain while the latter perishes. But it is evident that as long as the mind is not separated from reason and remains connected with it, the mind necessarily survives and lives. But by what force can it be separated? By bodily force, whose power is weaker, whose origin is inferior, whose order is more disparate? Not at all. Then by animate strength? But how so? Cannot a more powerful mind contemplate reason without separating another mind from it? Reason is not lacking in any mind which contemplates, if all minds contemplate; and since nothing is more powerful than reason itself, than which nothing is more immutable, by no means will there be a mind not joined to reason and yet more powerful than one which is so joined. It remains that either reason separates itself from mind, or else the mind itself is separated by will. But there is no envy in that nature, and, therefore, it offers itself for mind's enjoyment; and, what is more, whatever it joins to itself it causes to be, which is contrary to destruction. Moreover, it is too absurd for someone to say that the mind is separated from reason by the mind's own will, provided there can be any mutual separation of things which space does not contain. Indeed this can be said in contradiction to all we have argued above in meeting other opposition. What then? Should it be concluded that the mind is immortal? Or, even though it cannot be separated, can it perhaps be extinguished? But if the very strength of reason affects the mind by its connection (and it cannot fail to affect it), then it at once causes being to be ascribed to mind. For it is in great measure reason itself in which the supreme immutability is thought. Therefore, that which reason affects by virtue of itself it causes to exist in a certain respect. Hence the mind cannot be extinguished unless it be separated from reason, and it cannot be separated, as we have proved above. Therefore it cannot perish.

CHAPTER VII
AND IF THE MIND TENDS THROUGH SUBSTANCE
TOWARDS DEFECTION, STILL IT DOES NOT
ON THIS ACCOUNT PERISH

But that very turning away from reason by which stupidity enters the mind cannot occur without a defect in the mind. For if the mind has more being when turned towards reason and inhering in it, thus adhering to the unchangeable thing which is truth, both greatest and first; so when turned away from reason it has less being, which constitutes a defection. Moreover, every defect tends towards nothing [non-being], nor do we ever speak more properly of destruction than when that which was something becomes nothing. Therefore, to tend towards nothing [non-being] is to tend towards destruction. It is hard to say why this does not occur to the soul in which defect occurs. We grant all the above, but we deny that it follows that what tends towards nothing [non-being] perishes, that is, that it reaches nothing. This can be observed in the body also. For any body is part of the sensible world, and for this reason the larger it is and the more space it occupies the nearer it is to the universe; and the more it does this, the greater it is. For the whole is greater than the part. Hence, necessarily, it is less when it is diminished; that is, it suffers a defect when it is lessened. Moreover, it is lessened when something is taken from it by cutting away, and it follows from this that because of such subtraction it tends to nothing. But no cutting away leads to nothing as such. For every part which remains is a body, and whatever is a body occupies a place in some space. Nor would this be possible unless it were to have parts into which it might be cut again and again. Therefore, it can be infinitely diminished through infinite division, and hence can suffer defection and tend towards nothing, although it can never reach nothing. Further, this can be said and understood of space itself and of any interval whatever. For by taking, let us say, a half part from the limits, and always a half part from what is left, the interval is diminished and approaches a limit which yet it can in no mode attain. Accordingly, even less should it be feared that the mind may become nothing, for the mind is indeed better and more lively than the body.

CHAPTER VIII
JUST AS THAT CANNOT BE TAKEN FROM BODY BY
WHICH IT IS BODY, SO NEITHER CAN THAT BE TAKEN
FROM MIND BY WHICH IT IS MIND

But if that which causes the body to be is not in the matter of the body but in the form (which point is established by quite irrefutable reasoning, for a body is greater according as it has better form and is more excellent, and it is less according as it is uglier and is more deformed, which defect occurs not from a taking away of matter, about which enough has been said, but from a privation of form), then this should be questioned and discussed, lest someone assert that mind perishes through defect of form; for seeing that when it is stupid mind is deprived of some of its form, it may be believed that this privation can be increased so much as to deprive the mind of form in every mode, by this misfortune reducing it to nothing and causing it to perish. Hence, if we can succeed in showing that not even the body can be deprived of that by virtue of which it is body, perhaps we shall rightly maintain that the mind can much less have that taken from it by virtue of which it is mind. For whoever considers carefully will admit that any kind of mind whatever must be preferred to every body.

Let this, then, be the beginning of our argument, namely, that no thing makes or begets itself, unless it was before it existed: if the latter is false, the former is true. Again, that which has not been made or begotten, and yet is, must be everlasting. Whoever attributes this nature and this excellence to any body, errs indeed greatly. But why do we dispute? For even were we to attribute it to body we should be forced to attribute it much more to the mind. Thus if any body is everlasting, there is no mind which is not everlasting; seeing that any mind is to preferred to any body and eternal things to non-eternal things. But if it is truly said that the body is made, it was made by some maker, nor was the maker inferior to body. For an inferior maker would not have power to give to that which he was making whatever it is that makes it what it is. But the maker and the body are not equals, since it is necessary for a maker to have something better for making than that which he makes. For we do not make the absurd statement that the begetter is that thing which is begotten by him. Therefore, a whole body has been made by some force which is more powerful and better, or at least not corporeal. For if a body be made by a body, it cannot be made whole; for it is very true, as we stated in the beginning of this argument, that no thing can be made by itself. Moreover, this force or incorporeal nature being the producer of the whole body preserves the whole by its abiding power. For it did not make a thing and then vanish and desert the thing made. Indeed that substance which is not body is not, if I may speak thus, moved in space so that it can be separated from that substance which is localized; and this effecting strength cannot be idle, but preserves that which it has made, and does not allow it to lack the form by virtue of which it is to whatever extent it is. For since the thing made does not exist *per se*, if it is abandoned by that through which it exists, it will immediately cease to exist, and we cannot say that when the body was made it received the power to be sufficient by virtue of itself when it is deserted by its maker.

And if this is so, the mind which clearly excels the body has power to a greater degree. And thus the mind is proved immortal, if it can exist *per se*. For whatever exists thus must be incorruptible, and therefore unable to perish, since nothing abandons itself. But the changeability of the body is manifest, which the whole motion of the entire body indicates adequately. Hence, it is found by those who investigate carefully, in so far as such a nature can be investigated, that ordered changeableness imitates that which is unchangeable. Moreover, that which exists *per se* has no need of anything, not even of motion, since it has all it needs existing in itself; for all motion is towards another thing which is that which is lacked by that which is moved. Therefore, form is present in the whole body while a better nature which made it provides for and sustains it, hence, that changeability does not take away from a body its being a body, but causes it to pass from one form to another by a well-ordered motion. For not one of its parts is allowed to be reduced to nothing, since that effective power with its force, neither striving nor inactive, aims at a whole, permitting the body to be all which through the power it is, in so far as it is. Consequently, there should be no one so devoid of reason as not to be certain that the mind is better than the body, or when this has been granted, to think that it does not happen to the body that the body is not body, yet happens to the mind that it is not mind. If this does not happen, and a mind cannot exist unless it lives, surely a mind can never die.

CHAPTER IX
MIND IS LIFE, AND THUS IT CANNOT LACK LIFE

If anyone asserts that the mind ought not to fear that destruction in which that which was something becomes nothing, but ought to fear that in which we call those things dead which lack life, let him notice that there is no thing which lacks itself. Moreover, mind is a certain life, so that all which is animated lives. But every inanimate thing which can be animated is understood to be dead, that is, deprived of life. Hence the mind cannot die. For if anything can lack life, this thing is not mind which animates, but a thing which has been animated. If this is absurd, this kind of destruction should be feared much less by the mind, since destruction of life is surely not to be feared. For if the mind dies wholly when life abandons it, that very life which deserts it is understood much better as mind, as now mind is not something deserted by life, but the very life itself which deserted. For whatever dead thing is said to be abandoned by life, is understood to be deserted by the soul. Moreover, this life which deserts the things which die is itself the mind, and it does not abandon itself; hence the mind does not die.

CHAPTER X
MIND IS NOT THE ORGANIZATION OF BODY

Unless perhaps we ought to believe that life is some organization [*temperatio*] of the body, as some have held. It would never have seemed so to them if they had been able to see those things which exist truly and which remain unchangeable when the same mind has been freed from the habit of bodies and cleansed. For who has looked well within himself without having experienced that the more earnestly he had thought something, the more he was able to move and draw the attention of the mind away from the senses of the body? If the mind were an organization of the body, this would absolutely not happen. For a thing which did not have a nature of its own and was not a substance, but which like color and shape was in the body inseparably as in a subject, would not try in any way to turn itself away from that same body in order to perceive intelligible things; and only inasmuch as it could do this would it be able to look upon intelligible things and be made by this vision better and more excellent. Indeed, in no way can shape or color, or the very organization of the body, which is a certain mixture of four natures in which the same body consists, turn from the thing in which they are inseparably as in a subject. In comparison with these things, those things which the mind thinks when it turns away from the body are not wholly corporeal, and yet they exist, and that in great degree, for they maintain themselves always in the same mode. For nothing more absurd can be said than that those things which we see with the eyes exist, while those things which we perceive by the intellect do not; for it is mad to doubt that the intellect is incomparably superior to the eyes. Moreover, while these things which are thought maintain themselves in the same mode, when the mind sees them it shows well enough that it is joined to them in a certain miraculous and likewise incorporeal way, that is, not locally. For either they are in it, or it is in them. And whichever one of these is true, either the one is in the other as in a subject, or each one is a substance. But if the first is true, the mind is not in the body as in a subject, as color and shape are, since either it is substance itself or it is in another substance which is not body. Moreover, if the second is true, mind is not in body as in a subject, as color is in body, because the mind is a substance. Further, the organization of a body is in the body as in a subject, just as color is; therefore, mind is not the organization of the body, but the mind is life. No thing deserts itself, and that dies which is deserted by life. Therefore, the mind cannot die.

Aristotle

DE ANIMA

Aristotle's theory of the nature of the soul and the mind appear in *De Anima* (*On the Soul*), from which the following selection is taken.

BOOK I

3 . . . Now, in the first place, it is a mistake to say that the soul is a spatial magnitude. It is evident that Plato means the soul of the whole to be like the sort of soul which is called mind—not like the sensitive or the desiderative soul, for the movements of neither of these are circular. Now mind is one and continuous in the sense in which the process of thinking is so, and thinking is identical with the thoughts which are its parts; these have a serial unity like that of number, not a unity like that of a spatial magnitude. Hence mind cannot have that kind of unity either; mind is either without parts or is continuous in some other way than that which characterizes a spatial magnitude. How, indeed, if it were a spatial magnitude, could mind possibly think? Will it think with any one indifferently of its parts? In this case, the "part" must be understood either in the sense of a spatial magnitude or in the sense of a point (if a point *can* be called a part of a spatial magnitude). . . .

The view we have just been examining, in company with most theories about the soul, involves the following absurdity: they all join the soul to a body, or place it in a body, without adding any specification of the reason of their union, or of the bodily conditions required for it. Yet such explanation can scarcely be omitted; for some community of nature is presupposed by the fact that the one acts and the other is acted upon, the one moves and the other is moved; interaction always implies a *special* nature in the two interagents. All, however, that these thinkers do is to describe the specific characteristics of the soul; they do not try to determine anything about the body which is to contain it, as if it were possible, as in the Pythagorean myths, that any soul could be clothed upon with any body—an absurd view, for each body seems to have a form and shape of its own. It is as absurd as to say that the art of carpentry could embody itself in flutes; each art must use its tools, each soul its body.

4   There is yet another theory about soul, which has commended itself to many as no less probable than any of those we have hitherto mentioned, and has rendered public account of itself in the court of popular discussion. Its supporters say that the soul is a kind of harmony, for (a) harmony is a blend or composition of contraries, and (b) the body is compounded out of contraries. Harmony, however, is a certain proportion or composition of the constituents blended, and soul can be neither the one nor the other of these. Further, the power of originating movement cannot belong to a harmony, while almost all concur in regarding this as a principal attribute of soul. It is more appropriate to call health (or generally one of the good states of the body) a harmony than to predicate it of the soul. The absurdity becomes most apparent when we try to attribute the active and passive affections of the soul to a harmony; the necessary readjustment of their conceptions is difficult. Further, in using the word "harmony" we have one or other of two cases in our mind; the most proper sense is in relation to spatial magnitudes which have motion and position, where harmony means the disposition and cohesion of their parts in such a manner as to prevent the introduction into the whole of anything homogeneous with it, and the secondary sense, derived from the former, is that in which it means the ratio between the constituents so blended; in neither of these senses is it plausible to predicate it of soul. That soul is a harmony in the sense of the mode of composition of the parts of the body is a view easily refutable; for there are many composite parts and those variously compounded; of what bodily part is mind or the sensitive or the appetitive faculty the mode of composition? And what *is* the mode of composition which constitutes each of them? It is equally absurd to identify the soul with the ratio of the mixture; for the mixture which makes flesh has a different ratio between the elements from that which makes bone. The consequence of this view will therefore be that distributed throughout the whole body there will be many souls, since every one of the bodily parts is a different mixture of the elements, and the ratio of mixture is in each case a harmony, i.e. a soul. . . .

   That the soul cannot either be a harmony, or be moved in a circle, is clear from what we have said. Yet that it can be moved incidentally is, as we said above, possible, and even that in a sense it can move itself, i.e. in the sense that *the vehicle* in which it is can be moved, and moved by it; in no other sense can the soul be moved in space. More legitimate doubts might remain as to its movement in view of the following facts. We speak of the soul as being pained or pleased, being bold or fearful, being angry, perceiving, thinking. All these are regarded as modes of movement, and hence it might be inferred that the soul is moved. This, however, does not necessarily follow. We may admit to the full that being pained or pleased, or thinking, are movements (each of them a "being moved"), and that the movement is originated by the soul. For example we may regard anger or fear as such and such movements of the heart, and thinking as such and such another movement of that organ, or of some other; these modifications may arise either from changes of place in certain parts or from qualitative alterations (the special nature of the parts and the special modes of their changes being for our present purpose irrelevant). Yet to say that it is *the soul* which is angry is as inexact as it would be to say that it is the soul that weaves webs or builds houses. It is doubtless better to avoid saying that the soul pities or learns or thinks, and rather to say that it is the man who does this with his soul. What we mean is not that the movement is in the soul, but that sometimes it terminates in the soul and sometimes starts from it, sensation e.g. coming from without inwards, and reminiscence starting from the soul and terminating with the movements, actual or residual, in the sense organs.

The case of mind is different; it seems to be an independent substance implanted within the soul and to be incapable of being destroyed. If it could be destroyed at all, it would be under the blunting influence of old age. What really happens in respect of mind in old age is, however, exactly parallel to what happens in the case of the sense organs; if the old man could recover the proper kind of eye, he would see just as well as the young man. The incapacity of old age is due to an affection not of the soul but of its vehicle, as occurs in drunkenness or disease. Thus it is that in old age the activity of mind or intellectual apprehension declines only through the decay of some other inward part; mind itself is impassible. Thinking, loving, and hating are affections not of mind, but of that which has mind, so far as it has it. That is why, when this vehicle decays, memory and love cease; they were activities not of mind, but of the composite which has perished; mind is, no doubt, something more divine and impassible. That the soul cannot be moved is therefore clear from what we have said, and if it cannot be moved at all, manifestly it cannot be moved by itself. . . .

It must be all the same whether we speak of units or corpuscles; for if the spherical atoms of Democritus became points, nothing being retained but their being a quantum, there must remain in each a moving and a moved part, just as there is in what is continuous; what happens has nothing to do with the size of the atoms, it depends solely upon their being a quantum. That is why there must be something to originate movement in the units. If in the animal what originates movement is the soul, so also must it be in the case of the number, so that not the mover and the moved together, but the mover only, will be the soul. But how is it possible for one of the units to fulfil this function of originating movement? There must be *some* difference between such a unit and all the other units, and what difference can there be between one placed unit and another except a difference of position? If then, on the other hand, these psychic units within the body are different from the points *of* the body, there will be two sets of units both occupying the same place; for each unit will occupy a point. And yet, if there can be two, why cannot there be an infinite number? For if things can occupy an indivisible place, they must themselves be indivisible. If, on the other hand, the points of the body are identical with the units whose number is the soul, or if the number of the points in the body is the soul, why have not all bodies souls? For all bodies contain points or an infinity of points.

Further, how is it possible for these points to be isolated or separated from their bodies, seeing that lines cannot be resolved into points?

5   The result is, as we have said, that this view, while on the one side identical with that of those who maintain that soul is a subtle kind of body, is on the other entangled in the absurdity peculiar to Democritus' way of describing the manner in which movement is originated by soul. For if the soul is present throughout the whole percipient body, there must, if the soul be a kind of body, be two bodies in the same place; and for those who call it a number, there must be many points at one point, or every body must have a soul, unless the soul be a different sort of number—other, that is, than the sum of the points existing in a body. Another consequence that follows is that the animal must be moved by its number precisely in the way that Democritus explained its being moved by his spherical psychic atoms. What difference does it make whether we speak of small spheres or of large units, or, quite simply, of units in movement? One way or another, the movements of the animal must be due to their movements. Hence those who combine movement and number in the same subject lay themselves open to these and many other similar absurdities. It is impossible not only that these characters should give the definition of soul—it is impossible that they should even be attributes of it. The point is clear if the attempt be made to start from this as the account of soul and explain from it the affections and actions of the soul, e.g. reasoning, sensation, pleasure, pain, &c. For, to repeat what we have said earlier, movement and number do not facilitate even conjecture about the derivative properties of soul.

Such are the three ways in which soul has traditionally been defined; one group of thinkers declared it to be that which is most originative of movement because it moves itself, another group to be the subtlest and most nearly incorporeal of all kinds of body. We have now sufficiently set forth the difficulties and inconsistencies to which these theories are exposed. It remains now to examine the doctrine that soul is composed of the elements.

The reason assigned for this doctrine is that thus the soul may perceive or come to know everything that is, but the theory necessarily involves itself in many impossibilities. Its upholders assume that like is known only by like, and imagine that by declaring the soul to be composed of the elements they succeed in identifying the soul with all the things it is capable of apprehending. But the elements are not the only things it knows; there are many others, or, more exactly, an infinite number of others, formed out of the elements. Let us admit that the soul knows or perceives the elements out of which each of these composites is made up; but by what means will it know or perceive the composite whole, e.g. what God, man, flesh, bone (or any other compound) is? For each *is*, not merely the elements of which it is composed, but those elements combined in a determinate mode or ratio, as Empedocles himself says of bone,

> The kindly Earth in its broad-bosomed moulds
> Won of clear Water two parts out of eight
> And four of Fire; and so white bones were formed.

Nothing, therefore, will be gained by the presence of the elements in the soul, unless there be also present there the various formulae of proportion and the various compositions in accordance with them. Each element will indeed know its fellow outside, but there will be no knowledge of bone or man, unless they too are present in the constitution of the soul. The impossibility of this needs no pointing out; for who would suggest that stone or man could enter into the constitution of the soul? The same applies to "the good" and "the not-good," and so on. . . .

In general, we may ask, Why has not everything a soul, since everything either is an element, or is formed out of one or several or all of the elements? Each must certainly know one or several or all.

The problem might also be raised, What is that which unifies the elements into a soul? The elements correspond, it would appear, to the matter; what unites them, whatever it is, is the supremely important factor. But it is impossible that there should be something superior to, and dominant over, the soul (and *a fortiori* over the mind); it is reasonable to hold that mind is by nature most primordial and dominant, while their statement is that it is the elements which are first of all that is.

All, both those who assert that the soul, because of its knowledge or perception of what is, is compounded out of the elements, and those who assert that it is of all things the most originative of movement, fail to take into consideration all kinds of soul. In fact (1) not all beings that perceive can originate movement; there appear to be certain animals which are stationary, and yet local movement is the only one, so it seems, which the soul originates in animals. And (2) the same objection holds against all those who construct mind and the perceptive faculty out of the elements; for it appears that plants live, and yet are not endowed with locomotion or perception, while a large number of animals are without discourse of reason. Even if these points were waived and mind admitted to be a part of the soul (and so too the perceptive faculty), still, even so, there would be kinds and parts of soul of which they had failed to give any account. . . .

Certain thinkers say that soul is intermingled in the whole universe, and it is perhaps for that reason that Thales came to the opinion that all things are full of gods. This presents some difficulties: Why does the soul when it resides in air or fire not form an animal, while it does so when it resides in mixtures of the elements, and that although it is held to be of higher quality when contained in the former? (One might add the question, why the soul in air is maintained to be higher and more immortal than that in animals.) Both possible ways of replying to the former question lead to absurdity or paradox; for it is beyond paradox to say that fire or air is an animal, and it is absurd to refuse the name of animal to what has soul in it. The opinion that the elements have soul in them seems to have arisen from the doctrine that a whole must be homogeneous with its parts. If it is true that animals become animate by drawing into themselves a portion of what surrounds them, the partisans of this view are bound to say that the soul of the Whole too is homogeneous with all its parts. If the air sucked in is homogeneous, but soul heterogeneous, clearly while some part of soul will exist in the inbreathed air, some other part will not. The soul must either be homogeneous, or such that there are some parts of the Whole in which it is not to be found.

From what has been said it is now clear that knowing as an attribute of soul cannot be explained by soul's being composed of the elements, and that it is neither sound nor true to speak of soul as moved. But since (*a*) knowing, perceiving, opining, and further (*b*) desiring, wishing, and generally all other modes of appetition, belong to soul, and (*c*) the local movements of animals, and (*d*) growth, maturity, and decay are produced by the soul, we must ask whether each of these is an attribute of the soul as a whole, i.e. whether it is with the whole soul we think, perceive, move ourselves, act or are acted upon, or whether each of them requires a different part of the soul? So too with regard to life. Does it depend on one of the parts of soul? Or is it dependent on more than one? Or on all? Or has it some quite other cause?

Some hold that the soul is divisible, and that one part thinks, another desires. If, then, its nature admits of its being divided, what can it be that holds the parts together? Surely not the body; on the contrary it seems rather to be the soul that holds the body together; at any rate when the soul departs the body disintegrates and decays. If, then, there is something else which makes the soul one, this unifying agency would have the best right to the name of soul, and we shall have to repeat for it the question: Is *it* one or multipartite? If it is one, why not at once admit that "the soul" is one? If it has parts, once more the question must be put: What holds *its* parts together, and so *ad infinitum*?

The question might also be raised about the parts of the soul: What is the separate rôle of each in relation to the body? For, if the whole soul holds together the whole body, we should expect each part of the soul to hold together a part of the body. But this seems an impossibility; it is difficult even to imagine what sort of bodily part mind will hold together, or how it will do this. . . .

BOOK II

1 Let the foregoing suffice as our account of the views concerning the soul which have been handed on by our predecessors; let us now dismiss them and make as it were a completely fresh start, endeavouring to give a precise answer

to the question, What is soul? i.e. to formulate the most general possible definition of it.

We are in the habit of recognizing, as one determinate kind of what is, substance, and that in several senses, (a) in the sense of matter or that which in itself is not "a this" and (b) in the sense of form or essence, which is that precisely in virtue of which a thing is called "a this" and thirdly (c) in the sense of that which is compounded of both (a) and (b). Now matter is potentiality, form actuality; of the latter there are two grades related to one another as e.g. knowledge to the exercise of knowledge.

Among substances are by general consent reckoned bodies and especially natural bodies; for they are the principles of all other bodies. Of natural bodies some have life in them, others not; by life we mean self-nutrition and growth (with its correlative decay). It follows that every natural body which has life in it is a substance in the sense of a composite.

But since it is also a *body* of such and such a kind, viz. having life, the *body* cannot be soul; the body is the subject or matter, not what is attributed to it. Hence the soul must be a substance in the sense of the form of a natural body having life potentially within it. But substance is actuality, and thus soul is the actuality of a body as above characterized. Now the word actuality has two senses corresponding respectively to the possession of knowledge and the actual exercise of knowledge. It is obvious that the soul is actuality in the first sense, viz. that of knowledge as possessed, for both sleeping and waking presuppose the existence of soul, and of these waking corresponds to actual knowing, sleeping to knowledge possessed but not employed, and, in the history of the individual, knowledge comes before its employment or exercise.

That is why the soul is the first grade of actuality of a natural body having life potentially in it. The body so described is a body which is organized. The parts of plants in spite of their extreme simplicity are "organs"; e.g. the leaf serves to shelter the pericarp, the pericarp to shelter the fruit, while the roots of plants are analogous to the mouth of animals, both serving for the absorption of food. If, then, we have to give a general formula applicable to all kinds of soul, we must describe it as the first grade of actuality of a natural organized body. That is why we can wholly dismiss as unnecessary the question whether the soul and the body are one: it is as meaningless as to ask whether the wax and the shape given to it by the stamp are one, or generally the matter of a thing and that of which it is the matter. Unity has many senses (as many as "is" has), but the most proper and fundamental sense of both is the relation of an actuality to that of which it is the actuality.

We have now given an answer to the question, What is soul?—an answer which applies to it in its full extent. It is substance in the sense which corresponds to the definitive formula of a thing's essence. That means that it is "the essential whatness" of a body of the character just assigned. Suppose that what is literally an "organ" like an axe, were a *natural* body, its "essential whatness," would have been its essence, and so its soul; if this disappeared from it, it would have ceased to be an axe, except in name. As it is, it is just an axe; it wants the character which is required to make its whatness or form-ulable essence a soul; for that, it would have had to be a *natural* body of a particular kind, viz. one having *in itself* the power of setting itself in movement and arresting itself. Next, apply this doctrine in the case of the "parts" of the living body. Suppose that the eye were an animal—sight would have been its soul, for sight is the substance or essence of the eye which corresponds to the formula, the eye being merely the matter of seeing; when seeing is removed the eye is no longer an eye, except in name—it is no more a real eye than the eye of a statue or of a painted figure. We must now extend our consideration from the "parts" to the whole living body; for what the departmental sense is to the bodily part which is its organ, that the whole faculty of sense is to the whole sensitive body as such.

We must not understand by that which is "potentially capable of living" what has lost the soul it had, but only what still retains it; but seeds and fruits are bodies which possess the qualification. Consequently, while waking is actuality in a sense corresponding to the cutting and the seeing, the soul is actuality in the sense corresponding to the power of sight and the power in the tool; the body corresponds to what exists in potentiality; as the pupil *plus* the power of sight constitutes the eye, so the soul *plus* the body constitutes the animal.

From this it indubitably follows that the soul is inseparable from its body, or at any rate that certain parts of it are (if it has parts)—for the actuality of some of them is nothing but the actualities of their bodily parts. Yet some may be separable because they are not the actualities of any body at all. Further, we have no light on the problem whether the soul may not be the actuality of its body in the sense in which the sailor is the actuality of the ship.

This must suffice as our sketch or outline determination of the nature of soul.

2   Since what is clear or logically more evident emerges from what in itself is confused but more observable by us, we must reconsider our results from this point of view. For it is not enough for a definitive formula to express as most now do the mere fact; it must include and exhibit the ground also. At present definitions are given in a form analogous to the conclusion of a syllogism; e.g. What is squaring? The construction of an equilateral rectangle equal to a given oblong rectangle. Such a definition is in form equivalent to a conclusion. One that tells us that squaring is the discovery of a line which is a mean propor-tional between the two unequal sides of the given rectangle discloses the ground of what is defined.

We resume our inquiry from a fresh starting-point by calling attention to the fact that what has soul in it differs from what has not in that the former dis-plays life. Now this word has more than one sense, and provided any one alone of these is found in a thing we say that thing is living. Living, that is, may mean thinking or perception or local movement and rest, or movement in the sense of nutrition, decay and growth. Hence we think of plants also as living, for they are observed to possess in themselves an originative power through which they increase or decrease in all spatial directions; they grow up *and* down, and everything that grows increases its bulk alike in both directions or indeed in all, and continues to live so long as it can absorb nutriment.

This power of self-nutrition can be isolated from the other powers mentioned, but not they from it—in mortal beings at least. The fact is obvious in plants; for it is the only psychic power they possess.

This is the originative power the possession of which leads us to speak of things as *living* at all, but it is the possession of sensation that leads us for the first time to speak of living things as animals; for even those beings which possess no power of local movement but do possess the power of sensation we call animals and not merely living things.

The primary form of sense is touch, which belongs to all animals. Just as the power of self-nutrition can be isolated from touch and sensation generally, so touch can be isolated from all other forms of sense. (By the power of self-nutrition we mean that departmental power of the soul which is common to plants and animals: all animals whatsoever are observed to have the sense of touch.) What the explanation of these two facts is, we must discuss later. At present we must confine ourselves to saying that soul is the source of these phenomena and is characterized by them, viz. by the powers of self-nutrition, sensation, thinking, and motivity.

Is each of these a soul or a part of a soul? And if a part, a part in what sense? A part merely distinguishable by definition or a part distinct in local situation as well? In the case of certain of these powers, the answers to these questions are easy, in the case of others we are puzzled what to say. Just as in the case of plants which when divided are observed to continue to live though removed to a distance from one another (thus showing that in *their* case the soul of each individual plant before division was actually one, potentially many), so we notice a similar result in other varieties of soul, i.e. in insects which have been cut in two; each of the segments possesses both sensation and local movement; and if sensation, necessarily also imagination and appetition; for, where there is sensation, there is also pleasure and pain, and, where these, necessarily also desire.

We have no evidence as yet about mind or the power to think; it seems to be a widely different kind of soul, differing as what is eternal from what is perishable; it alone is capable of existence in isolation from all other psychic powers. All the other parts of soul, it is evident from what we have said, are, in spite of certain statements to the contrary, incapable of separate existence though, of course, distinguishable by definition. If opining is distinct from perceiving, to be capable of opining and to be capable of perceiving must be distinct, and so with all the other forms of living above enumerated. Further, some animals possess all these parts of soul, some certain of them only, others one only (this is what enables us to classify animals); the cause must be considered later. A similar arrangement is found also within the field of the senses; some classes of animals have all the senses, some only certain of them, others only one, the most indispensable, touch.

Since the expression "that whereby we live and perceive" has two meanings, just like the expression "that whereby we know"—that may mean either (*a*) knowledge or (*b*) the soul, for we can speak of knowing *by* or *with* either, and similarly that whereby we are in health may be either (*a*) health or (*b*) the body or some part of the body; and since of the two terms thus contrasted knowledge or health is the name of a form, essence, or ratio, or if we so express it an actuality of a recipient matter—knowledge of what is capable of knowing, health of what is capable of being made healthy (for the operation of that which is capable of originating change terminates and has its seat in what is changed or altered); further, since it is the soul by or with which primarily we live, perceive, and think:—it follows that the soul must be a ratio or formulable essence, not a matter or subject. For, as we said, the word substance has three meanings—form, matter, and the complex of both—and of these three what is called matter is potentiality, what is called form actuality. Since then the complex here is the living thing, the body cannot be the actuality of the soul; it is the soul which is the actuality of a certain kind of body. Hence the rightness of the view that the soul cannot be without a body, while it cannot *be* a body; it is not a body but something relative to a body. That is why it is *in* a body, and a body of a definite kind. It was a mistake, therefore, to do as former thinkers did, merely to fit it into a body without adding a definite specification of the kind or character of that body. Reflection confirms the observed fact; the actuality of any given thing can only be realized in what is already potentially that thing, i.e. in a matter of its own appropriate to it. From all this it follows that soul is an actuality or formulable essence of something that possesses a potentiality of being besouled.

René Descartes

PRINCIPLES OF PHILOSOPHY: REPLIES AND OBJECTIONS

Descartes gives a brief statement of his theory of the relation of mind and body in *Principles of Philosophy*. In two elaborations on this statement, he responds to problems raised by Antoine Arnauld in *The Reply to the Fourth Set of Objections*, and he answers difficulties raised by Princess Elizabeth of the Palatinate in a letter to her.

REPLY TO THE FOURTH SET OF OBJECTIONS

Reply to the First Part
The Nature of the Human Mind

I shall not take up time here by thanking my distinguished critic for bringing to my aid the authority of St. Augustine, and for expounding my arguments in a way which betokened a fear that others might not deem them strong enough.

I come first of all to the passage where my demonstration commences of how, *from the fact that I knew that nothing belongs to my essence* (i.e. to the essence of the mind alone) *beyond the fact that I am a thinking being, it follows that in actual truth nothing else does belong to it*. That was, to be sure, the place where I proved that God exists, that God, to wit, who can accomplish whatever I clearly and distinctly know to be possible.

For although much exists in me of which I am not yet conscious (for example in that passage I did, as a fact, assume that I was not yet aware that my mind had the power of moving the body, and that it was substantially united with it), yet since that which I do perceive is adequate to allow of my existing with it as my sole possession, I am certain that God could have created me without putting me in possession of those other attributes of which I am unaware. Hence it was that those additional attributes were judged not to belong to the essence of the mind.

For in my opinion nothing without which a thing can still exist is comprised in its essence, and although mind belongs to the essence of man, to be united to a human body is in the proper sense no part of the essence of mind. . . .

9   In order rightly to see what amount of certainty belongs to sense we must distinguish three grades as falling within it. To the first belongs the immediate affection of the bodily organ by external objects; and this can be nothing else than the motion of the particles of the sensory organs and the change of figure and position due to that motion. The second comprises the immediate mental result, due to the mind's union with the corporeal organ affected; such are the perceptions of pain, of pleasurable stimulation, of thirst, of hunger, of colours, of sound, savour, odour, cold, heat, and the like, which in the Sixth Meditation are stated to arise from the union and, as it were, the intermixture of mind and body. Finally the third contains all those judgments which, on the occasion of motions occurring in the corporeal organ, we have from our earliest years been accustomed to pass about things external to us.

René Descartes

LETTER TO PRINCESS ELIZABETH OF THE PALATINATE, MAY 21, 1643

Madame,

The honour your Highness does me in sending her commandments in writing is greater than I ever dared hope; and it is more consoling to my unworthiness than the other favour which I had hoped for passionately, which was to receive them by word of mouth. If I had been permitted to pay homage to you and offer you my very humble services when I was last at The Hague, I would have had too many wonders to admire at the same time. Seeing superhuman sentiments flowing from a body such as painters give to angels, I would have been ravished like a man coming fresh from earth to heaven. Thus I would hardly have been able to reply to your Highness, as she doubtless noticed when once before I had the honour of speaking with her. Your clemency has willed to comfort me by committing the traces of your thoughts to paper, so that I can read them many times, and grow accustomed to consider them. Thus I am less overwhelmed, but no less full of admiration, observing that it is not only at first sight that they seem perceptive, but that the more they are examined, the more judicious and solid they appear.

I may truly say that the question you ask is the one which may most properly be put to me in view of my published writings. There are two facts about the human soul on which depend all the things we can know of its nature. The first is that it thinks, the second is that it is united to the body and can act and be acted upon along with it. About the second I have said hardly anything; I have tried only to make the first well understood. For my principal aim was to prove the distinction between soul and body, and to this end only the first was useful, and the second might have been harmful. But because your Highness' vision is so clear that nothing can be concealed from her, I will try now to explain how I conceive the union of the soul and the body and how the soul has the power to move the body.

First I observe that there are in us certain primitive notions which are as it were models on which all our other knowledge is patterned. There are very few such notions. First, there are the most general ones, such as being, number, and duration, which apply to everything we can conceive. Then, as regards body in particular, we have only the notion of extension which entails the notions of shape and motion; and as regards soul in particular we have only the notion of thought, which includes the conceptions of the intellect and the inclinations of the will. Finally, as regards soul and body together, we have only the notion of their union, on which depends our notion of the soul's power to move the body, and the body's power to act on the soul and cause sensations and passions.

I observe next that all human scientific knowledge consists solely in clearly distinguishing these notions and attaching each of them only to the things to which it applies. For if we try to solve a problem by means of a notion that does not apply, we cannot help going wrong. Similarly we go wrong if we try to explain one of these notions by another, for since they are primitive notions, each of them can only be understood by itself. The use of our senses has made the notions of extension, shape, and movement more familiar to us than the others; and the main cause of our errors is that we commonly want to use these notions to explain matters to which they do not apply. For instance, we try to use our imagination to conceive the nature of the soul, or to conceive the way in which the soul moves the body after the manner in which one body is moved by another.

In the *Meditations* that your Highness condescended to read, I tried to give a conception of the notions which belong to the soul alone by distinguishing them from those that apply to the body alone. Accordingly, the next thing I must explain is how to conceive those that apply to the union of the soul with the body, and how to distinguish them from those which belong to the body alone or those which belong to the soul alone. At this point what I wrote at the end of my reply to the *Sixth Objections* may be useful. It is in our own soul that we must look for these simple notions. It possesses them all by nature, but it does not always sufficiently distinguish them from each other, or attach them to the objects to which they ought to be attached.

So I think that we have hitherto confounded the notion of the soul's power to act on the body with the power one body has to act on another. We have attributed both powers not to the soul, whose nature we did not yet know, but to the various qualities of bodies such as weight, heat etc. We imagined these qualities to be real, that is to say to have an existence distinct from that of bodies, and so to be substances, although we called them qualities. In order to conceive them we sometimes used notions we have for the purpose of knowing bodies, and sometimes used notions we have for the purpose of knowing the soul, depending on whether we were attributing to them something material or something immaterial. For instance, when we suppose that heaviness is a real quality of which all we know is that it has the power to move the body that possesses it towards the centre of the earth, we find no difficulty in conceiving how it moves the body nor how it is united to it. We do not suppose that the production of this motion takes place by a real contact between two surfaces, because we find by introspection that we have a specific notion to conceive it by. I think that we misuse this notion when we apply it to heaviness, which as I hope to show in my *Physics*, is not anything really distinct from body; but it was given us for the purpose of conceiving the manner in which the soul moves the body.

If I used more words to explain myself I would show that I had not realized the incomparable quality of your Highness' mind; but I would be too presumptuous if I dared to think that my reply should entirely satisfy her. I will try to avoid both errors by adding nothing for the present except that if I am capable of writing or saying anything which may give her pleasure, I will always count it a great privilege to take up my pen or to visit The Hague for that purpose; and that nothing in the world is so dear to me as the power of obeying her commands. I cannot here find any reason for observing the Hippocratic oath she enjoined on me since she has written nothing which does not deserve to be seen and admired by all. I will only say that as I prize infinitely your letter, I will treat it as misers treat their treasures. The more they prize them, the more they hide them, grudging the sight of them to the rest of the world and placing their supreme happiness in looking at them. So I will be glad to enjoy in solitude the benefit of looking at your letter; and my greatest ambition is to be able to call myself and to be your, etc.

Gottfried Leibniz

THE MONADOLOGY

Gottfried Wilhelm Leibniz (1646–1716) was one of the most brilliant mathematicians, scientists, and philosophers of his time. He worked as a diplomat for various German principalities while developing his philosophy. The best-known statement of his view of the mind-body relationship appears in *The Monadology*, from which the following selection is taken.

1. The Monad, of which we will speak here, is nothing else than a simple substance, which goes to make up composites; by simple, we mean without parts.

2. There must be simple substances because there are composites; for a composite is nothing else than a collection or *aggregatum* of simple substances.

3. Now, where there are no constituent parts there is possible neither extension, nor form, nor divisibility. These Monads are the true Atoms of nature, and, in fact, the Elements of things.

4. Their dissolution, therefore, is not to be feared and there is no way conceivable by which a simple substance can perish through natural means.

5. For the same reason there is no way conceivable by which a simple substance might, through natural means, come into existence, since it can not be formed by composition.

6. We may say then, that the existence of Monads can begin or end only all at once, that is to say, the Monad can begin only through creation and end only through annihilation. Composites, however, begin or end gradually.

7. There is also no way of explaining how a Monad can be altered or changed in its inner being by any other created thing, since there is no possibility of transposition within it, nor can we conceive of any internal movement which can be produced, directed, increased or diminished there within the substance, such as can take place in the case of composites where a change can occur among the parts. The Monads have no windows through which anything may

come in or go out. The Attributes are not liable to detach themselves and make an excursion outside the substance, as could *sensible species* of the Schoolmen. In the same way neither substance nor attribute can enter from without into a Monad.

8. Still Monads must needs have some qualities, otherwise they would not even be existences. And if simple substances did not differ at all in their qualities, there would be no means of perceiving any change in things. Whatever is in a composite can come into it only through its simple elements and the Monads, if they were without qualities, since they do not differ at all in quantity, would be indistinguishable one from another. For instance, if we imagine *a plenum* or completely filled space, where each part receives only the equivalent of its own previous motion, one state of things would not be distinguishable from another.

9. Each Monad, indeed, must be different from every other. For there are never in nature two beings which are exactly alike, and in which it is not possible to find a difference either internal or based on an intrinsic property.

10. I assume it as admitted that every created being, and consequently the created Monad, is subject to change, and indeed that this change is continuous in each.

11. It follows from what has just been said, that the natural changes of the Monad come from an internal principle, because an external cause can have no influence upon its inner being.

12. Now besides this principle of change there must also be in the Monad a manifoldness which changes. This manifoldness constitutes, so to speak, the specific nature and the variety of the simple substances.

13. This manifoldness must involve a multiplicity in the unity or in that which is simple. For since every natural change takes place by degrees, there must be something which changes and something which remains unchanged, and consequently there must be in the simple substance a plurality of conditions and relations, even though it has no parts.

14. The passing condition which involves and represents a multiplicity in the unity, or in the simple substance, is nothing else than what is called Perception. This should be carefully distinguished from Apperception or Consciousness, as will appear in what follows. In this matter the Cartesians have fallen into a serious error, in that they treat as nonexistent those perceptions of which we are not conscious. It is this also which has led them to believe that spirits alone are Monads and that there are no souls of animals or other Entelechies, and it has led them to make the common confusion between a protracted period of unconsciousness and actual death. They have thus adopted the Scholastic error that souls can exist entirely separated from bodies, and have even confirmed ill-balanced minds in the belief that souls are mortal.

15. The action of the internal principle which brings about the change or the passing from one perception to another may be called Appetition. It is true that

the desire (*l'appetit*) is not always able to attain to the whole of the perception which it strives for, but it always attains a portion of it and reaches new perceptions.

16. We, ourselves, experience a multiplicity in a simple substance, when we find that the most trifling thought of which we are conscious involves a variety in the object. Therefore all those who acknowledge that the soul is a simple substance ought to grant this multiplicity in the Monad. . . .

17. It must be confessed, however, that Perception, and that which depends upon it, are inexplicable by mechanical causes, that is to say, by figures and motions. Supposing that there were a machine whose structure produced thought, sensation, and perception, we could conceive of it as increased in size with the same proportions until one was able to enter into its interior, as he would into a mill. Now, on going into it he would find only pieces working upon one another, but never would he find anything to explain Perception. It is accordingly in the simple substance, and not in the composite nor in a machine that the Perception is to be sought. Furthermore, there is nothing besides perceptions and their changes to be found in the simple substance. And it is in these alone that all the internal activities of the simple substance can consist.

18. All simple substances or created Monads may be called Entelechies, because they have in themselves a certain perfection (ἔχουσι τὸ ἐντελές). There is in them a sufficiency (αὐτάρκεια) which makes them the source of their internal activities, and renders them, so to speak, incorporeal Automatons.

19. If we wish to designate as soul everything which has perceptions and desires in the general sense that I have just explained, all simple substances or created Monads could be called souls. But since feeling is something more than a mere perception I think that the general name of Monad or Entelechy should suffice for simple substances which have only perception, while we may reserve the term Soul for those whose perception is more distinct and is accompanied by memory.

20. We experience in ourselves a state where we remember nothing and where we have no distinct perception, as in periods of fainting, or when we are overcome by a profound, dreamless sleep. In such a state the soul does not sensibly differ at all from a simple Monad. As this state, however, is not permanent and the soul can recover from it, the soul is something more.

21. Nevertheless it does not follow at all that the simple substance is in such a state without perception. This is so because of the reasons given above; for it cannot perish, nor on the other hand would it exist without some affection and the affection is nothing else than its perception. When, however, there are a great number of weak perceptions where nothing stands out distinctively, we are stunned; as when one turns around and around in the same direction, a dizziness comes on, which makes him swoon and makes him able to distinguish nothing. Among animals, death can occasion this state for quite a period.

22. Every present state of a simple substance is a natural consequence of its preceding state, in such a way that its present is big with its future.

23. Therefore, since on awakening after a period of unconsciousness we become conscious of our perceptions, we must, without having been conscious of them, have had perceptions immediately before; for one perception can come in a natural way only from another perception, just as a motion can come in a natural way only from a motion.

24. It is evident from this that if we were to have nothing distinctive, or so to speak prominent, and of a higher flavor in our perceptions, we should be in a continual state of stupor. This is the condition of Monads which are wholly bare.

25. We see that nature has given to animals heightened perceptions, having provided them with organs which collect numerous rays of light or numerous waves of air and thus make them more effective in their combination. Something similar to this takes place in the case of smell, in that of taste and of touch, and perhaps in many other senses which are unknown to us. I shall have occasion very soon to explain how that which occurs in the soul represents that which goes on in the sense-organs.

26. The memory furnishes a sort of consecutiveness which imitates reason but is to be distinguished from it. We see that animals when they have the perception of something which they notice and of which they have had a similar previous perception, are led by the representation of their memory to expect that which was associated in the preceding perception, and they come to have feelings like those which they had before. For instance, if a stick be shown to a dog, he remembers the pain which it has caused him and he whines or runs away.

27. The vividness of the picture, which comes to him or moves him, is derived either from the magnitude or from the number of the previous perceptions. For, oftentimes, a strong impression brings about, all at once, the same effect as a long-continued habit or as a great many re-iterated, moderate perceptions.

28. Men act in like manner as animals, in so far as the sequence of their perceptions is determined only by the law of memory, resembling the *empirical physicians* who practice simply, without any theory, and we are empiricists in three-fourths of our actions. For instance, when we expect that there will be day-light to-morrow, we do so empirically, because it has always happened so up to the present time. It is only the astronomer who uses his reason in making such an affirmation.

29. But the knowledge of eternal and necessary truths is that which distinguishes us from mere animals and gives us reason and the sciences, thus raising us to a knowledge of ourselves and of God. This is what is called in us the Rational Soul or the Mind.

30. It is also through the knowledge of necessary truths and through abstractions from them that we come to perform Reflective Acts, which cause us

to think of what is called the I, and to decide that this or that is within us. It is thus, that in thinking upon ourselves we think of *being*, of *substance*, of the *simple* and *composite*, of a *material* thing and of God himself, conceiving that what is limited in us is in him without limits. These Reflective Acts furnish the principal objects of our reasonings. . . .

38. It is thus that the ultimate reason for things must be a necessary substance, in which the detail of the changes shall be present merely potentially, as in the fountain-head, and this substance we call God.

39. Now, since this substance is a sufficient reason for all the above mentioned details, which are linked together throughout, *there is but one God, and this God is sufficient.*

40. We may hold that the supreme substance, which is unique, universal and necessary with nothing independent outside of it, which is further a pure sequence of possible being, must be incapable of limitation and must contain as much reality as possible.

41. Whence it follows that God is absolutely perfect, perfection being understood as the magnitude of positive reality in the strict sense, when the limitations or the bounds of those things which have them are removed. There where there are no limits, that is to say, in God, perfection is absolutely infinite.

42. It follows also that created things derive their perfections through the influence of God, but their imperfections come from their own natures, which cannot exist without limits. It is in this latter that they are distinguished from God. An example of this original imperfection of created things is to be found in the natural inertia of bodies.

43. It is true, furthermore, that in God is found not only the source of existences, but also that of essences, in so far as they are real. In other words, he is the source of whatever there is real in the possible. This is because the Understanding of God is in the region of eternal truths or of the ideas upon which they depend, and because without him there would be nothing real in the possibilities of things, and not only would nothing be existent, nothing would be even possible.

44. For it must needs be that if there is a reality in essences or in possibilities or indeed in the eternal truths, this reality is based upon something existent and actual, and, consequently, in the existence of the necessary Being in whom essence includes existence or in whom possibility is sufficient to produce actuality. . . .

50. One created thing is more perfect than another when we find in the first that which gives an *a priori* reason for what occurs in the second. This is why we say that one acts upon the other.

51. In the case of simple substances, the influence which one Monad has upon another is only ideal. It can have its effect only through the mediation of God, in so far as in the Ideas of God each Monad can rightly demand that God, in regulating the others from the beginning of things, should have regarded it also. For, since one created Monad cannot have a physical influence upon the

inner being of another, it is only through this primal regulation that one can have dependence upon another.

52. It is thus that among created things action and passion are reciprocal. For God, in comparing two simple substances, finds in each one reasons obliging him to adapt the other to it; and consequently that which is active in certain respects is passive from another point of view,—active in so far as that which we distinctly know in it serves to give a reason for that which occurs in another, and passive in so far as the reason for what transpires in it is found in that which is distinctly known in another.

53. Now as there are an infinity of possible universes in the Ideas of God, and but one of them can exist, there must be a sufficient reason for the choice of God which determines him to select one rather than another.

54. And this reason is to be found only in the fitness or in the degree of perfection which these worlds possess, each possible thing having the right to claim existence in proportion to the perfection which it involves.

55. This is the cause for the existence of the greatest good; namely, that the wisdom of God permits him to know it, his goodness causes him to choose it and his power enables him to produce it.

56. Now, this interconnection, relationship, or this adaptation of all things to each particular one, and of each one to all the rest, brings it about that every simple substance has relations which express all the others and that it is consequently a perpetual living mirror of the universe.

57. And as the same city regarded from different sides appears entirely different, and is, as it were, multiplied perspectively, so, because of the infinite number of simple substances, there are a similar infinite number of universes which are, nevertheless, only the aspects of a single one, as seen from the special point of view of each Monad.

58. Through this means has been obtained the greatest possible variety, together with the greatest order that may be; that is to say, through this means has been obtained the greatest possible perfection.

59. This hypothesis, moreover, which I venture to call demonstrated, is the only one which fittingly gives proper prominence to the greatness of God. Monsieur Bayle recognized this when in his *Dictionary* (article "Rorarius"), he raised objections to it; indeed, he was inclined to believe that I attributed too much to God, and more than should be attributed. But he was unable to bring forward any reason why this universal harmony, which causes every substance to express exactly all others, through the relation which it has with them, is impossible.

60. Besides, in what has just been said, can be seen the *a priori* reasons why things cannot be otherwise than they are. It is because God, in ordering the whole, has had regard to every part and in particular to each Monad whose nature it is to represent. Therefore, nothing can limit it to represent merely a part of the things. It is nevertheless true, that this representation is, as regards the details of the whole universe, only a confused representation, and is dis-

tinct only as regards a small part of them, that is to say, as regards those things which are nearest or most in relation to each Monad. If the representation were distinct as to the details of the entire universe, each Monad would be a Deity. It is not in the object represented that the Monads are limited, but in the modifications of their knowledge of the object. In a confused way they reach out to infinity or to the whole, but are limited and differentiated in the degree of their distinct perceptions.

61. In this respect composites are like simple substances. For all space is filled up; therefore, all matter is connected; and in a plenum or filled space every movement has an effect upon bodies in proportion to their distance, so that not only is every body affected by those which are in contact with it, and responds in some way to whatever happens to them, but also by means of them the body responds to those bodies adjoining them, and their intercommunication can be continued to any distance at will. Consequently every body responds to all that happens in the universe, so that he who saw all, could read in each one what is happening everywhere, and even what has happened and what will happen. He can discover in the present what is distant both as regards space and as regards time; σύμπνοια πάντα, as Hippocrates said. A soul can, however, read in itself only what is there represented distinctly. It cannot all at once open up all its folds, because they extend to infinity.

62. Thus although each created Monad represents the whole universe, it represents more distinctly the body which specially pertains to it, and of which it constitutes the entelechy. And as the body expresses all the universe through the interconnection of all matter in the plenum, the soul also represents the whole universe in representing this body, which belongs to it in a particular way.

63. The body belonging to a Monad, which is its entelechy or soul, constitutes together with the entelechy what may be called a *living being*, and with a soul what is called an *animal*. Now, this body of a living being or of an animal is always organic, because every Monad is a mirror of the universe according to its own fashion, and, since the universe is regulated with perfect order, there must needs be order also in the representative, that is to say, in the perceptions of the soul and consequently in the body through which the universe is represented in the soul.

64. Therefore, every organic body of a living being is a kind of divine machine, or natural automaton, infinitely surpassing all artificial automatons. Because a machine constructed by man's skill is not a machine in each of its parts; for instance, the teeth of a brass wheel have parts or bits which to us are not artificial products and contain nothing in themselves to show the use to which the wheel was destined in the machine. The machines of nature, however, that is to say, living bodies, are still machines in their smallest parts *ad infinitum*. Such is the difference between nature and art, that is to say, between Divine art and ours.

65. The author of nature has been able to employ this divine and infinitely

marvellous artifice, because each portion of matter is not only, as the ancients recognized, infinitely divisible, but also because it is really divided without end, every part into other parts, each one of which has its own proper motion. Otherwise it would be impossible for each portion of matter to express all the universe.

66. Whence we see that there is a world of created things, of living beings, of animals, of entelechies, of souls, in the minutest particle of matter. . . .

78. These principles have furnished me the means of explaining on natural grounds the union, or, rather the conformity between the soul and the organic body. The soul follows its own laws, and the body has its laws. They are fitted to each other in virtue of the pre-established harmony between all substances, since they are all representations of one and the same universe.

79. Souls act in accordance with the laws of final causes through their desires, purposes and means. Bodies act in accordance with the laws of efficient causes or of motion. The two realms, that of efficient causes and that of final causes, are in harmony, each with the other.

80. Descartes saw that souls cannot at all impart force to bodies, because there is always the same quantity of force in matter. Yet, he thought that the soul could change the direction of bodies. This was, however, because at that time the law of nature, which affirms also the conservation of the same total direction in the motion of matter, was not known. If he had known that law, he would have fallen upon my system of Pre-established Harmony.

81. According to this system bodies act as if (to suppose the impossible) there were no souls at all, and souls act as if there were no bodies, and yet both body and soul act as if the one were influencing the other.

82. Although I find that essentially the same thing is true of all living things and animals, which we have just said, namely, that animals and souls begin from the very commencement of the world and that they come to an end no more than does the world, there is, as far as minds or rational souls are concerned nevertheless, this thing peculiar, that their little spermatic progenitors, as long as they remain such, have only ordinary or sensuous souls, but those of them which are, so to speak, elevated, attain by actual conception to human nature, and their sensuous souls are raised to the rank of reason and to the prerogative of minds.

83. Among the differences that there are between ordinary souls and spirits, some of which I have already instanced, there is also this that, while souls in general are living mirrors or images of the universe of created things, minds are also images of the Deity himself or of the author of nature. They are capable of knowing the system of the universe, and to imitate it somewhat by means of architectonic patterns, each mind being like a small divinity in its sphere.

84. Therefore, spirits are able to enter into a sort of social relationship with God, and with respect to them he is not only what an inventor is to his machine (as is his relation to the other created things), but he is also what a prince is to his subjects, and even what a father is to his children.

85. Whence it is easy to conclude that the totality of all the spirits must compose the city of God, that is to say, the most perfect state that is possible under the most perfect monarch.

86. This city of God, this truly universal monarchy, is a moral world within the natural world. It is what is noblest and most divine among the works of God. And in it consists in reality the glory of God, because he would have no glory were not his greatness and goodness known and wondered at by spirits. It is also in relation to this divine city that God properly has goodness. His wisdom and his power are shown everywhere.

87. As we established above that there is a perfect harmony between the two natural realms of efficient and final causes, it will be in place here to point out another harmony which appears between the physical realm of nature and the moral realm of grace, that is to say, between God, considered as the architect of the mechanism of the world and God considered as the Monarch of the divine city of spirits.

88. This harmony brings it about that things progress of themselves toward grace along natural lines, and that this earth, for example, must be destroyed and restored by natural means at those times when the proper government of spirits demands it, for chastisement in the one case and for a reward in the other.

89. We can say also that God, the Architect, satisfies in all respects God the Law-Giver, that therefore sins will bring their own penalty with them through the order of nature, and because of the very mechanical structure of things. And in the same way the good actions will attain their rewards in mechanical ways through their relation to bodies, although this cannot, and ought not, always to take place without delay.

90. Finally, under this perfect government, there will be no good action unrewarded and no evil action unpunished; everything should turn out for the well-being of the good; that is to say, of those who are not disaffected in this great state, who, after having done their duty, trust in Providence and who love and imitate, as is meet, the Author of all Good, delighting in the contemplation of his perfections according to the nature of that genuine, pure love which finds pleasure in the happiness of those who are loved. It is for this reason that wise and virtuous persons work in behalf of everything which seems comformable to the presumptive or antecedent will, and are, nevertheless, content with what God actually brings to pass through his secret, consequent and determining will, recognizing that if we were able to understand sufficiently well the order of the universe, we should find that it goes beyond all the desires of the wisest of us, and that it is impossible to have it better than it is, not only for all in general, but also for each one of us in particular, provided that we cleave as we should to the Author of all. For he is not only the Architect and the efficient cause of our being, but he is also our Lord and the Final Cause, who ought to be the whole goal of our will, and who, alone, can make our happiness.

David Hume

A TREATISE OF HUMAN NATURE

Hume applied his skeptical and empirical analysis to the problem of the relationship of the mind and body in Chapter 5 of
Book I, Part IV, of his *Treatise of Human Nature*.

First, I observe, that the word, action, according to this explication of it, can
never justly be apply'd to any perception, as deriv'd from a mind or thinking
substance. Our perceptions are all really different, and separable, and distinguishable from each other, and from every thing else, which we can imagine;
and therefore 'tis impossible to conceive, how they can be the action or abstract mode of any substance. The instance of motion, which is commonly
made use of to shew after what manner perception depends, as an action, upon
its substance, rather confounds than instructs us. Motion to all appearance
induces no real nor essential change on the body, but only varies its relation to
other objects. But betwixt a person in the morning walking in a garden with
company, agreeable to him; and a person in the afternoon inclos'd in a dungeon, and full of terror, despair, and resentment, there seems to be a radical
difference, and of quite another kind, than what is produc'd on a body by the
change of its situation. As we conclude from the distinction and separability of
their ideas, that external objects have a separate existence from each other; so
when we make these ideas themselves our objects, we must draw the same
conclusion concerning *them*, according to the precedent reasoning. At least it
must be confest, that having no idea of the substance of the soul, 'tis impossible for us to tell how it can admit of such differences, and even contrarieties of
perception without any fundamental change; and consequently can never tell
in what sense perceptions are actions of that substance. The use, therefore, of
the word, *action*, unaccompany'd with any meaning, instead of that of modification, makes no addition to our knowledge, nor is of any advantage to the
doctrine of the immateriality of the soul.

I add in the second place, that if it brings any advantage to that cause, it
must bring an equal to the cause of atheism. For do our Theologians pretend to

make a monopoly of the word, *action*, and may not the atheists likewise take possession of it, and affirm that plants, animals, men, &c. are nothing but particular actions of one simple universal substance, which exerts itself from a blind and absolute necessity? This you'll say is utterly absurd. I own 'tis unintelligible; but at the same time assert, according to the principles above-explain'd, that 'tis impossible to discover any absurdity in the supposition, that all the various objects in nature are actions of one simple substance, which absurdity will not be applicable to a like supposition concerning impressions and ideas.

From these hypotheses concerning the *substance* and *local conjunction* of our perceptions, we may pass to another, which is more intelligible than the former, and more important than the latter, *viz.* concerning the *cause* of our perceptions. Matter and motion, 'tis commonly said in the schools, however vary'd, are still matter and motion, and produce only a difference in the position and situation of objects. Divide a body as often as you please, 'tis still body. Place it in any figure, nothing ever results but figure, or the relation of parts. Move it in any manner, you still find motion or a change of relation. 'Tis absurd to imagine, that motion in a circle, for instance, shou'd be nothing but merely motion in a circle; while motion in another direction, as in an ellipse, shou'd also be a passion or moral reflexion: That the shocking of two globular particles shou'd become a sensation of pain, and that the meeting of two triangular ones shou'd afford a pleasure. Now as these different shocks, and variations, and mixtures are the only changes, of which matter is susceptible, and as these never afford us any idea of thought or perception, 'tis concluded to be impossible, that thought can ever be caus'd by matter.

Few have been able to withstand the seeming evidence of this argument; and yet nothing in the world is more easy than to refute it. We need only reflect on what has been prov'd at large, that we are never sensible of any connexion betwixt causes and effects, and that 'tis only by our experience of their constant conjunction, we can arrive at any knowledge of this relation. Now as all objects, which are not contrary, are susceptible of a constant conjunction, and as no real objects are contrary; I have inferr'd from these principles, that to consider the matter *a priori*, any thing may produce any thing, and that we shall never discover a reason, why any object may or may not be the cause of any other, however great, or however little the resemblance may be betwixt them. This evidently destroys the precedent reasoning concerning the cause of thought or perception. For tho' there appear no manner of connexion betwixt motion or thought, the case is the same with all other causes and effects. Place one body of a pound weight on one end of a lever, and another body of the same weight on another end; you will never find in these bodies any principle of motion dependent on their distances from the center, more than of thought and perception. If you pretend, therefore, to prove *a priori*, that such a position of bodies can never cause thought; because turn it which way you will, 'tis nothing but a position of bodies; you must by the same course of reasoning conclude, that it can never produce motion; since there is no more apparent connexion in the one case than in the other. But as this latter conclusion is contrary to evident experience, and as 'tis possible we may have a like experience in the operations of the mind, and may perceive a constant conjunction of thought and motion; you reason too hastily, when from the mere consideration of the ideas, you conclude that 'tis impossible motion can ever produce thought, or a different position of parts give rise to a different passion or reflexion. Nay 'tis not only possible we may have such an experience, but 'tis certain we have it; since every one may perceive, that the different dispositions of his body change his thoughts and sentiments. And shou'd it be said, that this depends on the union of soul and body; I wou'd answer, that we must separate the question concerning the substance of the mind from that concerning the cause of its thought; and that confining ourselves to the latter question we find by the comparing their ideas, that thought and motion are different from each other, and by experience, that they are constantly united; which being all the circumstances, that enter into the idea of cause and effect, when apply'd to the operations of matter, we may certainly conclude, that motion may be, and actually is, the cause of thought and perception.

There seems only this dilemma left us in the present case; either to assert, that nothing can be the cause of another, but where the mind can perceive the connexion in its idea of the objects: Or to maintain, that all objects, which we find constantly conjoin'd, are upon that account to be regarded as causes and effects. If we choose the first part of the dilemma, these are the consequences. *First*, We in reality affirm, that there is no such thing in the universe as a cause or productive principle, not even the deity himself; since our idea of that supreme Being is deriv'd from particular impressions, none of which contain any efficacy, nor seem to have *any* connexion with *any* other existence. As to what may be said, that the connexion betwixt the idea of an infinitely powerful being, and that of any effect, which he wills, is necessary and unavoidable; I answer, that we have no idea of a being endow'd with any power, much less of one endow'd with infinite power. But if we will change expressions, we can only define power by connexion; and then in saying, that the idea of an infinitely powerful being is connected with that of every effect, which he wills, we really do no more than assert, that a being, whose volition is connected with every effect, is connected with every effect; which is an identical proposition, and gives us no insight into the nature of this power or connexion. But, *secondly*, supposing, that the deity were the great and efficacious principle, which supplies the deficiency of all causes, this leads us into the grossest impieties and absurdities. For upon the same account, that we have recourse to him in natural operations, and assert that matter cannot of itself communicate motion, or produce thought, *viz.* because there is no apparent connexion betwixt these objects; I say, upon the very same account, we must acknowledge that the deity is the author of all our volitions and perceptions; since they have no more apparent connexion either with one another, or with the suppos'd but unknown substance of the soul. This agency of the supreme Being we know to have been asserted by several philosophers with relation to all the actions of the mind, except volition, or rather an inconsiderable part of volition; tho' 'tis easy to perceive, that this exception is a mere pretext, to avoid the dangerous consequences of that doctrine. If nothing be active but what has an apparent power, thought is in no case any more active than matter; and if this inactivity must make us have recourse to a deity, the supreme being is the real cause of all our actions, bad as well as good, vicious as well as virtuous.

Thus we are necessarily reduc'd to the other side of the dilemma, *viz.* that all objects, which are found to be constantly conjoin'd, are upon that account only to be regarded as causes and effects. Now as all objects, which are not contrary, are susceptible of a constant conjunction, and as no real objects are contrary; it follows, that for ought we can determine by the mere ideas, any thing may be the cause or effect of any thing; which evidently gives the advantage to the materialists above their antagonists.

To pronounce, then, the final decision upon the whole; the question concerning the substance of the soul is absolutely unintelligible: All our perceptions are not susceptible of a local union, either with what is extended or unextended; there being some of them of the one kind, and some of the other: And as the constant conjunction of objects constitutes the very essence of cause and effect, matter and motion may often be regarded as the causes of thought, as far as we have any notion of that relation.

'Tis certainly a kind of indignity to philosophy, whose sovereign authority ought every where to be acknowledg'd, to oblige her on every occasion to make apologies for her conclusions, and justify herself to every particular art and science, which may be offended at her. This puts one in mind of a king arraign'd for high-treason against his subjects. There is only one occasion, when philosophy will think it necessary and even honourable to justify herself, and that is, when religion may seem to be in the least offended; whose rights are as dear to her as her own, and are indeed the same. If any one, therefore, shou'd imagine that the foregoing arguments are any ways dangerous to religion, I hope the following apology will remove his apprehensions.

There is no foundation for any conclusion *a priori*, either concerning the operations or duration of any object, of which 'tis possible for the human mind to form a conception. Any object may be imagin'd to become entirely inactive, or to be annihilated in a moment; and 'tis an evident principle, *that whatever we can imagine, is possible.* Now this is no more true of matter, than of spirit; of an extended compounded substance, than of a simple and unextended. In both cases the metaphysical arguments for the immortality of the soul are equally inconclusive; and in both cases the moral arguments and those deriv'd from the analogy of nature are equally strong and convincing. If my philosophy, therefore, makes no addition to the arguments for religion, I have at least the satisfaction to think it takes nothing from them, but that every thing remains precisely as before.

B. WHAT IS THE NATURE OF THE EXTERNAL WORLD?

Bertrand Russell

A FREE MAN'S WORSHIP

Bertrand Russell (1872–1970) was perhaps the most important British philosopher of this century, making significant contributions in many areas of philosophy—logic, epistemology, metaphysics, ethics, and social and political thought. The following selection is from his essay "A Free Man's Worship," in which he presented a modern secular view of the physical world and humanity's place in it.

To Dr. Faustus in his study Mephistopheles told the history of the Creation, saying:

"The endless praises of the choirs of angels had begun to grow wearisome; for, after all, did He not deserve their praise? Had He not given them endless joy? Would it not be more amusing to obtain undeserved praise, to be worshipped by beings whom He tortured? He smiled inwardly, and resolved that the great drama should be performed.

"For countless ages the hot nebula whirled aimlessly through space. At length it began to take shape, the central mass threw off planets, the planets cooled, boiling seas and burning mountains heaved and tossed, from black masses of cloud hot sheets of rain deluged the barely solid crust. And now the first germ of life grew in the depths of the ocean, and developed rapidly in the fructifying warmth into vast forest trees, huge ferns springing from the damp mould, sea monsters breeding, fighting, devouring, and passing away. And from the monsters, as the play unfolded itself, Man was born, with the power of thought, the knowledge of good and evil, and the cruel thirst for worship. And Man saw that all is passing in this mad, monstrous world, that all is struggling to snatch, at any cost, a few brief moments of life before Death's inexorable decree. And Man said: 'There is a hidden purpose, could we but fathom it, and the purpose is good; for we must reverence something and in the visible world there is nothing worthy of reverence.' And Man stood aside from the struggle, resolving that God intended harmony to come out of chaos by human efforts. And when he followed the instincts which God had transmitted to him from his ancestry of beasts of prey, he called it Sin, and asked God to forgive him. But he doubted whether he could be justly forgiven, until he invented a divine Plan by which God's wrath was to have been appeased. And seeing the present was bad, he made it yet worse, that thereby the future might be better. And he gave God thanks for the strength that enabled him to forgo even the joys that were possible. And God smiled; and when he saw that Man had become perfect in renunciation and worship, he sent another sun through the sky, which crashed into Man's sun; and all returned again to nebula.

" 'Yes,' he murmured, 'it was a good play; I will have it performed again.' "

Such, in outline, but even more purposeless, more void of meaning, is the world which Science presents for our belief. Amid such a world, if anywhere, our ideals henceforward must find a home. That Man is the product of causes which had no prevision of the end they were achieving; that his origin, his growth, his hopes and fears, his loves and his beliefs, are but the outcome of accidental collocations of atoms; that no fire, no heroism, no intensity of thought and feeling, can preserve an individual life beyond the grave; that all the labours of the ages, all the devotion, all the inspiration, all the noonday brightness of human genius, are destined to extinction in the vast death of the solar system, and that the whole temple of Man's achievement must inevitably be buried beneath the debris of a universe in ruins—all these things, if not quite beyond dispute, are yet so nearly certain, that no philosophy which rejects them can hope to stand. Only within the scaffolding of these truths, only on the firm foundation of unyielding despair, can the soul's habitation henceforth be safely built.

How, in such an alien and inhuman world, can so powerless a creature as Man preserve his aspirations untarnished? A strange mystery it is that Nature, omnipotent but blind, in the revolutions of her secular hurryings through the abysses of space, has brought forth at last a child, subject still to her power, but gifted with sight, with knowledge of good and evil, with the capacity of judging all the works of his unthinking Mother. In spite of Death, the mark and seal of the parental control, Man is yet free, during his brief years, to examine, to criticize, to know, and in imagination to create. To him alone, in the world with which he is acquainted, this freedom belongs; and in this lies his superiority to the resistless forces that control his outward life.

The savage, like ourselves, feels the oppression of his impotence before the powers of Nature; but having in himself nothing that he respects more than Power, he is willing to prostrate himself before his gods, without inquiring whether they are worthy of his worship. Pathetic and very terrible is the long history of cruelty and torture, of degradation and human sacrifice, endured in the hope of placating the jealous gods: surely, the trembling believer thinks, when what is most precious has been freely given, their lust for blood must be appeased, and more will not be required. The religion of Moloch—as such creeds may be generically called—is in essence the cringing submission of the slave, who dare not, even in his heart, allow the thought that his master deserves no adulation. Since the independence of ideals is not yet acknowledged, Power may be freely worshipped, and receive an unlimited respect, despite its wanton infliction of pain.

But gradually, as morality grows bolder, the claim of the ideal world begins to be felt; and worship, if it is not to cease, must be given to gods of another kind than those created by the savage. Some, though they feel the demands of the ideal, will still consciously reject them, still urging that naked Power is worthy of worship. Such is the attitude inculcated in God's answer to Job out of the whirlwind: the divine power and knowledge are paraded, but of the divine goodness there is no hint. Such also is the attitude of those, who, in our own day, base their morality upon the struggle for survival, maintaining that the survivors are necessarily the fittest. But others, not content with an answer so repugnant to the moral sense, will adopt the position which we have become accustomed to regard as specially religious, maintaining that, in some hidden manner, the world of fact is really harmonious with the world of ideals. Thus Man creates God, all-powerful and all-good, the mystic unity of what is and what should be.

But the world of fact, after all, is not good; and, in submitting our judgment to it, there is an element of slavishness from which our thoughts must be purged. For in all things it is well to exalt the dignity of Man, by freeing him as far as possible from the tyranny of non-human Power. When we have realized that Power is largely bad, that man, with his knowledge of good and evil, is but a helpless atom in a world which has no such knowledge, the choice is again presented to us: Shall we worship Force, or shall we worship Goodness? Shall our God exist and be evil, or shall he be recognized as the creation of our own conscience?

Zeno of Elea

FRAGMENTS

The following selections are from the early Greek philosophers Zeno of Elea (c. 490 B.C.), Leucippus, and Democritus (c. 460 B.C.). Zeno presented a series of paradoxes that he encountered in attempting to explain the physical world. Leucippus and Democritus offered the earliest version of the atomic theory of matter.

PARADOXES ON PLURALITY

1

If what is had no magnitude, it would not even be. . . . But, if it is, each one must have a certain magnitude and a certain thickness, and must be at a certain distance from another, and the same may be said of what is in front of it; for it too, will have magnitude, and something will be in front of it. It is all the same to say this once and to say it always; for no such part of it will be the last, nor will one thing not be as compared with another. So, if things are a many, they must be both small and great, so small as not to have any magnitude at all, and so great as to be infinite.

2

For if it were added to any other thing it would not make it any larger; for nothing can gain in magnitude by the addition of what has no magnitude, and thus it follows at once that what was added was nothing. But if, when this is taken away from another thing, that thing is no less; and again, if, when it is added to another thing, that does not increase, it is plain that what was added was nothing, and what was taken away was nothing.

3

If things are a many, they must be just as many as they are, and neither more nor less. Now, if they are as many as they are, they will be finite in number.

If things are a many, they will be infinite in number; for there will always be other things between them, and others again between these. And so things are infinite in number.

4

If the unit is indivisible, it will, according to the proposition of Zeno, be nothing. That which neither makes anything larger by its addition to it, nor smaller by its subtraction from it, is not, he says, a real thing at all; for clearly what is real must be a magnitude. And, if it is a magnitude, it is corporeal; for that is corporeal which is in every dimension. The other things, *i.e.* the plane and the line, if added in one way will make things larger, added in another they will produce no effect; but the point and the unit cannot make things larger in any way.

5

If there is space, it will be in something; for all that is is in something, and what is in something is in space. So space will be in space, and this goes on *ad infinitum*, therefore there is no space.

PARADOXES ON MOTION

1

You cannot cross a race-course. You cannot traverse an infinite number of points in a finite time. You must traverse the half of any given distance before you traverse the whole, and the half of that again before you can traverse it. This goes on *ad infinitum*, so that there are an infinite number of points in any given space, and you cannot touch an infinite number one by one in a finite time.

2

Achilles will never overtake the tortoise. He must first reach the place from which the tortoise started. By that time the tortoise will have got some way ahead. Achilles must then make up that, and again the tortoise will be ahead. He is always coming nearer, but he never makes up to it.

3

The arrow in flight is at rest. For, if everything is at rest when it occupies a space equal to itself, and what is in flight at any given moment always occupies a space equal to itself it cannot move.

4

Half the time may be equal to double the time. Let us suppose three rows of bodies, one of which (A) is at rest while the other two (B, C) are moving with equal velocity in opposite directions (Fig. 1). By the time they are all in the same part of the course, B will have passed twice as many of the bodies in C as in A (Fig. 2).

FIGURE 1

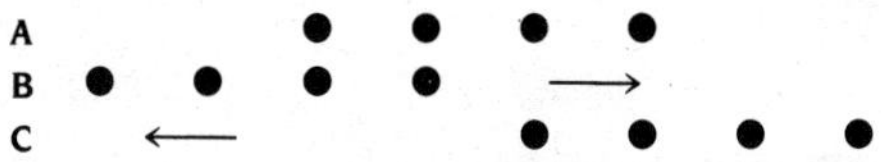

```
A         ●  ●  ●  ●
B  ●  ●  ●  ●        ⟶
C    ⟵         ●  ●  ●  ●
```

FIGURE 2

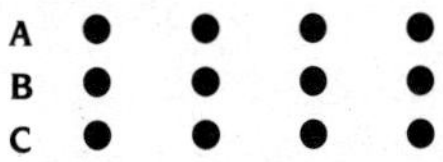

```
A  ●  ●  ●  ●
B  ●  ●  ●  ●
C  ●  ●  ●  ●
```

   Therefore the time which it takes to pass C is twice as long as the time it takes to pass A. But the time which B and C take to reach the position of A is the same. Therefore double the time is equal to the half.

Leucippus and Democritus
FRAGMENTS

Leukippos and Demokritos have decided about all things practically by the same method and on the same theory, taking as their starting-point what naturally comes first. Some of the ancients had held that the real must necessarily be one and immovable; for, said they, empty space is not real, and motion would be impossible without empty space separated from matter; nor, further, could reality be a many, if there were nothing to separate things. And it makes no difference if any one holds that the All is not continuous, but discrete, with its parts in contact (*the Pythagorean view*), instead of holding that reality is many, not one, and that there is empty space. For, if it is divisible at every point there is no one, and therefore no many, and the Whole is empty (*Zeno*); while, if we say it is divisible in one place and not in another, this looks like an arbitrary fiction; for up to what point and for what reason will part of the Whole be in this state and be full, while the rest is discrete? And, on the same grounds, they further say that there can be no motion. In consequence of these reasonings, then, going beyond perception and overlooking it in the belief that we ought to follow the argument, they say that the All is one and immovable (*Parmenides*), and some of them that it is infinite (*Melissos*), for any limit would be bounded by empty space. This, then, is the opinion they expressed about the truth, and these are the reasons which led them to do so. Now, so far as arguments go, this conclusion does seem to follow; but, if we appeal to facts, to hold such a view looks like madness. No one who is mad is so far out of his senses that fire and ice appear to him to be one; it is only things that are right, and things that appear right from habit, in which madness makes some people see no difference.

Leukippos, however, thought he had a theory which was in harmony with sense, and did not do away with coming into being and passing away, nor motion, nor the multiplicity of things. He conceded this to experience, while he conceded, on the other hand, to those who invented the One that motion was impossible without the void, that the void was not real, and that nothing of what was real was not real. "For," said he, "that which is strictly speaking real is an absolute *plenum*; but the *plenum* is not one. On the contrary, there are an infinite number of them, and they are invisible owing to the smallness of their bulk. They move in the void (for there is a void); and by their coming together they effect coming into being; by their separation, passing away."

Leukippos of Elea or Miletos (for both accounts are given of him) had associated with Parmenides in philosophy. He did not, however, follow the same path in his explanation of things as Parmenides and Xenophanes did, but, to all appearance, the very opposite. They made the All one, immovable, uncreated, and finite, and did not even permit us to search for *what is not*; he assumed innumerable and ever-moving elements, namely, the atoms. And he made their forms infinite in number, since there was no reason why they should be of one kind rather than another, and because he saw that there was unceasing becoming and change in things. He held, further, that *what is* is no more real than *what is not*, and that both are alike causes of the things that come into being; for he laid down that the substance of the atoms was compact and full, and he called them *what is*, while they moved in the void which he called *what is not*, but affirmed to be just as real as *what is*.

He [Leucippus] says that the All is infinite, and that it is part full, and part empty. These (the full and the empty), he says, are the elements. From them arise innumerable worlds and are resolved into them. The worlds come into being thus. There were borne along by "abscission from the infinite" many bodies of all sorts of figures "into a mighty void," and they being gathered together produce a single vortex. In it, as they came into collision with one another and were whirled round in all manner of ways, those which were alike were separated apart and came to their likes. But, as they were no longer able to revolve in equilibrium owing to their multitude, those of them that were fine went out to the external void, as if passed through a sieve; the rest stayed together, and becoming entangled with one another, ran down together, and made a first spherical structure. This was in substance like a membrane or skin containing in itself all kinds of bodies. And, as these bodies were borne round in a vortex, in virtue of the resistance of the middle, the surrounding membrane became thin, as the contiguous bodies kept flowing together from contact with the vortex. And in this way the earth came into being, those things which had been borne towards the middle abiding there. Moreover, the containing membrane was increased by the further separating out of bodies from outside; and, being itself carried round in a vortex, it further got possession of all with which it had come in contact. Some of these becoming entangled, produced a structure which was at first moist and muddy; but, when they had been dried and were revolving along with the vortex of the whole, they were then ignited and produced the substance of the heavenly bodies. The circle of the sun is the outermost, that of the moon is nearest to the earth, and those of the others are between these. And all the heavenly bodies are ignited because of the swiftness of their motion; while the sun is also ignited by the stars. But the moon only receives a small portion of fire. The sun and the moon are eclipsed . . . (And the obliquity of the zodiac is produced) by the earth being inclined towards the south; and the northern parts of it have constant snow and are cold and frozen. And the sun is eclipsed rarely, and the moon continually, because their circles are unequal. And just as there are comings into being of the world, so there are growths and decays and passings away in virtue of a certain necessity, of the nature of which he gives no clear account.

Aristotle

PHYSICS

Aristotle offered his criticism of ancient atomism and his solution to Zeno's paradoxes in the following excerpts from Books III, VI, and VIII of his *Physics*.

BOOK III

7   It is reasonable that there should not be held to be an infinite in respect of addition such as to surpass every magnitude, but that there should be thought to be such an infinite in the direction of division. For the matter and the infinite are contained inside what contains them, while it is the form which contains. It is natural too to suppose that in number there is a limit in the direction of the minimum, and that in the other direction every assigned number is surpassed. In magnitude, on the contrary, every assigned magnitude is surpassed in the direction of smallness, while in the other direction there is no infinite magnitude. The reason is that what is one is indivisible whatever it may be, e.g. a man is one man, not many. Number on the other hand is a plurality of "ones" and a certain quantity of them. Hence number must stop at the indivisible: for "two" and "three" are merely derivative terms, and so with each of the other numbers. But in the direction of largeness it is always possible to think of a larger number: for the number of times a magnitude can be bisected is infinite. Hence this infinite is potential, never actual: the number of parts that can be taken always surpasses any assigned number. But this number is not separable from the process of bisection, and its infinity is not a permanent actuality but consists in a process of coming to be, like time and the number of time.

With magnitudes the contrary holds. What is continuous is divided *ad infinitum*, but there is no infinite in the direction of increase. For the size which it can potentially be, it can also actually be. Hence since no sensible magnitude is infinite, it is impossible to exceed every assigned magnitude; for if it were possible there would be something bigger than the heavens.

The infinite is not the same in magnitude and movement and time, in the sense of a single nature, but its secondary sense depends on its primary sense, i.e. movement is called infinite in virtue of the magnitude covered by the movement (or alteration or growth), and time because of the movement. (I use these terms for the moment. Later I shall explain what each of them means, and also why every magnitude is divisible into magnitudes.)

Our account does not rob the mathematicians of their science, by disproving the actual existence of the infinite in the direction of increase, in the sense of the untraversable. In point of fact they do not need the infinite and do not use it. They postulate only that the finite straight line may be produced as far as they wish. It is possible to have divided in the same ratio as the largest quantity another magnitude of any size you like. Hence, for the purposes of proof, it will make no difference to them to have such an infinite instead, while its existence will be in the sphere of real magnitudes.

In the four-fold scheme of causes, it is plain that the infinite is a cause in the sense of matter, and that its essence is privation, the subject as such being what is continuous and sensible. All the other thinkers, too, evidently treat the infinite as matter—that is why it is inconsistent in them to make it what contains, and not what is contained. . . .

BOOK VI

2 Moreover, the current popular arguments make it plain that, if time is continuous, magnitude is continuous also, inasmuch as a thing passes over half a given magnitude in half the time taken to cover the whole: in fact without qualification it passes over a less magnitude in less time; for the divisions of time and of magnitude will be the same. And if either is infinite, so is the other, and the one is so in the same way as the other; i.e. if time is infinite in respect of its extremities, length is also infinite in respect of its extremities: if time is infinite in respect of divisibility, length is also infinite in respect of divisibility: and if time is infinite in both respects, magnitude is also infinite in both respects.

Hence Zeno's argument makes a false assumption in asserting that it is impossible for a thing to pass over or severally to come in contact with infinite things in a finite time. For there are two senses in which length and time and generally anything continuous are called "infinite": they are called so either in respect of divisibility or in respect of their extremities. So while a thing in a finite time cannot come in contact with things quantitatively infinite, it can come in contact with things infinite in respect of divisibility: for in this sense the time itself is also infinite: and so we find that the time occupied by the passage over the infinite is not a finite but an infinite time, and the contact with the infinites is made by means of moments not finite but infinite in number.

The passage over the infinite, then, cannot occupy a finite time, and the passage over the finite cannot occupy an infinite time: if the time is infinite the magnitude must be infinite also, and if the magnitude is infinite, so also is the time. This may be shown as follows. Let AB be a finite magnitude, and let us suppose that it is traversed in infinite time C, and let a finite period CD of the time be taken. Now in this period the thing in motion will pass over a certain segment of the magnitude: let BE be the segment that it has thus passed over. (This will be either an exact measure of AB or less or greater than an exact measure: it makes no difference which it is.) Then, since a magnitude equal to BE will always be passed over in an equal time, and BE measures the whole magnitude, the whole time occupied in passing over AB will be finite: for it will be divisible into periods equal in number to the segments into which the magnitude is divisible. Moreover, if it is the case that infinite time is not occupied in passing over every magnitude, but it is possible to pass over some magnitude, say BE, in a finite time, and if this BE measures the whole of which it is a part, and if an equal magnitude is passed over in an equal time, then it follows that the time like the magnitude is finite. That infinite time will not be occupied in passing over BE is evident if the time be taken as limited in one direction: for as the part will be passed over in less time than the whole, the time occupied in traversing this part must be finite, the limit in one direction being given. The same reasoning will also show the falsity of the assumption that infinite length can be traversed in a finite time. It is evident, then, from what has been said that neither a line nor a surface nor in fact anything continuous can be indivisible.

This conclusion follows not only from the present argument but from the consideration that the opposite assumption implies the divisibility of the indivisible. For since the distinction of quicker and slower may apply to motions occupying any period of time and in an equal time the quicker passes over a greater length, it may happen that it will pass over a length twice, or one and a half times, as great as that passed over by the slower: for their respective velocities may stand to one another in this proportion. Suppose, then, that the quicker has in the same time been carried over a length one and a half times as great as that traversed by the slower, and that the respective magnitudes are divided, that of the quicker, the magnitude ABCD, into three indivisibles, and that of the slower into the two indivisibles EF, FG. Then the time may also be divided into three indivisibles, for an equal magnitude will be passed over in an equal time. Suppose then that it is thus divided into JK, KL, LM. Again, since in the same time the slower has been carried over EF, FG, the time may also be similarly divided into two. Thus the indivisible will be divisible, and that which has no parts will be passed over not in an indivisible but in a greater time. It is evident, therefore, that nothing continuous is without parts. . . .

9   Zeno's reasoning, however, is fallacious, when he says that if everything when it occupies an equal space is at rest, and if that which is in locomotion is

always occupying such a space at any moment, the flying arrow is therefore motionless. This is false, for time is not composed of indivisible moments any more than any other magnitude is composed of indivisibles.

Zeno's arguments about motion, which cause so much disquietude to those who try to solve the problems that they present, are four in number. The first asserts the non-existence of motion on the ground that that which is in loco-motion must arrive at the half-way stage before it arrives at the goal. This we have discussed above.

The second is the so-called "Achilles," and it amounts to this, that in a race the quickest runner can never overtake the slowest, since the pursuer must first reach the point whence the pursued started, so that the slower must always hold a lead. This argument is the same in principle as that which depends on bisection, though it differs from it in that the spaces with which we successively have to deal are not divided into halves. The result of the argument is that the slower is not overtaken: but it proceeds along the same lines as the bisection-argument (for in both a division of the space in a certain way leads to the result that the goal is not reached, though the "Achilles" goes further in that it affirms that even the quickest runner in legendary tradition must fail in his pursuit of the slowest), so that the solution must be the same. And the axiom that that which holds a lead is never overtaken is false: it is not overtaken, it is true, while it holds a lead: but it is overtaken nevertheless if it is granted that it traverses the finite distance prescribed. These then are two of his arguments.

The third is that already given above, to the effect that the flying arrow is at rest, which result follows from the assumption that time is composed of moments: if this assumption is not granted, the conclusion will not follow.

The fourth argument is that concerning the two rows of bodies, each row being composed of an equal number of bodies of equal size, passing each other on a race-course as they proceed with equal velocity in opposite directions, the one row originally occupying the space between the goal and the middle point of the course and the other that between the middle point and the starting-post. This, he thinks, involves the conclusion that half a given time is equal to double that time. The fallacy of the reasoning lies in the assumption that a body occupies an equal time in passing with equal velocity a body that is in motion and a body of equal size that is at rest; which is false. For instance (so runs the argument), let A, A . . . be the stationary bodies of equal size, B, B . . . the bodies, equal in number and in size to A, A . . . , originally occupying the half of the course from the starting-post to the middle of the A's, and C, C, . . . those originally occupying the other half from the goal to the middle of the A's, equal in number, size, and velocity to B, B. . . . Then three consequences follow:

First, as the B's and the C's pass one another, the first B reaches the last C at the same moment as the first C reaches the last B. Secondly, at this moment the first C has passed all the A's, whereas the first B has passed only half the A's, and has consequently occupied only half the time occupied by the first C, since each of the two occupies an equal time in passing each A. Thirdly, at the same moment all the B's have passed all the C's: for the first C and the first B will simultaneously reach the opposite ends of the course, since (so says Zeno) the time occupied by the first C in passing each of the B's is equal to that occupied by it in passing each of the A's, because an equal time is occupied by both the first B and the first C in passing all the A's. This is the argument, but it presupposed the aforesaid fallacious assumption.

Nor in reference to contradictory change shall we find anything unanswerable in the argument that if a thing is changing from not-white, say, to white, and is in neither condition, then it will be neither white nor not-white: for the fact that it is not *wholly* in either condition will not preclude us from calling it white or not-white. We call a thing white or not-white not necessarily because it is wholly either one or the other, but because most of its parts or the most essential parts of it are so: not being in a certain condition is different from not being wholly in that condition. So, too, in the case of being and not-being and all other conditions which stand in a contradictory relation: while the changing thing must of necessity be in one of the two opposites, it is never wholly in either.

Again, in the case of circles and spheres and everything whose motion is confined within the space that it occupies, it is not true to say that the motion can be nothing but rest, on the ground that such things in motion, themselves and their parts, will occupy the same position for a period of time, and that therefore they will be at once at rest and in motion. For in the first place the parts do not occupy the same position for any period of time: and in the second place the whole also is always changing to a different position: for if we take the orbit as described from a point A on a circumference, it will not be the same as the orbit as described from B or C or any other point on the same circumference except in an accidental sense, the sense that is to say in which a musical man is the same as a man. Thus one orbit is always changing into another, and the thing will never be at rest. And it is the same with the sphere and everything else whose motion is confined within the space that it occupies. . . .

BOOK VIII

8 These and such-like, then, are the arguments for our conclusion that derive cogency from the fact that they have a special bearing on the point at issue. If we look at the question from the point of view of general theory, the same result would also appear to be indicated by the following arguments. Everything whose motion is continuous must, on arriving at any point in the course of its locomotion, have been previously also in process of locomotion to that point, if it is not forced out of its path by anything: e.g. on arriving at B a thing must also have been in process of locomotion to B, and that not merely when it

was near to B, but from the moment of its starting on its course, since there can be no reason for its being so at any particular stage rather than at an earlier one. So, too, in the case of the other kinds of motion. Now we are to suppose that a thing proceeds in locomotion from A to C and that at the moment of its arrival at C the continuity of its motion is unbroken and will remain so until it has arrived back at A. Then when it is undergoing locomotion from A to C it is at the same time undergoing also its locomotion to A from C: consequently it is simultaneously undergoing two contrary motions, since the two motions that follow the same straight line are contrary to each other. With this consequence there also follows another: we have a thing that is in process of change from a position in which it has not yet been: so, inasmuch as this is impossible, the thing must come to a stand at C. Therefore the motion is not a single motion, since motion that is interrupted by stationariness is not single.

Pierre Gassendi

SYNTAGMA PHILOSOPHICUM

Pierre Gassendi (1592–1655) was a French Catholic priest who
became a royal professor at the Collège de France. He revived
ancient atomism and sought to reconcile it with Christian belief. The selection is from his final work, the *Syntagma Philo-
sophicum.*

THE PHYSICS
SECTION I, BOOK III, CHAPTER 8

Atoms as the Primary Form of Matter

Hence, to present at last our conclusion that apparently the opinion of those
who maintain that atoms are the primary and universal material of all things
may be recommended above all others, I take pleasure in beginning with the
words of Aneponymus. After his opening remark that "There is no opinion so
false that it does not have some truth mixed in with it, but still the truth is
obscured by being mixed with the false," he then continues, "For in their assertion that the world is made up of atoms the Epicureans spoke the truth, but in
their assertion that these atoms had no beginning and that they flew about
separately in a great void, and then coalesced into four great bodies they were
telling fairy tales."[1] I say I take pleasure from these words for one can draw the
inference that there is nothing to prevent us from defending the opinion which
decides that the matter of the world and all the things contained in it is made
up of atoms, provided that we repudiate whatever falsehood is mixed in with it.
Therefore, in order to recommend the theory, we declare first that the idea that
atoms are eternal and uncreated is to be rejected and also the idea that they
are infinite in number and occur in any sort of shape; once this is done, it can
be admitted that atoms are the primary form of matter, which God created

---

[1]*Dialogus de substantiis physicis.*

finite from the beginning, which he formed into this visible world, which, finally, he ordained and permitted to undergo transformations out of which, in short, all the bodies which exist in the universe are composed. So stated, such an opinion has no evil in it which has not been corrected just as it is necessary to correct opinions in Aristotle and others which make matter eternal and uncreated in the same way, as others also make it infinite. In the meantime, this theory of matter has the advantage that it does not do a bad job of explaining how composition and resolution into the primary elemental particles is accomplished, and for what reason a thing is solid, or corporeal, how it becomes large or small, rarefied or dense, soft or hard, sharp or blunt, and so forth. For indeed these questions and others like them are not so clearly resolved in other theories where matter is considered as both infinitely divisible and either pure potentiality (as they say) or endowed with a certain shape from among a very small range of possibilities, or endowed with primary and secondary qualities, which either do not suffice to explain the variety in objects or are useless, as is clear from what I have already said.

Next we declare that the idea that atoms have impetus, or the power to move themselves inherent in their nature, is to be rejected and also its consequence that they have motion by which they have been wandering and have been impelled every which way for all time. It may then be admitted that atoms are mobile and active (*actuosas*) from the power of moving and acting which God instilled in them at their very creation, and which functions with his assent, for he compels all things just as he conserves all things. By this means such an opinion is also quite correct just as others which attribute motion and activity to matter must be corrected; to be specific, ones like Plato's, which holds that matter wandered without shape from eternity until its movement was reduced to order by the demiurge. . . .

There is need of an answer to the various sorts of objections which were usually urged against the position of the atomists and were carefully assembled by Lactantius. . . .

In regard to the sorts of objections that are found in Lactantius, among other things he asks first "Where do these tiny seeds come from, or what is their origin?" "For, if all things come from them," he says, "we will ask where they themselves come from." We can answer that they come from God, the author of all things; but since he is attacking the ancients, and above all Epicurus, they would not be able to make any other answer than what Aristotle, Plato, and other pagans did who, unwilling to accept creation, or production, from nothing, said therefore that matter did not have a cause, or efficient principle, hence that it was uncreated, not made, and eternal; that therefore it was inappropriate to ask what was the material from which primary matter was made since something is called primary only because there is nothing prior to it from which it is made. Hence Epicurus said specifically that there is nothing prior to the atoms and no one should insist on knowing from what underlying material they are formed. . . .

Next Lactantius argues, "if the seeds are round and smooth, surely they will not be able to take hold of each other in order to make some body. If anyone wants to bind together grain into a single conglomerate, the very smoothness of the grains themselves does not permit their joining into a solid." Now he was not unaware that all atoms were not considered round and smooth; he knew there were also angular and hooked ones, so I need say no more about the others. Epicurus had said that those with round or smooth surfaces could at least be caught onto if they could not catch onto each other and could be enclosed in the angles and hooks of the others and thus be joined into a single mass or solid. And this could well appear to be the cause of evaporation in which particles that are smooth, or less angular and hooked, set themselves free and fly away, but others enmeshed in the angles and hooks stay fast and do not set themselves free unless by several twists until they finally leave. And this may well be the reason why water evaporates far more rapidly than oil, why lead melts more quickly than silver, and other things of a similar nature which it would be pointless to list. But, Lactantius says, "if they project angles and hooks, atoms are divisible and severable and so can be cut and torn apart." From what I have already said, you can guess that Epicurus would reply that neither the angles and hooks nor the main body of the atom can be severed because they are solid through and through, lacking any admixture of void.

He makes the further objection that "it may be that atoms will do as long as it is a matter of small things, but when it is a question of the universe, it is a sign of sheer madness to increase their number and to say that it is formed from them"; and having made mention of the infinity of worlds, he says "What great power the atoms must have had to assemble such immeasurable masses from such tiny parts!" But if we conceive the entire earth as some part of the universe in such a way that the universe could be constructed from several masses like the earth, we surely would also understand that the entire earth is made up of several masses such as Mount Atlas or the Caucasian Mountains. But by the same reasoning we would realize that a mountain is made up of the accumulation of several masses either of vast chunks of earth or of boulders, and likewise that boulders are made up of rocks, and larger rocks of little ones, and finally they are made of molecules which are like grains of sand; so that nothing prevents us from conceiving the entire universe as composed of particles no larger than grains of sand.

On this basis I alluded earlier to a proof of Archimedes by which it was demonstrated invincibly that even if the grains of sand were so small that a poppy seed would divide up into ten thousand particles equal to them, not only fifty-two zeros placed in a row after a one (1,000,000,000 etc.) would suffice to express the number of those grains of sand which would be enough to produce the entire universe according to its generally accepted dimensions; but also sixty-four would do to express the number which are adequate to fill up that incredible vastness to which Aristarchus and Copernicus expand the universe. Now if you wish to proceed to the tiny dimensions of the atoms, imagine that every one of these particles is composed of ten hundred thousand of the most minute particles, then multiply this times the number with sixty-four zeros, and the number of the particles is expressed by no more than seventy zeros. And if you do not yet think that they are wholly beyond being divided into parts, split every one of them into ten hundred thousand; and then when you have made the multiplication, the resulting figure will not exceed seventy-six figures. Proceed further if you wish to, and note how easily figures will always be available by which you may finally express the number of atoms from which the universe could be constructed.

He pursues his objections, "If all things are made from indivisible particles, nothing would ever require a seed of its type, but would be made haphazardly by atoms rushing about and flying in different directions, and so plants, trees, fruit, and all things could be generated without soil, without roots, without moisture, and without seeds; birds could be generated without eggs, eggs without being laid, and so forth." And so he turns against Lucretius his own verses (already quoted once) as if he had no understanding of them

> If things are made from nothing, any breed
> Might bear another, no need for its seed.[2]

But the poet would answer in one word that all things are not made from all other things because not all atoms are the same, and therefore do not have the capacity to form into the same bodies. From the atoms there are first formed certain molecules of differing configurations which are the seeds of different things, and then every thing is woven and constructed from its own seeds in such a way that it is not and cannot be made from other seeds. And since the earth contains the seeds of plants, fruits, and trees, they cannot grow without the earth or without roots by which such seeds are assimilated as nourishment or without moisture in which these seeds are dissolved, and so on for the others.

Lactantius rises to his height and asks further "whether the atoms of fire lie concealed even in iron and flint or in a glass bowl full of water exposed to the sun, since it is well known that fire is generated by these." The poet will answer that not only atoms, but also seeds of fire lie in the flint, which needs only to be uncovered to spread out and make the flame appear. He says further that such seeds are contained not so much in the water as in the sun's rays projected through the water, so that they need only to be brought together to show their fire, which the configuration of the bowl can produce. The same thing can be said concerning a liquid in which vapor is condensed, and which Lactantius opposes with a similar argument.

Finally he gathers various arguments to show that "the senses, thought, memory, the mind, genius, reason, and the like cannot result from tiny seeds"

---

[2]*De rerum natura*, I, 159–160.

and to prove that "the universe and all things are the effects of the deliberation and providence of God, and not of the chance concurrence of atoms and things related to them." These are special considerations. The first sort belong to the third section in which it is denied that the mind and human reason are derived from the atoms or corporeal configurations; and in regard to the senses and the faculties dependent on them it will be explained, rightly or wrongly, how sensate things like animals can be born from insensate things such as atoms. And the second objection regards mostly the matter of the following book in which it will be shown to follow from our premisses that nothing was created without the deliberation and providence of God, and if atoms were the instrument used, they coalesced into the magnificent work of the universe not by a chance concurrence, but according to divine disposition. This much then was to be said about the primary elements of matter.

Pierre Gassendi

FIFTH OBJECTIONS TO DESCARTES' *MEDITATIONS*

Descartes and Gassendi clashed over their differing theories of the nature of matter. Gassendi summarized his objections to Descartes' *Meditations* in *Fifth Objections to Descartes'* Meditations, in which he addressed Descartes as "Mind." Descartes answered Gassendi's points in the selection that follows, from "Concerning Objections to the Sixth Meditation."

3. . . . *For finally you say*: And although possibly (or rather certainly, as I shall say in a moment) I possess a body with which I am very intimately conjoined, yet because on the one side I have a clear and distinct idea of myself, inasmuch as I am only a thinking and not an extended thing, and on the other I possess a distinct idea of body, inasmuch as it is only an extended and not a thinking thing; it is certain that I am really distinct from my body, and can exist without it.

So this was your objective, was it? Hence, since the whole of the difficulty hinges on this, we must halt awhile, in order to see how you manage to make this position good. The principal matter here in question is the distinction between you and body. But what body do you here mean? Plainly this solid body composed of members, the body to which, without doubt, the following words refer: I possess a body connected with myself and it is certain that I am distinct from my body, etc.

But now, O Mind, there is no difficulty about this body. There would be a difficulty, if with the greater part of philosophers I were to object that you were the realisation, the perfection, the activity, the form, the appearance, or, to use a popular fashion of speech, a mode of the body. They, forsooth, do not acknowledge that you are more distinct and separable from your body than figure, or any other mode. This, too, they maintain, whether you are the entire soul, or are besides also νοῦς δυνάμει, νοῦς παθητικός, *the potential intellect, or passive intellect, as they style it. But it pleases me to deal somewhat liberally with you and consider you as though you were the* νοῦς ποιητικός, *the active intellect, nay, even as* χωριστός, *i.e. capable of separate existence, though separable in another sense than they imagined.*

For since those philosophers assigned it to all men (if not rather to all things) as something common to them and as being the source of intellectual activity on the part of the potential intellect, exactly in the same way and with the same necessity as light supplies the eye with the opportunity of seeing (whence they were wont to compare it to the light of the sun, and hence to regard it as coming from without), I myself rather consider you (as you also are quite willing I should) as a certain special intellect exercising domination in the body.

Moreover I repeat that the difficulty is not as to whether you are separable or not from this body (whence, shortly before, I hinted that it was not necessary to recur to the power of God in order to secure the separability of those things which you apprehend as separate), but from the body which you yourself are: seeing that possibly you really are a subtle body diffused within that solid one, or occupying some seat within it. But you have not yet convinced us that you are anything absolutely incorporeal. Likewise, though in the second Meditation you proclaimed that you are not a wind, nor a fire, nor a vapour, nor a breath, do be advised of the warning I give you, that the statement thus announced has not been proved.

You said that you did not at that point dispute about those matters; but you have not subsequently discussed them, nor have you in any way proved that you are not a body of this kind. I had hoped that here you would make the matter good; but if you do discuss anything, if you do prove anything, your discussion and proof merely show that you are not the solid body, about which, as I have already said, there is no difficulty.

4. But, *you say,* I have on the one hand a clear and distinct idea of myself, in so far as I am merely a thinking thing and not extended, and on the other a distinct idea of body, in so far as it is an extended thing, but not one that thinks. *Firstly, however, in so far as the idea of body is concerned, there appears to be no need for spending much pains over it. For, if you indeed make this pronouncement about the idea of body universally, we must repeat our previous objection, namely that you have to prove that it is incompatible with the nature of body to be capable of thinking. Thus it would be a begging of the question when the problem was raised by you* as to whether you are a subtle body or not, *in a way that implied that thought is incompatible with body.*

But since you make that assertion and certainly treat only of that solid body, from which you maintain that you are separable and distinct, I do not on that account so much deny that you have an idea of yourself, as maintain that you could not possess it if you were really an unextended thing. For, I ask you, how do you think that you, an unextended subject, could receive into yourself the semblance or idea of a body which is extended? For, if such a semblance proceeds from the body, it is certainly corporeal and has parts outside of other parts, and consequently is corporeal. Or alternatively, whether or not its impression is due to some other source, since necessarily it always represents an extended body, it must still have parts and, consequently, be extended. Otherwise, if it has no parts, how will it represent parts? If it has no extension how will it represent extension? If devoid of figure, how represent an object possessing figure? If it has no position, how can it represent a thing which has upper and lower, right and left, and intermediate parts? If without variation, how represent the various colours, etc.? Therefore an idea appears not to lack extension utterly. But unless it is devoid of extension how can you, if unextended, be its subject? How will you unite it to you? How lay hold of it? How will you be able to feel it gradually fade and finally vanish away?

Next, relatively to your idea of yourself nothing is to be added to what has been already said, and especially in the second Meditation. For thence it is proved that, far from having a clear and distinct idea of yourself, you seem to be wholly without one. This is because, even though you recognise that you think, you do not know of what nature you, who think, are. Hence, since this operation alone is known to you, the chief matter is, nevertheless, hidden from you, namely, the substance which so operates. This brings up the comparison in which you may be likened to a blind man, who, on feeling heat, and being told that it proceeds from the sun, should think that he has a clear and distinct idea of the sun, inasmuch as, if anyone ask him what the sun is, he can reply: it is something which produces heat.

But, you will say, I here add not only that I am a thinking thing, but that I am a thing which is not extended. But not to mention that this is asserted without proof, since it is still in question, I ask firstly: for all that have you a clear and distinct idea of yourself? You say that you are not extended; but in so doing you say what you are not, not what you are. In order to have a clear and distinct idea, or, what is the same thing, a true and genuine idea of anything, is it not necessary to know the thing itself positively, and so to speak affirmatively, or does it suffice to know that it is not any other thing? Would it not then be a clear and distinct idea of Bucephalus, if one knew of him that he was not a fly?

But, not to urge this, my question is rather: are you not an extended thing, or are you not diffused throughout the body? I cannot tell what you will reply; for, though from the outset I recognised that you existed only in the brain, I formed that belief rather by conjecture than by directly following your opinion. I derived my conjecture from the statement which ensues, in which you assert, that you are not affected by all parts of the body, but only by the brain, or even by one of its smallest parts. But I was not quite certain whether you were found therefore only in the brain or in a part of it, since you might be found in the whole body, but be acted on at only one part. Thus it would be according to the popular belief, which takes the soul to be diffused through the entire body, while yet it is in the eye alone that it has vision.

Similarly the following words moved one to doubt: "and, although the whole mind seems to be united to the whole body," etc. You indeed do not there assert that you are united with the whole of the body, but you do not deny it. Howsoever it be, with your leave let me consider you firstly as diffused throughout the whole body. Whether you are the same as the soul, or something diverse from it, I ask you, O unextended thing, what you are that are spread from head to heel, or that are coextensive with the body, that have a like number of parts corresponding to its parts? Will you say that you are therefore unextended, because you are a whole in a whole, and are wholly in every part? I pray you tell me, if you maintain this, how you conceive it. Can a single thing thus be at the same time wholly in several parts? Faith assures us of this in the case of the sacred mystery (of the Eucharist). But the question here is relative to you, a natural object, and is indeed one relative to our natural light. Can we grasp how there can be a plurality of places without there being a plurality of objects located in them? Is not a hundred more than one? Likewise, if a thing is wholly in one place, can it be in others, unless it is itself outside itself, as place is outside place? Say what you will, it will at least be obscure and uncertain whether you are wholly in any part and not rather in the various parts of the body by means of your several parts. And since it is much more evident that nothing can exist as a whole in different places, it will turn out to be still more clear that you are not wholly in the single parts of your body but merely in the whole as a whole, and that you are so by means of your parts diffused through the whole and consequently that you have extension.

Secondly let us suppose that you are in the brain alone, or merely in some minute part of it. You perceive that the same thing is clearly an objection, since, however small that part be, it is nevertheless extended, and you are coextensive with it, and consequently are extended and have particular parts corresponding to its particular parts. Will you say that you take that part of the brain to be a point? That is surely incredible, but suppose it is a point. If it is indeed something Physical, the same difficulty remains, because such a point is extended and is certainly not devoid of parts. If it is a Mathematical point you know that it is given only by the imagination. But let it be given or let rather us feign that in the brain there is given a Mathematical point, to which you are united, and in which you exist. Now, see how useless a fiction this will turn out to be. For, if it is to be assumed, we must feign it to exist in such a way that you are at the meeting place of the nerves by which all the regions informed by the soul transmit to the brain the ideas or semblances of the things perceived by the senses. But firstly, the nerves do not all meet at one point, whether for the reason that, as the brain is continued into the spinal marrow, many nerves all over the back pass into that, or because those which extend to the middle of the head are not found to terminate in the same part of the brain. But let us assume that they all do meet; none the less they cannot all unite in a mathematical point, since they are bodies, not mathematical lines, and so able to meet in a mathematical point. And supposing we grant that they do so unite, it will be impossible for the spirits which pass through these to pass out of the nerves or to enter them, as being bodies; since body cannot be in or pass through what is not a place, as the mathematical point is. But though we should allow that the animal spirits do exist in or pass through what is not a place, nevertheless you, existing as you do in a point, in which there are neither right hand parts nor left hand, neither higher nor lower, nor anything similar, cannot judge as to whence they come nor what they report.

Moreover I say the same thing of those spirits which you must transmit in order to have feeling or to report tidings, and in order to move. I omit that we cannot grasp how you impress a motion upon them, you who are yourself in a point, unless you are really a body, or unless you have a body by which you are in contact with them and at the same time propel them. For, if you say that they are moved by themselves, and that you only direct their motion, remember that you somewhere else denied that the body is moved by itself; so that we must thence infer that you are the cause of that movement. Next, explain to us how such a direction can take place without some effort and so some motion on your part? How can there be effort directed towards anything, and motion on its part, without mutual contact of what moves and what is moved? How can there be contact apart from body, when (as is so clear to the natural light)

"Apart from body, naught touches or is touched?"

Yet why do I delay here when it is on you that the onus rests of proving that you are unextended and hence incorporeal? But neither do I think that you will find an argument in the fact that man is popularly said to consist of soul and body, inferring that if one part is *said to be body, the other must be declared not to be body. For, if you did so, you would give us an opportunity of drawing the distinction in such a way that man should be held to consist of a double body, viz. the solid one and the subtle one; and according to this scheme while the former retained the name body, the common term, the other would be given the name soul. I pass by the fact that the same thing would be said about the other animals, to which you have not granted a mind similar to your own; lucky they, if by your sanction they possess even a soul! Hence, therefore, when you conclude* that you are certain that you are really distinct from your body, *you see that that would be admitted, but that it would not therefore be conceded that you were incorporeal, and not rather a species of very subtle body distinct from your grosser body.*

You add *that hence you can exist apart from it? But after being conceded the point that you can exist apart from that grosser body in the same way as an odoriferous vapour does while passing out of an apple and dispersing into the air, what do you think you have gained? Something more certainly than the above mentioned Philosophers wish to prove, who believe that you wholly perish at death itself; being as it were like a figure which on the alteration of the superficies so disappears, that it may be said to be non-existent or wholly nothing. Indeed, since you were something corporeal as well, or a fine substance, you will not be said to vanish wholly at death, or wholly to pass into nothing, but to exist by means of your dispersed parts, howsoever much, on account of being thus drawn asunder, you are not likely to think any more, and will be said to be neither a thinking thing, nor a mind, nor a soul. Yet all these objections I bring, not in order to cast doubt on the conclusion you intend to prove, but merely by way of expressing my disagreement as to the cogency of the argument set forth by you.*

5. *In connection with this, you interpose several things tending to the same conclusion, on all of which we need not insist. One thing I note, and that is that you say* that nature teaches you by the sensation of pain, hunger, thirst, etc., that you are not lodged in the body as a sailor in a ship, but that you are very closely united with it and, so to speak, intermingled with it so as to compose one whole along with it. For if that were not the case, *you say,* "when my body is hurt, I who am merely a thinking thing would not feel pain, but should perceive the wound with the mere understanding, just as the sailor perceives by sight when something is damaged in his vessel, and when my body has need of food or drink, I should clearly understand this fact, and not have the confused feelings of hunger and thirst. For all these sensations of hunger, thirst, pain, etc. are in truth none other than certain confused modes of thought which are produced by the union and apparent intermingling of mind and body."

This is indeed quite right; but it still remains to be explained, how that union and apparent intermingling, *or* confusion, *can be found in you, if you are incorporeal, unextended and indivisible. For if you are not greater than a point, how can you be united with the entire body, which is of such great magnitude? How, at least, can you be united with the brain, or some minute part in it, which (as has been said) must yet have some magnitude or extension, however small it be? If you are wholly without parts, how can you mix or appear to mix with its minute subdivisions? For there is no mixture unless each of the things to be mixed* has parts that can mix with one another. Further, if you are discrete, how could you be involved with and form one thing along with matter itself? Again since conjunction or union exists between certain parts, ought there not to be a relation of similarity between parts of this sort? But what must the union of the corporeal with the incorporeal be thought to be? Do we conceive how stone and air are fused together, as in pumice stone, so as to become a fusion of uniform character? Yet the similarity between stone and air which itself is also a body, is greater than that between body and soul, or a wholly incorporeal mind.

René Descartes

MEDITATIONS ON FIRST PHILOSOPHY: REPLIES AND OBJECTIONS

CONCERNING THE OBJECTIONS TO THE SIXTH MEDITATION

1. I have already dealt with the objection *that material things as the objects of pure mathematics do not exist.*

Moreover it is false that the thinking of a Chiliagon is confused; for many deductions can be drawn from it most clearly and distinctly, which would not occur if it were perceived only in a confused manner or, as you say, merely *in respect of the force of the name.* But as a matter of fact we perceive the whole figure at the same time clearly although we are not able to imagine it as a whole at the same time; which proves that the two powers of understanding and imagining differ, not so much in respect of more and less, but as two wholly diverse modes of operation. Thus, in thinking, the mind employs itself alone, but in imagining it contemplates a corporeal form. And though geometrical figures are wholly corporeal, nevertheless the ideas by which they are understood, when they do not fall under the imagination, are not on that account to be reckoned corporeal.

Finally it is worthy of you alone, O flesh, to think *that the idea of God, of an Angel, and of the human mind, are corporeal, or after the fashion of the corporeal, derived forsooth from the human form, and from other very subtle, simple, and imperceptible objects, such as air or aether.* For whosoever thus represents God or the mind to himself, tries to imagine a thing which is not imageable, and constructs nothing but a corporeal idea to which he falsely assigns the name God or mind. For, in the true idea of mind, nothing is contained but thought and its attributes, of which none is corporeal.

2. In this passage you show very clearly that you rely on prejudices merely and never divest yourself of them, when you wish to make out that we suspect no falsity in matters in which we have never detected falsity; it is thus that, *when we behold a tower close at hand and touch it, we are sure that it is square,* if it appear to

be square; so too when we are really awake *we cannot doubt whether we are awake or dreaming*; and so forth. Now you have no reason to think that all the things in which error can reside have been noticed by you, and it could easily be proved that you sometimes are wrong about those things which you accept as certain. But when you come round to the position at which you state, *that at least we cannot doubt that things appear as they do*, you have returned to the true path; your statement is one that I have myself made in the second Meditation. But here the question raised concerned the reality of external objects, and in what you have contributed to this there is nothing correct.

3. I shall not here delay to notice your tedious and frequent repetitions of such statements as, e.g. *that I have failed to prove certain matters*, which nevertheless I have demonstrated; *that I have treated only of the solid body*, though I have dealt with every kind of matter, even of the subtlest; etc. What opposition other than a plain denial is merited by affirmations of this kind, which are not supported by reasons? Yet incidentally I should like to discover what argument you use to prove that I have treated of solid matter rather than of that which is subtle. Have I not said: "I *possess (a body) united with myself, and it is certain that I am distinct from my body*"? And I cannot see why these words are not equally applicable to an impalpable and to a solid body; nor do I think that anyone but you could fail to see this. Apart from this, in the second Meditation I made it evident that mind could be understood as an existing substance, though we did not understand anything to exist that was wind, or fire, or vapour, or breath, or anything else of a bodily nature however impalpable and refined. I said however that at that point I did not discuss whether it was in truth distinct from every kind of body; but in the present passage I did discuss the matter and proved my assertion. But you show that you have wholly failed to comprehend the controversy by your confusion of the issue as to what may be known of the soul with the question as to that which the soul really is.

4. Here you ask, *how I think that I, an unextended subject, can receive into myself the resemblance or idea of a thing which is extended*. I reply that no corporeal resemblance can be received in the mind, but that what occurs there is the pure thinking of a thing, whether it be corporeal or equally whether it be one that is incorporeal and lacking any corporeal semblance. But as to imagination, which can only be exercised in reference to corporeal things, my opinion is that it requires the presence of a semblance which is truly corporeal, and to which the mind applies itself, without, however, its being received in the mind.

Your statement *about the idea of the sun, which a blind man can derive merely from the sun's warmth*, is easily refuted. For the blind man can have a clear and distinct idea of the sun as a source of heat although he does not possess the idea of it as a source of light. Nor is your comparison of me to that blind man just: firstly, because the act of knowledge which apprehends a thing that thinks is much more extensive than our apprehension of a thing which warms, as it is much more than that of anything else, as was shown in its proper place; secondly, because no one can prove that that idea of the sun which the blind man forms, does not contain everything which can be learned of the sun, save those who, being endowed with sight, are aware in addition of its light and figure. You, however, not only know nothing more than I do of mind, but do not even have knowledge of the very thing I recognize in it; so that in this comparison it is rather you who play the part of blind man, while I, along with the whole human race, could at most be said to be one-eyed.

In adding that *the mind is not extended,* my intention was not thereby to explain what mind is, but merely to proclaim that those people are wrong who think that it is extended. In the same way if any people affirmed *that Bucephalus was Music,* it would not be idle of others to deny the statement. In good truth your subsequent attempts to prove that mind is extended because it makes use of a body which is extended, seem to employ no better reasoning than if you were to argue that because Bucephalus neighs and whinnies, and so utters sounds that are comparable with Music, it followed that Bucephalus is Music. For, though mind is united with the whole body, it does not follow that it itself is extended throughout the body, because it is not part of its notion to be extended, but merely to think. Neither does it apprehend extension by means of an extended semblance existing in it, although it images it by applying itself to a corporeal semblance which is extended, as has already been said. Finally there is no necessity for it itself to be a body although it has the power of moving body.

5. What you say at this point *relatively to the union of mind and body* is similar to what precedes. At no place do you bring an objection to my arguments; you only set forth the doubts which you think follow from my conclusions, though they arise merely from your wishing to subject to the scrutiny of the imagination matters which, by their own nature, do not fall under it. Thus when you wish to compare the union of mind and body with the mixture of two bodies, it is enough for me to reply that no such comparison ought to be set up, because the two things are wholly diverse, and we must not imagine that there are parts in mind because it is aware of parts in body. Whence do you derive the conclusion that everything which mind knows must exist in mind? If that were so, then, when it was aware of the magnitude of the earth, it would be obliged to have that object within it, and consequently would not only be extended but greater in extent than the whole world.

6. Here though you do not contradict me at all, you have nevertheless much to say; and hence the reader may discover that the number of your arguments is not to be inferred from any proportion between them and the prolixity of your words.

Up to this point we have had a discussion between mind and flesh, and, as was but natural, in many things they disagreed. But now, at the end, I catch sight of the real Gassendi, and look up to him as a man of great philosophical eminence. I salute him as a man noted for his intellectual candour and integrity of life, and shall endeavour, by employing all the courtesies which I can muster, to merit his friendship at all times. I therefore ask him not to take it amiss if, in replying to his objections, I have used a Philosophical freedom, since their entire contents caused me very great pleasure. Among other things I rejoiced that such a long and carefully composed dissertation contained nothing in opposition to my reasoning, nothing opposed even to my conclusions, to which I was not able very easily to reply.

George Berkeley

THREE DIALOGUES BETWEEN HYLAS AND PHILONOUS IN OPPOSITION TO SKEPTICS AND ATHEISTS

George Berkeley (1685–1753), Bishop of Cloyne in Ireland, developed a startling view known as *immaterialism*. He argued that matter, in the sense discussed by philosophers, was meaningless and that the world consisted only of minds and their ideas. In his *Three Dialogues between Hylas and Philonous* . . . , he set forth arguments for his view. Philonous ("lover of mind") represents Berkeley and Hylas ("matter") Berkeley's opponents.

HYLAS: I am glad to find there was nothing in the accounts I heard of you.

PHILONOUS: Pray, what were those?

HYLAS: You were represented in last night's conversation as one who maintained the most extravagant opinion that ever entered into the mind of man, to wit, that there is no such thing as *material substance* in the world.

PHILONOUS: That there is no such thing as what philosophers call "material substance," I am seriously persuaded; but if I were made to see anything absurd or skeptical in this, I should then have the same reason to renounce this that I imagine I have now to reject the contrary opinion.

HYLAS: What! Can anything be more fantastical, more repugnant to common sense or a more manifest piece of skepticism than to believe there is no such thing as matter?

PHILONOUS: Softly, good Hylas. What if it should prove that you, who hold there is, are, by virtue of that opinion, a greater skeptic and maintain more paradoxes and repugnancies to common sense than I who believe no such thing?

HYLAS: You may as soon persuade me the part is greater than the whole, as that, in order to avoid absurdity and skepticism, I should ever be obliged to give up my opinion in this point.

PHILONOUS: Well, then, are you content to admit that opinion for true which, upon examination, shall appear most agreeable to common sense and remote from skepticism?

HYLAS: With all my heart. Since you are for raising disputes about the plainest things in nature, I am content for once to hear what you have to say.

PHILONOUS: Pray, Hylas, what do you mean by a "skeptic"?

HYLAS: I mean what all men mean, one that doubts of everything.

PHILONOUS: He then who entertains no doubt concerning some particular point, with regard to that point cannot be thought a skeptic. . . . What think you of distrusting the senses, of denying the real existence of sensible things, or pretending to know nothing of them. Is not this sufficient to denominate a man a skeptic?

PHILONOUS: Shall we therefore examine which of us it is that denies the reality of sensible things or professes the greatest ignorance of them, since, if I take you rightly, he is to be esteemed the greatest skeptic?

HYLAS: That is what I desire.

PHILONOUS: What mean you by "sensible things"?

HYLAS: Those things which are perceived by the senses. Can you imagine that I mean anything else?

PHILONOUS: Pardon me, Hylas, if I am desirous clearly to apprehend your notions, since this may much shorten our inquiry. Suffer me then to ask you this further question. Are those things only perceived by the senses which are perceived immediately? Or may those things properly be said to be "sensible" which are perceived mediately, or not without the intervention of others?

HYLAS: I do not sufficiently understand you.

PHILONOUS: In reading a book, what I immediately perceive are the letters, but mediately, or by means of these, are suggested to my mind the notions of God, virtue, truth, etc. Now, that the letters are truly sensible things, or perceived by sense, there is no doubt; but I would know whether you take the things suggested by them to be so too.

HYLAS: No, certainly; it were absurd to think God or virtue sensible things, though they may be signified and suggested to the mind by sensible marks with which they have an arbitrary connection.

PHILONOUS: It seems then, that by "sensible things" you mean those only which can be perceived immediately by sense.

HYLAS: Right.

PHILONOUS: Does it not follow from this that, though I see one part of the sky red, another blue, and that my reason does thence evidently conclude there must be some cause of that diversity of colors, yet that cause cannot be said to be a sensible thing or perceived by the sense of seeing?

HYLAS: It does.

PHILONOUS: In like manner, though I hear variety of sounds, yet I cannot be said to hear the causes of those sounds.

HYLAS: You cannot.

PHILONOUS: And when by my touch I perceive a thing to be hot and heavy, I cannot say, with any truth or propriety, that I feel the cause of its heat or weight.

HYLAS: To prevent any more questions of this kind, I tell you once for all that by "sensible things" I mean those only which are perceived by sense, and that in truth the senses perceive nothing which they do not perceive immediately, for they make no inferences. The deducing therefore of causes or occasions from effects and appearances, which alone are perceived by sense, entirely relates to reason.

PHILONOUS: This point then is agreed between us—that *sensible things are those only which are immediately perceived by sense*. You will further inform me whether we immediately perceive by sight anything besides light and colors and figures; or by hearing, anything but sounds; by the palate, anything besides tastes; by smell, besides odors; or by the touch, more than tangible qualities.

HYLAS: We do not.

PHILONOUS: It seems, therefore, that if you take away all sensible qualities, there remains nothing sensible?

HYLAS: I grant it.

PHILONOUS: Sensible things therefore are nothing else but so many sensible qualities or combinations of sensible qualities?

HYLAS: Nothing else.

PHILONOUS: Heat is then a sensible thing?

HYLAS: Certainly.

PHILONOUS: Does the reality of sensible things consist in being perceived, or is it something distinct from their being perceived, and that bears no relation to the mind?

HYLAS: To *exist* is one thing, and to be *perceived* is another.

PHILONOUS: I speak with regard to sensible things only; and of these I ask, whether by their real existence you mean a subsistence exterior to the mind and distinct from their being perceived?

HYLAS: I mean a real absolute being, distinct from and without any relation to their being perceived.

PHILONOUS: Heat therefore, if it be allowed a real being, must exist without the mind?

HYLAS: It must.

PHILONOUS: Tell me, Hylas, is this real existence equally compatible to all degrees of heat, which we perceive, or is there any reason why we should attribute it to some and deny it to others? And if there be, pray let me know that reason.

HYLAS: Whatever degree of heat we perceive by sense, we may be sure the same exists in the object that occasions it.

PHILONOUS: What! the greatest as well as the least?

HYLAS: I tell you, the reason is plainly the same in respect of both: they are both perceived by sense; nay, the greater degree of heat is more sensibly perceived; and consequently, if there is any difference, we are more certain of its real existence than we can be of the reality of a lesser degree.

PHILONOUS: But is not the most vehement and intense degree of heat a very great pain?

HYLAS: No one can deny it.

PHILONOUS: And is any unperceiving thing capable of pain or pleasure?

HYLAS: No, certainly.

PHILONOUS: Is your material substance a senseless being or a being endowed with sense and perception?

HYLAS: It is senseless, without doubt.

PHILONOUS: It cannot, therefore, be the subject of pain?

HYLAS: By no means.

PHILONOUS: Nor, consequently, of the greatest heat perceived by sense, since you acknowledge this to be no small pain?

HYLAS: I grant it.

PHILONOUS: What shall we say then of your external object: is it a material substance or no?

HYLAS: It is a material substance with the sensible qualities inhering in it.

PHILONOUS: How then can a great heat exist in it, since you own it cannot in a material substance? I desire you would clear this point.

HYLAS: Hold, Philonous, I fear I was out in yielding intense heat to be a pain. It should seem rather that pain is something distinct from heat, and the consequence or effect of it.

PHILONOUS: Upon putting your hand near the fire, do you perceive one simple uniform sensation or two distinct sensations?

HYLAS: But one simple sensation.

PHILONOUS: Is not the heat immediately perceived?

HYLAS: It is.

PHILONOUS: And the pain?

HYLAS: True.

PHILONOUS: Seeing therefore they are both immediately perceived at the same time, and the fire affects you only with one simple or uncompounded idea, it follows that this same simple idea is both the intense heat immediately perceived and the pain; and, consequently, that the intense heat immediately perceived is nothing distinct from a particular sort of pain.

HYLAS: It seems so.

PHILONOUS: Again, try in your thoughts, Hylas, if you can conceive a vehement sensation to be without pain or pleasure.

HYLAS: I cannot.

PHILONOUS: Or can you frame to yourself an idea of sensible pain or pleasure, in general, abstracted from every particular idea of heat, cold, tastes, smells, etc.

HYLAS: I do not find that I can.

PHILONOUS: Does it not therefore follow that sensible pain is nothing distinct from those sensations or ideas—in an intense degree?

HYLAS: It is undeniable; and, to speak the truth, I begin to suspect a very great heat cannot exist but in a mind perceiving it.

PHILONOUS: What! are you then in that *skeptical* state of suspense, between affirming and denying?

HYLAS: I think I may be positive in the point. A very violent and painful heat cannot exist without the mind.

PHILONOUS: It has not therefore, according to you, any real being?

HYLAS: I own it.

PHILONOUS: Is it therefore certain that there is no body in nature really hot?

HYLAS: I have not denied there is any real heat in bodies. I only say there is no such thing as an intense real heat.

PHILONOUS: But did you not say before that all degrees of heat were equally real, or, if there was any difference, that the greater were more undoubtedly real than the lesser?

HYLAS: True; but it was because I did not then consider the ground there is for distinguishing between them, which I now plainly see. And it is this: because intense heat is nothing else but a particular kind of painful sensation, and pain cannot exist but in a perceiving being, it follows that no intense heat can really exist in an unperceiving corporeal substance. But this is no reason why we should deny heat in an inferior degree to exist in such a substance.

PHILONOUS: But how shall we be able to discern those degrees of heat which exist only in the mind from those which exist without it?

HYLAS: That is no difficult matter. You know the least pain cannot exist unperceived; whatever, therefore, degree of heat is a pain exists only in the mind. But as for all other degrees of heat nothing obliges us to think the same of them.

PHILONOUS: I think you granted before that no unperceiving being was capable of pleasure any more than of pain.

HYLAS: I did.

PHILONOUS: And is not warmth, or a more gentle degree of heat than what causes uneasiness, a pleasure?

HYLAS: What then?

PHILONOUS: Consequently, it cannot exist without the mind in any unper- ceiving substance, or body.

HYLAS: So it seems.

PHILONOUS: Since, therefore, as well those degrees of heat that are not pain- ful, as those that are, can exist only in a thinking substance, may we not conclude that external bodies are absolutely incapable of any degree of heat whatsoever? . . .

HYLAS: Well, since it must be so, I am content to yield this point and acknowledge that heat and cold are only sensations existing in our minds. But there still remain qualities enough to secure the reality of external things.

PHILONOUS: But what will you say, Hylas, if it shall appear that the case is the same with regard to all other sensible qualities, and that they can no more be supposed to exist without the mind than heat and cold?

HYLAS: Then, indeed, you will have done something to the purpose; but that is what I despair of seeing proved.

PHILONOUS: Let us examine them in order. What think you of tastes—do they exist without the mind, or no?

HYLAS: Can any man in his senses doubt whether sugar is sweet, or wormwood bitter?

PHILONOUS: Inform me, Hylas. Is a sweet taste a particular kind of pleasure or pleasant sensation, or is it not?

HYLAS: It is.

PHILONOUS: And is not bitterness some kind of uneasiness or pain?

HYLAS: I grant it.

PHILONOUS: If, therefore, sugar and wormwood are unthinking corporeal sub- stances existing without the mind, how can sweetness and bitter- ness, that is, pleasure and pain, agree to them?

HYLAS: Hold, Philonous. I now see what it was [that] deluded me all this time. You asked whether heat and cold, sweetness and bitterness, were not particular sorts of pleasure and pain; to which I an- swered simply that they were. Whereas I should have thus distin- guished: those qualities as perceived by us are pleasures or pains, but not as existing in the external objects. We must not therefore conclude absolutely that there is no heat in the fire or sweetness in the sugar, but only that heat or sweetness, as per- ceived by us, are not in the fire or sugar. What say you to this?

PHILONOUS: I say it is nothing to the purpose. Our discourse proceeded alto- gether concerning sensible things, which you defined to be "the things we immediately perceive by our senses." Whatever other qualities, therefore, you speak of, as distinct from these, I know nothing of them, neither do they at all belong to the point in dispute. You may, indeed, pretend to have discovered certain qualities which you do not perceive and assert those insensible qualities exist in fire and sugar. But what use can be made of this to your present purpose, I am at a loss to conceive. Tell me then once more, do you acknowledge that heat and cold, sweetness and bitterness (meaning those qualities which are perceived by the senses), do not exist without the mind?

HYLAS: I see it is to no purpose to hold out, so I give up the cause as to those mentioned qualities, though I profess it sounds oddly to say that sugar is not sweet.

PHILONOUS: But, for your further satisfaction, take this along with you: that which at other times seems sweet shall, to a distempered palate, appear bitter. And nothing can be plainer than that divers persons perceive different tastes in the same food, since that which one man delights in, another abhors. And how could this be if the taste was something really inherent in the food?

HYLAS: I acknowledge I know not how.

PHILONOUS: In the next place, odors are to be considered. And with regard to these I would fain know whether what has been said of tastes does not exactly agree to them? Are they not so many pleasing or displeasing sensations?

HYLAS: They are.

PHILONOUS: Can you then conceive it possible that they should exist in an unperceiving thing?

HYLAS: I cannot.

PHILONOUS: Or can you imagine that filth and ordure affect those brute animals that feed on them out of choice with the same smells which we perceive in them?

HYLAS: By no means.

PHILONOUS: May we not therefore conclude of smells, as of the other forementioned qualities, that they cannot exist in any but a perceiving substance or mind?

HYLAS: I think so.

PHILONOUS: Then as to sounds, what must we think of them, are they accidents really inherent in external bodies or not?

HYLAS: That they inhere not in the sonorous bodies is plain from hence; because a bell struck in the exhausted receiver of an air pump sends forth no sound. The air, therefore, must be thought the subject of sound.

PHILONOUS: What reason is there for that, Hylas?

HYLAS: Because, when any motion is raised in the air, we perceive a sound greater or lesser, in proportion to the air's motion; but without some motion in the air we never hear any sound at all.

PHILONOUS: And granting that we never hear a sound but when some motion is produced in the air, yet I do not see how you can infer from thence that the sound itself is in the air.

HYLAS: It is this very motion in the external air that produces in the mind the sensation of sound. For, striking on the drum of the ear, it causes a vibration which by the auditory nerves being communicated to the brain, the soul is thereupon affected with the sensation called "sound."

PHILONOUS: What! is sound then a sensation?

HYLAS: I tell you, as perceived by us it is a particular sensation in the mind.

PHILONOUS: And can any sensation exist without the mind?

HYLAS: No, certainly.

PHILONOUS: How then can sound, being a sensation, exist in the air if by the "air" you mean a senseless substance existing without the mind? . . .

HYLAS: To deal ingenuously, I do not like it. And, after the concessions already made, I had as well grant that sounds, too, have no real being without the mind.

PHILONOUS: And I hope you will make no difficulty to acknowledge the same of colors.

HYLAS: Pardon me; the case of colors is very different. Can anything be plainer than that we see them on the objects?

PHILONOUS: The objects you speak of are, I suppose, corporeal substances existing without the mind?

HYLAS: They are.

PHILONOUS: And have true and real colors inhering in them?

HYLAS: Each visible object has that color which we see in it.

PHILONOUS: How! is there anything visible but what we perceive by sight?

HYLAS: There is not.

PHILONOUS: And do we perceive anything by sense which we do not perceive immediately?

HYLAS: How often must I be obliged to repeat the same thing? I tell you, we do not.

PHILONOUS: Have patience, good Hylas, and tell me once more whether there is anything immediately perceived by the senses except sensible qualities. I know you asserted there was not; but I would now be informed whether you still persist in the same opinion.

HYLAS: I do.

PHILONOUS: Pray, is your corporeal substance either a sensible quality or made up of sensible qualities?

HYLAS: What a question that is! Who ever thought it was?

PHILONOUS: My reason for asking was, because in saying "each visible object has that color which we see in it," you make visible objects to be corporeal substances, which implies either that corporeal substances are sensible qualities or else that there is something besides sensible qualities perceived by sight; but as this point was formerly agreed between us, and is still maintained by you, it is a clear consequence that your corporeal substance is nothing distinct from sensible qualities.

HYLAS: You may draw as many absurd consequences as you please and endeavor to perplex the plainest things, but you shall never persuade me out of my senses. I clearly understand my own meaning.

PHILONOUS: I wish you would make me understand it, too. But, since you are unwilling to have your notion of corporeal substance examined, I shall urge that point no further. Only be pleased to let me know whether the same colors which we see exist in external bodies or some other.

HYLAS: The very same.

PHILONOUS: What! are then the beautiful red and purple we see on yonder clouds really in them? Or do you imagine they have in themselves any other form than that of a dark mist or vapor?

HYLAS: I must own, Philonous, those colors are not really in the clouds as they seem to be at this distance. They are only apparent colors.

PHILONOUS: "Apparent" call you them? How shall we distinguish these apparent colors from real?

HYLAS: Very easily. Those are to be thought apparent which, appearing only at a distance, vanish upon a nearer approach. . . .

PHILONOUS: The point will be past all doubt if you consider that, in case colors were real properties or affections inherent in external bodies, they could admit of no alteration without some change wrought in the very bodies themselves; but is it not evident from what has been said that, upon the use of microscopes, upon a change happening in the humors of the eye, or a variation of distance, without any manner of real alteration in the thing itself, the colors of any object are either changed or totally disappear? Nay, all other circumstances remaining the same, change but the situation of some objects and they shall present different colors to the eye. The same thing happens upon viewing an object in various degrees of light. And what is more known than that the same bodies appear differently colored by candlelight from what they do in the open day? Add to these the experiment of a prism which, separating the heterogeneous rays of light, alters the color of any object and will cause the whitest to appear of a deep blue or red to the naked eye. And now tell me whether you are still of opinion that every body has its true real color inhering in it; and if you think it has, I would fain know further from you what certain distance and position of the object, what peculiar texture and formation of the eye, what degree or kind of light is necessary for ascertaining that true color and distinguishing it from apparent ones.

HYLAS: I own myself entirely satisfied that they are all equally apparent and that there is no such thing as color really inhering in external bodies, but that it is altogether in the light. And what confirms me in this opinion is that in proportion to the light colors are still more or less vivid; and if there be no light, then are there no colors perceived. Besides, allowing there are colors on external objects, yet, how is it possible for us to perceive them? For no external body affects the mind unless it acts first on our organs of sense. But the only action of bodies is motion, and motion cannot be communicated otherwise than by impulse. A distant object, therefore, cannot act on the eye, nor consequently make itself or its properties perceivable to the soul. Whence it plainly follows that it is immediately some contiguous substance which, operating on the eye, occasions a perception of colors; and such is light.

PHILONOUS: How! is light then a substance?

HYLAS: I tell you, Philonous, external light is nothing but a thin fluid substance whose minute particles, being agitated with a brisk motion and in various manners reflected from the different surfaces of outward objects to the eyes, communicate different motions to the optic nerves; which, being propagated to the brain, cause therein various impressions, and these are attended with the sensations of red, blue, yellow, etc.

PHILONOUS: It seems, then, the light does no more than shake the optic nerves.

HYLAS: Nothing else.

PHILONOUS: And, consequent to each particular motion of the nerves, the mind is affected with a sensation which is some particular color.

HYLAS: Right.

PHILONOUS: And these sensations have no existence without the mind.

HYLAS: They have not.

PHILONOUS: How then do you affirm that colors are in the light, since by "light" you understand a corporeal substance external to the mind?

HYLAS: Light and colors, as immediately perceived by us, I grant cannot exist without the mind. But in themselves they are only the motions and configurations of certain insensible particles of matter.

PHILONOUS: Colors, then, in the vulgar sense, or taken for the immediate objects of sight, cannot agree to any but a perceiving substance.

HYLAS: That is what I say.

PHILONOUS: Well then, since you give up the point as to those sensible qualities which are alone thought colors by all mankind besides, you may hold what you please with regard to those invisible ones of the philosophers. It is not my business to dispute about them; only I would advise you to bethink yourself whether, considering the inquiry we are upon, it be prudent for you to affirm—"the red and blue which we see are not real colors, but certain unknown motions and figures which no man ever did or can see are truly so." Are not these shocking notions, and are not they subject to as many ridiculous inferences as those you were obliged to renounce before in the case of sounds?

HYLAS: I frankly own, Philonous, that it is in vain to stand out any longer. Colors, sounds, tastes, in a word, all those termed "secondary qualities," have certainly no existence without the mind. But by this acknowledgment I must not be supposed to derogate anything from the reality of matter or external objects; seeing it is no more than several philosophers maintain, who nevertheless are the farthest imaginable from denying matter. For the clearer understanding of this you must know sensible qualities are by philosophers divided into *primary* and *secondary*. The former are extension, figure, solidity, gravity, motion, and rest. And these they hold exist really in bodies. The latter are those above enumerated, or, briefly, all sensible qualities besides the primary, which they assert are only so many sensations or ideas existing nowhere but in the mind. But all this, I doubt not, you are already apprised of. For my part I have been a long time sensible there was such an opinion current among philosophers, but was never thoroughly convinced of its truth till now.

PHILONOUS: You are still then of opinion that *extension* and *figures* are inherent in external unthinking substances?

HYLAS: I am.

PHILONOUS: But what if the same arguments which are brought against secondary qualities will hold good against these also?

HYLAS: Why then I shall be obliged to think they too exist only in the mind.

PHILONOUS: Is it your opinion the very figure and extension which you perceive by sense exist in the outward object or material substance?

HYLAS: It is.

PHILONOUS: Have all other animals as good grounds to think the same of the figure and extension which they see and feel?

HYLAS: Without doubt, if they have any thought at all.

PHILONOUS: Answer me, Hylas. Think you the senses were bestowed upon all animals for their preservation and well-being in life? Or were they given to men alone for this end?

HYLAS: I make no question but they have the same use in all other animals.

PHILONOUS: If so, is it not necessary they should be enabled by them to perceive their own limbs and those bodies which are capable of harming them?

HYLAS: Certainly.

PHILONOUS: A mite therefore must be supposed to see his own foot, and things equal or even less than it, as bodies of some considerable dimension, though at the same time they appear to you scarce discernible or at best as so many visible points?

HYLAS: I cannot deny it.

PHILONOUS: And to creatures less than the mite they will seem yet larger?

HYLAS: They will.

PHILONOUS: Insomuch that what you can hardly discern will to another extremely minute animal appear as some huge mountain?

HYLAS: All this I grant.

PHILONOUS: Can one and the same thing be at the same time in itself of different dimensions?

HYLAS: That were absurd to imagine.

PHILONOUS: But from what you have laid down it follows that both the extension by you perceived and that perceived by the mite itself, as likewise all those perceived by lesser animals, are each of them the true extension of the mite's foot; that is to say, by your own principles you are led into an absurdity.

HYLAS: There seems to be some difficulty in the point.

PHILONOUS: Again, have you not acknowledged that no real inherent property of any object can be changed without some change in the thing itself?

HYLAS: I have.

PHILONOUS: But, as we approach to or recede from an object, the visible extension varies, being at one distance ten or a hundred times greater than at another. Does it not therefore follow from hence likewise that it is not really inherent in the object?

HYLAS: I own I am at a loss what to think.

PHILONOUS: Your judgment will soon be determined if you will venture to think as freely concerning this quality as you have done concerning the rest. Was it not admitted as a good argument that neither heat nor cold was in the water because it seemed warm to one hand and cold to the other?

HYLAS: It was.

PHILONOUS: Is it not the very same reasoning to conclude there is no extension or figure in an object because to one eye it shall seem little, smooth, and round, when at the same time it appears to the other great, uneven, and angular?

HYLAS: The very same. But does this latter fact ever happen?

PHILONOUS: You may at any time make the experiment by looking with one eye bare, and with the other through a microscope.

HYLAS: I know not how to maintain it, and yet I am loath to give up *extension*; I see so many odd consequences following upon such a concession.

PHILONOUS: Odd, say you? After the concessions already made, I hope you will stick at nothing for its oddness. But, on the other hand, should it not seem very odd if the general reasoning which includes all other sensible qualities did not also include extension? If it be allowed that no idea nor anything like an idea can exist in an unperceiving substance, then surely it follows that no figure or mode of extension, which we can either perceive or imagine, or have any idea of, can be really inherent in matter, not to mention the peculiar difficulty there must be in conceiving a material substance, prior to and distinct from extension, to be the *substratum* of extension. Be the sensible quality what it will—figure or sound or color—it seems alike impossible it should subsist in that which does not perceive it.

HYLAS: I give up the point for the present, reserving still a right to retract my opinion in case I shall hereafter discover any false step in my progress to it. . . .

PHILONOUS: For that matter, Hylas, you may take what time you please in reviewing the progress of our inquiry. You are at liberty to recover any slips you might have made, or offer whatever you have omitted which makes for your first opinion.

HYLAS: One great oversight I take to be this—that I did not sufficiently distinguish the *object* from the *sensation*. Now, though this latter may not exist without mind, yet it will not thence follow that the former cannot.

PHILONOUS: What object do you mean? The object of the senses?

HYLAS: The same.

PHILONOUS: It is then immediately perceived?

HYLAS: Right.

PHILONOUS: Make me to understand the difference between what is immediately perceived and a sensation.

HYLAS: The sensation I take to be an act of the mind perceiving; besides which there is something perceived, and this I call the "object." For example, there is red and yellow on that tulip. But then the act of perceiving those colors is in me only, and not in the tulip.

PHILONOUS: What tulip do you speak of? Is it that which you see?

HYLAS: The same.

PHILONOUS: And what do you see besides color, figure, and extension?

HYLAS: Nothing.

PHILONOUS: What you would say then is that the red and yellow are coexistent with the extension; is it not?

HYLAS: That is not all; I would say they have a real existence without the mind, in some unthinking substance.

PHILONOUS: That the colors are really in the tulip which I see is manifest. Neither can it be denied that this tulip may exist independent of your mind or mine; but that any immediate object of the senses—that is, any idea, or combination of ideas—should exist in an unthinking substance, or exterior to all minds, is in itself an evident contradiction. Nor can I imagine how this follows from what you said just now, to wit, that the red and yellow were on the tulip *you saw*, since you do not pretend to *see* that unthinking substance. . . .

HYLAS: I tell you extension is only a mode, and matter is something that supports modes. And is it not evident the thing supported is different from the thing supporting?

PHILONOUS: So that something distinct from, and exclusive of, extension is supposed to be the *substratum* of extension?

HYLAS: Just so.

PHILONOUS: Answer me, Hylas, can a thing be spread without extension, or is not the idea of extension necessarily included in *spreading*?

HYLAS: It is.

PHILONOUS: Whatsoever therefore you suppose spread under anything must have in itself an extension distinct from the extension of that thing under which it is spread?

HYLAS: It must.

PHILONOUS: Consequently, every corporeal substance being the *substratum* of extension must have in itself another extension by which it is qualified to be a *substratum*, and so on to infinity? And I ask whether this be not absurd in itself and repugnant to what you granted just now, to wit, that the *substratum* was something distinct from and exclusive of extension?

HYLAS: Aye, but, Philonous, you take me wrong. I do not mean that matter is *spread* in a gross literal sense under extension. The word "substratum" is used only to express in general the same thing with "substance."

PHILONOUS: Well then, let us examine the relation implied in the term "substance." Is it not that it stands under accidents?

HYLAS: The very same.

PHILONOUS: But that one thing may stand under or support another, must it not be extended?

HYLAS: It must.

PHILONOUS: Is not therefore this supposition liable to the same absurdity with the former?

HYLAS: You still take things in a strict literal sense; that is not fair, Philonous.

PHILONOUS: I am not for imposing any sense on your words; you are at liberty to explain them as you please. Only I beseech you, make me understand something by them. You tell me matter supports or stands under accidents. How! is it as your legs support your body?

HYLAS: No; that is the literal sense.

PHILONOUS: Pray let me know any sense, literal or not literal, that you understand it in.—How long must I wait for an answer, Hylas?

HYLAS: I declare I know not what to say. I once thought I understood well enough what was meant by matter's supporting accidents. But now, the more I think on it, the less can I comprehend it; in short, I find that I know nothing of it.

PHILONOUS: It seems then you have no idea at all, neither relative nor positive, of matter; you know neither what it is in itself nor what relation it bears to accidents?

HYLAS: I acknowledge it.

PHILONOUS: And yet you asserted that you could not conceive how qualities or accidents should really exist without conceiving at the same time a material support of them?

HYLAS: I did.

PHILONOUS: That is to say, when you conceive the real existence of qualities, you do withal conceive something which you cannot conceive?

HYLAS: It was wrong I own. But still I fear there is some fallacy or other. Pray, what think you of this? It is just come into my head that the ground of all our mistake lies in your treating of each quality by itself. Now I grant that each quality cannot singly subsist without the mind. Color cannot without extension, neither can figure without some other sensible quality. But, as the several qualities united or blended together form entire sensible things, nothing hinders why such things may not be supposed to exist without the mind.

PHILONOUS: Either, Hylas, you are jesting or have a very bad memory. Though, indeed, we went through all the qualities by name one after another, yet my arguments, or rather your concessions, nowhere tended to prove that the secondary qualities did not subsist each alone by itself, but that they were not *at all* without the mind. Indeed, in treating of figure and motion we concluded they could not exist without the mind, because it was impossible even in thought to separate them from all secondary qualities, so as to conceive them existing by themselves. But then this was not the only argument made use of upon that occasion. But (to pass by all that has been hitherto said and reckon it for nothing, if you will have it so) I am content to put the whole upon this issue. If you can conceive it possible for any mixture or combination of qualities, or any sensible object whatever, to exist without the mind, then I will grant it actually to be so.

HYLAS: If it comes to that the point will soon be decided. What more easy than to conceive a tree or house existing by itself, independent of, and unperceived by, any mind whatsoever? I do at this present time conceive them existing after that manner.

PHILONOUS: How say you, Hylas, can you see a thing which is at the same time unseen?

HYLAS: No, that were a contradiction.

PHILONOUS: Is it not as great a contradiction to talk of *conceiving* a thing which is *unconceived*?

HYLAS: It is.

PHILONOUS: The tree or house, therefore, which you think of is conceived by you?

HYLAS: How should it be otherwise?

PHILONOUS: And what is conceived is surely in the mind?

HYLAS: Without question, that which is conceived is in the mind.

PHILONOUS: How then came you to say you conceived a house or tree existing independent and out of all minds whatsoever?

HYLAS: That was I own an oversight, but stay, let me consider what led me into it.—It is a pleasant mistake enough. As I was thinking of a tree in a solitary place where no one was present to see it, methought that was to conceive a tree as existing unperceived or unthought of, not considering that I myself conceived it all the while. But now I plainly see that all I can do is to frame ideas in my own mind. I may indeed conceive in my own thoughts the idea of a tree, or a house, or a mountain, but that is all. And this is far from proving that I can conceive them *existing out of the minds of all spirits.* . . .

To speak the truth, Philonous, I think there are two kinds of objects: the one perceived immediately, which are likewise called "ideas"; the other are real things or external objects, perceived by the mediation of ideas which are their images and representations. Now I own ideas do not exist without the mind, but the latter sort of objects do. I am sorry I did not think of this distinction sooner; it would probably have cut short your discourse.

PHILONOUS: Are those external objects perceived by sense or by some other faculty?

HYLAS: They are perceived by sense.

PHILONOUS: How! is there anything perceived by sense which is not immediately perceived?

HYLAS: Yes, Philonous, in some sort there is. For example, when I look on a picture or statue of Julius Caesar, I may be said, after a manner, to perceive him (though not immediately) by my senses.

PHILONOUS: It seems then you will have our ideas, which alone are immediately perceived, to be pictures of external things: and that these also are perceived by sense inasmuch as they have a conformity or resemblance to our ideas?

HYLAS:	That is my meaning.
PHILONOUS:	And in the same way that Julius Caesar, in himself invisible, is nevertheless perceived by sight, real things, in themselves imperceptible, are perceived by sense.
HYLAS:	In the very same.
PHILONOUS:	Tell me, Hylas, when you behold the picture of Julius Caesar, do you see with your eyes any more than some colors and figures, with a certain symmetry and composition of the whole?
HYLAS:	Nothing else.
PHILONOUS:	And would not a man who had never known anything of Julius Caesar see as much?
HYLAS:	He would.
PHILONOUS:	Consequently, he has his sight and the use of it in as perfect a degree as you?
HYLAS:	I agree with you.
PHILONOUS:	Whence comes it then that your thoughts are directed to the Roman emperor, and his are not? This cannot proceed from the sensations or ideas of sense by you then perceived, since you acknowledge you have no advantage over him in that respect. It should seem therefore to proceed from reason and memory, should it not?
HYLAS:	It should. . . .
PHILONOUS:	My aim is only to learn from you the way to come at the knowledge of *material beings*. Whatever we perceive is perceived either immediately or mediately—by sense, or by reason and reflection. But, as you have excluded sense, pray show me what reason you have to believe their existence, or what *medium* you can possibly make use of to prove it, either to mine or your own understanding.
HYLAS:	To deal ingenuously, Philonous, now I consider the point, I do not find I can give you any good reason for it. But this much seems pretty plain, that it is at least possible such things may really exist. And as long as there is no absurdity in supposing them, I am resolved to believe as I did, till you bring good reasons to the contrary.
PHILONOUS:	What! is it come to this, that you only believe the existence of material objects, and that your belief is founded barely on the possibility of its being true? Then you will have me bring reasons against it, though another would think it reasonable the proof should lie on him who holds the affirmative. And, after all, this very point which you are now resolved to maintain, without any reason, is in effect what you have more than once during this discourse seen good reason to give up. But to pass over all

this—if I understand you rightly, you say our ideas do not exist without the mind, but that they are copies, images, or representations of certain originals that do?

HYLAS: You take me right.

PHILONOUS: They are then like external things?

HYLAS: They are.

PHILONOUS: Have those things a stable and permanent nature, independent of our senses, or are they in a perpetual change, upon our producing any motions in our bodies, suspending, exerting, or altering our faculties or organs of sense?

HYLAS: Real things, it is plain, have a fixed and real nature, which remains the same notwithstanding any change in our senses or in the posture and motion of our bodies; which indeed may affect the ideas in our minds, but it were absurd to think they had the same effect on things existing without the mind.

PHILONOUS: How then is it possible that things perpetually fleeting and variable as our ideas should be copies or images of anything fixed and constant? Or, in other words, since all sensible qualities, as size, figure, color, etc., that is, our ideas, are continually changing upon every alteration in the distance, medium, or instruments of sensation—how can any determinate material objects be properly represented or painted forth by several distinct things each of which is so different from and unlike the rest? Or, if you say it resembles some one only of our ideas, how shall we be able to distinguish the true copy from all the false ones?

HYLAS: I profess, Philonous, I am at a loss. I know not what to say to this.

PHILONOUS: But neither is this all. Which are material objects in themselves—perceptible or imperceptible?

HYLAS: Properly and immediately nothing can be perceived but ideas. All material things, therefore, are in themselves insensible and to be perceived only by their ideas.

PHILONOUS: Ideas then are sensible, and their archetypes or originals insensible?

HYLAS: Right.

PHILONOUS: But how can that which is sensible be like that which is insensible? Can a real thing, in itself *invisible*, be like a *color*, or a real thing which is not *audible* be like a *sound*? In a word, can anything be like a sensation or idea, but another sensation or idea?

HYLAS: I must own, I think not.

PHILONOUS: Is it possible there should be any doubt on the point? Do you not perfectly know your own ideas?

HYLAS: I know them perfectly, since what I do not perceive or know can be no part of my idea.

PHILONOUS: Consider, therefore, and examine them, and then tell me if there be anything in them which can exist without the mind, or if you can conceive anything like them existing without the mind?

HYLAS: Upon inquiry I find it is impossible for me to conceive or understand how anything but an idea can be like an idea. And it is most evident that *no idea can exist without the mind*.

PHILONOUS: You are, therefore, by your principles forced to deny the reality of sensible things, since you made it to consist in an absolute existence exterior to the mind. That is to say, you are a downright skeptic. So I have gained my point, which was to show your principles led to skepticism.

HYLAS: For the present I am, if not entirely convinced, at least silenced. . . .

THE SECOND DIALOGUE

HYLAS: I beg your pardon, Philonous, for not meeting you sooner. All this morning my head was so filled with our late conversation that I had not leisure to think of the time of the day, or indeed of anything else.

PHILONOUS: I am glad you were so intent upon it, in hopes if there were any mistakes in your concessions, or fallacies in my reasonings from them, you will now discover them to me.

HYLAS: I assure you I have done nothing ever since I saw you but search after mistakes and fallacies, and, with that view, have minutely examined the whole series of yesterday's discourse; but all in vain, for the notions it led me into, upon review, appear still more clear and evident; and the more I consider them, the more irresistibly do they force my assent.

PHILONOUS: And is not this, think you, a sign that they are genuine, that they proceed from nature and are comformable to right reason? Truth and beauty are in this alike, that the strictest survey sets them both off to advantage, while the false luster of error and disguise cannot endure being reviewed or too nearly inspected.

HYLAS: I own there is a great deal in what you say. Nor can anyone be more entirely satisfied of the truth of those odd consequences so long as I have in view the reasonings that lead to them. But when these are out of my thoughts, there seems, on the other hand, something so satisfactory, so natural and intelligible in the modern way of explaining things that I profess I know not how to reject it.

PHILONOUS: I know not what way you mean.

HYLAS: I mean the way of accounting for our sensations or ideas.

PHILONOUS: How is that?

HYLAS: It is supposed the soul makes her residence in some part of the brain, from which the nerves take their rise, and are thence extended to all parts of the body; and that outward objects, by the different impressions they make on the organs of sense, communicate certain vibrative motions to the nerves, and these, being filled with spirits, propagate them to the brain or seat of the soul, which, according to the various impressions or traces thereby made in the brain, is variously affected with ideas.

PHILONOUS: And call you this an explication of the manner whereby we are affected with ideas?

HYLAS: Why not, Philonous; have you anything to object against it?

PHILONOUS: I would first know whether I rightly understand your hypothesis. You make certain traces in the brain to be the causes or occasions of our ideas. Pray tell me whether by the "brain" you mean any sensible thing.

HYLAS: What else think you I could mean?

PHILONOUS: Sensible things are all immediately perceivable; and those things which are immediately perceivable are ideas, and these exist only in the mind. This much you have, if I mistake not, long since agreed to.

HYLAS: I do not deny it.

PHILONOUS: The brain therefore you speak of, being a sensible thing, exists only in the mind. Now I would fain know whether you think it reasonable to suppose that one idea or thing existing in the mind occasions all other ideas. And if you think so, pray how do you account for the origin of that primary idea or brain itself?

HYLAS: I do not explain the origin of our ideas by that brain which is perceivable to sense, this being itself only a combination of sensible ideas, but by another which I imagine.

PHILONOUS: But are not things imagined as truly *in the mind* as things perceived?

HYLAS: I must confess they are.

PHILONOUS: It comes, therefore, to the same thing; and you have been all this while accounting for ideas by certain motions or impressions in the brain, that is, by some alterations in an idea, whether sensible or imaginable it matters not.

HYLAS: I begin to suspect my hypothesis.

PHILONOUS: Besides spirits, all that we know or conceive are our own ideas. When, therefore, you say all ideas are occasioned by impressions in the brain, do you conceive this brain or no? If you do, then you talk of ideas imprinted in an idea causing that same idea, which is absurd. If you do not conceive it, you talk unintelligibly, instead of forming a reasonable hypothesis.

HYLAS: I now clearly see it was a mere dream. There is nothing in it.

PHILONOUS: You need not be much concerned at it, for, after all, this way of explaining things, as you called it, could never have satisfied any reasonable man. What connection is there between a motion in the nerves and the sensations of sound or color in the mind? Or how is it possible these should be the effect of that?

HYLAS: But I could never think it had so little in it as now it seems to have.

PHILONOUS: Well then, are you at length satisfied that no sensible things have a real existence, and that you are in truth an arrant *skeptic*?

HYLAS: It is too plain to be denied.

PHILONOUS: Look! are not the fields covered with a delightful verdure? Is there not something in the woods and groves, in the rivers and clear springs, that soothes, that delights, that transports the soul? At the prospect of the wide and deep ocean, or some huge mountain whose top is lost in the clouds, or of an old gloomy forest, are not our minds filled with a pleasing horror? Even in rocks and deserts is there not an agreeable wildness? How sincere a pleasure is it to behold the natural beauties of the earth! To preserve and renew our relish for them, is not the veil of night alternately drawn over her face, and does she not change her dress with the seasons? How aptly are the elements disposed! What variety and use in the meanest productions of nature! What delicacy, what beauty, what contrivance in animal and vegetable bodies! How exquisitely are all things suited, as well to their particular ends as to constitute apposite parts of the whole! And while they mutually aid and support, do they not also set off and illustrate each other? Raise now your thoughts from this ball of earth to all those glorious luminaries that adorn the high arch of heaven. The motion and situation of the planets, are they not admirable for use and order? Were those (miscalled "erratic") globes ever known to stray in their repeated journeys through the pathless void? Do they not measure areas round the sun ever proportioned to the times? So fixed, so immutable are the laws by which the unseen Author of Nature actuates the universe. How vivid and radiant is the luster of the fixed stars! How magnificent and rich that negligent profusion with which they appear to be scattered throughout the whole azure vault! Yet, if you take the telescope, it brings into your sight a new host of stars that escape the naked eye. Here they seem contiguous and minute, but to a nearer view, immense orbs of light at various distances, far sunk in the abyss of space. Now you must call imagination to your aid. The feeble narrow sense cannot descry innumerable worlds revolving round the central fires, and in those worlds the energy of an all-perfect Mind displayed in endless forms. But neither sense nor imagination are big enough to comprehend the boundless extent with all its glittering furniture. Though the laboring mind exert and strain each power to its utmost reach, there still stands out ungrasped a surplusage immeasurable. Yet all the vast bodies that compose this mighty frame, how distant and remote soever, are by some secret mechanism, some divine art and force linked in a mutual dependence and intercourse with each other, even with this earth, which was almost slipt from my thoughts and lost in the crowd of worlds. Is not the whole system immense, beautiful, glorious beyond expression and beyond thought! What treatment, then, do those philosophers deserve who would deprive these noble and delightful scenes of all reality? How should those principles be entertained that lead us to think all the visible beauty of the creation a false imaginary glare? To be plain, can you expect this skepticism of yours will not be thought extravagantly absurd by all men of sense?

HYLAS: Other men may think as they please, but for your part you have nothing to reproach me with. My comfort is you are as much a skeptic as I am.

PHILONOUS: There, Hylas, I must beg leave to differ from you.

HYLAS: What! have you all along agreed to the premises, and do you now deny the conclusion and leave me to maintain those paradoxes by myself which you led me into? This surely is not fair.

PHILONOUS: I deny that I agree with you in those notions that led to skepticism. You indeed said the *reality* of sensible thing consisted in an *absolute existence* out of the minds of spirits, or distinct from their being perceived. And, pursuant to this notion of reality, you are obliged to deny sensible things any real existence; that is, according to your definition, you profess yourself a skeptic. But I neither said nor thought the reality of sensible things was to be defined after that manner. To me it is evident, for the reasons you allow of, that sensible things cannot exist otherwise than in a mind or spirit. Whence I conclude, not that they have no real existence, but that, seeing they depend not on my thought and have an existence distinct from being perceived by me, *there must be some other mind wherein they exist.* As sure, therefore, as the sensible world really exists, so sure is there an infinite omnipresent Spirit, who contains and supports it. . . . Take here in brief my meaning: It is evident that the things I perceive are my own ideas, and that no idea can exist unless it be in a mind. Nor is it less plain that these ideas or things by me perceived, either themselves or their archetypes, exist independently of my mind; since I know myself not to be their author, it being out of my power to determine at pleasure what particular ideas I shall be affected with upon opening my eyes or ears. They must therefore exist in some other mind, whose will it is they should be exhibited to me. The things, I say, immediately perceived are ideas or, sensations, call them which you will. But how can any idea or sensation exist in, or be produced by, anything but a mind or spirit? This indeed is inconceivable; and to assert that which is inconceivable is to talk nonsense, is it not?

HYLAS: Without doubt.

PHILONOUS: But, on the other hand, it is very conceivable that they should exist in and be produced by a spirit, since this is no more than I daily experience in myself, inasmuch as I perceive numberless ideas, and, by an act of my will, can form a great variety of them and raise them up in my imagination; though, it must be confessed, these creatures of the fancy are not altogether so distinct, so strong, vivid, and permanent as those perceived by my senses, which latter are called "real things." From all which I conclude, *there is a Mind which affects me every moment with all the sensible impressions I perceive.* And from the variety, order, and manner of these I conclude the Author of them to be *wise, powerful, and good beyond comprehension.* Mark it well; I do not say: "I see things by perceiving that which represents them in the intelligible Substance of God." This I do not understand; but I say: "the things by me perceived are known by the understanding and produced by the will of an infinite Spirit." And is not all this most plain and evident? Is there any more in it than what a little observation of our own minds, and that which passes in them, not only enables us to conceive but also obliges us to acknowledge?

HYLAS: I think I understand you very clearly and own the proof you give of a Deity seems no less evident than it is surprising. But allowing that God is the supreme and universal cause of all things, yet may there not be still a third nature besides spirits and ideas? May we not admit a subordinate and limited cause of our ideas? In a word, may there not for all that be *matter*?

PHILONOUS: How often must I inculcate the same thing? You allow the things immediately perceived by sense to exist nowhere without the mind; but there is nothing perceived by sense which is not perceived immediately: therefore there is nothing sensible that exists without the mind. The matter, therefore, which you still insist on is something intelligible, I suppose something that may be discovered by reason, and not by sense.

HYLAS: You are in the right.

PHILONOUS: Pray let me know what reasoning your belief of matter is grounded on, and what this matter is in your present sense of it.

HYLAS: I find myself affected with various ideas whereof I know I am not the cause; neither are they the cause of themselves or of one another, or capable of subsisting by themselves, as being altogether inactive, fleeting, dependent beings. They have therefore some cause distinct from me and them, of which I pretend to know no more than that it is *the cause of my ideas*. And this thing, whatever it be, I call "matter."

PHILONOUS: Tell me, Hylas, has everyone a liberty to change the current proper signification annexed to a common name in any language? For example, suppose a traveler should tell you that in a certain country men pass unhurt through the fire; and, upon explaining himself, you found he meant by the word "fire" that which others call "water"; or, if he should assert that there are trees that walk upon two legs, meaning men by the term "trees." Would you think this reasonable?

HYLAS: No, I should think it very absurd. Common custom is the standard of propriety in language. And for any man to affect speaking improperly is to pervert the use of speech, and can never serve to a better purpose than to protract and multiply disputes where there is no difference in opinion.

PHILONOUS: And does not "matter," in the common current acceptation of the word, signify an extended, solid, movable, unthinking, inactive substance?

HYLAS: It does.

PHILONOUS: And has it not been made evident that no such substance can possibly exist? And though it should be allowed to exist, yet how can that which is *inactive* be a *cause*, or that which is *unthinking* be a *cause of thought*? You may, indeed, if you please, annex to the word "matter" a contrary meaning to what is vulgarly received, and tell me you understand by it an unextended, thinking, active being which is the cause of our ideas. But what else is this than to play with words and run into that very fault you just now condemned with so much reason? I do by no means find fault with your reasoning, in that you collect a cause from the phenomena; but I deny that the cause deducible by reason can properly be termed "matter."

HYLAS: There is indeed something in what you say. But I am afraid you do not thoroughly comprehend my meaning. I would by no means be thought to deny that God, or an infinite Spirit, is the Supreme Cause of all things. All I contend for is that, subordinate to the Supreme Agent, there is a cause of a limited and inferior nature which concurs in the production of our ideas, not by any act of will or spiritual efficiency, but by that kind of action which belongs to matter, viz., motion.

PHILONOUS: I find you are at every turn relapsing into your old exploded conceit, of a movable and consequently an extended substance existing without the mind. What! have you already forgotten you were convinced, or are you willing I should repeat what has been said on that head? In truth, this is not fair dealing in you still to suppose the being of that which you have so often acknowledged to have no being. . . .

HYLAS: I acknowledge it is possible we might perceive all things just as we do now, though there was no matter in the world; neither can I conceive, if there be matter, how it should produce any idea in our minds. And I do further grant you have entirely satisfied me that it is impossible there should be such a thing as matter in any of the foregoing acceptations. But still I cannot help supposing that there is *matter* in some sense or other. What that is I do not indeed pretend to determine.

PHILONOUS: I do not expect you should define exactly the nature of that unknown being. Only be pleased to tell me whether it is a substance—and if so, whether you can suppose a substance without accidents; or in case you suppose it to have accidents or qualities, I desire you will let me know what those qualities are, at least what is meant by "matter's supporting them"?

HYLAS: We have already argued on those points. I have no more to say to them. But, to prevent any further questions, let me tell you I at present understand by "matter" neither substance nor accident, thinking nor extended being, neither cause, instrument, nor occasion, but something entirely unknown, distinct from all these.

PHILONOUS: It seems then you include in your present notion of matter nothing but the general abstract idea of *entity*.

HYLAS: Nothing else, save only that I superadd to this general idea the negation of all those particular things, qualities, or ideas that I perceive, imagine, or in anywise apprehend.

PHILONOUS: Pray where do you suppose this unknown matter to exist?

HYLAS: Oh Philonous! now you think you have entangled me; for if I say it exists in place, then you will infer that it exists in the mind, since it is agreed that place or extension exists only in the mind; but I am not ashamed to own my ignorance. I know not where it exists; only I am sure it exists not in place. There is a negative answer for you. And you must expect no other to all the questions you put for the future about matter.

PHILONOUS: Since you will not tell me where it exists, be pleased to inform me after what manner you suppose it to exist, or what you mean by its "existence"?

HYLAS: It neither thinks nor acts, neither perceives nor is perceived.

PHILONOUS: But what is there positive in your abstracted notion of its existence?

HYLAS: Upon a nice observation, I do not find I have any positive notion or meaning at all. I tell you again, I am not ashamed to own my ignorance. I know not what is meant by its existence or how it exists.

PHILONOUS: Continue, good Hylas, to act the same ingenuous part and tell me sincerely whether you can frame a distinct idea of entity in general, prescinded from and exclusive of all thinking and corporeal beings, all particular things whatsoever.

HYLAS: Hold, let me think a little—I profess, Philonous, I do not find that I can. At first glance methought I had some dilute and airy notion of pure entity in abstract, but, upon closer attention, it has quite vanished out of sight. The more I think on it, the more am I confirmed in my prudent resolution of giving none but negative answers and not pretending to the least degree of any positive knowledge or conception of matter, its *where*, its *how*, its *entity*, or anything belonging to it.

PHILONOUS: When, therefore, you speak of the existence of matter, you have not any notion in your mind?

HYLAS: None at all.

PHILONOUS: Pray tell me if the case stands not thus: at first, from a belief of material substance, you would have it that the immediate objects existed without the mind; then, that they are archetypes; then, causes; next, instruments; then, occasions: lastly, *something in general*, which being interpreted proves *nothing*. So matter comes to nothing. What think you, Hylas, is not this a fair summary of your whole proceeding?

HYLAS: Be that as it will, yet I still insist upon it, that our not being able to conceive a thing is no argument against its existence.

PHILONOUS: That from a cause, effect, operation, sign, or other circumstance there may reasonably be inferred the existence of a thing not immediately perceived; and that it were absurd for any man to argue against the existence of that thing, from his having no direct and positive notion of it, I freely own. But where there is nothing of all this, where neither reason nor revelation induces us to believe the existence of a thing where we have not even a relative notion of it, where an abstraction is made from perceiving and being perceived, from spirit and idea, lastly, where there is not so much as the most inadequate or faint idea pretended to, I will not, indeed, thence conclude against the reality of any notion or existence of anything; but my inference shall be that you mean nothing at all, that you employ words to no manner of purpose, without any design or signification whatsoever. And I leave it to you to consider how mere jargon should be treated.

HYLAS: To deal frankly with you, Philonous, your arguments seem in themselves unanswerable, but they have not so great an effect on me as to produce that entire conviction, that hearty acquiescence, which attends demonstration. I find myself still relapsing into an obscure surmise of I know not what—*matter*. . . .

HYLAS: The reality of things cannot be maintained without supposing the existence of matter. And is not this, think you, a good reason why I should be earnest in its defense?

PHILONOUS: The reality of things! What things, sensible or intelligible?

HYLAS: Sensible things.

PHILONOUS: My glove, for example?

HYLAS: That or any other thing perceived by the senses.

PHILONOUS: But to fix on some particular thing, is it not a sufficient evidence to me of the existence of this *glove* that I see it and feel it and wear it? Or, if this will not do, how is it possible I should be assured of the reality of this thing which I actually see in this place by supposing that some unknown thing, which I never did or can see, exists after an unknown manner, in an unknown place, or in no place at all? How can the supposed reality of that which is intangible be a proof that anything tangible really exists? Or of that which is invisible, that any visible thing or, in general, of anything which is imperceptible, that a perceptible exists? Do but explain this and I shall think nothing too hard for you.

HYLAS: Upon the whole, I am content to own the existence of matter is highly improbable; but the direct and absolute impossibility of it does not appear to me.

PHILONOUS: But granting matter to be possible, yet, upon that account merely, it can have no more claim to existence than a golden mountain or a centaur.

HYLAS: I acknowledge it, but still you do not deny it is possible; and that which is possible, for aught you know, may actually exist.

PHILONOUS: I deny it to be possible; and have, if I mistake not, evidently proved, from your own concessions, that it is not. In the common sense of the word "matter," is there any more implied than an extended, solid, figured, movable substance existing without the mind? And have not you acknowledged, over and over, that you have seen evident reason for denying the possibility of such a substance?

HYLAS: True, but that is only one sense of the term "matter."

PHILONOUS: But is it not the only proper genuine received sense? And if matter in such a sense be proved impossible, may it not be thought with good grounds absolutely impossible? Else how could anything be proved impossible? Or, indeed, how could there be any proof at all one way or other to a man who takes the liberty to unsettle and change the common signification of words?

HYLAS: I thought philosophers might be allowed to speak more accurately than the vulgar, and were not always confined to the common acceptation of a term.

PHILONOUS: But this now mentioned is the common received sense among philosophers themselves. But, not to insist on that, have you not been allowed to take matter in what sense you pleased? And have you not used this privilege in the utmost extent, sometimes entirely changing, at others leaving out or putting into the definition of it whatever, for the present, best served your design, contrary to all the known rules of reason and logic? And has not this shifting, unfair method of yours spun out our dispute to an unnecessary length, matter having been particularly examined and by your own confession refuted in each of those senses? And can any more be required to prove the absolute impossibility of a thing than the proving it impossible in every particular sense that either you or anyone else understands it in?

HYLAS: But I am not so thoroughly satisfied that you have proved the impossibility of matter in the last most obscure abstracted and indefinite sense.

PHILONOUS: When is a thing shown to be impossible?

HYLAS: When a repugnancy is demonstrated between the ideas comprehended in its definition.

PHILONOUS: But where there are no ideas, there no repugnancy can be demonstrated between ideas?

HYLAS: I agree with you.

PHILONOUS: Now, in that which you call the obscure indefinite sense of the word "matter," it is plain, by your own confession, there was included no idea at all, no sense except an unknown sense, which is the same thing as none. You are not, therefore, to expect I should prove a repugnancy between ideas where there are no ideas, or the impossibility of matter taken in an *unknown* sense, that is, no sense at all. My business was only to show you meant *nothing*; and this you were brought to own. So that, in all your various senses, you have been shown either to mean nothing at all or, if anything, an absurdity. And if this be not sufficient to prove the impossibility of a thing, I desire you will let me know what is.

Bertrand Russell

PROBLEMS OF PHILOSOPHY

This chapter from Bertrand Russell's *Problems of Philosophy* gives a general presentation of the modern scientific view of the nature of the material world.

THE NATURE OF MATTER

In the preceding chapter we agreed, though without being able to find demonstrative reasons, that it is rational to believe that our sense-data—for example, those which we regard as associated with my table—are really signs of the existence of something independent of us and our perceptions. That is to say, over and above the sensations of colour, hardness, noise, and so on, which make up the appearance of the table to me, I assume that there is something else, *of* which these things are appearances. The colour ceases to exist if I shut my eyes, the sensation of hardness ceases to exist if I remove my arm from contact with the table, the sound ceases to exist if I cease to rap the table with my knuckles. But I do not believe that when all these things cease the table ceases. On the contrary, I believe that it is because the table exists continuously that all these sense-data will reappear when I open my eyes, replace my arm, and begin again to rap with my knuckles. The question we have to consider in this chapter is: What is the nature of this real table, which persists independently of my perception of it?

To this question physical science gives an answer, somewhat incomplete it is true, and in part still very hypothetical, but yet deserving of respect so far as it goes. Physical science, more or less unconsciously, has drifted into the view that all natural phenomena ought to be reduced to motions. Light and heat and sound are all due to wave-motions, which travel from the body emitting them to the person who sees light or feels heat or hears sound. That which has the wave-motion is either aether or "gross matter," but in either case is what the philosopher would call matter. The only properties which science assigns to it are position in space, and the power of motion according to the laws of motion. Science does not deny that it *may* have other properties; but if so, such other properties are not useful to the man of science, and in no way assist him in explaining the phenomena.

It is sometimes said that "light *is* a form of wave-motion," but this is misleading, for the light which we immediately see, which we know directly by means of our senses, is *not* a form of wave-motion, but something quite different—something which we all know if we are not blind, though we cannot describe it so as to convey our knowledge to a man who is blind. A wave-motion, on the contrary, could quite well be described to a blind man, since he can acquire a knowledge of space by the sense of touch; and he can experience a wave-motion by a sea voyage almost as well as we can. But this, which a blind man can understand, is not what we mean by *light*: we mean by *light* just that which a blind man can never understand, and which we can never describe to him.

Now this something, which all of us who are not blind know, is not, according to science, really to be found in the outer world: it is something caused by the action of certain waves upon the eyes and nerves and brain of the person who sees the light. When it is said that light *is* waves, what is really meant is that waves are the physical cause of our sensations of light. But light itself, the thing which seeing people experience and blind people do not, is not supposed by science to form any part of the world that is independent of us and our senses. And very similar remarks would apply to other kinds of sensations.

It is not only colours and sounds and so on that are absent from the scientific world of matter, but also *space* as we get it through sight or touch. It is essential to science that its matter should be in *a* space, but the space in which it is cannot be exactly the space we see or feel. To begin with, space as we see it is not the same as space as we get it by the sense of touch; it is only by experience in infancy that we learn how to touch things we see, or how to get a sight of things which we feel touching us. But the space of science is neutral as between touch and sight; thus it cannot be either the space of touch or the space of sight.

Again, different people see the same object as of different shapes, according to their point of view. A circular coin, for example, though we should always *judge* it to be circular, will *look* oval unless we are straight in front of it. When we judge that it *is* circular, we are judging that it has a real shape which is not its apparent shape, but belongs to it intrinsically apart from its appearance. But this real shape, which is what concerns science, must be in a real space, not the same as anybody's *apparent* space. The real space is public, the apparent space is private to the percipient. In different people's *private* spaces the same object seems to have different shapes; thus the real space, in which it has its real shape, must be different from the private spaces. The space of science, therefore, though *connected* with the spaces we see and feel, is not identical with them, and the manner of its connexion requires investigation.

We agreed provisionally that physical objects cannot be quite like our sense-data, but may be regarded as *causing* our sensations. These physical objects are in the space of science, which we may call "physical" space. It is important to notice that, if our sensations are to be caused by physical objects, there must be a physical space containing these objects and our sense-organs and nerves and brain. We get a sensation of touch from an object when we are in contact with it; that is to say, when some part of our body occupies a place in physical space quite close to the space occupied by the object. We see an object (roughly speaking) when no opaque body is between the object and our eyes in physical space. Similarly, we only hear or smell or taste an object when we are sufficiently near to it, or when it touches the tongue, or has some suitable position in physical space relatively to our body. We cannot begin to state what different sensations we shall derive from a given object under different circumstances unless we regard the object and our body as both in one physical space, for it is mainly the relative positions of the object and our body that determine what sensations we shall derive from the object.

Now our sense-data are situated in our private spaces, either the space of sight or the space of touch or such vaguer spaces as other senses may give us. If, as science and common sense assume, there is one public all-embracing physical space in which physical objects are, the relative positions of physical objects in physical space must more or less correspond to the relative positions of sense-data in our private spaces. There is no difficulty in supposing this to be the case. If we see on a road one house nearer to us than another, our other senses will bear out the view that is is nearer; for example, it will be reached sooner if we walk along the road. Other people will agree that the house which looks nearer to us is nearer; the ordnance map will take the same view; and thus everything points to a spatial relation between the houses corresponding to the relation between the sense-data which we see when we look at the houses. Thus we may assume that there is a physical space in which physical objects have spatial relations corresponding to those which the corresponding sense-data have in our private spaces. It is this physical space which is dealt with in geometry and assumed in physics and astronomy.

Assuming that there is physical space, and that it does thus correspond to private spaces, what can we know about it? We can know *only* what is required in order to secure the correspondence. That is to say, we can know nothing of what it is like in itself, but we can know the sort of arrangement of physical objects which results from their spatial relations. We can know, for example, that the earth and moon and sun are in one straight line during an eclipse, though we cannot know what a physical straight line is in itself, as we know the look of a straight line in our visual space. Thus we come to know much more about the *relations* of distances in physical space than about the distances themselves; we may know that one distance is greater than another, or that it is along the same straight line as the other, but we cannot have that immediate acquaintance with physical distances that we have with distances in our private spaces, or with colours or sounds or other sense-data. We can know all those things about physical space which a man born blind might know through other people about the space of sight; but the kind of things which a man born blind could never know about the space of sight we also cannot know about physical space. We can know the properties of the relations required to preserve the correspondence with sense-data, but we cannot know the nature of the terms between which the relations hold.

With regard to time, our *feeling* of duration or of the lapse of time is notoriously an unsafe guide as to the time that has elapsed by the clock. Times when we are bored or suffering pain pass slowly, times when we are agreeably occupied pass quickly, and times when we are sleeping pass almost as if they did not exist. Thus, in so far as time is constituted by duration, there is the same necessity for distinguishing a public and a private time as there was in the case of space. But in so far as time consists in an *order* of before and after, there is no need to make such a distinction; the time-order which events seem to have is, so far as we can see, the same as the time-order which they do have. At any rate no reason can be given for supposing that the two orders are not the same. The same is usually true of space: if a regiment of men are marching along a road, the *shape* of the regiment will look different from different points of view, but the men will appear arranged in the same *order* from all points of view. Hence we regard the *order* as true also in physical space, whereas the shape is only supposed to correspond to the physical space so far as is required for the preservation of the order.

In saying that the time-order which events *seem to have* is the same as the time-order which they *really have*, it is necessary to guard against a possible misunderstanding. It must not be supposed that the various states of different physical objects have the same time-order as the sense-data which constitute the perceptions of those objects. Considered as physical objects, the thunder and lightning are simultaneous; that is to say, the lightning is simultaneous with the disturbance of the air in the place where the disturbance begins, namely, where the lightning is. But the sense-datum which we call hearing the thunder does not take place until the disturbance of the air has travelled as far as to where we are. Similarly, it takes about eight minutes for the sun's light to reach us; thus, when we see the sun we are seeing the sun of eight minutes ago. So far as our sense-data afford evidence as to the physical sun they afford evidence as to the physical sun of eight minutes ago; if the physical sun had ceased to exist within the last eight minutes, that would make no difference to the sense-data which we call "seeing the sun." This affords a fresh illustration of the necessity of distinguishing between sense-data and physical objects.

What we have found as regards space is much the same as what we find in relation to the correspondence of the sense-data with their physical counterparts. If one object looks blue and another red, we may reasonably presume that there is some corresponding difference between the physical objects; if two objects both look blue, we may presume a corresponding similarity. But we cannot hope to be acquainted directly with the quality in the physical object which makes it look blue or red. Science tells us that this quality is a certain sort of wave-motion, and this sounds familiar, because we think of wave-motions in the space we see. But the wave-motions must really be in physical space, with which we have no direct acquaintance; thus the real wave-motions have not that familiarity which we might have supposed them to have. And what holds for colours is closely similar to what holds for other sense-data. Thus we find that, although the *relations* of physical objects have all sorts of knowable properties, derived from their correspondence with the relations of sense-data, the physical objects themselves remain unknown in their intrinsic nature, so far at least as can be discovered by means of the senses. The question remains whether there is any other method of discovering the intrinsic nature of physical objects.

The most natural, though not ultimately the most defensible, hypothesis to adopt in the first instance, at any rate as regards visual sense-data, would be that, though physical objects cannot, for the reasons we have been considering, be *exactly* like sense-data, yet they may be more or less like. According to this view, physical objects will, for example, really have colours, and we might, by good luck, see an object as of the colour it really is. The colour which an object seems to have at any given moment will in general be very similar, though not quite the same, from many different points of view; we might thus suppose the "real" colour to be a sort of medium colour, intermediate between the various shades which appear from the different points of view.

Such a theory is perhaps not capable of being definitely refuted, but it can be shown to be groundless. To begin with, it is plain that the colour we see depends only upon the nature of the light-waves that strike the eye, and is therefore modified by the medium intervening between us and the object, as well as by the manner in which light is reflected from the object in the direction of the eye. The intervening air alters colours unless it is perfectly clear, and any strong reflection will alter them completely. Thus the colour we see is a result of the ray as it reaches the eye, and not simply a property of the object from which the ray comes. Hence, also, provided certain waves reach the eye, we shall see a certain colour, whether the object from which the waves start has any colour or not. Thus it is quite gratuitous to suppose that physical objects have colours, and therefore there is no justification for making such a supposition. Exactly similar arguments will apply to other sense-data.

It remains to ask whether there are any general philosophical arguments enabling us to say that, if matter is real, it *must* be of such and such a nature. As explained above, very many philosophers, perhaps most, have held that whatever is real must be in some sense mental, or at any rate that whatever we can know anything about must be in some sense mental. Such philosophers are called "idealists." Idealists tell us that what appears as matter is really something mental; namely, either (as Leibniz held) more or less rudimentary minds, or (as Berkeley contended) ideas in the minds which, as we should commonly say, "perceive" the matter. Thus idealists deny the existence of matter as something intrinsically different from mind, though they do not deny that our sense-data are signs of something which exists independently of our private sensations. In the following chapter we shall consider briefly the reasons—in my opinion fallacious—which idealists advance in favour of their theory.

3
ETHICS

In metaphysics, logic, and epistemology, it is fairly easy to distinguish theoretical concerns from practical ones. For example, the metaphysical doctrine that no human being has free will raises issues that are primarily theoretical, that turn on what it means to say that one could have chosen to act differently from the way one did, that one's choices and actions are determined or caused by antecedent conditions, and that freedom and determinism, so interpreted, are logically compatible. These are all abstract issues whose direct practical consequences, if any, are seldom in the forefront of philosophical speculation.

In contrast, theoretical and practical issues are closely interwoven in ethics, sometimes called "moral philosophy." To be sure, ethics has a theoretical dimension that in principle can be abstracted from practical, concrete concerns, and some of the essays that follow have a pronounced theoretical emphasis. One in particular, the selection taken from G. E. Moore's *Principia Ethica*, is famous for its abstract treatment of moral questions. Moore points out that moral philosophers from the ancient Greeks to the twentieth century have concentrated on the question "What is the good life for man?" and have assumed almost universally that one should try to answer such a question by defining the term *good*. Moreover, they tend to assume that any correct answer lies in finding a psychological term equivalent to good, such as *pleasure, happiness,* or *satisfaction of desire*. Moore points out that the very effort to define *good* at all is misguided insofar as it assumes that any psychological or "naturalistic" term, such as pleasure, can mean the same thing as good. He called any such attempt at definition "the naturalistic fallacy," pointing out that if any sentence of the form "Pleasure is the only good" is not considered a truism like "Pleasure is the only pleasure," or "Good is the only good," it follows that no such term as *pleasure* or *happiness* can mean the same thing as "good." He concluded that "good" is *indefinable*, meaning that it cannot be explained or understood in nonmoral terms.

Whether Moore is right has been much debated since his essay appeared;

but our point now does not depend on deciding the question. We are stressing, rather, that though there are potential, long-range, practical implications stemming from his analysis—for example, that it would be a mistake for anyone to aim at pleasure if he wishes to lead a good life—the position Moore advances is mainly theoretical, turning on technical arguments. Philosophers have not objected to his theory because of its practical consequences, which for them are comparatively unimportant. Rather, they feel that his argumentation is invalid, so they have opposed it on highly technical grounds. It has thus been debated at an abstract rather than at an applied level.

Our aim in this chapter is to emphasize both the theoretical and applied sides of moral philosophy and to bring out how they are greatly intertwined. To do so, we have focused the readings on two questions: (1) Is abortion ever morally justified? (2) Is pleasure the main goal in life? The selections that deal with these issues are organized according to our usual sequence. They open with modern essays, then return to older sources to see how philosophers of the past have addressed these questions. We have chosen these selections because they identify and analyze the issues that are central to each problem. The readings should thus be of great interest to the student, since he or she will be able to follow the reasoning of master thinkers debating issues of the deepest human import.

The problem of abortion is easy to formulate but, as we shall see, difficult to resolve. By definition abortion is an interruption in the normal development of a pre-natal entity with the intention of terminating its existence. Not all invasive procedures interrupting the normal development of pre-natal entities are abortions. A Caesarian operation is such a medical procedure, but it is designed to *save* the life of the fetus.

As so posed, the problem of abortion's moral justifiability arises from two assumptions: (1) A pre-natal entity is an innocent being and (2) it is seemingly being given the ultimate punishment, namely, death. What moral system could possibly justify such an action against the innocent?

As the readings clearly bring out, the abortion issue is very complicated. Broadly speaking, we can distinguish two general types of answers. The first holds that pre-natal entities are undeveloped human beings and possibly even full-fledged persons having the essential properties that make us human, but that putting them to death is perfectly justifiable. Father John Connery, in the essay chosen from his book *Abortion: The Development of the Roman Catholic Perspective*, points out that abortion was a common practice in the Roman world and was not regarded as evil. In modern Japan, abortion is widely practiced. The reasons the Japanese give to support such a practice vary, but they typically include extreme overpopulation and the inability of households to support additional children. Unquestionably most persons who allow a child to be aborted do so reluctantly, arguing that when all factors are taken into consideration it is the only reasonable course of action.

This sort of justification, we stress, concedes that the aborted fetus is human. It simply states that sometimes killing the innocent is necessary and that there are overwhelming moral grounds that justify doing so. Analogies are drawn between abortion and war, which also results in the killing of infants and other innocent persons yet is justified by every civil society.

But more typically, those who justify abortion *deny* that one is engaged in killing the innocent. They draw a sharp line between abortion and infanticide. They claim that once the fetus has developed into a child (that is, has been born) it is both human and a person; and accordingly, infanticide is never justified, since this would amount to killing innocent persons. But they deny that the fetus is a human being (person). The arguments supporting this position become very subtle, and are advanced on both legal and moral grounds.

We have included the Supreme Court decision of 1973 that is the prevailing interpretation of law on the question of abortion. In *Rowe* v. *Wade* the Court held that fetuses are not "full legal persons" and that a woman has a right to an abortion, a right that is derived from the more general constitutional right to privacy. This decision had some qualifications. It stated that the general right to privacy is not absolute. Justice Blackmun specifically denied that a woman's right was absolute since "a state may properly assert important interests in safeguarding health, in maintaining medical standards, and in protecting *potential* life." Moreover, according to the Court, the state may also intervene after three months to protect the health of the woman, and the state can proscribe an abortion in the last ten weeks unless the mother's life or health is at stake. This landmark decision seems to be based upon the notion that at certain stages in its development the fetus is not a person and hence that the termination of the life of the fetus is not a case of killing innocent persons.

The supreme courts of various states have also ruled on abortion. In New York, for instance, abortion is legally permitted as late as the twenty-fourth week of pregnancy. In 1983 the Supreme Court nullified some state laws seeking to limit or regulate conditions under which some abortions could take place.

In general, those who say that abortion is morally justified while also holding that the killing of innocent persons is never morally justified must draw some sort of distinction between the fetus and a full-fledged human being, or human person. At the simplest level, some philosophers have claimed that the pre-natal entity is not human at all. Usually this position is held with respect to what is called the zygote (the fertilized cell less than a week old). These philosophers contend that the zygote (or conceptus or embryo) is only a "piece of tissue," comparable to a benign tumor, and that excising it has no moral implications, just as excising a tumor does not. This view, in effect, holds that the zygote is not a human being.

After about four weeks certain human features, including a face and incipient limbs, appear in the embryo, and by the eighth week brain functions can be detected. From the eighth week on, the entity is called a fetus. Some who say abortion is justified and does not amount to the killing of the innocent argue that though the fetus is *human*, it is not *a person*. Exactly what is meant by *person* is very complicated; some of the essays discuss this question in some detail. In some views, a person is a human being with a soul, a certain kind of psychic entity distinct from the body. Some religious people say it is the soul that goes to heaven after death, and for them baptism and other religious sacraments apply only to the soul. For such people, the question of when the soul appears is the fundamental issue with respect to the legitimacy of abortion. There are still other definitions of personhood, many of them developed by nonreligious defenders of abortion. Here we can summarize by saying that these people, while admitting that a pre-natal entity may be a human being or potential human being, deny that it is a person and accordingly deny that an innocent person is being killed.

Adherents of the extreme right-to-life position claim that abortion is *never* justified, even to save the life of the mother. They claim that from the moment of conception the object in the womb is a human being (and, some hold, a person with a human soul). They then argue that such human beings are innocent of any crime, so that any treatment of them must parallel the treatment of post-natal persons—infants and adults. If that is so, they argue, and if it is always morally unjust to kill post-natal human beings who are innocent of any crime, then it is unjust to kill the innocent unborn. The basic premise behind this position is that from the moment of conception the cell is a human being, although in its early stages a rudimentary or developing one, and that there is normally an unbroken continuity from the zygote to the mature, post-natal adult. This view draws no distinction between a zygote and a post-natal person with respect to humanity, and since the pre-natal entity is innocent, abortion is always morally wrong.

Let us turn now to the question of whether the good life is one of pleasure. Those who hold that it is are called hedonists (from the Greek word meaning "pleasure"). There are two forms of hedonism, psychological and ethical. Psychological and ethical hedonism are independent views. A philosopher could hold one of them without necessarily holding the other, and in the history of moral philosophy we find various combinations of these two principles. The psychological hedonist holds that *in fact* everyone is motivated by the desire to acquire pleasure; that this is our goal in life. Freud's defense of the so-called pleasure principle seems to share this view.

The ethical hedonist, on the other hand, argues that independent of what people *actually* aim at, they *should* aim at pleasure, which is the only thing worth having in its own right. The doctrine of Bentham and Mill that one ought to try to maximize the surplus of pleasure over pain in one's life seems to exemplify ethical hedonism. The basic argument of ethical hedonism is that pleasure, purified of everything else, produces an optimal feeling in the individual; pleasure produces feelings of well-being, contentment, and peace of mind. So being in a pleasant state is one of the maximum benefits that can accrue to a human being. Behind the argument lies the idea "Try it and see if you don't agree." Indeed, the argument goes on to say that the only reason for doing anything is to get pleasure out of doing it. Why do misers attempt to acquire and possess money? It is not the money that motivates them but the pleasure they get from possessing it. Why does Smith sacrifice himself for his family? It is because he ultimately gets pleasure out of doing so. If he didn't, he wouldn't do it (as Freud argued).

Many philosophers have disagreed with both theses of hedonism: that people strive to get pleasure and that pleasure is worth having in its own right. Bishop Joseph Butler (1662–1752), an English clergyman and author of the celebrated work *The Analogy of Religion* (1736), said that psychological hedonism is false. We do not seek pleasure, which cannot be identified, but things. If a man is hungry he does not seek pleasure but food; if thirsty, water to drink; if cold, warmth.

Even the classical Greek proponents of hedonism, Aristippus and Epicurus, recognized that pleasures can be divided into good and bad. Of course, if that is so, then *pleasure* and *good* cannot mean the same thing, which is the position Moore was to defend two thousand years later. But instead of abandoning ethical hedonism, Aristippus and Epicurus argued that a distinction can be made between pleasure and certain kinds of painful or uncomfortable consequences of obtaining such pleasure. If one gets pleasure from eating, and if one eats too much and becomes nauseated, it is the nausea that is bad, not the pleasure. One should simply eat more moderately and avoid the evil consequences of gluttony. Epicurus, for instance, modified the hedonic doctrine to argue that it was important to lead a life that was pleasant in the long run rather than to acquire intense momentary pleasures that had disagreeable accompaniments or consequences.

The basic problem with ethical hedonism, however, is that it runs counter to ordinary human experience. Most persons believe, as Aristotle did, that a good life should have *some* pleasure in it. If everything that happened to a person were unfortunate, that person's life could not be good by any measure. But persons of common sense believe that a life wholly concentrated upon the acquisition of pleasure is unbalanced in a different direction. They emphatically disagree with the late Mae West, who is reported to have said "Too much pleasure is not enough."

But now the reader should turn to the debate on this question personally and see where it leads.

A. IS ABORTION EVER MORALLY JUSTIFIED?

This is the entire 1973 United States Supreme Court decision of *Roe v. Wade*. It expresses the current legal interpretation of abortion in the United States.

SUPREME COURT OF THE UNITED STATES

Syllabus

ROE ET AL. *v.* WADE, DISTRICT ATTORNEY OF DALLAS COUNTY

APPEAL FROM THE UNITED STATES DISTRICT COURT FOR THE NORTHERN DISTRICT OF TEXAS

No. 70–18. Argued December 13, 1971—Reargued October 11, 1972—Decided January 22, 1973

A pregnant single woman (Roe) brought a class action challenging the constitutionality of the Texas criminal abortion laws, which proscribe procuring or attempting an abortion except on medical advice for the purpose of saving the mother's life. A licensed physician (Hallford), who had two state abortion prosecutions pending against him, was permitted to intervene. A childless married couple (the Does), the wife not being pregnant, separately attacked the laws, basing alleged injury on the future possibilities of contraceptive failure, pregnancy, unpreparedness for parenthood, and impairment of the wife's health. A three-judge District Court, which consolidated the actions, held that Roe and Hallford, and members of their classes, had standing to sue and presented justiciable controversies. Ruling that declaratory, though not injunctive, relief was warranted, the court declared the abortion statutes void as vague and overbroadly infringing those plaintiffs' Ninth and Fourteenth Amendment rights. The court ruled the Does' complaint not justiciable. Appellants directly appealed to this Court on the injunctive rulings, and appellee cross-appealed from the District Court's grant of declaratory relief to Roe and Hallford. Held:

1. While 28 U.S.C. § 1253 authorizes no direct appeal to this Court from the grant or denial of declaratory relief alone, review is not foreclosed when the case is properly before the Court on appeal from specific denial of injunctive

relief and the arguments as to both injunctive and declaratory relief are necessarily identical. P.8.

2. Roe has standing to sue; the Does and Hallford do not. Pp. 9–14.

ROE *v.* WADE

Syllabus

(a) Contrary to appellee's contention, the natural termination of Roe's pregnancy did not moot her suit. Litigation involving pregnancy, which is "capable of repetition, yet evading review," is an exception to the usual federal rule that an actual controversy must exist at review stages and not simply when the action is initiated. Pp. 9–10.

(b) The District Court correctly refused injunctive, but erred in granting declaratory, relief to Hallford, who alleged no federally protected right not assertable as a defense against the good-faith state prosecutions pending against him. *Samuels* v. *Mackell*, 401 U.S. 66.

(c) The Does' complaint, based as it is on contingencies, any one or more of which may not occur, is too speculative to present an actual case or controversy. Pp. 12–14.

3. State criminal abortion laws, like those involved here, that except from criminality only a life-saving procedure on the mother's behalf without regard to the stage of her pregnancy and other interest involved violate the Due Process Clause of the Fourteenth Amendment, which protects against state action the right to privacy, including a woman's qualified right to terminate her pregnancy. Though the State cannot override that right, it has legitimate interests in protecting both the pregnant woman's health and the potentiality of human life, each of which interests grows and reaches a "compelling" point at various stages of the woman's approach to term. Pp. 36–49.

(a) For the stage prior to approximately the end of the first trimester, the abortion decision and its effectuation must be left to the medical judgment of the pregnant woman's attending physician. Pp. 36–47.

(b) For the stage subsequent to approximately the end of the first trimester, the State, in promoting its interest in the health of the mother, may, if it chooses, regulate the abortion procedure in ways that are reasonably related to maternal health. Pp. 43–44.

(c) For the stage subsequent to viability the State, in promoting its interest in the potentiality of human life, may, if it chooses, regulate, and even proscribe, abortion except where necessary, in appropriate medical judgment, for the preservation of the life or health of the mother. Pp. 44–48.

4. The State may define the term "physician" to mean only a physician currently licensed by the State, and may proscribe any abortion by a person who is not a physician as so defined. Pp. 34–35, 48.

5. It is unnecessary to decide the injunctive relief issue since the Texas authorities will doubtless fully recognize the Court's ruling that the Texas criminal abortion statutes are unconstitutional. Pp. 51. 314 F. Supp. 1217, affirmed in part and reversed in part.

BLACKMUN, J., delivered the opinion of the Court, in which BURGER, C. J., and DOUGLAS, BRENNAN, STEWART, MARSHALL, and POWELL, JJ., joined. BURGER, C. J., and DOUGLAS and STEWART, JJ., filed concurring opinions. WHITE, J., filed a dissenting opinion, in which REHNQUIST, J., joined. REHNQUIST, J., filed a dissenting opinion.

VII

Three reasons have been advanced to explain historically the enactment of criminal abortion laws in the 19th century and to justify their continued existence.

It has been argued occasionally that these laws were the product of a Victorian social concern to discourage illicit sexual conduct. Texas, however, does not advance this justification in the present case, and it appears that no court or commentator has taken the argument seriously.[42] The appellants and *amici* contend, moreover, that this is not a proper state purpose at all and suggest that, if it were, the Texas statutes are overbroad in protecting it since the law fails to distinguish between married and unwed mothers.

A second reason is concerned with abortion as a medical procedure. When most criminal abortion laws were first enacted, the procedure was a hazardous one for the woman.[43] This was particularly true prior to the development of antisepsis. Antiseptic techniques, of course, were based on discoveries by Lister, Pasteur, and others first announced in 1867, but were not generally accepted and employed until about the turn of the century. Abortion mortality was high. Even after 1900, and perhaps until as late as the development of antibiotics in the 1940's, standard modern techniques such as dilation and curettage were not nearly so safe as they are today. Thus it has been argued that a State's real concern in enacting a criminal abortion law was to protect the pregnant woman, that is, to restrain her from submitting to a procedure that placed her life in serious jeopardy.

Modern medical techniques have altered this situation. Appellants and various *amici* refer to medical data indicating that abortion in early pregnancy, that is, prior to the end of first trimester, although not without its risk, is now relatively safe. Mortality rates for women undergoing early abortions, where the procedure is legal, appear to be as low as or lower than the rates for normal childbirth.[44] Consequently, any interest of the State in protecting the woman from an inherently hazardous procedure, except when it would be equally dangerous for her to forego it, has largely disappeared. Of course, important state interests in the area of health and medical standards do remain. The State has a legitimate interest in seeing to it that abortion, like any other medical procedure, is performed under circumstances that insure maximum safety for the patient. This interest obviously extends at least to the performing physician and his staff, to the facilities involved, to the availability of after-care, and to adequate provision for any complication or emergency that might arise. The prevalence of high mortality rates at illegal "abortion mills" strengthens, rather than weakens, the State's interest in regulating the conditions under which abortions are performed. Moreover, the risk to the woman increases as her pregnancy continues. Thus the State retains a definite interest in protecting the woman's own health and safety when an abortion is proposed at a late stage of pregnancy.

The third reason is the State's interest—some phrase it in terms of duty—in protecting prenatal life. Some of the argument for this justification rests on the theory that a new human life is present from the moment of conception.[45] The State's interest and general obligation to protect life then extends, it is argued, to prenatal life. Only when the life of the pregnant mother herself is at stake, balanced against the life she carries within her, should the interest of the embryo or fetus not prevail. Logically, of course, a legitimate state interest in this area need not stand or fall on acceptance of the belief that life begins at conception or at some other point prior to life birth. In assessing the State's interest, recognition may be given to the less rigid claim that as long as at least *potential* life is involved, the State may assert interests beyond the protection of the pregnant woman alone.

Parties challenging state abortion laws have sharply disputed in some courts the contention that a purpose of these laws, when enacted was to protect prenatal life.[46] Pointing to the absence of legislative history to support the contention, they claim that most state laws were designed solely to protect the woman. Because medical advances have lessened this concern, at least with respect to abortion in early pregnancy, they argue that with respect to such abortions the laws can no longer be justified by any state interest. There is some scholarly support for this view of original purpose.[47] The few state courts called upon to interpret their laws in the late 19th and early 20th centuries did focus on the State's interest in protecting the woman's health rather than in preserving the embryo and fetus.[48] Proponents of this view point out that in many States, including Texas,[49] by statute or judicial interpretation, the pregnant woman herself could not be prosecuted for self-abortion or for cooperating in an abortion performed upon her by another.[50] They claim that adoption of the "quickening" distinction through received common law and state statutes tacitly recognizes the greater health hazards inherent in late abortion and impliedly repudiates the theory that life begins at conception.

It is with these interests, and the weight to be attached to them, that this case is concerned.

VIII

The Constitution does not explicitly mention any right of privacy. In a line of decisions, however, going back perhaps as far as *Union Pacific R. Co. v. Botsford,* 141 U.S. 250, 251 (1891), the Court has recognized that a right of personal privacy, or a guarantee of certain areas or zones of privacy, does exist under the Constitution. In varying contexts the Court or individual Justices have indeed found at least the roots of that right in the First Amendment, *Stanley* v. *Georgia*, 394 U.S. 557, 564 (1969); in the Fourth and Fifth Amendments, *Terry* v. *Ohio*, 392 U.S. 1, 8–9 (1968), *Katz* v. *United States*, 389 U.S. 347, 350 (1967), *Boyd* v. *United States*, 116 U.S. 616 (1886), see *Olmstead* v. *United States*, 277 U.S. 438, 478 (1928) (Brandeis, J. dissenting); in the penumbras of the Bill of Rights, *Griswold* v. *Connecticut*, 381 U.S. 479, 484–485 (1965); in the Ninth Amendment, *id.*, at 486 (Goldberg, J., concurring); or in the concept of liberty guaranteed by the first section of the Fourteenth Amendment, see *Meyer* v. *Nebraska*, 262 U.S. 390, 399 (1923). These decisions make it clear that only personal rights that can be deemed "fundamental" or "implicit in the concept of ordered liberty," *Palko* v. *Connecticut*, 302 U.S. 319, 325 (1937), are included in this guarantee of personal privacy. They also make it clear that the right has some extension to activities relating to marriage, *Loving* v. *Virginia*, 388 U.S. 1, 12 (1967), procreation, *Skinner* v. *Oklahoma*, 316 U.S. 535, 541–542 (1942), contraception, *Eisenstadt* v. *Baird*, 405 U.S. 438, 453–454 (1972); *id.*, at 460, 463–465 (WHITE, J., concurring), family relationships, *Prince* v. *Massachusetts*, 321 U.S. 158, 166 (1944), and child rearing and education, *Pierce* v. *Society of Sisters*, 268 U.S. 510, 535 (1925), *Meyer* v. *Nebraska, supra.*

This right of privacy, whether it be founded in the Fourteenth Amendment's concept of personal liberty and restrictions upon state action, as we feel it is, or, as the District Court determined, in the Ninth Amendment's reservation of rights to the people, is broad enough to encompass a woman's decision whether or not to terminate her pregnancy. The detriment that the State would impose upon the pregnant woman by denying this choice altogether is apparent. Specific and direct harm medically diagnosable even in early pregnancy may be involved. Maternity, or additional offspring, may force upon the woman a distressful life and future. Psychological harm may be imminent. Mental and physical health may be taxed by child care. There is also the distress, for all concerned, associated with the unwanted child, and there is the problem of bringing a child into a family already unable, psychologically and otherwise, to care for it. In other cases, as in this one, the additional difficulties and continuing stigma of unwed motherhood may be involved. All these are factors the woman and her responsible physician necessarily will consider in consultation.

On the basis of elements such as these, appellants and some *amici* argue that the woman's right is absolute and that she is entitled to terminate her pregnancy at whatever time, in whatever way, and for whatever reason she alone chooses. With these we do not agree. Appellants' arguments that Texas either has no valid interest at all in regulating the abortion decision, or no interest strong enough to support any limitation upon the woman's sole determination, is unpersuasive. The Court's decisions recognizing a right of privacy also acknowledge that some state regulation in areas protected by that right is appropriate. As noted above, a state may properly assert important interests in safeguarding health, in maintaining medical standards, and in protecting potential life. At some point in pregnancy, these respective interests become sufficiently compelling to sustain regulation of the factors that govern the abortion decision. The privacy right involved, therefore, cannot be said to be absolute. In fact, it is not clear to us that the claim asserted by some *amici* that one has an unlimited right to do with one's body as one pleases bears a close relationship to the right of privacy previously articulated in the Court's decisions. The Court has refused to recognize an unlimited right of this kind in the past. *Jacobson* v. *Massachusetts*, 197 U.S. 11 (1905) (vaccination); *Buck* v. *Bell*, 274 U.S. 200 (1927) (sterilization).

We therefore conclude that the right of personal privacy includes the abortion decision, but that this right is not unqualified and must be considered against important state interests in regulation.

We note that those federal and state courts that have recently considered abortion law challenges have reached the same conclusion. A majority, in addition to the District Court in the present case, have held state laws unconstitutional, at least in part, because of vagueness or because of overbreadth and abridgement of rights. *Abele* v. *Markle*, 342 F. Supp. 800 (Conn. 1972), appeal pending; *Abele* v. *Markle*, —— F. Supp. —— (Conn. Sept. 20, 1972), appeal pending; *Doe* v. *Bolton*, 319 F. Supp. 1048 (ND Ga. 1970), appeal decided today, *post* ——; *Doe* v. *Scott*, 321 F. Supp. 1385 (ND Ill. 1971), appeal pending; *Poe* v. *Menghini*, 339 F. Supp. 986 (Kan. 1972); *YWCA* v. *Kugler*, 342 F. Supp. 1048 (NJ 1972); *Babbitz* v. *McCann*, 310 F. Supp. 293 (ED Wis. 1970), appeal dismissed, 400 U.S. 1 (1970); *People* v. *Belous*, 71 Cal. 2d 954, 458 P. 2d 194 (1969), cert. denied. 397 U.S. 915 (1970); *State* v. *Barquet*, 262 S. 2d 431 (Fla. 1972).

Others have sustained state statutes. *Crossen* v. *Attorney General*, 344 F. Supp. 587 (ED Ky. 1972), appeal pending; *Rosen* v. *Louisiana State Board of Medical Examiners*, 318 F. Supp. 1217 (ED La. 1970), appeal pending; *Corkey* v. *Edwards*, 322 F. Supp. 1248 (WDNC 1971), appeal pending; *Steinberg* v. *Brown*, 321 F. Supp. 741 (ND Ohio 1970); *Doe* v. *Rampton*, —— F. Supp. —— (Utah 1971), appeal pending; *Cheaney* v. *Indiana*, —— Ind. ——, 285 N.E. 2d 265 (1972); *Spears* v. *State*, 257 So. 2d 876 (Miss. 1972): *State* v. *Munson*, —— S.D. ——, 201 N.W. 2d 123 (1972), appeal pending.

Although the results are divided, most of these courts have agreed that the right of privacy, however based, is broad enough to cover the abortion decision; that the right, nonetheless, is not absolute and is subject to some limitations; and that at some point the state interests as to protection of health, medical standards, and prenatal life, become dominant. We agree with this approach.

Where certain "fundamental rights" are involved, the Court has held that regulation limiting these rights may be justified only by a "compelling state interest." *Kramer* v. *Union Free School District*, 395 U.S. 621, 627 (1969); *Shapiro* v. *Thompson*, 394 U.S. 618, 634 (1969); *Sherbert* v. *Verner*, 374 U.S. 398, 406 (1963), and that legislative enactments must be narrowly drawn to express only the legitimate state interests at stake. *Griswold* v. *Connecticut*, 381 U.S. 479, 485 (1965);

Aptheker v. *Secretary of State*, 378 U.S. 500, 508 (1964); *Cantwell* v. *Connecticut*, 310 U.S. 296, 307–308 (1940); see *Eisenstadt* v. *Baird*, 405 U.S. 438, 460, 463–464 (1972) (WHITE, J., concurring).

In the recent abortion cases cited above, courts have recognized these principles. Those striking down state laws have generally scrutinized the State's interest in protecting health and potential life and have concluded that neither interest justified broad limitations on the reasons for which a physician and his pregnant patient might decide that she should have an abortion in the early stages of pregnancy. Courts sustaining state laws have held that the State's determinations to protect health or prenatal life are dominant and constitutionally justifiable.

IX

The District Court held that the appelle failed to meet his burden of demonstrating that the Texas statute's infringement upon Roe's rights was necessary to support a compelling state interest, and that, although the defendant presented "several compelling justifications for state presence in the area of abortions," the statutes outstripped these justifications and swept "far beyond any areas of compelling state interest." 314 F. Supp., at 1222–1223. Appellant and appellee both contest that holding. Appellant, as has been indicated, claims an absolute right that bars any state imposition of criminal penalties in the area. Appellee argues that the State's determination to recognize and protect prenatal life from and after conception constitutes a compelling state interest. As noted above, we do not agree fully with either formulation.

A. The appellee and certain *amici* argue that the fetus is a "person" within the language and meaning of the Fourteenth Amendment. In support of this they outline at length and in detail the well-known facts of fetal development. If this suggestion of personhood is established, the appellant's case, of course, collapses, for the fetus' right to life is then guaranteed specifically by the Amendment. The appellant conceded as much on reargument.[51] On the other hand, the appellee conceded on reargument[52] that no case could be cited that holds that a fetus is a person within the meaning of the Fourteenth Amendment.

The Constitution does not define "person" in so many words. Section 1 of the Fourteenth Amendment contains three references to "person." The first, in defining "citizens," speaks of "persons born or naturalized in the United States." The word also appears both in the Due Process Clause and in the Equal Protection Clause. "Person" is used in other places in the Constitution: in the listing of qualifications for representatives and senators, Art. I, § 2, cl. 2, and § 3, cl. 3; in the Apportionment Clause, Art. I, § 2, cl. 3;[53] in the Migration and Importation provision, Art. I, § 9, cl. 1; in the Emolument Clause, Art. I, § 9, cl. 8; in the Electors provisions, Art. II, § 1, cl. 2, and the superseded cl. 3; in the provision outlining qualifications for the office of President, Art. II, § 1, cl. 5; in the Extradition provisions, Art. IV, § 2, cl. 2, and the superseded Fugitive Slave cl. 3; and in the Fifth, Twelfth, and Twenty-second Amendments as well as in §§ 2 and 3 of the Fourteenth Amendment. But in nearly all these instances, the use of the word is such that it has application only postnatally. None indicates, with any assurance, that it has any possible pre-natal application.[54]

All this, together with our observation, *supra*, that throughout the major portion of the 19th century prevailing legal abortion practices were far freer than they are today, persuades us that the word "person," as used in the Fourteenth Amendment, does not include the unborn.[55] This is in accord with the results reached in those few cases where the issue has been squarely presented. *McGarvey v. Magee-Womens Hospital*, 340 F. Supp. 751 (WD Pa. 1972); *Byrn v. New York City Health & Hospitals Corp.*, 31 N.Y. 2d 194, 286 N.E. 2d 887 (1972), appeal pending; *Abele v. Markle*, ‒‒‒‒ F. Supp. ‒‒‒‒ (Conn. Sept. 20, 1972), appeal pending. Compare *Cheaney v. Indiana*, ‒‒‒‒ Ind. ‒‒‒‒, 285 N.E. 265, 270 (1972); *Montana v. Rogers*, 278 F. 2d 68, 72 (CA7 1960), aff'd *sub nom. Montana v. Kennedy*, 366 U.S. 308 (1961); *Keeler v. Superior Court*, ‒‒‒‒ Cal. ‒‒‒‒, 470 P. 2d 617 (1970); *State v. Dickinson*, 23 Ohio App. 2d 259, 275 N.E. 2d 599 (1970). Indeed, our decision in *United States v. Vuitch*, 402 U.S. 62 (1971), inferentially is to the same effect, for we there would not have indulged in statutory interpretation favorable to abortion in specified circumstances if the necessary consequence was the termination of life entitled to Fourteenth Amendment protection.

This conclusion, however, does not of itself fully answer the contentions raised by Texas, and we pass on to other considerations.

B. The pregnant woman cannot be isolated in her privacy. She carries an embryo and, later, a fetus, if one accepts the medical definitions of the developing young in the human uterus. See Dorland's Illustrated Medical Dictionary, 478–479, 547 (24th ed. 1965). The situation therefore is inherently different from marital intimacy, or bedroom possession of obscene material, or marriage, or procreation, or education, with which *Eisenstadt, Giswold, Stanley, Loving, Skinner, Pierce,* and *Meyer* were respectively concerned. As we have intimated above, it is reasonable and appropriate for a State to decide that at some point in time another interest, that of health of the mother or that of potential human life, becomes significantly involved. The woman's privacy is no longer sole and any right of privacy she possesses must be measured accordingly.

Texas urges that, apart from the Fourteenth Amendment, life begins at conception and is present throughout pregnancy, and that, therefore, the State has a compelling interest in protecting that life from and after conception. We need not resolve the difficult question of when life begins. When those trained in the respective disciplines of medicine, philosophy, and theology are unable to arrive at any consensus, the judiciary, at this point in the development of man's knowledge, is not in a position to speculate as to the answer.

It should be sufficient to note briefly the wide divergence of thinking on this most sensitive and difficult question. There has always been strong support for the view that life does not begin until live birth. This was the belief of the Stoics.[56] It appears to be the predominant, though not the unanimous, attitude of the Jewish faith.[57] It may be taken to represent also the position of a large segment of the Protestant community, insofar as that can be ascertained; organized groups that have taken a formal position on the abortion issue have generally regarded abortion as a matter for the conscience of the individual and her family.[58] As we have noted, the common law found greater significance in quickening. Physicians and their scientific colleagues have regarded that event with less interest and have tended to focus either upon conception or upon live birth or upon the interim point at which the fetus becomes "viable," that is, potentially able to live outside the mother's womb, albeit with artificial aid.[59] Viability is usually placed at about seven months (28 weeks) but may occur earlier, even at 24 weeks.[60] The Aristotelian theory of "mediate anima-tion," that held sway throughout the Middle Ages and the Renaissance in Europe, continued to be official Roman Catholic dogma until the 19th century, despite opposition to this "ensoulment" theory from those in the Church who would recognize the existence of life from the moment of conception.[61] The latter is now, of course, the official belief of the Catholic Church. As one of the briefs *amicus* discloses, this is a view strongly held by many non-Catholics as well, and by many physicians. Substantial problems for precise definition of this view are posed, however, by new embryological data that purport to indi-cate that conception is a "process" over time, rather than an event, and by new medical techniques such as menstrual extraction, the "morning-after" pill, implantation of embryos, artificial insemination, and even artificial wombs.[62]

In areas other than criminal abortion the law has been reluctant to endorse any theory that life, as we recognize it, begins before live birth or to accord legal rights to the unborn except in narrowly defined situations and except when the rights are contingent upon live birth. For example, the traditional rule of tort law had denied recovery for prenatal injuries even though the child was born alive.[63] That rule has been changed in almost every jurisdiction. In most States recovery is said to be permitted only if the fetus was viable, or at least quick, when the injuries were sustained, though few courts have squarely so held.[64] In a recent development, generally opposed by the commentators, some States permit the parents of a stillborn child to maintain an action for wrongful death because of prenatal injuries.[65] Such an action, however, would appear to be one to vindicate the parents' interest and is thus consistent with the view that the fetus, at most, represents only the potentiality of life. Simi-larly, unborn children have been recognized as acquiring rights or interests by way of inheritance or other devolution of property, and have been represented by guardians *ad litem*.[66] Perfection of the interests involved, again, has generally been contingent upon live birth. In short, the unborn have never been recog-nized in the law as persons in the whole sense.

X

In view of all this, we do not agree that, by adopting one theory of life, Texas may override the rights of the pregnant woman that are at stake. We repeat, however, that the State does have an important and legitimate interest in preserving and protecting the health of the pregnant woman, whether she be a resident of the State or a nonresident who seeks medical consultation and treatment there, and that it has still *another* important and legitimate interest in protecting the potentiality of human life. These interests are separate and distinct. Each grows in substantiality as the woman approaches term and, at a point during pregnancy, each becomes "compelling."

With respect to the State's important and legitimate interest in the health of the mother, the "compelling" point, in the light of present medical knowledge, is at approximately the end of the first trimester. This is so because of the now established medical fact, referred to above at p. 34, that until the end of the first trimester mortality in abortion is less than mortality in normal childbirth. It follows that, from and after this point, a State may regulate the abortion procedure to the extent that the regulation reasonably relates to the preservation and protection of maternal health. Examples of permissible state regulation in this area are requirements as to the qualifications of the person who is to perform the abortion; as to the licensure of that person; as to the facility in which the procedure is to be performed, that is, whether it must be a hospital or may be a clinic or some other place of less-than-hospital status; as to the licensing of the facility; and the like.

This means, on the other hand, that, for the period of pregnancy prior to this "compelling" point, the attending physician, in consultation with his patient, is free to determine, without regulation by the State, that in his medical judgment the patient's pregnancy should be terminated. If that decision is reached, the judgment may be effectuated by an abortion free of interference by the State.

With respect to the State's important and legitimate interest in potential life, the "compelling" point is at viability. This is so because the fetus then presumably has the capability of meaningful life outside the mother's womb. State regulation protective of fetal life after viability thus has both logical and biological justifications. If the State is interested in protecting fetal life after viability, it may go so far as to proscribe abortion during that period except when it is necessary to preserve the life or health of the mother.

Measured against these standards, Art. 1196 of the Texas Penal Code, in restricting legal abortions to those "procured or attempted by medical advice for the purpose of saving the life of the mother," sweeps too broadly. The statute makes no distinction between abortions performed early in pregnancy and those performed later, and it limits to a single reason, "saving" the mother's life, the legal justification for the procedure. The statute, therefore, cannot survive the constitutional attack made upon it here.

This conclusion makes it unnecessary for us to consider the additional challenge to the Texas statute asserted on the grounds of vagueness. See *United States* v. *Vuitch*, 402 U.S. 62, 67–72 (1971).

XI

To summarize and to repeat:

1. A state criminal abortion statute of the current Texas type, that excepts

from criminality only a *life saving* procedure on behalf of the mother, without regard to pregnancy stage and without recognition of the other interests involved, is violative of the Due Process Clause of the Fourteenth Amendment.

(a) For the stage prior to approximately the end of the first trimester, the abortion decision and its effectuation must be left to the medical judgment of the pregnant woman's attending physician.

(b) For the stage subsequent to approximately the end of the first trimester, the State, in promoting its interest in the health of the mother, may, if it chooses, regulate the abortion procedure in ways that are reasonably related to maternal health.

(c) For the stage subsequent to viability the State, in promoting its interest in the potentiality of human life, may, if it chooses, regulate, and even proscribe, abortion except where it is necessary, in appropriate medical judgment, for the preservation of the life or health of the mother.

2. The State may define the term "physician," as it has been employed in the preceding numbered paragraphs of this Part XI of this opinion, to mean only a physician currently licensed by the State, and may proscribe any abortion by a person who is not a physician as so defined.

In *Doe* v. *Bolton, post,* procedural requirements contained in one of the modern abortion statutes are considered. That opinion and this one, of course, are to be read together.[67]

This holding, we feel, is consistent with the relative weights of the respective interests involved, with the lessons and example of medical and legal history, with the lenity of the common law, and with the demands of the profound problems of the present day. The decision leaves the State free to place increasing restrictions on abortion as the period of pregnancy lengthens, so long as those restrictions are tailored to the recognized state interests. The decision vindicates the right of the physician to administer medical treatment according to his professional judgment up to the points where important state interests provide compelling justifications for intervention. Up to those points the abortion decision in all its aspects is inherently, and primarily, a medical decision, and basic responsibility for it must rest with the physician. If an individual practitioner abuses the privilege of exercising proper medical judgment, the usual remedies, judicial and intra-professional, are available.

XII

Our conclusion that Art. 1196 is unconstitutional means, of course, that the Texas abortion statutes, as a unit, must fall. The exception of Art. 1196 cannot be stricken separately, for then the State is left with a statute proscribing all abortion procedures no matter how medically urgent the case.

Although the District Court granted plaintiff Roe declaratory relief, it stopped short of issuing an injunction against enforcement of the Texas statutes. The Court has recognized that different considerations enter into a federal court's decision as to declaratory relief, on the one hand, and injunctive relief, on the other. *Zwickler* v. *Koota.* 389 U.S. 241, 252–255 (1967); *Dombrowski* v.

Pfister, 380 U.S. 479 (1965). We are not dealing with a statute that, on its face, appears to abridge free expression, an area of particular concern under *Dombrowski* and refined in *Younger* v. *Harris*, 401 U.S., at 50.

We find it unnecessary to decide whether the District Court erred in withholding injunctive relief, for we assume the Texas prosecutorial authorities will give full credence to this decision that the present criminal abortion statutes of that State are unconstitutional.

The judgment of the District Court as to intervenor Hallford is reversed, and Dr. Hallford's complaint in intervention is dismissed. In all other respects the judgment of the District Court is affirmed. Costs are allowed to the appellee.

It is so ordered.

NOTES

NOTE: Where it is deemed desirable, a syllabus (headnote) will be released, as is being done in connection with this case, at the time the opinion is issued. The syllabus constitutes no part of the opinion of the Court but has been prepared by the Reporter of Decisions for the convenience of the reader. See *United States* v. *Detroit Lumber Co.*, 200 U.S. 321, 337.

[42]See, for example, YWCA v. *Kugler*, 342 F. Supp. 1048, 1074 (N.J. 1972); *Abele* v. *Markle*, 342 F. Supp. 800, 805–806 (Conn. 1972) (Newman, J., concurring), appeal pending; *Walsingham* v. *Florida*, 250 So. 2d 857, 863 (Ervin, J., concurring) (Fla. Supp. 1972); *State* v. *Gedicke*, 43 N.J.L. 86, 80 (Sup. St. 1881); Means II, at 381–382.

[43]See C. Haagensen & W. Lloyd, A Hundred Years of Medicine 19 (1943).

[44]Potts, Postconception Control of Fertility, 8 Int'l J. of G. & O. 957, 967 (1970) (England and Wales); Abortion Mortality, 20 Morbidity and Morality, 208, 209 (July 12, 1971) (U.S. Dept. of HEW, Public Health Service (New York City); Tietze, United States: Therapeutic Abortions, 1963–1968, 59 Studies in Family Planning 5, 7 (1970); Tietze, Mortality with Contraception and Induced Abortion, 45 Studies in Family Planning 6 (1969) (Japan, Czechoslovakia, Hungary); Tietze & Lehfeldt, Legal Abortion in Eastern Europe, 175 J.A.M.A. 1149, 1152 (April 1961). Other sources are discussed in Lader 17–23.

[45]See Brief of Amicus National Right to Life Foundation; R. Drinan, The Inviolability of the Right to Be Born, in Abortion and the Law 107 (D. Smith, editor, 1967); Louisell, Abortion, The Practice of Medicine, and the Due Process of Law, 16 UCLA L. Rev. 233 (1969); Noonan 1.

[46]See, *e.g.*, *Abele* v. *Markle*, 342 F. Supp. 800 (Conn. 1972), appeal pending.

[47]See discussions in Means I and Means II.

[48]See, *e.g.*, *State* v. *Murphy*, 27 N.J.L. 112, 114 (1858).

[49]*Watson* v. *State*, 9 Tex. App. 237, 244–245 (1880); *Moore* v. *State*, 37 Tex. Crim. R. 552, 561, 40 S.W. 287, 290 (1897); *Shaw* v. *State*, 73 Tex Crim. R. 337, 339, 165 S.W. 930, 931 (1914); *Fondren* v. *State*, 74 Tex. Crim. R. 552, 557, 169 S.W. 411, 414 (1914); *Gray* v. *State*, 77 Tex. Crim. R. 221, 229, 178 S.W. 337, 341 (1915). There is no immunity in Texas for the father who is not married to the mother. *Hammett* v. *State*, 84 Tex. Crim. R. 635, 209 S.W. 661 (1919); *Thompson* v. *State*,——Tex. Crim. R.——(1971), appeal pending.

[50]See *Smith* v. *State*, 33 Me. 48, 55 (1851); *In re Vince*, 2 N.J. 443, 450, 67 A. 2d 141, 144 (1949). A short discussion of the modern law on this issue is contained in the Comment to the ALI's Model Penal Code § 207.11, at 158 and nn. 35–37 (Tent. Draft No. 9, 1959).

[51]Tr. of Rearg. 20–21.

[52]Tr. of Rearg. 24.

[53]We are not aware that in the taking of any census under this clause, a fetus has even been counted.

[54]When Texas urges that a fetus is entitled to Fourteenth Amendment protection as a person, it faces a dilemma. Neither in Texas nor in any other State are all abortions prohibited. Despite broad proscription, an exception always exists. The exception contained in Art. 1196, for an abortion procured or attempted by medical advice for the purpose of saving the life of the mother, is typical. But if the fetus is a person who is not to be deprived of life without due process of law, and if the mother's condition is the sole determinant, does not the Texas exception appear to be out of line with the Amendment's command?

There are other inconsistencies between Fourteenth Amendment status and the typical abortion statute. It has already been pointed out, n. 49, *supra*, that in Texas the woman is not a principal or an accomplice with respect to an abortion upon her. If the fetus is a person, why is the woman not a principal or an accomplice? Further, the penalty for criminal abortion specified by Art. 1195 is significantly less than the maximum penalty for murder prescribed by Art. 1257 of the Texas Penal Code. If the fetus is a person, may the penalties be different?

[55]Cf. the Wisconsin abortion statute, defining "unborn child" to mean "a human being from the time of conception until it is born alive," Wis. Stat. § 940.04 (6) (1969), and the new Connecticut statute, Public Act No. 1, May 1972 Special Session, declaring it to be the public policy of the State and the legislative intent "to protect and preserve human life from the moment of conception."

[56]Edelstein 16.

[57]Lader 97–99; D. Feldman, Birth Control in Jewish Law 251–294 (1968). For a stricter view, see I. Jakobovits, Jewish Views on Abortion, in Abortion and the Law 124 (D. Smith ed. 1967).

[58]Amicus Brief for the American Ethical Union et al. For the position of the National Council of Churches and of other denominations, see Lader 99–101.

[59]L. Hellman & J. Pritchard, Williams Obstetrics 493 (14th ed. 1971); Dorland's Illustrated Medical Dictionary 1689 (24th ed. 1965).

[60]Hellman & Pritchard, *supra*, n. 58, at 493.

[61]For discussions of the development of the Roman Catholic position, see D. Callahan, Abortion: Law, Choice and Morality 409–447 (1970); Noonan 1.

[62]See D. Brodie, The New Biology and the Prenatal Child, 9 J. Fam. L. 391, 397 (1970); R. Gorney, The New Biology and the Future of Man, 15 UCLA L. Rev. 273 (1968); Note, Criminal Law——Abortion——The "Morning-After" Pill and Other Pre-Implantation Birth-Control Methods and the Law, 46 Ore. L. Rev. 211 (1967); G. Taylor, The Biological Time Bomb 32 (1968); A. Rosenfeld, The Second Genesis 138–139 (1969); G. Smith, Through a Test Tube Darkly: Artificial Insemination and the Law, 67 Mich. L. Rev. 127 (1968); Note, Artificial Insemination and the Law, U. Ill. L. F. 203 (1968).

[63]Prosser, Handbook of the Law of Torts 335–338 (1971); 2 Harper & James, The Law of Torts 1028–1031 (1956); Note, 63 Harv. L. Rev. 173 (1949).

[64]See cases cited in Prosser, *supra*, n. 62, at 336–338; Annotation, Action for Death of Unborn Child, 15 A.L.R. 3rd 992 (1967).

[65]Prosser, *supra*, n. 62, at 338; Note, The Law and the Unborn Child, 46 Notre Dame Law. 349, 354–360 (1971).

[66]D. Louisell, Abortion, The Practice of Medicine, and the Due Process of Law, 16 UCLA L. Rev. 233, 235–238 (1969); Note, 56 Iowa L. Rev. 994, 999–1000 (1971); Note, The Law and the Unborn Child, 46 Notre Dame Law. 349, 351–354 (1971).

[67]Neither in this opinion nor in *Doe* v. *Bolton, post*, do we discuss the father's rights, if any exist in the constitutional context, in the abortion decision. No paternal right has been asserted in either of the cases, and the Texas and the Georgia statutes on their face take no cognizance of the father. We are aware that some statutes recognize the father under certain circumstances. North Carolina, for example, 1B N.C. Gen. Stat. § 14–45.1 (Supp. 1971), requires written permission for the abortion from the husband when the woman is a married minor, that is, when she is less than 18 years of age, 41 N.C.A.G. 489 (1971); if the woman is an unmarried minor, written permission from the parents is required. We need not now decide whether provisions of this kind are constitutional.

John Connery

ABORTION: THE DEVELOPMENT OF THE ROMAN CATHOLIC PERSPECTIVE

In this essay taken from *The Development of the Roman Catholic Perspective*, Father John Connery (b. 1913) gives a brief history of the attitude of the Roman Catholic Church on the question of abortion.

The Christian tradition from the earliest days reveals a firm antiabortion attitude. There is no reason to believe that this was a Christian innovation. Strong evidence points to a continuity between this attitude and that of the Jews especially the early Jewish communities of pre-Christian times. But it contrasts markedly with the attitude and practice of the Roman world where the frequency of abortion, and particularly of infanticide, was noted even by pagan writers.

Early condemnations of abortion were generally associated with similar condemnations of infanticide, an indication that in the minds of the early Christians the two were closely related. The condemnation of abortion did not depend on and was not limited in any way by theories regarding the time of fetal animation. Even during the many centuries when Church penal and penitential practice was based on the theory of delayed animation, the condemnation of abortion was never affected by it. Whatever one would want to hold about the time of animation, or when the fetus became a human being in the strict sense of the term, abortion from the time of conception was considered wrong, and the time of animation was never looked on as a moral dividing line between permissible and immoral abortion. As long as what was aborted was destined to be a human being, it made no difference whether the abortion was induced before or after it became so. The final result was the same: a child was not born.

The current debate regarding abortion departs notably from the past in this respect. Many of those who argue in favor of abortion make the primary issue one of hominization. If the fetus is not yet a man, or a human being, or a person, or whatever terminology is used, it is entitled to less consideration. For many the time of hominization is the general dividing line between moral and immoral abortion. In the Christian tradition the distinction between the formed and unformed fetus (animated and unanimated) played no more than a secondary role, at least in reference to abortion. It was mainly used for purposes of legal classification and the grading of penances relative to the reconciliation of sinners.

Although the question when life begins, or when human life begins did not play a decisive role in determining the morality of abortion, it was of great interest to the ancients. What seems to be the more primitive approach held that the fetus did not become a human being until it was born. This was the judgment of the Jews in early biblical times. The Stoic philosopher associated life with breath and held that the fetus did not come alive until it began to breathe. Before it was born the fetus was considered to be part of the mother, and its development was explained in this way. The Aristotelian philosopher moved the beginnings of life back into the fetal period. In fact, the strict Aristotelian held that life began at the moment of conception (or perhaps even before, in some sense). But it was not human life at this stage. The human soul was not infused until the fetus was formed in the mother, and this occurred after forty days in the male fetus, ninety days in the female fetus. Aristotle also said that movement would be detected in an aborted fetus at the same times. According to the strict Aristotelian the fetus, before it was formed, had initially a vegetative soul, then a sensitive soul. But not all accepted this succession of souls. Some simply held that before the human soul was infused, the fetus was part of the mother. Others explained the growth and development of the fetus in the womb by the presence of a formative force in the semen. But there were a number of early Fathers who held the human soul was present right from the beginning. This was true not only of the traducianists, who maintained that the soul was transmitted in the semen just like the body, but also of some creationists, who held that the human soul was created when it was infused.

The question when life began was of decisive importance in classifying abortion as homicide. There is no evidence that early Christians ever associated the beginning of life with birth and therefore did not consider abortion at any time homicide. For centuries, however, the beginning of human life was associated with the formation of the fetus, an association which had its origin in the Septuagint as well as in Aristotle. In this context homicide was limited to the abortion of the formed fetus. Church practice in dealing with irregularities took this limitation into account, and spiritual penances were often graded according to whether the fetus was formed or unformed. But even though abortion of the unformed fetus was not considered real homicide, it was looked upon as anticipated homicide, or interpretive homicide, or homicide in intent, because it involved the destruction of a future man. It was always closely related to homicide.

It was not until the fourteenth century that the distinction between the formed and unformed (animated and unanimated) fetus was used as a basis for an exception to the general condemnation of abortion. A Dominican theologian, John of Naples, was the first to allow abortion of an unanimated fetus if necessary to save the mother's life. The basic reason for the allowance was precisely the fact that the unanimated fetus was not yet a human being. Some later authors questioned whether he was really advocating induced abortion or merely allowing treatment aimed at curing some maternal ailment. There is less ambiguity about authors such as Thomas Sanchez who argued that the fetus was a part of the mother, and in these circumstances, an unjust aggressor. If true, these arguments would justify induced abortion. In many respects the argumentation paralleled that used in the Hebrew tradition to justify dismembering the fetus at the time of delivery to save the mother's life. The only difference was that the dividing line was placed at term rather than at the time of formation.

The exception made by John of Naples had a respectable following, but it also met with opposition. The opposition stemmed from the objection that the arguments used would justify exceptions which no one wanted to make, such as, abortion of the animated fetus to save the mother, and abortion of the unanimated fetus, for other reasons. For a number of reasons, chief among which was the general acceptance of immediate animation, the whole issue of aborting the unanimated fetus to save the mother became obsolete.

Although some of the early church Fathers held immediate animation, theories of delayed animation formed the basis of church practice for many centuries. In the early seventeenth century a Belgian physician, Thomas Fienus, argued in favor of early animation. The argument was based on the need for a formative principle in the embryo right after conception. After ruling out other possibilities, Fienus concluded that this had to be a soul. It also had to be the same soul that was present in the fetus at the end of the developing process, since a succession of souls made no sense to Fienus. The opinion met initially with considerable opposition, but in the course of the next three centuries replaced the theory of delayed animation as the common opinion. It met with great favor from the medical profession, although the issue was more one of philosophy than of medicine. It was accepted in church practice in 1869 when Pius IX removed the limitation set in 1591 by Gregory XIV on excommunication for abortion. Even after immediate animation with a rational soul was commonly accepted there were still a few Aristotelians who continued to hold a succession of souls.

Some have seen in the doctrine of the Immaculate Conception a confirmation of the theory of immediate animation. Although this belief has a long history in the Church, it was not defined until 1854, a few centuries after the opinion was introduced by Thomas Fienus. A few theologians before that time saw in the dating of the feasts of the Immaculate Conception (Dec. 8) and the Nativity of the Blessed Virgin (Sept. 8) an implication regarding immediate animation. But even if one could draw some conclusion from this data, it would pertain only to the Blessed Virgin. But the dating of church feasts does not imply church teaching. Nor did the definition of the Immaculate Conception say anything about the time when the human soul was infused into the Blessed Virgin. All that was defined was that her soul was free from any taint of original sin from the moment of infusion, whenever that took place. The only opinion the Church has ever condemned was that which identified animation with the time of birth. It has never taught immediate animation. Even the fathers of Vatican II resisted efforts to elicit such a teaching statement in connection with its condemnation of abortion. And the most recent declaration (1974) on abortion from the Sacred Congregation for the Doctrine of the Faith made a similar bypass of the question.

Quite as meaningful historically as the issue of deliberately induced abortion was that of accidental abortion. In fact, there is good reason to believe that the case in Exodus was one of accidental abortion. During the Christian era the question of accidental abortion was resolved along the same general lines as accidental killing. The initial legislation freed anyone who was engaged in some necessary activity from responsibility for accidental killing, as long as there was no neglect. Soon the norm became the liceity of the person's act rather than its necessity. If the person was doing something licit and there was no neglect, he would not be responsible for a resulting death. The reader will remember the case of Placidus, and more particularly, that of the Carthusian monk, although in the latter case the more basic issue was that of animation. Initially, theologians and canonists held an individual responsible if the killing resulted from an action which was illicit for any reason. As the subject was more thoroughly considered, they demanded that there be more of a connection between the act and its liceity, and the resulting death. If the illicit act was not the actual cause of the death, or if the reason it was illicit had nothing to do with the danger of causing death, the death would not be imputed to the agent. The reader will recall the case of the cleric on horseback who was struck by another cleric and died from falling off his horse rather than from the blow itself. He will also recall the case of Placidus. The fact that he had stolen the horses (done something illicit) would not in itself make him responsible for the subsequent abortion.

The above reasoning may sound somewhat legalistic, but there is a realism underlying it which admits that not all killing can be reasonably avoided, and courageously confronts the issue of imputability. In the earlier description of accidental killing, the danger of causing death was not foreseen except perhaps in a confused sort of way. Eventually, however, cases arose in which it was quite possible to foresee clearly at least the danger of causing death. Would deaths in such cases be imputable? The question came up in the abortion discussion in connection with the use of remedies such as bloodletting, purgatives, and even bathing, which were prescribed for their therapeutic effects but which carried with them the danger of abortion if the woman was pregnant. The danger of causing an abortion was foreseen quite clearly when prescribing these remedies. Antonius de Corduba was the first theologian to maintain that since such remedies were by nature principally salutary, they could be prescribed when necessary to save the mother's life. But if they were principally lethal, they could not be prescribed. Later authors allowed the use of remedies even if they were only *equally* salutary. The Corduban distinction introduced a new dimension into the abortion discussion, but the distinction met with immediate acceptance. Eventually, it would become known simply as the distinction between *direct* and *indirect* abortion.

The claim is frequently made that the concern of the Catholic Church for the fetus was related chiefly to the question of baptism, that is, the eternal welfare of the fetus. History certainly testifies to the concern of the Church for the spiritual welfare of the fetus, but it testifies with equal clarity that the prior concern was with the taking of fetal life. It was because abortion constituted the taking of fetal life that it was condemned. If the one responsible for the abortion was also to blame for allowing the child to die without baptism, this was an additional fault. But even if the fetus could have been baptized after the abortion, the Church would not have condoned it. It is quite true that interest in baptism was primary in those cases where the abortion was considered accidental, and therefore indirect. If the fetus would have had an opportunity otherwise to be baptized, even accidental abortion to save the mother's life was not acceptable. Only a few theologians considered privation of baptism a primary barrier in abortion deliberately induced to save the mother's life. These were the theologians who held that it could be justified as self-defense against unjust aggression. If it prevented the baptism of the child, they would not allow it even in this case. Some nineteenth-century theologians offered as a reason for what they called *medical abortion* the fact that it would allow the child to be baptized. But again this was a secondary consideration. It was only after they had justified medical abortion as indirect killing that they offered this additional reason for allowing it. They would not have allowed direct killing to provide for the baptism of the child.

One of the most important controversies that arose was over craniotomy or embryotomy to save a mother's life. Those who argued in favor of these procedures maintained that the fetus in these circumstances was an unjust aggressor, even if only in a material sense. If this argument could be made, these procedures could be justified as legitimate self-defense. It will be remembered that St. Thomas and his followers did not allow an intention of killing the aggressor even in self-defense; only the state had this right. But he was satisfied that a private individual could achieve his goal of self-defense without intending to kill the assailant. The killing could be an accidental effect of the self-defense, and therefore *praeter intentionem* (unintentional). The proponents of craniotomy and embryotomy contended that all this would apply to these procedures, and the killing of the fetus would be an unintended effect. But the adversaries refused to consider the fetus an unjust aggressor in any sense. If the proponents of these procedures wanted to convince this group, they would have to justify it apart from a premise of unjust aggression.

No one in the tradition had ever justified intentional killing of an innocent (nonaggressor) person. But accidental killing even of a nonaggressor was not under certain circumstances imputed to the person who placed the act from which it resulted. The key question was whether it was sufficient that the killing of the fetus be *praeter intentionem* in the way St. Thomas required in reference to killing an unjust aggressor in self-defense. Some of the proponents of craniotomy wanted to extend St. Thomas' norm to cover a case where there was no aggression and allow acts of violence directed against an innocent person. The tradition, however, took a different approach to this case. It was more related to what St. Thomas and his predecessors had to say about accidental killing of an innocent person (2-2, q. 64, a. 8). What is clear is that when Corduba took up the question of abortion to save the mother's life he would not allow the type of act that might be proper in self-defense. Even though one might be able to claim that according to St. Thomas the killing even in this case was *praeter intentionem*, it was not permissible if the victim was a nonaggressor. If the act was *principaliter mortifera* it could not be condoned. Some of Corduba's successors qualified his principle somewhat, but none would allow action against a nonaggressor that was *principaliter mortifera*. One cannot get the kind of clarity about this issue he would like since there are at least three interpretations of the meaning of St. Thomas' article on self-defense. But it seems safe to say that the tradition allowed less when the victim was a nonaggressor than when there was unjust aggression, even though in both cases one might claim that the killing was *praeter intentionem*.

What is noteworthy is that none of these authors, with the exception perhaps of Apicella, tried to justify abortion or embryotomy to save the mother's life as an exception to the prohibition against direct killing of an innocent person. And even Apicella, admitting that a private individual did not have this right, felt that he had to introduce the state into the case to justify it. The rest all tried to justify it as accidental in some sense. It was undoubtedly their failure to do this convincingly that led to the condemnation of their opinions. It may be difficult in many cases to know where to draw the line between accidental and deliberate killing, but church authorities apparently felt that these theologians had gone over the line. And this seems to coincide with a common sense approach to the case. This may be the reason why theologians today who want to allow for induced abortion or embryotomy to save the mother's life are more inclined to argue for an exception to the general prohibition of direct killing of an innocent person.

This brings to a conclusion this study of the development of the Roman Catholic perspective on abortion. Curiously enough, the Church today finds itself in a position quite similar to the one which prevailed at the beginning of the Christian era. In those days it was surrounded by a society in which abortion (and infanticide) was practiced frequently. For the first one hundred and fifty years of its existence the Church had no support from the civil law in combating this evil. During the next eighteen hundred years this support was provided in the form of laws penalizing abortion. At the end of the nineteenth century Dr. Carl Capellmann credited Christian civilization with the achievement of almost eradicating abortion. Today, unfortunately, the trend has been reversed. The movement in the western world is toward liberalizing abortion legislation. In the United States laws protecting the fetus against abortion decisions by the mother have actually been declared unconstitutional. And in our present society the frequency of abortion is far greater than anything the Roman or ancient world ever knew or dreamed of. The early Church (together with the Jews) was able to present a common front against abortion in the pagan world. Can a divided Christianity repeat the performance of the early Church? Perhaps one can only respond, although hopefully, with the words of Hamlet: "Tis a consummation devoutly to be wished."

Plato

REPUBLIC

In this passage from the *Republic*, Plato not only argues for
eugenic marriages and the "disposing" of infants with defects
but also for the practice of abortion.

Is there anything better for a state than the generation in it of the best possible
women and men?

There is not.

And this, music and gymnastics applied as we described will effect.

Surely.

Then the institution we proposed is not only possible but the best for the
state.

That is so.

The women of the guardians, then, must strip, since they will be clothed with
virtue as a garment, and must take their part with the men in war and the other
duties of civic guardianship and have no other occupation. But in these very
duties lighter tasks must be assigned to the women than to the men because of
their weakness as a class. But the man who ridicules unclad women, exercising
because it is best that they should, "plucks the unripe fruit" of laughter and
does not know, it appears, the end of his laughter nor what he would be at. For
the fairest thing that is said or ever will be said is this, that the helpful is fair
and the harmful foul.

Assuredly.

In this matter, then, of the regulation of women, we may say that we have
surmounted one of the waves of our paradox and have not been quite swept
away by it in ordaining that our guardians and female guardians must have all
pursuits in common, but that in some sort the argument concurs with itself in
the assurance that what it proposes is both possible and beneficial.

It is no slight wave that you are thus escaping.

You will not think it a great one, I said, when you have seen the one that
follows.

Say on then and show me, said he.

This, said I, and all that precedes has for its sequel, in my opinion, the following law.

What?

That these women shall all be common to all these men, and that none shall cohabit with any privately, and that the children shall be common, and that no parent shall know its own offspring nor any child its parent.

This is a far bigger paradox than the other, and provokes more distrust as to its possibility and its utility.

I presume, said I, that there would be no debate about its utility, no denial that the community of women and children would be the greatest good, supposing it possible. But I take it that its possibility or the contrary would be the chief topic of contention.

Both, he said, would be right sharply debated.

You mean, said I, that I have to meet a coalition of arguments. But I expected to escape from one of them, and that if you agreed that the thing was beneficial, it would remain for me to speak only of its feasibility.

You have not escaped detection, he said, in your attempted flight, but you must render an account of both.

I must pay the penalty, I said, yet do me this much grace. Permit me to take a holiday, just as men of lazy minds are wont to feast themselves on their own thoughts when they walk alone. Such persons, without waiting to discover how their desires may be realized, dismiss that topic to save themselves the labor of deliberating about possibilities and impossibilities, assume their wish fulfilled, and proceed to work out the details in imagination, and take pleasure in portraying what they will do when it is realized, thus making still more idle a mind that is idle without that. I too now succumb to this weakness and desire to postpone and examine later the question of feasibility, but will at present assume that, and will, with your permission, inquire how the rulers will work out the details in practice, and try to show that nothing could be more beneficial to the state and its guardians than the effective operation of our plan. This is what I would try to consider first together with you, and thereafter the other topic, if you allow it.

I do allow it, he said. Proceed with the inquiry.

I think, then, said I, that the rulers, if they are to deserve that name, and their helpers likewise, will, the one, be willing to accept orders, and the other, to give them, in some things obeying our laws, and imitating them in others which we leave to their discretion.

Presumably.

You, then, the lawgiver, I said, have picked these men and similarly will select to give over to them women as nearly as possible of the same nature. And they, having houses and meals in common, and no private possessions of that kind, will dwell together, and being commingled in gymnastics and in all their life and education, will be conducted by innate necessity to sexual union. Is not what I say a necessary consequence?

Not by the necessities of geometry, he said, but by those of love, which are perhaps keener and more potent than the other to persuade and constrain the multitude.

They are, indeed, I said. But next, Glaucon, disorder and promiscuity in these unions or in anything else they do would be an unhallowed thing in a happy state and the rulers will not suffer it.

It would not be right, he said.

Obviously, then, we must arrange marriages, sacramental so far as may be. And the most sacred marriages would be those that were most beneficial.

By all means.

How, then, would the greatest benefit result? Tell me this, Glaucon. I see that you have in your house hunting dogs and a number of pedigreed cocks. Have you ever considered something about their unions and procreations?

What? he said.

In the first place, I said, among these themselves, although they are a select breed, do not some prove better than the rest?

They do.

Do you then breed from all indiscriminately, or are you careful to breed from the best?

From the best.

And, again, do you breed from the youngest or the oldest, or, so far as may be, from those in their prime?

From those in their prime.

And if they are not thus bred, you expect, do you not, that your birds' breed and hounds will greatly degenerate?

I do, he said.

And what of horses and other animals? I said. Is it otherwise with them?

It would be strange if it were, said he.

Gracious, said I, dear friend, how imperative, then, is our need of the highest skill in our rulers, if the principle holds also for mankind.

Well, it does, he said, but what of it?

This, said I, that they will have to employ many of those drugs of which we were speaking. We thought that an inferior physician sufficed for bodies that do not need drugs but yield to diet and regimen. But when it is necessary to prescribe drugs we know that a more enterprising and venturesome physician is required.

True, but what is the pertinency?

This, said I. It seems likely that our rulers will have to make considerable use of falsehood and deception for the benefit of their subjects. We said, I believe, that the use of that sort of thing was in the category of medicine.

And that was right, he said.

In our marriages, then, and the procreation of children, it seems there will be no slight need of this kind of "right."

How so?

It follows from our former admissions, I said, that the best men must cohabit with the best women in as many cases as possible and the worst with the worst in the fewest, and that the offspring of the one must be reared and that of the other not, if the flock is to be as perfect as possible. And the way in which all this is brought to pass must be unknown to any but the rulers, if, again, the herd of guardians is to be as free as possible from dissension.

Most true, he said.

We shall, then, have to ordain certain festivals and sacrifices, in which we shall bring together the brides and the bridegrooms, and our poets must compose hymns suitable to the marriages that then take place. But the number of the marriages we will leave to the discretion of the rulers, that they may keep the number of the citizens as nearly as may be the same, taking into account wars and diseases and all such considerations, and that, so far as possible, our city may not grow too great or too small.

Right, he said.

Certain ingenious lots, then, I suppose, must be devised so that the inferior man at each conjugation may blame chance and not the rulers.

Yes, indeed, he said.

And on the young men, surely, who excel in war and other pursuits we must bestow honors and prizes, and, in particular, the opportunity of more frequent intercourse with the women, which will at the same time be a plausible pretext for having them beget as many of the children as possible.

Right.

And the children thus born will be taken over by the officials appointed for this, men or women or both, since, I take it, the official posts too are common to women and men.

Yes.

The offspring of the good, I suppose, they will take to the pen or crèche, to certain nurses who live apart in a quarter of the city, but the offspring of the inferior, and any of those of the other sort who are born defective, they will properly dispose of in secret, so that no one will know what has become of them.

That is the condition, he said, of preserving the purity of the guardians' breed.

They will also supervise the nursing of the children, conducting the mothers to the pen when their breasts are full, but employing every device to prevent anyone from recognizing her own infant. And they will provide others who have milk if the mothers are insufficient. But they will take care that the mothers themselves shall not suckle too long, and the trouble of wakeful nights and similar burdens they will devolve upon the nurses, wet and dry.

You are making maternity a soft job for the women of the guardians.

It ought to be, said I, but let us pursue our design. We said that the offspring should come from parents in their prime.

True.

Do you agree that the period of the prime may be fairly estimated at twenty years for a woman and thirty for a man?

How do you reckon it? he said.

The women, I said, beginning at the age of twenty, shall bear for the state to the age of forty, and the man shall beget for the state from the time he passes his prime in swiftness in running to the age of fifty-five.

That is, he said, the maturity and prime for both of body and mind.

Then, if anyone older or younger than the prescribed age meddles with procreation for the state, we shall say that his error is an impiety and an injustice, since he is begetting for the city a child whose birth, if it escapes discovery, will not be attended by the sacrifices and the prayers which the priests and priestesses and the entire city prefer at the ceremonial marriages, that ever better offspring may spring from good sires and from fathers helpful to the state sons more helpful still. But this child will be born in darkness and conceived in foul incontinence.

Right, he said.

And the same rule will apply, I said, if any of those still within the age of procreation goes in to a woman of that age with whom the ruler has not paired him. We shall say that he is imposing on the state a baseborn, uncertified, and unhallowed child.

Most rightly, he said.

But when, I take it, the men and the women have passed the age of lawful procreation, we shall leave the men free to form such relations with whomsoever they please, except daughter and mother and their direct descendants and ascendants, and likewise the women, save with son and father, and so on, first admonishing them preferably not even to bring to light anything whatever thus conceived, but if they are unable to prevent a birth to dispose of it on the understanding that we cannot rear such an offspring.

All that sounds reasonable, he said, but how are they to distinguish one another's fathers and daughters, and the other degrees of kin that you have just mentioned?

They won't, said I, except that a man will call all male offspring born in the tenth and in the seventh month after he became a bridegroom his sons, and all female, daughters, and they will call him father. And, similarly, he will call their offspring his grandchildren and they will call his group grandfathers and grandmothers. And all children born in the period in which their fathers and mothers were procreating will regard one another as brothers and sisters. This will suffice for the prohibitions of intercourse of which we just now spoke. But the law will allow brothers and sisters to cohabit if the lot so falls out and the Delphic oracle approves.

Quite right, said he.

This, then, Glaucon, is the manner of the community of wives and children among the guardians. That it is consistent with the rest of our polity and by far the best way is the next point that we must get confirmed by the argument. Is not that so?

It is, indeed, he said.

St. Thomas Aquinas
SUMMA THEOLOGICA

Thomas Aquinas (1225–1274) discusses abortion in two passages from his monumental work, the Summa Theologica.

EIGHTH ARTICLE
WHETHER ONE IS GUILTY OF MURDER THROUGH KILLING SOMEONE BY CHANCE?

We proceed thus to the Eighth Article:—

Objection 1. It would seem that one is guilty of murder through killing someone by chance. For we read (Gen. iv. 23, 24) that Lamech slew a man in mistake for a wild beast, and that he was accounted guilty of murder. Therefore one incurs the guilt of murder through killing a man by chance.

Obj. 2. Further it is written (Exod. xxi. 22): If . . . one strike a woman with child, and she miscarry indeed . . . , if her death ensue thereupon, he shall render life for life. Yet this may happen without any intention of causing her death. Therefore one is guilty of murder through killing someone by chance.

Obj. 3. Further, the Decretals contain several canons prescribing penalties for unintentional homicide. Now penalty is not due save for guilt. Therefore he who kills a man by chance, incurs the guilt of murder.

On the contrary, Augustine says to Publicola (Ep. xlvii): When we do a thing for a good and lawful purpose, if thereby we unintentionally cause harm to anyone, it should by no means be imputed to us. Now it sometimes happens by chance that a person is killed as a result of something done for a good purpose. Therefore the person who did it is not accounted guilty.

I answer that, According to the Philosopher (Phys. ii. 6) chance is a cause that acts beside one's intention. Hence chance happenings, strictly speaking, are neither intended nor voluntary. And since every sin is voluntary, according to Augustine (De Vera Relig. xiv) it follows that chance happenings, as such, are not sins.

Nevertheless it happens that what is not actually and directly voluntary and intended, is voluntary and intended accidentally, according as that which removes an obstacle is called an accidental cause. Wherefore he who does not remove something whence homicide results whereas he ought to remove it, is in a sense guilty of voluntary homicide. This happens in two ways: first when a man causes another's death through occupying himself with unlawful things which he ought to avoid: secondly, when he does not take sufficient care. Hence, according to jurists, if a man pursue a lawful occupation and take due care, the result being that a person loses his life, he is not guilty of that person's death: whereas if he be occupied with something unlawful, or even with something lawful, but without due care, he does not escape being guilty of murder, if his action results in someone's death.

Reply Obj. 1. Lamech did not take sufficient care to avoid taking a man's life: and so he was not excused from being guilty of homicide.

Reply Obj. 2. He that strikes a woman with child does something unlawful: wherefore if there results the death either of the woman or of the animated fœtus, he will not be excused from homicide, especially seeing that death is the natural result of such a blow.

Reply Obj. 3. According to the canons a penalty is inflicted on those who cause death unintentionally, through doing something unlawful, or failing to take sufficient care. . . .

ELEVENTH ARTICLE
WHETHER A CHILD CAN BE BAPTIZED WHILE YET IN ITS MOTHER'S WOMB?

We proceed thus to the Eleventh Article:—

Objection 1. It seems that a child can be baptized while yet in its mother's womb. For the gift of Christ is more efficacious unto salvation than Adam's sin unto condemnation, as the Apostle says (Rom. v. 15). But a child while yet in its mother's womb is under sentence of condemnation on account of Adam's sin. For much more reason, therefore, can it be saved through the gift of Christ, which is bestowed by means of Baptism. Therefore a child can be baptized while yet in its mother's womb.

Obj. 2. Further, a child, while yet in its mother's womb, seems to be part of its mother. Now, when the mother is baptized, whatever is in her and part of her, is baptized. Therefore it seems that when the mother is baptized, the child in her womb is baptized.

Obj. 3. Further, eternal death is a greater evil than death of the body. But of two evils the less should be chosen. If, therefore, the child in the mother's womb cannot be baptized, it would be better for the mother to be opened, and the child to be taken out by force and baptized, than that the child should be eternally damned through dying without Baptism.

Obj. 4. Further, it happens at times that some part of the child comes forth first, as we read in Gen. xxxviii. 27: *In the very delivery of the infants, one put forth a hand, whereon the midwife tied a scarlet thread, saying: This shall come forth the first. But he drawing back his hand, the other came forth.* Now sometimes in such cases there is danger of death. Therefore it seems that that part should be baptized, while the child is yet in its mother's womb.

On the contrary, Augustine says (*Ep. ad Dardan.*): *No one can be born a second time unless he be born first.* But Baptism is a spiritual regeneration. Therefore no one should be baptized before he is born from the womb.

I answer that, It is essential to Baptism that some part of the body of the person baptized be in some way washed with water, since Baptism is a kind of washing, as stated above (Q. 66, A. 1). But an infant's body, before being born from the womb, can nowise be washed with water; unless perchance it be said that the baptismal water, with which the mother's body is washed, reaches the child while yet in its mother's womb. But this is impossible: both because the child's soul, to the sanctification of which Baptism is ordained, is distinct from the soul of the mother; and because the body of the animated infant is already formed, and consequently distinct from the body of the mother. Therefore the Baptism which the mother receives does not overflow on to the child which is in her womb. Hence Augustine says (*Cont. Julian.* vi): *If what is conceived within a mother belonged to her body, so as to be considered a part thereof, we should not baptize an infant whose mother, through danger of death, was baptized while she bore it in her womb. Since, then, it,* i.e. the infant, *is baptized, it certainly did not belong to the mother's body while it was in the womb.* It follows, therefore, that a child can nowise be baptized while in its mother's womb.

Reply Obj. 1. Children while in the mother's womb have not yet come forth into the world to live among other men. Consequently they cannot be subject to the action of man, so as to receive the sacrament, at the hands of man, unto salvation. They can, however, be subject to the action of God, in Whose sight they live, so as, by a kind of privilege, to receive the grace of sanctification; as was the case with those who were sanctified in the womb.

Reply Obj. 2. An internal member of the mother is something of hers by continuity and material union of the part with the whole: whereas a child while in its mother's womb is something of hers through being joined with, and yet distinct from her. Wherefore there is no comparison.

Reply Obj. 3. We should *not do evil that there may come good* (Rom. iii. 8). Therefore it is wrong to kill a mother that her child may be baptized. If, however, the mother die while the child lives yet in her womb, she should be opened that the child may be baptized.

Reply Obj. 4. Unless death be imminent, we should wait until the child has entirely come forth from the womb before baptizing it. If, however, the head, wherein the senses are rooted, appear first, it should be baptized, in cases of danger; nor should it be baptized again, if perfect birth should ensue. And seemingly the same should be done in cases of danger no matter what part of the body appear first. But as none of the exterior parts of the body belong to its integrity in the same degree as the head, some hold that since the matter is doubtful, whenever any other part of the body has been baptized, the child, when perfect birth has taken place, should be baptized with the form: *If thou art not baptized, I baptize thee,* etc.

Judith Jarvis Thomson

A DEFENSE OF ABORTION

Professor Judith Jarvis Thomson of the Massachusetts Institute of Technology here defends the practice of abortion under certain circumstances.

Most opposition to abortion relies on the premise that the fetus is a human being, a person, from the moment of conception. The premise is argued for, but, as I think, not well. Take, for example, the most common argument. We are asked to notice that the development of a human being from conception through birth into childhood is continuous; then it is said that to draw a line, to choose a point in this development and say "before this point the thing is not a person, after this point it is a person" is to make an arbitrary choice, a choice for which in the nature of things no good reason can be given. It is concluded that the fetus is, or anyway that we had better say it is, a person from the moment of conception. But this conclusion does not follow. Similar things might be said about the development of an acorn into an oak tree, and it does not follow that acorns are oak trees, or that we had better say they are. Arguments of this form are sometimes called "slippery slope arguments"—the phrase is perhaps self-explanatory—and it is dismaying that opponents of abortion rely on them so heavily and uncritically.

I am inclined to agree, however, that the prospects for "drawing a line" in the development of the fetus look dim. I am inclined to think also that we shall probably have to agree that the fetus has already become a human person well before birth. Indeed, it comes as a surprise when one first learns how early in its life it begins to acquire human characteristics. By the tenth week, for example, it already has a face, arms and legs, fingers and toes; it has internal organs, and brain activity is detectable.[1] On the other hand, I think that the premise is

---

[1] Daniel Callahan, *Abortion: Law, Choice and Morality* (New York, 1970), p. 373. This book gives a fascinating survey of the available information on abortion. The Jewish tradition is surveyed in David M. Feldman, *Birth Control in Jewish Law* (New York, 1968), Part 5, the Catholic tradition in John T. Noonan, Jr., "An Almost Absolute Value in History," in *The Morality of Abortion*, ed. John T. Noonan, Jr. (Cambridge, Mass., 1970).

false, that the fetus is not a person from the moment of conception. A newly fertilized ovum, a newly implanted clump of cells, is no more a person than an acorn is an oak tree. But I shall not discuss any of this. For it seems to me to be of great interest to ask what happens if, for the sake of argument, we allow the premise. How, precisely, are we supposed to get from there to the conclusion that abortion is morally impermissible? Opponents of abortion commonly spend most of their time establishing that the fetus is a person, and hardly any time explaining the step from there to the impermissibility of abortion. Perhaps they think the step too simple and obvious to require much comment. Or perhaps instead they are simply being economical in argument. Many of those who defend abortion rely on the premise that the fetus is not a person, but only a bit of tissue that will become a person at birth; and why pay out more arguments than you have to? Whatever the explanation, I suggest that the step they take is neither easy nor obvious, that it calls for closer examination than it is commonly given, and that when we do give it this closer examination we shall feel inclined to reject it.

I propose, then, that we grant that the fetus is a person from the moment of conception. How does the argument go from here? Something like this, I take it. Every person has a right to life. So the fetus has a right to life. No doubt the mother has a right to decide what shall happen in and to her body; everyone would grant that. But surely a person's right to life is stronger and more stringent than the mother's right to decide what happens in and to her body, and so outweighs it. So the fetus may not be killed; an abortion may not be performed.

It sounds plausible. But now let me ask you to imagine this. You wake up in the morning and find yourself back to back in bed with an unconscious violinist. A famous unconscious violinist. He has been found to have a fatal kidney ailment, and the Society of Music Lovers has canvassed all the available medical records and found that you alone have the right blood type to help. They have therefore kidnapped you, and last night the violinist's circulatory system was plugged into yours, so that your kidneys can be used to extract poisons from his blood as well as your own. The director of the hospital now tells you, "Look, we're sorry the Society of Music Lovers did this to you—we would never have permitted it if we had known. But still, they did it, and the violinist now is plugged into you. To unplug you would be to kill him. But never mind, it's only for nine months. By then he will have recovered from his ailment, and can safely be unplugged from you." Is it morally incumbent on you to accede to this situation? No doubt it would be very nice of you if you did, a great kindness. But do you *have* to accede to it? What if it were not nine months, but nine years? Or longer still? What if the director of the hospital says, "Tough luck, I agree, but you've now got to stay in bed, with the violinist plugged into you, for the rest of your life. Because remember this. All persons have a right to life, and violinists are persons. Granted you have a right to decide what happens in and to your body, but a person's right to life outweighs your right to decide what happens in and to your body. So you cannot ever be unplugged from him." I imagine you would regard this as outrageous, which suggests that something really is wrong with that plausible-sounding argument I mentioned a moment ago.

In this case, of course, you were kidnapped; you didn't volunteer for the operation that plugged the violinist into your kidneys. Can those who oppose abortion on the ground I mentioned make an exception for a pregnancy due to rape? Certainly. They can say that persons have a right to life only if they didn't come into existence because of rape; or they can say that all persons have a right to life, but that some have less of a right to life than others, in particular, that those who came into existence because of rape have less. But these statements have a rather unpleasant sound. Surely the question of whether you have a right to life at all, or how much of it you have, shouldn't turn on the question of whether or not you are the product of a rape. And in fact the people who oppose abortion on the ground I mentioned do not make this distinction, and hence do not make an exception in case of rape.

Nor do they make an exception for a case in which the mother has to spend the nine months of her pregnancy in bed. They would agree that would be a great pity, and hard on the mother; but all the same, all persons have a right to life, the fetus is a person, and so on. I suspect, in fact, that they would not make an exception for a case in which, miraculously enough, the pregnancy went on for nine years, or even the rest of the mother's life.

Some won't even make an exception for a case in which continuation of the pregnancy is likely to shorten the mother's life; they regard abortion as impermissible even to save the mother's life. Such cases are nowadays very rare, and many opponents of abortion do not accept this extreme view. All the same, it is a good place to begin: a number of points of interest come out in respect to it.

1. Let us call the view that abortion is impermissible even to save the mother's life "the extreme view." I want to suggest first that it does not issue from the argument I mentioned earlier without the addition of some fairly powerful premises. Suppose a woman has become pregnant, and now learns that she has a cardiac condition such that she will die if she carries the baby to term. What may be done for her? The fetus, being a person, has a right to life, but as the mother is a person too, so has she a right to life. Presumably they have an equal right to life. How is it supposed to come out that an abortion may not be performed? If mother and child have an equal right to life, shouldn't we perhaps flip a coin? Or should we add to the mother's right to life her right to decide what happens in and to her body, which everybody seems to be ready to grant—the sum of her rights now outweighing the fetus' right to life?

The most familiar argument here is the following. We are told that performing the abortion would be directly killing[2] the child, whereas doing nothing would not be killing the mother, but only letting her die. Moreover, in killing

---

[2]The term "direct" in the arguments I refer to is a technical one. Roughly, what is meant by "direct killing" is either killing as an end in itself, or killing as a means of some end, for example, the end of saving someone else's life. See footnote 5, p. 308, for an example of its use.

the child, one would be killing an innocent person, for the child has committed no crime, and is not aiming at his mother's death. And then there are a variety of ways in which this might be continued. (1) But as directly killing an innocent person is always and absolutely impermissible, an abortion may not be performed. Or, (2) as directly killing an innocent person is murder, and murder is always and absolutely impermissible, an abortion may not be performed.[3] Or, (3) as one's duty to refrain from directly killing an innocent person is more stringent than one's duty to keep a person from dying, an abortion may not be performed. Or, (4) if one's only options are directly killing an innocent person or letting a person die, one must prefer letting the person die, and thus an abortion may not be performed.[4]

Some people seem to have thought that these are not further premises which must be added if the conclusion is to be reached, but that they follow from the very fact that an innocent person has a right to life.[5] But this seems to me to be a mistake, and perhaps the simplest way to show this is to bring out that while we must certainly grant that innocent persons have a right to life, the theses in (1) through (4) are all false. Take (2), for example. If directly killing an innocent person is murder, and thus is impermissible, then the mother's directly killing the innocent person inside her is murder, and thus is impermissible. But it cannot seriously be thought to be murder if the mother performs an abortion on herself to save her life. It cannot seriously be said that she *must* refrain, that she *must* sit passively by and wait for her death. Let us look again at the case of you and the violinist. There you are, in bed with the violinist, and the director of the hospital says to you, "It's all most distressing, and I deeply sympathize, but you see this is putting an additional strain on your kidneys, and you'll be dead within the month. But you *have* to stay where you are all the same. Because unplugging you would be directly killing an innocent violinist,

---

[3]Cf. *Encyclical Letter of Pope Pius XI on Christian Marriage*, St. Paul Editions (Boston, n.d.), p. 32: "however much we may pity the mother whose health and even life is gravely imperiled in the performance of the duty allotted to her by nature, nevertheless what could ever be a sufficient reason for excusing in any way the direct murder of the innocent? This is precisely what we are dealing with here." Noonan (*The Morality of Abortion*, p. 43) reads this as follows: "What cause can ever avail to excuse in any way the direct killing of the innocent? For it is a question of that."

[4]The thesis in (4) [not included in this volume] is in an interesting way weaker than those in (1), (2), and (3): they rule out abortion even in cases in which both mother *and* child will die if the abortion is not performed. By contrast, one who held the view expressed in (4) could consistently say that one needn't prefer letting two persons die to killing one.

[5]Cf. the following passage from Pius XII, *Address to the Italian Catholic Society of Midwives*: "The baby in the maternal breast has the right to life immediately from God.—Hence there is no man, no human authority, no science, no medical, eugenic, social, economic or moral 'indication' which can establish or grant a valid juridical ground for a direct deliberate disposition of an innocent human life, that is a disposition which looks to its destruction either as an end or as a means to another end perhaps in itself not illicit.—The baby, still not born, is a man in the same degree and for the same reason as the mother" (quoted in Noonan, *The Morality of Abortion*, p. 45).

and that's murder, and that's impermissible." If anything in the world is true, it is that you do not commit murder, you do not do what is impermissible, if you reach around to your back and unplug yourself from that violinist to save your life.

The main focus of attention in writings on abortion has been on what a third party may or may not do in answer to a request from a woman for an abortion. This is in a way understandable. Things being as they are, there isn't much a woman can safely do to abort herself. So the question asked is what a third party may do, and what the mother may do, if it is mentioned at all, is deduced, almost as an afterthought, from what it is concluded that third parties may do. But it seems to me that to treat the matter in this way is to refuse to grant to the mother that very status of person which is so firmly insisted on for the fetus. For we cannot simply read off what a person may do from what a third party may do. Suppose you find yourself trapped in a tiny house with a growing child. I mean a very tiny house, and a rapidly growing child—you are already up against the wall of the house and in a few minutes you'll be crushed to death. The child on the other hand won't be crushed to death; if nothing is done to stop him from growing he'll be hurt, but in the end he'll simply burst open the house and walk out a free man. Now I could well understand it if a bystander were to say, "There's nothing we can do for you. We cannot choose between your life and his, we cannot be the ones to decide who is to live, we cannot intervene." But it cannot be concluded that you too can do nothing, that you cannot attack it to save your life. However innocent the child may be, you do not have to wait passively while it crushes you to death. Perhaps a pregnant woman is vaguely felt to have the status of house, to which we don't allow the right of self-defense. But if the woman houses the child, it should be remembered that she is a person who houses it.

I should perhaps stop to say explicitly that I am not claiming that people have a right to do anything whatever to save their lives. I think, rather, that there are drastic limits to the right of self-defense. If someone threatens you with death unless you torture someone else to death, I think you have not the right, even to save your life, to do so. But the case under consideration here is very different. In our case there are only two people involved, one whose life is threatened, and one who threatens it. Both are innocent: the one who is threatened is not threatened because of any fault, the one who threatens does not threaten because of any fault. For this reason we may feel that we bystanders cannot intervene. But the person threatened can.

In sum, a woman surely can defend her life against the threat to it posed by the unborn child, even if doing so involves its death. And this shows not merely that the theses in (1) through (4) are false; it shows also that the extreme view of abortion is false, and so we need not canvass any other possible ways of arriving at it from the argument I mentioned at the outset.

2. The extreme view could of course be weakened to say that while abortion is permissible to save the mother's life, it may not be performed by a third

party, but only by the mother herself. But this cannot be right either. For what we have to keep in mind is that the mother and the unborn child are not like two tenants in a small house which has, by an unfortunate mistake, been rented to both: the mother *owns* the house. The fact that she does adds to the offensiveness of deducing that the mother can do nothing from the supposition that third parties can do nothing. But it does more than this: it casts a bright light on the supposition that third parties can do nothing. Certainly it lets us see that a third party who says "I cannot choose between you" is fooling himself if he thinks this is impartiality. If Jones has found and fastened on a certain coat, which he needs to keep him from freezing, but which Smith also needs to keep him from freezing, then it is not impartiality that says "I cannot choose between you" when Smith owns the coat. Women have said again and again "This body is *my* body!" and they have reason to feel angry, reason to feel that it has been like shouting into the wind. Smith, after all, is hardly likely to bless us if we say to him, "Of course it's your coat, anybody would grant that it is. But no one may choose between you and Jones who is to have it."

We should really ask what it is that says "no one may choose" in the face of the fact that the body that houses the child is the mother's body. It may be simply a failure to appreciate this fact. But it may be something more interesting, namely the sense that one has a right to refuse to lay hands on people, even where it would be just and fair to do so, even where justice seems to require that somebody do so. Thus justice might call for somebody to get Smith's coat back from Jones, and yet you have a right to refuse to be the one to lay hands on Jones, a right to refuse to do physical violence to him. This, I think, must be granted. But then what should be said is not "no one may choose," but only "I cannot choose," and indeed not even this, but "I will not *act*," leaving it open that somebody else can or should, and in particular that anyone in a position of authority, with the job of securing people's rights, both can and should. So this is no difficulty. I have not been arguing that any given third party must accede to the mother's request that he perform an abortion to save her life, but only that he may.

I suppose that in some views of human life the mother's body is only on loan to her, the loan not being one which gives her any prior claim to it. One who held this view might well think it impartiality to say "I cannot choose." But I shall simply ignore this possibility. My own view is that if a human being has any just, prior claim to anything at all, he has a just, prior claim to his own body. And perhaps this needn't be argued for here anyway, since, as I mentioned, the arguments against abortion we are looking at do grant that the woman has a right to decide what happens in and to her body.

But although they do grant it, I have tried to show that they do not take seriously what is done in granting it. I suggest the same thing will reappear even more clearly when we turn away from cases in which the mother's life is at stake, and attend, as I propose we now do, to the vastly more common cases in which a woman wants an abortion for some less weighty reason than preserving her own life.

3. Where the mother's life is not at stake, the argument I mentioned at the outset seems to have a much stronger pull. "Everyone has a right to life, so the unborn person has a right to life." And isn't the child's right to life weightier than anything other than the mother's own right to life, which she might put forward as ground for an abortion?

This argument treats the right to life as if it were unproblematic. It is not, and this seems to me to be precisely the source of the mistake.

For we should now, at long last, ask what it comes to, to have a right to life. In some views having a right to life includes having a right to be given at least the bare minimum one needs for continued life. But suppose that what in fact *is* the bare minimum a man needs for continued life is something he has no right at all to be given? If I am sick unto death, and the only thing that will save my life is the touch of Henry Fonda's cool hand on my fevered brow, then all the same, I have no right to be given the touch of Henry Fonda's cool hand on my fevered brow. It would be frightfully nice of him to fly in from the West Coast to provide it. It would be less nice, though no doubt well meant, if my friends flew out to the West Coast and carried Henry Fonda back with them. But I have no right at all against anybody that he should do this for me. Or again, to return to the story I told earlier, the fact that for continued life that violinist needs the continued use of your kidneys does not establish that he has a right to be given the continued use of your kidneys. He certainly has no right against you that *you* should give him continued use of your kidneys. For nobody has any right to use your kidneys unless you give him such a right; and nobody has the right against you that you shall give him this right—if you do allow him to go on using your kidneys, this is a kindness on your part, and not something he can claim from you as his due. Nor has he any right against anybody else that *they* should give him continued use of your kidneys. Certainly he had no right against the Society of Music Lovers that they should plug him into you in the first place. And if you now start to unplug yourself, having learned that you will otherwise have to spend nine years in bed with him, there is nobody in the world who must try to prevent you, in order to see to it that he is given something he has a right to be given.

Some people are rather stricter about the right to life. In their view, it does not include the right to be given anything, but amounts to, and only to, the right not to be killed by anybody. But here a related difficulty arises. If everybody is to refrain from killing that violinist, then everybody must refrain from doing a great many different sorts of things. Everybody must refrain from slitting his throat, everybody must refrain from shooting him—and everybody must refrain from unplugging you from him. But does he have a right against everybody that they shall refrain from unplugging you from him? To refrain from doing this is to allow him to continue to use your kidneys. It could be argued that he has a right against us that *we* should allow him to continue to use your kidneys. That is, while he had no right against us that we should give him the use of your kidneys, it might be argued that he anyway has a right against us that we shall not now intervene and deprive him of the use of your kidneys. I shall come back to third-party interventions later. But certainly the violinist has no right against you that *you* shall allow him to continue to use your kidneys. As I said, if you do allow him to use them, it is a kindness on your part, and not something you owe him.

The difficulty I point to here is not peculiar to the right to life. It reappears in connection with all the other natural rights; and it is something which an adequate account of rights must deal with. For present purposes it is enough just to draw attention to it. But I would stress that I am not arguing that people do not have a right to life—quite to the contrary, it seems to me that the primary control we must place on the acceptability of an account of rights is that it should turn out in that account to be a truth that all persons have a right to life. I am arguing only that having a right to life does not guarantee having either a right to be given the use of or a right to be allowed continued use of another person's body—even if one needs it for life itself. So the right to life will not serve the opponents of abortion in the very simple and clear way in which they seem to have thought it would. . . .

Following the lead of the opponents of abortion, I have throughout been speaking of the fetus merely as a person, and what I have been asking is whether or not the argument we began with, which proceeds only from the fetus' being a person, really does establish its conclusion. I have argued that it does not.

But of course there are arguments and arguments, and it may be said that I have simply fastened on the wrong one. It may be said that what is important is not merely the fact that the fetus is a person, but that it is a person for whom the woman has a special kind of responsibility issuing from the fact that she is its mother. And it might be argued that all my analogies are therefore irrelevant—for you do not have that special kind of responsibility for that violinist, Henry Fonda does not have that special kind of responsibility for me. And our attention might be drawn to the fact that men and women both *are* compelled by law to provide support for their children. . . .

Surely we do not have any such "special responsibility" for a person unless we have assumed it, explicitly or implicitly. If a set of parents do not try to prevent pregnancy, do not obtain an abortion, and then at the time of birth of the child do not put it out for adoption, but rather take it home with them, then they have assumed responsibility for it, they have given it rights, and they cannot *now* withdraw support from it at the cost of its life because they now find it difficult to go on providing for it. But if they have taken all reasonable precautions against having a child, they do not simply by virtue of their biological relationship to the child who comes into existence have a special responsibility for it. They may wish to assume responsibility for it, or they may not wish to. And I am suggesting that if assuming responsibility for it would require large sacrifices, then they may refuse. A Good Samaritan would not refuse—or anyway, a Splendid Samaritan, if the sacrifices that had to be made were enormous. But then so would a Good Samaritan assume responsibility for that violinist; so would Henry Fonda, if he is a Good Samaritan, fly in from the West Coast and assume responsibility for me.

8. My argument will be found unsatisfactory on two counts by many of those who want to regard abortion as morally permissible. First, while I do argue that abortion is not impermissible, I do not argue that it is always permissible. There may well be cases in which carrying the child to term requires only Minimally Decent Samaritanism of the mother, and this is a standard we must not fall below. I am inclined to think it a merit of my account precisely that it does *not* give a general yes or a general no. It allows for and supports our sense that, for example, a sick and desperately frightened fourteen-year-old schoolgirl, pregnant due to rape, may *of course* choose abortion, and that any law which rules this out is an insane law. And it also allows for and supports our sense that in other cases resort to abortion is even positively indecent. It would be indecent in the woman to request an abortion, and indecent in a doctor to perform it, if she is in her seventh month, and wants the abortion just to avoid the nuisance of postponing a trip abroad. The very fact that the arguments I have been drawing attention to treat all cases of abortion, or even all cases of abortion in which the mother's life is not at stake, as morally on a par ought to have made them suspect at the outset.

Secondly, while I am arguing for the permissibility of abortion in some cases, I am not arguing for the right to secure the death of the unborn child. It is easy to confuse these two things in that up to a certain point in the life of the fetus it is not able to survive outside the mother's body; hence removing it from her body guarantees its death. But they are importantly different. I have argued that you are not morally required to spend nine months in bed, sustaining the life of that violinist; but to say this is by no means to say that if, when you unplug yourself, there is a miracle and he survives, you then have a right to turn round and slit his throat. You may detach yourself even if this costs him his life; you have no right to be guaranteed his death, by some other means, if unplugging yourself does not kill him. There are some people who will feel dissatisfied by this feature of my argument. A woman may be utterly devastated by the thought of a child, a bit of herself, put out for adoption and never seen or heard of again. She may therefore want not merely that the child be detached from her, but more, that it die. Some opponents of abortion are inclined to regard this as beneath contempt—thereby showing insensitivity to what is surely a powerful source of despair. All the same, I agree that the desire for the child's death is not one which anybody may gratify, should it turn out to be possible to detach the child alive.

At this place, however, it should be remembered that we have only been pretending throughout that the fetus is a human being from the moment of conception. A very early abortion is surely not the killing of a person, and so is not dealt with by anything I have said here.

B. IS PLEASURE THE MAIN GOAL OF LIFE?

Timothy Leary

POLITICS OF ECSTASY

In his Politics of Ecstasy, Timothy Leary (b. 1920) defends the use of pleasure-producing drugs as a way of life.

IT MAKES YOU FEEL SO GOOD

The evidence that LSD produces rapid, even sudden, cures for emotional disorders is threatening enough. Next comes the evidence that the process could be enjoyable, even ecstatic. That something which is "good for you" can also be pleasant is perhaps the most fearful pill of all for a puritan culture to swallow.

In a study by Savage, 85 percent reported "a very pleasant experience" and 81 percent "an experience of great beauty." Exactly two-thirds of Janiger's subjects claim "a very pleasant experience"; 70 percent of subjects in a study by Leary describe "wonderful, ecstatic or very pleasant" reactions.

"I cried for joy," says psychologist Wilson Van Deusen about his LSD session. "I will have enjoyed more living in the latter part of my life than most people ever know," says Cary Grant in summarizing his LSD results. "A possession by the spirit of wholeness," says philosopher Gerald Heard. "A repeated flow of beauty to heightened beauty from deeper to ever deeper meaning. Words like 'grace' and 'transfiguration' came to my mind," writes Aldous Huxley. "Extraordinary joy overcame me . . . a strong and beautiful feeling of eternity and infinity," chronicles Beringer, the famous Heidelberg neurologist. "A New Artificial Paradise," and "A Divine Plant" were the titles of papers by Havelock Ellis describing his mescal experiences.

Now such words as joy, ecstasy, grace, beauty, just don't exist in the psychiatric vocabulary. The poor psychiatrist has been given the sad task of looking for pathology. He's happiest when he's found problems and is usually bewildered when he comes face-to-face with the more meaningful experiences of life. This dilemma is nicely illustrated in a wistful comment by a well-known psychiatrist in the 1955 round table on LSD and mescaline sponsored by the American Psychiatric Association: "I should like to confess that my experience with mescaline was an exceedingly pleasant one. I found myself in my enthusiasm using words like 'mystical' and 'ecstatic,' until I found my colleagues raising their eyebrows at this, and looking at me askance; after which I simply described it as 'very pleasant.'"

LSD TURNS YOU ON TO GOD

That LSD produces ecstasy and sudden cure was probably reason enough for its being banned in America, but there was news ahead which increased the medical opposition. Evidence started turning up that psychedelic drugs produced religious experiences. Horrors! In the study by Savage, 90 percent of subjects claimed "a greater awareness of God or a higher power." Studies published by Leary revealed that over two-thirds of a sample of 67 ministers, monks, and rabbis reported the deepest spiritual experience of their lives. And in a double-blind, controlled study run on Good Friday, 1963, in the Boston University Chapel, 9 out of 10 divinity students shakingly recounted awesome mystical-religious experiences, and 2 of them promptly quit the ministry! "The drugs make an end run around Christ and go straight to the Holy Spirit," was the paradoxical comment of Theodore Gill, president of San Francisco's Presbyterian Theological Seminary. The words of William James, generally held to be the greatest psychologist America has ever produced, were remembered: "Looking back on my experiences [with nitrous oxide] they all converge toward an insight to which I cannot help ascribing some metaphysical significance."

According to *Time* magazine, "Clerics . . . charge that LSD zealots have become a clique of modern gnostics concerned only with furthering their private search for what they call 'inner freedom.' Others feel that the church should not quickly dismiss anything that has the power to deepen faith. Dr. W. T. Stace of Princeton, one of the nation's foremost students of mysticism, believes that LSD can change lives for the better. 'The fact that the experience was induced by drugs has no bearing on its validity,' he says."

POLICE CLUBS BOUNCING OFF OUR HEADS

At this point we remember Mr. Wasson's poignant account of the religious struggle between the Indians (who called the Mexican mushroom "God's flesh") and the agents of the Spanish Inquisition. *Esquire*'s Martin Mayer may have been saying more than he wished to reveal when he compared IFIF to a group of heretical Catholic converts, to fundamentalist Protestants, and to Christian Scientists in a context insulting to all three religious groups. Mr.

Mayer predicted that IFIF will end up like Catholic converts with "police clubs bouncing off their heads"; he may be telling us less about LSD than about the state of *his own* intolerance for any heretical deviation from *his* favored orthodoxies.

WE WANT TO HAVE FUN AND BE GOOD SCIENTISTS, TOO

Professor McClelland and Mr. Mayer make a great point of saying that IFIF is no longer a scientific group. The term "science" has apparently become a sacred term forbidden to innovating theorists and methodologists. It is true that we have often dispensed with the rituals of modern psychology. This is not because of naïveté or carelessness but from a thoughtful reconsideration of the philosophy of behavior and consciousness. Again, the popular press is not the place to discuss scholarly differences. Interested readers can find our criticisms and constructive alternatives in the scientific literature, consisting of new methods, forms, instruments and hypotheses designed and used by IFIF experimenters.

The accusation is also made that IFIF is anti-intellectual. It is true that we are most dissatisfied with the intellectual narrowness and naïveté of much of modern psychology and that we have taken as our central task the production of more effective and sophisticated concepts. We are indeed trying most energetically to outmode current theories of human nature as fast as we can. We do not see this as either rebellion or heresy but rather as the traditional goal of the intellectual-scientific game. We also believe that all human activities, including the scientific, are funny.

HAVE YOU OR HAVEN'T YOU? THAT IS THE QUESTION

The debate over psychedelic drugs invariably breaks down into two groups: those that have had the experience versus those that have not. As R. Gordon Wasson has pointed out with gentle sarcasm, "We are all divided into two classes: those who have taken the mushroom and are disqualified by the subjective experience, and those who have not taken the mushroom and are disqualified by their total ignorance of the subject." Or as comedian Dave Gardner puts it, "How are you gonna explain anything to anyone who hasn't ever?"

But we seem to need more than the inexperience-experience difference or our American puritanical heritage to explain why the "moral, religious, social" applications of psychedelic drugs can be experienced so freely and humorously in other countries and why such research is shut down in America with the undocumented cries of "morbidity," "mortality," "danger," "immoral."

GET YOUR STERILE, SURGICAL RUBBER GLOVES OFF MY SOUL, DOCTOR FARNSWORTH

The political role of medicine and psychiatry may have something to do with this difference. In other countries, physicians and psychiatrists are respected and well-paid members of the professional class. That and nothing more. In the United States these disciplines aspire to and lobby for a position of political and moral monopoly which is beyond criticism or debate. Dr. Dana Farnsworth, our psychiatric rival at Harvard, in his anti-LSD editorial in the *Journal of the American Medical Association* is bold enough to make this astounding statement: "The ingestion or injection or inhalation of any agent taken or given to alter a person's usual mental and emotional equilibrium must be looked upon as a medical procedure. These agents should, therefore, be under medical control. . . ." Snuff out your cigarette, boy, and forget your before-dinner martini, and throw out your wife's perfume bottle. Ladies and gentlemen, you've just lost a freedom you never realized you had to protect—the right to taste, smell, breathe or otherwise introduce into your own body anything which will change your mind or your mood. When we talk about "internal freedom" and "the politics of the nervous system," we are foreseeing and forewarning about invasions of personal liberty which no longer date to the brave new world of 1984. Our debate with psychiatrists about the use and control of psychedelic drugs involves the right, right now, of thoughtful Americans to change their own consciousness.

TRAINING FOR ECSTASY

A final clarification. Mr. Mayer and others have accused us of advocating indiscriminate availability and use of consciousness-expanding drugs. The facts are exactly to the contrary. IFIF has been more outspoken than any other group in the country in advocating the need for experience and training in the use of these extraordinarily powerful tools. The experience, however, must come from the drug itself, and the training must be specialized. No present medical or psychological degree qualifies for the job. A medical degree doesn't equip one to pilot a jet plane or to understand the incredible complexities of consciousness. The LSD experience is so novel and so powerful that the more you think you know about the mind, the more astounded and even frightened you'll be when your consciousness starts to flip you out of your mind. A new profession of psychedelic guides will inevitably develop to supervise these experiences. The training for this new profession will aim at producing the patience of a first-grade teacher, the humility and wisdom of a Hindu guru, the loving dedication of a minister-priest, the sensitivity of a poet, and the imagination of a science fiction writer.

DO YOU OR DON'T YOU?

The debate could and inevitably will be continued—in the press, in the scholarly journals, in conversations and within people's minds. Sooner or later everyone will have to answer for himself the simple basic question, do you or don't you? Do you want to turn on or don't you? Do you want to expand your awareness or not? Transcendence—becoming aware of a reality which lies outside of time, space and the beloved ego—has been a basic privilege and goal of man since earliest times. In our present age, writes Carl G. Jung in his autobiography, "man has been robbed of transcendence by the shortsightedness of the super-intellectual." A large number of serious and responsible citizens, along with a million or so young people, believe and have stated that transcendence can be brought about by the psychedelic chemicals, given suitable preparation and an appropriate setting.

But such a view has too many far-reaching consequences to be accepted on the basis of verbal debate. Each man must experience it for himself.

This article is unlikely to convince anyone or change anyone's opinion. If it will make some readers of E*squire* aware that a different view is possible than the one expressed in Mr. Mayer's article, our purpose will have been accomplished. Let us recall to mind the words Hermann Hesse, the Nobel Prize novelist and philosopher, wrote in *Siddhartha*:

> Words do not express thoughts very well; everything immediately becomes a little different, a little distorted, a little foolish. And yet it is also pleasing and seems right that what is of value and wisdom to one man seems nonsense to another.

Peace, Mr. Martin Mayer.

Aldous Huxley

BRAVE NEW WORLD

In *Brave New World*, British novelist Aldous Huxley (1894–1963) satirizes a way of life that depends on the pleasure-producing drug *soma*.

"Two thousand pharmacologists and bio-chemists were subsidized in A.F. 178."

"He does look glum," said the Assistant Predestinator, pointing at Bernard Marx.

"Six years later it was being produced commercially. The perfect drug."

"Let's bait him."

"Euphoric, narcotic, pleasantly hallucinant."

"Glum, Marx, glum." The clap on the shoulder made him start, look up. It was that brute Henry Foster. "What you need is a gramme of *soma*."

"All the advantages of Christianity and alcohol; none of their defects."

"Ford, I should like to kill him!" But all he did was to say, "No, thank you," and fend off the proffered tube of tablets.

"Take a holiday from reality whenever you like, and come back without so much as a headache or a mythology."

"Take it," insisted Henry Foster, "take it."

"Stability was practically assured."

"One cubic centimetre cures ten gloomy sentiments," said the Assistant Predestinator citing a piece of homely hypnopædic wisdom.

"It only remained to conquer old age."

"Damn you, damn you!" shouted Bernard Marx.

"Hoity-toity."

"Gonadal hormones, transfusion of young blood, magnesium salts . . ."

"And do remember that a gramme is better than a damn." They went out, laughing.

"All the physiological stigmata of old age have been abolished. And along with them, of course "

"Don't forget to ask him about that Malthusian belt," said Fanny.

"Along with them all the old man's mental peculiarities. Characters remain constant throughout a whole lifetime."

". . . two rounds of Obstacle Golf to get through before dark. I must fly."

"Work, play—at sixty our powers and tastes are what they were at seventeen. Old men in the bad old days used to renounce, retire, take to religion, spend their time reading, thinking—*thinking!*"

"Idiots, swine!" Bernard Marx was saying to himself as he walked down the corridor to the lift.

"Now—such is progress—the old men work, the old men copulate, the old men have no time, no leisure from pleasure, not a moment to sit down and think—or if ever by some unlucky chance such a crevice of time should yawn in the solid substance of their distractions, there is always *soma*, delicious *soma*, half a gramme for a half-holiday, a gramme for a week-end, two grammes for a trip to the gorgeous East, three for a dark eternity on the moon; returning whence they find themselves on the other side of the crevice, safe on the solid ground of daily labour and distraction, scampering from feely to feely, from girl to pneumatic girl, from Electromagnetic Golf course to . . ."

"But, Bernard, we shall be alone all night."
Bernard blushed and looked away. "I meant, alone for talking," he mumbled.
"Talking? But what about?" Walking and talking—that seemed a very odd way of spending an afternoon.

In the end she persuaded him, much against his will, to fly over to Amsterdam to see the Semi-Demi-Finals of the Women's Heavyweight Wrestling Championship.

"In a crowd," he grumbled. "As usual." He remained obstinately gloomy the whole afternoon; wouldn't talk to Lenina's friends (of whom they met dozens in the ice-cream *soma* bar between the wrestling bouts); and in spite of his misery absolutely refused to take the half-gramme raspberry sundae which she pressed upon him. "I'd rather be myself," he said. "Myself and nasty. Not somebody else, however jolly."

"A gramme in time saves nine," said Lenina, producing a bright treasure of sleep-taught wisdom.

Bernard pushed away the proffered glass impatiently.

"Now don't lose your temper," she said. "Remember, one cubic centimetre cures ten gloomy sentiments."

"Oh, for Ford's sake, be quiet!" he shouted.

Lenina shrugged her shoulders. "A gramme is always better than a damn," she concluded with dignity, and drank the sundae herself.

Epicurus

LETTER TO MENOECUS

> Though *epicureanism* is often used in popular speech as a syno-
> nym for a life of unremitting pleasure, Epicurus (341–270 B.C.)
> was much more cautious in his recommendations about the
> good life. He was at least as concerned with avoiding pain as
> with maximizing pleasure.

Accustom thyself to believe that death is nothing to us, for good and evil imply sentience, and death is the privation of all sentience; therefore a right under-standing that death is nothing to us makes the mortality of life enjoyable, not by adding to life an illimitable time, but by taking away the yearning after immortality. For life has no terrors for him who has thoroughly apprehended that there are no terrors for him in ceasing to live. Foolish, therefore, is the man who says that he fears death, not because it will pain when it comes, but because it pains in the prospect. Whatsoever causes no annoyance when it is present, causes only a groundless pain in the expectation. Death, therefore, the most awful of evils, is nothing to us, seeing that, when we are, death is not come, and, when death is come, we are not. It is nothing, then, either to the living or to the dead, for with the living it is not and the dead exist no longer. But in the world, at one time men shun death as the greatest of all evils, and at another time choose it as a respite from the evils in life. The wise man does not deprecate life nor does he fear the cessation of life. The thought of life is no offense to him, nor is the cessation of life regarded as an evil. And even as men choose of food not merely and simply the larger portion, but the more pleas-ant, so the wise seek to enjoy the time which is most pleasant and not merely that which is longest. And he who admonishes the young to live well and the old to make a good end speaks foolishly, not merely because of the desirable-ness of life, but because the same exercise at once teaches to live well and die well. Much worse is he who says that it were good not to be born, but when once one is born to pass with all speed through the gates of Hades. For if he truly believes this, why does he not depart from life? It were easy for him to do so, if once he were firmly convinced. If he speaks only in mockery, his words are foolishness, for those who hear believe him not.

We must remember that the future is neither wholly ours nor wholly not ours, so that neither must we count upon it as quite certain to come nor despair of it as quite certain not to come.

We must also reflect that of desires some are natural, others are groundless; and that of the natural some are necessary as well as natural, and some natural only. And of the necessary desires some are necessary if we are to be happy, some if the body is to be rid of uneasiness, some if we are even to live. He who has a clear and certain understanding of these things will direct every preference and aversion toward securing health of body and tranquillity of mind, seeing that this is the sum and end of a blessed life. For the end of all our actions is to be free from pain and fear, and, when once we have attained all this, the tempest of the soul is laid; seeing that the living creature has no need to go in search of something that is lacking, nor to look for anything else by which the good of the soul and of the body will be fulfilled. When we are pained because of the absence of pleasure, then, and then only, do we feel the need of pleasure. Wherefore we call pleasure the alpha and omega of a blessed life. Pleasure is our first and kindred good. It is the starting point of every choice and of every aversion, and to it we come back, inasmuch as we make feeling the rule by which to judge of every good thing. And since pleasure is our first and native good, for that reason we do not choose every pleasure whatsoever, but ofttimes pass over many pleasures when a greater annoyance ensures from them. And ofttimes we consider pains superior to pleasures when submission to the pains for a long time brings us as a consequence a greater pleasure. While therefore all pleasure because it is naturally akin to us is good, not all pleasure is choice-worthy, just as all pain is an evil and yet not all pain is to be shunned. It is, however, by measuring one against another, and by looking at the conveniences and inconveniences, that all these matters must be judged. Sometimes we treat the good as an evil, and the evil, on the contrary, as a good. Again, we regard independence of outward things as a great good, not so as in all cases to use little, but so as to be contented with little if we have not much, being honestly persuaded that they have the sweetest enjoyment of luxury who stand least in need of it, and that whatever is natural is easily procured and only the vain and worthless hard to win. Plain fare gives as much pleasure as a costly diet, when once the pain of want has been removed, while bread and water confer the highest possible pleasure when they are brought to hungry lips. To habituate one's self, therefore, to simple and inexpensive diet supplies all that is needful for health, and enables a man to meet the necessary requirements of life without shrinking, and it places us in a better condition when we approach at intervals a costly fare and renders us fearless of fortune.

When we say, then, that pleasure is the end and aim, we do not mean the pleasures of the prodigal or the pleasures of sensuality, as we are understood to do by some through ignorance, prejudice, or wilful misrepresentation. By pleasure we mean the absence of pain in the body and of trouble in the soul. It is not an unbroken succession of drinking bouts and of revelry, not sexual love, not the enjoyment of the fish and other delicacies of a luxurious table, which produce a pleasant life; it is sober reasoning, searching out the grounds of every choice and avoidance, and banishing those beliefs through which the greatest tumults take possession of the soul. Of all this the beginning and the greatest good is prudence. Wherefore prudence is a more precious thing even than philosophy; from it spring all the other virtues, for it teaches that we cannot lead a life of pleasure which is not also a life of prudence, honor, and justice; nor lead a life of prudence, honor, and justice, which is not also a life of pleasure. For the virtues have grown into one with a pleasant life, and a pleasant life is inseparable from them.

Who, then, is superior in thy judgement to such a man? He holds a holy belief concerning the gods, and is altogether free from the fear of death. He has diligently considered the end fixed by nature, and understands how easily the limit of good things can be reached and attained, and how either the duration or the intensity of evils is but slight. Destiny, which some introduce as sovereign over all things, he laughs to scorn, affirming rather that some things happen of necessity, others by chance, others through our own agency. For he sees that necessity destroys responsibility and that chance or fortune is inconstant; whereas our own actions are free, and it is to them that praise and blame naturally attach. It were better, indeed, to accept the legends of the gods than to bow beneath that yoke of destiny which the natural philosophers have imposed. The one holds out some faint hope that we may escape if we honor the gods, while the necessity of the naturalists is deaf to all entreaties. Nor does he hold chance to be a god, as the world in general does, for in the acts of a god there is no disorder; nor to be a cause, though an uncertain one, for he believes that no good or evil is dispensed by chance to men so as to make life blessed, though it supplies the starting-point of great good and great evil. He believes that the misfortune of the wise is better than the prosperity of the fool. It is better, in short, that what is well judged in action should not owe its successful issue to the aid of chance.

Exercise thyself in these and kindred precepts day and night, both by thyself and with him who is like unto thee; then never, either in waking or in dream, wilt thou be disturbed; but wilt live as a god among men. For man loses all semblance of mortality by living in the midst of immortal blessings.

Epicurus: Principal Doctrines

1. A blessed and eternal being has no trouble himself and brings no trouble upon any other being; hence he is exempt from movements of anger and partiality, for every such movement implies weakness.

2. Death is nothing to us; for the body, when it has been resolved into its elements, has no feeling, and that which has no feeling is nothing to us.

3. The magnitude of pleasure reaches its limit in the removal of all pain. When pleasure is present, so long as it is uninterrupted, there is no pain either of body or of mind or of both together.

4. Continuous pain does not last long in the flesh; on the contrary, pain, if extreme, is present a very short time, and even that degree of pain which barely outweighs pleasure in the flesh does not last for many days together. Illnesses of long duration even permit of an excess of pleasure over pain in the flesh.

5. It is impossible to live a pleasant life without living wisely and well and justly, and it is impossible to live wisely and well and justly without living pleasantly. Whenever any one of these is lacking, when, for instance, the man is not able to live wisely, though he lives well and justly, it is impossible for him to live a pleasant life.

Plato

PROTAGORAS

One of the most famous classical discussions of the pros and
cons of a life of pleasure is to be found in the section of Plato's
Protagoras reprinted here.

Well, said I, you speak of some men living well, and others badly?

He agreed.

Do you think then that a man would be living well who passed his life in pain
and vexation?

No.

But if he lived it out to the end with enjoyment, you would count him as
having lived well?

Yes.

Then to live pleasurably is good, to live painfully bad?

Yes, if one's pleasure is in what is honorable.

What's this, Protagoras? Surely you don't follow the common opinion that
some pleasures are bad and some pains good? I mean to say, in so far as they
are pleasant, are they not also good, leaving aside any consequence that they
may entail? And in the same way pains, in so far as they are painful, are bad?

I'm not sure Socrates, he said, whether I ought to give an answer as unqualified as your question suggests, and say that everything pleasant is good, and
everything painful evil. But with a view not only to my present answer but to
the whole of the rest of my life, I believe it is safest to reply that there are some
pleasures which are not good, and some pains which are not evil, others on the
other hand which are, and a third class which are neither evil nor good.

Meaning by pleasures, said I, what partakes of pleasure or gives it?

Certainly.

My question then is, whether they are not, qua pleasant, good. I am asking in
fact whether pleasure itself is not a good thing.

Let us, he replied, as you are so fond of saying yourself, investigate the
question; then if the proposition we are examining seems reasonable, and

pleasant and good appear identical, we shall agree on it. If not, that will be the time to differ.

Good, said I. Will you lead the inquiry or should I?

It is for you to take the lead, since you introduced the subject.

I wonder then, said I, if we can make it clear to ourselves like this. If a man were trying to judge, by external appearance, of another's health or some particular physical function, he might look at his face and hands and then say, "Let me see your chest and back too, so that I may make a more satisfactory examination." Something like this is what I want for our present inquiry. Observing that your attitude to the good and the pleasant is what you say, I want to go on something like this. Now uncover another part of your mind, Protagoras. What is your attitude to knowledge? Do you share the common view about that also? Most people think, in general terms, that it is nothing strong, no leading or ruling element. They don't see it like that. They hold that it is not the knowledge that a man possesses which governs him, but something else—now passion, now pleasure, now pain, sometimes love, and frequently fear. They just think of knowledge as a slave, pushed around by all the other affections. Is this your view too, or would you rather say that knowledge is a fine thing quite capable of ruling a man, and that if he can distinguish good from evil, nothing will force him to act otherwise than as knowledge dictates, since wisdom is all the reinforcement he needs?

Not only is this my view, replied Protagoras, but I above all men should think it shame to speak of wisdom and knowledge as anything but the most powerful elements in human life.

Well and truly answered, said I. But I expect you know that most men don't believe us. They maintain that there are many who recognize the best but are unwilling to act on it. It may be open to them, but they do otherwise. Whenever I ask what can be the reason for this, they answer that those who act in this way are overcome by pleasure or pain or some other of the things I mentioned just now.

Well, Socrates, it's by no means uncommon for people to say what is not correct.

Then come with me and try to convince them, and show what really happens when they speak of being overcome by pleasure and therefore, though recognizing what is best, failing to do it. If we simply declare, "You are wrong, and what you say is false," they will ask us, "If it is not being overcome by pleasure, what can it be? What do you two say it is? Tell us."

But why must we look into the opinions of the common man, who says whatever comes into his head?

I believe, I replied, that it will help us to find out how courage is related to the other parts of virtue. So if you are content to keep to our decision, that I should lead the way in whatever direction I think we shall best see the light, then follow me. Otherwise, if you wish, I shall give it up.

No, you are right, he said. Carry on as you have begun.

To return then, If they should ask us, "What is your name for what we called being worsted by pleasure?" I should reply, "Listen. Protagoras and I will try to explain it to you. We take it that you say this happens to you when, for example, you are overcome by the desire of food or drink or sex—which are pleasant things—and though you recognize them as evil, nevertheless indulge in them. They would agree. Then we should ask them, "In what respect do you call them evil? Is it because for the moment each of them provides its pleasure and is pleasant, or because they lay up for the future disease or poverty or suchlike? If they led to none of these things, but produced pure enjoyment, would they nevertheless be evils—no matter why or how they give enjoyment?" Can we expect any other answer than this, that they are not evil on account of the actual momentary pleasure which they produce, but on account of their consequences, disease and the rest?

I believe that would be their answer, said Protagoras.

"Well, to cause disease and poverty is to cause pain." They would agree, I think?

He nodded.

"So the only reason why these pleasures seem to you to be evil is, we suggest, that they result in pains and deprive us of future pleasures." Would they agree?

We both thought they would.

Now suppose we asked them the converse question. "You say also that pains may be good. You mean, I take it, such things as physical training, military campaigns, doctors' treatment involving cautery or the knife or drugs or starvation diet? These, you say, are good but painful?" Would they agree?

They would.

"Do you then call them good in virtue of the fact that at the time they cause extreme pain and agony, or because in the future there result from them health, bodily well-being, the safety of one's country, dominion over others, wealth?" The latter, I think they would agree.

Protagoras thought so too.

"And are they good for any other reason than that their outcome is pleasure and the cessation or prevention of pain? Can you say that you have any other end in mind, when you call them good, than pleasures or pains?" I think they would say no.

I too, said he.

"So you pursue pleasure as being good, and shun pain as evil?"

He agreed.

"Then your idea of evil is pain, and of good is pleasure. Even enjoying yourself you call evil whenever it leads to the loss of a pleasure greater than its own, or lays up pains that outweigh its pleasures. If it is in any other sense, or without anything else in mind, that you call enjoyment evil, no doubt you could tell us what it is, but you cannot."

I agree that they cannot, said Protagoras.

"Isn't it the same when we turn back to pain? To suffer pain you call good when it either rids us of greater pains than its own or leads to pleasures that outweigh them. If you have anything else in mind when you call the actual suffering of pain a good thing, you could tell us what it is, but you cannot."

True, said Protagoras.

"Now my good people," I went on, "if you ask me what is the point of all this rigmarole, I beg your indulgence. It isn't easy to explain the real meaning of what you call being overcome by pleasure, and any explanation is bound up with this point. You may still change your minds, if you can say that the good is anything other than pleasure, or evil other than pain. Is it sufficient for you to live life through with pleasure and without pain? If so, and you can mention no good or evil which cannot in the last resort be reduced to these, then listen to my next point.

"This position makes your argument ridiculous. You say that a man often recognizes evil actions as evil, yet commits them, under no compulsion, because he is led on and distracted by pleasure, and on the other hand that, recognizing the good, he refrains from following it because he is overcome by the pleasures of the moment. The absurdity of this will become evident if we stop using all these names together—pleasant, painful, good, and evil—and since they have turned out to be only two, call them by only two names—first of all good and evil, and only at a different stage pleasure and pain. Having agreed on this, suppose we now say that a man does evil though he recognizes it as evil. Why? Because he is overcome. By what? We can no longer say by pleasure, because it has changed its name to good. Overcome, we say. By what, we are asked. By the good, I suppose we shall say. I fear that if our questioner is ill-mannered, he will laugh and retort, What ridiculous nonsense, for a man to do evil, knowing it is evil and that he ought not to do it, because he is overcome by good. Am I to suppose that the good in you is or is not a match for the evil? Clearly we shall reply that the good is not a match; otherwise the man whom we speak of as being overcome by pleasure would not have done wrong. And in what way, he may say, does good fail to be a match for evil, or evil for good? Is it not by being greater or smaller, more or less than the other? We shall have to agree. Then by being overcome you must mean taking greater evil in exchange for lesser good.

"Having noted this result, suppose we reinstate the names pleasant and painful for the same phenomena, thus: A man does—*evil* we said before, but now we shall say *painful* actions, knowing them to be painful, because overcome by pleasures—pleasures, obviously, which were not a match for the pains. And what meaning can we attach to the phrase *not a match for*, when used of pleasure in relation to pain, except the excess or deficiency of one as compared with the other? It depends on whether one is greater or smaller, more or less intense than the other. If anyone objects that there is a great difference between present pleasure and pleasure or pain in the future, I shall reply that the difference cannot be one of anything else but pleasure and pain. So like an expert in weighing, put the pleasures and the pains together, set both the near and distant in the balance, and say which is the greater quantity. In weighing pleasures against pleasures, one must always choose the greater and the more; in weighing pains against pains, the smaller and the less; whereas in weighing pleasures against pains, if the pleasures exceed the pains, whether the distant, the near, or vice versa, one must take the course which brings those pleasures; but if the pains outweigh the pleasures, avoid it. Is this not so, good people?" I should say, and I am sure they could not deny it.

Protagoras agreed.

"That being so then, answer me this," I shall go on. "The same magnitudes seem greater to the eye from near at hand than they do from a distance. This is true of thickness and also of number, and sounds of equal loudness seem greater near at hand than at a distance. If now our happiness consisted in doing, I mean in choosing, greater lengths and avoiding smaller, where would lie salvation? In the art of measurement or in the impression made by appearances? Haven't we seen that the appearance leads us astray and throws us into confusion so that in our actions and our choices between great and small we are constantly accepting and rejecting the same things, whereas the metric art would have canceled the effect of the impression, and by revealing the true state of affairs would have caused the soul to live in peace and quiet and abide in the truth, thus saving our life?" Faced with these considerations, would people agree that our salvation would lie in the art of measurement?

He agreed that they would.

"Again, what if our welfare lay in the choice of odd and even numbers, in knowing when the greater number must rightly be chosen and when the less, whether each sort in relation to itself or one in relation to the other, and whether they were near or distant? What would assure us a good life then? Surely knowledge, and specifically a science of measurement, since the required skill lies in the estimation of excess and defect—or to be more precise, arithmetic, since it deals with odd and even numbers." Would people agree with us?

Protagoras thought they would.

"Well then," I shall say, "since our salvation in life has turned out to lie in the correct choice of pleasure and pain—more or less, greater or smaller, nearer or more distant—is it not in the first place a question of measurement, consisting as it does in a consideration of relative excess, defect, or equality?"

It must be.

"And if so, it must be a special skill or branch of knowledge."

Yes, they will agree.

"What skill, or what branch of knowledge it is, we shall leave till later; the fact itself is enough for the purposes of the explanation which you have asked for from Protagoras and me. To remind you of your question, it arose because we two agreed that there was nothing more powerful than knowledge, but that wherever it is found it always has the mastery over pleasure and everything else. You on the other hand, who maintain that pleasure often masters even the man who knows, asked us to say what this experience really is, if it is not being mastered by pleasure. If we had answered you straight off that it is ignorance, you would have laughed at us, but if you laugh at us now, you will be laughing at yourselves as well, for you have agreed that when people make a wrong choice of pleasures and pains—that is, of good and evil—the cause of their mistake is lack of knowledge. We can go further, and call it, as you have already agreed, a science of measurement, and you know yourselves that a wrong action which is done without knowledge is done in ignorance. So that is what being mastered by pleasure really is—ignorance, and most serious ignorance, the fault which Protagoras, Prodicus, and Hippias profess to cure. You on the other hand, because you believe it to be something else, neither go nor send your children to these Sophists, who are the experts in such matters. Holding that it is nothing that can be taught, you are careful with your money and withhold it from them—a bad policy both for yourselves and for the community."

That then is the answer we should make to the ordinary run of people, and I ask you—Hippias and Prodicus as well as Protagoras, for I want you to share our discussion—whether you think what I say is true.

They all agreed most emphatically that it was true.

You agree then, said I, that the pleasant is good and the painful bad. I ask exemption from Prodicus' precise verbal distinctions. Whether you call it pleasant, agreeable, or enjoyable, my dear Prodicus, or whatever name you like to apply to it, please answer in the sense of my request.

Prodicus laughed and assented, and so did the others.

Well, here is another point, I continued. All actions aimed at this end, namely a pleasant and painless life, must be fine actions, that is, good and beneficial.

They agreed.

Then if the pleasant is the good, no one who either knows or believes that there is another possible course of action, better than the one he is following, will ever continue on his present course when he might choose the better. To "act beneath yourself" is the result of pure ignorance; to "be your own master" is wisdom.

All agreed.

John Calvin

INSTITUTES OF THE CHRISTIAN RELIGION

Pleasure and sin are nearly interchangeable concepts in the writings of John Calvin (1509–1564). These are his comments on the doctrine of original sin.

BOOK SECOND
OF THE KNOWLEDGE OF GOD THE REDEEMER, IN CHRIST, AS FIRST MANIFESTED TO THE FATHERS, UNDER THE LAW, AND THEREAFTER TO US UNDER THE GOSPEL.

CHAPTER I
THROUGH THE FALL AND REVOLT OF ADAM, THE WHOLE HUMAN RACE MADE ACCURSED AND DEGENERATE. OF ORIGINAL SIN.

8. But lest the thing itself of which we speak be unknown or doubtful, it will be proper to define original sin (Calvin, in Conc. Trident. I., Dec. Sess. v.). I have no intention, however, to discuss all the definitions which different writers have adopted, but only to adduce the one which seems to me most accordant with truth. Original sin, then, may be defined a hereditary corruption and depravity of our nature, extending to all the parts of the soul, which first makes us obnoxious to the wrath of God, and then produces in us works which in Scripture are termed works of the flesh. This corruption is repeatedly designated by Paul by the term sin (Gal. v. 19); while the works which proceed from it, such as adultery, fornication, theft, hatred, murder, revellings, he terms, in the same way, the fruits of sin, though in various passages of Scripture, and even by Paul

himself, they are also termed sins. The two things, therefore, are to be distinctly observed—viz. that being thus perverted and corrupted in all the parts of our nature, we are, merely on account of such corruption, deservedly condemned by God, to whom nothing is acceptable but righteousness, innocence, and purity. This is not liability for another's fault. For when it is said, that the sin of Adam has made us obnoxious to the justice of God, the meaning is not, that we, who are in ourselves innocent and blameless, are bearing his guilt, but that since by his transgression we are all placed under the curse, he is said to have brought us under obligation. Through him, however, not only has punishment been derived, but pollution instilled, for which punishment is justly due. Hence Augustine, though he often terms it another's sin (that he may more clearly show how it comes to us by descent), at the same time asserts that it is each individual's own sin. And the Apostle most distinctly testifies, that "death passed upon all men, for that all have sinned" (Rom. v. 12); that is, are involved in original sin, and polluted by its stain. Hence, even infants bringing their condemnation with them from their mother's womb, suffer not for another's, but for their own defect. For although they have not yet produced the fruits of their own unrighteousness, they have the seed implanted in them. Nay, their whole nature is, as it were, a seed-bed of sin, and therefore cannot but be odious and abominable to God. Hence it follows, that it is properly deemed sinful in the sight of God; for there could be no condemnation without guilt. Next comes the other point—viz. that this perversity in us never ceases, but constantly produces new fruits, in other words, those works of the flesh which we formerly described; just as a lighted furnace sends forth sparks and flames, or a fountain without ceasing pours out water. Hence, those who have defined original sin as the want of the original righteousness which we ought to have had, though they substantially comprehend the whole case, do not significantly enough express its power and energy. For our nature is not only utterly devoid of goodness, but so prolific in all kinds of evil, that it can never be idle. Those who term it *concupiscence* use a word not very inappropriate, provided it were added (this, however, many will by no means concede), that everything which is in man, from the intellect to the will, from the soul even to the flesh, is defiled and pervaded with this concupiscence; or, to express it more briefly, that the whole man is in himself nothing else than concupiscence.

9. I have said, therefore, that all the parts of the soul were possessed by sin, ever since Adam revolted from the fountain of righteousness. For not only did the inferior appetites entice him, but abominable impiety seized upon the very citadel of the mind, and pride penetrated to his inmost heart (Rom. vii. 12; Book IV., chap. xv., sec. 10–12), so that it is foolish and unmeaning to confine the corruption thence proceeding to what are called sensual motions, or to call it an excitement, which allures, excites, and drags the single part which they call sensuality into sin. Here Peter Lombard has displayed gross ignorance (Lomb., Lib. ii. Dist. 21). When investigating the seat of corruption, he says it is in the flesh (as Paul declares), not properly, indeed, but as being more appar-

ent in the flesh. As if Paul had meant that only a part of the soul, and not the whole nature, was opposed to supernatural grace. Paul himself leaves no room for doubt, when he says, that corruption does not dwell in one part only, but that no part is free from its deadly taint. For, speaking of corrupt nature, he not only condemns the inordinate nature of the appetites, but, in particular, declares that the understanding is subjected to blindness, and the heart to depravity (Eph. iv. 17, 18). The third chapter of the Epistle to the Romans is nothing but a description of original sin. The same thing appears more clearly from the mode of renovation. For the spirit, which is contrasted with the old man, and the flesh, denotes not only the grace by which the sensual or inferior part of the soul is corrected, but includes a complete reformation of all its parts (Eph. iv. 23). And, accordingly, Paul enjoins not only that gross appetites be suppressed, but that we be renewed in the spirit of our mind (Eph. iv. 23), as he elsewhere tells us to be transformed by the renewing of our mind (Rom. xii. 2). Hence it follows, that that part in which the dignity and excellence of the soul are most conspicuous, has not only been wounded, but so corrupted, that mere cure is not sufficient. There must be a new nature. How far sin has seized both on the mind and heart, we shall shortly see. Here I only wish briefly to observe, that the whole man, from the crown of the head to the sole of the foot, is so deluged, as it were, that no part remains exempt from sin, and, therefore, everything which proceeds from him is imputed as sin. Thus Paul says, that all carnal thoughts and affections are enmity against God, and consequently death (Rom. viii. 7).

10. Let us have done, then, with those who dare to inscribe the name of God on their vices, because we say that men are born vicious. The divine workmanship, which they ought to look for in the nature of Adam, when still entire and uncorrupted, they absurdly expect to find in their depravity. The blame of our ruin rests with our own carnality, not with God, its only cause being our degeneracy from our original condition. And let no one here clamour that God might have provided better for our safety by preventing Adam's fall. This objection, which, from the daring presumption implied in it, is odious to every pious mind, relates to the mystery of predestination, which will afterwards be considered in its own place (Tertull. de Præscript. Calvin, Lib. de Predest.). Meanwhile, let us remember that our ruin is attributable to our own depravity, that we may not insinuate a charge against God himself, the Author of nature. It is true that nature has received a mortal wound, but there is a great difference between a wound inflicted from without, and one inherent in our first condition. It is plain that this wound was inflicted by sin; and, therefore, we have no ground of complaint except against ourselves. This is carefully taught in Scripture. For the Preacher says, "Lo, this only have I found, that God made man upright; but they have sought out many inventions" (Eccl. vii. 29). Since man, by the kindness of God, was made upright, but by his own infatuation fell away unto vanity, his destruction is obviously attributable only to himself (Athanas. in Orat. Cont. Idola.)

11. We say, then, that man is corrupted by a natural viciousness, but not by one which proceeded from nature. In saying that it proceeded not from nature, we mean that it was rather an adventitious event which befell man, than a substantial property assigned to him from the beginning. We, however, call it *natural* to prevent any one from supposing that each individual contracts it by depraved habit, whereas all receive it by a hereditary law. And we have authority for so calling it. For, on the same ground, the Apostle says, that we are "by nature the children of wrath" (Eph. ii. 3). How could God, who takes pleasure in the meanest of his works, be offended with the noblest of them all? The offence is not with the work itself, but the corruption of the work. Wherefore, if it is not improper to say that, in consequence of the corruption of human nature, man is naturally hateful to God, it is not improper to say, that he is naturally vicious and depraved. Hence, in the view of our corrupt nature, Augustine hesitates not to call those sins natural which necessarily reign in the flesh wherever the grace of God is wanting. This disposes of the absurd notion of the Manichees, who, imagining that man was essentially wicked, went the length of assigning him a different Creator, that they might thus avoid the appearance of attributing the cause and origin of evil to a righteous God.

G. E. Moore
PRINCIPIA ETHICA

G. E. Moore (1873–1958) argues in the following passage of his
Principia Ethica that pleasure and good are not the same thing
and, accordingly, that the good life is not identical with a life of
pleasure.

CHAPTER I.
THE SUBJECT-MATTER OF ETHICS.

1. It is very easy to point out some among our every-day judgments, with the
truth of which Ethics is undoubtedly concerned. Whenever we say, "So and so
is a good man," or "That fellow is a villain"; whenever we ask, "What ought I
to do?" or "Is it wrong for me to do like this?"; whenever we hazard such
remarks as "Temperance is a virtue and drunkenness a vice"—it is undoubtedly the business of Ethics to discuss such questions and such statements; to
argue what is the true answer when we ask what it is right to do, and to give
reasons for thinking that our statements about the character of persons or the
morality of actions are true or false. In the vast majority of cases, where we
make statements involving any of the terms "virtue," "vice," "duty," "right,"
"ought," "good," "bad," we are making ethical judgments; and if we wish to
discuss their truth, we shall be discussing a point of Ethics.

So much as this is not disputed; but it falls very far short of defining the
province of Ethics. That province may indeed be defined as the whole truth
about that which is at the same time common to all such judgments and
peculiar to them. But we have still to ask the question: What is it that is thus
common and peculiar? And this is a question to which very different answers
have been given by ethical philosophers of acknowledged reputation, and none
of them, perhaps, completely satisfactory.

2. If we take such examples as those given above, we shall not be far wrong
in saying that they are all of them concerned with the question of "conduct"—
with the question, what, in the conduct of us, human beings, is good, and what

is bad, what is right, and what is wrong. For when we say that a man is good, we commonly mean that he acts rightly; when we say that drunkenness is a vice, we commonly mean that to get drunk is a wrong or wicked action. And this discussion of human conduct is, in fact, that with which the name "Ethics" is most intimately associated. It is so associated by derivation; and conduct is undoubtedly by far the commonest and most generally interesting object of ethical judgments.

Accordingly, we find that many ethical philosophers are disposed to accept as an adequate definition of "Ethics" the statement that it deals with the question what is good or bad in human conduct. They hold that its enquiries are properly confined to "conduct" or to "practice"; they hold that the name "practical philosophy" covers all the matter with which it has to do. Now, without discussing the proper meaning of the word (for verbal questions are properly left to the writers of dictionaries and other persons interested in literature; philosophy, as we shall see, has no concern with them), I may say that I intend to use "Ethics" to cover more than this—a usage, for which there is, I think, quite sufficient authority. I am using it to cover an enquiry for which, at all events, there is no other word: the general enquiry into what is good.

Ethics is undoubtedly concerned with the question what good conduct is; but, being concerned with this, it obviously does not start at the beginning, unless it is prepared to tell us what is good as well as what is conduct. For "good conduct" is a complex notion: all conduct is not good; for some is certainly bad and some may be indifferent. And on the other hand, other things, beside conduct, may be good; and if they are so, then, "good" denotes some property, that is common to them and conduct; and if we examine good conduct alone of all good things, then we shall be in danger of mistaking for this property, some property which is not shared by those other things: and thus we shall have made a mistake about Ethics even in this limited sense; for we shall not know what good conduct really is. This is a mistake which many writers have actually made, from limiting their enquiry to conduct. And hence I shall try to avoid it by considering first what is good in general; hoping, that if we can arrive at any certainty about this, it will be much easier to settle the question of good conduct: for we all know pretty well what "conduct" is. This, then, is our first question: What is good? and What is bad? and to the discussion of this question (or these questions) I give the name of Ethics, since that science must, at all events, include it. . . .

6. What, then, is good? How is good to be defined? Now, it may be thought that this is a verbal question. A definition does indeed often mean the expressing of one word's meaning in other words. But this is not the sort of definition I am asking for. Such a definition can never be of ultimate importance in any study except lexicography. If I wanted that kind of definition I should have to consider in the first place how people generally used the word "good"; but my business is not with its proper usage, as established by custom. I should, indeed, be foolish, if I tried to use it for something which it did not usually

denote: if, for instance, I were to announce that, whenever I used the word "good," I must be understood to be thinking of that object which is usually denoted by the word "table." I shall, therefore, use the word in the sense in which I think it is ordinarily used; but at the same time I am not anxious to discuss whether I am right in thinking that it is so used. My business is solely with that object or idea, which I hold, rightly or wrongly, that the word is generally used to stand for. What I want to discover is the nature of that object or idea, and about this I am extremely anxious to arrive at an agreement.

But, if we understand the question in this sense, my answer to it may seem a very disappointing one. If I am asked "What is good?" my answer is that good is good, and that is the end of the matter. Or if I am asked "How is good to be defined?" my answer is that it cannot be defined, and that is all I have to say about it. But disappointing as these answers may appear, they are of the very last importance. To readers who are familiar with philosophic terminology, I can express their importance by saying that they amount to this: That propositions about the good are all of them synthetic and never analytic; and that is plainly no trivial matter. And the same thing may be expressed more popularly, by saying that, if I am right, then nobody can foist upon us such an axiom as that "Pleasure is the only good" or that "The good is the desired" on the pretence that this is "the very meaning of the word."

7. Let us, then, consider this position. My point is that "good" is a simple notion, just as "yellow" is a simple notion; that, just as you cannot, by any manner of means, explain to any one who does not already know it, what yellow is, so you cannot explain what good is. Definitions of the kind that I was asking for, definitions which describe the real nature of the object or notion denoted by a word, and which do not merely tell us what the word is used to mean, are only possible when the object or notion in question is something complex. You can give a definition of a horse, because a horse has many different properties and qualities, all of which you can enumerate. But when you have enumerated them all, when you have reduced a horse to his simplest terms, then you can no longer define those terms. They are simply something which you think of or perceive, and to any one who cannot think of or perceive them, you can never, by any definition, make their nature known. It may perhaps be objected to this that we are able to describe to others, objects which they have never seen or thought of. We can, for instance, make a man understand what a chimaera is, although he has never heard of one or seen one. You can tell him that it is an animal with a lioness's head and body, with a goat's head growing from the middle of its back, and with a snake in place of a tail. But here the object which you are describing is a complex object; it is entirely composed of parts, with which we are all perfectly familiar—a snake, a goat, a lioness; and we know, too, the manner in which those parts are to be put together, because we know what is meant by the middle of a lioness's back, and where her tail is wont to grow. And so it is with all objects, not previously known, which we are able to define: they are all complex; all composed of

parts, which may themselves, in the first instance, be capable of similar definition, but which must in the end be reducible to simplest parts, which can no longer be defined. But yellow and good, we say, are not complex: they are notions of that simple kind, out of which definitions are composed and with which the power of further defining ceases. . . .

12. Suppose a man says "I am pleased"; and suppose that is not a lie or a mistake but the truth. Well, if it is true, what does that mean? It means that his mind, a certain definite mind, distinguished by certain definite marks from all others, has at this moment a certain definite feeling called pleasure. "Pleased" *means* nothing but having pleasure, and though we may be more pleased or less pleased, and even, we may admit for the present, have one or another kind of pleasure; yet in so far as it is pleasure we have, whether there be more or less of it, and whether it be of one kind or another, what we have is one definite thing, absolutely indefinable, some one thing that is the same in all the various degrees and in all the various kinds of it that there may be. We may be able to say how it is related to other things: that, for example, it is in the mind, that it causes desire, that we are conscious of it, etc., etc. We can, I say, describe its relations to other things, but define it we can *not*. And if anybody tried to define pleasure for us as being any other natural object; if anybody were to say, for instance, that pleasure *means* the sensation of red, and were to proceed to deduce from that that pleasure is a colour, we should be entitled to laugh at him and to distrust his future statements about pleasure. Well, that would be the same fallacy which I have called the naturalistic fallacy. That "pleased" does not mean "having the sensation of red," or anything else whatever, does not prevent us from understanding what it does mean. It is enough for us to know that "pleased" does mean "having the sensation of pleasure," and though pleasure is absolutely indefinable, though pleasure is pleasure and nothing else whatever, yet we feel no difficulty in saying that we are pleased. The reason is, of course, that when I say "I am pleased," I do *not* mean that "I" am the same thing as "having pleasure." And similarly no difficulty need be found in my saying that "pleasure is good" and yet not meaning that "pleasure" is the same thing as "good," that pleasure *means* good, and that good *means* pleasure. If I were to imagine that when I said "I am pleased," I meant that I was exactly the same thing as "pleased," I should not indeed call that a naturalistic fallacy, although it would be the same fallacy as I have called naturalistic with reference to Ethics. The reason of this is obvious enough. When a man confuses two natural objects with one another, defining the one by the other, if for instance, he confuses himself, who is one natural object, with "pleased" or with "pleasure" which are others, then there is no reason to call the fallacy naturalistic. But if he confuses "good," which is not in the same sense a natural object, with any natural object whatever, then there is a reason for calling that a naturalistic fallacy; its being made with regard to "good" marks it as something quite specific, and this specific mistake deserves a name because it is so common.

Gilbert Ryle

PLEASURE

Gilbert Ryle (1900–1976) was professor of philosophy at Oxford University and the author of *The Concept of Mind*. We here reprint his essay on pleasure.

What sort of a difference is the difference between taking a walk which one enjoys and taking a walk to which one is indifferent?

(1) It might be suggested that it is, in genus if not in species, the sort of difference that there is between walking with a headache and walking without one; and that somewhat as one walker may recollect afterwards not only the ordinary acts and incidents of his walk, but also the steady or intermittent pains that he had had in his head while walking, so another walker who has enjoyed his walk might recall both the ordinary acts and incidents of his walk and also the steady pleasure or the intermittent pleasures that had been concomitant with the walk. It might even be suggested that as one walker may recollect that his headache had become specially acute just as he reached the canal, so another might recollect that his pleasure had become specially acute just as he reached the canal.

A person who made such a suggestion need not hold that to enjoy a walk is itself to have a special bodily sensation or series of bodily sensations concurrent with the walking. He might admit that while we can ask in which arm an agreeable or disagreeable tingle had been felt, we could not ask in which arm the agreeableness or disagreeableness of it had been felt. He might admit, too, that in the way in which pains yield to local or general anaesthetics, enjoyment and distaste are not the sorts of states or conditions for which anaesthetics are appropriate. But he might still suggest that pleasure is a non-bodily feeling, in supposedly the same generic sense of "feeling" as pain is a bodily feeling. If sophisticated enough, he might suggest that pleasure is a specific, introspectible *Erlebnis*, where a headache is a specific bodily *Erlebnis*. Now a sensation or *Erlebnis*, like a tingle, may be agreeable, disagreeable or neutral. If enjoying and disliking were correctly co-classified with such *Erlebnisse* or feelings, one would expect, by analogy, that one could similarly ask whether a person who had had the supposed pleasure-feeling or dislike-*Erlebnis* had liked or disliked having it. Enjoying or disliking a tingle would be, on this showing, having one bodily feeling plus one non-bodily feeling. Either, then, this non-bodily feeling is, in its turn, something that can be pleasant or unpleasant, which would require yet another non-bodily feeling . . . ; or the way or sense, if any, in which pleasure and distress are feelings is not in analogy with the way or sense in which tingles are feelings.

There are other places where the suggested analogy between pleasure and tingles collapses. If you report having a tingle in your arm, I can ask you to describe it. Is it rather like having an electric shock? Does it mount and subside like waves? Is it going on at this moment? But when you tell how much you are enjoying the smell of peat smoke in my room, you cannot even construe the parallel questions about your enjoyment. Nor is your inability to answer due merely to the very important fact that in order to attend to my questions you have to stop attending to the smell, and so cannot still be enjoying it. You cannot answer my questions even in retrospect. There is no phenomenon to describe, except the smell of the peat smoke.

(2) The enjoyment of a walk might, however, be co-classified by some, not with feelings like tingles, but with feelings like wrath, amusement, alarm and disappointment—which is a very different use of "feeling." It could be urged that though the walker would not naturally say that he had felt pleased all the time or had kept on feeling pleased, still he could quite naturally say such things as that he had felt as if he were walking on air, or that he had felt that he could go on for ever. These dicta, which would certainly suggest that he had enjoyed his walk, should, on this second view, be construed as reporting a passion or emotion, in that sense of those words in which a person who is scared, thrilled, tickled or surprised is in the grip of a more or less violent passion or emotion.

This second assimilation too collapses. The walker may enjoy his walk very much, but he is not, thereby, assailed or overcome by anything. A man may be too angry or surprised to think straight, but he cannot enjoy his walk too much to think straight. He can be perfectly calm while enjoying himself very much.

Panic, fury and mirth can be transports, convulsions or fits, but the enjoyment of the smell of peat smoke is not a paroxysm like these—not because it is very mild, where they are violent, but because it is not the sort of thing that can be resisted, whether successfully or unsuccessfully. It cannot be given way to, either. It is not a gale or a squall, but nor is it even a capful of wind. There is no conquering it or being conquered by it, though there is certainly such a thing as conquering or being conquered by the habit of indulging in something or the temptation to indulge in it.

(3) There is the third, though surely not the last, use of "feeling" in which moods or frames of mind like depression, cheerfulness, irritability and *insouci-*

ance are often called "feelings." Typically, though not universally, a mood lasts some hours or even a day or two, like the weather. But the mood of irritability is unlike the emotion or passion of anger, not only in its typical duration and not only in being more like squally weather than like a squall, but also in not having a particular object. A man is angry with his dog or his tie, but his irritability has no particular object, except, what comes to the same thing, the Scheme of Things in General. To be irritable is to be predisposed to lose one's temper with no matter which particular object. A person in a cheerful or energetic mood is predisposed to enjoy, *inter alia*, any walk that he may take; but what he enjoys is this particular walk. His enjoyment of it is not the fact that he is predisposed to enjoy any occupations or activities. Moreover, he enjoys his walk only while taking it, but he had felt cheerful or energetic, perhaps, ever since he got out of bed. So enjoying something is not the same sort of thing as being or feeling cheerful. On the contrary, the notion of being cheerful has to be explained in terms of the notion of pleasure, since to be cheerful is to be easy to please.

Sensations, emotional states and moods can, in principle, all be clocked. We can often say roughly how long a tingle or a headache lasted, very roughly how long a fit of rage or amusement lasted, and extremely roughly how long a mood of depression or cheerfulness lasted. But pleasure does not lend itself to such clockings. The walker can, indeed, say that he enjoyed his walk until it began to rain, two hours after he started out; or the diner can say that he enjoyed, though decreasingly, every bite of Stilton cheese that he took until satiety set in with the penultimate bite, and that this series of bites took about six minutes. But he cannot clock the duration of his enjoyment *against* the duration of the thing he enjoyed. He can, at best, divide the duration of the walk or meal into the parts which he enjoyed and the parts which he did not enjoy. The enjoyment of a walk is not a concomitant, e.g. an introspectible effect of the walking, such that there might be two histories, one the history of the walk, the other the history of its agreeableness to the walker. In particular there would be a glaring absurdity in the suggestion that the enjoyment of a walk might outlast the walk—unless all that was intended was that the walker enjoyed the walk and then enjoyed some after-effects or memories of the walk; or that the walk had made him cheerful for some time afterwards.

Psychologists nowadays often avoid idioms which suggest that enjoying a walk is having a special feeling while one walks, by speaking instead of the "hedonic tone" of the walker. This new idiom, apart from performing its one antiseptic function, does not by itself advance very much our conceptual enquiry. It does not make clear what sort of a thing pleasure is. Is the hedonic tone the sort of thing that could, conceivably, be induced by drugs or hypnosis—as Dutch courage and somnolence can be induced? Could a person be qualified by hedonic tone, without his doing or having anything in particular to enjoy doing or having? So let us try to make a more positive move of our own.

Sometimes I enjoy a smell, sometimes I dislike it, and very often I am quite indifferent to it. But I could not enjoy it, dislike it or be indifferent to it if I were totally oblivious or unaware of it. I cannot say, in retrospect, that I liked the smell but did not notice it. I could, of course, enjoy a complex of smells, views, cool air and running water without paying special heed to any one of them. But I could not have enjoyed just that complex while being totally oblivious of any one of those components of it. This "could not" is not a causal "could not." To say that a person had enjoyed the music, though too preoccupied to listen to it even as a background noise, would be to say something silly, not to report a *lusus naturae.* Unnoticed things, like ozone in the air, may certainly cause us to feel vigorous or cheerful. There may well be such an unnoticed cause of our being predisposed to enjoy, *inter alia,* the food and the music. But then we do not enjoy the ozone, but the food and the music; and of these we cannot be both oblivious and appreciative.

Similarly, when a person temporarily forgets his headache or tickle, he must cease, for that period, to be distressed by it. Being distressed by it entails not being oblivious of it. But just what is this connection between enjoying and attending, or between being oblivious and being undistressed? What, to begin with, is there to be said about the notions of attention and oblivion themselves?

When we consider the notion of attending, a subject which we consider far too seldom, we are apt to fancy that we have to do with some nuclear, one-piece notion; as if, for example, all attending were comparable with just switching on and aiming a torch in order to see what is there whether we see it or not. But in real life we use a wide variety of idioms for attending, most of which will not quite or even nearly do duty for one another. Some of these idioms correspond not too badly with the model of the torch-beam; others do not correspond with it at all.

For example, if at the prompting of someone else I come to notice a previously unnoticed smell, the way I become alive to the smell has some kinship with the way the hedgehog comes to be seen when the torch-beam is directed upon it. But then the way in which a strong smell so forces itself on my attention that I cannot *not* notice it is much more like a piece of barbed wire catching me than like an object being picked out by my exploring torch-beam.

When we describe someone as writing or driving carefully, we are describing him as attending to his task. But he is not, save *per accidens,* taking note of the things he is doing, since he is playing not an observer's part but an agent's part. He is taking pains to avoid, among other things, ambiguities or collisions, where noticing a strong smell does not involve taking pains at all.

Consider some other differences between the functions of such idioms as those of noticing, heed, being careful, being vigilant, concentrating, taking interest, being absorbed, giving one's mind to something, and thinking what one is doing. When excited or bored, I may not think what I am saying; but to say this is to say less than that I am talking recklessly. I may be interested in something when it would be too severe to say that I am concentrating on it;

and I may concentrate on something which fails to capture my interest. Attention is sometimes attracted, sometimes lent, sometimes paid and sometimes exacted.

Philosophers and psychologists sometimes speak of "acts" of attention. This idiom too is partially appropriate to certain contexts and quite inappropriate to others. When a person is actually bidden by someone else or by himself to attend, there is something which with some effort or reluctance he *does*. Where his attention had been wandering, it now settles; where he had been half-asleep, he is now wide awake; and this change he may bring about with a wrench. But the spectator at an exciting football match does not have to try to fasten or canalise his attention. To the question "How many acts of attention did you perform?" his proper answer would be "None." For no wrenches had occurred. His attention was fixed on the game but he went through no operations of fixing it. The same man, listening to a lecture, might perform a hundred operations of fixing his attention and still fail to keep his mind on what was being said. Acts of attending occur when attending is difficult. But sometimes attending is easy; and sometimes it is difficult, sometimes impossible not to attend.

Even where it is appropriate to speak of acts of attention, the word "act" carries very little of its ordinary luggage. In ordinary contexts we apply very multifarious criteria in determining what constitutes one act. Perhaps making one move in chess is performing one act; perhaps doing enough to warrant prosecution is performing one act; and perhaps getting from the beginning to the end of a speech without being side-tracked is one act. But a person who has, say, hummed a tune from beginning to end, not absentmindedly but on purpose and with some application, has not performed two acts or accomplished two tasks, one of humming plus one of giving his mind to reproducing the tune; or, at any rate, he has not performed two acts in that sense of "two acts" in which it would make sense to say that he might have done the second but omitted the first. Giving his mind to reproducing the tune is not doing something else, in the way in which a person sawing wood while humming is doing something else besides humming. We should say, rather, that a person who hums a tune with some concentration is humming in a different way from the way in which he hums automatically, for all that the difference might make no audible difference. It makes his humming a different sort of action, not a concomitance of separately performable actions.

I suggest that explicit talk about such things as heed, concentration, paying attention, care and so on occurs most commonly in instruction-situations and in accusation-situations, both of which are relatively small, though important, sections of discourse. Elsewhere, even when talking about human beings, we tend to make relatively few explicit mentions of these things, not because it would be irrelevant, but because it would be redundant to do so. The notions are already built into the meanings of lots of the biographical and critical expressions which we use in talking to people and about them. In partly the same way we do not often need to make explicit mention of the special functions of particular utensils and instruments; not because they have not got functions, but because the names of these utensils and instruments themselves generally tell us their functions. The gunsmith does not advertise "Guns to shoot with."

When, in our philosophising, we do remember how notions of care, vigilance, interest and the like are built into the meanings of lots of our biographical and critical expressions, we may still be tempted to assimilate all of these notions to the two special notions that are cardinal for pedagogues and disciplinarians, of *studying* and *conforming*. We then find that our resultant account of the spectator's interest in an exciting game has a smell of unreality about it. For he is not taking pains to improve his wits, or dutifully abiding by any rules. He is attending, but not in either of these special modes of attention. Being excited or interested is not being sedulous; it is, more nearly, not-having-to-be-sedulous.

The general point that I am trying to make is that the notion of *attending* or *giving one's mind to* is a polymorphous notion. The special point that I am trying to make is that the notion of *enjoying* is one variety in this genus, or one member of this clan, i.e. that the reason why I cannot, in logic, enjoy what I am oblivious of is the same as the reason why I cannot, in logic, spray my currant-bushes without gardening.

Let us consider again the moderately specific notion of *interest*. To be, at a particular moment, interested in something is certainly to be giving one's mind to it, though one can give one's mind to a task, without being interested in it. The notions of *being fascinated, carried away, being wrapped up in, excited, absorbed, puzzled, intrigued*, and many congeners, clearly tie up closely, though in different ways, with the notion of interest. Now to say that someone has been enjoying a smell or a walk at least suggests and maybe even implies that he has been interested in the smell or in the exercise and the incidents of the walk—not that he gave his mind to them in e.g., the sedulous way, but rather that his mind was taken up by them in a spontaneous way. This is, of course, not enough. Alarming, disgusting and surprising things capture my attention without my having to fix my attention on them. So do pains and tickles.

I should like, at this stage, to be able to answer these questions: What is it, in general, to give one's mind to something? What, more specifically, is it to give one's mind to something in the mode of being interested in it? What, finally, is it to give one's mind to something in that special dimension of interest which constitutes enjoyment? I cannot do this, but will throw out a few unscholastic remarks.

It will not, I think, be suggested that interest is either a separable process or activity or a peculiar feeling. Even if there are acts of attention, there are not acts of interest, or pangs of it either. *En passant*, it is just worth mentioning that a person might be, for a spell, wholly taken up with something, like a smell or a taste, though he would not claim that the smell or taste had been interesting—or of course boring either. We tend to reserve the adjective "interesting" for what provokes hypotheses or even for what would provoke hypotheses in the best people. A connoisseur might find a wine interesting; the ordinary diner might describe it as piquant or attractive or just nice.

Think of the partly metaphorical force of the expressions "absorbed" and "occupied." When the blotting-paper absorbs the ink, we picture the ink as unresisting and the blotting-paper as having the power. It thirstily imbibes every drop of the docile ink and will not give it up again. Somewhat similarly, when a child is absorbed in his game, he—every drop of him—is sucked up into the business of manipulating his clockwork trains. All his thoughts, all his talk, all his controllable muscular actions are those of his engine-drivers, signalmen and station-masters. His game is, for the moment, his whole world. He does not coerce or marshal himself into playing, as, maybe, his conscripted father does. Else there would be some drop of him which was recalcitrant to the blotting-paper. Yet when we say that he is wholly absorbed in his game, we do not accept the entire parallel of the ink and the blotting-paper. For the blotting-paper had been one thing and the ink-blot another. But the game which absorbs the child is nothing but the child himself, playing trains. He, the player, has, for the moment, sucked up, without resistance, every drop of himself that might have been on other businesses, or on no business at all.

Or think of the notion of occupation. Victorious troops occupy a city; its police, administration, communications and commerce are managed according to the policy or the whims of the victors. The citizens' public and private doings are subject to the permission and perhaps to the direction of their new masters. Yet there are different kinds of occupation. The city may be managed tyrannically, stiffly, amicably, paternally or fraternally; and while the citizens may feel like slaves or helots or infants, they might feel like adolescents who are being shown how to be free; how to manage themselves. Somewhat so a person who is occupied in reading may feel oppressed; but he may feel merely shepherded, or advised, or partnered, or trusted, or left to his own devices. But here again the parallel is only fragmentary, since here both the citizens and the occupying troops are the reader himself. He is under the control and he is the controller. It is his policy or his whim that directs and permits those doings of his own which, if he were unoccupied would otherwise be without these directions and permissions—and therefore be quite different doings.

There is an important objection which could be made against both of these attempted illustrations. It could be said that I have in fact been sketching an elucidation of the notions of absorption and occupation which fails for the reasons for which a *circulus in definiendo* ruins an attempted definition. To say that the child who is totally absorbed in a game has all his thoughts, conversation and controllable muscular movements sucked up into the one activity of playing trains would be simply to say that being absorbed in A involves not being absorbed in B, C or D. To say that a person who is occupied in reading brings and keeps all his doings under a unified control is only a long-winded way of saying that while he is engaged in reading, he is not engaged in bicycling or conversing; and these are truisms. I hope that I mean something less nugatory than this. A man who is not employed by one employer may not be employed by any other. He may be employable, but unemployed. Or he may be unemployable. Somewhat similarly, a person who is not taking an interest in A, need not be taking an interest in anything else. He may be inert, i.e. asleep or half-asleep. But he may not be inert and yet not be taking an interest in anything at all. He may be the victim of *ennui*, in which case he actively yawns, fidgets, wriggles, scratches, paces up and down and whistles; yet he may do all of these things absent-mindedly or mechanically. He is restless but not employed; energetic but not occupied. He does plenty of things, but not on purpose, carefully with zeal or enjoyment. He is accomplishing nothing, for he is essaying nothing. He is merely responding to stimuli. The right thing to say would perhaps be that the child's game sucks up not all his thoughts, conversation and controllable muscular movements but rather all his energies. These energies, when so sucked up, become the thinking, conversing and manipulating that constitute his playing. But this notion of energies seems a rather suspicious character.

What is the point of pressing analogies or even plays upon words like these? One point is this. Where, as here, unpicturesque discourse still eludes us, the harm done by subjugation to one picture is partly repaired by deliberately ringing the changes on two or three. If they are appropriate at all, they are likely to be appropriate in different ways and therefore to keep us reminded of features which otherwise we might forget. The analogy of the blotting-paper may remind us of what the analogy of the torch-beam would, by itself, shut out of our heads, namely the facts—the conceptual facts—that there can be attending where there is no switching on of attention, and that there can be attending where there is no question of exploring or discerning. The analogy of the military occupation of a city may keep us in mind of the conceptual facts, which the other analogies do not bring out, that giving one's mind to something may, but need not involve mutinousness, reluctance or even dull acquiescence. One's mind may be given readily and it may be given with zest. Not all control is oppression. Sometimes it is release. Both the analogy of the blotting-paper and the analogy of the fraternal military occupation are meant to indicate, in a very unprofessional way, the conceptual region in which pleasure is located. But, at best, the real work remains to do.

Sigmund Freud

BEYOND THE PLEASURE PRINCIPLE

In the writings of Sigmund Freud, the eminent Viennese
founder of psychoanalysis, we find a strong emphasis on the
role of pleasure in human activities.

I

In the theory of psycho-analysis we have no hesitation in assuming that the
course taken by mental events is automatically regulated by the pleasure principle. We believe, that is to say, that the course of those events is invariably set
in motion by an unpleasurable tension, and that it takes a direction such that
its final outcome coincides with a lowering of that tension—that is, with an
avoidance of unpleasure or a production of pleasure. In taking that course into
account in our consideration of the mental processes which are the subject of
our study, we are introducing an "economic" point of view into our work; and if,
in describing those processes, we try to estimate this "economic" factor in
addition to the "topographical" and "dynamic" ones, we shall, I think, be giving
the most complete description of them of which we can at present conceive,
and one which deserves to be distinguished by the term "metapsychological."

It is of no concern to us in this connection to enquire how far, with this
hypothesis of the pleasure principle, we have approached or adopted any particular, historically established, philosophical system. We have arrived at these
speculative assumptions in an attempt to describe and to account for the facts
of daily observation in our field of study. Priority and originality are not among
the aims that psycho-analytic work sets itself; and the impressions that underlie the hypothesis of the pleasure principle are so obvious that they can
scarcely be overlooked. On the other hand we would readily express our gratitude to any philosophical or psychological theory which was able to inform us
of the meaning of the feelings of pleasure and unpleasure which act so
imperatively upon us. But on this point we are, alas, offered nothing to our
purpose. This is the most obscure and inaccessible region of the mind, and,
since we cannot avoid contact with it, the least rigid hypothesis, it seems to
me, will be the best. We have decided to relate pleasure and unpleasure to the

quantity of excitation that is present in the mind but is not in any way "bound"; and to relate them in such a manner that unpleasure corresponds to an *increase* in the quantity of excitation and pleasure to a *diminution*. What we are implying by this is not a simple relation between the strength of the feelings of pleasure and unpleasure and the corresponding modifications in the quantity of excitation; least of all—in view of all we have been taught by psycho-physiology— are we suggesting any directly proportional ratio: the factor that determines the feeling is probably the amount of increase or diminution in the quantity of excitation *in a given period of time*. Experiment might possibly play a part here; but it is not advisable for us analysts to go into the problem further so long as our way is not pointed by quite definite observations.

We cannot, however, remain indifferent to the discovery that an investigator of such penetration as G. T. Fechner held a view on the subject of pleasure and unpleasure which coincides in all essentials with the one that has been forced upon us by psycho-analytic work. Fechner's statement is to be found contained in a small work, *Einige Ideen zur Schöpfungs- und Entwicklungsgeschichte der Organismen*, 1873 (Part XI, Supplement, 94), and reads as follows: "In so far as conscious impulses always have some relation to pleasure or unpleasure, pleasure and unpleasure too can be regarded as having a psycho-physical relation to conditions of stability and instability. This provides a basis for a hypothesis into which I propose to enter in greater detail elsewhere. According to this hypothesis, every psycho-physical motion rising above the threshold of consciousness is attended by pleasure in proportion as, beyond a certain limit, it approximates to complete stability, and is attended by unpleasure in proportion as, beyond a certain limit, it deviates from complete stability; while between the two limits, which may be described as qualitative thresholds of pleasure and unpleasure, there is a certain margin of aesthetic indifference. . . ."

The facts which have caused us to believe in the dominance of the pleasure principle in mental life also find expression in the hypothesis that the mental apparatus endeavours to keep the quantity of excitation present in it as low as possible or at least to keep it constant. This latter hypothesis is only another way of stating the pleasure principle; for if the work of the mental apparatus is directed towards keeping the quantity of excitation low, then anything that is calculated to increase that quantity is bound to be felt as adverse to the functioning of the apparatus, that is as unpleasurable. The pleasure principle follows from the principle of constancy: actually the latter principle was inferred from the facts which forced us to adopt the pleasure principle. Moreover, a more detailed discussion will show that the tendency which we thus attribute to the mental apparatus is subsumed as a special case under Fechner's principle of the "tendency towards stability," to which he has brought the feelings of pleasure and unpleasure into relation.

It must be pointed out, however, that strictly speaking it is incorrect to talk of the dominance of the pleasure principle over the course of mental processes. If such a dominance existed, the immense majority of our mental processes would have to be accompanied by pleasure or to lead to pleasure, whereas universal experience completely contradicts any such conclusion. The most that can be said, therefore, is that there exists in the mind a strong *tendency* towards the pleasure principle, but that that tendency is opposed by certain other forces or circumstances, so that the final outcome cannot always be in harmony with the tendency towards pleasure. We may compare what Fechner (1873, 90) remarks on a similar point: "Since however a tendency towards an aim does not imply that the aim is attained, and since in general the aim is attainable only by approximations. . . ."

If we turn now to the question of what circumstances are able to prevent the pleasure principle from being carried into effect, we find ourselves once more on secure and well-trodden ground and, in framing our answer, we have at our disposal a rich fund of analytic experience.

The first example of the pleasure principle being inhibited in this way is a familiar one which occurs with regularity. We know that the pleasure principle is proper to a *primary* method of working on the part of the mental apparatus, but that, from the point of view of the self-preservation of the organism among the difficulties of the external world, it is from the very outset inefficient and even highly dangerous. Under the influence of the ego's instincts of self-preservation, the pleasure principle is replaced by the *reality principle*. This latter principle does not abandon the intention of ultimately obtaining pleasure, but it nevertheless demands and carries into effect the postponement of satisfaction, the abandonment of a number of possibilities of gaining satisfaction and the temporary toleration of unpleasure as a step on the long indirect road to pleasure. The pleasure principle long persists, however, as the method of working employed by the sexual instincts, which are so hard to "educate," and, starting from those instincts, or in the ego itself, it often succeeds in overcoming the reality principle, to the detriment of the organism as a whole.

There can be no doubt, however, that the replacement of the pleasure principle by the reality principle can only be made responsible for a small number, and by no means the most intense, of unpleasurable experiences. Another occasion of the release of unpleasure, which occurs with no less regularity, is to be found in the conflicts and dissensions that take place in the mental apparatus while the ego is passing through its development into more highly composite organizations. Almost all the energy with which the apparatus is filled arises from its innate instinctual impulses. But these are not all allowed to reach the same phases of development. In the course of things it happens again and again that individual instincts or parts of instincts turn out to be incompatible in their aims or demands with the remaining ones, which are able to combine into the inclusive unity of the ego. The former are then split off from this unity by the process of repression, held back at lower levels of psychical development and cut off, to begin with, from the possibility of satisfaction. If they succeed subsequently, as can so easily happen with repressed sexual instincts, in struggling through, by roundabout paths, to a direct or to a substitutive satisfaction, that event, which would in other cases have been an opportunity for pleasure, is felt by the ego as unpleasure. As a consequence of the old conflict which ended in repression, a new breach has occurred in the pleasure principle at the very time when certain instincts were endeavouring, in accordance with the principle, to obtain fresh pleasure. The details of the process by which repression turns a possibility of pleasure into a source of unpleasure are not yet clearly understood or cannot be clearly represented; but there is no doubt that all neurotic unpleasure is of that kind—pleasure that cannot be felt as such.[1]

The two sources of unpleasure which I have just indicated are very far from covering the majority of our unpleasurable experiences. But as regards the remainder it can be asserted with some show of justification that their presence does not contradict the dominance of the pleasure principle. Most of the unpleasure that we experience is *perceptual* unpleasure. It may be perception of pressure by unsatisfied instincts; or it may be external perception which is either distressing in itself or which excites unpleasurable expectations in the mental apparatus—that is, which is recognized by it as a "danger." The reaction to these instinctual demands and threats of danger, a reaction which constitutes the proper activity of the mental apparatus, can then be directed in a correct manner by the pleasure principle or the reality principle by which the former is modified. This does not seem to necessitate any far-reaching limitation of the pleasure principle. Nevertheless the investigation of the mental reaction to external danger is precisely in a position to produce new material and raise fresh questions bearing upon our present problem.

[1]No doubt the essential point is that pleasure and unpleasure, being conscious feelings, are attached to the ego.

4
POLITICAL PHILOSOPHY

In this chapter our readings deal with two fundamental issues in political philosophy: Do citizens have the right to revolt against their government? Are there justifiable limits to free speech and publication? As usual, the readings begin with modern views, pro and con, of these questions, and then turn to earlier sources to see how philosophers of the past have perceived these matters. Let us try to identify the central issues in both cases.

The first question asks whether citizens are ever justified in disobeying their government, even to the point of revolution. The second question turns the issue around to ask whether government is ever justified in imposing limits on the right of a citizen to speak his or her mind on matters of public policy. When the questions are posed in this way, it is clear that one who raises such issues is thinking of a political situation in which such notions as legitimacy, rights, and obligations apply. To make this assumption is already to limit the scope of the discussion considerably because it presupposes that the governments in question have claims to legitimacy. How is this legitimacy to be determined?

Many, but not all, of the great political theorists of the past have contended that a government is legitimate only if it is created through a set of objective procedures that represent the will or choice of those persons who are being governed. To some theorists this assumption has directly implied that the government in question is democratic. In their view, a government is legitimate if the sources of power always reside with the people. In an ideal democracy, the government and the people are identical. All decisions are arrived at only after everyone has been consulted and has cast a vote. In general, the particular decision arrived at would be the will of the majority, as exercised through the formal procedure of the ballot box. The converse implication for this system is that the minority must accept that the majority position is the law of the land; it could not legitimately revolt against the majority position just because it has lost an election. So, in principle, it would seem that revolt against a legitimately constituted democratic government would always be illicit.

This pure theory would have to be modified by practical considerations. Except for very small states, such as the early city-states of Greece (Athens, Corinth, and the like), it is impossible to have a meaningful discussion about matters of public policy if everyone has to be consulted and then to vote. Even with modern, technologically advanced communications systems it would be technically infeasible to wait until everyone had a chance to hear all sides of an argument and contribute to it before a law could be implemented. Recognizing such practical exigencies, pure democracy as described above has had to be modified. No major countries in the world have *pure* democratic government. Those increasingly rare democracies (such as England, France, Italy, Canada, the United States) all have representative governments. These are systems in which the people retain power in principle but allow others to exercise it for them to carry out day-to-day affairs of government. In the United States, for instance, this system is a republic. Power at the federal level is invested in Representatives and Senators, who are entrusted with the power of making laws for the whole society, and in a President, who enforces the laws. In such a system power is not abandoned to the members of Congress or to the President but is given in trust. If they abuse it, then there are formal procedures for removing them from power through resignation or defeat at the polls. Most of the principles we have just described are to be found in the political philosophy of John Locke (1632–1704), in particular in his *Second Treatise on Civil Government*, one of the founding documents of democratic theory. We have reprinted large sections of this classic work in the readings.

Democracy, whether pure or representative, is sometimes called a system of self-government. The people govern and are governed—in short, they govern themselves. The model for such a concept of governance may be found in the common-sense notion of self-mastery or self-discipline, under which people learn to resist certain temptations and thus to exercise control over themselves. People govern themselves by passing laws after proper reflection and debate, so that the laws are proper and reasonable, and then committing themselves to obeying those laws. A simple example will suffice to explain the point. We all feel that the automobile speed limit should vary depending on circumstances. In a crowded downtown section of a city, the limit should be low—say 20 or 25 mph; on roads in the countryside, this limit ought to be raised. The figures arrived at should be the products of careful study; once society agrees to them, then all should obey them.

Autocracy differs from democracy in that *the source of authority* in society legitimately rests with a person or group rather than the people in toto. Historically, autocracy is the most common type of government, and in the present world there are more species of autocratic than of democratic government.

Though some democratic theorists have contended that no form of autocratic government is legitimate, others have argued just the opposite. In the selections that follow, we reprint parts of Plato's *Republic* and Hobbes' *Leviathan*. For different reasons, both defend autocratic forms of government.

In Plato's justification we find the strongest challenge to the idea that the people ought to have absolute authority. He assumes that not all persons alive at a given moment have equal talents. Some are stronger than others, some more intelligent, some better at playing musical instruments, and some better at ruling. According to Plato, those having the most talent for ruling should be selected out of the general population for this task. He proposes that a talent hunt be engaged in to find these people. In the *Republic* he lays down a complicated educational and testing procedure by which to make the prospective rulers the most intelligent and knowledgeable persons in society. Since these people make the best rulers, they should be given absolute authority to make binding decisions for society. If one allows everyone to cast an equal vote, and if most persons are incompetent to select the best public policies, the result will be incompetent government. A good society is one in which most persons are willing to acknowledge that a small minority are the rightful, most competent rulers and to accept their authority. Thus the majority of persons would have no say whatever in the operation of government.

Critics of Plato have argued that practical difficulties defeat the scheme. The main difficulty lies in choosing the rulers. Even the best educational systems may not produce those most able to rule. Plato's critics also charge that ruling is not a *direct* function of intelligence. Even intelligent and knowledgeable persons may turn out to be moral monsters, self-serving, hostile to the majority of people, and ultimately untrustworthy. These critics, usually of a democratic persuasion, say that it is unwise to give any person or group absolute power, only the people themselves. They quote Lord Acton's famous remark that "Power tends to corrupt; but absolute power corrupts absolutely."

We can now point out the different responses to our two fundamental questions from defenders of autocratic and democratic societies. Since there are different types of autocratic societies, the particular kind of response given might vary from type to type—but all of them will have something in common, and it is this feature we wish to bring out.

To the question "Do citizens have the right to revolt against their government?" autocratic theorists in general have said no. The Platonic argument would be simple. Revolt, by definition, would come from the nonruling class against the ruling class and thus would be mounted by those lacking the proper qualifications for ruling. The rebellion would replace competent by incompetent rule and would be totally unjustifiable. Hobbes, as the reader will discover, would modify this answer somewhat. Hobbes does not defend autocratic government on Platonic grounds—namely, that ideally those ruling should be the most competent to do so. Hobbes grew up in a time and place, seventeenth-century England, that were among the most turbulent in modern history. England was in almost continuous revolution rocked by internecine warfare and by rival groups seizing power. Hobbes argued in the face of these events that the most important feature that a society could provide for its people was stability and peace; accordingly, he held that ideally every person in society should give up the right to engage in war against others—should give up his individual power to a sovereign mutually acceptable to all. That sovereign should have absolute power, including the power to enforce peace, even if all civil rights were to be abrogated or annulled in the process. So for Hobbes, provided that the ruler maintained the peace, rebellion against him was always unjustified; it was only if he failed to do so that rebellion was legitimate. The Hobbesian account of society thus gives the ruler absolute power and the citizen only those rights granted to him by the ruler. This seems to be the exact opposite of the democratic view, where it is the people who possess ultimate power, which they transfer, for purposes of practical convenience, to their representatives. So Hobbes would say that citizens do not have the right to rebel against the Sovereign, provided that he maintains the peace.

There is surprisingly little unanimity in the answers given by democratic theorists to the question of whether rebellion is ever justified. Some defenders of pure democracy have argued that it is nonsensical to ask whether the people should rebel against themselves. If the people are both governors and governed, then who is left to rebel? To these people the only meaningful form of our question would be: Is a minority ever entitled to rise against the people? Their answer would be no.

But since pure democracy, as we have indicated previously, has hardly ever been realized in practice, the question in this form does not raise a realistic issue. It does, however, when a distinction is made between representatives who govern and the majority of the people, who are, in that sense, the governed. As Mill says in "On Liberty," "such phrases as 'self-government' and 'the power of the people over themselves' do not express the true state of the case." Modern democratic theorists like Noam Chomsky, Herbert Marcuse, and Barrington Moore as well as earlier proponents of this doctrine, among them Thomas Jefferson, have all expressed distrust of putting power into hands other than those of the people. They suspect that human nature is such that those in the possession of power will abuse it, and this includes members of the governing group, even if they are elected by the people. As Jefferson writes in a famous remark, "The tree of liberty should be refreshed by the blood of tyrants every twenty years." Some writers, notably Marcuse and Chomsky, have contended that morality and legitimacy of rule are to be sharply distinguished. A government may be democratic, they say, in the sense that all electoral processes have been observed, and yet be highly immoral. If all peaceful means to alter the political situation have been exhausted, and if such a government continues in power, then in special circumstances rebellion against such authority may be justified. But, of course, writers who hold this position agree that such circumstances are exceptional and the peaceful protest and legislative action are the preferred means of protest.

With respect to the question of free speech, the answers are much more predictable—though Marcuse is a surprising exception. Defenders of autocratic systems argue that there is no need for free speech. Not only are those being governed more or else incompetent to rule, so their opinions can be ignored, but, in fact, if allowed to voice views that run contrary to received public policy, they ultimately can damage the fabric of settled society, causing social unrest and even civil war. Accordingly, censorship and the suppression of free speech and the press have always been regarded as legitimate practices in nondemocratic (yet legitimate) forms of government.

The situation is, of course, entirely different in a democratic society. The basic reason there should be free speech, as Mill stresses in our selection, is that if the people wish to rule wisely, they should be exposed to all possible evidence and to discussion of all possible opinions concerning that evidence before making a decision about public policy. Since the people are the rulers, it would be wrong to withhold any possibly relevant material from them. So censorship in principle seems inconsistent with democratic theory: it would amount to the rulers putting restrictions on themselves, which is pointless.

In his essay "Repressive Tolerance" Herbert Marcuse challenges Mill's view. He argues that censorship of free speech is necessary if one is to preserve democracy. He contends that those who control the main media of communication in modern industrial societies can sway public opinion illegitimately. Instead of being neutral, fact-finding institutions, the media use their powerful positions for "propaganda" purposes. They are not interested in the pursuit of truth but in manipulating public opinion for their own purposes—to "moronize" the public, Marcuse says. Certain kinds of "propaganda" should be outlawed—racism, anti-Semitism, and certain kinds of fraudulent advertising on television. The difficulty with Marcuse's view is that people will differ, of course, as to what constitutes "unfair speech" or "propaganda," and if one constructs an institutional framework to decide such questions, one is developing a form of censorship that could be used for antisocial as well as beneficial purposes. However, Marcuse has raised some powerful points about unrestricted speech in a democratic society. His solutions to the difficulties are perhaps not acceptable, but then no one has come up with much better answers either.

Now we invite readers to examine these matters for themselves.

A. DO CITIZENS HAVE THE RIGHT TO REVOLT AGAINST THEIR GOVERNMENT?

Herbert Marcuse

THE PROBLEM OF VIOLENCE AND THE RADICAL OPPOSITION

In the following essay Herbert Marcuse (1898–1979) treats the question of the right to rebellion in a modern context.

Today radical opposition can be considered only in a global framework. Taken as an isolated phenomenon its nature is falsified from the start. I shall discuss this opposition with you in the global context with emphasis on the United States. You know that I hold today's student opposition to be a decisive factor of transformation: surely not, as I have been reproached, as an immediate revolutionary force, but as one of the strongest factors, one that can perhaps become a revolutionary force. Setting up connections between the student oppositions of various countries is therefore one of the most important strategic necessities of these years. There are scarcely any connections between the American and German student movements; the student opposition in the United States does not even possess an effective central organization. We must work for the establishment of such relations, and if in discussing the theme of this talk I mainly take the United States as an example, I do so in order to help prepare for the establishment of such relations. The student opposition in the United States is itself part of a larger opposition that is usually designated the ''New Left.''

I must begin by sketching briefly the principal difference between the New Left and the Old Left. The New Left is, with some exceptions, Neo-Marxist rather than Marxist in the orthodox sense; it is strongly influenced by what is called Maoism, and by the revolutionary movements in the Third World. Moreover, the New Left includes neo-anarchist tendencies, and it is characterized by a deep mistrust of the old leftist parties and their ideology. And the New Left is, again with exceptions, not bound to the old working class as the sole revolutionary agent. The New Left itself cannot be defined in terms of "class," consisting as it does of intellectuals, of groups from the civil rights movement, and of youth groups, especially the most radical elements of youth, including those who at first glance do not appear political at all, namely the hippies, to whom I shall return later. It is very interesting that this movement has as spokesmen not traditional politicians but rather such suspect figures as poets, writers, and intellectuals. If you reflect on this short sketch, you will admit that this circumstance is a real nightmare for "old Marxists." You have here an opposition that obviously has nothing to do with the "classical" revolutionary force: a nightmare, but one that corresponds to reality. I believe that this completely unorthodox constellation of the opposition is a true reflection of an authoritarian-democratic "achieving" society, of "one-dimensional society" as I have tried to describe it, whose chief characteristic is the integration of the dominated class on a very material and very real basis, namely on the basis of controlled and satisfied needs that in turn reproduce monopoly capitalism—a "controlled and repressed consciousness." The result of this constellation is the absence of the subjective necessity of a radical transformation whose objective necessity becomes ever more flagrant. And in these circumstances opposition is concentrated among the outsiders within the established order. First it is to "be found in the ghettos among the 'underprivileged,' whose vital needs even highly developed, advanced capitalism cannot and will not gratify. Second, the opposition is concentrated at the opposite pole of society, among those of the privileged whose consciousness and instincts break through or escape social control." I mean those social strata that, owing to their position and education, still have access to the facts and to the total structure of the facts—access that is truly hard to come by. These strata still have knowledge and consciousness of the continuously sharpening contradictions and of the price that the so-called affluent society extorts from its victims. In short, there is opposition at these two extreme poles of society, and I should like to describe them briefly:

The Underprivileged. In the United States the underprivileged are constituted in particular by national and racial minorities, which of course are mainly unorganized politically and often antagonistic among themselves (for example there are considerable conflicts in the large cities between blacks and Puerto Ricans). They are mostly groups that do not occupy a decisive place in the productive process and for this reason cannot be considered potentially revolutionary forces from the viewpoint of Marxian theory—at least not without allies. But in the global framework the underprivileged who must bear the entire weight of the system really are the mass basis of the national liberation struggle against neo-colonialism in the third world and against colonialism in the United States. Here, too, there is no effective association between national and racial minorities in the metropoles of capitalist society and the masses in the neo-colonial world who are already engaged in struggle against this society. These masses can perhaps now be considered the new proletariat and as such they are today a real danger for the world system of capitalism. To what extent the working class in Europe can still or again be counted among these groups of underprivileged is a problem that we must discuss separately; I cannot do so in the framework of what I have to say here today, but I should like to point out a fundamental distinction. What we can say of the American working class is that in their great majority the workers are integrated into the system and do not want a *radical* transformation, we probably cannot or not yet say of the European working class.

The Privileged. I should like to treat the second group that today opposes the system of advanced capitalism in two subdivisions. Let us first look at the so-called new working class, which is supposed to consist of technicians, engineers, specialists, scientists, etc., who are engaged in the productive process, albeit in a special position. Owing to their key position this group really seems to represent the nucleus of an objective revolutionary force, but at the same time it is a favorite child of the established system, which also shapes the consciousness of this group. Thus the expression "new working class" is at least premature.

Second, and practically the only subject of which I shall speak today, is the student opposition in its widest sense, including the so-called dropouts. As far as I can judge, the latter represent an important difference between the American and German student movements. In America many of the students who are in active opposition stop being students and, as a full-time occupation, organize the opposition. This contains a danger, but perhaps a positive advantage as well. I shall discuss the student opposition under three categories. We may ask first, what is this opposition directed against; second, what are its forms; and third, what are the prospects for the opposition?

First, what is the target of the opposition? This question must be taken extremely seriously, for we are dealing with opposition to a democratic, effectively functioning society that at least under normal circumstances does not operate with terror. Furthermore, and on this point we in the United States are quite clear, it is an opposition against the majority of the population, including the working class. It is an opposition against the system's ubiquitous pressure, which by means of its repressive and destructive productivity degrades everything, in an increasingly inhuman way, to the status of a commodity whose purchase and sale provide the sustenance and content of life; against the system's hypocritical morality and "values": and against the terror employed outside the metropolis. This opposition to the system as such was set off first by the civil rights movement and then by the war in Vietnam. As part of the civil rights movement students from the North went to the South in order to help blacks register for the vote. It was then that they saw for the first time how this free democratic system really looks, what the sheriffs really are up to, how murders and lynchings of blacks go unpunished though the criminals are well known. This acted as a traumatic experience and occasioned the political activation of students and the intelligentsia in general in the United States. Second, this opposition was augmented by the war in Vietnam. For these students the war revealed for the first time the essence of the established society: its innate need of expansion and aggression and the brutality of its fight against all liberation movements.

Unfortunately I have no time to discuss the question whether the war in Vietnam is an imperialist war. However, I should like to make a short observation here because the problem always comes up. If imperialism is understood in the old sense, that is that the United States is fighting for investments, then it is not an imperialist war even though this narrow aspect of imperialism is today already becoming an acute problem again. In the July 7, 1967, issue of *Newsweek*, for example, you can read that Vietnam represents twenty billion dollars worth of business, and this figure is growing every day. Despite this, however, we do not need to speculate on the applicability of a new definition of imperialism here, for leading spokesmen of the American government have pronounced upon it themselves. The aim in Vietnam is to prevent one of the world's strategically and economically most important areas from falling under Communist control. It is a question of a crucial struggle against all attempts at national liberation in all corners of the world, crucial in the sense that the success of the Vietnamese liberation struggle could give the signal for the activation of such liberation movements in other parts of the world much closer to the metropolis where gigantic investments have been made. If in this sense Vietnam is in no way just one more event of foreign policy but rather connected with the essence of the system, it is perhaps also a turning point in the development of the system, perhaps the beginning of the end. For what has been shown here is that the human will and the human body with the poorest weapons can keep in check the most efficient system of destruction of all times. This is a world-historical novelty.

I come now to the second question that I wanted to discuss, namely the forms of the opposition. We are speaking of the student opposition, and I should like to say from the start that we are not dealing with a politicization of the university, for the university is already political. You need think only of the extent to which the natural sciences, for example, and even such abstract disciplines as mathematics find immediate application today in production and in military strategy. You need think only of the extent to which the natural sciences and even sociology and psychology depend today on the financial support of the government and the large foundations, the extent to which the latter two fields have enrolled in the service of human control and market regulation. In this sense we can say that the university is already a political institution, and that at best the student opposition is an attempt at the anti-politicization, not the politicization of the university. Alongside positivist neutrality, which is pseudo-neutrality, it is necessary to provide a place in the curriculum and in the framework of intellectual discussion for its critique. That is why one of the main demands of the student opposition in the United States is a reform of the curriculum so that critical thought and knowledge are fully brought to bear on intellectual discussion—and not as agitation and propaganda. Where that is not possible, so-called "free universities" and "critical universities" are founded outside the university, as for example at Berkeley and at Stanford and now at some of the larger universities in the East. At these free universities courses and seminars are given about subjects that are not or only inadequately dealt with in the regular curriculum, such as Marxism, psychoanalysis, imperialism, foreign policy in the Cold War, and the ghettos.

Another form of student opposition is that of the famous teach-ins, sit-ins, be-ins, and love-ins. Here I should like to point only to the range of and tensions within the opposition: critical learning and teaching, concern with theory on the one hand, and, on the other, what can be referred to only as "existential community," or "doing one's own thing." I should like to say something about the meaning of this tension later, because in my opinion it expresses that fusion of political rebellion and sexual-moral rebellion which is an important factor in the opposition in America. It finds its most visible expression in the demonstration—unarmed demonstration—and there is no need to go hunting for occasions for such demonstrations. To seek confrontations only for their own sake is not only unnecessary, it is irresponsible. Confrontations are there. They do not have to be drummed up. Going out of the way to find them would falsify the opposition, for today it is in a defensive, not offensive, position. The occasions are there: for example, every escalation of the war in Vietnam; visits by representatives of war policies; picketing (as you know, a special form of American demonstration) factories in which napalm and other means of chemical warfare are produced. These demonstrations are organized and they are legal. Are such legal demonstrations confrontations with the institutionalized violence that is unleashed against the opposition? My answer is based on the American situation, but you will see that you can easily infer from it what applies to your own. These demonstrations are not confrontations when they remain within the framework of legality. But when they do so, they subject themselves to the institutionalized violence that autonomously determines the framework of legality and can restrict it to a suffocating minimum; for example, by applying laws such as those forbidding trespass on private or government property, interfering with traffic, disturbance of the peace, etc. Accordingly what was legal can become illegal from one minute to the next if a completely peaceful demonstration disturbs the peace or voluntarily or involuntarily trespasses on private property, and so on. In this situation confrontations with state power, with institutionalized violence, seem inevitable—unless opposition becomes a harmless ritual, a pacifier of conscience, and a star witness for the rights and freedoms available under the status quo. This was the experience of the civil rights movement: that the others practice the violence, that the others are the violence, and that against this violence legality is problematic from the very beginning. This will also be the experience of the student opposition as soon as the system feels threatened by it. And then the opposition is placed before the fatal decision:opposition as ritual event or opposition as resistance, i.e. civil disobedience.

I should like to say at least a few words about the right of resistance, because I am astonished again and again when I find out how little it has penetrated into people's consciousness that the recognition of the right of resistance, namely civil disobedience, belongs to the oldest and most sanctified elements of Western civilization. The idea that there is a right or law higher than positive law is as old as this civilization itself. Here is the conflict of rights before which every opposition that is more than private is placed. For the establishment has a legal monopoly of violence and the positive right, even the duty, to use this violence in its self-defense. In contrast, the recognition and exercise of a higher right and the duty of resistance, of civil disobedience, is a motive force in the historical development of freedom, a potentially liberating violence. Without this right of resistance, without activation of a higher law against existing law, we would still be today at the level of the most primitive barbarism. Thus I think that the concept of violence covers two different forms: the institutionalized violence of the established system and the violence of resistance, which is necessarily illegal in relation to positive law. It is meaningless to speak of the legality of resistance: no social system, even the freest, can constitutionally legalize violence directed against itself. Each of these forms has functions that conflict with those of the other. There is violence of suppression and violence of liberation; there is violence for the defense of life and violence of aggression. And both forms have been and will remain historical forces. So from the start the opposition is placed in the field of violence. Right stands against right, not only as abstract claim but as action. Again the *status quo* has the right to determine the limits of legality. This conflict of the two rights, of the right of resistance with institutionalized violence, brings with it the continual danger of clashing with the violence of the state unless the right of liberation is sacrificed to the right of the established order and unless, as in previous history, the number of victims of the powers that be continues to surpass those of the revolution. That means, however, that preaching nonviolence on principle reproduces the existing institutionalized violence. And in monopolistic industrial society this violence is concentrated to an unprecedented extent in the domination that penetrates the totality of society. In relation to this totality the right of liberation is in its immediate appearance a particular right. Thus the conflict of violence appears as a clash between general and particular or public and private violence, and in this clash the private violence will be defeated until it can confront the existing public power as a new general interest.

As long as the opposition does not have the social force of a new general interest, the problem of violence is primarily a problem of tactics. Can confrontation with the powers that be, in which the challenging force of the resistance loses, nevertheless in certain cases alter the constellation of power in favor of the opposition? In the discussion of this question one often-quoted argument is invalid, namely that through such confrontations the other side, the opponent, is strengthened. This happens anyway, regardless of such confrontations. It happens every time the opposition is activated, and the problem is to turn this strengthening of the opponent into a transitional stage. Then, however, the evaluation of the situation depends on the occasion of the confrontation and especially on the success of systematically executed programs of education and the organization of solidarity. Let me give an example from the United States. The opposition experiences the war against Vietnam as an attack on freedom, on life itself, that affects the entire society and that justifies the right of total defense. But the majority of the population still supports the government and the war, while the opposition is only diffusely and locally organized. The form of opposition that is still legal in this situation spontaneously develops into civil disobedience, into refusing military service and organizing this refusal. This is already illegal and makes the situation more acute. On the other hand the demonstrations are accompanied ever more systematically by educational work among the population. This is "community work." Students go into poor districts in order to activate the consciousness of the inhabitants, initially to eliminate the most obvious needs, such as the lack of the most primitive hygiene, etc. The students attempt to organize people for these immediate interests, but simultaneously to awaken the political consciousness of these districts. Such educational work, however, does not take place only in slums. There is also the famous "doorbell-ringing campaign," which involves discussing what is really going on with housewives and, when they are there, their husbands. This is particularly important before elections. I stress discussion with women because it has in fact turned out, as one might of course expect, that in general women are more accessible to humane arguments than men are. This is because women are not yet completely harnessed into the productive process. This educational work is very laborious and slow. Will it have success? The success is measurable—for example by the number of votes obtained by so-called "peace candidates" in local, state, and national elections.

Today a turn toward theory can be observed among the opposition, which is especially important in that the New Left, as I emphasized, began with a total suspicion of ideology. I believe that it is becoming more and more visible that every effort to change the system requires theoretical leadership. And in the United States and the student opposition today we find attempts not only to bridge the gap between the Old and the New Left but also to work out a critical theory of contemporary capitalism on a Neo-Marxist basis.

As the last aspect of the opposition I should like now to mention a new dimension of protest, which consists in the unity of moral-sexual and political rebellion. I should like to give you an illustration that I experienced as an eyewitness, which will show you the difference between what is happening in the United States and here. It was at one of the large anti-war demonstrations in Berkeley. The police, it is true, had permitted the demonstration, but forbidden access to the target of the demonstration, the military railroad station at

Oakland. This meant that, beyond a particular and clearly defined point, the demonstration would have become illegal by violating the police order. When thousands of students neared the point at which the forbidden road began they came upon a barricade consisting of about 10 rows of heavily armed policemen outfitted in black uniforms and steel helmets. The march approached this police barricade, and as usual there were several people at the head of the march who yelled that the demonstration should not stop but try instead to break through the police cordon, which naturally would have led to a bloody defeat without achieving any aim. The march itself had erected a counter-cordon, so that the demonstrators would first have had to break through their own cordon in order to cross that of the police. Naturally this did not happen. After two or three scary minutes the thousands of marchers sat down in the street, guitars and harmonicas appeared, people began "necking" and "petting," and so the demonstration ended. You may find this ridiculous, but I believe that a unity spontaneously and anarchically emerged here that perhaps in the end cannot fail to make an impression even on the enemy.

Let me speak for just a few minutes about the prospects of the opposition. I never said that the student opposition today is by itself a revolutionary force, nor have I ever seen in the hippies the "heir of the proletariat"! Only the national liberation fronts of the developing countries are today in a revolutionary struggle. But even they do not by themselves constitute an effective revolutionary threat to the system of advanced capitalism. All forces of opposition today are working at preparation and only at preparation—but toward necessary preparation for a possible crisis of the system. And precisely the national liberation fronts and the ghetto rebellion contribute to this crisis, not only as military but also as political and moral opponents—the living, human negation of the system. For the preparation and eventuality of such a crisis perhaps the working class, too, can be politically radicalized. But we must not conceal from ourselves that in this situation the question whether such radicalization will be to the left or the right is an open one. The acute danger of fascism or neo-fascism has not at all been overcome.

I have spoken of a possible crisis, of the eventuality of a crisis of the system. The forces that contribute to such a crisis would have to be discussed in great detail. I believe that we must see this crisis as the confluence of very disparate subjective and objective tendencies of an economic, political, and moral nature, in the East as well as the West. These forces are not yet organized on a basis of solidarity. They have no mass basis in the developed countries of advanced capitalism. Even the ghettos in the United States are in the initial stage of attempted politicization. And under these conditions it seems to me that the task of the opposition is first the liberation of consciousness outside of our own social group. For in fact the life of everyone is at stake, and today everyone is part of what Veblen called the "underlying population," namely the dominated. They must become conscious of the horrible policy of a system whose power and pressure grow with the threat of total annihilation. They must learn that the available productive forces are used for the reproduction of exploitation and oppression and that the so-called free world equips itself with military and police dictatorships in order to protect its surplus. This policy can in no way justify the totalitarianism of the other side, against which much can and must be said. But this totalitarianism is not expansive or aggressive and is still dictated by scarcity and poverty. This does not change the fact that it must be fought—but from the left.

Now the liberation of consciousness of which I spoke means more than discussion. It means, and in the current situation must mean, demonstrations, in the literal sense. The whole person must demonstrate his participation and his will to live, that is, his will to live in a pacified, human world. The established order is mobilized against this real possibility. And, if it harms us to have illusions, it is just as harmful, perhaps more harmful, to preach defeatism and quietism, which can only play into the hands of those that run the system. The fact is, that we find ourselves up against a system that from the beginning of the fascist period to the present has disavowed through its acts the idea of historical progress, a system whose internal contradictions repeatedly manifest themselves in inhuman and unnecessary wars and whose growing productivity is growing destruction and growing waste. Such a system is not immune. It is already defending itself against opposition, even that of intellectuals, in all corners of the world. And even if we see no transformation, we must fight on. We must resist if we still want to live as human beings, to work and be happy. In alliance with the system we can no longer do so.

Plato

CRITO

In the following selection from Plato's dialogue, the *Crito*, Socrates has been condemned to death by the Athenians. He argues with his disciple Crito that it is never right to disobey the legitimate laws of a society, including those that grant the state the right to put citizens to death for certain crimes. He refuses to accept provisions for escaping prison that Crito has tried to arrange.

CRITO: "If you leave the city, Socrates," the laws argue, "you shall return wrong for wrong and evil for evil, breaking your agreements and covenants with us, and injuring those whom you least ought to injure—yourself, your friends, your country, and us."

SOCRATES: That, my dear friend Crito, I do assure you, is what I seem to hear them saying . . . and the sound of their arguments rings so loudly in my head that I cannot hear the other side. However, if you think that you will do any good by it, say what you like.

CRITO: Socrates, I have nothing to say.

SOCRATES: Then, Crito, let us follow this course, since God points out the way. . . .

CRITO: . . . But look here, Socrates, it is still not too late to take my advice and escape. Your death means a double calamity for me. I shall not only lose a friend whom I can never possibly replace, but besides a great many people who don't know you and me very well will be sure to think that I let you down, because I could have saved you if I had been willing to spend the money. And what could be more contemptible than to get a name for thinking more of money than of your friends? Most people will never believe that it was you who refused to leave this place although we tried our hardest to persuade you.

SOCRATES: But my dear Crito, why should we pay so much attention to what "most people" think? The really reasonable people, who have more claim to be considered, will believe that the facts are exactly as they are.

CRITO: You can see for yourself, Socrates, that one has to think of popular opinion as well. Your present position is quite enough to show that the capacity of ordinary people for causing trouble is not confined to petty annoyances, but has hardly any limits if you once get a bad name with them.

SOCRATES: I only wish that ordinary people *had* an unlimited capacity for doing harm; then they might have an unlimited power for doing good, which would be a splendid thing, if it were so. Actually they have neither. They cannot make a man wise or stupid; they simply act at random.

CRITO: Have it that way if you like, but tell me this, Socrates. I hope that you aren't worrying about the possible effects on me and the rest of your friends, and thinking that if you escape we shall have trouble with informers for having helped you to get away, and have to forfeit all our property or pay an enormous fine, or even incur some further punishment? If any idea like that is troubling you, you can dismiss it altogether. We are quite entitled to run that risk in saving you, and even worse, if necessary. Take my advice, and be reasonable.

SOCRATES: All that you say is very much in my mind, Crito, and a great deal more besides.

CRITO: Very well, then, don't let it distress you. I know some people who are willing to rescue you from here and get you out of the country for quite a moderate sum. And then surely you realize how cheap these informers are to buy off; we shan't need much money to settle them, and I think you've got enough of my money for yourself already. And then even supposing that in your anxiety for my safety you feel that you oughtn't to spend my money, there are these foreign gentlemen staying in Athens who are quite willing to spend theirs. One of them, Simmias of Thebes, has actually brought the money with him for this very purpose, and Cebes and a number of others are quite ready to do the same. So, as I say, you mustn't let any fears on these grounds make you slacken your efforts to escape, and you mustn't feel any misgivings about what you said at your trial—that you wouldn't know what to do with yourself if you left this country. Wherever you go, there are plenty of places where you will find a welcome, and if you choose to go to Thessaly, I have friends there who will make much of you and give you complete protection, so that no one in Thessaly can interfere with you.

Besides, Socrates, I don't even feel that it is right for you to try to do what you are doing, throwing away your life when you might save it. You are doing your best to treat yourself in exactly the same way as your enemies would, or rather did, when they wanted to ruin you. What is more, it seems to me that you are letting your sons down too. You have it in your power to finish their bringing-up and education, and instead of that you are proposing to go off and desert them, and so far as you are concerned they will have to take their chance. And what sort of chance are they likely to get? The sort of thing that usually happens to orphans when they lose their parents. Either one ought not to have children at all, or one ought to see their upbringing and education through to the end. It strikes me that you are taking the line of least resistance, whereas you ought to make the choice of a good man and a brave one, considering that you profess to have made goodness your object all through life. Really, I am ashamed, both on your account and on ours, your friends'. It will look as though we had played something like a coward's part all through this affair of yours. First there was the way you came into court when it was quite unnecessary—that was the first act. Then there was the conduct of the defense—that was the second. And finally, to complete the farce, we get this situation, which makes it appear that we have let you slip out of our hands through some lack of courage and enterprise on our part, because we didn't save you, and you didn't save yourself, when it would have been quite possible and practicable, if we had been any use at all.

There, Socrates, if you aren't careful, besides the suffering there will be all this disgrace for you and us to bear. Come, make up your mind. Really it's too late for that now; you ought to have it made up already. There is no alternative; the whole thing must be carried through during this coming night. If we lose any more time, it can't be done; it will be too late. I appeal to you, Socrates, on every ground; take my advice and please don't be unreasonable!

SOCRATES: My dear Crito, I appreciate your warm feelings very much—that is, assuming that they have some justification. If not, the stronger they are, the harder they will be to deal with. Very well, then, we must consider whether we ought to follow your advice or not. You know that this is not a new idea of mine; it has always been my nature never to accept advice from any of my friends unless reflection shows that it is the best course that reason offers. I cannot abandon the principles which I used to hold in the past simply because this accident has happened to me; they seem to me to be much as they were, and I respect and regard the same principles now as before. So unless we can find better principles on this occasion, you can be quite sure that I shall not agree with you— not even if the power of the people conjures up fresh hordes of bogies to terrify our childish minds, by subjecting us to chains and executions and confiscations of our property.

Well, then, how can we consider the question most reasonably? Suppose that we begin by reverting to this view which you hold about people's opinions. Was it always right to argue that some opinions should be taken seriously but not others? Or was it always wrong? Perhaps it was right before the question of my death arose, but now we can see clearly that it was a mistaken persistence in a point of view which was really irresponsible nonsense. I should like very much to inquire into this problem, Crito, with your help, and to see whether the argument will appear in any different light to me now that I am in this position, or whether it will remain the same, and whether we shall dismiss it or accept it.

Serious thinkers, I believe, have always held some such view as the one which I mentioned just now, that some of the opinions which people entertain should be respected, and others should not. Now I ask you, Crito, don't you think that this is a sound principle? You are safe from the prospect of dying tomorrow, in all human probability, and you are not likely to have your judgment upset by this impending calamity. Consider, then, don't you think that this is a sound enough principle, that one should not regard all the opinions that people hold, but only some and not others? What do you say? Isn't that a fair statement?

CRITO: Yes, it is.

SOCRATES: In other words, one should regard the good ones and not the bad?

CRITO: Yes.

SOCRATES: The opinions of the wise being good, and the opinions of the foolish bad?

CRITO: Naturally.

SOCRATES: To pass on, then, what do you think of the sort of illustration that I used to employ? When a man is in training, and taking it seriously, does he pay attention to all praise and criticism and opinion indiscriminately, or only when it comes from the one qualified person, the actual doctor or trainer?

CRITO: Only when it comes from the one qualified person.

SOCRATES: Then he should be afraid of the criticism and welcome the praise of the one qualified person, but not those of the general public.

CRITO: Obviously.

SOCRATES: So he ought to regulate his actions and exercises and eating and drinking by the judgment of his instructor, who has expert knowledge, rather than by the opinions of the rest of the public.

CRITO: Yes, that is so.

SOCRATES: Very well. Now if he disobeys the one man and disregards his opinion and commendations, and pays attention to the advice of the many who have no expert knowledge, surely he will suffer some bad effect?

CRITO: Certainly.

SOCRATES: And what is this bad effect? Where is it produced? I mean, in what part of the disobedient person?

CRITO: His body, obviously; that is what suffers.

SOCRATES: Very good. Well now, tell me, Crito—we don't want to go through all the examples one by one—does this apply as a general rule, and above all to the sort of actions which we are trying to decide about, just and unjust, honorable and dishonorable, good and bad? Ought we to be guided and intimidated by the opinion of the many or by that of the one—assuming that there is someone with expert knowledge? Is it true that we ought to respect and fear this person more than all the rest put together, and that if we do not follow his guidance we shall spoil and mutilate that part of us which, as we used to say, is improved by right conduct and destroyed by wrong? Or is this all nonsense?

CRITO: No, I think it is true, Socrates.

SOCRATES: Then consider the next step. There is a part of us which is improved by healthy actions and ruined by unhealthy ones. If we spoil it by taking the advice of nonexperts, will life be worth living when this part is once ruined? The part I mean is the body. Do you accept this?

CRITO: Yes.

SOCRATES: Well, is life worth living with a body which is worn out and ruined in health?

CRITO: Certainly not.

SOCRATES: What about the part of us which is mutilated by wrong actions and benefited by right ones? Is life worth living with this part ruined? Or do we believe that this part of us, whatever it may be, in which right and wrong operate, is of less importance than the body?

CRITO: Certainly not.

SOCRATES: It is really more precious?

CRITO: Much more.

SOCRATES: In that case, my dear fellow, what we ought to consider is not so much what people in general will say about us but how we stand with the expert in right and wrong, the one authority, who represents the actual truth. So in the first place your proposition is not correct when you say that we should consider popular opinion in questions of what is right and honorable and good, or the opposite. Of course one might object, All the same, the people have the power to put us to death.

CRITO: No doubt about that! Quite true, Socrates. It is a possible objection.

SOCRATES: But so far as I can see, my dear fellow, the argument which we have just been through is quite unaffected by it. At the same time I should like you to consider whether we are still satisfied on this point, that the really important thing is not to live, but to live well.

CRITO: Why, yes.

SOCRATES: And that to live well means the same thing as to live honorably or rightly?

CRITO: Yes.

SOCRATES: Then in the light of this agreement we must consider whether or not it is right for me to try to get away without an official discharge. If it turns out to be right, we must make the attempt; if not, we must let it drop. As for the considerations you raise about expense and reputation and bringing up children, I am afraid, Crito, that they represent the reflections of the ordinary public, who put people to death, and would bring them back to life if they could, with equal indifference to reason. Our real duty, I fancy, since the argument leads that way, is to consider one question only, the one which we raised just now. Shall we be acting rightly in paying money and showing gratitude to these people who are going to rescue me, and in escaping or arranging the escape ourselves, or shall we really be acting wrongly in doing all this? If it becomes clear that such conduct is wrong, I cannot help thinking that the question whether we are sure to die, or to suffer any other ill effect for that matter, if we stand our ground and take no action, ought not to weigh with us at all in comparison with the risk of doing what is wrong.

CRITO: I agree with what you say, Socrates, but I wish you would consider what we ought to *do*.

SOCRATES: Let us look at it together, my dear fellow; and if you can challenge any of my arguments, do so and I will listen to you; but if you can't, be a good fellow and stop telling me over and over again that I ought to leave this place without official permission. I am very anxious to obtain your approval before I adopt the course which I have in mind. I don't want to act against your convictions. Now give your attention to the starting point of this inquiry—I hope that you will be satisfied with my way of stating it—and try to answer my questions to the best of your judgment.

CRITO: Well, I will try.

SOCRATES: Do we say that one must never willingly do wrong, or does it depend upon circumstances? Is it true, as we have often agreed before, that there is no sense in which wrongdoing is good or honorable? Or have we jettisoned all our former convictions in these last few days? Can you and I at our age, Crito, have spent all these years in serious discussions without realizing that we were no better than a pair of children? Surely the truth is just what we have always said. Whatever the popular view is, and whether the alternative is pleasanter than the present one or even harder to bear, the fact remains that to do wrong is in every sense bad and dishonorable for the person who does it. Is that our view, or not?

CRITO: Yes, it is.

SOCRATES: Then in no circumstances must one do wrong.

CRITO: No.

SOCRATES: In that case one must not even do wrong when one is wronged, which most people regard as the natural course.

CRITO: Apparently not.

SOCRATES: Tell me another thing, Crito. Ought one to do injuries or not?

CRITO: Surely not, Socrates.

SOCRATES: And tell me, is it right to do an injury in retaliation, as most people believe, or not?

CRITO: No, never.

SOCRATES: Because, I suppose, there is no difference between injuring people and wronging them.

CRITO: Exactly.

SOCRATES: So one ought not to return a wrong or an injury to any person, whatever the provocation is. Now be careful, Crito, that in making these single admissions you do not end by admitting something contrary to your real beliefs. I know that there are and always will be few people who think like this, and consequently between those who do think so and those who do not there can be no agreement on principle; they must always feel contempt when they observe one another's decisions. I want even you to consider very carefully whether you share my views and agree with me, and whether we can proceed with our discussion from the established hypothesis that it is never right to do a wrong or return a wrong or defend oneself against injury by retaliation, or whether you dissociate yourself from any share in this view as a basis for discussion. I have held it for a long time, and still hold it, but if you have formed any other opinion, say so and tell me what it is. If, on the other hand, you stand by what we have said, listen to my next point.

CRITO: Yes, I stand by it and agree with you. Go on.

SOCRATES: Well, here is my next point, or rather question. Ought one to fulfill all one's agreements, provided that they are right, or break them?

CRITO: One ought to fulfill them.

SOCRATES: Then consider the logical consequence. If we leave this place without first persuading the state to let us go, are we or are we not doing an injury, and doing it in a quarter where it is least justifiable? Are we or are we not abiding by our just agreements?

CRITO: I can't answer your question, Socrates. I am not clear in my mind.

SOCRATES: Look at it in this way. Suppose that while we were preparing to run away from here—or however one should describe it—the laws and constitution of Athens were to come and confront us and ask this question, Now, Socrates, what are you proposing to do? Can you deny that by this act which you are contemplating you intend, so far as you have the power, to destroy us, the laws, and the whole state as well? Do you imagine that a city can continue to exist and not be turned upside down, if the legal judgments which are pronounced in it have no force but are nullified and destroyed by private persons?

How shall we answer this question, Crito, and others of the same kind? There is much that could be said, especially by a professional advocate, to protest against the invalidation of this law which enacts that judgments once pronounced shall be binding. Shall we say, Yes, I do intend to destroy the laws, because the state wronged me by passing a faulty judgment at my trial? Is this to be our answer, or what?

CRITO: What you have just said, by all means, Socrates.

SOCRATES: Then what supposing the laws say, Was there provision for this in the agreement between you and us, Socrates? Or did you undertake to abide by whatever judgments the state pronounced?

If we expressed surprise at such language, they would probably say, Never mind our language, Socrates, but answer our questions; after all, you are accustomed to the method of question and answer. Come now, what charge do you bring against us and the state, that you are trying to destroy us? Did we not give you life in the first place? Was it not through us that your father married your mother and begot you? Tell us, have you any complaint against those of us laws that deal with marriage?

No, none, I should say.

Well, have you any against the laws which deal with children's upbringing and education, such as you had yourself? Are you not grateful to those of us laws which were instituted for this end, for requiring your father to give you a cultural and physical education?

Yes, I should say.

Very good. Then since you have been born and brought up and educated, can you deny, in the first place, that you were our child and servant, both you and your ancestors? And if this is so, do you imagine that what is right for us is equally right for you, and that whatever we try to do to you, you are justified in retaliating? You did not have equality of rights with your father, or your employer—supposing that you had had one—to enable you to retaliate. You were not allowed to answer back when you were scolded or to hit back when you were beaten, or to do a great many other things of the same kind. Do you expect to have such license against your country and its laws that if we try to put you to death in the belief that it is right to do so, you on your part will try your hardest to destroy your country and us its laws in return? And will you, the true devotee of goodness, claim that you are justified in doing so? Are you so wise as to have forgotten that compared with your mother and father and all the rest of your ancestors your country is something far more precious, more venerable, more sacred, and held in greater honor both among gods and among all reasonable men? Do you not realize that you are even more bound to respect and placate the anger of your country than your father's anger? That if you cannot persuade your country you must do whatever it orders, and patiently submit to any punishment that it imposes, whether it be flogging or imprisonment? And if it leads you out to war, to be wounded or killed, you must comply, and it is right that you should do so. You must not give way or retreat or abandon your position. Both in war and in the law courts and everywhere else you must do whatever your city and your country command, or else persuade them in accordance with universal justice, but violence is a sin even against your parents, and it is a far greater sin against your country.

What shall we say to this, Crito—that what the laws say is true, or not?

CRITO: Yes, I think so.

SOCRATES: Consider, then, Socrates, the laws would probably continue, whether it is also true for us to say that what you are now trying to do to us is not right. Although we have brought you into the world and reared you and educated you, and given you and all your fellow citizens a share in all the good things at our disposal, nevertheless by the very fact of granting our permission we openly proclaim this principle, that any Athenian, on attaining to manhood and seeing for himself the political organization of the state and us its laws, is permitted, if he is not satisfied with us, to take his property and go away wherever he likes. If any of you chooses to go to one of our colonies, supposing that he should not be satisfied with us and the state, or to emigrate to any other country, not one of us laws hinders or prevents him from going away wherever he likes, without any loss of property. On the other hand, if any one of you stands his ground when he can see how we administer justice and the rest of our public organization, we hold that by so doing he has in fact undertaken to do anything that we tell him. And we maintain that anyone who disobeys is guilty of doing wrong on three separate counts: first because we are his parents, and secondly because we are his guardians, and thirdly because, after promising obedience, he is neither obeying us nor persuading us to change our decision if we are at fault in any way, and although all our orders are in the form of proposals, not of savage commands, and we give him the choice of either persuading us or doing what we say, he is actually doing neither. These are the charges, Socrates, to which we say that you will be liable if you do what you are contemplating, and you will not be the least culpable of your fellow countrymen, but one of the most guilty.

If I asked why, they would no doubt pounce upon me with perfect justice and point out that there are very few people in Athens who have entered into this agreement with them as explicitly as I have. They would say, Socrates, we have substantial evidence that you are satisfied with us and with the state. You would not have been so exceptionally reluctant to cross the borders of your country if you had not been exceptionally attached to it. You have never left the city to attend a festival or for any other purpose, except on some military expedition. You have never traveled abroad as other people do, and you have never felt the impulse to acquaint yourself with another country or constitution. You have been content with us and with our city. You have definitely chosen us, and undertaken to observe us in all your activities as a citizen, and as the crowning proof that you are satisfied with our city, you have begotten children in it. Furthermore, even at the time of your trial you could have proposed the penalty of banishment, if you had chosen to do so—that is, you could have done then with the sanction of the state what you are now trying to do without.

But whereas at that time you made a noble show of indifference if you had to die, and in fact preferred death, as you said, to banishment, now you show no respect for your earlier professions, and no regard for us, the laws, whom you are trying to destroy. You are behaving like the lowest type of menial, trying to run away in spite of the contracts and undertakings by which you agreed to live as a member of our state. Now first answer this question. Are we or are we not speaking the truth when we say that you have undertaken, in deed if not in word, to live your life as a citizen in obedience to us?

What are we to say to that, Crito? Are we not bound to admit it?

CRITO: We cannot help it, Socrates.

SOCRATES: It is a fact, then, they would say, that you are breaking covenants and undertakings made with us, although you made them under no compulsion or misunderstanding, and were not compelled to decide in a limited time. You had seventy years in which you could have left the country, if you were not satisfied with us or felt that the agreements were unfair. You did not choose Sparta or Crete—

your favorite models of good government—or any other Greek or foreign state. You could not have absented yourself from the city less if you had been lame or blind or decrepit in some other way. It is quite obvious that you stand by yourself above all other Athenians in your affection for this city and for us its laws. Who would care for a city without laws? And now, after all this, are you not going to stand by your agreement? Yes, you are, Socrates, if you will take our advice, and then you will at least escape being laughed at for leaving the city.

We invite you to consider what good you will do to yourself or your friends if you commit this breach of faith and stain your conscience. It is fairly obvious that the risk of being banished and either losing their citizenship or having their property confiscated will extend to your friends as well. As for yourself, if you go to one of the neighboring states, such as Thebes or Megara, which are both well governed, you will enter them as an enemy to their constitution, and all good patriots will eye you with suspicion as a destroyer of law and order. Incidentally you will confirm the opinion of the jurors who tried you that they gave a correct verdict; a destroyer of laws might very well be supposed to have a destructive influence upon young and foolish human beings. Do you intend, then, to avoid well-governed states and the higher forms of human society? And if you do, will life be worth living? Or will you approach these people and have the impudence to converse with them? What arguments will you use, Socrates? The same which you used here, that goodness and integrity, institutions and laws, are the most precious possessions of mankind? Do you not think that Socrates and everything about him will appear in a disreputable light? You certainly ought to think so.

But perhaps you will retire from this part of the world and go to Crito's friends in Thessaly? That is the home of indiscipline and laxity, and no doubt they would enjoy hearing the amusing story of how you managed to run away from prison by arraying yourself in some costume or putting on a shepherd's smock or some other conventional runaway's disguise, and altering your personal appearance. And will no one comment on the fact that an old man of your age, probably with only a short time left to live, should dare to cling so greedily to life, at the price of violating the most stringent laws? Perhaps not, if you avoid irritating anyone. Otherwise, Socrates, you will hear a good many humiliating comments. So you will live as the toady and slave of all the populace, literally "roistering in Thessaly," as though you had left this country for Thessaly to attend a banquet there. And where will your discussions about goodness and uprightness be then, we should like to know? But of course you want to live for your children's sake, so that you may be able to bring them up and educate them. Indeed! By first taking them off to Thessaly and making foreigners of them, so that they may have that additional enjoyment? Or if that is not your intention, supposing that they are brought up here with you still alive, will they be better cared for and educated without you, because of course your friends will look after them? Will they look after your children if you go away to Thessaly, and not if you go away to the next world? Surely if those who profess to be your friends are worth anything, you must believe that they would care for them.

No, Socrates, be advised by us your guardians, and do not think more of your children or of your life or of anything else than you think of what is right, so that when you enter the next world you may have all this to plead in your defense before the authorities there. It seems clear that if you do this thing, neither you nor any of your friends will be the better for it or be more upright or have a cleaner conscience here in this world, nor will it be better for you when you reach the next. As it is, you will leave this place, when you do, as the victim of a wrong done not by us, the laws, but by your fellow men. But if you leave in that dishonorable way, returning wrong for wrong and evil for evil, breaking your agreements and covenants with us, and injuring those whom you least ought to injure—yourself, your friends, your country, and us—then you will have to face our anger in your lifetime, and in that place beyond when the laws of the other world know that you have tried, so far as you could, to destroy even us their brothers, they will not receive you with a kindly welcome. Do not take Crito's advice, but follow ours.

That, my dear friend Crito, I do assure you, is what I seem to hear them saying, just as a mystic seems to hear the strains of music, and the sound of their arguments rings so loudly in my head that I cannot hear the other side. I warn you that, as my opinion stands at present, it will be useless to urge a different view. However, if you think that you will do any good by it, say what you like.

CRITO: No, Socrates, I have nothing to say.

SOCRATES: Then give it up, Crito, and let us follow this course, since God points out the way.

Thomas Hobbes

LEVIATHAN

Thomas Hobbes (1588–1679) argues in the *Leviathan* that the sovereign's rights should be extensive, the citizen's minimal.

OF THE RIGHTS OF SOVERAIGNES BY INSTITUTION

A *Common-wealth* is said to be *Instituted*, when a *Multitude* of men do Agree, and *Covenant, every one, with every one*, that to whatsoever *Man*, or *Assembly of Men*, shall be given by the major part, the *Right* to *Present* the Person of them all, (that is to say, to be their *Representative*;) every one, as well he that *Voted for it*, as he that *Voted against it*, shall *Authorise* all the Actions and Judgements, of that Man, or Assembly of men, in the same manner, as if they were his own, to the end, to live peaceably amongst themselves, and be protected against other men.

From this Institution of a Common-wealth are derived all the *Rights*, and *Facultyes* of him, or them, on whom the Soveraigne Power is conferred by the consent of the People assembled.

First, because they Covenant, it is to be understood, they are not obliged by former Covenant to any thing repugnant hereunto. And Consequently they that have already Instituted a Common-wealth, being thereby bound by Covenant, to own the Actions, and Judgements of one, cannot lawfully make a new Covenant, amongst themselves, to be obedient to any other, in any thing whatsoever, without his permission. And therefore, they that are subjects to a Monarch, cannot without his leave cast off Monarchy, and return to the confusion of a disunited Multitude; nor transferre their Person from him that beareth it, to another Man, or other Assembly of men: for they are bound, every man to every man, to Own, and be reputed Author of all, that he that already is their Soveraigne, shall do, and judge fit to be done: so that any one man dissenting, all the rest should break their Covenant made to that man, which is injustice: and they have also every man given the Soveraignty to him that beareth their Person; and therefore if they depose him, they take from him that which is his own, and so again it is injustice. Besides, if he that attempteth to depose his

Soveraign, be killed, or punished by him for such attempt, he is author of his own punishment, as being by the Institution, Author of all his Soveraign shall do: And because it is injustice for a man to do any thing, for which he may be punished by his own authority, he is also upon that title, unjust. And whereas some men have pretended for their disobedience to their Soveraign, a new Covenant, made, not with men, but with God; this also is unjust: for there is no Covenant with God, but by mediation of some body that representeth Gods Person; which none doth but Gods Lieutenant, who hath the Soveraignty under God. But this pretence of Covenant with God, is so evident a lye, even in the pretenders own consciences, that it is not onely an act of an unjust, but also of a vile, and unmanly disposition.

Secondly, Because the Right of bearing the Person of them all, is given to him they make Soveraigne, by Covenant onely of one to another, and not of him to any of them; there can happen no breach of Covenant on the part of the Soveraigne; and consequently none of his Subjects, by any pretence of forfeiture, can be freed from his Subjection. That he which is made Soveraigne maketh no Covenant with his Subjects beforehand, is manifest; because either he must make it with the whole multitude, as one party to the Covenant; or he must make a severall Covenant with every man. With the whole, as one party, it is impossible; because as yet they are not one Person; and if he make so many severall Covenants as there be men, those Covenants after he hath the Soveraignty are voyd, because what act soever can be pretended by any one of them for breach thereof, is the act both of himselfe, and of all the rest, because done in the Person, and by the Right of every one of them in particular. Besides, if any one, or more of them, pretend a breach of the Covenant made by the Soveraigne at his Institution; and others, or one other of his Subjects, or himselfe alone, pretend there was no such breach, there is in this case, no Judge to decide the controversie: it returns therefore to the Sword again; and every man recovereth the right of Protecting himselfe by his own strength, contrary to the designe they had in the Institution. It is therefore in vain to grant Soveraignty by way of precedent Covenant. The opinion that any Monarch receiveth his Power by Covenant, that is to say on Condition, proceedeth from want of understanding this easie truth, that Covenants being but words, and breath, have no force to oblige, contain, constrain, or protect any man, but what it has from the publique Sword; that is, from the untyed hands of that Man, or Assembly of men that hath the Soveraignty, and whose actions are avouched by them all, and performed by the strength of them all, in him united. But when an Assembly of men is made Soveraigne; then no man imagineth any such Covenant to have past in the Institution; for no man is so dull as to say, for example, the People of *Rome*, made a Covenant with the Romans, to hold the Soveraignty on such or such conditions; which not performed, the Romans might lawfully depose the Roman People. That men see not the reason to be alike in a Monarchy, and in a Popular Government, proceedeth from the ambition of some, that are kinder to the government of an Assembly, whereof they may hope to participate, than of Monarchy, which they despair to enjoy.

Thirdly, because the major part hath by consenting voices declared a Soveraigne; he that dissented must now consent with the rest; that is, be contented to avow all the actions he shall do, or else justly be destroyed by the rest. For if he voluntarily entered into the Congregation of them that were assembled, he sufficiently declared thereby his will (and therefore tacitely covenanted) to stand to what the major part should ordayne: and therefore if he refuse to stand thereto, or make Protestation against any of their Decrees, he does contrary to his Covenant, and therfore unjustly. And whether he be of the Congregation, or not; and whether his consent be asked, or not, he must either submit to their decrees, or be left in the condition of warre he was in before; wherein he might without injustice be destroyed by any man whatsoever.

Fourthly, because every Subject is by this Institution Author of all the Actions, and Judgments of the Soveraigne Instituted; it followes, that whatsoever he doth, it can be no injury to any of his Subjects; nor ought he to be by any of them accused of Injustice. For he that doth any thing by authority from another, doth therein no injury to him by whose authority he acteth: But by this Institution of a Common-wealth, every particular man is Author of all the Soveraigne doth; and consequently he that complaineth of injury from his Soveraigne, complaineth of that whereof he himselfe is Author; and therefore ought not to accuse any man but himselfe; no nor himselfe of injury; because to do injury to ones selfe, is impossible. It is true that they that have Soveraigne power, may commit Iniquity; but not Injustice, or Injury in the proper signification.

Fifthly, and consequently to that which was sayd last, no man that hath Soveraigne power can justly be put to death, or otherwise in any manner by his Subjects punished. For seeing every Subject is Author of the actions of his Soveraigne; he punisheth another, for the actions committed by himselfe.

And because the End of this Institution, is the Peace and Defence of them all; and whosoever has right to the End, has right to the Means; it belongeth of Right, to whatsoever Man, or Assembly that hath the Soveraignty, to be Judge both of the meanes of Peace and Defence; and also of the hindrances, and disturbances of the same; and to do whatsoever he shall think necessary to be done, both before hand, for the preserving of Peace and Security, by prevention of Discord at home and Hostility from abroad; and, when Peace and Security are lost, for the recovery of the same. And therefore,

Sixthly, it is annexed to the Soveraignty, to be Judge of what Opinions and Doctrines are averse, and what conducing to Peace; and consequently, on what occasions, how farre, and what, men are to be trusted withall, in speaking to Multitudes of people; and who shall examine the Doctrines of all bookes before they be published. For the Actions of men proceed from their Opinions; and in the well governing of Opinions, consisteth the well governing of mens Actions, in order to their Peace, and Concord. And though in matter of Doctrine, nothing ought to be regarded but the Truth; yet this is not repugnant to regulating of the same by Peace. For Doctrine repugnant to Peace, can no more be True, than Peace and Concord can be against the Law of Nature. It is true, that in a Common-wealth, where by the negligence, or unskilfullnesse of Governours, and Teachers, false Doctrines are by time generally received; the contrary Truths may be generally offensive: Yet the most sudden, and rough busling in of a new Truth, that can be, does never breake the Peace, but only somtimes awake the Warre. For those men that are so remissely governed, that they dare take up Armes, to defend, or introduce an Opinion, are still in Warre; and their condition not Peace, but only a Cessation of Armes for feare of one another; and they live as it were, in the procincts of battaile continually. It belongeth therefore to him that hath the Soveraign Power, to be Judge, or constitute all Judges of Opinions and Doctrines, as a thing necessary to Peace, thereby to prevent Discord and Civill Warre.

Seventhly, is annexed to the Soveraigntie, the whole power of prescribing the Rules, whereby every man may know, what Goods he may enjoy and what Actions he may doe, without being molested by any of his fellow Subjects: And this is it men call *Propriety*. For before constitution of Soveraign Power (as hath already been shewn) all men had right to all things; which necessarily causeth Warre: and therefore this Proprietie, being necessary to Peace, and depending on Soveraign Power, is the Act of that Power, in order to the publique peace. These Rules of Propriety (or *Meum* and *Tuum*) and of *Good*, *Evill*, *Lawfull*, and *Unlawfull* in the actions of Subjects, are the Civill Lawes, that is to say, the Lawes of each Common-wealth in particular; though the name of Civill Law be now restrained to the antient Civill Lawes of the City of *Rome*; which being the head of a great part of the World, her Lawes at that time were in these parts the Civill Law.

Eighthly, is annexed to the Soveraigntie, the Right of Judicature; that is to say, of hearing and deciding all Controversies, which may arise concerning Law, either Civill, or Naturall, or concerning Fact. For without the decision of Controversies, there is no protection of one Subject, against the injuries of another; the Lawes concerning *Meum* and *Tuum* are in vaine; and to every man remaineth, from the naturall and necessary appetite of his own conservation, the right of protecting himselfe by his private strength, which is the condition of Warre; and contrary to the end for which every Common-wealth is instituted.

Ninthly, is annexed to the Soveraignty, the Right of making Warre, and Peace with other Nations, and Common-wealths; that is to say, of Judging when it is for the publique good, and how great forces are to be assembled, armed, and payd for that end; and to levy mony upon the Subjects, to defray the expenses thereof. For the Power by which the people are to be defended, consisteth in their Armies; and the strength of an Army, in the union of their strength under one Command; which Command the Soveraign Instituted, therefore hath; because the command of the *Militia*, without other Institution, maketh him that hath it Soveraign. And therefore whosoever is made Generall of an Army, he that hath the Soveraign Power is always Generallissimo.

Tenthly, is annexed to the Soveraignty, the choosing of all Councellours, Ministers, Magistrates, and Officers, both in Peace, and War. For seeing the

Soveraign is charged with the End, which is the common Peace and Defence; he is understood to have Power to use such Means, as he shall think most fit for his discharge.

Eleventhly, to the Soveraign is committed the Power of Rewarding with riches, or honour; and of Punishing with corporall, or pecuniary punishment, or with ignominy every Subject according to the Law he hath formerly made; or if there be no Law made, according as he shall judge most to conduce to the encouraging of men to serve the Common-wealth, or deterring of them from doing dis-service to the same.

Lastly, considering what values men are naturally apt to set upon themselves; what respect they look for from others; and how little they value other men; from whence continually arise amongst them, Emulation, Quarrells, Factions, and at last Warre, to the destroying of one another, and diminution of their strength against a Common Enemy; It is necessary that there be Lawes of Honour, and a publique rate of the worth of such men as have deserved, or are able to deserve well of the Common-wealth; and that there be force in the hands of some or other, to put those Lawes in execution. But it hath already been shewn, that not onely the whole *Militia*, or forces of the Common-wealth; but also the Judicature of all Controversies, is annexed to the Soveraignty. To the Soveraign therefore it belongeth also to give titles of Honour; and to appoint what Order of place, and dignity, each man shall hold; and what signes of respect, in publique or private meetings, they shall give to one another.

These are the Rights, which make the Essence of Soveraignty; and which are the markes, whereby a man may discern in what Man, or Assembly of men, the Soveraign Power is placed, and resideth. For these are incommunicable, and inseparable. The Power to coyn Mony; to dispose of the estate and persons of Infant heires; to have præemption in Markets; and all other Statute Præroga- tives, may be transferred by the Soveraign; and yet the Power to protect his Subjects be retained. But if he transferre the *Militia*, he retains the Judicature in vain, for want of execution of the Lawes: Or if he grant away the Power of raising Mony; the *Militia* is in vain: or if he give away the government of Doc- trines, men will be frighted into rebellion with the feare of Spirits. And so if we consider any one of the said Rights, we shall presently see, that the holding of all the rest, will produce no effect, in the conservation of Peace and Justice, the end for which all Common-wealths are Instituted. And this division is it, whereof it is said, *a Kingdome divided in it selfe cannot stand*: For unlesse this divi- sion precede, division into opposite Armies can never happen. If there had not first been an opinion received of the greatest part of *England*, that these Powers were divided between the King, and the Lords, and the House of Commons, the people had never been divided, and fallen into this Civill Warre; first between those that disagreed in Politiques; and after between the Dissenters about the liberty of Religion; which have so instructed men in this point of Soveraign Right, that there be few now (in *England*,) that do not see, that these Rights are inseparable, and will be so generally acknowledged, at the next return of Peace;

and so continue, till their miseries are forgotten; and no longer, except the vulgar be better taught than they have hetherto been.

And because they are essentiall and inseparable Rights, it follows necessarily, that in whatsoever, words any of them seem to be granted away, yet if the Soveraign Power it selfe be not in direct termes renounced, and the name of Soveraign no more given by the Grantees to him that Grants them, the Grant is voyd: for when he has granted all he can, if we grant back the Soveraignty, all is restored, as inseparably annexed thereunto.

This great Authority being Indivisible, and inseparably annexed to the Soveraignty, there is little ground for the opinion of them, that say of Soveraign Kings, though they be *singulis majores*, of greater Power than every one of their Subjects, yet they be *Universis minores*, of lesse power than them all together. For if by *all together*, they mean not the collective body as one person, then *all together*, and *every one*, signifie the same; and the speech is absurd. But if by *all together*, they understand them as one Person (which person the Soveraign bears,) then the power of all together, is the same with the Soveraigns power; and so again the speech is absurd: which absurdity they see well enough, when the Soveraignty is in an Assembly of the people; but in a Monarch they see it not; and yet the power of Soveraignty is the same in whomsoever it be placed. . . .

To come now to the particulars of the true Liberty of a Subject; that is to say, what are the things, which though commanded by the Soveraign, he may neverthelesse, without Injustice, refuse to do; we are to consider, what Rights we passe away, when we make a Common-wealth; or (which is all one,) what Liberty we deny our selves, by owning all the Actions (without exception) of the Man, or Assembly we make our Soveraign. For in the act of our *Submission*, consisteth both our *Obligation*, and our *Liberty*; which must therefore be inferred by arguments taken from thence; there being no Obligation on any man, which ariseth not from some Act of his own; for all men equally, are by Nature Free. And because such arguments, must either be drawn from the expresse words, I *Authorise all his Actions*, or from the Intention of him that submitteth himselfe to his Power, (which Intention is to be understood by the End for which he so submitteth;) The Obligation, and Liberty of the Subject, is to be derived, either from those Words, (or others equivalent;) or else from the End of the Institution of Soveraignty; namely, the Peace of the Subjects within themselves, and their Defence against a common Enemy.

First therefore, seeing Soveraignty by Institution, is by Covenant of every one to every one; and Soveraignty by Acquisition, by Covenants of the Vanquished to the Victor, or Child to the Parent: It is manifest, that every Subject has Liberty in all those things, the right whereof cannot by Covenant be transferred. . . . Covenants, not to defend a mans own body, are voyd. Therefore,

If the Soveraign command a man (though justly condemned,) to kill, wound, or mayme himselfe; or not to resist those that assault him; or to abstain from the use of food, ayre, medicine, or any other thing, without which he cannot live; yet hath that man the Liberty to disobey.

If a man be interrogated by the Soveraign, or his Authority, concerning a crime done by himselfe, he is not bound (without assurance of Pardon) to confesse it; because no man . . . can be obliged by Covenant to accuse him-selfe.

Again, the Consent of a Subject to Soveraign Power, is contained in these words, I *Authorise, or take upon me, all his actions*; in which there is no restriction at all, of his own former naturall Liberty: For by allowing him to *kill me*, I am not bound to kill my selfe when he commands me. 'Tis one thing to say, *Kill me, or my fellow, if you please*; another thing to say, I *will kill my selfe, or my fellow*. It followeth therefore, that

No man is bound by the words themselves, either to kill himselfe, or any other man; And consequently, that the Obligation a man may sometimes have, upon the Command of the Soveraign to execute any dangerous, or dishonour-able Office, dependeth not on the Words of our Submission; but on the Inten-tion; which is to be understood by the End thereof. When therefore our refusall to obey, frustrates the End for which the Soveraignty was ordained; then there is no Liberty to refuse: otherwise there is.

Upon this ground, a man that is commanded as a Souldier to fight against the enemy, though his Soveraign have Right enough to punish his refusall with death, may neverthelesse in many cases refuse, without Injustice; as when he substituteth a sufficient Souldier in his place: for in this case he deserteth not the service of the Common-wealth. And there is allowance to be made for natural timorousnesse, not onely to women, (of whom no such dangerous duty is expected,) but also to men of feminine courage. When Armies fight, there is on one side, or both, a running away; yet when they do it not out of trechery, but fear, they are not esteemed to do it unjustly, but dishonourably. For the same reason, to avoyd battell, is not Injustice, but Cowardise. But he that inrowleth himselfe a Souldier, or taketh imprest mony, taketh away the excuse of a timorous nature; and is obliged, not onely to go to the battell, but also not to run from it, without his Captaines leave. And when the Defence of the Common-wealth, requireth at once the help of all that are able to bear Arms, every one is obliged; because otherwise the Institution of the Common-wealth, which they have not the purpose, or courage to preserve, was in vain.

To resist the Sword of the Common-wealth, in defence of another man, guilty, or innocent, no man hath Liberty; because such Liberty, takes away from the Soveraign, the means of Protecting us; and is therefore destructive of the very essence of Government. But in case a great many men together, have already resisted the Soveraign Power unjustly, or committed some Capitall crime, for which every one of them expecteth death, whether have they not the Liberty then to joyn together, and assist, and defend one another? Certainly they have: For they but defend their lives, which the Guilty man may as well do, as the Innocent. There was indeed injustice in the first breach of their duty. Their bearing of Arms subsequent to it, though it be to maintain what they have done, is no new unjust act. And if it be onely to defend these persons, it is not unjust at all. But the offer of Pardon taketh from them, to whom it is offered the plea of self-defence, and maketh their perseverence in assisting, or defending the rest, unlawfull.

As for other Lyberties, they depend on the silence of the Law. In cases where the Sovereign has prescribed no rule, there the Subject hath the Liberty to do, or forbeare, according to his own discretion. And therefore such Liberty is in some places more, and in some lesse; and in some times more, in other times lesse, according as they that have the Soveraignty shall think most convenient. As for Example, there was a time, when in *England* a man might enter in to his own Land, (and dispossesse such as wrongfully possessed it) by force. But in after-times, that Liberty of Forcible entry, was taken away by a Statute made (by the King) in Parliament. And in some places of the world, men have the Liberty of many wives: in other places, such Liberty is not allowed.

If a Subject have a controversie with his Soveraigne, of Debt, or of right of possession of lands or goods, or concerning any service required at his hands, or concerning any penalty corporall, or pecuniary, grounded on a precedent Law; He hath the same Liberty to sue for his right, as if it were against a Subject; and before such Judges, as are appointed by the Sovereign. For seeing the Sovereign demandeth by force of a former Law, and not by vertue of his Power; he declareth thereby, that he requireth no more, than shall appear to be due by that Law. The sute therefore is not contrary to the will of the Sovereign; and consequently the Subject hath the Liberty to demand the hearing of his Cause; and sentence, according to that Law. But if he demand, or take any thing by pretence of his Power; there lyeth, in that case, no action of Law; for all that is done by him in Vertue of his Power, is done by the Authority of every subject, and consequently, he that brings an action against the Sovereign, brings it against himselfe.

If a Monarch, or Soveraign Assembly, grant Liberty to all, or any of his Subjects; which Grant standing, he is disabled to provide for their safety, the Grant is voyd; unlesse he directly renounce, or transferre the Soveraignty to another. For in that he might openly, (if it had been his will,) and in plain termes, have renounced, or transferred it, and did not; it is to be understood it was not his will; but that the Grant proceeded from ignorance of the repugnancy between such a Liberty and the Soveraign Power; and therefore the Soveraignty is still retayned; and consequently all those Powers, which are necessary to the exercising thereof; such as are the Power of Warre, and Peace, of Judicature, of appointing Officers, and Councellours, of levying Mony, and the rest named in the 18th Chapter.

The Obligation of Subjects to the Soveraign is understood to last as long, and no longer, than the power lasteth, by which he is able to protect them. For the right men have by Nature to protect themselves, when none else can protect them, can by no Covenant be relinquished. The Soveraignty is the Soule of the Common-wealth; which once departed from the Body, the members doe no more receive their motion from it. The end of Obedience is Protection; which, wheresoever a man seeth it, either in his own, or in anothers sword, Nature applyeth his obedience to it, and his endeavour to maintaine it. And though Soveraignty, in the intention of them that make it, be immortall; yet is it in its own nature, not only subject to violent death, by forreign war; but also through the ignorance, and passions of men, it hath in it, from the very institution, many seeds of a natural mortality, by Intestine Discord.

If a Subject be taken prisoner in war; or his person, or his means of life be within the Guards of the enemy, and hath his life and corporall Libertie given him, on condition to be Subject to the Victor, he hath Libertie to accept the condition; and having accepted it, is the subject of him that took him; because he had no other way to preserve himselfe. The case is the same, if he be deteined on the same termes, in a forreign country. But if a man be held in prison, or bonds, or is not trusted with the libertie of his bodie; he cannot be understood to be bound by Covenant to subjection; and therefore may, if he can, make his escape by any means whatsoever.

If a Monarch shall relinquish the Soveraignty, both for himself, and his heires; His Subjects returne to the absolute Libertie of Nature; because, though Nature may declare who are his Sons, and who are the nerest of his Kin; yet it dependeth on his own will, (as hath been said in the precedent chapter,) who shall be his Heyr. If therefore he will have no Heyre, there is no Soveraignty, nor Subjection. The case is the same, if he dye without known Kindred, and without declaration of his Heyre. For then there can no Heire be known, and consequently no Subjection be due.

If the Soveraign Banish his Subject; during the Banishment, he is not Subject. But he that is sent on a message, or hath leave to travell, is still Subject; but it is, by Contract between Soveraigns, not by vertue of the covenant of Subjection. For whosoever entreth into anothers dominion, is Subject to all the Lawes thereof; unlesse he have a privilege by the amity of the Soveraigns, or by speciall licence.

If a Monarch subdued by war, render himself Subject to the Victor; his Subjects are delivered from their former obligation, and become obliged to the Victor. But if he be held prisoner, or have not the liberty of his own Body; he is not understood to have given away the Right of Soveraigntie; and therefore his Subjects are obliged to yield obedience to the Magistrates formerly placed, governing not in their own name, but in his. For, his Right remaining, the question is only of the Administration; that is to say, of the Magistrates and Officers; which, if he have not means to name, he is supposed to approve those, which he himself had formerly appointed.

John Locke

SECOND TREATISE ON CIVIL GOVERNMENT

John Locke (1632–1704) was one of the founders of democratic theory. In these passages from his *Second Treatise on Civil Government*, he talks about the rights of citizens to overthrow despotic government.

OF THE DISSOLUTION OF GOVERNMENT

211. He that will with any clearness speak of the dissolution of government ought in the first place to distinguish between the dissolution of the society and the dissolution of the government. That which makes the community and brings men out of the loose state of nature into one politic society is the agreement which everybody has with the rest to incorporate and act as one body, and so be one distinct commonwealth. The usual and almost only way whereby this union is dissolved is the inroad of foreign force making a conquest upon them; for in that case, not being able to maintain and support themselves as one entire and independent body, the union belonging to that body which consisted therein must necessarily cease, and so every one return to the state he was in before, with a liberty to shift for himself and provide for his own safety, as he thinks fit, in some other society. Whenever the society is dissolved, it is certain the government of that society cannot remain. Thus conquerors' swords often cut up governments by the roots and mangle societies to pieces, separating the subdued or scattered multitude from the protection of and dependence on that society which ought to have preserved them from violence. The world is too well instructed in, and too forward to allow of, this way of dissolving of governments to need any more to be said of it; and there wants not much argument to prove that where the society is dissolved, the government cannot remain—that being as impossible as for the frame of a house to subsist when the materials of it are scattered and dissipated by a whirlwind, or jumbled into a confused heap by an earthquake.

212.   Besides this overturning from without, governments are dissolved from within.

First, when the legislative is altered. Civil society being a state of peace amongst those who are of it, from whom the state of war is excluded by the umpirage which they have provided in their legislative for the ending all differences that may arise amongst any of them, it is in their legislative that the members of a commonwealth are united and combined together into one coherent living body. This is the soul that gives form, life, and unity to the commonwealth; from hence the several members have their mutual influence, sympathy, and connection; and, therefore, when the legislative is broken or dissolved, dissolution and death follows; for the essence and union of the society consisting in having one will, the legislative, when once established by the majority, has the declaring and, as it were, keeping of that will. The constitution of the legislative is the first and fundamental act of society, whereby provision is made for the continuation of their union under the direction of persons and bonds of laws made by persons authorized thereunto by the consent and appointment of the people, without which no one man or number of men amongst them can have authority of making laws that shall be binding to the rest. When any one or more shall take upon them to make laws, whom the people have not appointed so to do, they make laws without authority, which the people are not therefore bound to obey; by which means they come again to be out of subjection and may constitute to themselves a new legislative as they think best, being in full liberty to resist the force of those who without authority would impose anything upon them. Everyone is at the disposure of his own will when those who had by the delegation of the society the declaring of the public will are excluded from it, and others usurp the place who have no such authority or delegation.

213.   This being usually brought about by such in the commonwealth who misuse the power they have, it is hard to consider it aright, and know at whose door to lay it, without knowing the form of government in which it happens. Let us suppose then the legislative placed in the concurrence of three distinct persons:

(1) A single hereditary person having the constant supreme executive power, and with it the power of convoking and dissolving the other two within certain periods of time.

(2) An assembly of hereditary nobility.

(3) An assembly of representatives chosen *pro tempore* by the people. Such a form of government supposed, it is evident,

214.   First, that when such a single person or prince sets up his own arbitrary will in place of the laws which are the will of the society declared by the legislative, then the legislative is changed; for that being in effect the legislative whose rules and laws are put in execution and required to be obeyed.

When other laws are set up, and other rules pretended and enforced than what the legislative constituted by the society have enacted, it is plain that the legislative is changed. Whoever introduces new laws, not being thereunto authorized by the fundamental appointment of the society, or subverts the old, disowns and overturns the power by which they were made, and so sets up a new legislative.

215.   Secondly, when the prince hinders the legislative from assembling in its due time, or from acting freely pursuant to those ends for which it was constituted, the legislative is altered; for it is not a certain number of men, no, nor their meeting, unless they have also freedom of debating and leisure of perfecting what is for the good of the society, wherein the legislative consists. When these are taken away or altered so as to deprive the society of the due exercise of their power, the legislative is truly altered; for it is not names that constitute governments but the use and exercise of those powers that were intended to accompany them, so that he who takes away the freedom or hinders the acting of the legislative in its due seasons in effect takes away the legislative and puts an end to the government.

216.   Thirdly, when, by the arbitrary power of the prince, the electors or ways of election are altered without the consent and contrary to the common interest of the people, there also the legislative is altered; for if others than those whom the society has authorized thereunto do choose, or in another way than what the society has prescribed, those chosen are not the legislative appointed by the people.

217.   Fourthly, the delivery also of the people into the subjection of a foreign power, either by the prince or by the legislative, is certainly a change of the legislative, and so a dissolution of the government; for the end why people entered into society being to be preserved one entire, free, independent society, to be governed by its own laws, this is lost whenever they are given up into the power of another.

218.   Why in such a constitution as this the dissolution of the government in these cases is to be imputed to the prince is evident. Because he, having the force, treasure, and offices of the state to employ, and often persuading himself, or being flattered by others, that as supreme magistrate he is incapable of control—he alone is in a condition to make great advances toward such changes, under pretense of lawful authority, and has it in his hands to terrify or suppress opposers as factious, seditious, and enemies to the government. Whereas no other part of the legislative or people is capable by themselves to attempt any alteration of the legislative, without open and visible rebellion apt enough to be taken notice of, which, when it prevails, produces effects very little different from foreign conquest. Besides, the prince in such a form of

government having the power of dissolving the other parts of the legislative, and thereby rendering them private persons, they can never in opposition to him or without his concurrence alter the legislative by a law, his consent being necessary to give any of their decrees that sanction. But yet, so far as the other parts of the legislative in any way contribute to any attempt upon the government, and do either promote or not, what lies in them, hinder such designs, they are guilty and partake in this, which is certainly the greatest crime men can be guilty of one toward another.

219. There is one way more whereby such a government may be dissolved, and that is when he who has the supreme executive power neglects and abandons that charge, so that the laws already made can no longer be put in execution. This is demonstratively to reduce all to anarchy, and so effectually to dissolve the government; for laws not being made for themselves, but to be by their execution the bonds of the society, to keep every part of the body politic in its due place and function, when that totally ceases, the government visibly ceases, and the people become a confused multitude, without order or connection. Where there is no longer the administration of justice for the securing of men's rights, nor any remaining power within the community to direct the force to provide for the necessities of the public, there certainly is no government left. Where the laws cannot be executed, it is all one as if there were no laws; and a government without laws is, I suppose, a mystery in politics, inconceivable to human capacity and inconsistent with human society.

220. In these and the like cases, when the government is dissolved, the people are at liberty to provide for themselves by erecting a new legislative, differing from the other by the change of persons or form, or both, as they shall find it most for their safety and good; for the society can never by the fault of another lose the native and original right it has to preserve itself, which can only be done by a settled legislative, and a fair and impartial execution of the laws made by it. But the state of mankind is not so miserable that they are not capable of using this remedy till it be too late to look for any. To tell people they may provide for themselves by erecting a new legislative, when by oppression, artifice, or being delivered over to a foreign power, their old one is gone, is only to tell them they may expect relief when it is too late and the evil is past cure. This is in effect no more than to bid them first be slaves, and then to take care of their liberty; and when their chains are on, tell them they may act like freemen. This, if barely so, is rather mockery than relief; and men can never be secure from tyranny if there be no means to escape it till they are perfectly under it; and therefore it is that they have not only a right to get out of it, but to prevent it.

221. There is, therefore, secondly, another way whereby governments are dissolved, and that is when the legislative or the prince, either of them, act contrary to their trust.

First, the legislative acts against the trust reposed in them when they endeavor to invade the property of the subject, and to make themselves or any part of the community masters or arbitrary disposers of the lives, liberties, or fortunes of the people.

222. The reason why men enter into society is the preservation of their property; and the end why they choose and authorize a legislative is that there may be laws made and rules set as guards and fences to the properties of all the members of the society to limit the power and moderate the dominion of every part and member of the society; for since it can never be supposed to be the will of the society that the legislative should have a power to destroy that which every one designs to secure by entering into society, and for which the people submitted themselves to legislators of their own making. Whenever the legislators endeavor to take away and destroy the property of the people, or to reduce them to slavery under arbitrary power, they put themselves into a state of war with the people who are thereupon absolved from any further obedience, and are left to the common refuge which God has provided for all men against force and violence. Whensoever, therefore, the legislative shall transgress this fundamental rule of society, and either by ambition, fear, folly, or corruption, endeavor to grasp themselves, or put into the hands of any other, an absolute power over the lives, liberties, and estates of the people, by this breach of trust they forfeit the power the people had put into their hands for quite contrary ends, and it devolves to the people, who have a right to resume their original liberty and, by the establishment of a new legislative, such as they shall think fit, provide for their own safety and security, which is the end for which they are in society. What I have said here concerning the legislative in general holds true also concerning the supreme executor, who having a double trust put in him—both to have a part in the legislative and the supreme execution of the law—acts against both when he goes about to set up his own arbitrary will as the law of the society. He acts also contrary to his trust when he either employs the force, treasure, and offices of the society to corrupt the representatives and gain them to his purposes, or openly pre-engages the electors and prescribes to their choice such whom he has by solicitations, threats, promises, or otherwise won to his designs, and employs them to bring in such who have promised beforehand what to vote and what to enact. Thus to regulate candidates and electors, and new-model the ways of election, what is it but to cut up the government by the roots, and poison the very fountain of public security? For the people, having reserved to themselves the choice of their representatives, as the fence to their properties, could do it for no other end but that they might always be freely chosen, and, so chosen, freely act and advise as the necessity of the commonwealth and the public good should upon examination and mature debate be judged to require. This those who give their votes before they hear the debate and have weighed the reasons on all sides are not capable of doing. To prepare such an assembly as this, and endeavor to

set up the declared abettors of his own will for the true representatives of the people and the lawmakers of the society, is certainly as great a breach of trust and as perfect a declaration of a design to subvert the government as is possible to be met with. To which if one shall add rewards and punishments visibly employed to the same end, and all the arts of perverted law made use of to take off and destroy all that stand in the way of such a design, and will not comply and consent to betray the liberties of their country, it will be past doubt what is doing. What power they ought to have in the society who thus employ it contrary to the trust that went along with it in its first institution is easy to determine; and one cannot but see that he who has once attempted any such thing as this cannot any longer be trusted.

223. To this perhaps it will be said that, the people being ignorant and always discontented, to lay the foundation of government in the unsteady opinion and uncertain humor of the people is to expose it to certain ruin; and no government will be able long to subsist if the people may set up a new legislative whenever they take offense at the old one. To this I answer: Quite the contrary. People are not so easily got out of their old forms as some are apt to suggest. They are hardly to be prevailed with to amend the acknowledged faults in the frame they have been accustomed to. And if there be any original defects, or adventitious ones introduced by time or corruption, it is not an easy thing to get them changed, even when all the world sees there is an opportunity for it. This slowness and aversion in the people to quit their old constitutions has in the many revolutions which have been seen in this kingdom, in this and former ages, still kept us to, or after some interval of fruitless attempts still brought us back again to, our old legislative of king, lords, and commons; and whatever provocations have made the crown be taken from some of our princes' heads, they never carried the people so far as to place it in another line.

224. But it will be said this hypothesis lays a ferment for frequent rebellion. To which I answer:

First, no more than any other hypothesis; for when the people are made miserable, and find themselves exposed to the ill-usage of arbitrary power, cry up their governors as much as you will for sons of Jupiter, let them be sacred or divine, descended or authorized from heaven, give them out for whom or what you please, the same will happen. The people generally ill-treated, and contrary to right, will be ready upon any occasion to ease themselves of a burden that sits heavy upon them. They will wish and seek for the opportunity, which in the change, weakness, and accidents of human affairs seldom delays long to offer itself. He must have lived but a little while in the world who has not seen examples of this in his time, and he must have read very little who cannot produce examples of it in all sorts of governments in the world.

225. Secondly, I answer, such revolutions happen not upon every little mismanagement in public affairs. Great mistakes in the ruling part, many wrong

and inconvenient laws, and all the slips of human frailty will be born by the people without mutiny or murmur. But if a long train of abuses, prevarications, and artifices, all tending the same way, make the design visible to the people, and they cannot but feel what they lie under and see whither they are going, it is not to be wondered that they should then rouse themselves and endeavor to put the rule into such hands which may secure to them the ends for which government was at first erected, and without which ancient names and specious forms are so far from being better that they are much worse than the state of nature or pure anarchy—the inconveniences being all as great and as near, but the remedy farther off and more difficult.

226.   Thirdly, I answer that this doctrine of a power in the people of providing for their safety anew by a new legislative, when their legislators have acted contrary to their trust by invading their property, is the best fence against rebellion, and the probablest means to hinder it; for rebellion being an opposition, not to persons, but authority which is founded only in the constitutions and laws of the government, those, whoever they be, who by force break through, and by force justify their violation of them, are truly and properly rebels; for when men, by entering into society and civil government, have excluded force and introduced laws for the preservation of property, peace, and unity amongst themselves, those who set up force again in opposition to the laws do *rebellare*—that is, bring back again the state of war—and are properly rebels; which they who are in power, by the pretense they have to authority, the temptation of force they have in their hands, and the flattery of those about them, being likeliest to do, the properest way to prevent the evil is to show them the danger and injustice of it who are under the greatest temptation to run into it.

227.   In both the forementioned cases, when either the legislative is changed or the legislators act contrary to the end for which they were constituted, those who are guilty are guilty of rebellion; for if any one by force takes away the established legislative of any society, and the laws of them made pursuant to their trust, he thereby takes away the umpirage which every one had consented to for a peaceable decision of all their controversies, and a bar to the state of war amongst them. They who remove or change the legislative take away this decisive power which nobody can have but by the appointment and consent of the people, and so destroying the authority which the people did, and nobody else can, set up, and introducing a power which the people has not authorized, they actually introduce a state of war which is that of force without authority; and thus by removing the legislative established by the society—in whose decisions the people acquiesced and united as to that of their own will—they unite the knot and expose the people anew to the state of war. And if those who by force take away the legislative are rebels, the legislators themselves, as has been shown, can be no less esteemed so, when they who were set up for

the protection and preservation of the people, their liberties and properties, shall by force invade and endeavor to take them away; and so they putting themselves into a state of war with those who made them the protectors and guardians of their peace, are properly, and with the greatest aggravation, *rebellantes*, rebels.

228.   But if they who say "it lays a foundation for rebellion" mean that it may occasion civil wars or intestine broils, to tell the people they are absolved from obedience when illegal attempts are made upon their liberties or properties, and may oppose the unlawful violence of those who were their magistrates when they invade their properties contrary to the trust put in them, and that therefore this doctrine is not allowed, being so destructive to the peace of the world; they may as well say, upon the same ground, that honest men may not oppose robbers or pirates because this may occasion disorder or bloodshed. If any mischief come in such cases, it is not to be charged upon him who defends his own right, but on him that invades his neighbor's. If the innocent honest man must quietly quit all he has, for peace's sake, to him who will lay violent hands upon it, I desire it may be considered what a kind of peace there will be in the world, which consists only in violence and rapine, and which is to be maintained only for the benefit of robbers and oppressors. Who would not think it an admirable peace betwixt the mighty and the mean when the lamb without resistance yielded his throat to be torn by the imperious wolf. Polyphemus' den gives us a perfect pattern of such a peace and such a government, wherein Ulysses and his companions had nothing to do but quietly to suffer themselves to be devoured. And no doubt Ulysses, who was a prudent man, preached up passive obedience, and exhorted them to a quiet submission by representing to them of what concernment peace was to mankind, and by showing the inconveniences which might happen if they should offer to resist Polyphemus, who had now the power over them.

229.   The end of government is the good of mankind. And which is best for mankind? That the people should be always exposed to the boundless will of tyranny, or that the rulers should be sometimes liable to be opposed when they grow exorbitant in the use of their power and employ it for the destruction and not the preservation of the properties of their people?

Thomas Jefferson

LETTER TO JAMES MADISON JANUARY 30, 1787

In three remarkable letters, Thomas Jefferson (1743–1826), third president of the United States, claims that revolution is a good thing—a medicine necessary for the sound health of government.

Those characters, wherein fear predominates over hope, may . . . conclude too hastily, that nature has formed man insusceptible of any other government than that of force, a conclusion not founded in truth nor experience. Societies exist under three forms, sufficiently distinguishable. 1. Without government, as among our Indians. 2. Under governments, wherein the will of everyone has a just influence; as is the case in England, in a slight degree, and in our States, in a great one. 3. Under governments of force; as is the case in all other monarchies, and in most of the other republics. To have an idea of the curse of existence under these last, they must be seen. It is a government of wolves over sheep. It is a problem, not clear in my mind, that the first condition is not the best. But I believe it to be inconsistent with any great degree of population. The second state has a great deal of good in it. The mass of mankind under that, enjoys a precious degree of liberty and happiness. It has its evils, too; the principal of which is the turbulence to which it is subject. But weigh this against the oppressions of monarchy, and it becomes nothing. *Malo periculosam libertatem quam quietam servitutem.* Even this evil is productive of good. It prevents the degeneracy of government, and nourishes a general attention to the public affairs. I hold it, that a little rebellion, now and then, is a good thing, and as necessary in the political world as storms in the physical. Unsuccessful rebellions, indeed, generally establish the encroachments on the rights of the people, which have produced them. An observation of this truth should render honest republican governors so mild in their punishment of rebellions, as not to discourage them too much. It is a medicine necessary for the sound health of government.

Thomas Jefferson

LETTER TO BENJAMIN HAWKINS AUGUST 4, 1787

I am astonished at some people's considering a kingly government as a refuge. Advise such to read the fable of the frogs who solicited Jupiter for a king. If that does not put them to rights, send them to Europe to see something of the trappings of monarchy, and I will undertake that every man shall go back thoroughly cured. If all the evils which can arise among us, from the republican form of our government, from this day to the day of judgment, could be put into a scale against what this country suffers from its monarchical form in a week, or England in a month, the latter would preponderate. Consider the contents of the Red Book in England, or the Almanac Royal in France, and say what a people gain by monarchy. No race of kings has ever presented above one man of common sense in twenty generations. The best they can do is to leave things to their ministers; and what are their ministers but a committee, badly chosen? If the king ever meddles, it is to do harm.

Thomas Jefferson

LETTER TO WILLIAM S. SMITH
NOVEMBER 13, 1787

The British ministry have so long hired their gazetteers to repeat, and model into every form, lies about our being in anarchy, that the world has at length believed them, the English nation has believed them, the ministers themselves have come to believe them, and what is more wonderful, we have believed them ourselves. Yet where does this anarchy exist? Where did it ever exist, except in the single instance of Massachusetts? And can history produce an instance of rebellion so honorably conducted? I say nothing of its motives. They were founded in ignorance, not wickedness. God forbid we should ever be twenty years without such a rebellion. The people cannot be all, and always, well informed. The part which is wrong will be discontented, in proportion to the importance of the facts they misconceive. If they remain quiet under such misconceptions, it is a lethargy, the forerunner of death to the public liberty. We have had thirteen States independent for eleven years. There has been one rebellion. That comes to one rebellion in a century and a half, for each State. What country before, ever existed a century and a half without a rebellion? And what country can preserve its liberties, if its rulers are not warned from time to time, that their people preserve the spirit of resistance? Let them take arms. The remedy is to set them right as to facts, pardon and pacify them. What signify a few lives lost in a century or two? The tree of liberty must be refreshed from time to time, with the blood of patriots and tyrants. It is its natural manure.

Karl Marx and Friedrich Engels
COMMUNIST MANIFESTO

The *Communist Manifesto*, written by Karl Marx (1818–1883) and
Friedrich Engels (1820–1895), is a stirring call for working people to rise and cast off their chains.

A spectre is haunting Europe—the spectre of Communism. All the powers of
old Europe have entered into a holy alliance to exorcise this spectre: Pope and
Tsar, Metternich and Guizot, French Radicals and German police-spies.

Where is the party in opposition that has not been decried as communistic
by its opponents in power? Where is the Opposition that has not hurled back
the branding reproach of Communism, against the more advanced opposition
parties, as well as against its reactionary adversaries?

Two things result from this fact:

I. Communism is already acknowledged by all European powers to be itself
a power.

II. It is high time that Communists should openly, in the face of the whole
world, publish their views, their aims, their tendencies, and meet this nursery
tale of the spectre of Communism with a manifesto of the party itself.

To this end, Communists of various nationalities have assembled in London,
and sketched the following manifesto, to be published in the English, French,
German, Italian, Flemish and Danish languages:

I: BOURGEOIS AND PROLETARIANS

The history of all hitherto existing society is the history of class struggles.

Freeman and slave, patrician and plebeian, lord and serf, guild-master and
journeyman, in a word, oppressor and oppressed, stood in constant opposition
to one another, carried on an uninterrupted, now hidden, now open fight, a
fight that each time ended, either in a revolutionary reconstitution of society at
large, or in the common ruin of the contending classes.

In the earlier epochs of history, we find almost everywhere a complicated arrangement of society into various orders, a manifold gradation of social rank. In ancient Rome we have patricians, knights, plebeians, slaves; in the Middle Ages, feudal lords, vassals, guild-masters, journeymen, apprentices, serfs; in almost all of these classes, again, subordinate gradations.

The modern bourgeois society that has sprouted from the ruins of feudal society has not done away with class antagonisms. It has but established new classes, new conditions of oppression, new forms of struggle in place of the old ones.

Our epoch, the epoch of the bourgeoisie, possesses, however, this distinctive feature: it has simplified the class antagonisms. Society as a whole is more and more splitting up into two great hostile camps, into two great classes directly facing each other—bourgeoisie and proletariat.

From the serfs of the Middle Ages sprang the chartered burghers of the earliest towns. From these burgesses the first elements of the bourgeoisie were developed.

The discovery of America, the rounding of the Cape, opened up fresh ground for the rising bourgeoisie. The East-Indian and Chinese markets, the colonisation of America, trade with the colonies, the increase in the means of exchange and in commodities generally, gave to commerce, to navigation, to industry, an impulse never before known, and thereby, to the revolutionary element in the tottering feudal society, a rapid development.

The feudal system of industry, in which industrial production was monopolised by closed guilds, now no longer sufficed for the growing wants of the new markets. The manufacturing system took its place. The guild-masters were pushed aside by the manufacturing middle class; division of labour between the different corporate guilds vanished in the face of division of labour in each single workshop.

Meantime the markets kept ever growing, the demand ever rising. Even manufacture no longer sufficed. Thereupon, steam and machinery revolutionised industrial production. The place of manufacture was taken by the giant, modern industry, the place of the industrial middle class, by industrial millionaires, the leaders of whole industrial armies, the modern bourgeois.

Modern industry has established the world market, for which the discovery of America paved the way. This market has given an immense development to commerce, to navigation, to communication by land. This development has, in its turn, reacted on the extension of industry; and in proportion as industry, commerce, navigation, railways extended, in the same proportion the bourgeoisie developed, increased its capital, and pushed into the background every class handed down from the Middle Ages.

We see, therefore, how the modern bourgeoisie is itself the product of a long course of development, of a series of revolutions in the modes of production and of exchange.

Each step in the development of the bourgeoisie was accompanied by a corresponding political advance of that class. An oppressed class under the sway of the feudal nobility, an armed and self-governing association in the mediæval commune; here independent urban republic (as in Italy and Germany), there taxable "third estate" of the monarchy (as in France); afterwards, in the period of manufacture proper, serving either the semi-feudal or the absolute monarchy as a counterpoise against the nobility, and, in fact, cornerstone of the great monarchies in general, the bourgeoisie has at last, since the establishment of Modern Industry and of the world market, conquered for itself, in the modern representative State, exclusive political sway. The executive of the modern State is but a committee for managing the common affairs of the whole bourgeoisie.

The bourgeoisie, historically, has played a most revolutionary part.

The bourgeoisie, wherever it has got the upper hand, has put an end to all feudal, patriarchal, idyllic relations. It has pitilessly torn asunder the motley feudal ties that bound man to his "natural superiors," and has left no other nexus between man and man than naked self-interest, than callous "cash payment." It has drowned the most heavenly ecstasies of religious fervour, of chivalrous enthusiasm, of philistine sentimentalism, in the icy water of egotistical calculation. It has resolved personal worth into exchange value, and in place of the numberless indefeasible chartered freedoms, has set up that single, unconscionable freedom—Free Trade. In one word, for exploitation, veiled by religious and political illusions, it has substituted naked, shameless, direct, brutal exploitation.

The bourgeoisie has stripped of its halo every occupation hitherto honoured and looked up to with reverent awe. It has converted the physician, the lawyer, the priest, the poet, the man of science, into its paid wage-labourers.

The bourgeoisie has torn away from the family its sentimental veil, and has reduced the family relation to a mere money relation.

The bourgeoisie has disclosed how it came to pass that the brutal display of vigour in the Middle Ages, which reactionaries so much admire, found its fitting complement in the most slothful indolence. It has been the first to show what man's activity can bring about. It has accomplished wonders far surpassing Egyptian pyramids, Roman aqueducts, and Gothic cathedrals; it has conducted expeditions that put in the shade all former Exoduses of nations and crusades.

The bourgeoisie cannot exist without constantly revolutionising the instruments of production, and thereby the relations of production, and with them the whole relations of society. Conservation of the old modes of production in unaltered form, was, on the contrary, the first condition of existence for all earlier industrial classes. Constant revolutionising of production, uninterrupted disturbance of all social conditions, everlasting uncertainty and agitation distinguish the bourgeois epoch from all earlier ones. All fixed, fast-frozen relations, with their train of ancient and venerable prejudices and opinions, are swept away, all new-formed ones become antiquated before they can ossify. All that is solid melts into air, all that is holy is profaned, and man is at last compelled to face with sober senses his real conditions of life and his relations with his kind.

The need of a constantly expanding market for its products chases the bourgeoisie over the whole surface of the globe. It must nestle everywhere, settle everywhere, establish connections everywhere.

The bourgeoisie has through its exploitation of the world market given a cosmopolitan character to production and consumption in every country. To the great chagrin of reactionaries, it has drawn from under the feet of industry the national ground on which it stood. All old-established national industries have been destroyed or are daily being destroyed. They are dislodged by new industries, whose introduction becomes a life and death question for all civilised nations, by industries that no longer work up indigenous raw material, but raw material drawn from the remotest zones; industries whose products are consumed, not only at home, but in every quarter of the globe. In place of the old wants, satisfied by the production of the country, we find new wants, requiring for their satisfaction the products of distant lands and climes. In place of the old local and national seclusion and self-sufficiency, we have intercourse in every direction, universal inter-dependence of nations. And as in material, so also in intellectual production. The intellectual creations of individual nations become common property. National one-sidedness and narrow-mindedness become more and more impossible, and from the numerous national and local literatures there arises a world literature.

The bourgeoisie, by the rapid improvement of all instruments of production, by the immensely facilitated means of communication, draws all, even the most barbarian, nations into civilisation. The cheap prices of its commodities are the heavy artillery with which it batters down all Chinese walls, with which it forces the barbarians' intensely obstinate hatred of foreigners to capitulate. It compels all nations, on pain of extinction, to adopt the bourgeois mode of production; it compels them to introduce what it calls civilisation into their midst, i.e., to become bourgeois themselves. In one word, it creates a world after its own image.

The bourgeoisie has subjected the country to the rule of the towns. It has created enormous cities, has greatly increased the urban population as compared with the rural, and has thus rescued a considerable part of the population from the idiocy of rural life. Just as it has made the country dependent on the towns, so it has made barbarian and semi-barbarian countries dependent on the civilised ones, nations of peasants on nations of bourgeois, the East on the West.

The bourgeoisie keeps more and more doing away with the scattered state of the population, of the means of production, and of property. It has agglomerated population, centralised means of production, and has concentrated property in a few hands. The necessary consequence of this was political centralisation. Independent, or but loosely connected provinces, with separate interests, laws, governments and systems of taxation, become lumped together into one nation, with one government, one code of laws, one national class interest, one frontier and one customs tariff.

The bourgeoisie, during its rule of scarce one hundred years, has created more massive and more colossal productive forces than have all preceding generations together. Subjection of nature's forces to man, machinery, application of chemistry to industry and agriculture, steam-navigation, railways, electric telegraphs, clearing of whole continents for cultivation, canalisation of rivers, whole populations conjured out of the ground—what earlier century had even a presentiment that such productive forces slumbered in the lap of social labour?

We see then; the means of production and of exchange, on whose foundation the bourgeoisie built itself up, were generated in feudal society. At a certain stage in the development of these means of production and of exchange, the conditions under which feudal society produced and exchanged, the feudal organisation of agriculture and manufacturing industry, in one word, the feudal relations of property became no longer compatible with the already developed productive forces; they became so many fetters. They had to be burst asunder; they were burst asunder.

Into their place stepped free competition, accompanied by a social and political constitution adapted to it, and by the economical and political sway of the bourgeois class.

A similar movement is going on before our own eyes. Modern bourgeois society with its relations of production, of exchange and of property, a society that has conjured up such gigantic means of production and of exchange, is like the sorcerer who is no longer able to control the powers of the nether world whom he has called up by his spells. For many a decade past the history of industry and commerce is but the history of the revolt of modern productive forces against modern conditions of production, against the property relations that are the conditions for the existence of the bourgeoisie and of its rule. It is enough to mention the commercial crises that by their periodical return put the existence of the entire bourgeois society on its trial, each time more threateningly. In these crises a great part not only of the existing products, but also of the previously created productive forces, are periodically destroyed. In these crises there breaks out an epidemic that, in all earlier epochs, would have seemed an absurdity—the epidemic of over-production. Society suddenly finds itself put back into a state of momentary barbarism; it appears as if a famine, a universal war of devastation had cut off the supply of every means of subsistence; industry and commerce seem to be destroyed. And why? Because there is too much civilisation, too much means of subsistence, too much industry, too much commerce. The productive forces at the disposal of society no longer tend to further the development of the conditions of bourgeois property; on the contrary, they have become too powerful for these conditions, by which they are fettered, and so soon as they overcome these fetters, they bring disorder into the whole of bourgeois society, endanger the existence of bourgeois property. The conditions of bourgeois society are too narrow to comprise the wealth created by them. And how does the bourgeoisie get over these crises? On the one hand by enforced destruction of a mass of productive forces; on the other, by the conquest of new markets, and by the more thorough exploitation of the old ones. That is to say, by paving the way for more extensive and more destructive crises, and by diminishing the means whereby crises are prevented.

The weapons with which the bourgeoisie felled feudalism to the ground are now turned against the bourgeoisie itself.

But not only has the bourgeoisie forged the weapons that bring death to itself; it has also called into existence the men who are to wield those weapons—the modern working class—the proletarians.

In proportion as the bourgeoisie, i.e., capital, is developed, in the same proportion is the proletariat, the modern working class, developed—a class of labourers, who live only so long as they find work, and who find work only so long as their labour increases capital. These labourers, who must sell themselves piece-meal, are a commodity, like every other article of commerce, and are consequently exposed to all the vicissitudes of competition, to all the fluctuations of the market.

Owing to the extensive use of machinery and to division of labour, the work of the proletarians has lost all individual character, and, consequently, all charm for the workman. He becomes an appendage of the machine, and it is only the most simple, most monotonous, and most easily acquired knack, that is required of him. Hence, the cost of production of a workman is restricted, almost entirely, to the means of subsistence that he requires for his maintenance, and for the propagation of his race. But the price of a commodity, and therefore, also of labour, is equal to its cost of production. In proportion, therefore, as the repulsiveness of the work increases, the wage decreases. Nay, more, in proportion as the use of machinery and division of labour increases, in the same proportion the burden of toil also increases, whether by prolongation of the working hours, by increase of the work exacted in a given time, or by increased speed of the machinery, etc.

Modern industry has converted the little workshop of the patriarchal master into the great factory of the industrial capitalist. Masses of labourers, crowded into the factory, are organised like soldiers. As privates of the industrial army they are placed under the command of a perfect hierarchy of officers and sergeants. Not only are they slaves of the bourgeois class, and of the bourgeois state; they are daily and hourly enslaved by the machine, by the overlooker, and, above all, by the individual bourgeois manufacturer himself. The more openly this despotism proclaims gain to be its end and aim, the more petty, the more hateful and the more embittering it is.

The less the skill and exertion of strength implied in manual labour, in other words, the more modern industry becomes developed, the more is the labour of men superseded by that of women. Differences of age and sex have no longer any distinctive social validity for the working class. All are instruments of labour, more or less expensive to use, according to their age and sex.

No sooner is the exploitation of the labourer by the manufacturer so far at an end that he receives his wages in cash than he is set upon by the other portions of the bourgeoisie, the landlord, the shopkeeper, the pawnbroker, etc.

The lower strata of the middle class—the small tradespeople, shopkeepers, and retired tradesmen generally, the handicraftsmen and peasants—all these sink gradually into the proletariat, partly because their diminutive capital does not suffice for the scale on which modern industry is carried on, and is swamped in the competition with the large capitalists, partly because their specialised skill is rendered worthless by new methods of production. Thus the proletariat is recruited from all classes of the population.

The proletariat goes through various stages of development. With its birth begins its struggle with the bourgeoisie. At first the contest is carried on by individual labourers, then by the work people of a factory, then by the operatives of one trade, in one locality, against the individual bourgeois who directly exploits them. They direct their attacks not against the bourgeois conditions of production, but against the instruments of production themselves: they destroy imported wares that compete with their labour, they smash to pieces machinery, they set factories ablaze, they seek to restore by force the vanished status of the workman of the Middle Ages.

At this stage the labourers still form an incoherent mass scattered over the whole country, and broken up by their mutual competition. If anywhere they unite to form more compact bodies, this is not yet the consequence of their own active union, but of the union of the bourgeoisie, which class, in order to attain its own political ends, is compelled to set the whole proletariat in motion, and is moreover yet, for a time, able to do so. At this stage, therefore, the proletarians do not fight their enemies, but the enemies of their enemies, the remnants of absolute monarchy, the landowners, the non-industrial bourgeois, the petty bourgeoisie. Thus the whole historical movement is concentrated in the hands of the bourgeoisie; every victory so obtained is a victory for the bourgeoisie.

But with the development of industry the proletariat not only increases in number; it becomes concentrated in greater masses, its strength grows, and it feels that strength more. The various interests and conditions of life within the ranks of the proletariat are more and more equalised, in proportion as machinery obliterates all distinctions of labour, and nearly everywhere reduces wages to the same low level. The growing competition among the bourgeois, and the resulting commercial crises, make the wages of the workers ever more fluctuating. The unceasing improvement of machinery, ever more rapidly developing, makes their livelihood more and more precarious; the collisions between individual workmen and individual bourgeois take more and more the character of collisions between two classes. Thereupon the workers begin to form combinations (trades' unions) against the bourgeois; they club together in order to keep up the rate of wages; they found permanent associations in order to make provision beforehand for these occasional revolts. Here and there the contest breaks out into riots.

Now and then the workers are victorious, but only for a time. The real fruit of their battles lies, not in the immediate result, but in the ever expanding union of the workers. This union is helped on by the improved means of communication that are created by modern industry, and that place the workers of different localities in contact with one another. It was just this contact that was needed to centralise the numerous local struggles, all of the same character, into one national struggle between classes. But every class struggle is a political struggle. And that union, to attain which the burghers of the Middle Ages, with their miserable highways, required centuries, the modern proletarians, thanks to railways, achieve in a few years.

This organisation of the proletarians into a class, and consequently into a political party, is continually being upset again by the competition between the workers themselves. But it ever rises up again, stronger, firmer, mightier. It compels legislative recognition of particular interests of the workers, by taking advantage of the divisions among the bourgeoisie itself. Thus the ten-hours' bill in England was carried.

Altogether, collisions between the classes of the old society further in many ways the course of development of the proletariat. The bourgeoisie finds itself involved in a constant battle. At first with the aristocracy; later on, with those portions of the bourgeoisie itself, whose interests have become antagonistic to the progress of industry; at all times with the bourgeoisie of foreign countries. In all these battles it sees itself compelled to appeal to the proletariat, to ask for its help, and thus to drag it into the political arena. The bourgeoisie itself, therefore, supplies the proletariat with its own elements of political and general education, in other words, it furnishes the proletariat with weapons for fighting the bourgeoisie.

Further, as we have already seen, entire sections of the ruling classes are, by the advance of industry, precipitated into the proletariat, or are at least threatened in their conditions of existence. These also supply the proletariat with fresh elements of enlightenment and progress.

Finally, in times when the class struggle nears the decisive hour, the process of dissolution going on within the ruling class, in fact within the whole range of old society, assumes such a violent, glaring character that a small section of the ruling class cuts itself adrift and joins the revolutionary class, the class that holds the future in its hands. Just as, therefore, at an earlier period, a section of the nobility went over to the bourgeoisie, so now a portion of the bourgeoisie goes over to the proletariat, and, in particular, a portion of the bourgeois ideologists, who have raised themselves to the level of comprehending theoretically the historical movement as a whole.

Of all the classes that stand face to face with the bourgeoisie to-day, the proletariat alone is a really revolutionary class. The other classes decay and finally disappear in the face of modern industry; the proletariat is its special and essential product.

The lower middle class, the small manufacturer, the shopkeeper, the artisan, the peasant, all these fight against the bourgeoisie, to save from extinction their existence as fractions of the middle class. They are therefore not revolutionary, but conservative. Nay, more, they are reactionary, for they try to roll back the wheel of history. If by chance they are revolutionary, they are so only in view of their impending transfer into the proletariat; they thus defend not their present, but their future interests; they desert their own standpoint to place themselves at that of the proletariat.

The "dangerous class," the social scum, that passively rotting mass thrown off by the lowest layers of old society, may, here and there, be swept into the movement by a proletarian revolution; its conditions of life, however, prepare it far more for the part of a bribed tool of reactionary intrigue.

In the conditions of the proletariat, those of old society at large are already virtually swamped. The proletarian is without property; his relation to his wife and children has no longer anything in common with the bourgeois family relations; modern industrial labour, modern subjection to capital, the same in England as in France, in America as in Germany, has stripped him of every trace of national character. Law, morality, religion, are to him so many bourgeois prejudices, behind which lurk in ambush just as many bourgeois interests.

All the preceding classes that got the upper hand, sought to fortify their already acquired status by subjecting society at large to their conditions of appropriation. The proletarians cannot become masters of the productive forces of society, except by abolishing their own previous mode of appropriation, and thereby also every other previous mode of appropriation. They have nothing of their own to secure and to fortify; their mission is to destroy all previous securities for, and insurances of, individual property.

All previous historical movements were movements of minorities, or in the interest of minorities. The proletarian movement is the self-conscious, independent movement of the immense majority, in the interest of the immense majority. The proletariat, the lowest stratum of our present society, cannot stir, cannot raise itself up, without the whole superincumbent strata of official society being sprung into the air.

Though not in substance, yet in form, the struggle of the proletariat with the bourgeoisie is at first a national struggle. The proletariat of each country must, of course, first of all settle matters with its own bourgeoisie.

In depicting the most general phases of the development of the proletariat, we traced the more or less veiled civil war, raging within existing society, up to the point where that war breaks out into open revolution, and where the violent overthrow of the bourgeoisie lays the foundation for the sway of the proletariat.

Hitherto, every form of society has been based, as we have already seen, on the antagonism of oppressing and oppressed classes. But in order to oppress a class, certain conditions must be assured to it under which it can, at least, continue its slavish existence. The serf, in the period of serfdom, raised himself to membership in the commune, just as the petty bourgeois, under the yoke of feudal absolutism, managed to develop into a bourgeois. The modern labourer, on the contrary, instead of rising with the progress of industry, sinks deeper and deeper below the conditions of existence of his own class. He becomes a pauper, and pauperism develops more rapidly than population and wealth. And here it becomes evident that the bourgeoisie is unfit any longer to be the ruling class in society and to impose its conditions of existence upon society as an over-riding law. It is unfit to rule because it is incompetent to assure an existence to its slave within his slavery, because it cannot help letting him sink into such a state, that it has to feed him, instead of being fed by him. Society can no longer live under this bourgeoisie; in other words, its existence is no longer compatible with society.

The essential condition for the existence and for the sway of the bourgeois class is the formation and augmentation of capital; the condition for capital is wage-labour. Wage-labour rests exclusively on competition between the labourers. The advance of industry, whose involuntary promoter is the bourgeoisie, replaces the isolation of the labourers, due to competition, by their revolutionary combination, due to association. The development of modern industry, therefore, cuts from under its feet the very foundation on which the bourgeoisie produces and appropriates products. What the bourgeoisie therefore produces, above all, are its own grave-diggers. Its fall and the victory of the proletariat are equally inevitable.

II: PROLETARIANS AND COMMUNISTS

In what relation do the Communists stand to the proletarians as a whole?

The Communists do not form a separate party opposed to other working class parties.

They have no interests separate and apart from those of the proletariat as a whole.

They do not set up any sectarian principles of their own, by which to shape and mould the proletarian movement.

The Communists are distinguished from the other working class parties by this only: 1. In the national struggles of the proletarians of the different countries, they point out and bring to the front the common interests of the entire proletariat, independently of all nationality. 2. In the various stages of development which the struggle of the working class against the bourgeoisie has to pass through, they always and everywhere represent the interests of the movement as a whole.

The Communists, therefore, are on the one hand, practically, the most advanced and resolute section of the working class parties of every country, that section which pushes forward all others; on the other hand, theoretically, they have over the great mass of the proletariat the advantage of clearly understanding the line of march, the conditions, and the ultimate general results of the proletarian movement.

The immediate aim of the Communists is the same as that of all the other proletarian parties: formation of the proletariat into a class, overthrow of the bourgeois supremacy, conquest of political power by the proletariat.

The theoretical conclusions of the Communists are in no way based on ideas or principles that have been invented, or discovered, by this or that would-be universal reformer.

They merely express, in general terms, actual relations springing from an existing class struggle, from a historical movement going on under our very eyes. The abolition of existing property relations is not at all a distinctive feature of Communism.

All property relations in the past have continually been subject to historical change consequent upon the change in historical conditions.

The French revolution, for example, abolished feudal property in favour of bourgeois property.

The distinguishing feature of Communism is not the abolition of property generally but the abolition of bourgeois property. But modern bourgeois private property is the final and most complete expression of the system of producing and appropriating products that is based on class antagonisms, on the exploitation of the many by the few.

In this sense, the theory of the Communists may be summed up in the single sentence: Abolition of private property.

B. ARE THERE JUSTIFIABLE LIMITS TO FREE SPEECH AND PUBLICATION?

Aryeh Neier

DEFENDING MY ENEMY

In *Defending My Enemy*, Aryeh Neier (b. 1937) describes taking one of the hardest cases for any civil libertarian—defending the right to free speech for a group of American Nazis—and argues that this is just the sort of case that makes the concept of free speech in a democracy meaningful.

PROLOGUE

"My only hope," said a letter I received from a man in Boston, "is that if we are both forced into a march some day to some crematorium, *you* will be at the head of the parade, at which time you will in your rapture have an opportunity to sing hosannas in praise of freedom of speech for your tormentors."

I have received many similar letters. They were provoked by the efforts of the American Civil Liberties Union, which I served as executive director, to secure free speech for a group of American Nazis who said they wanted to march in Skokie, Illinois. The most succinct letter was from the man who proposed a motto for the ACLU: "The First Amendment *über Alles.*"

While it was painful to receive those letters, one woman's message of support was more disturbing. "I love free speech," she wrote, "more than I detest the Nazis." Like the people who denounced me, she thought a choice had to be made between upholding free speech and fighting the Nazis. She just made a different choice.

I made no such choice. I supported free speech for Nazis when they wanted to march in Skokie in order to defeat Nazis. Defending my enemy is the only way to protect a free society against the enemies of freedom. If that seems to be a paradox, I hope it will not be when you finish reading this book.

My reasons for hating Nazis are personal as well as philosophical. I could have written back to the man who expressed his hope that I would head the parade to the crematorium, saying that I narrowly missed dying there.

I am a Jew, born in Berlin. My parents were *Ostjuden* (Jews from Eastern Europe) who left their families in Poland and went to Berlin in the years after World War I. The 1920s were good years for them. They built comfortable lives. But by the time I was born, in 1937, the world of my parents was crumbling. Although many of his friends had already left, my father, Wolf Neier, who was then employed by the Berlin Jewish Community as a teacher of Hebrew, stayed on in Berlin. We did leave, finally, in 1939, at what was probably for us the last possible moment. We escaped to England. My ten-year-old sister, Esther, went by herself. My father traveled separately from my mother and me. I got out of Germany in August 1939, days before the outbreak of World War II in Europe.

We were not reunited immediately. The British took time to separate refugees from spies and saboteurs. After my father survived that sifting process, he had to find a job and earn some money to reassemble the family. I spent a year in a hostel for refugee children. It is an experience I recall vividly. The hostel was a miserable place. I hated it.

Not long after the family was reunited in London, our house was destroyed in a bombing attack. We were evacuated to a Midlands town and, after a period of boarding in the home of a gracious and generous English family, found a place of our own to live.

When the war ended, my parents discovered what had happened to their families. Almost everyone was dead. Only fragmentary information was available on how they had been murdered. My father's mother had been shot and killed early in the war, soon after the Germans overran the village in Poland where she lived. Two of my mother's brothers had survived in Bergen-Belsen until the end, only to be killed on the eve of the camp's liberation. Others died along the way.

In Northampton, England, where I spent the years immediately after the war, a friend of my parents established a group home for Jewish boys who had survived the death camps. My father and my sister became their teachers. I spent much of my time with them and they became my friends. They were the first death-camp survivors I met. I learned a little about how they escaped the crematoria. Yosie, who was only fourteen when he came to England and looked much younger, had lived in the woods for four years, much of that time entirely by himself. Janek lived because he entertained the camp guards with his singing and accordion playing. Another survived—I now deduce from his appearance and by recalling what the others said at the time—because the guards found him so beautiful.

I recite my own background to suggest why I am unwilling to put anything, even love of free speech, ahead of detestation of the Nazis. Many residents of Skokie, Illinois, have far better grounds for detesting the Nazis. They themselves experienced the death camps. I know those horrors only through the words of others. They watched the Nazis kill members of their families. I was too young ever to know the members of my family who died in the camps and I was hundreds of miles away in England when they died. I could not bring myself to advocate freedom of speech in Skokie if I did not believe that the chances are best for preventing a repetition of the Holocaust in a society where every incursion on freedom is resisted. Freedom has its risks. Suppression of freedom, I believe, is a sure prescription for disaster.

In describing my childhood brushes with Nazi terror, I do not hope to mitigate the anger of the man who wants to see me lead the parade to the crematorium. It would do no good. Most Jews know other Jews who are so filled with self-hatred that they are the worst anti-Semites. I have been put in that category, I suppose, by many of the letter writers who denounce me so bitterly for defending free speech for Nazis.

The most frequently repeated line of all in the many letters about Skokie that I received was: "How can you, a Jew, defend freedom for Nazis?"

In thinking about the answer to that question during the many months when the letters poured in, I found my own sense of Jewishness deepening. The response I made, perhaps illustrating a trait reputed to be characteristic of Jews, most often began with a question: "How can I, a Jew, refuse to defend freedom, even for Nazis?"

Freedom is no certain protection. The risks are clear. If the Nazis are free to speak, they may win converts. It is possible that they will win so many adherents that they will attain the power to abolish freedom and to destroy me.

John Milton's view that truth will prevail in a free and open encounter with falsehood is my view, too. I want to keep encounters between ideas free and open, expecting to give truth the edge. But I cannot accept Milton's principle as infallible. In this century that has seen so much evil, I must be wary of putting too much faith in any principle of human behavior. And I must examine with care the alternatives that are available to me. My freedom—and my life—may depend on the choice.

The alternative to freedom is power. If I could be certain that I could wipe out Nazism *and* all comparable threats to my safety by the exercise of power, perhaps I would be tempted to choose that course. But we Jews have little power. We are few in number. We are known by the world as a separate race and a separate religion. Only Jews are doubly marked as a people apart.

The rest of the world is suspicious of us Jews. We are like each other and we will stick by each other, the world believes. If a scapegoat is needed for any evil, look among Jews and accuse all Jews. If a Jew took part in the Crucifixion, all Jews are Christ killers. If a Captain Dreyfus is a traitor, all Jews are traitors. If a Karl Marx—despite his childhood baptism—is a Jew, all Jews are revolutionaries. If a Jew lends money, all Jews are usurers. If one Jew is a participant in a financial scandal, the Jews are manipulating the economy. Because he is identified as a Jew, the Jew captures attention. There are Jews everywhere. We can be blamed for everything.

Because we Jews are uniquely vulnerable, I believe we can win only brief respite from persecution in a society in which encounters are settled by power. As a Jew, therefore, concerned with my own survival and the survival of the

Jews—the two being inextricably linked—I want restraints placed on power. The restraints that matter most to me are those which ensure that I cannot be squashed by power, unnoticed by the rest of the world. If I am in danger, I want to cry out to my fellow Jews and to all those I may be able to enlist as my allies. I want to appeal to the world's sense of justice. I want restraints which prohibit those in power from interfering with my right to speak, my right to publish, or my right to gather with others who also feel threatened. Those in power must not be allowed to prevent us from assembling and joining our voices together so we can speak louder and make sure that we are heard. To defend myself, I must restrain power with freedom, even if the temporary beneficiaries are the enemies of freedom.

Albert Camus said, "Freedom is the concern of the oppressed, and her natural protectors have always come from among the oppressed." It is a matter of self-interest. The oppressed are the victims of power. If they are to end their oppression, they must either win freedom or take power themselves. Many of those who have suffered oppression prefer to take power themselves. One-fifth of all the Jews in the world have sought refuge in their own homeland, Israel. It is a place where Jews hope their oppression will end because there, they make the rules. They have the power. Some Jews have sought refuge in other countries, in scattered communities where most of their neighbors are also Jews. Because Jews loom large in the population of a town such as Skokie, it is also a place where they hope their oppression will end because they can make the rules and exercise the power there. Skokie, in that sense, is a microcosmic reflection of Israel. It is a place where the Jews believe they should be able to defend themselves against invasion.

Only heroic efforts have enabled Israel to resist invasion and to survive contests of power with hostile neighbors. Even those most determined to vindicate Israel's interests through displays of force must know that it is only a question of time until that will no longer suffice to preserve Israel against destruction. Israel requires restraints on the power of its neighbors before it is too late. The sword alone will not ensure the survival of Israel.

Other refuges for the Jews, such as Skokie, have far tinier chances for survival in contests based solely on the exercise of power. Skokie cannot be an independent nation. It is governed by the laws and practices of the state of Illinois and of the United States of America. Seventy thousand people, many of them commuters to Chicago, cannot build a wall around themselves to keep out threatening ideas. Skokie requires other protections. Jews and friends of Jews may hold power in Skokie, but they do not hold power in the rest of the country. Nor will they ever. The Jews in Skokie require restraints on power to guard themselves. Keeping a few Nazis off the streets of Skokie will serve Jews poorly if it means that the freedoms to speak, publish, or assemble any place in the United States are thereby weakened.

In Robert Bolt's play A *Man for All Seasons*, Sir Thomas More asks Roper, "What would you do? Cut a great road through law to get after the devil?"

Roper answers, "I'd cut down every law in England to do that." "Oh?" says More. "And when the last law was down and the devil turned around on you— where would you hide, Roper, the laws all being flat? . . . D'you really think you could stand upright in the wind that would blow then? Yes, I'd give the devil benefit of law for my own safety's sake."

Jews cannot hide from the Nazis in Skokie. For their own safety's sake, they must give the devil—the Nazis—benefit of law. It is dangerous to let the Nazis have their say. But it is more dangerous by far to destroy the laws that deny anyone the power to silence Jews if Jews should need to cry out to each other and to the world for succor. Jews have been persecuted too many times in history for anyone to assert that their sufferings are at an end. When the time comes for Jews to speak, to publish, and to march in behalf of their own safety, Illinois and the United States must not be allowed to interfere. The Nazis, I respond to those who ask how I, a Jew, can defend freedom for Nazis, must be free to speak because Jews must be free to speak and because I must be free to speak.

I received many thousands of letters of denunciation. By contrast, there were only a few hundred letters of support. As in the case of the woman who loves free speech more than she detests Nazis, not all the letters of support were entirely reassuring. But some of the support made up for the bitter attacks. One of my favorites was a letter from a doctor in New York City who expressed a stronger commitment to the defense of free speech for the Nazis. "I defend the right to express all or any unpopular opinions," said the doctor, "but, as my grandfather would say, they should only drop dead."

The Nazis never marched in Skokie. They announced that march in a successful effort to maintain their visibility during a period when they were prevented from holding demonstrations in Marquette Park, the section of Chicago where they make their headquarters and enjoy the greatest support. The legal battle against the restrictions on free speech in Marquette Park was fought with little public notice at the same time that the highly publicized struggle over Skokie was underway. Just a few days before the Skokie march was scheduled to take place in June 1978, the legal obstacles to demonstrations in Marquette Park were cleared away. Having achieved their original goal, the Nazis cancelled the Skokie march. As they knew very well, if they had gone forward with it, they would have looked ridiculous. The Nazis might have mustered twenty or thirty people to take part in their march while some fifty thousand people were scheduled to participate in a giant counterdemonstration organized by leaders of Skokie's community of concentration-camp survivors.

Even though the Skokie march never took place, Skokie remains the symbolic battleground. During the fifteen months between the time the Nazis first announced their intention to march in Skokie and the time they called off their march after their legal right to hold it was upheld, it was the subject of a great public debate. That debate continues. Almost every daily newspaper in the country published editorials about Skokie. With a few exceptions, the press sided with the American Civil Liberties Union in defending free speech. Letters-to-the-editor columns were heavily weighted on the other side. Syndicated columnists seemed to divide about equally. Skokie has been an inflammatory issue on hundreds of call-in radio shows around the country. It has been a leading topic of sermons in churches and synagogues. United States Senators have stated their views in the *Congressional Record*. Skokie has provoked fierce debates in schools, offices, community centers, old-age homes, restaurants, living rooms, and wherever else people gather. In the debates I heard, almost everyone said they were for free speech. The questions that divided people are whether American Nazis have forfeited their right to speak by identifying themselves with an ideology that produced the Holocaust. And even if the Nazis should be allowed to speak, they could be banned, couldn't they, from a town that is a haven for victims of Nazism? The debates I heard were rarely calm. Many were dominated by intense emotional outbursts. In some cases, it seemed as though the bitterness expressed would do permanent damage to relationships between people.

Why has Skokie become a symbol and a rallying point? The Nazi attempt to march in Skokie, Illinois, raised no novel legal questions. The arguments for and against free speech in Skokie are identical to those in hundreds of other court cases. Nor, regrettably, is there anything novel in the spectacle of a group of Americans who choose to strut in storm-trooper uniforms with swastika armbands. In the past two decades, such sights have become a familiar part of the urban landscape. The Nazis have no more adherents today and represent no greater a political threat today than during any part of that period. Nor is there anything unusual about a Nazi attempt to march in a place where their mere appearance is a calculated insult to the memory of the victims of Nazism. Like many other dissident groups, the Nazis are intentionally provocative, hoping to attract attention and to trap their enemies into ugly and discrediting responses.

Skokie is, nevertheless, a crisis point for American freedom and it will remain a classic case in the annals of law. The emergence of the Skokie case as a cause célèbre lies in part in its timing. Skokie comes at a moment when American Jews fear that they—and Israel—will be betrayed by the Western democracies. Will the need for Arab oil and petrodollars take precedence over Jewish interests? Skokie symbolizes the reemergence of the ultimate threat to Jewish existence. The world stood by and watched the Nazis destroy the Jews. It could happen again.

Skokie also comes at a moment of special fragility in the uneasy alliance between people with a primary commitment to left-wing politics and people with a primary commitment to civil liberties. The civil rights movement of the 1960s and the antiwar movement and opposition to Richard Nixon forged that alliance. Those are all past. Skokie and related cases shattered that alliance.

Finally, Skokie comes at a moment when liberalism is in sharp decline. It is getting difficult to find any candidate for public office willing to identify himself or herself as a liberal. One of the most frequently repeated lines around is the definition of a conservative as "a liberal who has been mugged." Defense of free speech for Nazis in Skokie, many people believe, is a prime example of liberal naiveté, roughly comparable to inviting a mugger home for dinner. Do not defend the enemy.

Whatever the reasons, Skokie has sent shock waves through many American institutions. Jewish organizations and other groups that have tried to maintain their traditional commitment to free speech find themselves out of step with their own constituencies. Some have taken refuge in silence while others discover special circumstances in Skokie which make it different from every other case of a group attempting to express its views in a place where its doctrines are anathema. Even the nation's leading free-speech organization, the American Civil Liberties Union, has watched a substantial part of its own membership quitting in angry protest over the ACLU's defense of the rights of Nazis who want to march in Skokie. . . .

Herbert Marcuse

REPRESSIVE TOLERANCE

Herbert Marcuse believes in democracy but holds—very unusually for a democrat—that certain kinds of restrictions must be placed on freedom of speech.

This essay examines the idea of tolerance in our advanced industrial society. The conclusion reached is that the realization of the objective of tolerance would call for intolerance toward prevailing policies, attitudes, opinions, and the extension of tolerance to policies, attitudes, and opinions which are outlawed or suppressed. In other words, today tolerance appears again as what it was in its origins, at the beginning of the modern period—a partisan goal, a subversive liberating notion and practice. Conversely, what is proclaimed and practiced as tolerance today, is in many of its most effective manifestations serving the cause of oppression.

The author is fully aware that, at present, no power, no authority, no government exists which would translate liberating tolerance into practice, but he believes that it is the task and duty of the intellectual to recall and preserve historical possibilities which seem to have become utopian possibilities—that it is his task to break the concreteness of oppression in order to open the mental space in which this society can be recognized as what it is and does.

Tolerance is an end in itself. The elimination of violence, and the reduction of suppression to the extent required for protecting man and animals from cruelty and aggression are preconditions for the creation of a humane society. Such a society does not yet exist; progress toward it is perhaps more than before arrested by violence and suppression on a global scale. As deterrents against nuclear war, as police action against subversion, as technical aid in the fight against imperialism and communism, as methods of pacification in neo-colonial massacres, violence and suppression are promulgated, practiced, and defended by democratic and authoritarian governments alike, and the people subjected to these governments are educated to sustain such practices as necessary for the preservation of the status quo. Tolerance is extended to policies, conditions, and modes of behavior which should not be tolerated because they are impeding, if not destroying, the chances of creating an existence without fear and misery.

This sort of tolerance strengthens the tyranny of the majority against which authentic liberals protested. The political locus of tolerance has changed: while it is more or less quietly and constitutionally withdrawn from the opposition, it is made compulsory behavior with respect to established policies. Tolerance is turned from an active into a passive state, from practice to nonpractice: laissez-faire the constituted authorities. It is the people who tolerate the government, which in turn tolerates opposition within the framework determined by the constituted authorities.

Tolerance toward that which is radically evil now appears as good because it serves the cohesion of the whole on the road to affluence or more affluence. The toleration of the systematic moronization of children and adults alike by publicity and propaganda, the release of destructiveness in aggressive driving, the recruitment for and training of special forces, the impotent and benevolent tolerance toward outright deception in merchandising, waste, and planned obsolescence are not distortions and aberrations, they are the essence of a system which fosters tolerance as a means for perpetuating the struggle for existence and suppressing the alternatives. The authorities in education, morals, and psychology are vociferous against the increase in juvenile delinquency; they are less vociferous against the proud presentation, in word and deed and pictures, of ever more powerful missiles, rockets, bombs—the mature delinquency of a whole civilization.

According to a dialectical proposition it is the whole which determines the truth—not in the sense that the whole is prior or superior to its parts, but in the sense that its structure and function determine every particular condition and relation. Thus, within a repressive society, even progressive movements threaten to turn into their opposite to the degree to which they accept the rules of the game. To take a most controversial case: the exercise of political rights (such as voting, letter-writing to the press, to Senators, etc., protest-demonstrations with a priori renunciation of counterviolence) in a society of total administration serves to strengthen this administration by testifying to the existence of democratic liberties which, in reality, have changed their content and lost their effectiveness. In such a case, freedom (of opinion, of assembly, of speech) becomes an instrument for absolving servitude. And yet (and only here the dialectical proposition shows its full intent) the existence and practice of these liberties remain a precondition for the restoration of their original oppositional function, provided that the effort to transcend their (often self-imposed) limitations is intensified. Generally, the function and value of tolerance depend on the equality prevalent in the society in which tolerance is practiced. Tolerance itself stands subject to overriding criteria: its range and its limits cannot be defined in terms of the respective society. In other words, tolerance is an end in itself only when it is truly universal, practiced by the rulers as well as by the ruled, by the lords as well as by the peasants, by the sheriffs as well as by their victims. And such universal tolerance is possible only when no real or alleged enemy requires in the national interest the education and training of people in military violence and destruction. As long as these conditions do not prevail, the conditions of tolerance are "loaded": they are determined and defined by the institutionalized inequality (which is certainly compatible with constitutional equality), i.e., by the class structure of society. In such a society, tolerance is *de facto* limited on the dual ground of legalized violence or suppression (police, armed forces, guards of all sorts) and of the privileged position held by the predominant interests and their "connections."

These background limitations of tolerance are normally prior to the explicit and judicial limitations as defined by the courts, custom, governments, etc. (for example, "clear and present danger," threat to national security, heresy). Within the framework of such a social structure, tolerance can be safely practiced and proclaimed. It is of two kinds: (1) the passive toleration of entrenched and established attitudes and ideas even if their damaging effect on man and nature is evident; and (2) the active, official tolerance granted to the Right as well as to the Left, to movements of aggression as well as to movements of peace, to the party of hate as well as to that of humanity. I call this non-partisan tolerance "abstract" or "pure" inasmuch as it refrains from taking sides—but in doing so it actually protects the already established machinery of discrimination.

The tolerance which enlarged the range and content of freedom was always partisan—intolerant toward the protagonists of the repressive status quo. The issue was only the degree and extent of intolerance. In the firmly established liberal society of England and the United States, freedom of speech and assembly was granted even to the radical enemies of society, provided they did not make the transition from word to deed, from speech to action.

Relying on the effective background limitations imposed by its class structure, the society seemed to practice general tolerance. But liberalist theory had already placed an important condition on tolerance: it was "to apply only to human beings in the maturity of their faculties." John Stuart Mill does not only speak of children and minors; he elaborates: "Liberty, as a principle, has no application to any state of things anterior to the time when mankind have become capable of being improved by free and equal discussion." Anterior to that time, men may still be barbarians, and "despotism is a legitimate mode of government in dealing with barbarians, provided the end be their improvement, and the means justified by actually effecting that end." Mill's often-quoted words have a less familiar implication on which their meaning depends: the internal connection between liberty and truth. There is a sense in which truth is the end of liberty, and liberty must be defined and confined by truth. Now in what sense can liberty be for the sake of truth? Liberty is self-determination, autonomy—this is almost a tautology, but a tautology which results from a whole series of synthetic judgments. It stipulates the ability to determine one's own life: to be able to determine what to do and what not to do, what to suffer and what not. But the subject of this autonomy is never the contingent, private individual as that which he actually is or happens to be; it is rather the individual as a human being who is capable of being free with the others. And the problem of making possible such a harmony between every individual liberty and the other is not that of finding a compromise between competitors, or between freedom and law, between general and individual interest, common and private welfare in an *established* society, but of *creating* the society in which man is no longer enslaved by institutions which vitiate self-determination from the beginning. In other words, freedom is still to be created even for the freest of the existing societies. And the direction in which it must be sought, and the institutional and cultural changes which may help to attain the goal are, at least in developed civilization, *comprehensible*, that is to say, they can be identified and projected, on the basis of experience, by human reason.

In the interplay of theory and practice, true and false solutions become distinguishable—never with the evidence of necessity, never as the positive, only with the certainty of a reasoned and reasonable chance, and with the persuasive force of the negative. For the true positive is the society of the future and therefore beyond definition and determination, while the existing positive is that which must be surmounted. But the experience and understanding of the existent society may well be capable of identifying what is *not* conducive to a free and rational society, what impedes and distorts the possibilities of its creation. Freedom is liberation, a specific historical process in theory and practice, and as such it has its right and wrong, its truth and falsehood.

The uncertainty of chance in this distinction does not cancel the historical objectivity, but it necessitates freedom of thought and expression as preconditions of finding the way to freedom—it necessitates *tolerance*. However, this tolerance cannot be indiscriminate and equal with respect to the contents of expression, neither in word nor in deed; it cannot protect false words and wrong deeds which demonstrate that they contradict and counteract the possibilities of liberation. Such indiscriminate tolerance is justified in harmless debates, in conversation, in academic discussion; it is indispensable in the scientific enterprise, in private religion. But society cannot be indiscriminate where the pacification of existence, where freedom and happiness themselves are at stake: here, certain things cannot be said, certain ideas cannot be expressed, certain policies cannot be proposed, certain behavior cannot be permitted without making tolerance an instrument for the continuation of servitude.

The danger of "destructive tolerance" (Baudelaire), of "benevolent neutrality" toward *art* has been recognized: the market, which absorbs equally well (although with often quite sudden fluctuations) art, anti-art, and non-art, all possible conflicting styles, schools, forms, provides a "complacent receptacle, a friendly abyss" (Edgar Wind, *Art and Anarchy* [New York: Knopf, 1964], p. 101) in which the radical impact of art, the protest of art against the established reality is swallowed up. However, censorship of art and literature is regressive under all circumstances. The authentic oeuvre is not and cannot be a prop of oppression, and pseudo-art (which can be such a prop) is not art. Art stands against history, withstands history which has been the history of oppression, for art subjects reality to laws other than the established ones: to the laws of the Form which creates a different reality—negation of the established one even where art depicts the established reality. But in its struggle with history, art subjects itself to history: history enters the definition of art and enters into the distinction between art and pseudo-art. Thus it happens that what was once art becomes pseudo-art. Previous forms, styles, and qualities, previous modes of protest and refusal cannot be recaptured in or against a different society. There are cases where an authentic oeuvre carries a regressive political message—Dostoevski is a case in point. But then, the message is canceled by the oeuvre itself: the regressive political content is absorbed, *aufgehoben* in the artistic form: in the work as literature.

Tolerance of free speech is the way of improvement, of progress in liberation, *not* because there is no objective truth, and improvement must necessarily be a compromise between a variety of opinions, but because there *is* an objective truth which can be discovered, ascertained only in learning and comprehending that which is and that which can be and ought to be done for the sake of improving the lot of mankind. This common and historical "ought" is not immediately evident, at hand: it has to be uncovered by "cutting through," "splitting," "breaking asunder" (*dis-cutio*) the given material—separating right and wrong, good and bad, correct and incorrect. The subject whose "improvement" depends on a progressive historical practice is each man as man, and this universality is reflected in that of the discussion, which a priori does not exclude any group or individual. But even the all-inclusive character of liberalist tolerance was, at least in theory, based on the proposition that men were (potential) *individuals* who could learn to hear and see and feel by themselves, to develop their own thoughts, to grasp their true interests and rights and capabilities, also against established authority and opinion. This was the rationale of free speech and assembly. Universal toleration becomes questionable when its rationale no longer prevails, when tolerance is administered to manipulated and indoctrinated individuals who parrot, as their own, the opinion of their masters, for whom heteronomy has become autonomy.

The telos of tolerance is truth. It is clear from the historical record that the authentic spokesmen of tolerance had more and other truth in mind than that of propositional logic and academic theory. John Stuart Mill speaks of the truth which is persecuted in history and which does *not* triumph over persecution by virtue of its "inherent power," which in fact has no inherent power "against the dungeon and the stake." And he enumerates the "truths" which were cruelly and successfully liquidated in the dungeons and at the stake: that of Arnold of Brescia, of Fra Dolcino, of Savonarola, of the Albigensians, Waldensians, Lollards, and Hussites. Tolerance is first and foremost for the sake of the heretics—the historical road toward *humanitas* appears as heresy: target of persecution by the powers that be. Heresy by itself, however, is no token of truth.

The criterion of progress in freedom according to which Mill judges these movements is the Reformation. The evaluation is *ex post*, and his list includes opposites (Savonarola too would have burned Fra Dolcino). Even the ex post evaluation is contestable as to its truth: history corrects the judgment—too late. The correction does not help the victims and does not absolve their executioners. However, the lesson is clear: intolerance has delayed progress and has prolonged the slaughter and torture of innocents for hundreds of years. Does this clinch the case for indiscriminate, "pure" tolerance? Are there historical conditions in which such toleration impedes liberation and multiplies the victims who are sacrificed to the status quo? Can the indiscriminate guaranty of political rights and liberties be repressive? Can such tolerance serve to contain qualitative social change?

I shall discuss this question only with reference to political movements, attitudes, schools of thought, philosophies which are "political" in the widest sense—affecting the society as a whole, demonstrably transcending the sphere of privacy. Moreover, I propose a shift in the focus of the discussion: it will be concerned not only, and not primarily, with tolerance toward radical extremes, minorities, subversives, etc., but rather with tolerance toward majorities, toward official and public opinion, toward the established protectors of freedom. In this case, the discussion can have as a frame of reference only a democratic society, in which the people, as individuals and as members of political and other organizations, participate in the making, sustaining, and changing policies. In an authoritarian system, the people do not tolerate—they suffer established policies.

Under a system of constitutionally guaranteed and (generally and without too many and too glaring exceptions) practiced civil rights and liberties, opposition and dissent are tolerated unless they issue in violence and/or in exhortation to and organization of violent subversion. The underlying assumption is that the established society is free, and that any improvement, even a change in the social structure and social values, would come about in the normal course of events, prepared, defined, and tested in free and equal discussion, on the open marketplace of ideas and goods.* Now in recalling John Stuart Mill's passage, I drew attention to the premise hidden in this assumption: free and

---

*I wish to reiterate for the following discussion that, *de facto*, tolerance is *not* indiscriminate and "pure" even in the most democratic society. The "background limitations" stated on page 417 restrict tolerance before it begins to operate. The antagonistic structure of society rigs the rules of the game. Those who stand against the established system are a priori at a disadvantage, which is not removed by the toleration of their ideas, speeches, and newspapers.

equal discussion can fulfill the function attributed to it only if it is *rational*—expression and development of independent thinking, free from indoctrination, manipulation, extraneous authority. The notion of pluralism and countervailing powers is no substitute for this requirement. One might in theory construct a state in which a multitude of different pressures, interests, and authorities balance each other out and result in a truly general and rational interest. However, such a construct badly fits a society in which powers are and remain unequal and even increase their unequal weight when they run their own course. It fits even worse when the variety of pressures unifies and coagulates into an overwhelming whole, integrating the particular countervailing powers by virtue of an increasing standard of living and an increasing concentration of power. Then, the laborer, whose real interest conflicts with that of management, the common consumer whose real interest conflicts with that of the producer, the intellectual whose vocation conflicts with that of his employer find themselves submitting to a system against which they are powerless and appear unreasonable. The ideas of the available alternatives evaporates into an utterly utopian dimension in which it is at home, for a free society is indeed unrealistically and undefinably different from the existing ones. Under these circumstances, whatever improvement may occur "in the normal course of events" and without subversion is likely to be improvement in the direction determined by the particular interests which control the whole.

By the same token, those minorities which strive for a change of the whole itself will, under optimal conditions which rarely prevail, be left free to deliberate and discuss, to speak and to assemble—and will be left harmless and helpless in the face of the overwhelming majority, which militates against qualitative social change. This majority is firmly grounded in the increasing satisfaction of needs, and technological and mental coordination, which testify to the general helplessness of radical groups in a well-functioning social system.

Within the affluent democracy, the affluent discussion prevails, and within the established framework, it is tolerant to a large extent. All points of view can be heard: the Communist and the Fascist, the Left and the Right, the white and the Negro, the crusaders for armament and for disarmament. Moreover, in endlessly dragging debates over the media, the stupid opinion is treated with the same respect as the intelligent one, the misinformed may talk as long as the informed, and propaganda rides along with education, truth with falsehood. This pure toleration of sense and nonsense is justified by the democratic argument that nobody, neither group nor individual, is in possession of the truth and capable of defining what is right and wrong, good and bad. Therefore, all contesting opinions must be submitted to "the people" for its deliberation and choice. But I have already suggested that the democratic argument implies a necessary condition, namely, that the people must be capable of deliberating and choosing on the basis of knowledge, that they must have access to authentic information, and that, on this basis, their evaluation must be the result of autonomous thought.

In the contemporary period, the democratic argument for abstract tolerance tends to be invalidated by the invalidation of the democratic process itself. The liberating force of democracy was the chance it gave to effective dissent, on the individual as well as social scale, its openness to qualitatively different forms of government, of culture, education, work—of the human existence in general. The toleration of free discussion and the equal right of opposites was to define and clarify the different forms of dissent: their direction, content, prospect. But with the concentration of economic and political power and the integration of opposites in a society which uses technology as an instrument of domination, effective dissent is blocked where it could freely emerge: in the formation of opinion, in information and communication, in speech and assembly. Under the rule of monopolistic media—themselves the mere instruments of economic and political power—a mentality is created for which right and wrong, true and false are predefined wherever they affect the vital interests of the society. This is, prior to all expression and communication, a matter of semantics: the blocking of effective dissent, of the recognition of that which is not of the Establishment which begins in the language that is publicized and administered. The meaning of words is rigidly stabilized. Rational persuasion, persuasion to the opposite is all but precluded. The avenues of entrance are closed to the meaning of words and ideas other than the established one—established by the publicity of the powers that be, and verified in their practices. Other words can be spoken and heard, other ideas can be expressed, but, at the massive scale of the conservative majority (outside such enclaves as the intelligentsia), they are immediately "evaluated" (i.e. automatically understood) in terms of the public language—a language which determines "a priori" the direction in which the thought process moves. Thus the process of reflection ends where it started: in the given conditions and relations. Self-validating, the argument of the discussion repels the contradiction because the antithesis is redefined in terms of the thesis. For example, thesis: we work for peace; antithesis: we prepare for war (or even: we wage war); unification of opposites: preparing for war *is* working for peace. Peace is redefined as necessarily, in the prevailing situation, including preparation for war (or even war) and in this Orwellian form, the meaning of the word "peace" is stabilized. Thus, the basic vocabulary of the Orwellian language operates as a priori categories of understanding: preforming all content. These conditions invalidate the logic of tolerance which involves the rational development of meaning and precludes the closing of meaning. Consequently, persuasion through discussion and the equal presentation of opposites (even where it is really equal) easily lose their liberating force as factors of understanding and learning; they are far more likely to strengthen the established thesis and to repel the alternatives.

Impartiality to the utmost, equal treatment of competing and conflicting issues is indeed a basic requirement for decision-making in the democratic process—it is an equally basic requirement for defining the limits of tolerance.

But in a democracy with totalitarian organization, objectivity may fulfill a very different function, namely, to foster a mental attitude which tends to obliterate the difference between true and false, information and indoctrination, right and wrong. In fact, the decision between opposed opinions has been made before the presentation and discussion get under way—made, not by a conspiracy or a sponsor or a publisher, not by any dictatorship, but rather by the "normal course of events," which is the course of administered events, and by the mentality shaped in this course. Here, too, it is the whole which determines the truth. Then the decision asserts itself, without any open violation of objectivity, in such things as the make-up of a newspaper (with the breaking up of vital information into bits interspersed between extraneous material, irrelevant items, relegating of some radically negative news to an obscure place), in the juxtaposition of gorgeous ads with unmitigated horrors, in the introduction and interruption of the broadcasting of facts by overwhelming commercials. The result is a *neutralization* of opposites, a neutralization, however, which takes place on the firm grounds of the structural limitation of tolerance and within a preformed mentality. When a magazine prints side by side a negative and a positive report on the FBI, it fulfills honestly the requirements of objectivity: however, the chances are that the positive wins because the image of the institution is deeply engraved in the mind of the people. Or, if a newscaster reports the torture and murder of civil rights workers in the same unemotional tone he uses to describe the stock market or the weather, or with the same great emotion with which he says his commercials, then such objectivity is spurious—more, it offends against humanity and truth by being calm where one should be enraged, by refraining from accusation where accusation is in the facts themselves. The tolerance expressed in such impartiality serves to minimize or even absolve prevailing intolerance and suppression. If objectivity has anything to do with truth, and if truth is more than a matter of logic and science, then this kind of objectivity is false, and this kind of tolerance inhuman. And if it is necessary to break the established universe of meaning (and the practice enclosed in this universe) in order to enable man to find out what is true and false, this deceptive impartiality would have to be abandoned. The people exposed to this impartiality are no *tabulae rasae*, they are indoctrinated by the conditions under which they live and think and which they do not transcend. To enable them to become autonomous, to find by themselves what is true and what is false for man in the existing society, they would have to be freed from the prevailing indoctrination (which is no longer recognized as indoctrination). But this means that the trend would have to be reversed: they would have to get information slanted in the opposite direction. For the facts are never given immediately and never accessible immediately; they are established, "mediated" by those who made them; the truth, "the whole truth" surpasses these facts and requires the rupture with their appearance. This rupture—prerequisite and token of all freedom of thought and of speech—

cannot be accomplished within the established framework of abstract tolerance and spurious objectivity because these are precisely the factors which precondition the mind *against* the rupture.

The factual barriers which totalitarian democracy erects against the efficacy of qualitative dissent are weak and pleasant enough compared with the practices of a dictatorship which claims to educate the people in the truth. With all its limitations and distortions, democratic tolerance is under all circumstances more humane than an institutionalized intolerance which sacrifices the rights and liberties of the living generations for the sake of future generations. The question is whether this is the only alternative. I shall presently try to suggest the direction in which an answer may be sought. In any case, the contrast is not between democracy in the abstract and dictatorship in the abstract.

Democracy is a form of government which fits very different types of society (this holds true even for a democracy with universal suffrage and equality before the law), and the human costs of a democracy are always and everywhere those exacted by the society whose government it is. Their range extends all the way from normal exploitation, poverty, and insecurity to the victims of wars, police actions, military aid, etc., in which the society is engaged—and not only to the victims within its own frontiers. These considerations can never justify the exacting of different sacrifices and different victims on behalf of a future better society, but they do allow weighing the costs involved in the perpetuation of an existing society against the risk of promoting alternatives which offer a reasonable chance of pacification and liberation. Surely, no government can be expected to foster its own subversion, but in a democracy such a right is vested in the people (i.e. in the majority of the people). This means that the ways should not be blocked on which a subversive majority could develop, and if they are blocked by organized repression and indoctrination, their reopening may require apparently undemocratic means. They would include the withdrawal of toleration of speech and assembly from groups and movements which promote aggressive policies, armament, chauvinism, discrimination on the grounds of race and religion, or which oppose the extension of public services, social security, medical care, etc. Moreover, the restoration of freedom of thought may necessitate new and rigid restrictions on teachings and practices in the educational institutions which, by their very methods and concepts, serve to enclose the mind within the established universe of discourse and behavior—thereby precluding a priori a rational evaluation of the alternatives. And to the degree to which freedom of thought involves the struggle against inhumanity, restoration of such freedom would also imply intolerance toward scientific research in the interest of deadly "deterrents," of abnormal human endurance under inhuman conditions, etc. I shall presently discuss the question as to who is to decide on the distinction between liberating and repressive, human and inhuman teachings and practices; I have already suggested that this distinction is not a matter of value-preference but of rational criteria.

While the reversal of the trend in the educational enterprise at least could conceivably be enforced by the students and teachers themselves, and thus be self-imposed, the systematic withdrawal of tolerance toward regressive and repressive opinions and movements could only be envisaged as results of large-scale pressure which would amount to an upheaval. In other words, it would presuppose that which is still to be accomplished: the reversal of the trend. However, resistance at particular occasions, boycott, non-participation at the local and small-group level may perhaps prepare the ground. The subversive character of the restoration of freedom appears most clearly in that dimension of society where false tolerance and free enterprise do perhaps the most serious and lasting damage, namely, in business and publicity. Against the emphatic insistence on the part of spokesmen for labor, I maintain that practices such as planned obsolescence, collusion between union leadership and management, slanted publicity are not simply imposed from above on a powerless rank and file, but are *tolerated* by them—and by the consumer at large. However, it would be ridiculous to speak of a possible withdrawal of tolerance with respect to these practices and to the ideologies promoted by them. For they pertain to the basis on which the repressive affluent society rests and reproduces itself and its vital defenses—their removal would be that total revolution which this society so effectively repels.

To discuss tolerance in such a society means to re-examine the issue of violence and the traditional distinction between violent and non-violent action. The discussion should not, from the beginning, be clouded by ideologies which serve the perpetuation of violence. Even in the advanced centers of civilization, violence actually prevails: it is practiced by the police, in the prisons and mental institutions, in the fight against racial minorities; it is carried, by the defenders of metropolitan freedom, into the backward countries. This violence indeed breeds violence. But to refrain from violence in the face of vastly superior violence is one thing, to renounce a priori violence against violence, on ethical or psychological grounds (because it may antagonize sympathizers) is another. Non-violence is normally not only preached to but exacted from the weak—it is a necessity rather than a virtue, and normally it does not seriously harm the case of the strong. (Is the case of India an exception? There, passive resistance was carried through on a massive scale, which disrupted, or threatened to disrupt, the economic life of the country. Quantity turns into quality: on such a scale, passive resistance is no longer passive—it ceases to be non-violent. The same holds true for the General Strike.) Robespierre's distinction between the terror of liberty and the terror of despotism, and his moral glorification of the former belongs to the most convincingly condemned aberrations, even if the white terror was more bloody than the red terror. The comparative evaluation in terms of the number of victims is the quantifying approach which reveals the man-made horror throughout history that made violence a necessity. In terms of historical function, there is a difference between revolutionary and reactionary violence, between violence practiced by the oppressed and by the oppressors. In terms of ethics, both forms of violence are inhuman and evil—but since when is history made in accordance with ethical standards? To start applying them at the point where the oppressed rebel against the oppressors, the have-nots against the haves is serving the cause of actual violence by weakening the protest against it.

> Comprenez enfin ceci: si la violence a commencé ce soir, si l'exploitation ni l'oppression n'ont jamais existé sur terre, peut-être la non-violence affichée peut apaiser la querelle. Mais si le régime tout entier et jusqu'à vos non-violentes pensées sont conditionnées par une oppression millénaire, votre passivité ne sert qu'à vous ranger du côté des oppresseurs. (Sartre, Preface to Frantz Fanon, *Les Damnés de la Terre*, Paris: Maspéro, 1961, p. 22).

The very notion of false tolerance, and the distinction between right and wrong limitations on tolerance, between progressive and regressive indoctrination, revolutionary and reactionary violence demand the statement of criteria for its validity. These standards must be prior to whatever constitutional and legal criteria are set up and applied in an existing society (such as "clear and present danger," and other established definitions of civil rights and liberties), for such definitions themselves presuppose standards of freedom and repression as applicable or not applicable in the respective society: they are specifications of more general concepts. By whom, and according to what standards, can the political distinction between true and false, progressive and regressive (for in this sphere, these pairs are equivalent) be made and its validity be justified? At the outset, I propose that the question cannot be answered in terms of the alternative between democracy and dictatorship, according to which, in the latter, one individual or group, without any effective control from below, arrogate to themselves the decision. Historically, even in the most democratic democracies, the vital and final decisions affecting the society as a whole have been made, constitutionally or in fact, by one or several groups without effective control by the people themselves. The ironical question: who educates the educators (i.e. the political leaders) also applies to democracy. The only authentic alternative and negation of dictatorship (with respect to this question) would be a society in which "the people" have become autonomous individuals, freed from the repressive requirements of a struggle for existence in the interest of domination, and as such human beings choosing their government and determining their life. Such a society does not yet exist anywhere. In the meantime, the question must be treated *in abstracto*—abstraction, not from the historical possibilities, but from the realities of the prevailing societies.

I suggested that the distinction between true and false tolerance, between progress and regression can be made rationally on empirical grounds. The real possibilities of human freedom are relative to the attained stage of civilization. They depend on the material and intellectual resources available at the respective stage, and they are quantifiable and calculable to a high degree. So are, at the stage of advanced industrial society, the most rational ways of using these resources and distributing the social product with priority on the satisfaction of vital needs and with a minimum of toil and injustice. In other words, it is possible to define the direction in which prevailing institutions, policies, opinions would have to be changed in order to improve the chance of a peace which is not identical with cold war and a little hot war, and a satisfaction of needs which does not feed on poverty, oppression, and exploitation. Consequently, it is also possible to identify policies, opinions, movements which would promote this chance, and those which would do the opposite. Suppression of the regressive ones is a prerequisite for the strengthening of the progressive ones.

The question, who is qualified to make all these distinctions, definitions, identifications for the society as a whole, has now one logical answer, namely, everyone "in the maturity of his faculties" as a human being, everyone who has learned to think rationally and autonomously. The answer to Plato's educational dictatorship is the democratic educational dictatorship of free men. John Stuart Mill's conception of the *res publica* is not the opposite of Plato's: the liberal too demands the authority of Reason not only as an intellectual but also as a political power. In Plato, rationality is confined to the small number of philosopher-kings; in Mill, every rational human being participates in the discussion and decision—but only as a rational being. Where society has entered the phase of total administration and indoctrination, this would be a small number indeed, and not necessarily that of the elected representatives of the people. The problem is not that of an educational dictatorship, but that of breaking the tyranny of public opinion and its makers in the closed society.

However, granted the empirical rationality of the distinction between progress and regression, and granted that it may be applicable to tolerance, and may justify strongly discriminatory tolerance on political grounds (cancellation of the liberal creed of free and equal discussion), another impossible consequence would follow. I said that, by virtue of its inner logic, withdrawal of tolerance from regressive movements, and discriminatory tolerance in favor of progressive tendencies would be tantamount to the "official" promotion of subversion. The historical calculus of progress (which is actually the calculus of the prospective reduction of cruelty, misery, suppression) seems to involve the calculated choice between two forms of political violence: that on the part of the legally constituted powers (by their legitimate action, or by their tacit consent, or by their inability to prevent violence), and that on the part of potentially subversive movements. Moreover, with respect to the latter, a policy of unequal treatment would protect radicalism on the Left against that on the Right. Can the historical calculus be reasonably extended to the justification of one form of violence as against another? Or better (since "justification" carries a moral connotation), is there historical evidence to the effect that the social origin and impetus of violence (from among the ruled or the ruling classes, the have or the have-nots, the Left or the Right) is in a demonstrable relation to progress (as defined above)?

With all the qualifications of a hypothesis based on an "open" historical record, it seems that the violence emanating from the rebellion of the oppressed classes broke the historical continuum of injustice, cruelty, and silence for a brief moment, brief but explosive enough to achieve an increase in the scope of freedom and justice, and a better and more equitable distribution of misery and oppression in a new social system—in one word: progress in civilization. The English civil wars, the French Revolution, the Chinese and the Cuban Revolutions may illustrate the hypothesis. In contrast, the one historical change from one social system to another, marking the beginning of a new period in civilization, which was *not* sparked and driven by an effective movement "from below," namely, the collapse of the Roman Empire in the West, brought about a long period of regression for long centuries, until a new, higher period of civilization was painfully born in the violence of the heretic revolts of the thirteenth century and in the peasant and laborer revolts of the fourteenth century.[1]

With respect to historical violence emanating from among ruling classes, no such relation to progress seems to obtain. The long series of dynastic and imperialist wars, the liquidation of Spartacus in Germany in 1919, Fascism and Nazism did not break but rather tightened and streamlined the continuum of suppression. I said emanating "from among ruling classes": to be sure, there is hardly any organized violence from above that does not mobilize and activate mass support from below; the decisive question is, on behalf of and in the interest of which groups and institutions is such violence released? And the answer is not necessarily ex post: in the historical examples just mentioned, it could be and was anticipated whether the movement would serve the revamping of the old order or the emergence of the new.

Liberating tolerance, then, would mean intolerance against movements from the Right, and toleration of movements from the Left. As to the scope of this tolerance and intolerance: . . . it would extend to the stage of action as well as of discussion and propaganda, of deed as well as of word. The traditional criterion of clear and present danger seems no longer adequate to a stage where the whole society is in the situation of the theater audience when somebody cries: "fire." It is a situation in which the total catastrophy could be triggered off any moment, not only by a technical error, but also by a rational miscalculation of risks, or by a rash speech of one of the leaders. In past and different circumstances, the speeches of the Fascist and Nazi leaders were the immediate prologue to the massacre. The distance between the propaganda and the action, between the organization and its release on the people had

---

[1]In modern times, fascism has been a consequence of the transition to industrial society *without* a revolution. See Barrington Moore's forthcoming book *Social Origins of Dictatorship and Democracy*.

become too short. But the spreading of the word could have been stopped before it was too late: if democratic tolerance had been withdrawn when the future leaders started their campaign, mankind would have had a chance of avoiding Auschwitz and a World War.

The whole post-fascist period is one of clear and present danger. Consequently, true pacification requires the withdrawal of tolerance before the deed, at the stage of communication in word, print, and picture. Such extreme suspension of the right of free speech and free assembly is indeed justified only if the whole of society is in extreme danger. I maintain that our society is in such an emergency situation, and that it has become the normal state of affairs. Different opinions and "philosophies" can no longer compete peacefully for adherence and persuasion on rational grounds: the "marketplace of ideas" is organized and delimited by those who determine the national and the individual interest. In this society, for which the ideologists have proclaimed the "end of ideology," the false consciousness has become the general consciousness—from the government down to its last objects. The small and powerless minorities which struggle against the false consciousness and its beneficiaries must be helped: their continued existence is more important than the preservation of abused rights and liberties which grant constitutional powers to those who oppress these minorities. It should be evident by now that the exercise of civil rights by those who don't have them presupposes the withdrawal of civil rights from those who prevent their exercise, and that liberation of the Damned of the Earth presupposes suppression not only of their old but also of their new masters.

Withdrawal of tolerance from regressive movements *before* they can become active; intolerance even toward thought, opinion, and word, and finally, intolerance in the opposite direction, that is, toward the self-styled conservatives, to the political Right—these anti-democratic notions respond to the actual development of the democratic society which has destroyed the basis for universal tolerance. The conditions under which tolerance can again become a liberating and humanizing force have still to be created. When tolerance mainly serves the protection and preservation of a repressive society, when it serves to neutralize opposition and to render men immune against other and better forms of life, then tolerance has been perverted. And when this perversion starts in the mind of the individual, in his consciousness, his needs, when heteronomous interests occupy him before he can experience his servitude, then the efforts to counteract his dehumanization must begin at the place of entrance, there where the false consciousness takes form (or rather: is systematically formed)—it must begin with stopping the words and images which feed this consciousness. To be sure, this is censorship, even precensorship, but openly directed against the more or less hidden censorship that permeates the free media. Where the false consciousness has become prevalent in national and popular behavior, it translates itself almost immediately into practice: the safe distance between ideology and reality, repressive thought and repressive

action, between the word of destruction and the deed of destruction is danger-
ously shortened. Thus, the break through the false consciousness may provide
the Archimedean point for a larger emancipation—at an infinitesimally small
spot, to be sure, but it is on the enlargement of such small spots that the
chance of change depends.

The forces of emancipation cannot be identified with any social class which,
by virtue of its material condition, is free from false consciousness. Today, they
are hopelessly dispersed throughout the society, and the fighting minorities
and isolated groups are often in opposition to their own leadership. In the
society at large, the mental space for denial and reflection must first be recre-
ated. Repulsed by the concreteness of the administered society, the effort of
emancipation becomes "abstract"; it is reduced to facilitating the recognition
of what is going on, to freeing language from the tyranny of the Orwellian
syntax and logic, to developing the concepts that comprehend reality. More
than ever, the proposition holds true that progress in freedom demands progress in the *consciousness* of freedom. Where the mind has been made into a
subject-object of politics and policies, intellectual autonomy, the realm of
"pure" thought has become a matter of *political education* (or rather: counter-
education).

This means that previously neutral, value-free, formal aspects of learning
and teaching now become, on their own grounds and in their own right, political: learning to know the facts, the whole truth, and to comprehend it is radical
criticism throughout, intellectual subversion. In a world in which the human
faculties and needs are arrested or perverted, autonomous thinking leads into
a "perverted world": contradiction and counter-image of the established world
of repression. And this contradiction is not simply stipulated, is not simply the
product of confused thinking or phantasy, but is the logical development of the
given, the existing world. To the degree to which this development is actually
impeded by the sheer weight of a repressive society and the necessity of making a living in it, repression invades the academic enterprise itself, even prior to
all restrictions on academic freedom. The pre-empting of the mind vitiates
impartiality and objectivity: unless the student learns to think in the opposite
direction, he will be inclined to place the facts into the predominant framework
of values. Scholarship, i.e. the acquisition and communication of knowledge,
prohibits the purification and isolation of facts from the context of the whole
truth. An essential part of the latter is recognition of the frightening extent to
which history was made and recorded by and for the victors, that is, the extent
to which history was the development of oppression. And this oppression is in
the facts themselves which it establishes; thus they themselves carry a negative value as part and aspect of their facticity. To treat the great crusades *against*
humanity (like that against the Albigensians) with the same impartiality as the
desperate struggles *for* humanity means neutralizing their opposite historical
function, reconciling the executioners with their victims, distorting the record.
Such spurious neutrality serves to reproduce acceptance of the dominion of

the victors in the consciousness of man. Here, too, in the education of those who are not yet maturely integrated, in the mind of the young, the ground for liberating tolerance is still to be created.

Education offers still another example of spurious, abstract tolerance in the guise of concreteness and truth: it is epitomized in the concept of self-actualization. From the permissiveness of all sorts of license to the child, to the constant psychological concern with the personal problems of the student, a large-scale movement is under way against the evils of repression and the need for being oneself. Frequently brushed aside is the question as to what has to be repressed before one can be a self, oneself. The individual potential is first a negative one, a portion of the potential of his society: of aggression, guilt feeling, ignorance, resentment, cruelty which vitiate his life instincts. If the identity of the self is to be more than the immediate realization of this potential (undesirable for the individual as human being), then it requires repression and sublimation, conscious transformation. This process involves at each stage (to use the ridiculed terms which here reveal their succinct concreteness) the negation of the negation, mediation of the immediate, and identity is no more and no less than this process. "Alienation" is the constant and essential element of identity, the objective side of the subject—and not, as it is made to appear today, a disease, a psychological condition. Freud well knew the difference between progressive and regressive, liberating and destructive repression. The publicity of self-actualization promotes the removal of the one and the other, it promotes existence in that immediacy which, in a repressive society, is (to use another Hegelian term) bad immediacy (*schlechte Unmittelbarkeit*). It isolates the individual from the one dimension where he could "find himself": from his political existence, which is at the core of his entire existence. Instead, it encourages non-conformity and letting-go in ways which leave the real engines of repression in the society entirely intact, which even strengthen these engines by substituting the satisfactions of private and personal rebellion for a more than private and personal, and therefore more authentic, opposition. The desublimation involved in this sort of self-actualization is itself repressive inasmuch as it weakens the necessity and the power of the intellect, the catalytic force of that unhappy consciousness which does not revel in the archetypal personal release of frustration—hopeless resurgence of the Id which will sooner or later succumb to the omnipresent rationality of the administered world—but which recognizes the horror of the whole in the most private frustration and actualizes itself in this recognition.

I have tried to show how the changes in advanced democratic societies, which have undermined the basis of economic and political liberalism, have also altered the liberal function of tolerance. The tolerance which was the great achievement of the liberal era is still professed and (with strong qualifications) practiced, while the economic and political process is subjected to an ubiquitous and effective administration in accordance with the predominant interests. The result is an objective contradiction between the economic and political structure on the one side, and the theory and practice of toleration on the other. The altered social structure tends to weaken the effectiveness of tolerance toward dissenting and oppositional movements and to strengthen conservative and reactionary forces. Equality of tolerance becomes abstract, spurious. With the actual decline of dissenting forces in the society, the opposition is insulated in small and frequently antagonistic groups who, even where tolerated within the narrow limits set by the hierarchical structure of society, are powerless while they keep within these limits. But the tolerance shown to them is deceptive and promotes coordination. And on the firm foundations of a coordinated society all but closed against qualitative change, tolerance itself serves to contain such change rather than to promote it.

These same conditions render the critique of such tolerance abstract and academic, and the proposition that the balance between tolerance toward the Right and toward the Left would have to be radically redressed in order to restore the liberating function of tolerance becomes only an unrealistic speculation. Indeed, such a redressing seems to be tantamount to the establishment of a "right of resistance" to the point of subversion. There is not, there cannot be any such right for any group or individual against a constitutional government sustained by a majority of the population. But I believe that there is a "natural right" of resistance for oppressed and overpowered minorities to use extralegal means if the legal ones have proved to be inadequate. Law and order are always and everywhere the law and order which protect the established hierarchy; it is nonsensical to invoke the absolute authority of this law and this order against those who suffer from it and struggle against it—not for personal advantages and revenge, but for their share of humanity. There is no other judge over them than the constituted authorities, the police, and their own conscience. If they use violence, they do not start a new chain of violence but try to break an established one. Since they will be punished, they know the risk, and when they are willing to take it, no third person, and least of all the educator and intellectual, has the right to preach them abstention.

Arthur M. Schlesinger, Jr.

AMERICA 1968: THE POLITICS OF VIOLENCE

Arthur M. Schlesinger, Jr. (b. 1917), a distinguished American historian, disagrees with the analysis given in the preceding selection by Marcuse. We reprint part of his essay "America 1968: The Politics of Violence."

The world today is asking a terrible question—a question which every citizen of this Republic should be putting to himself: what sort of people are we, we Americans?

And the answer which much of the world is bound to return is that we are today the most frightening people on this planet.

We are a frightening people because for three years we have been devastating a small country on the other side of the world in a war which bears no rational relationship to our national security or our national interest.

We are a frightening people because we have already in this decade murdered the two of our citizens who stood preeminently before the world as the embodiments of American idealism—and because last night we tried to murder a third.

We are a frightening people because the atrocities we commit hardly touch our official self-righteousness, our invincible conviction of our moral infallibility.

The ghastly things we do to our own people, the ghastly things we do to other people—these must at last compel us to look searchingly at ourselves and our society before hatred and violence rush us on to more evil and finally tear our nation apart.

We cannot take the easy course and blame everyone but ourselves for the things we do. We cannot blame the epidemic of murder at home on deranged and solitary individuals separate from the rest of us. For these individuals are plainly weak and suggestible men, stamped by our society with a birthright of hatred and a compulsion toward violence.

We cannot blame our epidemic of murder abroad on the wickedness of those who will not conform to our views of how they should behave and how they should live. For the zeal with which we have pursued an irrational war suggests the internal impulses of hatred and violence demanding outlet and shaping our foreign policy to their ends.

We must recognize that the evil is in us, that it springs from some dark, intolerable tension in our history and our institutions. It is almost as if a primal curse had been fixed on our nation, perhaps when we first began the practice of killing and enslaving those whom we deemed our inferiors because their skin was another color. We are a violent people with a violent history, and the instinct for violence has seeped into the bloodstream of our national life.

We are also, at our best, a generous and idealistic people. Our great leaders—Lincoln most of all—have perceived both the destructive instinct and the moral necessity of transcending destruction if we are going to have any sort of rational and decent society. They have realized how fragile the membranes of our civilization are, stretched so thin over a nation so disparate in its composition, so tense in its interior relationships, so cunningly enmeshed in underground fears and antagonisms, so entrapped by history in the ethos of violence.

Now, as our nation grows more centralized, our energy more concentrated, our inner tensions more desperate, our frustrations in our own land and in the world more embittered, we can no longer regard hatred and violence as accidents and aberrations, as nightmares which will pass away when we awake. We must see them as organic in our national past; we must confront them; we must uncover the roots of hatred and violence and, through self-knowledge, move toward self-control. And we must exert every effort in the meantime to protect and strengthen the membranes of civility against the impulses of destruction.

In this effort, a special responsibility lies on our intellectual community. For one can expect primitive emotions on the part of those who occupy the right wing of our national politics. But the intellectual community should be the particular custodian of the life of reason. It should be the particular champion of discipline and restraint. It should be the particular enemy of hatred and violence.

Little is more dismaying than the way in which some, a few, in the intellectual community have rejected the life of reason, have succumbed to the national susceptibility for hatred and violence, have, indeed, begun themselves to exalt hatred and violence as if primitivism in emotion constituted a higher morality. I do not suggest that such intellectuals are responsible for the atrocities committed at home and abroad. I do suggest that they have contributed to the atmosphere which has begun to legitimize hatred and violence. I do suggest that they are reinforcing the assault on civility and hastening the decomposition of the American social process.

Some wonder, no doubt, whether that social process is worth saving. But the alternative to process is anarchy, where those who use the means of violence win out; and the intellectual community will always lose in this competition. Our process, with all its defects, is a process of change—peaceful change—on which all decency and rationality depend. . . .

The very weight of these contradictions has produced a rush of despair about libertarian democracy itself. By libertarian democracy I mean simply the system in which the rule of the majority at any given time rests on the guarantee of the right of minorities to convert themselves into new majorities. Such a system assumes political action to be in its essence a rational process—that is, a deliberate choice of means to achieve desired ends. As a rational process, libertarian democracy requires the widest possible freedom of discussion and debate; and this implies, of course, a considerable indulgence of wrongheadedness and imbecility along the way.

This has been the American theory, as laid down, for example, in the Constitution and the Bill of Rights. And, in the course of our national history, libertarian democracy has led to many useful results. It has also led to many frustrations. It has left problems unsolved, wrongs unredressed, and sinners unpunished. It cannot be relied upon to produce rapid and conclusive change. The very insistence on reasonableness and due process has seemed at times a pretext for inaction and therefore a mask for injustice. This has been particularly the case in recent years. From the moment we started bombing North Vietnam in February 1965, our government appeared rigidly and sanctimoniously unresponsive to reasoned criticism of its course. Increasingly persuaded that change was impossible within the constitutional order, people started to turn to civil disobedience, emotional agitation, and even violent protest. A sense began to arise that libertarian democracy itself was impotent in the new world of economic, military, and intellectual corporatism. One saw a growing conviction, especially among the young, that party politics were a façade and a fake. One saw a growing cynicism about democratic institutions, a growing defection from the democratic process. In due course, the spreading sense of the impotence of libertarian democracy generated a creed systematically and candidly opposed to libertarian democracy.

The new creed has two parts. The first part is an attempt to clear away what its theorists regard as the noxious rubbish of the Bill of Rights. The new creed thus perceives the First Amendment as the keystone, not of liberty, but of a wicked apparatus of tolerance employed by an oppressive social order to thwart basic change. I do not wish to do this new doctrine an injustice, so I will state in the words of its leading advocate—that is, Herbert Marcuse—its belief that it is *necessary* and *right*, as a matter of principle, to suppress views with which one disagrees and to howl down those who utter such views.

Mr. Marcuse begins with the proposition that contemporary society has absorbed and abolished the historic means of social revolution. It has done this through an ingenious and despicable combination of welfarism, tolerance, and manipulation. Capitalism, in short, subverts potential opponents by offering a measure of apparent economic security and personal freedom.

Mr. Marcuse is determined to expose this state of affairs. As he sees it, any improvement in the condition of the powerless and the oppressed only plays into the hands of the rulers—and is therefore to be regretted. And the device of tolerance is particularly evil because it renders "the traditional ways and means of protest ineffective—perhaps even dangerous because they preserve the illusion of popular sovereignty."

The way to revive the hope of social change, Mr. Marcuse suggests, is therefore to do away with tolerance: "Certain things cannot be said, certain ideas cannot be expressed, certain policies cannot be proposed, certain behavior cannot be permitted without making tolerance an instrument for the continuation of servitude." He is commendably specific about what he would forbid. His program, as he states it,

> would include the withdrawal of toleration of speech and assembly from groups and movements which promote aggressive policies, armament, chauvinism, discrimination on the grounds of race and religions, or which oppose the extension of public services, medical care, etc. Moreover, the restoration of freedom of thought may necessitate new and rigid restrictions on teachings and practices in the educational institutions.

Mr. Marcuse's call for the forcible suppression of false ideas is, I have suggested, only the first part of the new creed. Nor is such an assault on the Bill of Rights new, even for radicals. The Stalinists of the 'thirties, for example, had no compunction in arguing in much the same way that civil freedom should be denied those who resist the Stalinist truth. What particularly distinguishes the New Left of the 'sixties from previous American radicalisms is the second part of its creed—and here not the summons to revolution, which again is familiar, but the refusal to state revolutionary goals except in the most abstract and empty language. To put it more precisely, what distinguishes the New Left is not only its unwillingness to define what it aims for after the revolution but its belief that such reticence is a virtue.

On its positive side, the new creed becomes, so to speak, a kind of existentialism in politics—a primitive kind, no doubt, but still rooted in some manner in the existential perception that man dwells in an absurd universe and defines himself through his choices. In extreme cases, this perception may lead to *voyages au bout de la nuit*: as Nietzsche said, "Nihilism represents the ultimate logical conclusion of our great values and ideals—because we must experience nihilism before we can find out what value these 'values' really had." In its serious form, existentialism can lead to an immense and intense sense of individual responsibility as every man realizes that only he can provide his own escape from the enveloping nothingness around him. In its vulgar form, however, with which we are dealing here, existential politics becomes the notion that we must feel and act before we think; it is the illusion that the experience of feeling and action will produce the insight and the policy.

Existential politics in this form springs much more from Sorel than from Kierkegaard. Georges Sorel, you will recall, drew a distinction between myths, which, he said, were "not descriptions of things, but expressions of a determination to act," and utopias, which were intellectual products, the work of theorists who "seek to establish a model to which they can compare existing society." Sorel regarded utopias—that is, rational programs—as contemptible. The myth must be the basis of action; the myth would produce the revolution, which would thereafter produce its own program; and "the myth," Sorel emphasized, "must be judged as a means of acting on the present; any attempt to discuss how far it can be taken literally as future history is devoid of sense." So, in the footsteps of Sorel, the New Leftists believe in the omnipotence of the deed and the irrelevance of the goal. The political process is no longer seen as the deliberate choice of means to move toward a desired end. Where libertarian democracy had ideally demanded means consistent with the end, and where the Stalinist left of the 'thirties contended that the end justified the means, the New Left propounds a different doctrine: that the means create the end.

Let us not ignore the attractions of the existential approach. After all, there are many absurdities in our world. Our country has never undertaken anything more absurd in its history than the Vietnam war. After all, a man does make himself by his decisions. After all, our conventional liberalism is to a discouraging degree a liberalism of promises and excuses. After all, social renewal can only come from personal commitment.

All these things help explain, I think, the appeal of the new creed. Yet this creed contains so much in the way of fakery and fallacy—to put it bluntly, it is so preposterous and so depraved—that I do not see how it can be long entertained by any serious democrat.

Let us look first at the negative part; the demand for the forcible suppression of false ideas. This immediately raises a self-evident question: how is one to tell which ideas are admissible and which are to be suppressed? "In the interplay of theory and practice," Mr. Marcuse replies, "true and false solutions become distinguishable. . . . Freedom is liberation, a specific historical process in theory and practice, and as such it has its right and wrong, its truth and falsehood." But who is to make this determination? What agency is the repository of final judgment on truth and falsehood? Here, alas, Mr. Marcuse lets us down. His standards are hopelessly vague, and in the end he places his confidence in what he mystically calls "the democratic educational dictatorship of free men."

This is not very satisfactory; so let us pursue the question a step further. I suppose that the new creed does not expect to make such judgments through a man. But, if not through a man, these judgments must be made through a mechanism, which means through men. Such a mechanism would plainly have to have an extraordinary degree of power. What assurance can there ever be that this power would be used disinterestedly—that is, for the good and the true, should there ever be a means of defining the good and the true—rather than in the interests of the men operating the mechanism? What will this mechanism become—what have such mechanisms ever become—but a means for the suppression of all criticism of the manipulators of the mechanism? So the mechanism, in the end, rests on an assumption of human infallibility.

But the assumption of human infallibility has never been justified in the long and varied history of mankind. It implies the rule of those whom Mr. Dooley long ago defined as men who do what they think "th' Lord wud do if He only knew the facts in th' case"—and Mr. Dooley was defining a fanatic.

Not only do men who claim infallibility in politics do far more evil than good; but the systematic suppression of supposedly false ideas would deeply constrict and impoverish human knowledge and understanding. "There is no error so crooked," Tupper said, "but it hath in it some lines of truth." Or, as Norman Mailer recently put it, "Sometimes a profound idea is buried in a particularly ugly notion." Human creativity takes a marvelous and sinister diversity of forms. How dare anyone assume the right to censor and deny the unlimited freedom of human expression? "I tolerate with the utmost latitude the right of others to differ from me in opinion without imputing to them criminality," wrote Jefferson. "I know too well the weakness and uncertainty of human reason to wonder at its different result."

The demand for the forcible suppression of "false" ideas would be an enormously effective way of calling a halt to human progress. Nor does the other half of the new creed make any more sense: that is, the conviction that one should feel and act first and think later, that the means create the end. The kind of action supremely required to strike through the mask of official society, we are told, is violence. Without violence, official society, in its present sophisticated condition, will calmly co-opt and emasculate the opposition. Only violence will force official society to drop the smiling mask of tolerance and reveal its inner viciousness. More than this, violence becomes a means of social and individual redemption. As Frantz Fanon has written, "Violence is a cleaning force. It frees the native from his inferiority complex and from his despair and inaction; it makes him fearless and restores his self-respect. . . . Violence alone, violence committed by the people, violence organized and educated by its leaders, makes it possible for the masses to understand social truths."

Plato

REPUBLIC

In these passages from the *Republic*, Plato defends censorship.

BOOK II

You know, I [Socrates] said, that we begin by telling children stories which, though not wholly destitute of truth, are in the main fictitious; and these stories are told them when they are not of an age to learn gymnastics.

Very true. . . .

You know also that the beginning is the most important part of any work, especially in the case of a young and tender thing; for that is the time at which the character is being formed and the desired impression is more readily taken.

Quite true.

And shall we just carelessly allow children to hear any casual tales which may be devised by casual persons, and receive into their minds ideas for the most part the very opposite of those which we should wish them to have when they are grown up?

We cannot.

Then the first thing will be to establish a censorship of the writers of fiction, and let the censors receive any tale of fiction which is good, and reject the bad; and we will desire mothers and nurses to tell their children the authorised ones only. Let them fashion the mind with such tales, even more fondly than they mould the body with their hands; but most of those which are now in use must be discarded. . . .

BOOK X

. . . we have not yet brought forward the heaviest count in our accusation:— the power which poetry has of harming even the good (and there are very few who are not harmed), is surely an awful thing?

Yes, certainly, if the effect is what you say.

Hear and judge: The best of us, as I conceive, when we listen to a passage of Homer, or one of the tragedians, in which he represents some pitiful hero who is drawling out his sorrows in a long oration, or weeping, and smiting his breast—the best of us, you know, delight in giving way to sympathy, and are in raptures at the excellence of the poet who stirs our feelings most.

Yes, of course I know.

But when any sorrow of our own happens to us, then you may observe that we pride ourselves on the opposite quality—we would fain be quiet and patient; this is the manly part, and the other which delighted us in the recitation is now deemed to be the part of a woman.

Very true, he said.

Now can we be right in praising and admiring another who is doing that which any one of us would abominate and be ashamed of in his own person?

No, he said, that is certainly not reasonable.

Nay, I said, quite reasonable from one point of view.

What point of view?

If you consider, I said, that when in misfortune we feel a natural hunger and desire to relieve our sorrow by weeping and lamentation, and that this feeling which is kept under control in our own calamities is satisfied and delighted by the poets;—the better nature in each of us, not having been sufficiently trained by reason or habit, allows the sympathetic element to break loose because the sorrow is another's; and the spectator fancies that there can be no disgrace to himself in praising and pitying any one who comes telling him what a good man he is, and making a fuss about his troubles; he thinks that the pleasure is a gain, and why should he be supercilious and lose this and the poem too? Few persons ever reflect, as I should imagine, that from the evil of other men something is communicated to themselves. And so the feeling of sorrow which has gathered strength at the sight of the misfortunes of others is with difficulty repressed in our own.

How very true.

And does not the same hold also of the ridiculous? There are jests which you would be ashamed to make yourself, and yet on the comic stage, or indeed in private, when you hear them, you are greatly amused by them, and are not at all disgusted at their unseemliness;—the case of pity is repeated;—there is a principle in human nature which is disposed to raise a laugh, and this which you once restrained by reason, because you were afraid of being thought a buffoon, is now let out again; and having stimulated the risible faculty at the theatre, you are betrayed unconsciously to yourself into playing the comic poet at home.

Quite true, he said.

And the same may be said of lust and anger and all the other affections, of desire and pain and pleasure, which are held to be inseparable from every action—in all of them poetry feeds and waters the passions instead of drying them up; she lets them rule, although they ought to be controlled, if mankind are ever to increase in happiness and virtue.

I cannot deny it.

Therefore, Glaucon, I said, whenever you meet with any of the eulogists of Homer declaring that he has been the educator of Hellas, and that he is profitable for education and for the ordering of human things, and that you should take him up again and again and get to know him and regulate your whole life according to him, we may love and honour those who say these things—they are excellent people as far as their lights extend; and we are ready to acknowledge that Homer is the greatest of poets and first of tragedy writers; but we must remain firm in our conviction that hymns to the gods and praises of famous men are the only poetry which ought to be admitted into our State. For if you go beyond this and allow the honeyed muse to enter, either in epic or lyric verse, not law and the reason of mankind, which by common consent have ever been deemed best, but pleasure and pain will be the rulers in our State.

That is most true, he said.

And now since we have reverted to the subject of poetry, let this our defence serve to show the reasonableness of our former judgment in sending away out of our State an art having the tendencies which we have described, for reason constrained us.

We too are inspired by that love of poetry which the education of noble States has implanted in us, and therefore we would have her appear at her best and truest; but so long as she is unable to make good her defence, this argument of ours shall be a charm to us, which we will repeat to ourselves while we listen to her strains; that we may not fall away into the childish love of her which captivates the many. At all events we are well aware that poetry being such as we have described is not to be regarded seriously as attaining to the truth; and he who listens to her, fearing for the safety of the city which is within him, should be on his guard against her seductions and make our words his law.

Yes, he said, I quite agree with you.

Yes, I said, my dear Glaucon, for great is the issue at stake, greater than appears, whether a man is to be good or bad. And what will any one be profited if under the influence of honour or money or power, aye, or under the excitement of poetry, he neglect justice and virtue?

Thomas Hobbes

LEVIATHAN

Thomas Hobbes argues in *Leviathan* that the supposed right to
freedom of speech and press must be sharply curtailed.

It is annexed to the sovereignty to be judge of what opinions and doctrines are
averse and what conducing to peace; and consequently, on what occasions,
how far, and what men are to be trusted withal, in speaking to multitudes of
people, and who shall examine the doctrines of all books before they be published. For the actions of men proceed from their opinions, and in the well
governing of opinions consisteth the well-governing of men's actions, in order
to their peace and concord. And though in matter of doctrine nothing ought to
be regarded but the truth; yet this is not repugnant to regulating the same by
peace. For doctrine repugnant to peace can be no more true than peace and
concord can be against the law of Nature. It is true that in a commonwealth,
where, by the negligence or unskillfulness of governors and teachers, false
doctrines are by time generally received; the contrary truths may be generally
offensive. Yet the most sudden and rough bursting in of a new truth that can
be, does never break the peace, but only sometimes awake the war. For those
men that are so remissly governed, that they dare take up arms to defend or
introduce an opinion, are still in war; and their condition not peace, but only a
cessation of arms for fear of one another; and they live, as it were, in the
precincts of battle continually. It belongeth therefore to him that hath the
sovereign power to be judge, or constitute all judges of opinions and doctrines,
as a thing necessary to peace, thereby to prevent discord and civil war.

John Stuart Mill

ON LIBERTY

A celebrated modern defense of freedom of thought and speech is to be found in "On Liberty" by John Stuart Mill (1806–1873).

The time, it is to be hoped, is gone by, when any defense would be necessary of the "liberty of the press" as one of the securities against corrupt or tyrannical government. No argument, we may suppose, can now be needed, against permitting a legislature or an executive, not identified in interest with the people, to prescribe opinions to them, and determine what doctrines or what arguments they shall be allowed to hear. This aspect of the question, besides, has been so often and so triumphantly enforced by preceding writers, that it needs not be specially insisted on in this place. . . . it is not, in constitutional countries, to be apprehended, that the government, whether completely responsible to the people or not, will often attempt to control the expression of opinion, except when in doing so it makes itself the organ of the general intolerance of the public. Let us suppose, therefore, that the government is entirely at one with the people, and never thinks of exerting any power of coercion unless in agreement with what it conceives to be their voice. But I deny the right of the people to exercise such coercion, either by themselves or by their government. The power itself is illegitimate. The best government has no more title to it than the worst. It is as noxious, or more noxious, when exerted in accordance with public opinion, than when in opposition to it. If all mankind minus one were of one opinion, and only one person were of the contrary opinion, mankind would be no more justified in silencing that one person, than he, if he had the power, would be justified in silencing mankind. . . . the peculiar evil of silencing the expression of an opinion is, that it is robbing the human race; posterity as well as the existing generation; those who dissent from the opinion, still more than those who hold it. If the opinion is right, they are deprived of the opportunity of exchanging error for truth: if wrong, they lose, what is almost as great a benefit, the clearer perception and livelier impression of truth, produced by its collision with error.

. . . The opinion which it is attempted to suppress by authority may possibly be true. Those who desire to suppress it, of course deny its truth; but they are not infallible. They have no authority to decide the question for all mankind, and exclude every other person from the means of judging. To refuse a hearing to an opinion, because they are sure that it is false, is to assume that *their* certainty is the same thing as *absolute* certainty. All silencing of discussion is an assumption of infallibility. Its condemnation may be allowed to rest on this common argument, not the worse for being common.

Unfortunately for the good sense of mankind, the fact of their fallibility is far from carrying the weight in their practical judgment, which is always allowed to it in theory; for while every one well knows himself to be fallible, few think it necessary to take any precautions against their own fallibility, or admit the supposition that any opinion, of which they feel very certain, may be one of the examples of the error to which they acknowledge themselves to be liable. . . . for in proportion to a man's want of confidence in his own solitary judgment, does he usually repose, with implicit trust, on the infallibility of "the world" in general. And the world, to each individual, means the part of it with which he comes in contact; his party, his sect, his church, his class of society: the man may be called, by comparison, almost liberal and large-minded to whom it means anything so comprehensive as his own country or his own age. Nor is his faith in this collective authority at all shaken by his being aware that other ages, countries, sects, churches, classes, and parties have thought, and even now think, the exact reverse. He devolves upon his own world the responsibility of being in the right against the dissentient worlds of other people; and it never troubles him that mere accident has decided which of these numerous worlds is the object of his reliance, and that the same causes which make him a Churchman in London, would have made him a Buddhist or Confucian in Pekin. Yet it is as evident in itself, as any amount of argument can make it, that ages are no more infallible than individuals; every age having held many opinions which subsequent ages have deemed not only false but absurd; and it is as certain that many opinions, now general, will be rejected by future ages, as it is that many, once general, are rejected by the present.

Complete liberty of contradicting and disproving our opinion, is the very condition which justifies us in assuming its truth for purposes of action; and on no other terms can a being with human faculties have any rational assurance of being right. . . .

There must be discussion, to show how experience is to be interpreted. Wrong opinions and practices gradually yield to fact and argument: but facts and arguments, to produce any effect on the mind, must be brought before it. Very few facts are able to tell their own story, without comments to bring out their meaning. The whole strength and value, then, of human judgment, depending on the one property, that it can be set right when it is wrong, reliance can be placed on it only when the means of setting it right are kept constantly at hand. . . . Strange it is, that men should admit the validity of the arguments for free discussion, but object to their being "pushed to an extreme"; not seeing that unless the reasons are good for an extreme case, they are not good for any case. Strange that they should imagine that they are not assuming infallibility, when they acknowledge that there should be free discussion on all subjects which can possibly be *doubtful*, but think that some particular principle or doctrine should be forbidden to be questioned because it is so *certain*, that is, because *they are certain* that it is certain. To call any proposition certain, while there is any one who would deny its certainty if permitted, but who is not permitted, is to assume that we ourselves, and those who agree with us, are the judges of certainty, and judges without hearing the other side.

Mankind can hardly be too often reminded, that there was once a man named Socrates, between whom and the legal authorities and public opinion of his time, there took place a memorable collision. Born in an age and country abounding in individual greatness, this man has been handed down to us by those who best knew both him and the age, as the most virtuous man in it; while *we* know him as the head and prototype of all subsequent teachers of virtue. . . . This acknowledged master of all the eminent thinkers who have since lived—whose fame, still growing after more than two thousand years, all but outweighs the whole remainder of the names which make his native city illustrious—was put to death by his countrymen, after a judicial conviction, for impiety and immorality. Impiety, in denying the gods recognized by the State; indeed his accuser asserted (see the *Apologia*) that he believed in no gods at all. Immorality, in being, by his doctrines and instructions, a "corrupter of youth." Of these charges the tribunal, there is every ground for believing, honestly found him guilty, and condemned the man who probably of all then born had deserved the best of mankind, to be put to death as a criminal.

To pass from this to the only other instance of judicial iniquity, the mention of which, after the condemnation of Socrates, would not be an anti-climax: the event which took place on Calvary rather more than eighteen hundred years ago. The man who left on the memory of those who witnessed his life and conversation, such an impression of his moral grandeur, that eighteen subsequent centuries have done homage to him as the Almighty in person, was ignominiously put to death, as what? As a blasphemer. Men did not merely mistake their benefactor; they mistook him for the exact contrary of what he was, and treated him as that prodigy of impiety, which they themselves are now held to be, for their treatment of him. The feelings with which mankind now regard these lamentable transactions, especially the later of the two, render them extremely unjust in their judgment of the unhappy actors. These were, to all appearance, not bad men—not worse than men commonly are, but rather the contrary; men who possessed in a full, or somewhat more than a full measure, the religious, moral, and patriotic feelings of their time and people. . . .

Let us now pass to the second division of the argument, and dismissing the supposition that any of the received opinions may be false, let us assume them to be true, and examine into the worth of the manner in which they are likely to be held, when their truth is not freely and openly canvassed. However unwillingly a person who has a strong opinion may admit the possibility that his opinion may be false, he ought to be moved by the consideration that however true it may be, if it is not fully, frequently, and fearlessly discussed, it will be held as a dead dogma, not a living truth.

It |the necessity of free discussion| is illustrated in the experience of almost all ethical doctrines and religious creeds. They are full of meaning and vitality to those who originate them, and to the direct disciples of the originators. Their meaning continues to be felt in undiminished strength, and is perhaps brought out into even fuller consciousness, so long as the struggle lasts to give the doctrine or creed an ascendancy over other creeds. At last it either prevails, and becomes the general opinion, or its progress stops; it keeps possession of the ground it has gained, but ceases to spread further. When either of these results has become apparent, controversy on the subject flags, and gradually dies away. The doctrine has taken its place, if not as a received opinion, as one of the admitted sects or divisions of opinion: those who hold it have generally inherited, not adopted it; and conversion from one of these doctrines to another, being now an exceptional fact, occupies little place in the thoughts of their professors. Instead of being, as at first, constantly on the alert either to defend themselves against the world, or to bring the world over to them, they have subsided into acquiescence, and neither listen, when they can help it, to arguments against their creed, nor trouble dissentients (if there be such) with arguments in its favor. From this time may usually be dated the decline in the living power of the doctrine.

. . . We have hitherto considered only two possibilities: that the received opinion may be false, and some other opinion, consequently, true; or that, the received opinion being true, a conflict with the opposite error is essential to a clear apprehension and deep feeling of its truth. But there is a commoner case than either of these; when the conflicting doctrines, instead of being one true and the other false, share the truth between them; and the nonconforming opinion is needed to supply the remainder of the truth, of which the received doctrine embodies only a part. Popular opinions . . . are often true, but seldom or never the whole truth. They are a part of the truth; sometimes a greater, sometimes a smaller part, but exaggerated, distorted, and disjoined from the truths by which they ought to be accompanied and limited. Heretical opinions, on the other hand, are generally some of these suppressed and neglected truths, bursting the bonds which kept them down, and either seeking reconciliation with the truth contained in the common opinion, or fronting it as enemies. . . .

Truth, in the greater practical concerns of life, is so much a question of the reconciling and combining of opposites, that very few have minds sufficiently capacious and impartial to make the adjustment with an approach to correctness, and it has to be made by the rough process of a struggle between combatants fighting under hostile banners. On any of the great questions, . . . if either of the two opinions has a better claim than the other, not merely to be tolerated, but to be encouraged and countenanced, it is the one which happens at the particular time and place to be in a minority. That is the opinion which, for the time being, represents the neglected interests, the side of human well-being which is in danger of obtaining less than its share.

. . . Since there are few mental attributes more rare than that judicial faculty which can sit in intelligent judgment between two sides of a question, of which only one is represented by an advocate before it, truth has no chance but in proportion as every side of it, every opinion which embodies any fraction of the truth, not only finds advocates, but is so advocated as to be listened to.

We have now recognized the necessity to the mental well-being of mankind (on which all their other well-being depends) of freedom of opinion, and freedom of the expression of opinion, on four distinct grounds; which we will now briefly recapitulate.

First, if any opinion is compelled to silence, that opinion may, for aught we can certainly know, be true. To deny this is to assume our own infallibility.

Secondly, though the silenced opinion be an error, it may, and very commonly does, contain a portion of truth; and since the general or prevailing opinion on any subject is rarely or never the whole truth, it is only by the collision of adverse opinions that the remainder of the truth has any chance of being supplied.

Thirdly, even if the received opinion be not only true, but the whole truth, unless it is suffered to be, and actually is, vigorously and earnestly contested, it will, by most of those who receive it, be held in the manner of a prejudice, with little comprehension or feeling of its rational grounds. And not only this, but, fourthly, the meaning of the doctrine itself will be in danger of being lost, or enfeebled, and deprived of its vital effect on the character and conduct: the dogma becoming a mere formal profession, inefficacious for good, but cumbering the ground, and preventing the growth of any real and heart-felt conviction, from reason or personal experience.

Anthony Comstock

TRAPS FOR THE YOUNG

Anthony Comstock (1844–1915) tried in his writings to expose
the dangers of "lust" and licentious literature. The following is
a passage from his *Traps for the Young.*

This moral vulture [obscenity] steals upon our youth in the home, school, and
college, silently striking its terrible talons into their vitals, and forcibly bearing
them away on hideous wings to shame and death. Like a cancer, it fastens itself
upon the imagination, and sends down into the future life thousands of roots,
poisoning the nature, enervating the system, destroying self-respect, fettering
the will power, defiling the mind, corrupting the thoughts, leading to secret
practises of most foul and revolting character, until the victim tires of life, and
existence is scarcely endurable. It sears the conscience, hardens the heart, and
damns the soul. It leads to lust and lust breeds unhallowed living, and sinks
man, made in the image of God, below the level of the beasts. There is no force
at work in the community more insidious, more constant in its demands, or
more powerful and far reaching than lust. *It is the constant companion of all other
crimes.* It is honeycombing society. Like a frightful monster, it stands peering
over the sleeping child, to catch its first thoughts on awakening. This is especially true when the eye of youth has been defiled with scenes of lasciviousness
in the weekly criminal papers, or by their offspring obscene books and pictures.
The peace of the family is wrecked, homes desolated, and society degraded,
while it curses more and more each generation born into the world.

Think of the homes that are wrecked by unbridled passion, of the curse that
falls upon any community when there is spread before the eyes of all classes by
the newspaper gossip, the inner secrets of those whited sepulchres, those
moral monsters, who, stripped of all sense of shame, parade their foul living in
the courts. . . .

I repeat, *lust is the boon companion of all other crimes.* There is no evil so extensive,
none doing more to destroy the institutions of free America. It sets aside the

laws of God and morality; marriage bonds are broken, most sacred ties severed, State laws ignored, and dens of infamy plant themselves in almost every community, and then reaching out like immense cuttlefish, draw in, from all sides, our youth to destruction. . . .

Many a parent sends away the child [to school] pure, fresh, and vigorous. He comes back, after a few years' absence, with pale cheeks, lustreless and sunken eyes, enervated body, moody, nervous, and irritable—a moral wreck—and the parents mourn "that the child has studied too hard." If they could get at the real trouble, it would be found that the child has fallen into one of those lust-traps, or death traps by mail. Habits thus formed many a youth promises himself he will check at a certain date; that when he is a man, or twenty-one years of age, he will stop his vicious practises. Ah! silly boy, the shackles of habit you will never be able to throw off by your own unaided strength. The longer indulgence continues, the weaker you become to will and do against the force within. The standard of self-respect is being constantly lowered, and the will weakened. *The time to stop is before you begin.*

Where does this evil exist? Where are the traps set? I reply, everywhere. Children of all grades in society, institutions of learning in all sections of the land, and the most select homes, are invaded by the evil of licentious literature.

John Ciardi

WHAT IS PORNOGRAPHY?

Former editor of the *Saturday Review* John Ciardi (b. 1916) argues that the novel *Fanny Hill* is pornographic but that it should not be banned for being such.

John Cleland's memoirs of a woman of pleasure (often known as *Fanny Hill*) has been published in the United States by G. P. Putnam's Sons, and its publication certainly opens a new level of discussion in the ever-raging debate on book censorship.

The book banners have defended censorship on the grounds that "pornographic literature" tends to incite the young to lewd, lascivious, indecent, and generally parental behavior. There have been minor variations on this theme, but as a regular thing the expressed concern of the censors has been the teen-ager rather than the adult and the fear has been that "pornography"— whatever one intends by the word—will damage the sensibilities, habits, and moral standards of adolescents.

For myself I must believe that the sensibilities of the young are determined not by their reading habits but by the tone of the society in which they live, and that their habits and moral standards are determined by the persuasions of what gets called their "peer group," countered (as one may hope) by the example set for them by their parents. Reading, to be sure, can be a far-reaching influence upon thoughtful adolescents but it is not their reading habits that determine their attitudes toward life, sex, and social responsibility. It is, rather, their attitudes that determine their reading habits.

So persuaded, I have defended one banned book after another because I believed in each case that the author was seriously (with or without talent, but seriously) trying to give form to his impressions of life as he had found it to be.

The now practically forgotten furor over four-letter words in World War II novels is relevant. Any man trying to set on paper what he experienced in the dog-face army of our hope inevitably has a problem. Civilians, as a general thing, do not permit themselves the kind of Anglo-Saxon points of emphasis that pepper G.I. talk. And a good thing, too. Yet a man who has been there and who wants to describe how it really was, cannot help but feel dishonest if he censors the talk. (I cannot resist noting, after a random survey of "sexy" titles sold under the counter along 42nd Street in New York City, that genuine pornography seems to avoid all four-letter words and to render its sexier passages in high flights of pseudo-poetic verbiage full of cosmic mixed metaphors.) The serious writer's urge to be realistic, on the other hand, is an inextricable part of his esthetic seriousness. He is likely, in fact, to become impassioned at the civilian protestations and to argue that if Aunt Jane can let the boys fight, die, and be bored for her freedom, she can humping damn well be made to listen to the vocabulary of her freedom as it was exercised in the crotch-deep mud of the stinking fact there are no parades for.

One may disagree with what the author takes to be necessary reality, but those who decry the honesty of such an author's seriousness must certainly open themselves to the charge of refusing reality. For the artist to concur in the parental habit of sweeping sex under the rug is to destroy his sense of honesty. The parents did, after all, beget their children by some sort of sexual approximation, though evidently in half-guilt about the whole thing, and in terror of admitting any approximate reality to the discussion. By and large Americans have managed to make "sex" a dirty word. Collaterally, the American parent has been ever ready to unload some of his own guilt feelings onto a vaguely defined idea of "pornography." All of us, alas, live in a social conspiracy to commit sexual hypocrisy. In defending the freedom of serious writers to describe life as they think they have observed it, I have, as I believe, defended a necessary honesty.

In the past, however, my defense has always been of books written with a serious intent to give form to an idea of reality. No such claim, as I see it, can be made for Cleland's *Memoirs*.

The book, elegantly styled to the mannerisms of eighteenth-century diction, is derived from the picaresque novel by way of the episodic sexual adventures of such a female rogue as DeFoe's Moll Flanders, and from the simpering protestations of such a roguish and self-seeking hypocrite as Richardson's Pamela.

The *Memoirs*, that is to say, has an admirable ancestry. By now, moreover, it is an established literary curiosity, and Cleland's skill as a stylist, as an observer of human motives, and as a reporter of the fads of his age can be argued to provide the literary historian with some valuable, if incidental, footnotes.

With all scholarly details in place, however, and with all incidental stylistic merits recognized, the book still remains an overt piece of pornography. It was conceived and written with no intent but to titillate the reader by ringing the sexual changes in minute (and yet evasive) detail, the author's catalogue of sexual variations being limited only (and considerably) by his own lack of imagination. (He might at least have read the classics and given Roman substance to English mannerism.) With Cleland's series of sexual encounters there is no effort to depict the lives of men and women seriously. The details of sexuality are, in fact, suggestively exaggerated. The seeming naïveté of Fanny's memoirs is not the result of simplicity, but is an artful coloration of the tone, clearly designed to heighten the suggestiveness of the sexual narration. And the author himself could not have begun to believe that life in a London brothel was remotely as he described it.

I am not well disposed, let me say, to banning any book. I believe that parents who have reared their children in sympathy, and yet within a sense of this world as it goes, have nothing to fear from what the children read. And it is always likely—it seems, in fact, certain—that any statute framed to suppress pornography will be used to suppress the work of serious writers. It is, I believe, socially irresponsible to let moral indignation bring about statutes that cannot, by their nature, be responsibly phrased to cover all cases. The only consequence of such statutes is that the good will be damned with the bad—a clear affront to the legal principle that it is better for a hundred guilty persons to go free than to punish one innocent person. These, I submit, are ponderable reasons for opposing legal censorship of any sort, and I must take them to be sufficient.

But to the specific question "Is the *Memoirs* a pornographic book?" I can give only one answer.

It certainly is: it was written as such, it has had a clandestine history in which all scholars have held it to be such, and such it is today and will be to the dark end of time's last bookshelf.

5
PHILOSOPHY OF RELIGION

This chapter deals with two issues central to the philosophy of religion: Does God exist? How can evil exist if God is all-wise, all-powerful, and all-good? The reading materials that follow start from modern debates on these questions and then turn to earlier essays by great philosophers of the past. Our own discussion will begin with the first question, "Does God exist?"

The concept of God that is part and parcel of the Judeo-Christian tradition is a unique one; indeed, some religions—Buddhism, for example—do not have the notion of a divine being at all. For Buddhists, the Buddha was not a God in the Western sense; rather they perceived him as an exceptionally wise man whose precepts about life were profound, yet simple to understand. He is worshiped because he formulated a code of life that inspired emulation. In Western terms he might be regarded as an exceptionally enlightened prophet. The idea central to Judaism and Christianity that there is only one God is also not a universal conception. The Babylonians, Egyptians, Greeks, and Romans, among others, worshiped a plurality of gods. Indeed, their gods were often conceived with a human appearance and character traits: they were loving, quarrelsome, aggressive, and warlike. They differed from humans essentially in their immortality.

In the Judeo-Christian tradition, God is the sole creator of the universe. He is invisible, intangible, and possessed of infinitely powerful attributes. This conception is virtually unique in human history, so that there is little wonder that the existence question has arisen mainly in Western culture. Since God is not accessible in any way to the senses, there is no way by direct observation to prove that He exists. Of course, there are written materials that make this assertion. These are regarded by devotees of these religions as sacred texts whose authenticity is beyond question. Others have challenged this point of view, arguing that books are written by humans and that such appeals are not decisive.

In general, philosophers have sought other ways of establishing that God, as so conceived, does exist. These range from appeals to very unusual personal experiences such as revelations or mystic insights to powerful and articulate logical arguments. Our readings cover a broad segment, though not all, of this range of approaches. Our emphasis will be upon argumentation, broadly construed. We will examine three of the most common and famous arguments that philosophers have advanced to prove that God exists.

The first is called the argument from design, an example of which will be found in a selection taken from Isaac Newton's *Principia Mathematica*. Newton, one of the greatest scientists of all time, felt that the uniform laws that nature exhibits, in particular the laws of planetary motion, could not be accidental products. As he wrote, "This most beautiful system of the sun, planets, and comets could only proceed from the counsel and dominion of an intelligent and powerful Being." A similar argument is expressed by one of the protagonists of Hume's "Dialogues Concerning Natural Religion," Cleanthes. His argument rests upon an analogy. It claims that the universe is analogous to a giant machine. Since all machines are created by someone rational, it follows that the universe must have been created by someone rational—God. Accordingly, God exists.

Each element of the argument is supported by evidence. Cleanthes holds that machines are always created by rational creatures—we never find a watch or an automobile that just grew naturally, as, say, a tree or plant might. And this seems like a very plausible contention. Second, Cleanthes argues that the universe is like a machine, and this assertion he also supports by evidence. A simple example will illustrate the power of this point, which is similar to Newton's. In the eighteenth century, a German astronomer named Johann Bode discovered a relationship between the size of the planets and their distance from the sun, and that this relationship could be expressed quite precisely in terms of a simple arithmetical progression (Newton uses similar examples from astronomy). What Bode's Law seems to show is that the solar system resembles a massive machine, with every part standing in a specific relationship to every other part, all in accordance with discoverable mathematical formulae. This view was strengthened in the nineteenth century when John Adams and Urbain Jean Joseph Leverrier, working independently, noticed certain irregularities in the predicted orbit of Uranus. Assuming the truth of physical laws they inferred that there must still be another planet beyond Uranus, and the discovery of Neptune by telescopic observation confirmed this prediction. What this example seems to show is that the universe exhibits the kind of regularity and predictability we find in machines. If the motor in our car begins to run irregularly, we can predict, if we have mechanical knowledge, where the source of the difficulty is likely to lie. Is there any difference between a prediction about the irregularity of a planet's orbit and that of a motor? Not according to Newton and Cleanthes—though, of course, the universe is larger and enormously more complicated. But they would say that these are only differences of degree, not of kind. So the fact that we can predict from a knowledge of one part of the system what must be the case elsewhere shows that the universe is a kind of machine. And if so, it must have a designer, since all machines, as we have already established, are produced by rational beings. Therefore, God exists.

This type of argument has been called an argument from experience. It rests upon past experience that every machine we have ever found has been created by an intelligent being and upon our experience of the sort of regularities that make something into a machine. As such, the argument at most could establish only with a high degree of probability that God exists. This conclusion does not *necessarily* follow, as it would in a purely logical argument.

Other philosophers have tried to develop stronger arguments that establish that there is a God with absolute certainty. One of the most famous of such arguments is the ontological argument of St. Anselm of Canterbury (1033–1109). It is to be found in its entirety in our selection from his *Proslogium*. Anselm's statement of the argument is very complicated. We might try to summarize it as follows. It is what logicians call an indirect argument, or a reductio ad absurdum. The basic idea is that for the reasons given earlier one cannot directly prove that there is a God, so one should approach the matter indirectly. One proves that the hypothesis that God does *not* exist leads to a contradiction, which means that the hypothesis in question is false. From this it follows that the negation of the hypothesis is true, and so it is true that God exists. Anselm's argument begins by drawing a distinction between things that exist only in the mind and things that exist in reality. He says that before a painter begins a painting, that painting exists in his mind. After he finishes the painting, it exists in reality. All persons have at least a minimal conception of God in their minds. Without necessarily fully knowing what God is, even a fool knows that nothing could be greater than God. Suppose one assumes that God exists only in the mind but not in reality. Then it would be possible to conceive of a being just like the one that exists in the mind, but which also exists in reality. This being would then have an additional feature—existing in reality—and would be greater than God. But this contradicts the premise that nothing can be greater than God; and one arrived at such a result only by assuming that God did not exist in reality. Accordingly, that assumption must be false, and God must exist in reality.

Anselm's argument is very clever. It does not rely upon any sort of observational evidence or an appeal to past experience. It holds that reason, *unassisted*, can prove there must be a God. This is a remarkable and powerful claim, and, of course, it has been challenged by philosophers since it first appeared (although we will not discuss criticisms of the argument here).

A third type of argument mixes reason and experience. Kant called it the cosmological proof. This argument has been accepted by the Catholic Church as providing a rational proof that God exists. In our group of readings we include a brief selection from Thomas Aquinas (1225–1274), greatest of the scholastic philosophers. Thomas provided five arguments—the so-called "five ways"—to demonstrate on rational grounds that God exists. Three of his five ways are variations of Kant's cosmological proof. The simplest is what Aquinas calls the argument from efficient causation. The argument starts with the statement that in the observable world we never find a case of something causing itself; this would entail that it precedes itself, which is not possible. Moreover, if one eliminates a cause, one eliminates an effect. We note that an event occurring today, say, is a last event in a series and had an immediately preceding cause, and that it itself had a cause, and so on. If it were possible to go on to infinity, that would mean there was no first (original) cause, and, if so, there could have been no second, third, and so on, up to the last event we just noticed. But since there is a last event, there must then be a beginning to the causal series: an event that is uncaused—and this we call God.

This is a mixed argument in that it begins with an appeal to evidence. We find, on the basis of evidence, that no event occurs without a cause; we find that if we remove the cause, we remove the effect; and we find that X, which we have just witnessed, is a last event. From these sorts of observations, the argument infers *logically* that there must be a first cause, which is itself uncaused. If there were not, the sequence of causes and effects would regress infinitely, which means that there would be no first cause; and if no first, then no succeeding effect; and if no succeeding effect, then no last effect. But there is a last effect and therefore there must be a first cause.

According to Kant, the only possible formal arguments for the existence of God are variants of the argument from design, the ontological proof, and the cosmological proof. But other philosophers have offered considerations for believing God's existence that differ from any of the above. Such considerations have been advanced by Blaise Pascal (1623–1662) in a selection from his *Pensées*; by William James, the American psychologist and philosopher (1842–1910) in his *Will to Believe*; and by Sören Kierkegaard (1813–1855) in his *Philosophical Fragments*. Though their specific proposals differ in various ways, the three philosophers agree that there can be no decisive proof, on the basis of either pure reason or evidence of the senses, that God exists.

Pascal's position is that the common man is in the position of a gambler. He is facing the question of whether there is a God or not. The stakes are high. If there is, he has everything to win and nothing to lose. If there is no God, he loses only what he puts into his commitment to abide by God's rules. James is in broad agreement with Pascal, but differs in emphasizing that what is at stake cannot be characterized in game-like language. At stake, rather, is a momentous life commitment. For James a momentous commitment is one that would change one's life. Some momentous commitments are forced—we either do them or reject them—like getting married, having children, becoming space pilots, and so on. Other commitments are not forced. I don't have to decide one way or another, so they are not momentous. One is not forced to take a stand about whether there is life on Mars. But one is forced to take a stand on the basic religious question, and the stand, James says, makes a real difference. Moreover, one is faced with what James calls a "forced option." One cannot refuse either to make the commitment or to withhold it—as one could refuse to bet. By refusing to make a commitment, one is exercising one possible option, that of denying that there is a God. But for James this is foolish; for if one refuses to make such a commitment and it should turn out that there is a God, one has indeed lost everything. James thus argues that on pragmatic grounds one should reconstruct one's life on the assumption that there is a God; and this will ultimately prove a useful and productive hypothesis. Even if in some ontological sense it should turn out that there is no God, acting as if there were will have enhanced one's life, so one will have been justified in following this course.

Kierkegaard's view is more radical than either of the above. He holds that no rational considerations of any sort are relevant to the question—including betting or evidence. Indeed, he holds that because of God's nature no kind of evidence could establish His existence. The matter is an ultimate mystery. In this situation one must simply make a commitment that goes beyond reason—one must take a "plunge into absurdity." One believes, as Tertullian had said in the third century, "because it is absurd." For Kierkegaard, to believe without reason is the true test of genuine religious commitment.

The question of God's existence is directly connected to the second question our readings cover—the problem of evil. This problem arises for a person who wishes to be an orthodox adherent to the familiar monotheistic religions such as Judaism and Christianity. These religions, as we have pointed out, hold that there is one all-wise, all-powerful, and all-good God. But if one accepts this description of the divinity, how can one explain the existence of evil? As the Greek philosopher Epicurus pointed out, if God is all-wise and all-powerful and if evil exists, He must not be benevolent. For being all-wise, He would have known how to prevent evil, and being all-powerful, He surely could have prevented it. It would seem that He must have *allowed* evil to exist and thus could not be all-good. Again, if one wishes to hold that God is all-good and that there is evil, then one cannot hold that God is all-wise and all-powerful. If He is all-good, then He would desire a world in which there is no evil. But if evil exists, then God either did not know how to prevent its occurrence or was not powerful enough to do so.

This problem appears in one of the world's oldest existing literatures, the Holy Scriptures, in particular in the Book of Job. There the problem is posed as one of God's justice. Job is depicted as a holy, sin-free man, to whom horrible things happen. How can God allow this? Either God is not powerful enough to prevent this from happening, or not wise enough to know how, or not good enough to want to. At the end of this beautifully written work, Job grovels in the dust, conceding that he cannot explain this mystery and asking for God's forgiveness for having questioned Him.

A variety of solutions to the problem will be found in the selections that follow. Some philosophers have held that what appears to be evil *really* isn't; if finite human beings had God's scope and vision they could see that what appears to be evil may really be a blessing in disguise. Another possibility is to modify or reinterpret the characteristics ordinarily ascribed to God. One might hold that as compared with humans, God's attributes seem "infinite," but that even these are limited. So that wise, good, and powerful though he is, there are some constraints on him and that evil arises because of such limitations.

An interesting attempt to solve the difficulty holds that though God is infinitely wise, powerful, and good, evil exists because when God created man, He created man in His image. God thus gave him free will, the power to act in ways that are unpredictable. But to say that man is free is to say that he is ultimately responsible for the *moral* (as opposed to physical) evils that beset him. By giving man freedom, God thus allowed for a world in which evil could exist. He could have prevented evil, but this would have entailed altering human character in a way that would now be unrecognizable.

Whether any of these solutions resolve the puzzle is a question we now set for readers to answer for themselves.

A. DOES GOD EXIST?

Jean-Paul Sartre

EXISTENTIALISM AS A HUMANISM

Jean-Paul Sartre (1905–1980), one of the founders of existentialism, here argues for a form of atheism.

Atheistic existentialism, of which I am a representative, declares with greater consistency that if God does not exist there is at least one being whose existence comes before its essence, a being which exists before it can be defined by any conception of it. That being is man or, as Heidegger has it, the human reality. What do we mean by saying that existence precedes essence? We mean that man first of all exists, encounters himself, surges up in the world—and defines himself afterwards. If man as the existentialist sees him is not definable, it is because to begin with he is nothing. He will not be anything until later, and then he will be what he makes of himself. Thus, there is no human nature, because there is no God to have a conception of it. Man simply is. Not that he is simply what he conceives himself to be, but he is what he wills, and as he conceives himself after already existing—as he wills to be after that leap towards existence. Man is nothing else but that which he makes of himself. That is the first principle of existentialism. And this is what people call its "subjectivity" using the word as a reproach against us. But what do we mean to say by this, but that man is of a greater dignity than a stone or a table? For we mean to say that man primarily exists—that man is, before all else, something which propels itself towards a future and is aware that it is doing so. Man is, indeed, a project which possesses a subjective life, instead of being a kind of moss, or a fungus or a cauliflower. Before that projection of the self nothing exists, not even in the heaven of intelligence: man will only attain existence when he is what he purposes to be. Not, however, what he may wish to be. For what we usually understand by wishing or willing is a conscious decision taken—much more often than not—after we have made ourselves what we are. I may wish to join a party, to write a book or to marry—but in such a case what is usually called my will is probably a manifestation of a prior and more spontaneous decision. If, however, it is true that existence is prior to essence, man

459

is responsible for what he is. Thus, the first effect of existentialism is that it puts every man in possession of himself as he is, and places the entire responsibility for his existence squarely upon his own shoulders. And, when we say that man is responsible for himself, we do not mean that he is responsible only for his own individuality, but that he is responsible for all men. The word "subjectivism" is to be understood in two senses, and our adversaries play upon only one of them. Subjectivism means, on the one hand, the freedom of the individual subject and, on the other, that man cannot pass beyond human subjectivity. It is the latter which is the deeper meaning of existentialism. When we say that man chooses himself, we do mean that every one of us must choose himself; but by that we also mean that in choosing for himself he chooses for all men. For in effect, of all the actions a man may take in order to create himself as he wills to be, there is not one which is not creative, at the same time, of an image of man such as he believes he ought to be. To choose between this or that is at the same time to affirm the value of that which is chosen; for we are unable ever to choose the worse. What we choose is always the better; and nothing can be better for us unless it is better for all. If, moreover, existence precedes essence and we will to exist at the same time as we fashion out image, that image is valid for all and for the entire epoch in which we find ourselves. Our responsibility is thus much greater than we had supposed, for it concerns mankind as a whole. If I am a worker, for instance, I may choose to join a Christian rather than a Communist trade union. And if, by that membership, I choose to signify that resignation is, after all, the attitude that best becomes a man, that man's kingdom is not upon this earth, I do not commit myself alone to that view. Resignation is my will for everyone, and my action is, in consequence, a commitment on behalf of all mankind. Or if, to take a more personal case, I decide to marry and to have children, even though this decision proceeds simply from my situation, from my passion or my desire, I am thereby committing not only myself, but humanity as a whole, to the practice of monogamy. I am thus responsible for myself and for all men, and I am creating a certain image of man as I would have him to be. In fashioning myself I fashion man.

This may enable us to understand what is meant by such terms—perhaps a little grandiloquent—as anguish, abandonment and despair. As you will soon see, it is very simple. First, what do we mean by anguish? The existentialist frankly states that man is in anguish. His meaning is as follows—When a man commits himself to anything, fully realising that he is not only choosing what he will be, but is thereby at the same time a legislator deciding for the whole of mankind—in such a moment a man cannot escape from the sense of complete and profound responsibility. There are many, indeed, who show no such anxiety. But we affirm that they are merely disguising their anguish or are in flight from it. Certainly, many people think that in what they are doing they commit no one but themselves to anything: and if you ask them, "What would happen if everyone did so?'' they shrug their shoulders and reply, ''Everyone does not do so.'' But in truth, one ought always to ask oneself what would happen if everyone did as one is doing, nor can one escape from that disturbing thought except by a kind of self-deception. The man who lies in self-excuse, by saying ''Everyone will not do it'' must be ill at ease in his conscience, for the act of lying implies the universal value which it denies. By its very disguise his anguish reveals itself. This is the anguish that Kierkegaard called ''the anguish of Abraham.'' You know the story: An angel commanded Abraham to sacrifice his son: and obedience was obligatory, if it really was an angel who had appeared and said, ''Thou, Abraham, shalt sacrifice thy son.'' But anyone in such a case would wonder, first, whether it was indeed an angel and secondly, whether I am really Abraham. Where are the proofs? A certain mad woman who suffered from hallucinations said that people were telephoning to her, and giving her orders. The doctor asked, ''But who is it that speaks to you?'' She replied: ''He says it is God.'' And what, indeed, could prove to her that it was God? If an angel appears to me, what is the proof that it is an angel; or, if I hear voices, who can prove that they proceed from heaven and not from hell, or from my own subconsciousness or some pathological condition? Who can prove that they are really addressed to me?

Who, then, can prove that I am the proper person to impose, by my own choice, my conception of man upon mankind? I shall never find any proof whatever; there will be no sign to convince me of it. If a voice speaks to me, it is still I myself who must decide whether the voice is or is not that of an angel. If I regard a certain course of action as good, it is only I who choose to say that it is good and not bad. There is nothing to show that I am Abraham: nevertheless I also am obliged at every instant to perform actions which are examples. Everything happens to every man as though the whole human race had its eyes fixed upon what he is doing and regulated its conduct accordingly. So every man ought to say, ''Am I really a man who has the right to act in such a manner that humanity regulates itself by what I do.'' If a man does not say that, he is dissembling his anguish. Clearly, the anguish with which we are concerned here is not one that could lead to quietism or inaction. It is anguish pure and simple, of the kind well known to all those who have borne responsibilities. When, for instance, a military leader takes upon himself the responsibility for an attack and sends a number of men to their death, he chooses to do it and at bottom he alone chooses. No doubt he acts under a higher command, but its orders, which are more general, require interpretation by him and upon that interpretation depends the life of ten, fourteen or twenty men. In making the decision, he cannot but feel a certain anguish. All leaders know that anguish. It does not prevent their acting, on the contrary it is the very condition of their action, for the action presupposes that there is a plurality of possibilities, and in choosing one of these, they realise that it has value only because it is chosen. Now it is anguish of that kind which existentialism describes, and moreover, as we shall see, makes explicit through direct responsibility towards other men who are concerned. Far from being a screen which could separate us from action, it is a condition of action itself.

And when we speak of "abandonment"—a favourite word of Heidegger—we only mean to say that God does not exist, and that it is necessary to draw the consequences of his absence right to the end. The existentialist is strongly opposed to a certain type of secular moralism which seeks to suppress God at the least possible expense. Towards 1880, when the French professors endeavoured to formulate a secular morality, they said something like this:—God is a useless and costly hypothesis, so we will do without it. However, if we are to have morality, a society and a law-abiding world, it is essential that certain values should be taken seriously; they must have an *à priori* existence ascribed to them. It must be considered obligatory *a priori* to be honest, not to lie, not to beat one's wife, to bring up children and so forth; so we are going to do a little work on this subject, which will enable us to show that these values exist all the same, inscribed in an intelligible heaven although, of course, there is no God. In other words—and this is, I believe, the purport of all that we in France call radicalism—nothing will be changed if God does not exist; we shall rediscover the same norms of honesty, progress and humanity, and we shall have disposed of God as an out-of-date hypothesis which will die away quietly of itself. The existentialist, on the contrary, finds it extremely embarrassing that God does not exist, for there disappears with Him all possibility of finding values in an intelligible heaven. There can no longer be any good *à priori*, since there is no infinite and perfect consciousness to think it. It is nowhere written that "the good" exists, that one must be honest or must not lie, since we are now upon the plane where there are only men. Dostoievsky once wrote "If God did not exist, everything would be permitted"; and that, for existentialism, is the starting point. Everything is indeed permitted if God does not exist, and man is in consequence forlorn, for he cannot find anything to depend upon either within or outside himself. He discovers forthwith, that he is without excuse. For if indeed existence precedes essence, one will never be able to explain one's action by reference to a given and specific human nature; in other words, there is no determinism—man is free, man *is* freedom. Nor, on the other hand, if God does not exist, are we provided with any values or commands that could legitimise our behaviour. Thus we have neither behind us, nor before us in a luminous realm of values, any means of justification or excuse. We are left alone, without excuse. That is what I mean when I say that man is condemned to be free. Condemned, because he did not create himself, yet is nevertheless at liberty, and from the moment that he is thrown into this world he is responsible for everything he does.

St. Anselm
PROSLOGIUM

St. Anselm (1034–1109) was Archbishop of Canterbury and author of the *Proslogium*, in which we find perhaps the earliest version of the ontological proof of the existence of God.

CHAPTER II

Truly there is a God, although the fool hath said in his heart, There is no God.

And so, Lord, do thou, who dost give understanding to faith, give me, so far as thou knowest it to be profitable, to understand that thou art as we believe; and that thou art that which we believe. And, indeed, we believe that thou art a being than which nothing greater can be conceived. Or is there no such nature, since the fool hath said in his heart, there is no God? (Psalms xiv. i). But, at any rate, this very fool, when he hears of this being of which I speak—a being than which nothing greater can be conceived—understands what he hears, and what he understands is in his understanding; although he does not understand it to exist.

For, it is one thing for an object to be in the understanding, and another to understand that the object exists. When a painter first conceives of what he will afterwards perform, he has it in his understanding, but he does not yet understand it to be, because he has not yet performed it. But after he has made the painting, he both has it in his understanding, and he understands that it exists, because he has made it.

Hence, even the fool is convinced that something exists in the understanding, at least, than which nothing greater can be conceived. For, when he hears of this, he understands it. And whatever is understood, exists in the understanding. And assuredly that, than which nothing greater can be conceived, cannot exist in the understanding alone. For, suppose it exists in the understanding alone: then it can be conceived to exist in reality; which is greater.

Therefore, if that, than which nothing greater can be conceived, exists in the understanding alone, the very being, than which nothing greater can be conceived, is one, than which a greater can be conceived. But obviously this is impossible. Hence, there is no doubt that there exists a being, than which nothing greater can be conceived, and it exists both in the understanding and in reality.

CHAPTER III

God cannot be conceived not to exist.—God is that, than which nothing greater can be conceived.—That which can be conceived not to exist is not God.

And it assuredly exists so truly, that it cannot be conceived not to exist. For, it is possible to conceive of a being which cannot be conceived not to exist; and this is greater than one which can be conceived not to exist. Hence, if that, than which nothing greater can be conceived, can be conceived not to exist, it is not that, than which nothing greater can be conceived. But this is an irreconcilable contradiction. There is, then, so truly a being than which nothing greater can be conceived to exist, that it cannot even be conceived not to exist; and this being thou art, O Lord, our God.

So truly, therefore, dost thou exist, O Lord, my God, that thou canst not be conceived not to exist; and rightly. For, if a mind could conceive of a being better than thee, the creature would rise above the Creator; and this is most absurd. And, indeed, whatever else there is, except thee alone, can be conceived not to exist. To thee alone, therefore, it belongs to exist more truly than all other beings, and hence in a higher degree than all others. For, whatever else exists does not exist so truly, and hence in a less degree it belongs to it to exist. Why, then, has the fool said in his heart, there is no God (Psalms xiv. 1), since it is so evident, to a rational mind, that thou dost exist in the highest degree of all? Why, except that he is dull and a fool?

Thomas Aquinas

SUMMA THEOLOGICA

St. Thomas Aquinas is generally regarded as the greatest Catholic philosopher. In selected passages from his *Summa Theologica*, we find his "five ways," or proofs of the existence of God.

QUESTION 2. WHETHER THERE IS A GOD

Under the first of these questions there are three points of inquiry:

1. is it self-evident that there is a God?
2. can it be made evident?
3. is there a God?

Article 1. Is it self-evident that there is a God?

THE FIRST POINT: 1. It seems self-evident that there is a God. For things are said to be self-evident to us when we are innately aware of them, as, for example, first principles. Now as Damascene says when beginning his book, *the awareness that God exists is implanted by nature in everybody*. That God exists is therefore self-evident.

2. Moreover, a proposition is self-evident if we perceive its truth immediately upon perceiving the meaning of its terms: a characteristic, according to Aristotle, of first principles of demonstration. For example, when we know what wholes and parts are, we know at once that wholes are always bigger than their parts. Now once we understand the meaning of the word "God" it follows that God exists. For the word means "that than which nothing greater can be meant." Consequently, since existence in thought and fact is greater than existence in thought alone, and since, once we understand the word "God," he exists in thought, he must also exist in fact. It is therefore self-evident that there is a God.

3. Moreover, it is self-evident that truth exists, for even denying it would admit it. Were there no such thing as truth, then it would be true that there is no truth; something then is true, and therefore there is truth. Now God is truth itself; I *am the way, the truth and the life*. That there is a God, then, is self-evident.

On the other hand, nobody can think the opposite of a self-evident proposition, as Aristotle's discussion of first principles makes clear. But the opposite of the proposition "God exists" can be thought, for *the fool* in the psalms *said in his heart: There is no God*. That God exists is therefore not self-evident.

REPLY: A self-evident proposition, though always self-evident in itself, is sometimes self-evident to us and sometimes not. For a proposition is self-evident when the predicate forms part of what the subject means; thus it is self-evident that man is an animal, since being an animal is part of the meaning of man. If therefore it is evident to everybody what it is to be this subject and what it is to have such a predicate, the proposition itself will be self-evident to everybody. This is clearly the case with first principles of demonstration, which employ common terms evident to all, such as "be" and "not be," "whole" and "part." But if what it is to be this subject or have such a predicate is not evident to some people, then the proposition, though self-evident in itself, will not be so to those to whom its subject and predicate are not evident. And this is why Boethius can say that *certain notions are* self-evident and *commonplaces only to the learned, as, for example, that only bodies can occupy space.*

I maintain then that the proposition "God exists" is self-evident in itself, for, as we shall see later, its subject and predicate are identical, since God is his own existence. But, because what it is to be God is not evident to us, the proposition is not self-evident to us, and needs to be made evident. This is done by means of things which, though less evident in themselves, are nevertheless more evident to us, by means, namely, of God's effects.

Hence: 1. The awareness that God exists is not implanted in us by nature in any clear or specific way. Admittedly, man is by nature aware of what by nature he desires, and he desires by nature a happiness which is to be found only in God. But this is not, simply speaking, awareness that there is a God, any more than to be aware of someone approaching is to be aware of Peter, even should it be Peter approaching: many, in fact, believe the ultimate good which will make us happy to be riches, or pleasure, or some such thing.

2. Someone hearing the word "God" may very well not understand it to mean "that than which nothing greater can be thought," indeed, some people have believed God to be a body. And even if the meaning of the word "God" were generally recognized to be "that than which nothing greater can be thought," nothing thus defined would thereby be granted existence in the world of fact, but merely as thought about. Unless one is given that something in fact exists than which nothing greater can be thought—and this nobody denying the existence of God would grant—the conclusion that God in fact exists does not follow.

3. It is self-evident that there exists truth in general, but it is not self-evident to us that there exists a First Truth.

Article 2. Can it be made evident?

THE SECOND POINT: 1. That God exists cannot, it seems, be made evident. For that God exists is an article of faith, and since, as St. Paul says, faith is concerned with *the unseen*, its propositions cannot be demonstrated, that is made evident. It is therefore impossible to demonstrate that God exists.

2. Moreover, the central link of demonstration is a definition. But Damascene tells us that we cannot define what God is, but only what he is not. Hence we cannot demonstrate that God exists.

3. Moreover, if demonstration of God's existence were possible, this could only be by arguing from his effects. Now God and his effects are incommensurable; for God is infinite and his effects finite, and the finite cannot measure the infinite. Consequently, since effects incommensurate with their cause cannot make it evident, it does not seem possible to demonstrate that God exists.

On the other hand, St Paul tells us that *the hidden things of God can be clearly understood from the things that he has made*. If so, one must be able to demonstrate that God exists from the things that he has made, for knowing whether a thing exists is the first step towards understanding it.

REPLY: There are two types of demonstration. One, showing "why," follows the natural order of things among themselves, arguing from cause to effect; the other, showing "that," follows the order in which we know things, arguing from effect to cause (for when an effect is more apparent to us than its cause, we come to know the cause through the effect). Now any effect of a cause demonstrates that that cause exists, in cases where the effect is better known to us, since effects are dependent upon causes, and can only occur if the causes already exist. From effects evident to us, therefore, we can demonstrate what in itself is not evident to us, namely, that God exists.

Hence: 1. The truths about God which St. Paul says we can know by our natural powers of reasoning—that God exists, for example—are not numbered among the articles of faith, but are presupposed to them. For faith presupposes natural knowledge, just as grace does nature and all perfections that which they perfect. However, there is nothing to stop a man accepting on faith some truth which he personally cannot demonstrate, even if that truth in itself is such that demonstration could make it evident.

2. When we argue from effect to cause, the effect will take the place of a definition of the cause in the proof that the cause exists; and this especially if the cause is God. For when proving anything to exist, the central link is not what that thing is (we cannot even ask what it is until we know that it exists), but rather what we are using the name of the thing to mean. Now when demonstrating from effects that God exists, we are able to start from what the word

"God" means, for, as we shall see, the names of God are derived from these effects.

3. Effects can give comprehensive knowledge of their cause only when commensurate with it: but, as we have said, any effect whatever can make it clear that a cause exists. God's effects, therefore, can serve to demonstrate that God exists, even though they cannot help us to know him comprehensively for what he is.

Article 3. Is there a God?

THE THIRD POINT: 1. It seems that there is no God. For if, of two mutually exclusive things, one were to exist without limit, the other would cease to exist. But by the word "God" is implied some limitless good. If God then existed, nobody would ever encounter evil. But evil is encountered in the world. God therefore does not exist.

2. Moreover, if a few causes fully account for some effect, one does not seek more. Now it seems that everything we observe in this world can be fully accounted for by other causes, without assuming a God. Thus natural effects are explained by natural causes, and contrived effects by human reasoning and will. There is therefore no need to suppose that a God exists.

On the other hand, Scripture represents God as declaring, I *am who am*.

REPLY: There are five ways in which one can prove that there is a God.

The first and most obvious way is based on change. Some things in the world are certainly in process of change: this we plainly see. Now anything in process of change is being changed by something else. This is so because it is characteristic of things in process of change that they do not yet have the perfection towards which they move, though able to have it; whereas it is characteristic of something causing change to have that perfection already. For to cause change is to bring into being what was previously only able to be, and this can only be done by something that already is: thus fire, which is actually hot, causes wood, which is able to be hot, to become actually hot, and in this way causes change in the wood. Now the same thing cannot at the same time be both actually x and potentially x, though it can be actually x and potentially y: the actually hot cannot at the same time be potentially hot, though it can be potentially cold. Consequently, a thing in process of change cannot itself cause that same change; it cannot change itself. Of necessity therefore anything in process of change is being changed by something else. Moreover, this something else, if in process of change, is itself being changed by yet another thing; and this last by another. Now we must stop somewhere, otherwise there will be no first cause of the change, and, as a result, no subsequent causes. For it is only when acted upon by the first cause that the intermediate causes will produce the change: if the hand does not move the stick, the stick will not move anything else. Hence one is bound to arrive at some first cause of change not itself being changed by anything, and this is what everybody understands by God.

The second way is based on the nature of causation. In the observable world causes are found to be ordered in series; we never observe, nor ever could, something causing itself, for this would mean it preceded itself, and this is not possible. Such a series of causes must however stop somewhere; for in it an earlier member causes an intermediate and the intermediate a last (whether the intermediate be one or many). Now if you eliminate a cause you also eliminate its effects, so that you cannot have a last cause, nor an intermediate one, unless you have a first. Given therefore no stop in the series of causes, and hence no first cause, there would be no intermediate causes either, and no last effect, and this would be an open mistake. One is therefore forced to suppose some first cause, to which everyone gives the name "God."

The third way is based on what need not be and on what must be, and runs as follows. Some of the things we come across can be but need not be, for we find them springing up and dying away, thus sometimes in being and sometimes not. Now everything cannot be like this, for a thing that need not be, once was not; and if everything need not be, once upon a time there was nothing. But if that were true there would be nothing even now, because something that does not exist can only be brought into being by something already existing. So that if nothing was in being nothing could be brought into being, and nothing would be in being now, which contradicts observation. Not everything therefore is the sort of thing that need not be; there has got to be something that must be. Now a thing that must be, may or may not owe this necessity to something else. But just as we must stop somewhere in a series of causes, so also in the series of things which must be and owe this to other things. One is forced therefore to suppose something which must be, and owes this to no other thing than itself; indeed it itself is the cause that other things must be.

The fourth way is based on the gradation observed in things. Some things are found to be more good, more true, more noble, and so on, and other things less. But such comparative terms describe varying degrees of approximation to a superlative; for example, things are hotter and hotter the nearer they approach what is hottest. Something, therefore, is the truest and best and most noble of things, and hence the most fully in being; for Aristotle says that the truest things are the things most fully in being. Now *when many things possess some property in common, the one most fully possessing it causes it in the others: fire,* to use Aristotle's example, *the hottest of all things, causes all other things to be hot.* There is something therefore which causes in all other things their being, their goodness, and whatever other perfection they have. And this we call "God."

The fifth way is based on the guidedness of nature. An orderedness of actions to an end is observed in all bodies obeying natural laws, even when they lack awareness. For their behaviour hardly ever varies, and will practically always turn out well; which shows that they truly tend to a goal, and do not merely hit it by accident. Nothing however that lacks awareness tends to a goal, except under the direction of someone with awareness and with understanding; the arrow, for example, requires an archer. Everything in nature, therefore, is directed to its goal by someone with intelligence, and this we call "God."

Hence: 1. As Augustine says, *Since God is supremely good, he would not permit any evil at all in his works, unless he were sufficiently almighty and good to bring good even from evil.* It is therefore a mark of the limitless goodness of God that he permits evils to exist, and draws from them good.

2. Natural causes act for definite purposes under the direction of some higher cause, so that their effects must also be referred to God as the first of all causes. In the same manner contrived effects must likewise be referred back to a higher cause than human reasoning and will, for these are changeable and can cease to be, and, as we have seen, all changeable things and things that can cease to be require some first cause which cannot change and of itself must be.

Isaac Newton

PRINCIPIA MATHEMATICA

In this passage from his *Principia Mathematica*, Isaac Newton (1642–1727) puts forth a version of the argument from design based upon astronomical evidence.

I. GENERAL SCHOLIUM

The hypothesis of vortices is pressed with many difficulties. That every planet by a radius drawn to the sun may describe areas proportional to the times of description, the periodic times of the several parts of the vortices should observe the square of their distances from the sun; but that the periodic times of the planets may obtain the 3/2th power of their distances from the sun, the periodic times of the parts of the vortex ought to be as the 3/2th power of their distances. That the smaller vortices may maintain their lesser revolutions about Saturn, Jupiter, and other planets, and swim quietly and undisturbed in the greater vortex of the sun, the periodic times of the parts of the sun's vortex should be equal; but the rotation of the sun and planets about their axes, which ought to correspond with the motions of their vortices, recede far from all these proportions. The motions of the comets are exceedingly regular, are governed by the same laws with the motions of the planets, and can by no means be accounted for by the hypothesis of vortices; for comets are carried with very eccentric motions through all parts of the heavens indifferently, with a freedom that is incompatible with the notion of a vortex.

Bodies projected in our air suffer no resistance but from the air. Withdraw the air, as is done in Mr. Boyle's vacuum, and the resistance ceases; for in this void a bit of fine down and a piece of solid gold descend with equal velocity. And the same argument must apply to the celestial spaces above the earth's atmosphere; in these spaces, where there is no air to resist their motions, all bodies will move with the greatest freedom; and the planets and comets will constantly pursue their revolutions in orbits given in kind and position, according to the laws above explained; but though these bodies may, indeed, continue in their orbits by the mere laws of gravity, yet they could by no means have at first derived the regular position of the orbits themselves from those laws.

The six primary planets are revolved about the sun in circles concentric with the sun, and with motions directed toward the same parts and almost in the same plane. Ten moons are revolved about the earth, Jupiter, and Saturn, in circles concentric with them, with the same direction of motion, and nearly in the planes of the orbits of those planets; but it is not to be conceived that mere mechanical causes could give birth to so many regular motions, since the comets range over all parts of the heavens in very eccentric orbits; for by that kind of motion they pass easily through the orbs of the planets, and with great rapidity; and in their aphelions, where they move the slowest and are detained the longest, they recede to the greatest distances from each other, and hence suffer the least disturbance from their mutual attractions. This most beautiful system of the sun, planets, and comets could only proceed from the counsel and dominion of an intelligent and powerful Being. And if the fixed stars are the centers of other like systems, these, being formed by the like wise counsel, must be all subject to the dominion of One, especially since the light of the fixed stars is of the same nature with the light of the sun and from every system light passes into all the other systems; and lest the systems of the fixed stars should, by their gravity, fall on each other, he hath placed those systems at immense distances from one another.

This Being governs all things, not as the soul of the world, but as Lord over all; and on account of his dominion he is wont to be called "Lord God" παντοκράτωρ, or "Universal Ruler"; for "God" is a relative word and has a respect to servants; and Deity is the dominion of God, not over his own body, as those imagine who fancy God to be the soul of the world, but over servants. The Supreme God is a Being eternal, infinite, absolutely perfect, but a being, however perfect, without dominion, cannot be said to be "Lord God"; for we say "my God," "your God," "the God of Israel," "the God of Gods," and "Lord of Lords," but we do not say "my Eternal," "your Eternal," "the Eternal of Israel," "the Eternal of Gods"; we do not say "my Infinite," or "my Perfect": these are titles which have no respect to servants. The word "God"[1] usually signifies "Lord," but every lord is not a God. It is the dominion of a spiritual being which constitutes a God; a true, supreme, or imaginary dominion makes a true, supreme, or imaginary God. And from his true dominion it follows that the true God is a living, intelligent, and powerful Being; and, from his other perfections, that he is supreme or most perfect. He is eternal and infinite, omnipotent and omniscient; that is, his duration reaches from eternity to eternity; his presence

---

[1]Dr. Pocock derives the Latin word "*Deus*" from the Arabic "*du*" (in the oblique case "*di*"), which signifies "Lord." And in this sense princes are called "gods," Psalm lxxxii. ver. 6; and John x. ver. 35. And Moses is called a "god" to his brother Aaron, and a "god" to Pharaoh (Exodus iv. ver. 16; and vii. ver. 1). And in the same sense the souls of dead princes were formerly, by the Heathens, called "gods," but falsely, because of their want of dominion.

from infinity to infinity; he governs all things and knows all things that are or can be done. He is not eternity and infinity, but eternal and infinite; he is not duration or space, but he endures and is present. He endures forever and is everywhere present; and, by existing always and everywhere, he constitutes duration and space. Since every particle of space is *always*, and every indivisible moment of duration is *everywhere*, certainly the Maker and Lord of all things cannot be *never* and *nowhere*. Every soul that has perception is, though in different times and in different organs of sense and motion, still the same indivisible person. There are given successive parts in duration, coexistent parts in space, but neither the one nor the other in the person of a man or his thinking principle; and much less can they be found in the thinking substance of God. Every man, so far as he is a thing that has perception, is one and the same man during his whole life, in all and each of his organs of sense. God is the same God, always and everywhere. He is omnipresent not *virtually* only but also *substantially*; for virtue cannot subsist without substance. In him[2] are all things contained and moved, yet neither affects the other; God suffers nothing from the motion of bodies, bodies find no resistance from the omnipresence of God. It is allowed by all that the Supreme God exists necessarily, and by the same necessity he exists *always* and *everywhere*. Whence also he is all similar, all eye, all ear, all brain, all arm, all power to perceive, to understand, and to act; but in a manner not at all human, in a manner not at all corporeal, in a manner utterly unknown to us. As a blind man has no idea of colors, so have we no idea of the manner by which the all-wise God perceives and understands all things. He is utterly void of all body and bodily figure, and can therefore neither be seen nor heard nor touched; nor ought he to be worshiped under the representation of any corporeal thing. We have ideas of his attributes, but what the real substance of anything is we know not. In bodies we see only their figures and colors, we hear only the sounds, we touch only their outward surfaces, we smell only the smells and taste the savors, but their inward substances are not to be known either by our senses or by any reflex act of our minds; much less, then, have we any idea of the substance of God. We know him only by his most wise and excellent contrivances of things and final causes; we admire him for his perfections, but we reverence and adore him on account of his dominion, for we adore him as his servants; and a god without dominion, providence, and final causes is nothing else but Fate and Nature. Blind metaphysical necessity, which is certainly the same always and everywhere, could produce no variety of things. All that diversity of natural things which we find suited to different

[2]This was the opinion of the Ancients. So Pythagoras, in *Cicer. de* Nat. *Deor.* lib. i. Thales, Anaxagoras, Virgil, *Georg.* lib. iv. ver. 220; and *Aeneid*, lib. vi. ver. 721. *Philo Allegor*, at the beginning of lib. i. Aratus, in his *Phaenom*, at the beginning. So also the sacred writers: as St. Paul, Acts xvii. ver. 27, 28. St. John's Gosp. chap. xiv. ver. 2. Moses, in Deuteronomy iv. ver. 39; and x. ver. 14. David, Psalm cxxxix. ver. 7, 8, 9. Solomon, I Kings viii. ver. 27. Job xxii. ver. 12, 13, 14. Jeremiah, xxiii. ver. 23, 24. The Idolaters supposed the sun, moon, and stars, the souls of men, and other parts of the world to be parts of the Supreme God, and therefore to be worshiped; but erroneously.

times and places could arise from nothing but the ideas and will of a Being necessarily existing. But, by way of allegory, God is said to see, to speak, to laugh, to love, to hate, to desire, to give, to receive, to rejoice, to be angry, to fight, to frame, to work, to build; for all our notions of God are taken from the ways of mankind by a certain similitude, which, though not perfect, has some likeness, however. And thus much concerning God, to discourse of whom from the appearances of things does certainly belong to natural philosophy.

Hitherto we have explained the phenomena of the heavens and of our sea by the power of gravity, but have not yet assigned the cause of this power. This is certain, that it must proceed from a cause that penetrates to the very centers of the sun and planets, without suffering the least diminution of its force; that operates not according to the quantity of the surfaces of the particles upon which it acts (as mechanical causes used to do), but according to the quantity of the solid matter which they contain, and propagates its virtue on all sides to immense distances, decreasing always as the inverse square of the distances. Gravitation toward the sun is made up out of the gravitations toward the several particles of which the body of the sun is composed, and in receding from the sun decreases accurately as the inverse square of the distances as far as the orbit of Saturn, as evidently appears from the quiescence of the aphelion of the planets; nay, and even to the remotest aphelion of the comets, if those aphelions are also quiescent. But hitherto I have not been able to discover the cause of those properties of gravity from phenomena, and I frame no hypotheses; for whatever is not deduced from the phenomena is to be called a hypothesis, and hypotheses, whether metaphysical or physical, whether of occult qualities or mechanical, have no place in experimental philosophy. In this philosophy particular propositions are inferred from the phenomena and afterward rendered general by induction. Thus it was that the impenetrability, the mobility, and the impulsive force of bodies, and the laws of motion and of gravitation, were discovered. And to us it is enough that gravity does really exist and act according to the laws which we have explained, and abundantly serves to account for all the motions of the celestial bodies and of our sea.

And now we might add something concerning a certain most subtle spirit which pervades and lies hid in all gross bodies, by the force and action of which spirit the particles of bodies attract one another at near distances and cohere, if contiguous; and electric bodies operate to greater distances, as well repelling as attracting the neighboring corpuscles; and light is emitted, reflected, refracted, inflected, and heats bodies; and all sensation is excited, and the members of animal bodies move at the command of the will, namely, by the vibrations of this spirit, mutually propagated along the solid filaments of the nerves, from the outward organs of sense to the brain and from the brain into the muscles. But these are things that cannot be explained in few words; nor are we furnished with that sufficiency of experiments which is required to an accurate determination and demonstration of the laws by which this electric and elastic spirit operates.

David Hume

DIALOGUES CONCERNING NATURAL RELIGION

In Hume's *Dialogues Concerning Natural Religion*, published post-humously, three characters—Demea, Cleanthes, and Philo—argue the validity of proofs for the existence of God. In this selection from Part II of the *Dialogues*, we find Philo's criticisms of Cleanthes' version of the argument from design.

Good God! cried Demea, interrupting him, where are we? Zealous defenders of religion allow, that the proofs of a Deity fall short of perfect evidence! And you, Philo, on whose assistance I depended, in proving the adorable mysterious-ness of the divine nature, do you assent to all these extravagant opinions of Cleanthes? For what other name can I give them? Or why spare my censure, when such principles are advanced, supported by such an authority, before so young a man as Pamphilus?

You seem not to apprehend, replied Philo, that I argue with Cleanthes in his own way; and by showing him the dangerous consequences of his tenets, hope at last to reduce him to our opinion. But what sticks most with you, I observe, is the representation which Cleanthes has made of the argument *a posteriori*; and finding that that argument is likely to escape your hold and vanish into air, you think it so disguised that you can scarcely believe it to be set in its true light. Now, however much I may dissent, in other respects, from the dangerous prin-ciples of Cleanthes, I must allow, that he has fairly represented that argument; and I shall endeavour so to state the matter to you, that you will entertain no farther scruples with regard to it.

Were a man to abstract from every thing which he knows or has seen, he would be altogether incapable, merely from his own ideas, to determine what kind of scene the universe must be, or to give the preference to one state or situation of things above another. For as nothing, which he clearly conceives, could be esteemed impossible or implying a contradiction, every chimera of his fancy would be upon an equal footing; nor could he assign any just reason, why he adheres to one idea or system, and rejects the others, which are equally possible.

Again; after he opens his eyes, and contemplates the world, as it really is, it would be impossible for him, at first, to assign the cause of any event; much less, of the whole of things or of the universe. He might set his fancy a rambling; and she might bring him in an infinite variety of reports and representations. These would all be possible; but being all equally possible, he would never, of himself, give a satisfactory account for his preferring one of them to the rest. Experience alone can point out to him the true cause of any phenomenon.

Now according to this method of reasoning, Demea, it follows (and is, indeed, tacitly allowed by Cleanthes himself) that order, arrangement, or the adjustment of final causes is not, of itself, any proof of design; but only so far as it has been experienced to proceed from that principle. For aught we can know *a priori*, matter may contain the source or spring of order originally, within itself, as well as mind does; and there is no more difficulty in conceiving, that the several elements, from an internal unknown cause, may fall into the most exquisite arrangement, than to conceive that their ideas, in the great, universal mind, from a like internal, unknown cause, fall into that arrangement. The equal possibility of both these suppositions is allowed. By experience we find (according to Cleanthes), that there is a difference between them. Throw several pieces of steel together, without shape or form; they will never arrange themselves so as to compose a watch: Stone, and mortar, and wood, without an architect, never erect a house. But the ideas in a human mind, we see, by an unknown, inexplicable œconomy, arrange themselves so as to form the plan of a watch or house. Experience, therefore, proves, that there is an original principle of order in mind, not in matter. From similar effects we infer similar causes. The adjustment of means to ends is alike in the universe, as in a machine of human contrivance. The causes, therefore, must be resembling.

I was from the beginning scandalised, I must own, with this resemblance, which is asserted, between the Deity and human creatures; and must conceive it to imply such a degradation of the supreme Being as no sound theist could endure. With your assistance, therefore, Demea, I shall endeavour to defend what you justly call the adorable mysteriousness of the divine nature, and shall refute this reasoning of Cleanthes; provided he allows, that I have made a fair representation of it.

When Cleanthes had assented, Philo, after a short pause, proceeded in the following manner.

That all inferences, Cleanthes, concerning fact, are founded on experience, and that all experimental reasonings are founded on the supposition, that similar causes prove similar effects, and similar effects similar causes; I shall not, at present, much dispute with you. But observe, I entreat you, with what extreme caution all just reasoners proceed in the transferring of experiments to similar cases. Unless the cases be exactly similar, they repose no perfect confidence in applying their past observation to any particular phenomenon. Every alteration of circumstances occasions a doubt concerning the event; and it requires new experiments to prove certainly, that the new circumstances are of no moment or importance. A change in bulk, situation, arrangement, age, disposition of the air, or surrounding bodies; any of these particulars may be attended with the most unexpected consequences: And unless the objects be quite familiar to us, it is the highest temerity to expect with assurance, after any of these changes, an event similar to that which before fell under our observation. The slow and deliberate steps of philosophers, here, if any where, are distinguished from the precipitate march of the vulgar, who, hurried on by the smallest similitude, are incapable of all discernment or consideration.

But can you think, Cleanthes, that your usual phlegm and philosophy have been preserved in so wide a step as you have taken, when you compared to the universe houses, ships, furniture, machines; and from their similarity in some circumstances inferred a similarity in their causes? Thought, design, intelligence, such as we discover in men and other animals, is no more than one of the springs and principles of the universe, as well as heat or cold, attraction or repulsion, and a hundred others, which fall under daily observation. It is an active cause, by which some particular parts of nature, we find, produce alterations on other parts. But can a conclusion, with any propriety, be transferred from parts to the whole? Does not the great disproportion bar all comparison and inference? From observing the growth of a hair, can we learn any thing concerning the generation of a man? Would the manner of a leaf's blowing, even though perfectly known, afford us any instruction concerning the vegetation of a tree?

But allowing that we were to take the *operations* of one part of nature upon another for the foundation of our judgment concerning the *origin* of the whole (which never can be admitted) yet why select so minute, so weak, so bounded a principle as the reason and design of animals is found to be upon this planet? What peculiar privilege has this little agitation of the rain which we call thought, that we must thus make it the model of the whole universe? Our partiality in our own favour does indeed present it on all occasions: But sound philosophy ought carefully to guard against so natural an illusion.

So far from admitting, continued Philo, that the operations of a part can afford us any just conclusion concerning the origin of the whole, I will not allow any one part to form a rule for another part, if the latter be very remote from the former. Is there any reasonable ground to conclude, that the inhabitants of other planets possess thought, intelligence, reason, or any thing similar to these faculties in men? When nature has so extremely diversified her manner of operation in this small globe; can we imagine, that she incessantly copies herself throughout so immense a universe? And if thought, as we may well suppose, be confined merely to this narrow corner, and has even there so limited a sphere of action; with what propriety can we assign it for the original cause of all things? The narrow views of a peasant, who makes his domestic œconomy the rule for the government of kingdoms, is in comparison a pardonable sophism.

But were we ever so much assured, that a thought and reason, resembling the human, were to be found throughout the whole universe, and were its activity elsewhere vastly greater and more commanding than it appears in this globe: Yet I cannot see, why the operations of a world, constituted, arranged, adjusted, can with any propriety be extended to a world, which is in its embryo-state, and is advancing towards that constitution and arrangement. By observation, we know somewhat of the œconomy, action, and nourishment of a finished animal; but we must transfer with great caution that observation to the growth of a fœtus in the womb, and still more, to the formation of an animalcule in the loins of its male parent. Nature, we find, even from our limited experience, possesses an infinite number of springs and principles, which incessantly discover themselves on every change of her position and situation. And what new and unknown principles would actuate her in so new and unknown a situation as that of the formation of a universe, we cannot, without the utmost temerity, pretend to determine.

[A very small part of this great system, during a very short time, is very imperfectly discovered to us: And do we thence pronounce decisively concerning the origin of the whole?]

Admirable conclusion! Stone, wood, brick, iron, brass have not, at this time, in this minute globe of earth, an order or arrangement without human art and contrivance: Therefore the universe could not originally attain its order and arrangement, without something similar to human art. But is a part of nature a rule for another part very wide of the former? Is it a rule for the whole? Is a very small part a rule for the universe? Is nature in one situation, a certain rule for nature in another situation, vastly different from the former?

And can you blame me, Cleanthes, if I here imitate the prudent reserve of Simonides, who, according to the noted story, being asked by Hiero, *What God was*? desired a day to think of it, and then two days more; and after that manner continually prolonged the term, without ever bringing in his definition or description? Could you even blame me, if I had answered at first, *that I did not know*, and was sensible that this subject lay vastly beyond the reach of my faculties? You might cry out sceptic and raillier as much as you pleased: But having found, in so many other subjects, much more familiar, the imperfections and even contradictions of human reason, I never should expect any success from its feeble conjectures, in a subject, so sublime, and so remote from the sphere of our observation. When two *species* of objects have always been observed to be conjoined together, I can *infer*, by custom, the existence of one wherever I *see* the existence of the other: And this I call an argument from experience. But how this argument can have place, where the objects, as in the present case, are single, individual, without parallel, or specific resemblance, may be difficult to explain. And will any man tell me with a serious countenance, that an orderly universe must arise from some thought and art, like the human; because we have experience of it? To ascertain this reasoning, it were requisite, that we had experience of the origin of worlds; and it is not sufficient surely, that we have seen ships and cities arise from human art and contrivance. . . .

Philo was proceeding in this vehement manner, somewhat between jest and earnest, as it appeared to me; when he observed some signs of impatience in Cleanthes, and then immediately stopped short. What I had to suggest, said Cleanthes, is only that you would not abuse terms, or make use of popular expressions to subvert philosophical reasonings. You know, that the vulgar often distinguish reason from experience, even where the question relates only to matter of fact and existence; though it is found, where that *reason* is properly analysed, that it is nothing but a species of experience. To prove by experience the origin of the universe from mind is not more contrary to common speech than to prove the motion of the earth from the same principle. And a caviller might raise all the same objections to the Copernican system, which you have urged against my reasonings. Have you other earths, might he say, which you have seen to move? Have. . . .

Yes! cried Philo, interrupting him, we have other earths. Is not the moon another earth, which we see to turn round its centre? Is not Venus another earth, where we observe the same phenomenon? Are not the revolutions of the sun also a confirmation, from analogy, of the same theory? All the planets, are they not earths, which revolve about the sun? Are not the satellites moons, which move round Jupiter and Saturn, and along with these primary planets, round the sun? These analogies and resemblances, with others, which I have not mentioned, are the sole proofs of the Copernican system: And to you it belongs to consider, whether you have any analogies of the same kind to support your theory.

In reality, Cleanthes, continued he, the modern system of astronomy is now so much received by all enquirers, and has become so essential a part even of our earliest education, that we are not commonly very scrupulous in examining the reasons upon which it is founded. It is now become a matter of mere curiosity to study the first writers on that subject, who had the full force of prejudice to encounter, and were obliged to turn their arguments on every side, in order to render them popular and convincing. But if we peruse Galilæo's famous Dialogues concerning the system of the world, we shall find, that that great genius, one of the sublimest that ever existed, first bent all his endeavours to prove, that there was no foundation for the distinction commonly made between elementary and celestial substances. The schools, proceeding from the illusions of sense, had carried this distinction very far; and had established the latter substances to be ingenerable, incorruptible, unalterable, impassible; and had assigned all the opposite qualities to the former. But Galilæo, beginning with the moon, proved its similarity in every particular to the earth; its convex figure, its natural darkness when not illuminated, its density, its distinction into solid and liquid, the variations of its phases, the mutual illuminations of the earth and moon, their mutual eclipses, the inequalities of the lunar surface, &c. After many instances of this kind, with regard to all the planets, men plainly saw, that these bodies became proper objects of experience; and that the similarity of their nature enabled us to extend the same arguments and phenomena from one to the other.

In this cautious proceeding of the astronomers, you may read your own condemnation, Cleanthes; or rather may see, that the subject in which you are engaged exceeds all human reason and enquiry. Can you pretend to show any such similarity between the fabric of a house, and the generation of a universe? Have you ever seen nature in any such situation as resembles the first arrangement of the elements? Have worlds ever been formed under your eye? and have you had leisure to observe the whole progress of the phenomenon, from the first appearance of order to its final consummation? If you have, then cite your experience, and deliver your theory.

William James

THE WILL TO BELIEVE

William James (1842–1910) was an American philosopher and psychologist intensely interested in religion. In "The Will to Believe," he presents a view similar to that of Blaise Pascal (1623–1662), who in his *Pensées* proposed that one should wager that God exists. If wrong, one has lost nothing; if right, one has gained everything.

In the recently published Life by Leslie Stephen of his brother, Fitz-James, there is an account of a school to which the latter went when he was a boy. The teacher, a certain Mr. Guest, used to converse with his pupils in this wise: "Gurney, what is the difference between justification and sanctification?—Stephen, prove the omnipotence of God!" etc. In the midst of our Harvard freethinking and indifference we are prone to imagine that here at your good old orthodox College conversation continues to be somewhat upon this order; and to show you that we at Harvard have not lost all interest in these vital subjects, I have brought with me tonight something like a sermon on justification by faith to read to you—I mean an essay in justification *of* faith, a defence of our right to adopt a believing attitude in religious matters, in spite of the fact that our merely logical intellect may not have been coerced. "The Will to Believe," accordingly, is the title of my paper.

I have long defended to my own students the lawfulness of voluntarily adopted faith; but as soon as they have got well imbued with the logical spirit, they have as a rule refused to admit my contention to be lawful philosophically, even though in point of fact they were personally all the time chock-full of some faith or other themselves. I am all the while, however, so profoundly convinced that my own position is correct, that your invitation has seemed to me a good occasion to make my statements more clear. Perhaps your minds will be more open than those with which I have hitherto had to deal. I will be as little technical as I can, though I must begin by setting up some technical distinctions that will help us in the end.

I

Let us give the name of *hypothesis* to anything that may be proposed to our belief; and just as the electricians speak of live and dead wires, let us speak of any hypothesis as either *live* or *dead*. A live hypothesis is one which appeals as a real possibility to him to whom it is proposed. If I ask you to believe in the Mahdi, the notion makes no electric connection with your nature—it refuses to scintillate with any credibility at all. As an hypothesis it is completely dead. To an Arab, however (even if he be not one of the Mahdi's followers), the hypothesis is among the mind's possibilities: it is alive. This shows that deadness and liveness in an hypothesis are not intrinsic properties, but relations to the individual thinker. They are measured by his willingness to act. The maximum of liveness in an hypothesis means willingness to act irrevocably. Practically, that means belief; but there is some believing tendency wherever there is willingness to act at all.

Next, let us call the decision between two hypotheses an *option*. Options may be of several kinds. They may be—first, *living* or *dead*; secondly, *forced* or *avoidable*; thirdly, *momentous* or *trivial*; and for our purposes we may call an option a *genuine* option when it is of the forced, living, and momentous kind.

1. A living option is one in which both hypotheses are live ones. If I say to you: "Be a theosophist or be a Mohammedan," it is probably a dead option, because for you neither hypothesis is likely to be alive. But if I say: "Be an agnostic or be a Christian," it is otherwise: trained as you are, each hypothesis makes some appeal, however small, to your belief.

2. Next, if I say to you: "Choose between going out with your umbrella or without it," I do not offer you a genuine option, for it is not forced. You can easily avoid it by not going out at all. Similarly, if I say, "Either love me or hate me," "Either call my theory true or call it false," your opinion is avoidable. You may remain indifferent to me, neither loving nor hating, and you may decline to offer any judgment as to my theory. But if I say, "Either accept this truth or go without it," I put on you a forced option, for there is no standing place outside of the alternative. Every dilemma based on a complete logical disjunction, with no possibility of not choosing, is an option of this forced kind.

3. Finally, if I were Dr. Nansen and proposed to you to join my North Pole expedition, your option would be momentous; for this would probably be your only similar opportunity, and your choice now would either exclude you from the North Pole sort of immortality altogether or put at least the chance of it into your hands. He who refuses to embrace a unique opportunity loses the prize as surely as if he tried and failed. *Per contra*, the option is trivial when the opportunity is not unique, when the stake is insignificant, or when the decision is reversible if it later proved unwise. Such trivial options abound in the scientific life. A chemist finds an hypothesis live enough to spend a year in its verification: he believes in it to that extent. But if his experiments prove inconclusive either way, he is quit for his loss of time, no vital harm being done.

It will facilitate our discussion if we keep all these distinctions well in mind.

II

The next matter to consider is the actual psychology of human opinion. When we look at certain facts, it seems as if our passional and volitional nature lay at the root of all our convictions. When we look at others, it seems as if they could do nothing when the intellect had once said its say. Let us take the latter facts up first.

Does it not seem preposterous on the very face of it to talk of our opinions being modifiable at will? Can our will either help or hinder our intellect in its perceptions of truth? Can we, by just willing it, believe that Abraham Lincoln's existence is a myth, and that the portraits of him in *McClure's Magazine* are all of some one else? Can we, by any effort of our will, or by any strength of wish that it were true, believe ourselves well and about when we are roaring with rheumatism in bed, or feel certain that the sum of the two one-dollar bills in our pocket must be a hundred dollars? We can *say* any of these things, but we are absolutely impotent to believe them; and of just such things is the whole fabric of the truths that we do believe in made up—matters of fact, immediate or remote, as Hume said, and relations between ideas, which are either there or not there for us if we see them so, and which if not there cannot be put there by any action of our own.

In Pascal's *Thoughts* there is a celebrated passage known in literature as Pascal's wager. In it he tries to force us into Christianity by reasoning as if our concern with truth resembled our concern with the stakes in a game of chance. Translated freely his words are these: You must either believe or not believe that God is—which will you do? Your human reason cannot say. A game is going on between you and the nature of things which at the day of judgment will bring out either heads or tails. Weigh what your gains and your losses would be if you should stake all you have on heads, or God's existence: if you win in such case, you gain eternal beatitude; if you lose, you lose nothing at all. If there were an infinity of chances, and only one for God in this wager, still you ought to stake your all on God; for though you surely risk a finite loss by this procedure, any finite loss is reasonable, even a certain one is reasonable, if there is but the possibility of infinite gain. Go, then, and take holy water, and have masses said; belief will come and stupefy your scruples—*Cela vous fera croire et vous abêtira.* Why should you not? At bottom, what have you to lose?

You probably feel that when religious faith expresses itself thus, in the language of the gaming-table, it is put to its last trumps. Surely Pascal's own personal belief in masses and holy water had far other springs; and this celebrated page of his is but an argument for others, a last desperate snatch at a weapon against the hardness of the unbelieving heart. We feel that a faith in masses and holy water adopted wilfully after such a mechanical calculation would lack the inner soul of faith's reality; and if we were ourselves in the place of the Deity, we should probably take particular pleasure in cutting off believers of this pattern from their infinite reward. It is evident that unless there be some pre-existing tendency to believe in masses and holy water, the option offered to the will by Pascal is not a living option. Certainly no Turk ever took to masses and holy water on its account; and even to us Protestants these means of salvation seem such foregone impossibilities that Pascal's logic, invoked for them specifically, leaves us unmoved. As well might the Mahdi write to us, saying, "I am the Expected One whom God has created in his effulgence. You shall be infinitely happy if you confess me; otherwise you shall be cut off from the light of the sun. Weigh, then, your infinite gain if I am genuine against your finite sacrifice if I am not!" His logic would be that of Pascal; but he would vainly use it on us, for the hypothesis he offers us is dead. No tendency to act on it exists in us to any degree.

The talk of believing by our volition seems, then, from one point of view, simply silly. From another point of view it is worse than silly, it is vile. When one turns to the magnificent edifice of the physical sciences, and sees how it was reared; what thousands of disinterested moral lives of men lie buried in its mere foundations; what patience and postponement, what choking down of preference, what submission to the icy laws of outer fact are wrought into its very stones and mortar; how absolutely impersonal it stands in its vast augustness—then how besotted and contemptible seems every little senti-mentalist who comes blowing his voluntary smoke-wreaths, and pretending to decide things from out of his private dream! Can we wonder if those bred in the rugged and manly school of science should feel like spewing such subjectivism out of their mouths? The whole system of loyalties which grow up in the schools of science go dead against its toleration; so that it is only natural that those who have caught the scientific fever should pass over to the opposite extreme, and write sometimes as if the incorruptibly truthful intellect ought positively to prefer bitterness and unacceptableness to the heart in its cup.

> It fortifies my soul to know
> That though I perish, Truth is so—

sings Clough, while Huxley exclaims: "My only consolation lies in the reflection that, however bad our posterity may become, so far as they hold by the plain rule of not pretending to believe what they have no reason to believe, because it may be to their advantage so to pretend [the word 'pretend' is surely here redundant], they will not have reached the lowest depth of immorality." And that delicious *enfant terrible* Clifford writes: "Belief is desecrated when given to unproved and unquestioned statements for the solace and private pleasure of the believer. . . . Whoso would deserve well of his fellows in this matter will guard the purity of his belief with a very fanaticism of jealous care, lest at any time it should rest on an unworthy object, and catch a stain which can never be wiped away. . . . If [a] belief has been accepted on insufficient evidence [even though the belief be true, as Clifford on the same page explains] the pleasure is a stolen one. . . . It is sinful because it is stolen in defiance of our duty to mankind. That duty is to guard ourselves from such beliefs as from a pestilence which may shortly master our own body and then spread to the rest of the town. . . . It is wrong always, everywhere, and for every one, to believe anything upon insufficient evidence." . . .

VIII

And now, after all this introduction, let us go straight at our question. I have said, and now repeat it, that not only as a matter of fact do we find our passional nature influencing us in our opinions, but that there are some options between opinions in which this influence must be regarded both as an inevitable and as a lawful determinant of our choice.

I fear here that some of you my hearers will begin to scent danger, and lend an inhospitable ear. Two first steps of passion you have indeed had to admit as necessary—we must think so as to avoid dupery, and we must think so as to gain truth; but the surest path to those ideal consummations, you will probably consider, is from now onwards to take no further passional step.

Well, of course, I agree as far as the facts will allow. Wherever the option between losing truth and gaining it is not momentous, we can throw the chance of *gaining truth* away, and at any rate save ourselves from any chance of *believing falsehood*, by not making up our minds at all till objective evidence has come. In scientific questions, this is almost always the case; and even in human affairs in general, the need of acting is seldom so urgent that a false belief to act on is better than no belief at all. Law courts, indeed, have to decide on the best evidence attainable for the moment, because a judge's duty is to make law as well as to ascertain it, and (as a learned judge once said to me) few cases are worth spending much time over: the great thing is to have them decided on *any* acceptable principle, and got out of the way. But in our dealings with objective nature we obviously are recorders, not makers, of the truth; and decisions for the mere sake of deciding promptly and getting on to the next business would be wholly out of place. Throughout the breadth of physical nature facts are what they are quite independently of us, and seldom is there any such hurry about them that the risks of being duped by believing a premature theory need be faced. The questions here are always trivial options, the hypotheses are hardly living (at any rate not living for us spectators), the choice between believing truth or falsehood is seldom forced. The attitude of sceptical balance is therefore the absolutely wise one if we would escape mistakes. What difference, indeed, does it make to most of us whether we have or have not a theory of the Röntgen rays, whether we believe or not in mind-stuff, or have a conviction about the causality of conscious states? It makes no difference. Such options are not forced on us. On every account it is better not to make them, but still keep weighing reasons *pro et contra* with an indifferent hand.

I speak, of course, here of the purely judging mind. For purposes of discovery such indifference is to be less highly recommended, and science would be far less advanced than she is if the passionate desires of individuals to get their own faiths confirmed had been kept out of the game. See for example the sagacity which Spencer and Weismann now display. On the other hand, if you want an absolute duffer in an investigation, you must, after all, take the man who has no interest whatever in its results: he is the warranted incapable, the positive fool. The most useful investigator, because the most sensitive observer, is always he whose eager interest in one side of the question is balanced by an equally keen nervousness lest he become deceived. Science has organized this nervousness into a regular *technique*, her so-called method of verification; and she has fallen so deeply in love with the method that one may even say she has ceased to care for truth by itself at all. It is only truth as technically verified that interests her. The truth of truths might come in merely affirmative form, and she would decline to touch it. Such truth as that, she might repeat with Clifford, would be stolen in defiance of her duty to mankind. Human passions, however, are stronger than technical rules. "Le cœur a ses raisons," as Pascal says, "que la raison ne connaît pas"; and however indifferent to all but the bare rules of the game the umpire, the abstract intellect, may be, the concrete players who furnish him the materials to judge of are usually, each one of them, in love with some pet "live hypothesis" of his own. Let us agree, however, that wherever there is no forced option, the dispassionately judicial intellect with no pet hypothesis, saving us, as it does, from dupery at any rate, ought to be our ideal.

The question next arises: Are there not somewhere forced options in our speculative questions, and can we (as men who may be interested at least as much in positively gaining truth as in merely escaping dupery) always wait with impunity till the coercive evidence shall have arrived? It seems *a priori* improbable that the truth should be so nicely adjusted to our needs and powers as that. In the great boarding-house of nature, the cakes and the butter and the syrup seldom come out so even and leave the plates so clean. Indeed, we should view them with scientific suspicion if they did.

IX

Moral questions immediately present themselves as questions whose solution cannot wait for sensible proof. A moral question is a question not of what sensibly exists, but of what is good, or would be good if it did exist. Science can tell us what exists; but to compare the *worths*, both of what exists and of what does not exist, we must consult not science, but what Pascal calls our heart. Science herself consults her heart when she lays it down that the infinite ascertainment of fact and correction of false belief are the supreme goods for man. Challenge the statement, and science can only repeat it oracularly, or else prove it by showing that such ascertainment and correction bring man all sorts of other goods which man's heart in turn declares. The question of having moral beliefs at all or not having them is decided by our will. Are our moral preferences true or false, or are they only odd biological phenomena, making things good or bad for *us*, but in themselves indifferent? How can your pure intellect decide? If your heart does not *want* a world of moral reality, your head will assuredly never make you believe in one. Mephistophelian scepticism, indeed, will satisfy the head's play-instincts much better than any rigorous idealism can. Some men (even at the student age) are so naturally cool-hearted that the moralistic hypothesis never has for them any pungent life, and in their supercilious presence the hot young moralist always feels strangely ill at ease. The appearance of knowingness is on their side, of *naïveté* and gullibility on his. Yet, in the inarticulate heart of him, he clings to it that he is not a dupe, and that there is a realm in which (as Emerson says) all their wit and intellectual superiority is no better than the cunning of a fox. Moral scepticism can no more be refuted or proved by logic than intellectual scepticism can. When we stick to it that there *is* truth (be it of either kind), we do so with our whole nature, and resolve to stand or fall by the results. The sceptic with his whole nature adopts the doubting attitude; but which of us is the wiser, Omniscience only knows.

Turn now from these wide questions of good to a certain class of questions of fact, questions concerning personal relations, states of mind between one man and another. *Do you like me or not?*—for example. Whether you do or not depends, in countless instances, on whether I meet you half-way, am willing to assume that you must like me, and show you trust and expectation. The previous faith on my part in your liking's existence is in such cases what makes your liking come. But if I stand aloof, and refuse to budge an inch until I have objective evidence, until you shall have done something apt, as the absolutists say, *ad extorquendum assensum meum*, ten to one your liking never comes. How many women's hearts are vanquished by the mere sanguine insistence of some man that they *must* love him! he will not consent to the hypothesis that they cannot. The desire for a certain kind of truth here brings about that special truth's existence; and so it is in innumerable cases of other sorts. Who gains promotions, boons, appointments, but the man in whose life they are seen to play the part of live hypotheses, who discounts them, sacrifices other things for their sake before they have come, and takes risks for them in advance? His faith acts on the powers above him as a claim, and creates its own verification.

A social organism of any sort whatever, large or small, is what it is because each member proceeds to his own duty with a trust that the other members will simultaneously do theirs. Wherever a desired result is achieved by the co-operation of many independent persons, its existence as a fact is a pure consequence of the precursive faith in one another of those immediately concerned. A government, an army, a commercial system, a ship, a college, an athletic team, all exist on this condition, without which not only is nothing achieved, but nothing is even attempted. A whole train of passengers (individually brave enough) will be looted by a few highwaymen, simply because the latter can count on one another, while each passenger fears that if he makes a movement of resistance, he will be shot before any one else backs him up. If we believed that the whole car-full would rise at once with us, we should each severally rise, and train-robbing would never even be attempted. There are, then, cases where a fact cannot come at all unless a preliminary faith exists in its coming. And *where faith in a fact can help create the fact*, that would be an insane logic which should say that faith running ahead of scientific evidence is the "lowest kind of immorality" into which a thinking being can fall. Yet such is the logic by which our scientific absolutists pretend to regulate our lives!

X

In truths dependent on our personal action, then, faith based on desire is certainly a lawful and possibly an indispensable thing.

But now, it will be said, these are all childish human cases, and have nothing to do with great cosmical matters, like the question of religious faith. Let us then pass on to that. Religions differ so much in their accidents that in discussing the religious question we must make it very generic and broad. What then do we now mean by the religious hypothesis? Science says things are; morality says some things are better than other things; and religion says essentially two things.

First, she says that the best things are the more eternal things, the overlapping things, the things in the universe that throw the last stone, so to speak, and say the final word. "Perfection is eternal"—this phrase of Charles Secrétan seems a good way of putting this first affirmation of religion, an affirmation which obviously cannot yet be verified scientifically at all.

The second affirmation of religion is that we are better off even now if we believe her first affirmation to be true.

Now, let us consider what the logical elements of this situation are *in case the religious hypothesis in both its branches be really true.* (Of course, we must admit that possibility at the outset. If we are to discuss the question at all, it must involve a living option. If for any of you religion be a hypothesis that cannot, by any living possibility, be true, then you need go no farther. I speak to the "saving remnant" alone.) So proceeding, we see, first, that religion offers itself as a *momentous* option. We are supposed to gain, even now, by our belief, and to lose by our non-belief, a certain vital good. Secondly, religion is a *forced* option, so far as that good goes. We cannot escape the issue by remaining sceptical and waiting for more light, because, although we do avoid error in that way *if religion be untrue*, we lose the good, *if it be true*, just as certainly as if we positively chose to disbelieve. It is as if a man should hesitate indefinitely to ask a certain woman to marry him because he was not perfectly sure that she would prove an angel after he brought her home. Would he not cut himself off from that particular angel-possibility as decisively as if he went and married some one else? Scepticism, then, is not avoidance of option; it is option of a certain particular kind of risk. *Better risk loss of truth than chance of error*—that is your faith-vetoer's exact position. He is actively playing his stake as much as the believer is; he is backing the field against the religious hypothesis, just as the believer is backing the religious hypothesis against the field. To preach scepticism to us as a duty until "sufficient evidence" for religion be found, is tantamount therefore to telling us, when in presence of the religious hypothesis, that to yield to our fear of its being error is wiser and better than to yield to our hope that it may be true. It is not intellect against all passions, then; it is only intellect with one passion laying down its law. And by what, forsooth, is the supreme wisdom of this passion warranted? Dupery for dupery, what proof is there that dupery through hope is so much worse than dupery through fear? I, for one, can see no proof; and I simply refuse obedience to the scientist's command to imitate his kind of option, in a case where my own stake is important enough to give me the right to choose my own form of risk. If religion be true and the evidence for it be still insufficient, I do not wish, by putting your extinguisher upon my nature (which feels to me as if it had after all some business in this matter), to forfeit my sole chance in life of getting upon the winning side—that chance depending, of course, on my willingness to run the risk of acting as if my passional need of taking the world religiously might be prophetic and right.

All this is on the supposition that it really may be prophetic and right, and that, even to us who are discussing the matter, religion is a live hypothesis which may be true. Now, to most of us religion comes in a still further way that makes a veto on our active faith even more illogical. The more perfect and more eternal aspect of the universe is represented in our religions as having personal form. The universe is no longer a mere *It* to us, but a *Thou*, if we are religious; and any relation that may be possible from person to person might be possible here. For instance, although in one sense we are passive portions of the universe, in another we show a curious autonomy, as if we were small active centres on our own account. We feel, too, as if the appeal of religion to us were made to our own active good-will, as if evidence might be forever withheld from us unless we met the hypothesis half-way. To take a trivial illustration; just as a man who in a company of gentlemen made no advances, asked a warrant for every concession, and believed no one's word without proof, would cut himself off by such churlishness from all the social rewards that a more trusting spirit would earn—so here, one who should shut himself up in snarling logicality and try to make the gods extort his recognition willy-nilly, or not get it at all, might cut himself off forever from his only opportunity of making the gods' acquaintance. This feeling, forced on us we know not whence, that by obstinately believing that there are gods (although not to do so would be so easy both for our logic and our life) we are doing the universe the deepest service we can, seems part of the living essence of the religious hypothesis. If the hypothesis *were* true in all its parts, including this one, then pure intellectualism, with its veto on our making willing advances, would be an absurdity; and some participation of our sympathetic nature would be logically required. I, therefore, for one, cannot see my way to accepting the agnostic rules for truth-seeking, or wilfully agree to keep my willing nature out of the game. I cannot do so for this plain reason, that *a rule of thinking which would absolutely prevent me from acknowledging certain kinds of truth if those kinds of truth were really there, would be an irrational rule.* That for me is the long and short of the formal logic of the situation, no matter what the kinds of truth might materially be.

I confess I do not see how this logic can be escaped. But sad experience makes me fear that some of you may still shrink from radically saying with me, *in abstracto*, that we have the right to believe at our own risk any hypothesis that is live enough to tempt our will. I suspect, however, that if this is so, it is because you have got away from the abstract logical point of view altogether, and are thinking (perhaps without realizing it) of some particular religious hypothesis which for you is dead. The freedom to "believe what we will" you apply to the case of some patent superstition; and the faith you think of is the faith defined by the schoolboy when he said, "Faith is when you believe something that you know ain't true." I can only repeat that this is misapprehension. In *concreto*, the freedom to believe can only cover living options which the intellect of the individual cannot by itself resolve; and living options never seem absurdities to him who has them to consider. When I look at the religious question as it really puts itself to concrete men, and when I think of all the possibilities which both practically and theoretically it involves, then this command that we shall put a stopper on our heart, instincts, and courage, and *wait*—acting of course meanwhile more or less as if religion were *not* true[1]—till doomsday, or till such time as our intellect and senses working together may have raked in evidence enough—this command, I say, seems to me the queerest idol ever manufactured in the philosophic cave. Were we scholastic absolutists, there might be more excuse. If we had an infallible intellect with its objective certitudes, we might feel ourselves disloyal to such a perfect organ of knowledge in not trusting to it exclusively, in not waiting for its releasing word. But if we are empiricists, if we believe that no bell in us tolls to let us know for certain when truth is in our grasp, then it seems a piece of idle fantasticality to preach so solemnly our duty of waiting for the bell. Indeed we *may* wait if we will—I hope you do not think that I am denying that—but if we do so, we do so at our peril as much as if we believed. In either case we *act*, taking our life in our hands. No one of us ought to issue vetoes to the other, nor should we bandy words of abuse. We ought, on the contrary, delicately and profoundly to respect one another's mental freedom: then only shall we bring about the intellectual republic; then only shall we have that spirit of inner tolerance without which all

---

[1] Since belief is measured by action, he who forbids us to believe religion to be true, necessarily also forbids us to act as we should if we did believe it to be true. The whole defence of religious faith hinges upon action. If the action required or inspired by the religious hypothesis is in no way different from that dictated by the naturalistic hypothesis, then religious faith is a pure superfluity, better pruned away, and controversy about its legitimacy is a piece of idle trifling, unworthy of serious minds. I myself believe, of course, that the religious hypothesis gives to the world an expression which specifically determines our reactions, and makes them in a large part unlike what they might be on a purely naturalistic scheme of belief.

our outer tolerance is soulless, and which is empiricism's glory; then only shall we live and let live, in speculative as well as in practical things.

I began by a reference to Fitz-James Stephen; let me end by a quotation from him. "What do you think of yourself? What do you think of the world? . . . These are questions with which all must deal as it seems good to them. They are riddles of the Sphinx, and in some way or other we must deal with them. . . . In all important transactions of life we have to take a leap in the dark. . . . If we decide to leave the riddles unanswered, that is a choice; if we waver in our answer, that, too, is a choice: but whatever choice we make, we make it at our peril. If a man chooses to turn his back altogether on God and the future, no one can prevent him; no one can show beyond reasonable doubt that he is mistaken. If a man thinks otherwise and acts as he thinks, I do not see that any one can prove that *he* is mistaken. Each must act as he thinks best; and if he is wrong, so much the worse for him. We stand on a mountain pass in the midst of whirling snow and blinding mist, through which we get glimpses now and then of paths which may be deceptive. If we stand still we shall be frozen to death. If we take the wrong road we shall be dashed to pieces. We do not certainly know whether there is any right one. What must we do? 'Be strong and of a good courage.' Act for the best, hope for the best, and take what comes. . . . If death ends all, we cannot meet death better."[2]

[2]*Liberty, Equality, Fraternity*, p. 353, 2d edition. London, 1874.

Alfred J. Ayer

CRITIQUE OF ETHICS AND THEOLOGY

Logical positivism, or logical empiricism, was a doctrine developed in Vienna in the 1920s and 1930s. A British representative of this movement was A. J. Ayer (b. 1910). In this provocative essay he argues that all religious statements are meaningless.

This mention of God brings us to the question of the possibility of religious knowledge. We shall see that this possibility has already been ruled out by our treatment of metaphysics. But, as this is a point of considerable interest, we may be permitted to discuss it at some length.

It is now generally admitted, at any rate by philosophers, that the existence of a being having the attributes which define the god of any non-animistic religion cannot be demonstratively proved. To see that this is so, we have only to ask ourselves what are the premises from which the existence of such a god could be deduced. If the conclusion that a god exists is to be demonstratively certain, then these premises must be certain; for, as the conclusion of a deductive argument is already contained in the premises, any uncertainty there may be about the truth of the premises is necessarily shared by it. But we know that no empirical proposition can ever be anything more than probable. It is only *a priori* propositions that are logically certain. But we cannot deduce the existence of a god from an *a priori* proposition. For we know that the reason why *a priori* propositions are certain is that they are tautologies. And from a set of tautologies nothing but a further tautology can be validly deduced. It follows that there is no possibility of demonstrating the existence of a god.

What is not so generally recognised is that there can be no way of proving that the existence of a god, such as the God of Christianity, is even probable. Yet this also is easily shown. For if the existence of such a god were probable, then the proposition that he existed would be an empirical hypothesis. And in that case it would be possible to deduce from it, and other empirical hypotheses, certain experiential propositions which were not deducible from those other hypotheses alone. But in fact this is not possible. It is sometimes claimed, indeed, that the existence of a certain sort of regularity in nature constitutes sufficient evidence for the existence of a god. But if the sentence "God exists" entails no more than that certain types of phenomena occur in certain sequences, then to assert the existence of a god will be simply equivalent to asserting that there is the requisite regularity in nature; and no religious man would admit that this was all he intended to assert in asserting the existence of a god. He would say that in talking about God, he was talking about a transcendent being who might be known through certain empirical manifestations, but certainly could not be defined in terms of those manifestations. But in that case the term "god" is a metaphysical term. And if "god" is a metaphysical term, then it cannot be even probable that a god exists. For to say that "God exists" is to make a metaphysical utterance which cannot be either true or false. And by the same criterion, no sentence which purports to describe the nature of a transcendent god can possess any literal significance.

It is important not to confuse this view of religious assertions with the view that is adopted by atheists, or agnostics.[1] For it is characteristic of an agnostic to hold that the existence of a god is a possibility in which there is no good reason either to believe or disbelieve; and it is characteristic of an atheist to hold that it is at least probable that no god exists. And our view that all utterances about the nature of God are nonsensical, so far from being identical with, or even lending any support to, either of these familiar contentions, is actually incompatible with them. For if the assertion that there is a god is nonsensical, then the atheist's assertion that there is no god is equally nonsensical, since it is only a significant proposition that can be significantly contradicted. As for the agnostic, although he refrains from saying either that there is or that there is not a god, he does not deny that the question whether a transcendent god exists is a genuine question. He does not deny that the two sentences "There is a transcendent god" and "There is no transcendent god" express propositions one of which is actually true and the other false. All he says is that we have no means of telling which of them is true, and therefore ought not to commit ourselves to either. But we have seen that the sentences in question do not express propositions at all. And this means that agnosticism also is ruled out.

Thus we offer the theist the same comfort as we gave to the moralist. His assertions cannot possibly be valid, but they cannot be invalid either. As he says nothing at all about the world, he cannot justly be accused of saying anything false, or anything for which he has insufficient grounds. It is only when the theist claims that in asserting the existence of a transcendent god he is expressing a genuine proposition that we are entitled to disagree with him.

[1] This point was suggested to me by Professor H. H. Price.

It is to be remarked that in cases where deities are identified with natural objects, assertions concerning them may be allowed to be significant. If, for example, a man tells me that the occurrence of thunder is alone both necessary and sufficient to establish the truth of the proposition that Jehovah is angry, I may conclude that, in his usage of words, the sentence "Jehovah is angry" is equivalent to "It is thundering." But in sophisticated religions, though they may be to some extent based on men's awe of natural process which they cannot sufficiently understand, the "person" who is supposed to control the empirical world is not himself located in it; he is held to be superior to the empirical world, and so outside it; and he is endowed with super-empirical attributes. But the notion of a person whose essential attributes are non-empirical is not an intelligible notion at all. We may have a word which is used as if it named this "person," but, unless the sentences in which it occurs express propositions which are empirically verifiable, it cannot be said to symbolize anything. And this is the case with regard to the word "god," in the usage in which it is intended to refer to a transcendent object. The mere existence of the noun is enough to foster the illusion that there is a real, or at any rate a possible entity corresponding to it. It is only when we enquire what God's attributes are that we discover that "God," in this usage, is not a genuine name.

It is common to find belief in a transcendent god conjoined with belief in an after-life. But, in the form which it usually takes, the content of this belief is not a genuine hypothesis. To say that men do not ever die, or that the state of death is merely a state of prolonged insensibility, is indeed to express a significant proposition, though all the available evidence goes to show that it is false. But to say that there is something imperceptible inside a man, which is his soul or his real self, and that it goes on living after he is dead, is to make a metaphysical assertion which has no more factual content than the assertion that there is a transcendent god.

It is worth mentioning that, according to the account which we have given of religious assertions, there is no logical ground for antagonism between religion and natural science. As far as the question of truth or falsehood is concerned, there is no opposition between the natural scientist and the theist who believes in a transcendent god. For since the religious utterances of the theist are not genuine propositions at all, they cannot stand in any logical relation to the propositions of science. Such antagonism as there is between religion and science appears to consist in the fact that science takes away one of the motives which make men religious. For it is acknowledged that one of the ultimate sources of religious feeling lies in the inability of men to determine their own destiny; and science tends to destroy the feeling of awe with which men regard an alien world, by making them believe that they can understand and anticipate the course of natural phenomena, and even to some extent control it. The fact that it has recently become fashionable for physicists themselves to be sympathetic towards religion is a point in favour of this hypothesis. For this sympathy towards religion marks the physicists' own lack of confidence in the validity of their hypotheses, which is a reaction on their part from the anti-religious dogmatism of nineteenth-century scientists, and a natural outcome of the crisis through which physics has just passed.

It is not within the scope of this enquiry to enter more deeply into the causes of religious feeling, or to discuss the probability of the continuance of religious belief. We are concerned only to answer those questions which arise out of our discussion of the possibility of religious knowledge. The point which we wish to establish is that there cannot be any transcendent truths of religion. For the sentences which the theist uses to express such "truths" are not literally significant.

An interesting feature of this conclusion is that it accords with what many theists are accustomed to say themselves. For we are often told that the nature of God is a mystery which transcends the human understanding. But to say that something transcends the human understanding is to say that it is unintelligible. And what is unintelligible cannot significantly be described. Again, we are told that God is not an object of reason but an object of faith. This may be nothing more than an admission that the existence of God must be taken on trust, since it cannot be proved. But it may also be an assertion that God is the object of a purely mystical intuition, and cannot therefore be defined in terms which are intelligible to the reason. And I think there are many theists who would assert this. But if one allows that it is impossible to define God in intelligible terms, then one is allowing that it is impossible for a sentence both to be significant and to be about God. If a mystic admits that the object of his vision is something which cannot be described, then he must also admit that he is bound to talk nonsense when he describes it.

For his part, the mystic may protest that his intuition does reveal truths to him, even though he cannot explain to others what these truths are; and that we who do not possess this faculty of intuition can have no ground for denying that it is a cognitive faculty. For we can hardly maintain *a priori* that there are no ways of discovering true propositions except those which we ourselves employ. The answer is that we set no limit to the number of ways in which one may come to formulate a true proposition. We do not in any way deny that a synthetic truth may be discovered by purely intuitive methods as well as by the rational method of induction. But we do say that every synthetic proposition, however it may have been arrived at, must be subject to the test of actual experience. We do not deny *a priori* that the mystic is able to discover truths by his own special methods. We wait to hear what are the propositions which embody his discoveries, in order to see whether they are verified or confuted by our empirical observations. But the mystic, so far from producing propositions which are empirically verified, is unable to produce any intelligible propositions at all. And therefore we say that his intuition has not revealed to him any facts. It is no use his saying that he has apprehended facts but is unable to express them. For we know that if he really had acquired any information, he would be able to express it. He would be able to indicate in some way or other how the genuineness of his discovery might be empirically determined. The fact that he cannot reveal what he "knows," or even himself devise an empirical test to validate his "knowledge," shows that his state of mystical intuition is not a genuinely cognitive state. So that in describing his vision the mystic does not give us any information about the external world; he merely gives us indirect information about the condition of his own mind.

These considerations dispose of the argument from religious experience, which many philosophers still regard as a valid argument in favour of the existence of a god. They say that it is logically possible for men to be immediately acquainted with God, as they are immediately acquainted with a sense-content, and that there is no reason why one should be prepared to believe a man when he says that he is seeing a yellow patch, and refuse to believe him when he says that he is seeing God. The answer to this is that if the man who asserts that he is seeing God is merely asserting that he is experiencing a peculiar kind of sense-content, then we do not for a moment deny that his assertion may be true. But, ordinarily, the man who says that he is seeing God is saying not merely that he is experiencing a religious emotion, but also that there exists a transcendent being who is the object of this emotion; just as the man who says that he sees a yellow patch is ordinarily saying not merely that his visual sense-field contains a yellow sense-content, but also that there exists a yellow object to which the sense-content belongs. And it is not irrational to be prepared to believe a man when he asserts the existence of a yellow object, and to refuse to believe him when he asserts the existence of a transcendent god. For whereas the sentence "There exists here a yellow-coloured material thing" expresses a genuine synthetic proposition which could be empirically verified, the sentence "There exists a transcendent god" has, as we have seen, no literal significance.

We conclude, therefore, that the argument from religious experience is altogether fallacious. The fact that people have religious experiences is interesting from the psychological point of view, but it does not in any way imply that there is such a thing as religious knowledge, any more than our having moral experiences implies that there is such a thing as moral knowledge. The theist, like the moralist, may believe that his experiences are cognitive experiences, but, unless he can formulate his "knowledge" in propositions that are empirically verifiable, we may be sure that he is deceiving himself. It follows that those philosophers who fill their books with assertions that they intuitively "know" this or that moral or religious "truth" are merely providing material for the psycho-analyst. For no act of intuition can be said to reveal a truth about any matter of fact unless it issues in verifiable propositions. And all such propositions are to be incorporated in the system of empirical propositions which constitutes science.

B. HOW CAN EVIL EXIST IF GOD IS ALL-WISE, ALL-POWERFUL, AND ALL-GOOD?

Antony Flew

DIVINE OMNIPOTENCE AND HUMAN FREEDOM

In the following essay, Antony Flew (b. 1921) discusses the problem of evil and its relationship to the free-will problem.

Either God cannot abolish evil or he will not: if he cannot then he is not all-powerful; if he will not then he is not all-good.

The dilemma is much older than this, St. Augustine's formulation of it. Perhaps the most powerful of all sceptical arguments, it has appealed especially to the clearest and most direct minds, striking straight and decisively to the heart of the matter. It was, for instance, central to J. S. Mill's rejection of Christianity and he returns to it repeatedly and often angrily throughout his *Three Essays on Religion*:[1] e.g.

> . . . the impossible problem of reconciling infinite benevolence and justice with infinite power in the Creator of such a world as this. The attempt to do so not only involves absolute contradiction in an intellectual point of view but exhibits to excess the revolting spectacle of a jesuitical defence of moral enormities (pp. 186–7).

[1]Longman's, 1874. This is a powerful and lucid book, original particularly in that Mill, though rejecting the Christian revelation and consequently not "incumbered with the necessity of admitting the omnipotence of the Creator" (p. 186), was still, in spite of Hume and Darwin, sufficiently impressed with the argument to design to explore at length the idea of a finite God, allowing "a large balance of probability in favour of creation by intelligence" (p. 174). Though this book made a considerable contemporary impact it seems to have been curiously neglected since: for it has never been reprinted (the R.P.A. to note); and even such a philosophical scholar as Professor A. N. Prior overlooked the essay on "Nature," which is centrally relevant to the theme of his *Logic and the Basis of Ethics* (O.U.P., 1949).

These are robust words, but not quite final.

(1) Several determined attempts have been made to escape from the dilemma. One favourite—which might be dubbed the Free-will Defence—runs like this. The first move is to point out: "Nothing which implies contradiction falls under the omnipotence of God"[2]; that is, Even God cannot do what is *logically* impossible; that is, If you make up a self-contradictory, a nonsense, sentence it won't miraculously become sense just because you have put the word "God" as its subject. The third formulation is greatly superior to the other two, because it brings out the nature of *logical* impossibility. It should appeal to theologians, as being free of the unwanted and of course entirely incorrect[3] suggestion that "being unable to do the logically impossible" is some sort of limitation on or weakness in Omnipotence, whereas the only limitation lies in men who contradict themselves and talk nonsense about God.[4] The second move in this defence is to claim: "God gave men free-will"; and this necessarily implies the possibility of doing evil as well as good, that is to say that there would be a contradiction in speaking, it would be nonsense to speak, of creatures with freedom to choose good or evil but not able to choose evil. (Which, no blame to him, is what his creatures men have done). This may be followed by a third rather less common move: to point out that certain good things, viz. certain virtues, logically presuppose: not merely beings with freedom of choice (which alone are capable of either virtue or vice), and consequently the possibility of evil; but also the actual occurrence of certain evils. Thus what we might call the second-order goods of sympathetic feeling and action logically could not occur without (at least the appearance of) the first-order evils of suffering or misfortune. And the moral good of forgiveness presupposes the prior occurrence of (at least the appearance of) some lower-order evil to be forgiven. This may be already a second-order moral evil such as callousness, thus making the forgiveness a third-order good. Here one recalls: O *felix culpa quae tantum ac talem meruit habere redemptorem.*

The upshot is that there are certain goods, e.g. moral virtues, which logically presuppose the possibility of correlative evils, and others, e.g. the virtues of forgiveness and sympathetic action, which logically presuppose the actuality (or at least the appearance) of certain evils, in this case the doing of injuries and the suffering of misfortunes. Thus it would not make sense to suggest that God might have chosen to achieve these goods without the possibility in the one case, the actuality in the other, of the correlative and presupposed evils.

[2]Aquinas *Summa Theologica*, I, Q. XXV, Art. 4.

[3]Which misled a philosopher of the calibre of M'Taggart: see his *Some Dogmas of Religion* (Arnold, 1906 and 1930), §166, where he attacks and rejects the whole notion of omnipotence on these misguided grounds.

[4]Professor C. S. Lewis is one of the very few theologians to have made the point in this superior way, using the "formal mode of speech" (*The Problem of Pain*: Bles, 1940, p. 16). Credit where this is due; especially as we shall later be assailing other parts of the book in successive footnotes.

Unfortunately men have chosen to misuse their freedom by choosing to exploit the possibility of wrongdoing necessarily involved in the possibility of right-doing. But this is not God's fault: or at any rate it does not show that God *cannot* be both all-powerful and all-good. It is this Free-will Defence we propose to examine.

(2) It is a powerful defence: which has satisfied many believers; and routed or at least rattled many sceptics. The usual counters are: First: to point out that by no means all the evil in the world can be traced back to an origin in human wickedness, nor shown to make possible any higher-order goods. The obvious and least disputable example is animal pain before the emergence of *homo sapiens*; which cannot be the result of human wickedness because it preceded it; and which cannot have made possible any second-order good, because it preceded the arrival of any beings capable of such second-order goods and evils. Second: to note the injustice of the allocation of the first-order nonmoral evils. The unfortunate idiom which talks of "Man's sin, and its consequences for Man" at least seems to involve a doctrine of the rightness of collective responsibility,[5] and certainly tends complacently to conceal that the worst consequences of the wickedness of a Hitler fall not on him or other conspicuously guilty men but on their victims. Third: to say that a God who is prepared to allow such a volume of evil as there actually is in the world, because this is the necessary price of securing certain special goods which have been and will be achieved, cannot after all possibly be called good. To call such a being, ruthlessly paying an enormous price in evil means to attain his good ends, himself good is mere flattery: "worthy only of those whose slavish fears make them offer the homage of lies to a Being who, they profess to think, is incapable of being deceived and holds all falsehood in abomination" (Mill, *loc. cit.*, p. 52); and justifying Hobbes' claim that "in the attributes we give to God, we are not to consider the signification of philosophical truth; but the signification of pious intention, to do him the greatest honour we are able" (*Leviathan*, Ch. XXXI, Everyman, p. 195); Fourth: to warn the religious apologist meticulously to avoid any pretence that God could be limited by the laws of his own Universe. Thus the suggestion that suffering, as a matter of fact, can refine characters as nothing else can is not merely doubtfully true but also, in this context, blasphemous. For the notion of causally necessary means to ends, as opposed to that of logically necessary preconditions, cannot apply to creative omnipotence.[6]

These counter-attacks have not the simple seemingly decisive force of the original dilemma. Against the first it is possible to suggest, and impossible definitively to dispose of, the possibility that whatever evil does not ultimately

---

[5]See, for instance, the strictures on it of Professor H. D. Lewis in his *Morals and The New Theology* (Gollancz, 1947), *passim*, and his *Morals and Revelation* (Allen & Unwin, 1951), Ch. II and V.

[6]See Mill, *loc. cit.*, pp. 176–7: where Mill goes on to draw the conclusion that arguments to design square ill with this notion.

originate in human wickedness originates in the wickedness of evil spirits beginning before man began.[7] Against the third it is possible to appeal to the fact that no man knows what will be the ultimate sum of good to place in the scales against the absolutely enormous, but perhaps relatively trifling and in any case also unknown, ultimate sum of evil.[8] And the Christian can complain that the epithet "ruthless" neglects a vital implication of the incarnation doctrine; that God pities and shares the sufferings of his creatures.

There thus seem to be ways out of a dilemma which presented Christianity as a simultaneous belief in two logically incompatibles and to a more defensible position where great faith is still called for, but no longer a faith in what is known to be not merely untrue but an "absolute contradiction." The sceptic has apparently been forced to abandon his clear-cut knock-down refutation and to resort to arguing: that there need not have been so much and/or certain kinds of evil to get the good; that if there need, or in any case, it were better not to have had the goods which could only be bought at such a price. Such arguments may still constitute a formidable challenge; but they do leave the believer with some freedom of manœuvre.

(3) This account in terms of move and counter-move is only a crudely stylized cartoon, without the panoply of distinctions and refinements required to do justice to the full complexity of the logical situation. But its purpose is

---

[7]This idea is taken very seriously indeed by C. S. Lewis (*loc. cit.*, pp. 121f.). To make this more than just another desperate *ad hoc* expedient of apologetic it is necessary to produce independent reason for launching such an hypothesis (if "hypothesis" is not too flattering a term for it). We cannot here embark on the important question of what sort of reason there could be: but for stimulating suggestions see John Wisdom, *Other Minds* (Blackwell, 1952).

[8]See, for instance, I. M. Crombie in Chapter VI (ii) above. C. S. Lewis was again driven to a desperate manœuvre (*loc. cit.*, pp. 103–4): "We must never make the problem of pain worse than it is by vague talk of 'the unimaginable sum of human misery.' Suppose that I have a toothache of intensity x: and suppose that you, who are seated behind me, also begin to have a toothache of intensity x. You may if you choose say that the total amount of pain in the room is now $2x$. But you must remember that no one is suffering $2x$: search all time and all space and you will not find that composite pain in anyone's consciousness. There is no such thing as a sum of suffering, for no one suffers it. When we have reached the maximum that a single person can suffer, we have, no doubt, reached something very horrible, but we have reached all the suffering there ever can be in the universe. The addition of a million fellow sufferers adds no more pain." But this is fantastic. The facts that no one can suffer more than they can, and that the calculus of arithmetic cannot be applied to the field of pain (or pleasure) as fully and precisely as Bentham would have liked, provide not the slightest reason for saying that it makes no sense to use such expressions as "sum of pain" in the rough-and-ready way in which people do in fact use them. They surely use them: *not* as part of some impossible piece of applied mathematics from which a numerical value for a sum of pains of different people, durations and intensities might be derived (Benthan himself sensibly refrained from such an enterprise: see, e.g. *Principles of Morals and Legislation* Ch. IV); *but* simply to bring out such truisms as that, all other things being equal, it's a worse business if two people have toothache than if one does, and worse still if there is an epidemic. It is thus preposterous for Lewis to maintain that "the addition of a million fellow sufferers adds no more pain": and monstrous thereby to imply, presumably, that this addition makes no value difference.

merely to set the stage for the launching of a further, new, or at least unusual, sceptical counter-attack. This is directed at the key position of the whole Free-will Defence: the idea that there is a contradiction involved in saying that God might have made people so that they always in fact *freely* chose the right. If there is no contradiction here then Omnipotence might have made a world inhabited by wholly virtuous people; the Free-will Defence is broken-backed; and we are back again with the original intractable antinomy. . . .

(4) We cannot hope here even to begin to meet objections to the theses of (3) based on the rejection of our fundamental idea that freedom and universal causal determinism are not necessarily incompatible. But suppose now that someone accepting it raised the objection that what has been shown is: *not* that there is no "contradiction in speaking of *God* so arranging things that all men would always as a matter of fact freely choose to do the right"; *but* that there is no contradiction in the idea of men always freely doing the right although all their behaviour without exception followed (i.e. could be sub-sumed under or fitted into) universal laws of nature, although it was deter-mined by (i.e. completely predictable on the basis of) those laws, and although the notion of caused cause was applicable to it all. The nerve of the distinction lies in the *personality* of God, which makes a crucial difference: in the former case a *quasi-personal* being has *fixed* everything that everyone will do, and choose, and suffer; in the latter case it has not been *fixed*, but it is just the fact that people will make precisely those decisions which they will make and not those alternative decisions which they could have made if they had had the mind to. The former is the doctrine of predestination:[9] the latter of determinism.[10]

Now, the argument would run, whereas the latter is perhaps compatible with human freedom and the fair ascription of responsibility to human agents; the former certainly is not. For consider the phenomenon of post-hypnotic sugges-tion: described in this quotation from Knight and Knight, A *Modern Introduction to Psychology* (University Tutorial Press, 1948), p. 212:

> A subject is hypnotized, and is told that after a precise time interval . . . he is to carry out some series of actions. . . . When he is awakened from the hypnotic trance he remembers nothing of these instructions. Nevertheless, when the pre-scribed time is up, he will carry out the programme in every detail. If he is asked why he is behaving in this curious fashion, he will usually produce some highly ingenious rationalization. . . .

Now, it might be said, predestinationism makes out that all of us, all the time, whether we know it or not, *both* when by ordinary standards we are acting freely and could help doing what we choose to do, *and* when we are acting

---

[9]"God from all eternity did by the most wise and holy counsel of his own will, freely and un-changeably ordain whatsoever comes to pass" (*Westminster Confession*, 1649).

[10]Notice that we have been careful in our choice of phrases above to avoid any of the pre-destinarian suggestions which are often confusingly incorporated in determinist formulations.

under compulsion, have no choice, or are not acting at all but are asleep or paralysed; all of us are, really and ultimately, as it were acting out the irresistible suggestions of the Great Hypnotist. And this idea surely is incompatible with that of our being free agents, properly accountable for what we do. Hence there is after all "a contradiction in speaking of God so arranging things that all men always as a matter of fact freely choose to do the right."

(*a*) This objection is apparently conclusive. Yet it involves a crucial and subtle mistake: the actual logical situation is exceedingly hard to determine categorically; but the uncertainty is not about whether or not sceptical attack can be warded off but about which and how many positions have to be yielded to it.

Now certainly if we were to discover that a person or group of people, whom previously we had thought to be acting freely and therefore to be properly accountable in law and morals for what they misdid, had in fact been acting out the suggestions of some master-hypnotist, then we should need to reconsider all questions of their accountability in the light of this fresh information. It would not prove that they were not in any degree responsible, even if we knew that this hypnotist's suggestions were irresistible.[11] For there would remain the question whether they willingly put themselves in his power knowing what this might involve: here the analogy is with the man who knows that he is "not responsible for what he does" when he is drunk but who could have helped getting into that state (see Aristotle, *Nicomachean Ethics*, III, v, §8: 1113 B 31ff.). What our information would be sufficient to prove is that there was someone else besides the apparent agent, namely the hypnotist, who is at least as responsible, at least an accessory before the fact: here the analogy is to the boss who sends one of his gang to do a job, or to the man who sets a booby-trap leaving it where his victim will certainly spring it.

But the case of predestination, where the hypnotist would be not a human being but God, is essentially different. First, because here there is no question of any of us being in any way responsible for allowing ourselves to fall under the spell of this hypnotist. Second, because here it is not a matter of some being divinely hypnotized and some not; or of all being so for part of the time, and part not; but of absolutely everyone from the beginning to the end of time being hypnotized all the time. The first reaction to the idea of God, the Great Hypnotist, is that this would mean that no one ever was or had been or would be *really* responsible, that none of the people whom we should otherwise have been certain could have helped doing things *really* could. And so on. But this is at least very misleading. Certainly it would be monstrous to suggest that anyone, *however truly responsible in the eyes of men*, could fairly be called to account and punished by the God who had rigged his every move. All the bitter words which have ever been written against the wickedness of the God of predestination-

---

[11]It is said that this is not in fact the case with any actual hypnotist: though the evidence is conflicting; and in any case irrelevant to our argument here.

ism—especially when he is also thought of as filling Hell with all but the elect—are amply justified.[12] But this is not sufficient to show that every use of any of the phrases "acted freely," "had a choice," "made his own decisions" and so forth as applied to any human being must have been wrong, if predestinationism is true. Again remember the Argument of the Paradigm Case. The *meaning* of these phrases has been given in terms of certain familiar human situations, and the differences between these. No new information, not even the supposed item of theological fact that we are created by Omnipotence, can possibly show that such phrases cannot correctly be applied to such situations, or that there do not subsist between these situations the differences they were introduced to mark.[13] The position seems to be that: while there is no "contradiction in speaking of God as so arranging things that all men always as a matter of fact freely choose to do the right"; the idea of God arraigning and punishing anyone who freely chose the wrong, if he so arranges things that his victim does so act, "outrages . . . the most ordinary justice and humanity."[14]

(*b*) If the objector prefers to go on maintaining—and we should only very hesitantly suggest he was wrong—that this idea that we are all of us always as it were acting out the divine post-hypnotic suggestions is incompatible with saying that all of us sometimes act of our own free will, then two possibilities are open to him: both of which equally involve the annihilation of the Free-will Defence. He can say that God exists and as his creatures we simply cannot be free: for what the doctrine of creation[15] means is that all power is from God,

---

[12]"The recognition, for example, of the object of highest worship in a being who could make a Hell; and who could create countless generations of human beings with the certain foreknowledge that he was creating them for this fate. . . . Any other of the outrages to the most ordinary justice and humanity involved in the common Christian conception of the moral character of God sinks into insignificance beside this dreadful idealization of wickedness" (*Three Essays on Religion*, pp. 113–14). Cf. the *Westminster Confession*, "By the decree of God, for the manifestation of His glory, some men and angels are predestinated unto everlasting life, and others foreordained to everlasting death." On these issues I can find no difference of substance between Calvinism and Roman Catholicism: Calvin stated with harsh clarity and without equivocation what is implicit in conciliar pronouncements.

[13]A dim realization of this may have been what enabled the Calvinists to think that "God from all eternity did . . . freely and unchangeably ordain whatsoever comes to pass. Yet . . . thereby" is no "violence offered to the will of the creatures." What was wrong was to suggest that in such a case: "neither is God the author of sin"; that *God* could fairly hold men accountable (quotes from the *Westminster Confession*).

[14]Calvin scarcely pretended otherwise: the damned were damned "by a just and irreprehensible, but incomprehensible judgment." In thus seeing and accepting the implications of omnipotence he showed himself to have both a clearer head and a stronger—shall we say?—stomach than most believers.

[15]See Ch. IX: we are concerned here with what I there call the theological sense of "creation"; which neither entails nor is entailed by the also questionably significant proposition that the Universe was made by God in the beginning of time. (On this last phrase see M. Scriven in *Brit. J. Phil. Science*, 1954 and on the absence of the two-way entailment see St. Thomas's *de aeternitate mundi contra murmurantes*.)

that all things and creatures are always and utterly dependent on God, for their beginning and preservation, in and for their powers, their activities, and their limitations.[16] If he says this then clearly he cannot use the central move of the Free-will Defence "to justify the ways of God to man." Furthermore if he continues to hold, as he must, with Kant and everybody else, that morality presupposes freedom then he has left no room for higher-order, or any order, moral goods attainable by man. The alternative option consists in reversing the argument[17] to produce a new proof of God's non-existence, an inverted Kantian postulate of practical reason. Thus he can say that since we clearly *are* free agents on some occasions we *cannot* be God's creatures; and hence there *cannot* be a creator God. In which case the question of defence, free-will or any other, does not arise.

(*c*) Besides saying that the idea that we all always as it were act out the suggestions of the Divine Hypnotist is or is not compatible with saying that all of us sometimes act of our own free-will there is a third possibility. We might argue that the whole notion of an omnipotent creator God is logically vicious. If this is so the problem of evil cannot arise, since the notions of God as either all-powerful, or all-good or as even existing at all will all be equally vicious. This is a position to which the present writer is very much inclined;[18] and the difficulties which arise in attempts to reconcile divine omnipotence with human freedom might be taken as an indication that the former notion ought to come under suspicion. We cannot here examine this position; and fortunately it is sufficient to make three points only. First, even if it is correct it by no means follows that there cannot be any right and wrong about such theological arguments as those we have been deploying: for our propositions may nevertheless be sound or unsound in much the same sort of way as those of proposed *reductiones ad absurdum* in geometry; which also and similarly make use of expressions which are, strictly, non-significant. Second, if it is correct the practical consequences here may seem very much the same as those presented by the second option of (4) (*b*) above. For the question whether it is that the Universe has as a matter of fact no creator or that this suggestion does not even make sense is clearly academic. Third our concentration at the end of (4) (*a*) above on the moral monstrosity of the doctrine of a Hell-filling creator must not be allowed to conceal from us that we were there dealing with only one and an evaluative aspect of the much more general fact that there is absurdity in

---

[16]C. S. Lewis puts it nicely, without I think realizing how disastrous this doctrine is for what he wants to say about human responsibility: |Men| "wanted some corner in the universe of which they could say to God, 'This is our business not yours.' But there is no such corner. They wanted to be nouns, but they were, and eternally must be, mere adjectives" (*loc. cit.*, p. 68).

[17]On this move compare Smart in Ch. III above and Descartes: "Some indeed might be found who would be disposed rather to deny the existence of a being so powerful than to believe that there is nothing certain" (*Meditation*, I).

[18]See, for instance, my share of Ch. IX below, *ad fin*.

the notion of any transactions at all between creatures and their Creator. It is not merely that his "punishing" his creatures is morally repellent, but that it does not deserve to be called punishment at all.[19] Again it is not that only the notion of punishment is inapplicable but that a similar absurdity infects all concepts which apply originally only to transactions between autonomous and responsible human beings if we try to transfer them to describe possible trans- actions between Creator and creatures. Thus to speak of a creature "praising," "promising," "being rewarded by," "injuring," or "defying" his Creator is equally to misuse language: it is far more inappropriate than to use these words unescorted by warning inverted commas of the "activities" of a ven- triloquist's dummy; because the ventriloquist at most *fashioned* but he did not *create* his dummy.[20] Though this is not to dispose of that whole range of ques- tions: Are those propositions which seem to be about men's actual or hypo- thetical transactions with God, if transformed into psychological and other sorts of propositions about the universe, as a matter of fact true?[21]

(5) Finally a few words on the pictures associated with the Free-will Defence. These do much to ease the "double-think"[22] which goes on here when people hold *both* that our faults, though curiously and arbitrarily[23] not our virtues, are to be laid not at God's but at our door because he made us free agents; *and* that all power is in God's hands all the time, that every move, every thought of his creatures depends on him for its initiation and conservation, and presumably therefore that he could change the heart of any man at any time if he wanted him to reverse his wants.

The picture of the Great Father and his (mainly prodigal) sons is attractive; but quite inappropriate here, where the Father is supposed to represent Om- nipotence and the sons are human beings. It seems suitable, because it does take account of the manifest facts of human freedom and responsibility to one another. But it is radically inappropriate to the relation between Creator and creature. A human father has only limited knowledge and limited powers. Once he has begotten and reared his sons there is usually precious little he can do about it if he doesn't like the way they behave. So that, as he had no means of knowing before their conception how radically prodigal they would be, and so

[19]See my "The Justification of Punishment" in *Philosophy*, 1954, on what a standard case of punish- ment necessarily involves.

[20]On the possibility that the doctrine of the incarnation circumvents this difficulty see Ch. X and Ch. XI.

[21]See for the sort of "desupernaturalization" we have in mind: Lucretius, quoted in Ch. VI (i) A, and John Wisdom, "Gods" *ad fin.*, in *Logic and Language*, First Series (ed. Antony Flew: Blackwell, 1951).

[22]See Ch. VI (i) D above for the definition of this term, quoted.

[23]Perhaps the elusive doctrine of the negativity of evil seems to some people to remove the arbitrariness: but surely if you take creation seriously it cannot do this? For who is there but God who could have left the gaps?

long as he did his best to bring them up in the way they should go, there are usually no grounds for ascribing responsibility to him. But the position with an omnipotent Creator must be different. There can be no question of ignorance or of inability to do anything about it or of creatures being even temporarily autonomous. On the contrary the doctrine of creation necessarily involves that God is as it were accessory before during and after the fact to every human action. Or rather, "accessory" is a ludicrously weak word for the source and ground of all being and power.[24] Again, a human father may fairly and without absurdity reward or punish his sons and they can without absurdity or inverted commas be said to defy, promise or injure him. But these relations cannot subsist between a Creator and creatures. The analogy offered by the picture breaks down in precisely the respects which are crucial.

The only picture which begins to do justice to this situation is the one we have already offered, that of the Great Hypnotist with all his creatures acting out, usually unknowingly, his commands. To fail to appreciate this is to fail to take the theological doctrine of creation seriously. And this, as both Mill[25] and Calvin[26] in their very different ways were at pains to point out, is what most believers most of the time do. Similarly to suggest that God might himself have limited his power is to fail in the same way: for if the limitation is real it must involve that the Universe is now to that extent out of control, and contains things independent of God; which is precisely what the doctrine of creation denies.[27] But this picture, though it represents perhaps as well as may be the relations of creatures and Creator, misrepresents the relations of creature to creature by suggesting that none of us could very properly hold another responsible or be held responsible by him. (All this section (5) is assuming the position of (4) (a) above.)

(6) *Summary.* We first posed the dilemma and then (1) outlined the three elements of the Free-will Defence and (2) four counter-moves usually made against it. In (3) we argued that there was no contradiction in saying that God could have made men so that they all always freely chose the right, but indicated that this did not definitely dispose of the matter, since the apologist

---

[24]See C. S. Lewis again, as quoted above, on our being adjectives and never nouns.

[25]See *loc. cit.*, pp. 39–40 and 115–16.

[26]See *Institutes*, Bk. II, Ch. 4 and Bk. III, Ch. 21.

[27]Consider here C. S. Lewis' speculation that "the 'annihilation' of a soul" may not be "intrinsically possible" (*loc. cit.*, p. 113). This idea no doubt seems more plausible dressed in the idiom of "intrinsic impossibility": but Lewis has elsewhere (pp. 15ff.) rightly pointed out that only *logical* impossibility could without contradiction be said to apply to God (see (1) above): and it is therefore wholly irrelevant to try to support this present arbitrary piece of special pleading by an appeal to the fact that we have no experience of the *annihilation* as opposed to the *transformation* of *matter*. Which is in any case a curious appeal to come from one who certainly wishes to claim that it makes sense to speak of *creatio ex nihilo*: both in the "popular" and in the "theological" senses distinguished in Ch. IX below.

could regroup the two remaining elements in the Free-will Defence for a further, albeit rather desperate, stand. In (4) we considered the suggestion that while determinism may be compatible with human responsibility predestinationism is not: concluding, tentatively, that this is not so, but only because and in so far as a creator could and must be taken as outwith the range of human transactions. This section was awkward and unsteady: but not in any way to comfort the orthodox. Finally in (5) we pointed out how a favourite picture used to illustrate the relation of Creator to his creatures misleads believers to overlook those radically disruptive implications of the creation doctrine to which the possible objection of (4) had led us.

Steven S. Schwarzschild, Emil L. Fackenheim, Richard H. Popkin, George Steiner, and Elie Wiesel

JEWISH VALUES IN THE POST-HOLOCAUST FUTURE: A SYMPOSIUM

In the following symposium, four speakers discuss the meaning and implications of the Nazi destruction of the Jewish community in Europe during the Second World War.

STEVEN S. SCHWARZSCHILD

We meet in order to try to explore together a problem which we believe to be important for Judaism, for the Jewish people, and therefore for the world. Permit me to attempt a definition and explanation of the problem that we have set for ourselves in the phrase, "Jewish values in the post-Holocaust future."

In the face of new facts language always fails. The catastrophe that overwhelmed European Jewry, and therewith the people of Israel as a whole, during the reign of Nazism was and will forever remain an absolute *novum*—the enactment of absolute human and historical evil. We speak of it as "the Holocaust." But there have been other holocausts, and they were nothing like this. In such a linguistic perplexity Jews usually, and rightly, turn to Hebrew as the one language that is in accord with their spirit and with the reality of their experiences. Thus we try the word *sho'ah*. But there have been other *sho'ot*, and they cannot compare quantitatively or qualitatively, in very principle, with the human bestiality and immorality that exercised themselves upon us. Thus it turns out at the very beginning of our conversation, as I doubt not its further course will prove over and over again, that because the Jewish experience of the 30's and 40's was truly *sui generis*, all speaking about it and its consequences will be thoroughly inadequate. Perhaps silence would be the only proper posture toward it.

But this would be too simple. The Holocaust is so agonizing, even *ex post facto*, precisely because it is the ultimate paradox. It imposes silence even while it demands speech. George Steiner's latest book, which deals largely with this problematic, expresses the paradox in its very title, *Language and Silence.* We have to try to live in the world and with the people that went through and, in one way or another, participated in that great purgatory. And human living means language. But surely henceforth—and this is the first premise of our conversation this afternoon—human language, and all that it implies in understanding, values and aims, must be fundamentally different from what it was before. We hold that, in the perspective of what our eyes have seen, the world, history, and the role of Israel in these must be totally reevaluated by Jews as well as by non-Jews. Our understanding of them, and therefore the words which we use for them, must be completely revised.

We are saying that a new age has begun. Christians think that the watershed of human history occurred on Calvary. The French Revolution wanted to start counting the years anew beginning with 1789. There was a whole generation of European intellectuals who thought, and some still dare think, that the First World War changed the face of the earth. Jews, to the contrary, have always insisted on measuring time in such a way as to proclaim their belief that God's original will for man has been and still to this day is continuously operative. I doubt that even now we would be prepared to sacrifice the unity of history any more than the unity of God Himself. But we must confess that the unity of history is different from what we may previously have thought it to be. We know not what it is. We are deeply puzzled as to how to redirect it. To try to find the beginnings of answers to this question is, perhaps, our chief concern here.

The post-Holocaust world is fundamentally different from the previous world. Many of the sensitive writers, Jewish and Gentile, have been saying this, with varying degrees of success, for two decades. Some few thinkers have tried to tackle the implications of this recognition, however gingerly. Many Jews, in Israel and the Diaspora, have acted on it almost instinctively. But religious thinkers have overwhelmingly shied away from this truth. As far as Christian thinkers are concerned, the astounding and—at least to me—almost as frightening fact as the Holocaust itself is the influential sector of opinion which asserts a new and unbounded—of all things!—optimism about man and history. With very few exceptions, Jewish religious thinkers have tended to avoid the issue altogether. The most favorable interpretation of this latter fact that I can think of is that, perhaps, they hesitate to rock the life-boat in which the captain and the few survivors of the disaster are trying to save themselves.

But the questions imperiously demand a hearing. In 1949 I put them something like this to an audience of Jewish D.P.'s and survivors in the center of Europe: What new knowledge of God has risen out of the chimneys of Auschwitz? What do we know now about man that we did not know before he created Maidanek? By what values shall we try to live that have been seared into our flesh in Bergen-Belsen? What new Jewish actions have been commanded by the loudspeakers in Buchenwald? What new words have been pressed on our lips by the whips and boots of Theresienstadt? In short, what will the world of tomorrow have to look like which we now know to be, to be able to be, and to have been what Rousset called *l'univers concentrationnaire*?

To conclude the explication of our title-phrase, we want to concentrate on the "future." We do not primarily want to ask how we and the world have in fact been affected by what has happened, nor what our present condition is as a result (though these are, of course, indispensable and important preliminary questions). We *are* asking, and asking in all seriousness: Knowing what we do, having become what we are, seeing the world as it is—by what values are we to act among ourselves and in relationship to the world at large in our future? We hold—and this is the second premise of our conversation—that this future of ours is perforce a future different from all other futures that have ever been, in that it is, as they were not, a "post-Holocaust future." Specifically, we put these three questions, in a very tentative and optional fashion, to the four main participants in the conversation: 1) What seems to you to be the present condition of the human world in the perspective of the Holocaust? 2) What do you hold to be the demands made upon us and upon the world by having to live after the Holocaust has taken place? 3) In this light, what do you think will have to be the world in the future?

These questions can also be phrased in terms of the time and place in which we happen to be assembled. Today is Purim. This is a day preeminently suited to the consideration of the role of a tried and saved Israel in the world and in God's providence. By a rather rare coincidence, in 1967 it is also the Christian Easter. I venture to suggest, without wishing to spell it out, that the coincidence of Purim and Easter could lead to more useful and perceptive reflections on the role of Christianity in the tragic Jewish theodicy than the more frequent coincidence of Passover and Easter. Furthermore, a few short blocks from where we are meeting in New York City, a "be-in" is taking place right now in Central Park, with colored balloons, gift-candies, guitars, young people with long hair and somewhat unconventional clothes. I, for one, want to ask what our relationship is and ought to be to the world of established institutions and beliefs in which the Holocaust took place—and what is and should it be to the new, rebellious, youthful, alienated world that, in large measure, like the remnant of Israel itself, has fallen heir to its poisoned wells?

Our four panelists come from very various backgrounds and disciplines. But they have this in common: they are profoundly concerned and literate Jews, and in their lives and work they have given testimony to their sensitivity to the historic centrality of the Holocaust. We shall begin our proceedings with opening statements by the members of the panel.

EMIL L. FACKENHEIM

Our topic today has two presuppositions which, I take it, we are not going to question but will simply take for granted. First, there is a unique and unprecedented crisis in the period of Jewish history which needs to be faced by all Jews, from the Orthodox at one extreme to the secularists at the other. (Thus I take it that we are not going to discuss the various forms of Judaism and Jewishness as though nothing had happened.) Second, whatever our response to the present crisis, it will be, in any case, a stubborn persistence in our Jewishness, not an attempt to abandon it or escape from it. (Thus I take it that we shall leave dialogues with Jews who do not want to be Jews for another day.)

How shall we understand the crisis of this period in Jewish history? We shall, I think, be misled if we think in the style of the social sciences which try to grasp the particular in terms of the universal. We shall then, at best, understand the present Jewish crisis only in terms of the universal Western or human crisis, thus failing to grasp its uniqueness; at worst we shall abuse such an understanding as a means of escaping into the condition of contemporary-man-in-general. Instead of relying on the sociological mind, we must rely on the historical mind, which moves from the particular to the universal. But the historical mind, too, has its limitations. Thus no contemporary Jewish historian at the time of the destruction of the First or the Second Temple could have fully understood the world-historical significance of that event, if only because, in the midst of the crisis, he was not yet on the other side of it. We, too, are in the midst of the contemporary crisis, and hence unable fully to understand it. As for our attitude toward the future, this cannot be one of understanding or prediction, but only one of commitment and, possibly, faith.

How shall we achieve such fragmentary understanding of our present crisis as is possible while we are still in the midst of it? A crisis as yet unended can only be understood in terms of contradictions as yet resolved. Jewish existence today is permeated by three main contradictions:

1. The American Jew of today is a "universalist," if only because he has come closer to the full achievement of equal status in society than any other Jew in the history of the Diaspora; yet this development coincides with the resurrection of Jewish "particularism" in the rebirth of a Jewish nation.

2. The Jew of today is committed to modern "secularism," as the source of his emancipation; yet his future survival as Jew depends on past religious resources. Hence even the most Orthodox Jew of today is a secularist insofar as, and to the extent that, he participates in the political and social processes of society. And even the most secularist Jew is religious insofar as, and to the extent that, he must fall back on the religious past in his struggle for a Jewish future.

3. Finally—and this is by far the most radical contradiction, and one which threatens to engulf the other two—the Jew in two of the three main present centers of Jewry, America and Israel, is at home in the modern world, for he has found a freedom and autonomy impossible in the pre-modern world. Yet he is but twenty-five years removed from a catastrophe unequaled in all of Jewish history—a catastrophe which in its distinctive characterizations is modern in nature.

These are the three main contradictions. Merely to state them is to show

how false it would be for us to see our present Jewish crisis as nothing more than an illustration of the general Western or human crisis. I will add to the general point nothing more than the mere listing of two specific examples. First, we may have a problem with "secularity," like our Christian neighbors. But our problem is not theirs, if only because for us—who have "celebrated" the secular city since the French Revolution—the time for such celebrating is past since the Holocaust. Second, while we have our problems with academically inspired atheism and agnosticism, they are central at best only for Jews who want to be men-in-general. For the authentic Jew who faces up to his singled-out Jewish condition—even for the authentic agnostic or atheistic Jew—a merely academically inspired doubt in God must seem sophomoric when he, after Auschwitz, must grapple with despair.

We must, then, take care lest we move perversely in responding to our present crisis. We must first face up and respond to our Jewish singled-out condition. Only thus and then can we hope to enter authentically into an understanding of and relation with other manifestations of a present crisis which is doubtless universal.

In groping for authentic responses to our present Jewish crisis, we do well to begin with responses which have already occurred. I believe that there are two such responses: first, a commitment to Jewish survival; second, a commitment to Jewish unity.

I confess I used to be highly critical of Jewish philosophies which seemed to advocate no more than survival for survival's sake. I have changed my mind. I now believe that, in this present, unbelievable age, even a mere collective commitment to Jewish group-survival for its own sake is a momentous response, with the greatest implications. I am convinced that future historians will understand it, not, as our present detractors would have it, as the tribal response-mechanism of a fossil, but rather as a profound, albeit as yet fragmentary, act of faith, in an age of crisis to which the response might well have been either flight in total disarray or complete despair.

The second response we have already found is a commitment to Jewish unity. This, to be sure, is incomplete and must probably remain incomplete. Yet it is nonetheless real. Thus the American Council for Judaism is an anachronism, as is, I venture to say, an Israeli nationalism which would cut off all ties with the Diaspora. No less anachronistic is a Jewish secularism so blind in its worship of the modern secular world as wholly to spurn the religious resources of the Jewish past; likewise, an Orthodoxy so untouched by the modern secular world as to have remained in a pre-modern ghetto.

Such, then, are the responses to the present crisis in Jewish history which we have already found, in principle however inadequately in practice. And their implications are even now altogether momentous. Whether aware of what we have decided or not, we have made the collective decision to endure the contradiction of present Jewish existence. We have collectively rejected the option, either of "checking out" of Jewish existence altogether or of so avoiding the present contradictions as to shatter Jewish existence into fragments.

But the question now is whether we can go beyond so fragmentary a commitment. In the present situation, this question becomes: can we confront the Holocaust, and yet not despair? Not accidentally has it taken twenty years for us to face this question, and it is not certain that we can face it yet. The contradiction is too staggering, and every authentic escape is barred. We are bidden to turn present and future life into death, as the price of remembering death at Auschwitz. And we are forbidden to affirm present and future life, as the price of forgetting Auschwitz.

We have lived in this contradiction for twenty years without being able to face it. Unless I am mistaken, we are now beginning to face it, however fragmentarily and inconclusively. And from this beginning confrontation there emerges what I will boldly term a 614th commandment: *the authentic Jew of today is forbidden to hand Hitler yet another, posthumous victory.* (This formulation is terribly inadequate, yet I am forced to use it until one more adequate is found. First, although no anti-Orthodox implication is intended, as though the 613 commandments stood necessarily in need of change, we must face the fact that something radically new has happened. Second, although the commandment should be positive rather than negative, we must face the fact that Hitler did win at least one victory—the murder of six million Jews. Third, although the very name of Hitler should be erased rather than remembered, we cannot disguise the uniqueness of his evil under a comfortable generality, such as persecution-in-general, tyranny-in-general, or even the-demonic-in-general.)

I think the authentic Jew of today is beginning to hear the 614th commandment. And he hears it whether, as agnostic, he hears no more, or whether, as believer, he hears the voice of the *metzaveh* (the commander) in the *mitzvah* (the commandment). Moreover, it may well be the case that the authentic Jewish agnostic and the authentic Jewish believer are closer today than at any previous time.

To be sure, the agnostic hears no more than the *mitzvah*. Yet if he is Jewishly authentic, he cannot but face the fragmentariness of his hearing. He cannot, like agnostics and atheists all around him, regard this *mitzvah* as the product of self-sufficient human reason, realizing itself in an ever-advancing history of autonomous human enlightenment. The 614th commandment must be, to him, an abrupt and absolute *given*, revealed in the midst of total catastrophe.

On the other hand, the believer, who bears the voice of the *metzaveh* in the *mitzvah*, can hardly hear anything more than the *mitzvah*. The reasons which made Martin Buber speak of an eclipse of God are still compelling. And if, nevertheless, a bond between Israel and the God of Israel can be experienced in the abyss, this can hardly be more than the *mitzvah* itself.

The implications of even so slender a bond are momentous. If the 614th commandment is binding upon the authentic Jew, then we are, first, commanded to survive as Jews, lest the Jewish people perish. We are commanded, second, to remember in our very guts and bones the martyrs of the Holocaust, lest their memory perish. We are forbidden, thirdly, to deny or despair of God, however much we may have to contend with Him or with belief in Him, lest

Judaism perish. We are forbidden, finally, to despair of the world as the place which is to become the kingdom of God, lest we help make it a meaningless place in which God is dead or irrelevant and everything is permitted. To abandon any of these imperatives, in response to Hitler's victory at Auschwitz, would be to hand him yet other, posthumous victories.

How can we possibly obey these imperatives? To do so requires the endurance of intolerable contradictions. Such endurance cannot but bespeak an as yet unutterable faith. If we are capable of this endurance, then the faith implicit in it may well be of historic consequence. At least twice before—at the time of the destruction of the First and of the Second Temples—Jewish endurance in the midst of catastrophe helped transform the world. We cannot know the future, if only because the present is without precedent. But this ignorance on our part can have no effect on our present action. The uncertainty of what will be may not shake our certainty of what we must do.

RICHARD H. POPKIN

The Holocaust focuses attention for all of us who are survivors on what we are and what we are trying to preserve in the post-Holocaust world. The motto of the Yad Vashem Memorial in Jerusalem is "Remember." Many of us have been brought back to a living Judaism and to living in Jewish history through remembering the Holocaust. I think one of our problems at this stage is trying to find our future in terms of what we are remembering, in terms of what our past can have been.

An aspect of this is trying to come to terms with the Holocaust itself. In the twenty years since 1945, we have not been able to see it as people have the previous Holocaust—the expulsion from Spain and the Spanish Inquisition— as some sort of indication of the immediate triumph of Judaism. A work written in the middle of the sixteenth century, A *Consolation for the Tribulations of Israel*, pictures the then greatest Jewish catastrophe as partly something which the Jews deserved because of their backsliding, partly as the result of the viciousness of the outside world, but most importantly of all, as an indication that something tremendous was about to occur in Judaism. About a hundred years after this work, others were written in the same vein, indicating that the whole trend of European history, including the catastrophe of the Spanish Jews, pointed to and would bring about the triumph of Judaism.

I think in our situation the catastrophe has been so great that no one has dared to see it in sixteenth-century terms. We try to see it in terms of European history. I think we have as yet been unable to come to grips with the Holocaust because we cannot understand how European civilization could have marched triumphantly through Enlightenment to the Holocaust. For all of us who are survivors, one of our duties is to try to find the past that fits our present and our possible future. Our present is, in considerable part, one which finds Jews flourishing in the United States, in a manner unprecedented in Diaspora history. Our present also includes the living State of Israel and the Jewish nation restored to the Land of Israel after two thousand years. Our present, too, includes three million Jews submerged in Russia. What sort of a past do we have to go with this present and a possible future?

There is the story of a Spanish bishop, in the sixteenth century, who was asked by his nephew of Jewish origin: What must he do in order to apply for a position with the government? (At that juncture in Spanish history, anybody with Jewish blood could not possibly get a government job.) The bishop wrote back: "My dear nephew, you have first to make the most crucial decision of all. You have to decide who your parents were." The bishop then proceeded to show his nephew how a man in his position decides what his past has been in order to have a future.

I think that in the post-Holocaust world we are looking for the roots to our present and our future. The usual picture we have of Jewish history makes Meah Shearim, the Orthodox quarter of Jerusalem, intelligible as the distinct source of our present and possible future. Jewish studies, however, in the last twenty or thirty years have indicated that there are far wider ramifications to our past. Judaism has not always been a rigid group of Orthodox people, maintaining a tradition, living apart from the world. There have been very important instances of a creative, living, changing, developing Judaism in the world, in the secular world, the world of nations, functioning within it and contributing to it. In recent history, the most important such cases are the Spanish and the Dutch experiences—the Spanish experience of the 15th and 16th centuries, and the Dutch one of the 17th century. Until very recently, neither the Christian nor the Jewish perspective saw much of a meaningful place for a creative, living, developing Judaism in a secular world of nations. To the outside world, the Jews seemed to be only the Jewish "problem." To the Jews, their present and possible future fate seemed to be to live apart from a secular world of nations, and not making any contribution to it.

I have been interested to find that wherever I have spoken about the history of the Spanish Jews, somebody has always raised the question: was Columbus Jewish? This question is always raised with fear, trepidation, hope, and interest. I have tried to figure out why this particular case, of all possibilities, preoccupies people. They don't ask whether Cervantes was Jewish, or Saint Teresa; it's always Columbus. The people who ask this are extremely hopeful that the answer is in the affirmative, but they seem to feel, with fear and trembling, that something is going to be revealed no matter what the answer is. I think this indicates, in part, a desire to see a very important development in the world as having a meaning in Jewish history. Somehow, if the answer as to whether Columbus was Jewish is "yes," then this will open up new possibilities for future Jewish experience.

Jewish history in the early part of the twentieth century is largely what Negro history is at the present time, an attempt to find, to prove, that we were and are there—that Jews were present at the various great moments of the world's history, that they were not just living in ghettos, that they did make contributions. I think the next stage is to find our significance in the Western historical experience. Spain and Holland come closest to the present state of the world; there Jews also played a tremendous role in the total life of the society at large.

Spain is not just the land of Maimonides, but is, above all, the land in which an enormous number of Jews took part in secular society, in a religious Christian society, and were often its leaders. In Holland, the first place in the Western world where Judaism could be practiced freely, one finds another instance of Judaism flourishing within and as part of a dynamic secular society. Up to now, what has appeared of most interest to everyone about the Dutch case is not what the Jews did within the Jewish community as part of the Dutch society, but rather what happened to the few renegades who were thrown out of the Jewish community. Spinoza and Uriel Da Costa have been seen as meaningful figures. I think that in looking for parallels to our present situation we have to look not just to the people who were thrown out or who were unable to live within the Jewish society in a national secular world, but for those who were able to and did make contributions in such a world.

In stressing the importance of Spain and Holland as possible indications of what we are up against and what we may be going towards, one has, of course, to realize the monumental differences between our present situation and the previous ones. In Spain, after the forced conversions, the Jews partook in society unwillingly. They were forced into the Christian society, and, having been forced into it, were able to play a very dynamic, very tragic role in what transpired in 16th- and 17th-century Spain. In Holland they refused to become part of the Dutch world, refused to become precursors of an American-type of experience, but insisted on carrying on a Spanish-type of American experience. What would have happened to them had they been allowed to live freely in Spain? But it is true that in each of these cases, what happened to the preservation of Judaism, its continuity and its development, with the full force of secular influence upon it, is much more revealing for our present than to consider those aspects of Jewish history which tended to remain static and to preserve a certain type of Orthodoxy in a certain type of society.

If one accepts, as I do, Judah Halevi's view, that Jewish history is the "inner core" of world history, what we are and what we are going to be may become crucial not just for our own future but for a universal future. In trying to figure out what we are, I think we have to go back to the many aspects of what we have been and to see the directions in which these may lead us. The Western world of which we are a part must some day come to terms with the Holocaust as a part of its history. I think part of the Jewish mission is to lead the way in trying to work out and present a meaningful world in a post-Holocaust world. American-Jewish writers right now lead the way in showing the meaninglessness of modern life. Perhaps it is possible that we can also find the other side, through the restudying of our past and finding the teachers who can help us now. Our future will be formed in part from what meaningful roots we can find in our heritage.

I think that what is now going on at the Hebrew University is an indication of the problem of finding our roots and our future—of finding our roots close to both the most developed aspects of the Western world and in the study of our Jewish past. These two have been fused before, in part, in Spain and Holland, but under peculiarly different circumstances. Perhaps in the freedom that America and Israel allow in the free exploration and development of Judaism, we can again find a creative and vital fusion in which Judaism will become, in a new form, the beacon light to the nations.

GEORGE STEINER

I am honestly not certain that there is much to add. I imagine that the point is that no Jew, including all of us up here, can speak well for any other Jew. The Diaspora and the lack of a dogmatic eschatology make of Judaism a multiplicity of personal choices. I cannot really understand the formulation of the subject too thoroughly: I am not sure I know what I would want to say about the values of Judaism after the Holocaust, but I do feel I would like to say something about the values of one particular Jew.

Yet, at the same time, there is a cohesion of all Jews, a very curious mutual recognition in the moment of meeting. Jewishness, as distinct from Judaism, is an almost physical code of antennae, which reach out across national and linguistic barriers and even through the mask of assimilation. Anyone who has traveled in the world knows the curious, haunting swiftness with which, however you are dressed, however you behave, the other Jew in the community finds you out. I believe I would know a Chinese Jew were I to meet him in the crowd in Canton.

Why? There are tricks of eye and step that are possibly the remembrance burned into the skin of the long hunt. We have been on the run a long, long time. But the principle of recognition, recognizance, of knowing again, of locating ourselves in the secret mirror of the man we meet, that may lie deeper. We touch here on that most unpleasant and important of subjects—the matter of race, about which American Jews, it seems to me, very often exhibit a very understandable gingerliness. That question is presently moving into a new and problematic light. In the present state of inquiry into the structure and stabilities of the genetic code, only a very foolhardy man would be dogmatic about racial differences and characteristics or about the way in which social habituations penetrate psychosomatic patterns. It is conceivable—I say no more than that it is conceivable—that when Jews meet, be they Unitarian or Williamsburg, Cantonese or Moroccan, they know each other as do animals of a cognate species. Simply because one's enemies say certain things, they need not be lies. That is the fascination of the truth. Hence, I think that our question is a two-fold one: the values of one particular Jew; and the values of belonging, whether we would or not, to that somewhat mysterious community of historical, racial awareness which we call Jewishness.

I believe that the most coherent position towards one's own identity results from an attempt to bring these two questions into living reciprocity. To do this, I would like to try for myself simply to rephrase the issue. I am not very sanguine nor well-informed about the values of Judaism after Auschwitz. But I do have strong feelings about the value of being a Jew after Auschwitz. We are survivors of a very careful program of total elimination, compounded of direct action, Nazism, about which in this room there is no need to say anything whatever, and of indifference, about which there will be a need to say a great deal more, because this is one of the chapters hardly written about, hardly discussed, except by the specialists. One thinks of the fifty above-quota visas offered in this country in 1937, when 100,000 children could have been saved. One thinks of the position of England, the country where I make my home. One thinks of the frontiers closed in France. And it is my conviction that had Hitler not made a foolish military move, had Hitler stopped, let us say, after Czechoslovakia and said: "I really stick to my promise now. That's enough. I won't invade, I won't attack; you let me do internally what I wish"—then the ski-slopes of Garmisch would be full of tourists to this day, a few miles away from the concentration camps. In other words, Nazism is not a unique demonism; it almost carried out what the world by and large was prepared to see carried out. The historians support this in detail, for in the beginning the Nazis watched closely whether there would be reflexes, whether there would be counter-moves; and it was only when it appeared that the world did not give a damn, that the Nazis began implementing the full plan. Thus we are survivors, not only of one particular doctrinal bestiality, but also of a very widespread, let us call it at its most courteous, indifference. Men are always accomplices to whatever leaves them indifferent.

If we are survivors, survivors bear scars, but they also have privileges. I imagine that Lazarus had license to make bad jokes, to pick his nose at dinner, and to be occasionally tactless after his wondrous return to the living. Interestingly, we know almost nothing about his behavior afterwards. This is surely a much more interesting problem than his resurrection; and I daresay that three days in a Galilean tomb was less of death than two nights in the ditch at Babi Yar or three days in the cesspool at Treblinka.

Outside Israel, the Jew continues to be a guest among men, more or less welcome, more or less accepted, but a guest nevertheless. To say that I believe this to be the case also in America—and I have said it—is to invite not only misunderstanding but obvious malaise and unhappiness for both parties in the conversation, so I will therefore limit myself to only one point. To say that a large Gentile community, which is also today almost the most nationalist on earth in many of its aspects, is different from all other such communities in history is to say that history makes a quantum jump; is to say that there are fundamental ontological, metaphysical discontinuities, and that it cannot happen here or there for some fundamental metaphysical reason. I plead guilty to not believing this. I do not think history makes quantum jumps. I think that where there are powerful categories of similitude, history has recognizable patterns and dangers.

This is entirely my own belief, and I do not want to press it upon you. But Auschwitz has made the Jew a guest with certain privileges of indelicacy, of irritancy, of subversion. I think he must try to make creative the malaise which his hosts will experience, whatever his behavior. That malaise remains, behave he as deferentially and as urbanely as he may. And if this is so, let us make this malaise creative, productive, fruitful. I think we must do this by the simplest injunction (usually ascribed to Nietzsche, but actually, forgive the small pedantry, a quote from Pindar): "Labor to become what you are." I think we must refuse to be other than what we are. That is to say, we must not accept the fiction, and it is a fiction, of assured permanent residence, of acceptance, of entrance into the Gentile nation. We must not accept it if the price is nationalism, national patriotism, in any militant sense. The Jew must, I think, rejoice in the distrust of his nationalist host and say: "Yes, I am potentially disloyal to any policy that I believe evil or inhuman. 'My country right or wrong' is a slogan for barbarism. My city is that of man; my citizenship, that of human possibility. I am not a tree, to exult in rootedness"—rootedness, I must say, is a word that always jars me in the mouth of a Jew—"but a man, endowed with the marvel of legs, with the knowledge that there are many languages in which fathers can teach their children, and that frontiers are a cruel myth which have again and again been closed to me for my destruction." Now, for the Jew of genius it has long been true that exile is home. Marx, of course, lies buried in Hampstead and Freud in Golders Green; if I remember rightly, the ashes of Einstein were scattered in New Jersey. We are not a people for cemeteries and plots of ground. Even in death Moses was a delightfully displaced person. What was the fate of the exceptional has, I think, through the Holocaust, become our common privilege. A Jew who is a nationalist in a Gentile community is aping his own destroyers. Quite simply, men have made us guests among them; let us teach them, so far as our example may, to be guests of each other. For if they do not learn it, civilization as we know it may go to violent destruction.

Here is where I think the peculiar uniqueness of our task lies, because I wonder whether any nation in history, any people, race or tribe, has a greater obligation to live and teach this lesson of common humanity, this refusal to consider a passport as anything but a contract, renegotiable at all times, in the light of conscience, than the Jews, who *may* have launched upon history and ourselves the murderous boomerang of arrogance and nationalistic fervor. For it is in Judaism that we find claims which the Hellenic world did not put forth. We know today that Nazism subtly mimed the millenary claims and the myth of singular election in the Judaism of the Pentateuch. In a way that I do not think we have yet fully understood, there was between the Nazis, the core of the

Nazis, and the Jews a kind of hideous relationship of parody. When I am reminded, as we have just been, of Judah Halevi's statement that Jewish history is the core of universal history, it reminds me of nothing more than the Chinese claims of the Middle Kingdom as being alone human; and there are other claims that go back as far. So, to the extent that we may be responsible for having spoken of being a people exalted, a people divinely elect against others, certainly during the time of Joshua and the Judges, to that extent the boomerang sought us out and nearly destroyed us totally. Perhaps the instruction of that is that we must never again accept those claims and those nationalisms.

The value of being a Jew after the Holocaust is a tremendous one. I think it is extremely appropriate that we should be meeting on Purim, a day of pleasure, of noise and rejoicing, because the value of being a Jew after the Holocaust is the value of being a man who has experienced to the uttermost the bestiality of man. We have very few surprises ahead of us. We know in our charred marrow what men can become when they yield their reason to a flag and put their feet in boots. The value of being a Jew is to try to make truth one's locale and free inquiry one's native tongue. I suspect it is the deep conflict between this aim and the anguishing political and strategic necessities of the day which accounts for the grave malaise in Israel. To be a Jew is to rejoice in the links stronger than any political loyalty, which may connect us with the most audacious that is being thought and said, which connects us with the linguistics of Noam Chomsky and the anthropology of Claude Lévi-Strauss, with the physics of Rabi and the music of Schoenberg, the poetics of Kafka and the mathematics of Kantor. And though I would yield, of course, to Professor Popkin's deep knowledge of the richness of the Orthodox community in Amsterdam, I will not let him expel Spinoza; he is one we want to keep. When moored—please, not anchored—in the uncertain haven of a nationalist community (and what Gentile communities are not deeply nationalist?), this is a citizenship which we must try to make ours—a citizenship of protest.

Let me conclude quite simply. I think we all carry with us, each of us, from childhood on, some totemic or talismanic figure. Mine is a man called Marc Bloch, probably the greatest medieval historian ever, the man who, with Tawney, founded the modern way of thinking about agricultural and economic history in France. Marc Bloch escaped in the debacle in 1940, got to England, and came to a college in my own University, where, having escaped with his life, he was warned not to go back under any circumstances. Marc Bloch there wrote a small book called *Etrange Défaite* ("Strange Defeat"), the deepest book written on the collapse of France in 1940, merciless and pitiless. It was the work of a man who had thought it through and saw the rottenness and the horror of France and of the nation that had been his. He left the manuscript with Sir Dennis Brogan and went back into France. He joined the underground in a gay and amused way, skeptical even then about his colleagues and their naivetés and how they were running affairs. He was captured and tortured a long time, and he did not say a word. He was taken out near Grenoble to be shot with other hostages. Among those who were about to be killed with him, Bloch saw a boy of only fourteen or fifteen, an FFI courier who had been picked up by the Germans. He saw that the child was terribly afraid, and he asked the Germans for permission that they be shot together. Marc Bloch took the child by the hand, and the last thing he was heard to say—this has been authenticated by witnesses—was: "Now, you must listen to me. It will not hurt very much." They went out together, and he was speaking to the boy right to the end.

The values of that moment, the historian's training, the gift of humanity— these belong to all men, not alone to the Jews. But the Jew, I think, may have the uncomfortable obligation and privilege of practicing them right now pretty constantly and at whatever price of discomfort.

ELIE WIESEL

I have listened to my fellow-panelists, and found in their theses, as they relate to the Holocaust, both conviction and affirmation, which I wish I could share with them. But I cannot.

Since today is Purim, a reference to the Midrash might be in order; it is relevant to our subject. What, ask the Rabbis, is the difference between Hanukka and Purim? Both holidays celebrate victories—the survival of our people—but yet they are not of the same nature. Hanukka: The Greeks sought to absorb Judea spiritually; some Jews responded favorably, and assimilation became fashionable; but then the Maccabees rose up in arms in the battle against Hellenism. Purim is a different story. When Haman planned to extermi- nate the Jews, the Jews, led by Mordecai, proclaimed three days of prayer and fasting. The question is asked: Why did the Jews oppose spiritual resistance to physical threat and physical resistance to spiritual threat? The Midrash ex- plains this paradox in the following way: The Jewish people entered into a covenant with God. We are to protect His Torah, and He, in turn, assumes responsibility for Israel's presence in the world. Thus, when our spirituality— the Torah—was in danger, we used force in protecting it; but when our physical existence was threatened, we simply reminded God of His duties and promises deriving from the covenant.

Well, it seems that, for the first time in our history, this very covenant was broken. That is why the Holocaust has terrifying theological implications. Whether we want it or not, because of its sheer dimensions, the event tran- scends man and involves more than him alone. It can be explained neither with God nor without Him. Everything that happened then and there was linked to finality, to total experience. Everybody concerned was totally committed to his condition: the murderer to his crime, the victim to his fate, the bystander to his indifference. All men became identified with their image, their absolute. They turned into gods.

But then, the covenant was equally revoked with regard to the relationship between Jew and man. For the first time in our history, the Jewish people was totally abandoned. God's failure was matched by man's. The world was divided—with some rare exceptions—into assassins, victims, and indifferent onlookers. Our friends belonged to the latter category. Intellectuals who, today, speak up against the war in Vietnam, against discrimination and poverty, ought to remember their predecessors who spoke up in protest against Nazism and evil, but who somehow failed to comprehend what was done to Jews. There were no protests, no mass demonstrations, no show of solidarity; in his all-out war against Jews, Hitler was convinced that he faced no enemy, no resistance.

Man's failure was then political and spiritual as well. George Steiner refers to it in his *Language and Silence*. Cold-blood murder and culture did not exclude each other. If the Holocaust proved anything, it is that it is possible for a person both to love poems and kill children; many Germans cried when listening to Mozart, when playing Haydn, when quoting Goethe and Schiller—but remained quite unemotional and casual when torturing and shooting children. Their act had no effect on their spirit; the idea had no bearing on the source of inspiration. Heidegger served as Chancellor of the Freiburg University under the Nazis. Karl Orff, the composer, was Goebbels' favorite musician. As for Von Karajan, he did not lose his talent when conducting in Berlin and elsewhere, wearing a Nazi-uniform.

Something then must be wrong not only with their concept of evil, but with man's as well.

Something must also be wrong with our own people and its concept of its own mission. Judged from within, we did not emerge as victors. The universal failure is, to a certain extent, our failure. Never before have so many Jews been abandoned by so many Jews. The massacre in Europe had almost no bearing on American Jewish life. The annihilation of thousands of Eastern European communities was almost not at all reflected in what was going on in the thousands of American Jewish communities. Tea parties, card games, musical soirées continued to take place. Of course, money was raised, but entertainment was not omitted from the program. In certain free countries in Europe, the situation was not better—perhaps, even worse. When consulted by their governments whether to bring in refugees, some communal leaders had to answer, and their answer was less than enthusiastic.

As a consequence, the whole world remained closed to Jews, trapped inside Europe. Dr. Popkin spoke of the Spanish Inquisition. Things, however, were different then. Chased from Spain, chased from Holland, the Jews could go somewhere else. There was always one door open, somewhere. But not this time. We know from history that when one Jewish community encountered persecution anywhere, all others rose to its aid. When one Jew was in danger, all others tried to save him. The Maharam of Rothenberg spent years away from home, paying ransom for individual prisoners. *Pidyon shvuyim* (the redemption of captives) is a *mitzvah*; so is *hatzalat nefashot* (the saving of lives). Nothing of this sort was accomplished in the last war. The victims were abandoned even by their own people.

After failures of such magnitude, after such defeats on all counts, what is left? What can one do now? How can one speak of Jewish values when we know what was done to them and to those who believed in them?

I presume that the expression, "Jewish values in the post-Holocaust future" means: what lesson do they offer all men? In other words: in what way have these values changed, and to what extent could they become universal?

My question is: why should we at all care for all men? Why should we teach them anything, since we know already how they usually tend to reward us? Furthermore: if these values should apply to what Emil Fackenheim called the community of Israel—how can one still have faith even in it? Where was the community of Israel then? Where is it now? What if someone told you that it has to be created and built anew?

How can one define Jewish values today when we have not yet come to grips, not with the Holocaust—one never comes to terms with it—but with its tale? The full story of the Holocaust has not yet been told. All that we know is fragmentary, perhaps even untrue. Perhaps, what we tell about what happened and what really happened has nothing to do one with the other. We want to remember. But remember what? And what for? Does any one know the answer to this?

During the war, some Jews attempted to escape and to survive for one reason only: to tell the story. Cynics were amazed and asked them: What for? The world does not deserve your sacrifice or your tale; it won't even believe you. But the cynics themselves were among those who tried, for the same reason, to preserve the tale. That very reason was, ironically, invoked by the Judenrat: let the few remain and transmit what happened to the many. *Echad ba'ir ushnayim b'mishpacha*—"let one person bear witness for his whole town, and two for their entire family." For deep down people lived and died in fear: perhaps the last Jew will disappear, and the tale will die with him. But then—so what? Let it not be told! Perhaps the "post-Holocaust future" does not deserve its past! Why were we so concerned with mankind which chose to ignore our fate?

Yet, we are concerned. We do try to put the experience into words. But can we? That is my question. Language is poor and inadequate. The moment it is told, the experience turns into betrayal. The Oral Tradition had to remain oral. The Kotzker Rebbe said: the Oral Torah that we know is not the real one; the true *Torah shē-b'al peh* remained oral and secret.

That is our problem, that is my fear: perhaps whatever we try to write and say about Jewish values and Jewish experience has no relationship to either.

St. Augustine

CONFESSIONS

In his remarkable autobiography, the *Confessions*, St. Augustine
(A.D. 354–430) discusses his efforts to free himself from a life of
evil and sin.

[XII.] 21. Alypius indeed kept me from marrying; alleging, that so could we by
no means with undistracted leisure live together in the love of wisdom, as we
had long desired. For himself was even then most pure in this point, so that it
was wonderful; and that the more, since in the outset of his youth he had
entered into that course, but had not stuck fast therein; rather had he felt
remorse and revolting at it, living thenceforth until now most continently. But I
opposed him with the examples of those, who as married men had cherished
wisdom, and served God acceptably, and retained their friends, and loved them
faithfully. Of whose greatness of spirit I was far short; and bound with the
disease of the flesh, and its deadly sweetness, drew along my chain, dreading
to be loosed, and as if my wound had been fretted, put back his good persuasions, as it were the hand of one that would unchain me. Moreover, by me did
the serpent speak unto Alypius himself, by my tongue weaving and laying in his
path pleasurable snares, wherein his virtuous and free feet might be entangled.
  22. For when he wondered that I, whom he esteemed not slightly, should
stick so fast in the birdlime of that pleasure, as to protest (so oft as we discussed it) that I could never lead a single life; and urged in my defence when I
saw him wonder, that there was great difference between his momentary and
scarce-remembered knowledge of that life, which so he might easily despise,
and my continued acquaintance whereto if but the honourable name of marriage were added, he ought not to wonder why I could not contemn that course;
he began also to desire to be married; not as overcome with desire of such
pleasure, but out of curiosity. For he would fain know, he said, what that should
be, without which my life, to him so pleasing, would to me seem not life but a
punishment. For his mind, free from that chain, was amazed at my thraldom;

and through that amazement was going on to a desire of trying it, thence to the trial itself, and thence perhaps to sink into that bondage whereat he wondered, seeing he was willing to *make a covenant with death*; and, *he that loves danger, shall fall into it.* For whatever honour there be in the office of well-ordering a married life, and a family, moved us but slightly. But me for the most part the habit of satisfying an insatiable appetite tormented, while it held me captive; him, an admiring wonder was leading captive. So were we, until Thou, O Most High, not forsaking our dust, commiserating us miserable, didst come to our help, by wondrous and secret ways.

[XIII.] 23. Continual effort was made to have me married. I wooed, I was promised, chiefly through my mother's pains, that so once married, the health-giving baptism might cleanse me, towards which she rejoiced that I was being daily fitted, and observed that her prayers, and Thy promises, were being fulfilled in my faith. At which time verily, both at my request and her own longing, with strong cries of heart she daily begged of Thee, that Thou wouldest by a vision discover unto her something concerning my future marriage; Thou never wouldest. She saw indeed certain vain and phantastic things, such as the energy of the human spirit, busied thereon, brought together; and these she told me of, not with that confidence she was wont, when Thou shewedst her any thing, but slighting them. For she could, she said, through a certain feeling, which in words she could not express, discern betwixt Thy revelations, and the dreams of her own soul. Yet the matter was pressed on, and a maiden asked in marriage, two years under the fit age; and, as pleasing, was waited for.

[XIV.] 24. And many of us friends conferring about, and detesting the turbulent turmoils of human life, had debated and now almost resolved on living apart from business and the bustle of men; and this was to be thus obtained; we were to bring whatever we might severally procure, and make one household of all; so that through the truth of our friendship nothing should belong especially to any; but the whole thus derived from all, should as a whole belong to each, and all to all. We thought there might be some ten persons in this society; some of whom were very rich, especially Romanianus our townsman, from childhood a very familiar friend of mine, whom the grievous perplexities of his affairs had brought up to court; who was the most earnest for this project; and therein was his voice of great weight, because his ample estate far exceeded any of the rest. We had settled also, that two annual officers, as it were, should provide all things necessary, the rest being undisturbed. But when we began to consider whether the wives, which some of us already had, others hoped to have, would allow this, all that plan, which was being so well moulded, fell to pieces in our hands, was utterly dashed and cast aside. Thence we betook us to sighs, and groans, and our steps to follow the *broad and beaten ways* of the world; for many thoughts were in our heart, *but Thy counsel standeth for ever.* Out of which counsel Thou didst deride ours, and preparedst Thine own; purposing to *give us meat in due season, and to open Thy hand, and to fill our souls with blessing.*

[XV.] 25. Meanwhile my sins were being multiplied, and my concubine being torn from my side as a hindrance to my marriage, my heart which clave unto her was torn and wounded and bleeding. And she returned to Afric, vowing unto Thee never to know any other man, leaving with me my son by her. But unhappy I, who could not imitate a very woman, impatient of delay, inasmuch as not till after two years was I to obtain her I sought, not being so much a lover of marriage, as a slave to lust, procured another, though no wife, that so by the servitude of an enduring custom, the disease of my soul might be kept up and carried on in its vigor or even augmented, into the dominion of marriage. Nor was that my wound cured, which had been made by the cutting away of the former, but after inflammation and most acute pain, it mortified, and my pains became less acute, but more desperate.

[XVI.] 26. To Thee be praise, glory to Thee, Fountain of mercies. I was becoming more miserable, and Thou nearer. Thy right hand was continually ready to pluck me out of the mire, and to wash me throughly, and I knew it not; nor did any thing call me back from a yet deeper gulf of carnal pleasures, but the fear of death, and of Thy judgment to come; which amid all my changes, never departed from my breast. And in my disputes with my friends Alypius and Nebridius, of the nature of good and evil, I held that Epicurus had in my mind won the palm, had I not believed, that after death there remained a life for the soul, and places of requital according to men's deserts, which Epicurus would not believe. And I asked, "were we immortal, and to live in perpetual bodily pleasure, without fear of losing it, why should we not be happy, or what else should we seek?" not knowing that great misery was involved in this very thing, that, being thus sunk and blinded, I could not discern that light of excellence and beauty, to be embraced for its own sake, which the eye of flesh cannot see, and is seen by the inner man. Nor did I, unhappy, consider from what source it sprung, that even on these things, foul as they were, I with pleasure discoursed with my friends, nor could I, even according to the notions I then had of happiness, be happy without friends, amid what abundance soever of carnal pleasures. And yet these friends I loved for themselves only, and I felt that I was beloved of them again for myself only. . . .

. . . so conceived I Thy creation, itself finite, full of Thee, the Infinite; and I said, Behold God, and behold what God hath created; and God is good, yea, most mightily and incomparably better than all these: but yet He, the Good, created them good; and see how He environeth and full-fils them. Where is evil then, and whence, and how crept it in hither? What is its root, and what its seed? Or hath it no being? Why then fear we and avoid what is not? Or if we fear it idly, then is that very fear evil, whereby the soul is thus idly goaded and racked. Yea, and so much a greater evil, as we have nothing to fear, and yet do fear. Therefore either is that evil which we fear, or else evil is, that we fear. Whence is it then? seeing God, the Good, hath created all these things good. He indeed, the greater and chiefest Good, hath created these lesser goods; still both Creator and created, all are good. Whence is evil? Or, was there some evil matter of which He made, and formed, and ordered it, yet left something in it, which He did not convert into good? Why so then? Had He no might to turn and change the whole, so that no evil should remain in it, seeing He is Allmighty? Lastly, why would He make any thing at all of it, and not rather by the same Allmightiness cause it not to be at all? Or, could it then be, against His will? Or if it were from eternity, why suffered He it so to be for infinite spaces of times past, and was pleased so long after to make something out of it? Or if He were suddenly pleased now to effect somewhat, this rather should the Allmighty have effected, that this evil matter should not be, and He alone be, the whole, true, sovereign, and infinite Good. Or if it was not good that He who was good, should not also frame and create something that were good, then, that evil matter being taken away and brought to nothing, He might form good matter, whereof to create all things. For He should not be Allmighty, if He might not create something good without the aid of that matter which Himself had not created. These thoughts I revolved in my miserable heart, overcharged with most gnawing cares, lest I should die ere I had found the truth; yet was the faith of Thy Christ our Lord and Saviour, professed in the Church Catholic, firmly fixed in my heart, in many points, indeed, as yet unformed, and fluctuating from the rule of doctrine; yet did not my mind utterly leave it, but rather daily took in more and more of it.

8. By this time also had I rejected the lying divinations and impious dotages of the astrologers. Let Thine own mercies, out of my very inmost soul, confess unto Thee for this also, O my God. For Thou, Thou altogether, (for who else calls us back from the death of all errors, save the Life which cannot die, and the Wisdom which needing no light enlightens the minds that need it, whereby the universe is directed, down to the whirling leaves of trees?) Thou madest provision for my obstinacy wherewith I struggled against Vindicianus, an acute old man, and Nebridius, a young man of admirable talents; the first vehemently affirming, and the latter often (though with some doubtfulness) saying, "That there was no such art whereby to foresee things to come, but that men's conjectures were a sort of lottery, and that out of many things, which they said should come to pass, some actually did, unawares to them who spake it, who stumbled upon it, through their oft speaking." Thou providedst then a friend for me, no negligent consulter of the astrologers; nor yet well skilled in those arts, but (as I said) a curious consulter with them, and yet knowing something, which he said he had heard of his father, which how far it went to overthrow the estimation of that art, he knew not. This man then, Firminus by name, having had a liberal education, and well taught in Rhetoric, consulted me, as one very dear to him, what, according to his so-called constellations, I thought on certain affairs of his, wherein his worldly hopes had risen, and I, who had herein now begun to incline towards Nebridius' opinion, did not altogether refuse to conjecture, and tell him what came into my unresolved mind; but added, that I was now almost persuaded, that these were but empty and ridiculous follies.

Thereupon he told me, that his father had been very curious in such books, and had a friend as earnest in them as himself, who with joint study and conference fanned the flame of their affections to these toys, so that they would observe the moments, whereat the very dumb animals, which bred about their houses, gave birth, and then observed the relative position of the heavens, thereby to make fresh experiments in this so-called art. He said then that he had heard of his father, that what time his mother was about to give birth to him, Firminus, a woman-servant of that friend of his father's, was also with child, which could not escape her master, who took care with most exact diligence to know the births of his very puppies. And so it was, that (the one for his wife, and the other for his servant, with the most careful observation, reckoning days, hours, nay, the lesser divisions of the hours,) both were delivered at the same instant; so that both were constrained to allow the same constellations, even to the minutest points, the one for his son, the other for his new-born slave. For so soon as the women began to be in labour, they each gave notice to the other what was fallen out in their houses, and had messengers ready to send to one another, so soon as they had notice of the actual birth, of which they had easily provided, each in his own province, to give instant intelligence. Thus then the messengers of the respective parties met, he averred, at such an equal distance from either house, that neither of them could make out any difference in the position of the stars, or any other minutest points; and yet Firminus, born in a high estate in his parents' house, ran his course through the gilded paths of life, was increased in riches, raised to honours; whereas that slave continued to serve his masters, without any relaxation of his yoke, as Firminus, who knew him, told me.

9. Upon hearing and believing these things, told by one of such credibility, all that my resistance gave way; and first I endeavoured to reclaim Firminus himself from that curiosity, by telling him, that upon inspecting his constellations, I ought, if I were to predict truly, to have seen in them, parents eminent among their neighbours, a noble family in its own city, high birth, good education, liberal learning. But if that servant had consulted me upon the same constellations, since they were his also, I ought again (to tell him too truly) to see in them a lineage the most abject, a slavish condition, and every thing else, utterly at variance with the former. Whence then if I spake the truth, I should, from the same constellations, speak diversely, or if I spake the same, speak falsely: thence it followed most certainly, that whatever, upon consideration of the constellations, was spoken truly, was spoken not out of art, but chance; and whatever spoken falsely, was not out of ignorance in the art, but the failure of the chance.

Moses Maimonides

GUIDE OF THE PERPLEXED

The medieval Jewish theologian Moses Maimonides (1135–
1204) discusses the question of evil.

Often it occurs to the imagination of the multitude that there are more evils in
the world than there are good things. As a consequence, this thought is contained in many sermons and poems of all the religious communities, which say
that it is surprising if good exists in the temporal, whereas the evils of the
temporal are numerous and constant. This error is not found only among the
multitude, but also among those who deem that they know something.

Rāzī has written a famous book, which he has entitled "Divine Things." He
filled it with the enormity of his ravings and his ignorant notions. Among them
there is a notion that he has thought up, namely, that there is more evil than
good in what exists; if you compare man's well-being and his pleasures in the
time span of his well-being with the pains, the heavy sufferings, the infirmities,
the paralytic afflictions, the wretchedness, the sorrows, and the calamities that
befall him, you find that his existence—he means the existence of man—is a
punishment and a great evil inflicted upon him. He began to establish this
opinion by inductively examining these misfortunes, so as to oppose all that is
thought by the adherents of the truth regarding the beneficence and manifest
munificence of the deity and regarding His being, may He be exalted, the
absolute good and regarding all that proceeds from Him being indubitably an
absolute good. The reason for this whole mistake lies in the fact that this
ignoramus and those like him among the multitude consider that which exists
only with reference to a human individual. Every ignoramus imagines that all
that exists exists with a view to his individual sake; it is as if there were nothing
that exists except him. And if something happens to him that is contrary to
what he wishes, he makes the trenchant judgment that all that exists is an evil.
However, if man considered and represented to himself that which exists and
knew the smallness of his part in it, the truth would become clear and manifest

to him. For this extensive raving entertained by men with regard to the multitude of evils in the world is not said by them to hold good with regard to the angels or with regard to the spheres and the stars or with regard to the elements and the minerals and the plants composed of them or with regard to the various species of animals, but their whole thought only goes out to some individuals belonging to the human species. If someone has eaten bad food and consequently was stricken with leprosy, they are astonished how this great ill has befallen him and how this great evil exists. They are also astonished when one who frequently copulates is stricken blind, and they think it a marvelous thing the calamity of blindness that has befallen such a man and other such calamities.

Now the true way of considering this is that all the existent individuals of the human species and, all the more, those of the other species of the animals are things of no value at all in comparison with the whole that exists and endures. It has made this clear, saying: *Man is like unto vanity, and so on. Man, that is a worm; and the son of man, that is a maggot. How much less in them that dwell in houses of clay, and so on. Behold, the nations are as a drop of a bucket, and so on.* There are also all the other passages figuring in the texts of the books of the prophets concerning this sublime and grave subject, which is most useful in giving man knowledge of his true value, so that he should not make the mistake of thinking that what exists is in existence only for the sake of him as an individual. According to us, on the other hand, what exists is in existence because of the will of its Creator; and among the things that are in existence, the species of man is the least in comparison to the superior existents—I refer to the spheres and the stars. As far as comparison with the angels is concerned, there is in true reality no relation between man and them. Man is merely the most noble among the things that are subject to generation, namely, in this our nether world; I mean to say that he is the noblest thing that is composed of the elements. Withal his existence is for him a great good and a benefit on the part of God because of the properties with which He has singled him out and perfected him. The greater part of the evils that befall its individuals are due to the latter, I mean the deficient individuals of the human species. It is because of evils that we have produced ourselves of our free will; but we attribute them to God, may He be exalted above this; just as He explains in His book, saying: *Is corruption His? No; His children's is the blemish, and so on.* Solomon too has explained this, saying: *The foolishness of man perverteth his way; and his heart fretteth against the Lord.* The explanation of this lies in the fact that all the evils that befall man fall under one of three species.

The first species of evil is that which befalls man because of the nature of coming-to-be and passing-away, I mean to say because of his being endowed with matter. Because of this, infirmities and paralytic afflictions befall some individuals either in consequence of their original natural disposition, or they supervene because of changes occurring in the elements, such as corruption of the air or a fire from heaven and a landslide. We have already explained that divine wisdom has made it obligatory that there should be no coming-to-be except through passing-away. Were it not for the passing-away of the individuals, the coming-to-be relating to the species would not continue. Thus that pure beneficence, that munificence, that activity causing good to overflow, are made clear. He who wishes to be endowed with flesh and bones and at the same time not be subject to impressions and not to be attained by any of the concomitants of matter merely wishes, without being aware of it, to combine two contraries, namely, to be subject to impressions and not to be subject to them. For if he were not liable to receive impressions, he would not have been generated, and what exists of him would have been one single individual and not a multitude of individuals belonging to one species. Galen has put it well in the third of the book of "Utilities," saying: Do not set your mind on the vain thought that it is possible that out of menstrual blood and sperm there should be generated a living being that does not die, is not subject to pain, is in perpetual motion, or is as brilliant as the sun. This dictum of Galen draws attention to one particular case falling under a general proposition. That proposition is as follows: Everything that is capable of being generated from any matter whatever, is generated in the most perfect way in which it is possible to be generated out of that specific matter; the deficiency attaining the individuals of the species corresponds to the deficiency of the particular matter of the individual. Now the ultimate term and the most perfect thing that may be generated out of blood and sperm is the human species with its well-known nature consisting in man's being a living, rational, and mortal being. Thus this species of evils must necessarily exist. Withal you will find that the evils of this kind that befall men are vey few and occur only seldom. For you will find cities, existing for thousands of years, that have never been flooded or burned. Also thousands of people are born in perfect health whereas the birth of an infirm human being is an anomaly, or at least—if someone objects to the word anomaly and does not use it—such an individual is very rare; for they do not form a hundredth or even a thousandth part of those born in good health.

The evils of the second kind are those that men inflict upon one another, such as tyrannical domination of some of them over others. These evils are more numerous than those belonging to the first kind, and the reasons for that are numerous and well known. The evils in question also come from us. However, the wronged man has no device against them. At the same time, there is no city existing anywhere in the whole world in which evil of this kind is in any way widespread and predominant among the inhabitants of that city; but its existence is also rare—in the cases, for instance, when one individual surprises another individual and kills him or robs him by night. This kind of evil becomes common, reaching many people, only in the course of great wars; and such events too do not form the majority of occurrences upon the earth taken as a whole.

The evils of the third kind are those that are inflicted upon any individual among us by his own action; this is what happens in the majority of cases, and these evils are much more numerous than those of the second kind. All men lament over evils of this kind; and it is only seldom that you find one who is not guilty of having brought them upon himself. He who is reached by them deserves truly to be blamed. To him one may say what has been said: *This hath been to you of your own doing.* It has also been said: *He doeth it that would destroy his own soul. Solomon* has said about evils of this kind: *The foolishness of man perverteth his way, and so on.* He also has explained with reference to evils of this kind that they are done by man to himself; his dictum being: *Behold, this only have I found, that God made man upright; but they have sought out many thoughts;* these thoughts are those that have been vanquished by these evils. About this kind it has also been said: *For affliction cometh not forth from the dust, neither doth trouble spring out of the ground.* Immediately afterwards it is explained that this sort of evil is brought into existence by man, for it is said: *For man is born unto trouble, and so on.* This kind of consequent upon all vices, I mean concupiscence for eating, drinking, and copulation, and doing these things with excess in regard to quantity or irregularly or when the quality of the foodstuffs is bad. For this is the cause of all corporeal and psychical diseases and ailments. With regard to the diseases of the body, this is manifest. With regard to the diseases of the soul due to this evil regimen, they arise in two ways: In the first place, through the alteration necessarily affecting the soul in consequence of the alteration of the body, the soul being a corporeal faculty—it having already been said that the moral qualities of the soul are consequent upon the temperament of the body. And in the second place, because of the fact that the soul becomes familiarized with, and accustomed to, unnecessary things and consequently acquires the habit of desiring things that are unnecessary either for the preservation of the individual or for the preservation of the species; and this desire is something infinite. For whereas all necessary things are restricted and limited, that which is superfluous is unlimited. If, for instance, your desire is directed to having silver plate, it would be better if it were of gold; some have crystal plate; and perhaps plate is procured that is made out of emeralds and rubies, whenever these stones are to be found. Thus every ignoramus who thinks worthless thoughts is always sad and despondent because he is not able to achieve the luxury attained by someone else. In most cases such a man exposes himself to great dangers, such as arise in sea voyages and the service of kings; his aim therein being to obtain these unnecessary luxuries. When, however, he is stricken by misfortunes in these courses he has pursued, he complains about God's decree and predestination and begins to put the blame on the temporal and to be astonished at the latter's injustice in not helping him to obtain great wealth, which would permit him to procure a great deal of wine so as always to be drunk and a number of concubines adorned with gold and precious stones of various kinds so as to move him to copulate more than he is able so as to experience pleasure—as if the end of existence consisted merely in the pleasure of such an ignoble man. The error of the multitude has arrived at the point where they impute to the Creator deficiency of power because of His having produced that which exists and endowed it with a nature entailing, according to their imagination, these great evils; inasmuch as this nature does not help every vicious man to achieve the satisfaction of his vice so that his corrupt soul should reach the term of its demand, which, according to what we have explained, has no limit. On the other hand, men of excellence and knowledge have grasped and understood the wisdom manifested in that which exists, as *David* has set forth, saying: *All the paths of the Lord are mercy and truth unto such as keep His covenant and His testimonies*. By this he says that those who keep to the nature of that which exists, keep the commandments of the Law, and know the ends of both, apprehend clearly the excellency and the true reality of the whole. For this reason they take as their end that for which they were intended as men, namely, apprehension. And because of the necessity of the body, they seek what is necessary for it, *bread to eat, and raiment to put on*, without any luxury. If one restricts oneself to what is necessary, this is the easiest of things and may be obtained with a very small effort. Whatever in it that is seen as difficult and hard for us is due to the following reason: when one endeavors to seek what is unnecessary, it becomes difficult to find even what is necessary. For the more frequently hopes cling to the superfluous, the more onerous does the matter become; forces and revenues are spent for what is unnecessary and that which is necessary is not found. You ought to consider the circumstances in which we are placed with regard to its being found. For the more a thing is necessary for a living being, the more often it may be found and the cheaper it is. On the other hand, the less necessary it is, the less often it is found and it is very expensive. Thus, for instance, the necessary for man is air, water, and food. But air is the most necessary, for nobody can be without it for a moment without perishing. As for water, one can remain without it for a day or two. Accordingly air is indubitably easier to find and cheaper than water. Water is more necessary than food, for certain people may remain, if they drink and do not eat, for four or five days without food. Accordingly in every city you find water more frequently and at a cheaper price than food. Things are similar with regard to foodstuffs; those that are most necessary are easier to find at a given place and cheaper than the unnecessary. Regarding musk, amber, rubies, and emeralds, I do not think that anyone of sound intellect can believe that man has strong need for them unless it be for medical treatment; and even in such cases, they and other similar things can be replaced by numerous herbs and earths.

This is a manifestation of the beneficence and munificence of God, may He be exalted, shown even with regard to this weak living creature. Regarding manifestations of His justice, may He be exalted, and of the equality established by Him between them, they are very evident. For within the domain of natural generation and corruption, there is no case in which an individual animal belonging to any species by having a special faculty possessed only by him or by having an additional part of the body. For all natural, psychic, and animal faculties and all the parts that are found in one particular individual are also found, as far as essence is concerned, in another—even though there be accidentally a deficiency because of something that has supervened and that is not according to nature. But this is rare, as we have made clear. There in no way exists a relation of superiority and inferiority between individuals conforming to the course of nature except that which follows necessarily from the differences in the disposition of the various kinds of matter; this being necessary on account of the nature of the matter of the particular species and not specially intended for one individual rather than another. As for the fact that one individual possesses many sachets and clothes adorned with gold whereas another lacks these superfluities of life, there is no injustice and no inequity in this. He who has obtained these luxuries has not gained thereby an increment in his substance. He has only obtained a false imagining or a plaything. And he who lacks the superfluities of life is not necessarily deficient. *And he that gathered much had nothing over, and he that gathered little had no lack; they gathered every man according to his eating.* This is what happens for the most part at every time and at every place. And, as we have made clear, no attention should be paid to anomalies.

Through the two considerations that have been set forth, His beneficence, may He be exalted, with regard to His creatures will become clear to you, in that He brings into existence what is necessary according to its order of importance and in that He makes individuals of the same species equal at their creation. With a view to this true consideration, the Master of those who know says: *For all His ways are judgment.* And David says: *All the paths of the Lord are mercy and truth, and so on,* as we have made clear. David also says explicitly: *The Lord is good to all; and His tender mercies are over all His works.* For His bringing us into existence is absolutely the great good, as we have made clear, and the creation of the governing faculty in the living beings is an indication of His mercifulness with regard to them, as we have made clear.

Baruch Spinoza

ETHICS

In this section of the E*thics*, Baruch Spinoza (1632–1677) discusses freedom and evil in relation to God.

APPENDIX TO BOOK 1

In the foregoing I have explained the nature and properties of God. I have
shown that he necessarily exists, that he is one: that he is, and acts solely by
the necessity of his own nature; that he is the free cause of all things, and how
he is so; that all things are in God, and so depend on him, that without him
they could neither exist nor be conceived; lastly, that all things are predeter-
mined by God, not through his free will or absolute fiat, but from the very
nature of God or infinite power. I have further, where occasion offered, taken
care to remove the prejudices, which might impede the comprehension of my
demonstrations. Yet there still remain misconceptions not a few, which might
and may prove very grave hindrances to the understanding of the concatena-
tion of things, as I have explained it above. I have therefore thought it worth
while to bring these misconceptions before the bar of reason.

All such opinions spring from the notion commonly entertained, that all
things in nature act as men themselves act, namely, with an end in view. It is
accepted as certain, that God himself directs all things to a definite goal (for it
is said that God made all things for man, and man that he might worship him).
I will, therefore, consider this opinion, asking first, why it obtains general credence, and why all men are naturally so prone to adopt it? secondly, I will point
out its falsity; and, lastly, I will show how it has given rise to prejudices about
good and bad, right and wrong, praise and blame, order and confusion, beauty
and ugliness, and the like. However, this is not the place to deduce these
misconceptions from the nature of the human mind: it will be sufficient here, if
I assume as a starting point, what ought to be universally admitted, namely,
that all men are born ignorant of the causes of things, that all have the desire
to seek for what is useful to them, and that they are conscious of such desire.

Herefrom it follows, first, that men think themselves free inasmuch as they are conscious of their volitions and desires, and never even dream, in their ignorance, of the causes which have disposed them so to wish and desire. Secondly, that men do all things for an end, namely, for that which is useful to them, and which they seek. Thus it comes to pass that they only look for a knowledge of the final causes of events, and when these are learned, they are content, as having no cause for further doubt. If they cannot learn such causes from external sources, they are compelled to turn to considering themselves, and reflecting what end would have induced them personally to bring about the given event, and thus they necessarily judge other natures by their own. Further, as they find in themselves and outside themselves many means which assist them not a little in their search for what is useful, for instance, eyes for seeing, teeth for chewing, herbs and animals for yielding food, the sun for giving light, the sea for breeding fish, &c. they come to look on the whole of nature as a means for obtaining such conveniences. Now as they are aware, their they found these conveniences and did not make them they think they have cause for believing, that some other being has made them for their use. As they look upon things as means, they cannot believe them to be self-created; but, judging from the means which they are accustomed to prepare for themselves, they are bound to believe in some ruler or rulers of the universe endowed with human freedom, who have arranged and adapted everything for human use. They are bound to estimate the nature of such rulers (having no information on the subject) in accordance with their own nature, and therefore they assert that the gods ordained everything for the use of man, in order to bind man to themselves and obtain from him the highest honour. Hence also it follows, that everyone thought out for himself, according to his abilities, a different way of worshipping God, so that God might love him more than his fellows, and direct the whole course of nature for the satisfaction of his blind cupidity and insatiable avarice. Thus the prejudice developed into superstition, and took deep root in the human mind; and for this reason everyone strove most zealously to understand and explain the final causes of things; but in their endeavour to show that nature does nothing in vain, *i.e.*, nothing which is useless to man, they only seem to have demonstrated that nature, the gods, and men are all mad together. Consider, I pray you, the result: among the many helps of nature they were bound to find some hindrances, such as storms, earthquakes, diseases, &c.: so they declared that such things happen, because the gods are angry at some wrong done them by men, or at some fault committed in their worship. Experience day by day protested and showed by infinite examples, that good and evil fortunes fall to the lot of pious and impious alike; still they would not abandon their inveterate prejudice, for it was more easy for them to class such contradictions among other unknown things of whose use they were ignorant, and thus to retain their actual and innate condition of ignorance, than to destroy the whole fabric of their reasoning and start afresh. They therefore laid down as an axiom, that God's judgments far transcend human understanding. Such a doctrine might well have sufficed to conceal the truth from the human race for all eternity, if mathematics had not furnished another standard of verity in considering solely the essence and properties of figures without regard to their final causes. There are other reasons (which I need not mention here) besides mathematics, which might have caused men's minds to be directed to these general prejudices, and have led them to the knowledge of the truth.

I have now sufficiently explained my first point. There is no need to show at length, that nature has no particular goal in view, and that final causes are mere human figments. This, I think, is already evident enough, both from the causes and foundations on which I have shown such prejudice to be based, and also from Prop. xvi., and the Corollary of Prop. xxxii., and, in fact, all those propositions in which I have shown, that everything in nature proceeds from a sort of necessity, and with the utmost perfection. However, I will add a few remarks, in order to overthrow this doctrine of a final cause utterly. That which is really a cause it considers as an effect, and *vice versâ*: it makes that which is by nature first to be last, and that which is highest and most perfect to be most imperfect. Passing over the questions of cause and priority as self-evident, it is plain from Props. xxi., xxii., xxiii. that that effect is most perfect which is produced immediately by God; the effect which requires for its production several intermediate causes is, in that respect, more imperfect. But if those things which were made immediately by God were made to enable him to attain his end, then the things which come after, for the sake of which the first were made, are necessarily the most excellent of all.

Further, this doctrine does away with the perfection of God: for, if God acts for an object, he necessarily desires something which he lacks. Certainly, theologians and metaphysicians draw a distinction between the object of want and the object of assimilation; still they confess that God made all things for the sake of himself, not for the sake of creation. They are unable to point to anything prior to creation, except God himself, as an object for which God should act, and are therefore driven to admit (as they clearly must), that God lacked those things for whose attainment he created means, and further that he desired them.

We must not omit to notice that the followers of this doctrine, anxious to display their talent in assigning final causes, have imported a new method of argument in proof of their theory—namely, a reduction, not to the impossible but to ignorance; thus showing that they have no other method of exhibiting their doctrine. For example, if a stone falls from a roof on to someone's head, and kills him, they will demonstrate by their new method, that the stone fell in order to kill the man; for, if it had not by God's will fallen with that object, how could so many circumstances (and there are often many concurrent circumstances) have all happened together by chance? Perhaps you will answer that the event is due to the facts that the wind was blowing, and the man was walking that way. "But why," they will insist, "was the wind blowing, and why was the man at that very time walking that way?" If you again answer, that the wind had then sprung up because the sea had begun to be agitated the day before, the weather being previously calm, and that the man had been invited by a friend, they will again insist: "But why was the sea agitated, and why was the man invited at that time?" So they will pursue their questions from cause to cause, till at last you take refuge in the will of God—in other words, the sanctuary of ignorance. So, again, when they survey the frame of the human body, they are amazed; and being ignorant of the causes of so great a work of art, conclude that it has been fashioned, not mechanically, but by divine and supernatural skill, and has been so put together that one part shall not hurt another.

Hence anyone who seeks for the true causes of miracles, and strives to understand natural phenomena as an intelligent being, and not to gaze at them like a fool, is set down and denounced as an impious heretic by those, whom the masses adore as the interpreters of nature and the gods. Such persons know that, with the removal of ignorance, the wonder which forms their only available means for proving and preserving their authority would vanish also. But I now quit this subject, and pass on to my third point.

After men persuaded themselves, that everything which is created is created for their sake, they were bound to consider as the chief quality in everything that which is most useful to themselves, and to account those things the best of all which have the most beneficial effect on mankind. Further, they were bound to form abstract notions for the explanation of the nature of things, such as *goodness, badness, order, confusion, warmth, cold, beauty, deformity,* and so on; and from the belief that they are free agents arose the further notions *praise* and *blame, sin* and *merit.*

I will speak of these latter hereafter, when I treat of human nature; the former I will briefly explain here.

Everything which conduces to health and the worship of God they have called *good,* everything which hinders these objects they have styled *bad;* and inasmuch as those who do not understand the nature of things do not verify phenomena in any way, but merely imagine them after a fashion, and mistake their imagination for understanding, such persons firmly believe that there is an *order* in things, being really ignorant both of things and their own nature. When phenomena are of such a kind, that the impression they make on our senses requires little effort of imagination, and can consequently be easily remembered, we say that they are *well-ordered;* if the contrary, that they are *ill-ordered* or *confused.* Further, as things which are easily imagined are more pleasing to us, men prefer order to confusion—as though there were any order in nature, except in relation to our imagination—and say that God has created all things in order; thus, without knowing it, attributing imagination to God, unless, indeed, they would have it that God foresaw human imagination, and arranged everything, so that it should be most easily imagined. If this be their theory, they would not, perhaps, be daunted by the fact that we find an infinite number of phenomena, far surpassing our imagination, and very many others which confound its weakness. But enough has been said on this subject. The other abstract notions are nothing but modes of imagining, in which the imagination is differently affected, though they are considered by the ignorant as the chief attributes of things, inasmuch as they believe that everything was created for the sake of themselves; and, according as they are affected by it, style it good or bad, healthy or rotten and corrupt. For instance, if the motion which objects we see communicate to our nerves be conducive to health, the objects causing it are styled *beautiful*; if a contrary motion be excited, they are styled *ugly*.

Things which are perceived through our sense of smell are styled fragrant or fetid; if through our taste, sweet or bitter, full-flavoured or insipid; if through our touch, hard or soft, rough or smooth, &c.

Whatsoever affects our ears is said to give rise to noise, sound, or harmony. In this last case, there are men lunatic enough to believe, that even God himself takes pleasure in harmony; and philosophers are not lacking who have persuaded themselves, that the motion of the heavenly bodies gives rise to harmony—all of which instances sufficiently show that everyone judges of things according to the state of his brain, or rather mistakes for things the forms of his imagination. We need no longer wonder that there have arisen all the controversies we have witnessed, and finally scepticism: for, although human bodies in many respects agree, yet in very many others they differ; so that what seems good to one seems bad to another; what seems well ordered to one seems confused to another; what is pleasing to one displeases another, and so on. I need not further enumerate, because this is not the place to treat the subject at length, and also because the fact is sufficiently well known. It is commonly said: "So many men, so many minds; everyone is wise in his own way; brains differ as completely as palates." All of which proverbs show, that men judge of things according to their mental disposition, and rather imagine than understand: for, if they understood phenomena, they would, as mathematics attest, be convinced, if not attracted, by what I have urged.

We have now perceived, that all the explanations commonly given of nature are mere modes of imagining, and do not indicate the true nature of anything, but only the constitution of the imagination; and, although they have names, as though they were entities, existing externally to the imagination, I call them entities imaginary rather than real; and, therefore, all arguments against us drawn from such abstractions are easily rebutted.

Many argue in this way. If all things follow from a necessity of the absolutely perfect nature of God, why are there so many imperfections in nature? such, for instance, as things corrupt to the point of putridity, loathsome deformity, confusion, evil, sin, &c. But these reasoners are, as I have said, easily confuted, for the perfection of things is to be reckoned only from their own nature and power; things are not more or less perfect, according as they delight or offend human senses, or according as they are serviceable or repugnant to mankind.

To those who ask why God did not so create all men, that they should be governed only by reason, I give no answer but this: because matter was not lacking to him for the creation of every degree of perfection from highest to lowest; or, more strictly, because the laws of his nature are so vast, as to suffice for the production of everything conceivable by an infinite intelligence, as I have shown in Prop. xvi.

Such are the misconceptions I have undertaken to note; if there are any more of the same sort, everyone may easily dissipate them for himself with the aid of a little reflection.

ACKNOWLEDGMENTS

For permission to reprint copyrighted material the editors are indebted to the following:

Barnes and Noble Books. "Pleasure" from *Collected Essays*, Vol. II, by Gilbert Ryle, 1971.

Basic Books, Inc. From *Conjectures and Refutations: The Growth of Scientific Knowledge* by Karl R. Popper. © 1963 by Karl R. Popper. From *Studies in Hysteria* by Josef Breuer and Sigmund Freud. Published in the United States of America by Basic Books, Inc., Publishers, by arrangement with The Hogarth Press, Ltd. Reprinted by permission of Basic Books, Inc., Publishers.

Beacon Press. "The Problem of Violence and the Radical Opposition" from *Five Lectures* by Herbert Marcuse; copyright © 1970 by Herbert Marcuse. "Repressive Tolerance" by Herbert Marcuse from *A Critique of Pure Tolerance*; copyright © 1965, 1969 by Herbert Marcuse. Reprinted by permission of Beacon Press.

Chatto & Windus and Mrs. Laura Huxley. From *Brave New World* by Aldous Huxley. Copyright 1932, 1960 by Aldous Huxley.

Cambridge University Press. From *Phaedrus* by Plato, edited by R. Hackforth, published by Cambridge University Press, New York, 1952.

Dover Publications, Inc. From *Language, Truth, and Logic* by A. J. Ayer, 1952 Dover Publications, Inc. N.Y. From *Ethics* by Spinoza, translated by R. H. Elwes. Used with the permission of the publisher.

E. P. Dutton. From *Defending My Enemy* by Aryeh Neier, 1979.

Harper & Row, Publishers, Inc. From *Brave New World* by Aldous Huxley. Copyright 1932, 1960 by Aldous Huxley. From *The Myth of Mental Illness* by Thomas S. Szasz, M.D. Copyright © 1961 by Harper & Row, Publishers, Inc. Reprinted by permission of Harper & Row, Publishers, Inc.

Harvard University Press and *The Loeb Classical Library* for an excerpt from the *Republic* by Plato, translated by Paul Shorey, 1930.

Houghton Mifflin Company. From *Crisis of Confidence* by Arthur Schlesinger. Copyright © 1967, 1968, 1969 by Arthur M. Schlesinger, Jr. Reprinted by permission of Houghton Mifflin Company.

Humanities Press Inc. From *Scepticism* by Arne Naess, 1968. Reprinted by permission of Humanities Press Inc., Atlantic Highlands, N.J. 07716.

Johnson Reprint Corporation. From *Selected Works of Pierre Gassendi*. © Johnson Reprint Corporation, New York, N.Y. Reprinted by permission of Johnson Reprint Corporation.

Loyola University Press. From *The Development of the Roman Catholic Perspective* by John Connery, 1977. Reprinted with permission of Loyola University Press, Chicago.

Macmillan Publishing Co., Inc. From "Divine Omnipotence and Human Freedom" by Antony Flew. Reprinted with permission of Macmillan Publishing Company from *New Essays in Philosophical Theology*, edited by Antony Flew and Alasdair MacIntyre (New York: Macmillan, 1955).

William Morrow & Company. From *Moodswing: The Third Revolution in Psychiatry* by Ronald R. Fieve, M.D. Copyright © 1975 by Ronald R. Fieve. Abridged by permission of William Morrow & Company.

NLB/Verso Editions, London. From *Against Method* by Paul Feyerabend, 1975.

W. W. Norton & Company, Inc., Sigmund Freud Copyrights Ltd, The Institute of Psycho-Analysis, and The Hogarth Press Ltd. From *Beyond the Pleasure Principle* by Sigmund

Freud; from *The Standard Edition of the Complete Psychological Works of Sigmund Freud*, translated and edited by James Strachey. Copyright © 1961 by James Strachey. Used by permission.

Oxford University Press. From *The Problems of Philosophy* by Bertrand Russell (1912). Reprinted by permission of Oxford University Press.

Philosophical Library, New York. From *Existentialism and Humanism* by Jean-Paul Sartre.

Prentice-Hall, Inc. From Saint Aurelius Augustine's *Concerning the Teacher and On the Immortality of the Soul*, translated by George G. Leckie, © 1938, renewed 1966, pp. 56–76. Reprinted by permission of Prentice-Hall, Inc., Englewood Cliffs, N.J.

Princeton University Press. From "A Defense of Abortion" by Judith Jarvis Thomson, *Philosophy and Public Affairs*, Vol. 1, No. 1 (Fall 1971). Copyright © 1971 by Princeton University Press. Reprinted by permission of Princeton University Press.

The Putnam Publishing Group. From *The Politics of Ecstasy* by Timothy Leary. Copyright © 1968 by The League for Spiritual Discovery, Inc. Reprinted by permission of G. P. Putnam's Sons.

Saturday Review and John Ciardi. "What Is Pornography" by John Ciardi, from *Saturday Review*, July 13, 1963. Copyright © 1963 by *Saturday Review*. Reprinted by permission of the author.

University Books/Lyle Stuart Inc. "Telepathy" from *Encyclopaedia of Psychic Science*. Reprinted by arrangement with Lyle Stuart.

University of Chicago Press. From *The Structure of Scientific Revolutions* by Thomas Kuhn, 1962. From *Guide of the Perplexed* by Moses Maimonides.